PULPIT POLITICS;

OR,

ECCLESIASTICAL LEGISLATION ON SLAVERY,

IN ITS

DISTURBING INFLUENCES

ON THE

AMERICAN UNION.

BY PROF. DAVID CHRISTY,

NEGRO UNIVERSITIES PRESS
NEW YORK

Originally published in 1862
by Faran & McLean, Publishers

Reprinted 1969 by
Negro Universities Press
A Division of Greenwood Publishing Corp.
New York

SBN 8371-1284-2

INTRODUCTION.

In a former work — COTTON IS KING — the author has discussed the *Economical Relations of American Slavery.* That production was written in a conservative spirit, and with the view of laying before the public, North and South, the facts necessary to demonstrate the inestimable value of the Union, and the wide-spread ruin that must follow its dissolution.

In another volume — ETHIOPIA — written with the design of promoting *African Colonization,* the author attempted to show, among other things, that, of all the population torn from Africa by the slave-trade and consigned to slavery, the colored people of the United States alone had made sufficient progress to justify the hope that any portion of the race were capable of carrying back a Christian civilization to the land of their fathers.

The present volume — PULPIT POLITICS — aims at presenting the *Ecclesiastical Legislation on Slavery, at the North, in its disturbing influences upon the American Union.* The aim here is equally conservative ; the design being to place before the people all that is known on the subject of slavery, in its bearings on the moral progress of the African race. By this means it is believed that the public will be able to judge, with greater accuracy, how far the action of the Churches may have been in accordance, strictly, with the legitimate duties of the Gospel ministry; or how far it may have partaken of a fanatical character, calculated unnecessarily to disturb the peace of the Church, and endanger the safety of the Union.

In selecting a title for this work — Pulpit Politics — it is not intended to bring the charge of political preaching against the

iii

majority of clergymen. The moral mania of abolitionism has by no means been universally prevalent among the members of the sacred profession. On the contrary, there have been very many of them, who have acted on the principle that the kingdom of their Divine Master "is not of this world;" and who have, consequently, resolutely opposed all ecclesiastical legislation in civil affairs.

If it be claimed as a right, that the divine shall review the action of the civilian; it is equally the right of the civilian to review the action of the divine. In the pulpit, proclaiming the Gospel of peace, the minister is sacred; on the stump, or in the pulpit, announcing his political opinions, he is only a politician; and, there, his sacred character does not attach to him. Hence it is, that a political parson is always treated as a mere politician, and rightfully loses his influence as a divine.

The class of clergymen who have conducted the controversy on slavery, and forced many of the Churches into the vortex of abolitionism, have long been directing attention to civil affairs, and asking for changes in the Constitution and laws of the country in relation to that institution. In turn, it is now proposed to bring the action of the Churches, in reference to emancipation, before the bar of public opinion, there to be judged as to the wisdom of their policy, by the fruits it has borne.

If it shall be found, on contrasting the condition of the African race throughout the world, that fewer obstacles to their evangelization exist in the United States than anywhere else; if it shall be found, indeed, that no obstacles to the accomplishment of that object exist, except such as have been created by the inconsiderate zeal of clergymen themselves; then the country must be convinced that the agitation in favor of emancipation has been uncalled for, and not necessary to the discharge of any christian duty toward the colored people; and that Christian ministers, therefore, have been inexcusable in agitating the subject of slavery, so as to distract and divide the Churches, and lead to the ruin of the country.

A word in reference to the causes which gave to abolitionism its early advantages and rapid growth. When the work of foreign missions had been fairly commenced, the hope began to be entertained that the progress of the Gospel would be equally as rapid as its extension over the world had been in Apostolic times. This expectation did not originate with the less informed but zealous-minded christian. It was the out-growth of a high intelligence, a deep-toned piety, a broad philanthropy, and a strong faith in the promises of God. But the mind that conceived it was unendowed with the knowledge of future events, and knew nothing of the purposes of the Almighty — knew nothing of the obstacles to the extension of the Gospel existing among the heathen. On this point, almost a half century since, the declaration was made, "that the energies of Christendom, wisely directed, and attended with the blessing of the Spirit, might send the Gospel over the world in a quarter of a century." This hopeful sentiment was uttered in connection with the action of the American Board of Commissioners for Foreign Missions, and was, at first, only the expression of an individual; * but it was accepted by the Prudential Committee of the Board, and formally adopted by the Board itself, at its meeting in 1816.† The pulpit of America was then strongly represented from the Theological Schools of Great Britain. The missions in the West Indies had been greatly hindered, in their success among the slaves, by the hostility of the planters. In consequence of this, slavery, among the British people, was considered incompatible with the progress of the Gospel. This view, based upon the results in the West Indies alone, seems to have been adopted by the American ministry without examination, and accepted as a theory of universal application. Gradually diffused as a floating sentiment upon the surface of society, it led to a common conviction that, in some way not explainable, slavery was an evil which demanded eradication as a preliminary step to the evangelization of the African race. Those holding this opinion, seem to have adopted a logic something like this : As slavery can not prevail under the universal domination of the Gospel, therefore the abolition of slavery is essential to the world's conversion to Christianity. In this way they failed to view the Gospel as a curative remedy for human degradation and indolence, and as capable of lifting the lowly of the race to an elevation where

---

* Rev. Dr. Worcester, as quoted in the Memorial Volume of the Board, 1861.
† Memorial Volume, pages 130, 131.

slavery might no longer be necessary to the promotion of industry, and would, therefore, become a useless institution among men.

The christian men who then entertained these views, never counseled violence as a means of overthrowing American slavery; and uniformly expressed their aversion to the aims and actions of the abolitionists. But in admitting that slavery presented obstacles to the progress of the Gospel, and that emancipation was a measure that should be promoted by all lawful means, they were but preparing a soil upon which the abolitionists could sow their seed, and reap an abundant harvest.

That a radical error prevailed upon this question, among good men, is demonstrated by the history of foreign missions during the last half century. The spread of the Gospel in heathen countries, has made no such rapid progress as the projectors of foreign missionary enterprises anticipated would attend the labors of the good men sent forth to that work. The facts in this volume will show, that slavery in America, by freeing its subjects from all connection with heathen superstitions and idolatries, and in having trained them in the use of the English language, has accomplished, for four millions of people, once barbarous, what all the foreign missions in the world have done for less than one-fifth of that number of heathen; and that the actual number of converts, among the colored people of the Slave States, is nearly double that of all the converts in the whole of the heathen missions of Protestant Christendom.

The burden of the ecclesiastical legislation of the United States on slavery, has been based upon the theories started in Great Britain. It is well, therefore, that some allusion should be made to them here. The principal one, as argued by Mr. BUXTON, in 1823, and stated by Mr. CANNING, is as follows: "The continuance of slavery, and the principles of the Christian religion are incompatible." * In the course of the debates Mr. CANNING said:

"Religion ought to control the acts and to regulate the consciences of governments, as well as of individuals; but when it is put forward to serve a political purpose, however laudable, it is done, I think, after the example of ill times; and I can not but remember the ill objects

---

* Canning's Select Speeches, page 409.

to which in those times such a practice was applied. . . . . . . If it be meant that in the Christian religion there is a special denunciation of slavery — that slavery and Christianity can not exist together — I think the honorable gentleman himself must admit that the proposition is historically false; and again I must say, that I can not consent to the confounding, for a political purpose, what is morally true with what is historically false. One peculiar characteristic of the Christian dispensation, if I must venture in this place upon such a theme, is, that it has accommodated itself to all states of society, rather than that it has selected any particular state of society for the peculiar exercise of its influence. If it has added lustre to the sceptre of the sovereign, it has equally been the consolation of the slave. It applies to all ranks of life, to all conditions of men; and the sufferings of this world, even to those upon whom they press most heavily, are rendered comparatively indifferent by the prospect of compensation in the world of which Christianity affords the assurance. True it certainly is, that Christianity generally tends to elevate, not to degrade, the character of man; but it is not true, in the specific sense conveyed in the honorable gentleman's Resolution; it is not true, that there is that in the Christian religion which makes it impossible that it should coëxist with slavery in the world. Slavery has been known in all times, and under all systems of religion, whether true or false.* . . . .

"The honorable gentleman can not wish more than I do, that under this gradual operation, under this widening diffusion of light and liberality, the spirit of the Christian religion may effect all the objects he has at heart. But it seems to me that it is not, for the practical attainment of his objects, desirable that that which may be the influencing spirit should be put forward as the active agent. When Christianity was introduced into the world, it took its root amidst the galling slavery of the Roman Empire; more galling in many respects (though not precisely of the same character,) than that of which the honorable gentleman, in common, I may say, with every friend of humanity, complains. Slavery at that period gave to the master the power of life and death over his bondsman: this is undeniable — known to every body. '*Ita servus homo est!*' are the words put by Juvenal into the mouth of the fine lady who calls upon her husband to crucify his slave. If the evils of this dreadful system nevertheless gradually vanished before the gentle but certain influence of Christianity, and if the great author of the system trusted rather to this

---

* Canning's Select Speeches, pages 403, 404.

gradual operation of the principle than to any immediate or direct precept, I think parliament would do more wisely rather to rely upon the like operation of the same principle, than to put forward the authority of Christianity in at least a questionable shape. The name of Christianity ought not to be thus used, unless we are prepared to act in a much more summary manner than the honorable gentleman himself proposes."

In referring to the dangers of the measure proposed, Mr. CANNING gave the following eloquent and prophetic warning of the consequences of removing the shackles from the barbarous negro, and instead of emancipation urged a system of religious instruction for his moral elevation :

"Sir, we must remember that we are dealing with a being, possessing the form and strength of a man, but the intellect only of a child. To turn him loose in the manhood of his physical strength, in the maturity of his physical passions, but in the infancy of his uninstructed reason, would be to raise up a creature resembling the splendid fiction of romance ; the hero of which can sketch a human form, with all the corporeal capabilities of a man, and with the thews and sinews of a giant ; but being unable to impart to the work of his hands a perception of right and wrong, he finds too late that he has only created a more than mortal power of doing mischief, and himself recoils from the monster of his own creation." *

It is time that the slavery question was disposed of forever. Its agitation has done a fatal work. The Church is in fragments ; the nation in ruins. If the author's labors will tend to the healing of the divisions in the one, and the reconstruction of the other, he will be amply compensated for his toil.

---

* Canning's Select Speeches, page 421.

CONTENTS.

CHAPTER I.

CHAPTER II.

SECTION I.

CHAPTER III

SECTION V.

SECTION VI.

SECTION VII.

SECTION VIII.

Ecclesiastical legislation on slavery designed to transfer the subject to the arena
of politics, 426; the scheme successful, 426; the basis laid was accepted by abolitionists, 426; this action created alarm at the South, 427; measures adopted to
counteract the dangers threatened, 427; Nullification and the Tariff a pretext,
427; abolition claimed the right to use both moral and political means for the
overthrow of slavery, 429; the principles of the Liberty party, and also of the
Garrisonians, 430; abolitionism in the Presidential campaigns, 430; abolition
Convention of 1841 in Ohio, and its resolutions and address, 431–434; abolition
Convention in New York, its ultra resolutions advising negroes to steal, etc., 434;
opinions of Mr. Birney in 1843, 435; in 1844, 436; speech of Mr. Chase, 437–440;
South-Western Liberty Convention, 1845, at Cincinnati, 440; speech of Mr. Birney, of Mr. Wills, of Judge Stevens, resolutions, address, 440–442; remarks on
the incendiary productions of these men, 442–451; notice of the dogma that
"slavery is the creature of local law," 443; Hon. J. W. Stevenson on this point,
443; he quotes Lord Stowell as repudiating the doctrine, 444; he notices other
cases illustrative of his views, 445–448; Mr. Clay on abolitionism, 448; argument of Charles O'Connor in Lemmon case, 451–45C.

SECTION II.

THE SLAVERY AGITATION IN CONGRESS.. 456

Abolition in 1835, the offspring of ecclesiastical action, 456; political abolitionism
not then organized, 456; abolition used as a means of promoting the sectional
interests of New England, 456; General Jackson's condemnation of abolition in
his message, 457; abolition petitions in Congress, 458; debates upon them, 459–485.

CHAPTER I.

BRITISH THEORIES ON AFRICAN EVANGELIZATION, AS DERIVED FROM
THE EFFECTS OF THE SLAVE TRADE AND BRITISH COLONIAL
SLAVERY.

THE condition of Africa had long enlisted the sympathies of
the benevolent, before anything was attempted for the moral and
social elevation of its inhabitants. Its degradation was known
to be extreme, but its true situation was involved in mystery.
To the traffic in slaves was attributed much of its wretchedness.
Time, however, showed that the iron despotism of its kings,
the absoluteness of its domestic slavery, the objects of its idolatrous worship, the modes of performing its religious rites, its cruel
superstitions, its degrading customs, its human sacrifices, its can-
nibalism, must have dated their origin far back beyond the commencement of the slave trade. This traffic, it became evident, had
not originated the greatest evils under which Africa suffered, but
was itself one of the natural fruits of the social and moral degradation previously existing.

At length the darkness of that barbarism was to be penetrated
by the light of civilization, and the attempt made to lift the African up to the level of the Caucasian. This effort was not a
voluntary one, springing spontaneously from the mind of the
philanthropist, and undertaken out of pure sympathy for Africa.
The people were forced into action, for its accomplishment, in
such a manner as God only can lead men into important measures for human progress. It was inaugurated by the adoption
of such schemes, and conducted in such a way, as seemed best
adapted to determine the question, whether the black man can be

(17)

made the equal of the white. It was begun, too, at the very moment when the white man, on the American continent, was commencing his attempt at solving the mighty problem of man's capability of self-government. It was a most important moment, this, when the first steps were taken towards the redemption of Africa. * None, for a moment, supposed that the task could be performed in a thousand years to come. The work was an untried one — such a work as had never before been attempted upon earth. Nations had conquered nations — had destroyed their captives or enslaved them — but never had the strong devoted themselves to the elevation of the weak. Two thousand years had the whites struggled, unaided, to gain the boon of constitutional freedom; and, even then, but a single nation had succeeded. Could the blacks do more — could they advance, at a single stride, from barbarism to civilization! We shall see.

On the 22d May, 1772, Lord Mansfield decided the celebrated Somersett case, and pronounced it unlawful to hold a slave in Great Britain. † Previously to this date many slaves had been introduced into English families, and, on running away, had been delivered up to their masters, by order of the court of King's Bench, under Lord Mansfield; but now the poor African, no longer hunted as a beast of prey in the streets of London, slept under his roof, miserable as it might be, in perfect security. ‡

To Granville Sharp belonged the honor of this achievement. By the decision referred to, about 400 negroes were thrown upon

---

* We refer, of course, to the first efforts which had been productive of favorable results. Earlier attempts had been made to introduce the Gospel into Africa, but without success. On this point, Mr. Tracy, in his History of Colonization and Missions, says:

"Catholic missionaries labored for two hundred and forty-one years, but every vestige of their influence has been gone for many generations. The Moravians, beginning in 1736, toiled for thirty-four years, making five attempts, at a cost of eleven lives, and effected nothing. An English attempt, at Bulama Island, in 1792, partly missionary in its character, was abandoned in two years, with a loss of one hundred lives. A mission sent to the Foulahs, from England, in 1795, returned without commencing its labors. The London, Edinburgh and Glasgow Society, commenced three stations in 1797, which were extinct in three years, and five of the six missionaries dead."

† See subsequent notices of the opinions of Lords Mansfield and Stowell.

‡ Clarkson's History of the Slave Trade.

their own resources. Without any one to care for them, they soon found themselves to be but mere outcasts, with none to protect or employ them. In despair, they flocked to Mr. Sharp, as their patron; but, considering their numbers, and his limited means, it was impossible for him to afford them adequate relief. To those thus emancipated, others, discharged from the army and navy, were afterwards added, who, by their improvidence, were reduced to extreme distress. After much reflection, Mr. Sharp determined to colonize them in Africa; but, possessing only a limited fortune, it was impossible for him to effect this object without aid from others. That aid could not be obtained; and fifteen years passed away before any thing could be accomplished. By this time, the blacks — indigent, unemployed, despised, forlorn, vicious — had become such nuisances as to make it necessary they should be sent somewhere, and no longer suffered to infest the streets of London. * At length the Government came to the aid of Mr. Sharp, and supplied the means of their transportation and support. †

In April, 1787, these African freemen, to the number of 400, were put on shipboard for Africa; and bidding farewell to the soil of Britain, where freedom had wrought no good for them, were landed, in the following month, at Sierra Leone. The next year a few new emigrants arrived, and, after much difficulty and suffering and a great reduction of their numbers, the colony was considered as established.

In March, 1792, a reinforcement of 1,131 colored persons, arrived at Sierra Leone. These men were fugitive slaves, who had joined the English during the American Revolutionary war, and had been promised lands in Nova Scotia; but the Government having failed to meet its pledge, in consequence of the opposition of the whites, and the climate proving unfavorable, they sought a refuge in Africa, to which they were removed under the care of Mr. Clarkson.

The control of the colony soon passed from the hands of Mr. Sharp, to those of a Company. When this change occurred, the liberal system of government adopted by Mr. Sharp, which ad-

* Wadstrom, p. 220.
† Memoirs of Granville Sharp.

mitted colored men to a share in its administration, was super-
seded by more rigid laws, excluding them from voting and from
office. This led the American blacks to rebel, and they were
only subjected to the control of the Governor, after a hard fought
battle, in which he was aided by some natives, and by 550 free
negroes from Jamaica, who landed on the day of the engagement. Three of the rebel leaders were captured and afterwards
executed — thus extinguishing this little spark of democracy in
the colony. The 550 maroons (mulattoes) who thus arrived so
opportunely to the aid of the Governor, were a set of turbulent
freemen, of the mountains of Jamaica, who had first been shipped
to Nova Scotia, and thence to Sierra Leone.

On the first of January, 1808, the Government relieved the
Company from its difficulties, by assuming the sovereignty of
Sierra Leone. In this year the slave trade was prohibited, and
the colony became necessary to the crown in carrying out its
purposes towards Africa.

With this introductory historical sketch of the foundation of
Sierra Leone, the way is prepared to enter upon the missionary
history of the colony, and to determine how far the opinions of
British Christians, on the subject of slavery, have been influenced
by that important event — an event purely providential, and not
of man's devising.

Missions for the benefit of this colony had been first attempted
in 1792, again in 1795, and again in 1797: but all these efforts
had failed. In 1804, the Church Missionary Society sent out its
missionaries, with orders to seek for stations among the natives
outside of the territory of the colony ; because of the opposition
within it, which had originated from the efforts to coerce the colonists into subjection to the authorities; and because of the prevalence of the slave trade, at that time a legal traffic for British
subjects within its limits, as well as to all other nations throughout the whole of Africa. But the efforts of these missionaries
also failed, and they had to await further developments.

In 1808, when the slave trade was abolished by Great Britain,
this same mission commenced ten stations as directed, but were
unable to sustain them. The natives, not under the control of
the colony, but interested in the slave trade, burned the mission

houses and churches, destroyed the growing crops of the missionaries, threatened their lives, and otherwise persecuted them.

When England abandoned the traffic in slaves, it so happened that she thereby only surrendered its monopoly into the hands of France, Portugal, and Spain, who had tropical territory which demanded an increase of labor. Hence, there was no diminution of its extent, or abatement of its horrors, but a vast increase of both : and, although the missions from 1792 to 1808 had failed, both in and out of the colony, yet 'the continuance of the traffic, beyond its limits, after 1808, drove the missionaries within its jurisdiction, in the hopes of better protection. But these out-stations were not wholly abandoned until after a long struggle to sustain them — the last one having been maintained until 1818.

In 1811, the English Wesleyans sent out a missionary to the Nova Scotia blacks, in Sierra Leone ; who was successful in establishing a mission among them on a permanent basis. The Church Missionary Society also continued its labors with success, directing its efforts, mainly, to the improvement of the natives. These natives have been of two classes : first, those living in the colony and its vicinity ; and, second, those recaptured from slave ships, after the system of an armed repression of the slave trade had been adopted. But no missions could succeed, until after the suppression of that traffic had been effected in Sierra Leone, and British authority began to exert a controlling influence upon the coast. This led to the conviction, that Africa could not be evangelized while the slave trade prevailed. The present naval force, on that coast, had no existence then, nor until many years after the traffic in slaves was prohibited ; while, at the same time, the demand for slaves was so great as to give the utmost activity to the trade. This is clearly indicated by the fact, that while the entire exports of slaves from Africa, from 1798 to 1810, numbered 85,000 annually, they had increased, in 1815, to 106,000 annually ; or more than 20,000 annually over the former exports. *

These results led British Christians to the conclusion, that the slave trade could not be suppressed and Africa christianized, except by the destruction of the markets for slaves. Destroy the demand, argued the English people, and the supply will cease.

* See Parliamentary Reports.

But this demand could only be destroyed by universal emancipation; and, therefore, it was urged, that all the enslaved must be set free — that West India slavery must be abolished.

To reconcile the nation, generally, to the proposed measure of abolition in the colonies, arguments were offered on the economical aspects of the question. The theory was broached, that free labor was doubly profitable over slave labor — that one freeman working under the stimulus of wages, was worth two slaves toiling beneath the lash. As a result of the prohibition of the slave trade, in cutting off the ordinary supplies of labor, the exports from the islands had fallen off thirty-three per cent. Freedom, it was nevertheless urged, would fully restore their prosperity; and, thus, emancipation would not only be the discharge of a moral duty, but it would also be a profitable measure. In this way, the war against slavery became a popular movement in Great Britain, and was zealously prosecuted, until, in 1833, the emancipation act was carried in Parliament.

The results of emancipation upon the prosperity of the Islands, as well as upon the slave trade and emancipation at large, have been very different from what was anticipated by the people of England. These points will receive attention as we progress. It need only be remarked here, in addition to what has been already stated, that the exports of slaves from Africa, according to Parliamentary Reports, were increased immediately after West India Emancipation, or from 1835 to 1839, to 135,800 annually; being 50,800 more than were exported yearly, when the crusade against the slave trade was commenced by Mr. Wilberforce.

The theory that the evangelization of Africa could not be effected during the existence of the slave trade, had very many facts to sustain it, and it became the universal creed of Christendom. It lay at the foundation of the organization of the American Colonization Society; and, twenty-five years later, in connection with commercial objects, it put in motion the costly, yet fatal Niger expedition. From this belief, there was but a step to the conviction that the African race, at large, could not be christianized as long as they remained in bondage.

This theory, too, had then much to give it support, as is apparent from the results of missionary efforts in the West Indies.

Look at the facts recorded in the general history of missions; and also at the testimony of individuals familiar with the condition of the Islands. The Rev. J. M. PHILLIPPO, for twenty years a missionary in Jamaica, and who has written its history, says:

" Upwards of 120 years after Jamaica had become an appendage of the British crown, scarcely an effort had been made to instruct the slaves in the great doctrines and duties of Christianity; and although, in 1696, at the instance of the mother country, an act was passed by the local legislature, directing that all slave owners should instruct their negroes, and have them baptized ' when fit for it,' it is evident, from the very terms in which the act was expressed, that it was designed to be, as it afterwards proved, a dead letter — a mere political manœuvre, intended to prevent the parent state from interfering in the management of the slaves."

From this time to 1770, a period of 74 years, the question of slave instruction in Jamaica received no attention. When, in 1770, Parliament put certain questions to Mr. Weddeburn, as to the actual state of religious instruction of slaves in the island, he replied: " There are a few properties on which there are Moravian parsons; but, in general, there is no religious instruction." The same testimony was borne at the same time by Mr. Fuller, agent of Jamaica, and two others, who, when asked " what religious instructions are there for the negro slaves," answered, " we know of none such in Jamaica."

The Rev. Dr. Coke, who was sent out on a missionary exploration, in 1787, says:

" When I first landed in Jamaica, the form of Godliness was hardly visible; and its power, except in some few solitary instances, was totally unknown. Iniquity prevailed in all its forms. Both whites and blacks, to the number of between 300,000 and 400,000, were evidently living without hope and without God in the world. The language of the Apostle seems strikingly descriptive of their entire depravity: ' There is none righteous, no, not one; there is none that understandeth, there is none that seeketh after God. Their throats are an open sepulchre; with their tongue they have used deceit; the poison of asps is under their lips; their feet are swift to shed blood, and the way of peace they have not known."

In 1796, Mr. Edwards, the historian of the West Indies, in his place in the House of Commons, when speaking of sending missionaries to a certain point in Jamaica, said:

"I speak from my own knowledge when I say, that they are cannibals, and that instead of listening to a missionary, they would certainly *eat* him."

The introduction of the Gospel into Jamaica, as well as into the other West India Islands, met with the most rancorous opposition from the planters, who, with some honorable exceptions, viewed the religious instruction of the slaves as "incompatible with the existence of slavery." The work of missions therefore, though begun in Jamaica, by the Baptists in 1814, and by the Methodists in 1789 and again in 1815, made but little progress, being resolutely opposed until about 1820. In 1824, the Moravians, who had commenced so far back as 1754, had four stations and four missionaries; the Wesleyans eight stations and eight missionaries; and the Baptists five stations and five missionaries.

Though overawed by the mother country, the planters still manifested bitter hostility to the religious instruction of the slaves. In 1824, they renewed their persecutions of the missionaries, and in 1832, on a partial insurrection of the blacks — beginning in December, 1831 — their wrath overflowing all bounds, they commenced an indiscriminate destruction of the mission property. In this frightful crusade against the Gospel, they destroyed no less than 14 chapels, with private houses and other property, belonging to the Baptists, amounting in value to $115,250; and 6 chapels belonging to the Methodists, and property worth $30-000. Every species of cruelty and insult was inflicted upon the missionaries.

The emancipation act of the following year, 1833, going into effect August 1, 1834, by which the slaves became apprentices and afterwards, in 1838, were set entirely free, forever put it out of the power of the planters to repeat such acts of violence and injustice. The missions have since been continued among the colored people of the British West Indies, with varying results, as we shall hereafter see.

To gain a true idea of the varied conditions of the population of the several British West India Islands, a more definite statement must be made. The principal facts are taken from NEWCOMB'S ENCYCLOPÆDIA OF MISSIONS, second revised edition, New York, 1858. *

ANTIGUA, settled in 1632, had a total population, in 1846, of 83,726, of whom 23,350 were blacks. The Gospel was introduced into this island in 1760, by one of its leading public men, Mr. Gilbert, who had become a convert to Christianity, under the preaching of Mr. Wesley, during a visit to England. Nearly 200 persons were united in Christian fellowship under his superintendence; but while thus zealously employed, for the good of his own slaves and that of others, he was removed by death, and the flock left as sheep without a shepherd. In the prosecution of his labors, he was encountered by bitter hostility. His loss to these converts was supplied by a pious shipwright, who for about eight years kept them together, until Dr. Coke, in 1786, supplied a permanent missionary to the island.

This mission appears to have enjoyed, for many years, an almost uninterrupted prosperity, until 1826, when all the missionaries, with part of their families, 13 in all, perished at sea, in returning from a district meeting held in St. Christophers.

ST. VINCENTS, settled in 1763, had, in 1846, a population of 26,533, of whom 18,114 were blacks. The first missionary was introduced into St. Vincents in 1787, by Dr. Coke. At first the mission was successful, and the opposition, for several years, was confined to some lawless individuals; but at length the arm of authority was turned against the mission, and the Colonial Assembly passed certain laws calculated to root out the Wesleyans from the island. The law was extremely severe, including banishment and death, under certain circumstances. The majority of the people, however, were opposed to the law, and it remained in force but a short time — the king having vetoed it, as contrary to the principles of toleration. While it was in force, however, the missionary was arrested, imprisoned, and banished. Before the passage of this law, the converts numbered about 1,000; but,

---

* The dates of the settlements of the islands, severally, with the number of the population, are taken from the MISSIONARY GUIDE BOOK, 1846, London, which gives, as its authority, MURRAY'S ENCYCLOPÆDIA OF GEOGRAPHY. — *Newcomb.*

soon afterward, were reduced one-half by the dispersions which followed. In 1794, two missionaries were sent out to renew the work; and many returning from their wanderings, the congregation began to increase. But the spirit of hostility was rather smothered than subdued. In March, 1797, a mob, headed by a magistrate, attacked the Methodist chapel, threw down the railings, broke the lamps, pulled down the communion rails, and tore the Bible in pieces. About a year after, an attempt was made upon the lives of the missionaries. Their house was broken open in the night, and some ruffians, armed with cutlasses, entered the sleeping apartments, turned up the bed and searched for them in every corner. Happily, the missionaries, anticipating the attack, had taken refuge for the night at the dwelling of a friend.

BARBADOS, settled in 1624, had a population in 1846, of 120,-000, of whom 66,000 were blacks. The mission work, among the slaves, was commenced in 1788, but the missionary soon met with violent opposition, on the ground that he was disseminating among the negroes, notions incompatible with their condition as slaves. Repeated attempts were made by the mob to interrupt the meetings for worship, in which they conducted themselves in the most violent and outrageous manner. An appeal to the magistrate for redress proving fruitless, the dwelling of the missionary was attacked with stones, and his wife struck with violence. His successor, in 1791, found the prejudices so far dispelled, that he had access to more estates than he could visit. Persecution had now nearly ceased, but it had given place to a settled contempt for divine things. But, in October, 1823, intelligence was received that an insurrection had broken out among the slaves of Jamaica, and the Methodist missionaries were accused of being accessory to it, by teaching sedition under pretence of giving instruction. The intelligence raised a storm of wrath against the mission here, and every indignity was heaped on the missionary. A mob assembled and tore down the chapel, and the life of the missionary being in danger, he left the island for St. Vincents. These outrages led to a censure upon the inhabitants by the British House of Commons; and, to relieve themselves of the odium, 94 of the principal men signed a declaration, expressing their regret at the occurrence, and their approbation of the sentiments of the House. But, in 1826, when another missionary arrived, placards were posted up, calling upon the mob to tar and feather him, and the president refused him a license to preach. Yet, afterward, he proceeded in his work without molestation, a new chapel was erected, the prejudice against the Methodists subsided, and a prosperous mission was established.

VIRGIN ISLANDS, settled in 1660, had 7,731 inhabitants in 1846, of whom 4,318 were blacks. The mission work was begun, in this group of islands, in 1789. A large society was soon collected at Tortola, and, other missionaries arriving, the work was extended to Spanish Town, and other islets in the vicinity. But, in December, 1805, a most brutal outrage was committed, by a mob, on one of the missionaries at Tortola, by which he came near losing his life. This was done in revenge for an alleged publication in England, respecting the morals of the people of the island. Before the commencement of this mission, every species of wickedness prevailed among the negroes; but since the Gospel entered, their superstitious practices have been abandoned. No early statistics of membership are given, but, in 1853, the church in Tortola, is said to have had 1,604 members.

BERMUDAS, settled in 1612, had a population, in 1846, of 8,-720, of whom 3,314 were blacks. These are a numerous cluster of small islands, included in the West Indies, and belonging to the British. A mission was commenced on Somer's Island, in 1779, which had to encounter the prejudices of the whites and the heathenish superstitions of the blacks: the latter being found under the slavish dominion of witchcraft, as it prevails in Africa; but it was not long before the Gospel began to exert its influence. Yet this was no sooner manifested, than the hostility of the whites was aroused. Laws were passed similar to those in Jamaica; and the missionary was imprisoned six months in the common jail, by which his health was so impaired that he was recalled, and the island left destitute of the Gospel for six years. In 1808, another missionary visited the island, but found the society previously gathered by the first missionary dispersed. Obtaining permission from the governor, he commenced his labors, but without any great success. In 1853, the Church members numbered 445

BAHAMAS, settled in 1783, had a population, in 1846, of 18,718, of whom 7,734 were blacks. These islands are the most western of the West Indies, extending along the coast of Florida, toward Cuba. The first mission, in these islands, was commenced in 1800 ; and though a law had been previously enacted, prohibiting the instruction of slaves, the missionary, having obtained permission to preach, soon succeeded in raising a small society. Other missionaries arriving, the work was successfully extended to several of the islands, where a great reformation followed their labors. But, in 1816, the legislature passed an act prohibiting, under severe penalties, meetings for divine worship earlier than sun-rise and later than sun-set, thus depriving the slaves of the privilege of attending. After a few years, however, the legislature retraced its steps, and repealed the restrictions which had been laid upon the poor negroes. In 1853, the Methodist mission, in the Bahamas, had 2,800 members.

Besides the missions already noticed, the Methodists established many others, the details of which are not given in the work from which we quote.

As the final result of the whole labors of the Methodists, in the West Indies, including Hayti, Guiana, and some of the Dutch and Danish Islands, their church members, in 1853, numbered 48,589. This included the converts among the coolies, for whom missionaries have been appointed.

In noticing the results of the missionary efforts in Jamaica, the Baptist missions were referred to as having suffered along with the Methodists. The Baptists entered that field in 1814. Encouraged by early indications of success, the Society pressed forward in its work, increasing the number of its laborers and forming new stations, till, at the annual meeting of the missionaries at Falmouth, in April, 1831, the number of members reported was 10,838. The year following, the terrible mob violence, already noticed, broke up all their missions and destroyed their property. But they were again soon reorganized, and the churches continued to prosper to such a degree, that they were never in a better condition than when the emancipation act was carried into full effect in 1838. In 1841, the number of members had increased to 27,706; and, in Jamaica, in 1842, the ministers unanimously resolved, as an appropriate commemoration at once of the day of freedom and the jubilee of the mission, to detach themselves from the funds of the parent society, after the first of August ensuing. This proved to be an ill-advised measure, and injurious to the cause of missions.

The Baptists extended their missions to some of the other islands, particularly after the passage of the emancipation act; but, as our aim in this part of our investigations is, chiefly, to trace the progress of the Gospel under slavery, we shall not add further details here, but leave them to be noticed hereafter. The population of Jamaica, in 1846, was 380,000 of whom 255,290 were blacks, the remainder being mulattoes and whites.

The Island of St. Thomas, settled in 16—, had, in 1846, a population of 5,080, of whom 4,500 were blacks. In 1732, the Moravians commenced their mission in this island; and in 1736, three persons were baptized. In 1738, a negro named Mingo was baptized, and became a zealous assistant. Through his preaching an awakening took place over the whole island. But the planters opposed the work, and persecuted and imprisoned the missionaries. Count Zinzendorf, however, who unexpectedly arrived in the island, procured their liberation. The missions were extended to the other Danish islands, St. Croix and St. Jan; and the work progressed, until, in 1832, a centennary jubilee was held, and the important and encouraging fact was reported, that during that period, 37,000 souls had been baptized in these islands. All this work was accomplished under slavery, as emancipation, in the Danish islands, was not effected until 1848.

The Island of St. Jan, in 1846, had a population of 2,430, of whom 2,250 were blacks; and St. Croix 31,387, of whom 29,164 were blacks.

There are, at the present time, in the three Danish islands, St. Thomas, St. Croix, and St. Jan, belonging to the Moravians, 8 stations, 35 laborers, and 9,398 converts, of whom 2,892 are communicants.

In Jamaica, the Moravians, in 1804, fifty years from the founding of the mission, were able to report but 938 negroes as having been baptized. In 1831 and '32, as before stated, they greatly suffered from mob violence. In 1851, in a review of the Jamaica mission, the *Moravian Church Miscellany* represents it as comprising 13 stations, and the negroes, in connection with the churches, as numbering 13,388, young and old.

In ANTIGUA, a mission was commenced by the Moravians in 1756, which had to endure much persecution from the planters; yet, in 1788, they numbered more than 6,000 converts. In 1823, there had been received into the Church, within the preceding fifty years, 16,099 converts, young and old. In 1826, the number of slaves receiving instruction was 14,823; and, at the present time, the number of members reported is 8,000, there having been some diminution attributed to the encroachments of other denominations. The Moravians also established missions in ST. KITTS, BARBADOS, and DUTCH GUIANA, with varying success.

The Church Missionary Society; the Society for the propagation of the Gospel; the London Missionary Society; and the United Scotch Presbyterian Church, have all established missions in the West Indies—a portion of them previous to emancipation, but, mainly, since that epoch. The statistics of their operations, previous to 1833, are not accessible.

In closing the history of the Methodist missions in Jamaica, up to the period of emancipation, the writer from whom we quote, says : *

"The emancipation of the negroes was quickly followed by very important changes. The Sabbath was observed with hallowed strictness. Nothing was to be seen on that day but decently dressed people going to and from their places of worship; congregations were increased and multiplied; old chapels were enlarged, and new ones erected. Education was also greatly extended. A great change took place also in the public opinion of Jamaica, as to the Methodist missionaries. Formerly no names were too vile, no treatment too bad for them ; even their chapels were shut up or razed to the ground as public nuisances. Yet within five years after the late insurrection, the House of Assembly of Jamaica made a grant of £500 to aid in the erection of a Methodist chapel in Kingston; and, during the discussion of the subject, the highest eulogiums were pronounced on the usefulness of the Wesleyan missionaries. The Common Council of Kingston, and several of the parochial vestries, followed the example of the Assembly, and made grants for similar purposes."

* Encyclopædia of Missions.

The Bishop of Barbados, too, thus described the results :

" First. Wives and husbands hitherto living on different estates began to live together.

" Second. The number of marriages greatly increased. One of his clergy had married ten couple a week, since the first of August.

" Third. The schools greatly increased ; a hundred were added in one district.

. " Fourth. The planters complain that their whole weeding gang (children), instead of going to work, go to school.

" Fifth. All the young women cease to work in the field, and are learning female employment.

" Sixth. Friendly societies for mutual relief have increased.

" Seventh. The work of the clergymen is doubled. One of the chapels which held three hundred is being enlarged, so as to contain nine hundred, and still will not be large enough."

Under these encouragements, the missionaries pressed onward in their work, so that in six years after full emancipation, 1844, they had a membership, in Jamaica, numbering 26,585. But 1853 shows a falling off in the members to 19,478. This astonishing result is thus accounted for, in the work from which we continue to quote : *

" Yet, though at the first the prospects seemed to brighten, after a few years they grew worse. Many of the colored people purchased small lots of land, sometimes in the mountains, built cottages, and cultivated the ground for a living. Many left their old homes and sought employment elsewhere, often at a distance from the house of God. Many grew worldly-minded, made money the great object of their pursuit, and sought for happiness in earthly things. Some even returned to their vile heathenish practices, which, it was hoped, they had utterly forgotten."

In justice to our common humanity, it must be stated that —

" In some of the colonies, there were not only no persecuting laws, but the missionaries were greatly encouraged, both by the local government, and by the owners of slaves. Even in those islands where they met with persecution, they had many friends among the planters and others of the white inhabitants. Some built chapels on their estates,

---

* Encyclopædia of Missions.

and others subscribed handsomely to their erection in the neighborhood." *

It will now be apparent, that so far as the influence upon the blacks was concerned, the missionary success in Jamaica, while the work could be prosecuted peacefully, was fully equal to that of any other missions in any part of the heathen world. The history of these missions proves, that slaves are not rendered inaccessible to the Gospel, merely because of their subjection to slavery; but that, wherever the master favors the work, encouraging success is to be expected. When closely analyzed, the motives prompting British Christians to urge emancipation so vehemently, appear to have originated in the belief, not that the blacks were incapable of christianization under slavery, but that, while slavery prevailed, the masters would continue to interrupt the mission work, and thus render the conversion of the slaves impracticable.

It may be very easy, at this day, to point out defects in the measures of British Christians, for giving the Gospel to the West India slaves; but it must be remembered, that they were engaging in a work in which the lights of experience afforded no aid. Where the moral gloom appeared the darkest, there they first attempted to let in the rays of the Sun of Righteousness. Had the masters been first brought under the influence of the Gospel, like the christian master of Antigua, Mr. GILBERT, they would have been most efficient auxiliaries in the work of instruction among the negroes. All masters could not have become teachers, but all would have given the missionaries free access to their slaves. Under this state of things, British Christians would not have felt that emancipation was indispensable to the conversion of the blacks; and the churches, effecting their object under existing laws, would not have demanded the abolition of slavery. But the opposite course having been pursued — the throne having been invoked to constrain the masters, and force them to allow the instruction of their slaves — a position of antagonism was produced between the churches and the planters, producing re-

---

* Encyclopædia of Missions, p. 770.

sults, as we shall see, that have been ruinous to all the best interests of both whites and blacks.

Another subject needs examination here, as it is connected with the British theory that slavery is unfavorable to an increase of population.

Twenty-six years after England conquered the island of Jamaica, 1696, up to which time the importation of slaves still continued, the whites numbered 15,198, and the slaves 9,500. At the end of an additional forty-six years, 1742, during nearly the whole of which period the monopoly of the slave trade was held by England, the whites numbered 14,000, and the slaves 100,000. The annual importation of slaves into Jamaica, now reached 16,-000, so that at the end of another twenty-eight years, 1770, they numbered 200,000, while the whites had scarcely increased 2,000. These numbers show, that from 1742 to 1770, the number of slaves who sunk under the lash of the Jamaica task-master, must have been 248,000, or almost 9,000 annually. The whole number of slaves imported into this island by the English, up to 1808, when the slave trade was forbidden, was 850,000, to which must be added the 40,000 previously imported by the Spaniards, making the total number of Africans transported to Jamaica, amount to 890,000. And yet the startling truth must be told, that when the census was taken, in 1835, under the emancipation act, so as to determine the distribution of compensation to the masters, instead of there having been any increase on the numbers imported, they amounted to only 311,692.

But Jamaica was not alone in this wholesale destruction of human life. Taking the whole of the British West India Colonies, and the most astonishing results are presented. The total importation of slaves into these islands — including Jamaica — up to 1808, was 1,700,000, while the number left for emancipation, including their descendants, was but 660,000. *

Such are the leading facts upon which British philanthropists based their theories upon slavery, in its effects upon population and upon African evangelization. We shall again have occasion to refer to these theories.

---

* See Compend of U. S. Census, 1850, — also " Ethiopia."

But whence originated the white men, who so resolutely opposed the introduction of the Gospel into the West Indies, and impiously attempted to shut out the light of heaven from the darkened souls of its slaves ?　In answer to this question, we shall draw, briefly, upon the history of Jamaica, before referred to, by Rev. Mr. Phillippo, as a type of the whole:

" The Island of Jamaica, discovered in 1492, was settled by a colony of Spaniards in 1509, who, by their oppressions and savage cruelties, in less than fifty years wholly exterminated the native Indian population, originally numbering from 80,000 to 100,000.　African slaves seem to have been introduced at an early day as substitutes for the natives ; and up to 1655, when the English, then at war with Spain, took possession of the island, 40,000 slaves had been imported by the Spaniards, only 1,500 of whom were then surviving.　Jamaica, by this change of masters, was not much improved in its social and moral condition, which, under the 146 years of Spanish rule, had been deplorable.　It now became the rendezvous of buccaneers and piratical crusaders, a desperate band of men from all the maritime powers of Europe, who continued to perpetrate almost every degree of wickedness, both on sea and land, until 1760, when peace was made with Spain, and a more vigorous administration of law attempted."

The English people deduced four theories from the facts detailed :

1. That the Slave Trade is incompatible with African evangelization.

2. That Slavery, wherever it prevails, is adverse to an increase of population.

3. That Slavery presents an insuperable barrier to the evangelization of the Africans subjected to its control.

4. That Free Labor is more profitable than slave labor — the labor of one freeman, under the stimulus of wages, being more productive than that of two slaves, toiling under the dread of the lash.

These propositions we propose to examine, in detail, in the following pages, so as to judge of their applicability to American Slavery.

CHAPTER II.

EXAMINATION OF THE ERRORS IN THE BRITISH THEORIES, AS APPLIED TO AMERICAN SLAVERY BEFORE WEST INDIA EMANCIPATION.

In turning from the consideration of the results of British Colonial Slavery, to inquire into the results of American Slavery, * some very striking facts are presented, which show a well-marked diversity in the two systems. The theories entertained by the English, were of slow growth, and not fully adopted until near the period of West India Emancipation. To form a correct judgment in relation to American slavery, and to fairly contrast it with the British system, a period must be embraced of equal extent to that required to form the English theories. They were four in number, as stated in the close of the preceding chapter; and, with a view to the more distinct understanding of the whole of the questions to be examined, we may consider them in separate sections :

Section I. — That the Slave Trade is incompatible with African Evangelization.

This theory was fully sustained by the effects of the slave trade upon Africa itself. Looking at the question from that point of view alone, it was a logical deduction from the facts then revealed in the history of that traffic. It presented no redeeming trait in its character, and not a solitary circumstance connected with its prosecution, that tended, in the slightest degree, to work the least

---

* The term " American Slavery," unless otherwise stated, applies to that of the United States.

improvement in the moral condition of its subjects. On land, it greatly aggravated the warlike disposition of the natives, and caused the soil of Africa to whiten with human bones. In the holds of the slave ships, despair and death were ever present, and hope and joy never entered.

But when a broader view of the subject is taken, the hand of God is perceivable in this wonderful movement. Africa was sunk in the deepest moral darkness, and had wholly forgotten the only Creator. Among her gods were gods of blood, and human beings the offerings sacrificed upon their altars. Wars were waged to multiply captives, that the number of sacrifices might be enlarged, and the anger of the deities more fully appeased or their favor more certainly secured. The slave trader presented himself in the midst of the worshipers, and offered a price for the victims. Superstition, overpowered by cupidity, accepting gold instead of blood, dropped the sacrificial knife, and the devoted one gladly went into slavery to escape the impending horrible death.

The Portuguese took the lead among European nations in the traffic in slaves. The first experiment was made in 1442. It proved successful, and many private adventurers soon afterward embarked in the trade. In 1481, the king of Portugal, taking the title of Lord of Guinea, erected many forts on the African coast for the protection of the traffic. As early as 1503, a few negro slaves had been sent into St. Domingo; and, in 1511, Ferdinand had permitted them to be imported in great numbers. In 1518, some Genoese merchants, who had purchased the monopoly of the traffic in slaves from a favorite of Charles, commenced their transportation from Africa to America, * and brought the slave trade into that regular form which it long maintained. The French next obtained its monopoly, and kept it until it yielded them, according to Spanish official accounts, the sum of $204,-000,000. In 1713, the English, at the treaty of Utrecht, secured it for thirty years; but Spain, in 1739, purchased the British right, for the remaining four years, by the payment of $500,000. The Dutch also participated in the traffic; and, in 1620, intro-

---

* "America" here refers to the West Indies, Mexico, South America, Brazil, &c.

duced the first slaves into the North American Colonies. In 1808, the traffic in slaves was prohibited by both the United States and Great Britain.

In the earlier years of the slave trade, the Christian world was in no condition to send the Gospel to heathen lands. In 1516, says an eminent historian, "Religion was regarded only as an instrument of government." * The Reformation, then only beginning, was long in making such progress as enabled Protestant Christians to engage in attempts to propagate their religion. They were more concerned for themselves, and for their children, than for the world at large ; as it was long doubtful whether they could maintain their ground in opposition to the power wielded against them. These were days of darkness and discouragement, but light and hope at length arose, and Christians began to put on their armor to battle for the extension of the kingdom of Christ. It was not until near the close of the 18th century, that Christian missions were vigorously commenced, by some of the British churches; and it was only in 1812, that the first American missionaries went into their fields in Asia. Six years earlier, the father of our Foreign Missionary scheme, SAMUEL J. MILLS, recorded this memorable sentence : "I think I can trust myself in the hands of God, and all that is dear to me ; but I long to have the time arrive, when the Gospel shall be preached to the *poor Africans*." A few years later brought around the organization of the African Colonization Society ; and Mr. Mills offered himself, as an explorer, to find a highway for the colored man's return to the land of his fathers. He accomplished his object, 1817, only to find his grave, on the return voyage, in the midst of the sea.

The Christian Church had now become awakened to the importance of extending the Gospel to the heathen throughout the world. Asia, with its pagan inhabitants and its false religions, was not unknown to the Christians of Europe and America. But Africa, with its barbarous hordes and murderous religious rites, was known only to the slave trader. Much had to be learned in relation to the mode of conducting Christian missions. In turning over the historic page, it was found that —

---

* D'Aubigné's History of the Reformation.

" Christianity, at first, went wherever a preparation had been made for its reception by the scattering and settlement of the Jewish race, and by the preëxistent diffusion of the scriptures of the Old Testament, in the Greek language. Within *these* limits the Gospel seated itself, and there it held its position with more or less of continuity ; and beyond the same limits it was, indeed, carried forth, and it won its triumphs ; but soon it lost its hold ; soon it retreated, and disappeared, leaving only some scattered and scarcely appreciable fragments on its spots, to denote the course it had taken." *

If primitive Christianity could only sustain itself permanently, in the midst of the civilized races of men, what security was there that, in the 18th and 19th centuries, it could be extended among the barbarous tribes of Africa, or of any other country ? Whether the founders of modern missions had doubts upon this subject or not, they wisely resolved, in sending out missionaries, that the school and the church should be inseparable. This was the more necessary, as, in every field occupied, whether in Asia, Africa, the Islands of the Sea, or among the Indians of North America, a strange language had to be studied before the missionary could deliver his message of salvation.

But what was God doing, while man was thus tardily preparing for the evangelization of the world? British and American Christians, enjoying religious freedom, and using a common language, were the most active and zealous in promoting the work of missions. The slave trade had brought to their doors its thousands of thousands of Africans, who, under slavery, had been taught the English language, and were thus prepared to be instructed, directly, by the Christian teacher, who knew only his mother tongue. Many Christians, both English and American, beheld the hand of God in this movement, and accepted it as a Providential dispensation, bringing within their reach a race of men otherwise inaccessible to the Gospel. Others, equally devoted to the cause of Christ, and anxious to extend his kingdom among men, consecrated themselves to the work in Africa itself. The barbarism of that benighted people was thus assailed at the two extremes. In the West Indies the teachers were few, and met

---

* Isaac Taylor's Wesley and Methodism, p. 293.

with opposition; while, in the United States they were numerous, with none to interrupt their labors. The results among the enslaved Africans were most encouraging; but the results in Africa itself were not so successful. The efforts to plant the Gospel in that barbarous land led to the discovery of many facts of significant import, which convey lessons of instruction not to be overlooked. The climate of Africa proved itself so unfavorable to the health of white men, that only a few of the missionaries could labor long in that field. It was farther found, that the men and women of mature years were incapable of comprehending moral or religious truths; and that, from the degraded condition of the population, it was impracticable to elevate the youth to the practice of a sound christian morality, except by carefully excluding them from the society of the natives. To do this, the teacher had to exert a despot's power, as the only means of restraining them from the ways of evil. He had to limit their liberties, as the only means by which he could preserve their morals. To let them run at will, rendered his teachings powerless for good, and ensured their moral destruction. * These results were nothing new in the history of the workings of fallen human nature. Neglected children, in the midst of a vicious population, whatever their color, always run to ruin. No exemption from the workings of this law prevails in Africa, any more than in other lands; on the contrary, the fatal results, in that country, to the unrestrained youth, are only the more certain, because of the greater degradation of its population.

These facts include lessons of grave importance. God rules among the children of men. He, alone, knows how to carry out measures sufficiently broad to secure the accomplishment of his purposes. He seemed to have decreed the redemption of Africa. To effect that work, it was necessary that Africans themselves should be educated for the execution of the task: for in its climate the white man sickens and dies, where the black man may dwell in safety. The slave trader carried away the sons of Africa, and placed them in contact with British and American civilization; where the restraints of slavery forced them to ac-

---

* See the Report of Bishop Scott, on his return from Liberia.

quire a knowledge of agriculture, mechanical arts, literature, science, and religion. The hand of God is as plainly discernible in this dispensation of his Providence, towards the African race, as it was in sending Jacob into Egypt with his sons, and permitting the enslavement of their posterity, that they might afterward rise above their former pastoral condition. Without the knowledge of the arts, sciences, and agriculture, acquired by them under Egyptian slavery, the people of Israel never could have become a great nation.

Such is precisely the condition of the black race of men. Africa had slumbered on, for thousands of years, in sloth and pollution. The slave trade came as a means of mental excitation to her people. Carried away from a life of indolence to one of active industry, the intellect of the negro became awakened under the very chains which bound him. Visited by the disciples of Jesus, he found that human sympathy was a reality. Amazed at the discovery, he listened with joy to the story of redeeming love. Convinced, from past experience, that mankind are in open rebellion against God, and that each individual heart is depraved and sinful, he willingly accepted the offered salvation. This accomplished, that same Providence which permitted the slave trader to bring him away from Africa, now influences the master's heart to send his Christian slave back to the land of his fathers, with the tidings of salvation to its people. *

Again, we repeat: Providence, unquestionably, designs to teach a lesson to Christians, by the permission of the African slave trade and African slavery By the introduction of these two

---

* Among the Episcopal missionaries who went to Abbeokuta, in 1846, was the Rev. Samuel Crowther, a native of Yoruba, who had been captured by the Fellatahs, in 1821, and sold to the traders at Lagos. Shipped on board a slaver for Brazil, recaptured by an English cruizer, educated at Sierra Leone, ordained to the ministry of the Gospel in England, he had now returned, after twenty-five years of absence from his native land, to proclaim the way of salvation to his relatives and countrymen; and he had the inexpressible gratification of finding his mother and two sisters, soon after his arrival, and of being instrumental in the conversion of his mother to Christianity. "Ethiopia," p. 215.

Mr. Crowther, although carried off by the slave traders, was never enslaved—being recaptured before reaching Brazil. Other similar instances have occurred, where the captives have returned, after having endured many years of slavery.

great elements of progress, into connection with modern civilization, not only were the Christian nations awakened to the importance of commerce and manufactures, as means of national aggrandizement, but they were made acquainted with the condition of Africa and its population. The abject state of its people was not the effect of their subjection to a superior race; but the deep degradation into which they had sunk was the result of their own doings. The slave trade, in some respects, had rendered African society less bloody in its customs, while in others, perhaps, it had increased its rapacity. But all these things were to be swept away before the dawn of the millennial glory, and the Gospel brought to bear upon Africa as upon other lands. How was this to be done? The fatality of its climate to the white man, would effectually prevent his rendering much aid in the work, as a resident missionary. And, again, the delays that would be imposed upon him, in the study of a new language, would increase the difficulties attending the introduction of the Gospel among that people. Foreseeing these, and all other obstacles to African evangelization, as also the action of the Church in behalf of the African race, events, under Providence, were so ordered, that the barbarian was brought to the Christian, instead of awaiting the tardier and more dangerous plan of the Christian going to the barbarian.

But this was not all. The removal of the African from his own country, to take his place beside the christian teacher, in a distant land, so far anticipated the awakening of the Church to a sense of her duty, that the slave, using a foreign tongue, was taught the Christian's language, and prepared to comprehend the teachings of the Gospel, before the message of salvation reached his ears. Here was a very mysterious providence, requiring not the aids of inspiration for its interpretation. And more than this was effected. These children of Africa, instead of roving hither and thither at will, were compelled to remain, from year to year, on the same estates, thus allowing each succeeding Sabbath to present the same persons to the religious teacher — a condition of restraint that could not be secured in Africa, and which, attended with Christian instruction, was more favorable to moral improvement than any elsewhere afforded to the colored race.

And, yet, there were those in the United States, as well as in the West Indies, who refused to accept this providential revelation of the Divine will to the Church. But this refusal was from very different motives, and by very different classes of persons. In the West Indies, the opposition to giving Christian instruction to the blacks, came from the slave owners; in the United States, it came from the ministers of the Gospel. In the former case, it has been reckoned as purely Satanic in its origin; in the latter, its results have been sufficiently disastrous to indicate that it had a similarity of origin. With us, whole denominations, nearly, shrunk back from the task of giving the Gospel to the slaves, except on condition that the master would first set them free. This was not exactly the form of the proposition, but practically it amounted to the same thing. In the early days of slavery, there were no regular missionaries, as now, among the blacks. The ministers could not be supported except by the patronage of the master; and he would not pay a ministry that cast him out of the church. The ministers, therefore, had to leave, and both master and slave were suffered to remain without the means of grace; or, else, were forced to seek some other denominational connection, where their relations were understood and recognized.

And what has been the history of these religious bodies, who thus refused the Gospel to the poor barbarian slave, unless they could, at the same time, place him on terms of legal equality with his civilized master? What has become of these professed ambassadors of Christ, who could stand aside and see the poor bondman sink to perdition, without offering him the salvation that would lead him to heaven, except on the condition that they could first secure to him his personal freedom on earth? We shall call upon one of the aged ministers of the Gospel, to answer this question.* He once took the lead, as we shall see hereafter, in the anti-slavery movement in his Church. In the *Christian Instructor,* of Philadelphia, October, 1861, we find him saying:

"The truth must be spoken at all hazards. There is but 'one body;' Christ has but one Church on earth. But it is sadly rent and dis-

---

* Rev. David McDill, D. D., now of Illinois.

figured by divisions, so that it does not appear to be ' one.' Its glory is sadly sullied with envying and strife.

"And the divisions, and their accompanying envyings and strifes, have been greatly multiplied within the last half century, though we have been accustomed to regard it as the era of Bible and Missionary Societies, as well as of greatly increased Christian activity and enterprise. The writer can look back to a time within his remembrance, when there was one Baptist, one Methodist, one Associate, one Associate Reformed, one Reformed, and one General Assembly Presbyterian Church.

"How is it now—how has it been during the period of which we have just spoken? The Baptist Church has divided into three parties, the Methodists into three, the Associate into three, the Associate Reformed into three or four, the Reformed into four, the General Assembly Presbyterian into six, viz: The Cumberland Presbyterians, the Old School Presbyterians, the New School Presbyterians, the Free Church Presbyterians, the Old School Presbyterians South, and the New School Presbyterians South. True, some of these parties continued but for a little time, but still, they were divisions, and they existed long enough to produce some strife, and some scandal. Instead of preaching Christ, and him crucified, they were under a kind of necessity which led them too often to inveigh against the errors and corruptions of all the others, especially of those who came the nearest to themselves in faith and practice, and from whom they had separated, to convince all that the schism was not causeless, and that they were the only party or ' church' which was fashioned according to the pattern shown in the Mount. Thus the attention of many was, in a sad degree, directed to some 'peculiarities,' and turned away from the vital truths of the Gospel. Without inquiring who was to blame, or who was not to blame, for causing these divisions, have we not reason to regard Christ as addressing us—we mean the body of professing Christians—and putting the question to our consciences : Whereas, there are among you envying, and strife, and divisions, are ye not carnal? . . . . . . We are not to look for much more Christian union, till the Church in all her branches become less carnal and more spiritual."

But lest any one should imagine, as some have done, that the advancement made by the negro race under slavery is a necessary result of that system, and is not due, alone, to the Christian instruction they have received, in connection with slavery, it is only necessary to refer to the condition of the slaves in those countries where they have not enjoyed the teachings of the Gospel. In all such cases, their barbarism is yet complete, and they are left as monuments to admonish Christendom that nothing, save their careful moral instruction, can ever elevate them to the level of the civilized races. Indeed, before this volume is complete, it will be demonstrated, that freedom and slavery are both alike powerless in the redemption of the African race, where careful Christian training is not employed; and more than this will be proved, as the facts will show that, in their present condition, wherever freedom prevails, and they are left unprotected and un-restrained, they are, generally, so far incapable of caring for themselves and their offspring, that they are every where tending to extinction, instead of advancing in numbers and intelligence.

It would seem, then, that THE MISSION OF THE SLAVE TRADE, considered in a Providential point of view, when all the facts before us are taken into account, has been to bring African bar-barism into contact with Christian civilization, as a preliminary step toward the ultimate evangelization of the negro race. Nor has this work of negro instruction been required, without an equivalent being rendered. The contact of civilization and bar-barism, in this case, has been of such a nature as to be of the greatest possible advantage, in an economical point of view, for a long series of years, to the nations engaged in tropical and sub-tropical cultivation; and it was only after centuries had elapsed, during which the moral instruction of the negroes had been neglected, that the nations so acting were deprived of their slaves, and their tropical possessions involved in ruin. A noted example is found in the loss of Hayti by the French; and an equally strik-ing one exists in England's losses in her West India colonies. In these islands, the planters very generally refused the religious teacher any access to their slaves; and a whirlwind of excitement raised in England, nearly three hundred years after the introduc-tion of slavery, swept away their property interest in the black man forever.

The United States, as we shall see, has most fully met the designs of Providence in permitting the slave trade; as from the first, the religious instruction of the slaves has been an object of attention. Nor has she been content with the home instruction only of her slaves. By means of the Colonization Society, she has taken the preliminary steps necessary to the ultimate evan-gelization of Africa, thus aiming at obeying the teachings of Providence, as connected with the permission of the slave trade to the civilized nations.

But we must conclude our remarks on this head. The theory under consideration — that the slave trade is incompatible with African evangelization — may be considered as sustained, only so far as its direct action upon Africa is concerned; but it is subject to modifications, so far as relates to its indirect action, and sup-plies a grand example of the manner in which the Almighty can bring good out of evil. The history of the slave trade, while revealing to us the heaven-daring wickedness of the people of Africa, affords a striking illust tion of the general truth, that when God has designs of mercy toward a wicked people, He visits them with judgments which are adapted to secure their repent-ance and lead them back to Himself.

SECTION II.—THAT SLAVERY, WHEREVER IT PREVAILS, IS AD-VERSE TO AN INCREASE OF POPULATION. *

A brief review of the history of American Slavery, will demon-strate that this theory is not of general application, however true it may have been as applied to British Colonial Slavery.

The act of Congress prohibiting the slave trade, took effect in 1808. The act of the British Parliament, to the same effect, went into operation at the same time. The two nations made an equal start in attempting to arrest that traffic. The importation of slaves into the United States, at this date, including the periods before and after their independence, was about 400,000.† The importation into the British West Indies, including the period in which they were under Spanish rule, was 1,700,000. ‡   After

---

* The reader may not understand the laws of population; it may, therefore, be remarked, that in all prosperous communities, the births are from four to six per cent. per annum, and the deaths from two to three per cent., giving an increase, annually, of from two to three per cent. to the population.

† Compend. of U. S. Census, 1850.

‡ Of this number the Spaniards imported 40,000.

1808, the traffic in slaves could no longer be prosecuted under the sanction of law in either country, and their importation was discontinued.

The United States census for 1830, shows that our African population at that date had increased to 2,328,642, of whom 319,599 were freemen, being an *increase* on the 400,000 originally imported of more than 1,900,000. The census of the British West Indies, taken in 1835, under the emancipation act, shows that these islands, at that date, had a negro population of only 660,000, being a *decrease* of more than 1,000,000 on the number originally imported. *

From these facts, the difference in the American and the British systems of slavery, in their effects upon the increase of population, can be readily inferred; and it will be easy to perceive, also, how the American and the Englishman — like the two knights of old, when looking at the opposite sides of the bi-colored shield — should have adopted antagonistic theories on this question.

It is only in the light of these facts, that any satisfactory explanation can be given, why that eminent philanthropist, Sir THOMAS FOWELL BUXTON, in 1831, when commenting on the enormous decrease of the slave population in the West Indies, should have employed this language:

"Where the blacks are free they increase. But let there be a change in only one circumstance, let the population be the same in every respect, only let them be slaves instead of freemen, and the current is immediately stopped." †

Here is the theory of a British philanthropist, based upon the workings of slavery under British rule. Must the American accept this theory, because a philanthropist is its author? Must he let it pass unquestioned, while five distinct American census returns stamp it as erroneous? Why did not Mr. BUXTON examine these returns, before announcing his theory? Why did he not state the true cause of the constant decrease of the slave

---

* See Compend. of U. S. Census, 1850.
† North British Review, August, 1848.

population in the West Indies, and its corresponding rapid increase in the United States? The cause of this difference in
results, could have been easily explained. In the West Indies,
the disparity in the sexes, and the neglect of infants, produced a
continuous decrease of population; while in the United States,
the care taken of infants by white women, and the equality of
the sexes among the slaves, produced the enormous increase given
above. Added to this, was another feature in the history of the
two systems of slavery — the British and American — which
marks, in a striking manner, their difference of effect upon human
life. Before the cultivation of cotton and sugar had assumed
any very prominent position in the commerce of the United
States — indeed, before any regular exports of cotton had commenced — provision had been made for the abolition of the slave
trade. The American planter, therefore, when regular exports
had commenced, and were rapidly increasing, was placed in a
position in which his reliance for an increase of labor had to
depend, entirely, on the natural increase of his slaves already in
possession. And, even had he been desirous of greatly increasing his laborers, by importations from Africa, between the periods
of the adoption of the Constitution and the prohibition of the
slave trade, he could not have done so, as the Revolution had left
him too little money to effect that object. The care of the slave
children thus became a matter of great importance to the American master. Quite different, however, was the situation in which
the English planter had been placed in the West Indies. There,
for a century before the prohibition of the traffic in slaves, tropical cultivation by slave labor had been conducted with great
profit. To secure to herself the advantages of this cultivation,
Great Britain, in 1713, by the treaty of Utrecht, obtained the
monopoly of the slave trade for thirty years. The great activity
with which the traffic was prosecuted, at this period, is referred
to elsewhere. Such was the ease, then, with which slaves could
be procured from Africa, that it became much less expensive to
import them, than to raise them on the plantations. The labor
of the mother in the field was vastly more valuable than her
services in the nursery. Again, as the most aggravated feature
in the whole system, it was found that, by over-working, a slave

could be made to produce as much in four or five years, as, by ordinary labor, he would do in eight or ten. The aim of the planter — or rather of his overseer, the owner of the estate being usually a non-resident — was, therefore, to get the greatest possible amount of work out of the slave in the least possible time !

Such was West India slavery as compared with that of America. It will now be apparent to the most superficial thinker, that the theory under consideration received a sad proof of its truth in the history of British Colonial slavery; but that it is wholly untrue, as applied to the slavery of the United States.

SECTION III.—THAT SLAVERY PRESENTS AN INSUPERABLE BARRIER TO THE EVANGELIZATION OF THE AFRICANS SUBJECTED TO ITS CONTROL.

We shall limit the investigations under this head, in the present chapter, to the period preceding West India Emancipation, so that the contrast between British slavery and American slavery, as retarding or promoting the conversion of the colored people, can be more clearly made out, and the differences in the results be better understood. When this is done, the contrast can be continued in another chapter; so as to show the difference in the missionary success under freedom, in the West Indies and other parts of the world, and under slavery in the United States. The claims set up for emancipation as an economical measure, must also be considered, in connection with the question of its moral advantages.

More than this, however, will be necessary, to illustrate the whole of the bearings of American slavery, and to determine whether, in the present condition of the colored people, their subjection to servitude does or does not present a barrier to their christianization. This point, fortunately, can be determined more readily in connection with American slavery, than with the operations of the system of African bondage anywhere else; because the work of emancipation began, in the United States, at an early day, and soon a large number of colored people, in a state of freedom, appeared in the community. Thus, the two classes — slaves and freemen — have existed together ever since the origin of the government — the first census, in 1790, showing a free colored population of nearly 60,000. The fact that a large portion of the freedmen have been wholly separated from the slave population, by a geographical line, makes the task of tracing the results the more easily performed. In this field of investigation, as well as in that concerning the West Indies, many collateral topics must be introduced, in illustration of the subject under consideration. The character of these discussions may be inferred from the following statement of the subjects examined:

1. The Christian character of the early immigrants of the North American Colonies; their estimate of the influence of barbarism upon free institutions; and the diversity of the means adopted to avoid the evils anticipated by an increase of the negro population.

2. Opinions of Revolutionary statesmen upon the subject of negro slavery, and the propriety and prospects of general emancipation.

3. Effects of emancipation upon the negroes of the United States, previous to the period of West India Emancipation.

4. Contrast of the results of freeing the blacks in the North, with the continuation of them in slavery in the South.

5. Deductions from the facts stated.

With this approximate statement of the topics to be examined, we may proceed with our investigations:

1. *The Christian character of the early immigrants of the North American Colonies; their estimate of the influence of barbarism upon free institutions; and the diversity of the means adopted to avoid the evils anticipated by an increase of the negro population.*

As, in closing the preceding chapter, the godless character of the white settlers in Jamaica is referred to as contributing, mainly, to the hindrance of the Christian missions among its black population, so, in approaching the investigation of the facts relating to the favorable influence which American Slavery has exerted over the cause of the Gospel among our African population, it will be necessary to refer to the Christian character of the early white settlers of this country, as contributing, chiefly, to the greater success here.

Like the white settlers of Jamaica, numbers of the earlier emigrants to America, were exiles from the country of their birth — not as criminals, self-exiled, to escape the punishment justly due for crime, but exiles on account of their religious belief. The intolerant zeal for religious uniformity, prevailing in Europe, compelled many of its population to flee from persecution to this country, where they could worship God according to the dictates of their own consciences. No lengthened eulogy of these men is needed — the Christian character of the majority of them being a matter of history. With them the school house and the church — the sources of intelligence and morality — were objects of the first importance. They believed that the perpetuity of the free institutions they hoped to found, would depend, not upon any magic in the mere possession of freedom, but in the intelligence and morality of their posterity.

These were not the men to deny the Gospel to any human being. On the contrary, the Indian and the African both received attention, and both were instructed in the Christian faith. But while they labored for the moral elevation of these children of barbarism, they refused to admit them to the privileges of citizenship. No morbid sentimentality, upon the subject of human rights, could induce them to overlook the dangers into which they might precipitate themselves, by conferring upon savage men, or even the half-civilized, equal privileges in the government of the country.

Time rolled on, and the period of the American Revolution approached. The slave trade, forced upon the colonies by the mother country, was revealing, more and more, the difficulties attendant upon the presence of a barbarous population in the midst of a civilized people. At the North, where slave labor in the field proved to be profitless, it was felt to be a grievous burden. So fully had this sentiment fixed itself upon the public mind, especially in the northern colonies, that there was no difficulty in securing an expression of opinion hostile to the slave trade. It was not so much because the negroes were held as slaves, that the colonists objected to their importation, as because their barbarism presented a barrier to the prosperity of the country. This was the true state of public opinion.

An opportunity for the expression of these sentiments was presented, when the Boston Port Bill passed the British Parliament. All commerce was at once destroyed, and various meetings were immediately called, to consider the best plan to be pursued for the redress of grievances. The measures finally adopted, by the colonies, were designed mainly to be retaliatory upon the commerce of Great Britain. Accompanying the resolutions adopted by the Colonists generally, were another class of resolutions upon the question of the slave trade. These were passed in many of the counties of Virginia, in some of the Colonial conventions, and, finally, in those of the Continental Congress, in which the slave trade, and the purchase of additional slaves, were specially referred to as measures to be at once discontinued. In substance they declare, as the sentiment of the people :

"That the African trade is injurious to the colonies; that it obstructs the population of them by freemen; that it prevents the immigration of manufacturers and other useful emigrants from Europe from settling among them; that it is dangerous to virtue and the welfare of the population; that it occasions an annual increase of the balance of trade against them; that they most earnestly wished to see an entire stop put to such a wicked, cruel, and unlawful traffic; that they would not purchase any slaves hereafter to be imported; nor hire their vessels, nor sell their commodities or manufactures to those who are concerned in their importation. South Carolina and Georgia did not follow the example of Virginia; and North Carolina, in resolving against the slave trade, but acquiesced in the non-intercourse policy, until the grievances complained of should be remedied." *

The plan adopted by the Colonists, to force Great Britain to terms, included the policy of non-intercourse. Her foreign commerce had then a value of but *eighty millions of dollars per annum*, nearly one-half of which, directly and indirectly, was dependent upon her North American and West India colonies, and the African slave trade. The colonies resolved not to import or consume any British manufactures, or West India products; and not to export to the mother country, or the West Indies, any

* Cotton is King embraces, in detail, the facts on this subject.

of their own productions. *   The non-importation of negroes formed a part of this policy.

" The North American colonies could not have devised a measure so alarming to Great Britain, and so well calculated to force Parliament into the repeal of her obnoxious laws, as this policy of non-intercourse. It would deprive the West Indies of their ordinary supplies of provisions, and force them to suspend their usual cultivation, to produce their own food.   It would cause not only the cessation of imports from Great Britain into the West Indies, on account of the inability of its people to pay, but would, at once, check all demand for slaves, both in the sugar islands and in North America — thus creating a loss to the mother country, in the African trade alone, of three and a half millions of dollars, and putting in peril one-half of the commerce of England." †

These details are necessary to enable the reader to understand the true nature of the opposition to the slave trade existing at that period.

Another remark, in this connection, upon a different point: That the emancipation of the negroes was not contemplated by those, in general, who voted for the non-intercourse resolutions, is evident from the subsequent action of Virginia, where the greater portion of the meetings were held.   They could not have intended to enfranchise men, whom they declared to be obstacles in the way of public prosperity, and as dangerous to the morals of the people.   Nor could the signers of the Declaration of Independence have designed to include the Indians and negroes, in the assertion that " all men are created equal; " because these same men, in afterwards adopting the Constitution, deliberately excluded the Indians from citizenship, and forever fixed the negro in a condition of servitude, under that Constitution, by including him, as a slave, in the article fixing the ratio of Congressional representation on the basis of five negroes equaling three white men.   The phrase — " all men are created equal " — could, therefore, have meant nothing more than the declaration of a general principle, asserting the equality of the Colonists, before God, with those who claimed it as a divine right to lord it over them.   The Indians were men as well as the negroes.   Both

* See American Archives, vol. I.   † Cotton is King, page 233, 3d edition.

were within the territory over which the United Colonies claimed jurisdiction. The exclusion of both from citizenship, under the Constitution, is conclusive that neither was intended to be embraced in the Declaration of Independence, with any reference to their admission to an equality with the whites, in the government about to be established.

The successful issue of the American Revolution, left the people highly elated with their achievement. Exalted ideas of the value of personal freedom prevailed, and its power in remedying all human ills was believed to be almost omnipotent. Every measure, therefore, which promised an enlargement of human liberty, was readily accepted by the public. For a time, the maxims of the fathers — that intelligence and morality are essential to the success of free government — seem to have been overlooked. This, however, was true only in reference to the North; and even there, the public sympathy was not extended to the Indian, but limited to the negro.

It was under these circumstances, and during the prevalence of these opinions, that the Legislatures of the Northern States commenced their legislation on the subject of slavery. The Revolution had closed, the treaty of peace had been signed, Sept. 3, 1783, and the new Constitution adopted, March 4, 1789.

In 1780, Pennsylvania and Massachusetts passed their measures for the abolition of slavery : the latter by a Constitutional provision, and the former by a legislative act — the one making emancipation *immediate*, the other *gradual*. Eight years later, Connecticut and Rhode Island followed their example. The work of emancipation, begun by the four States named, continued to progress, so that in fifteen years from the adoption of the Federal Constitution, New Hampshire, Vermont, New York, and New Jersey had also enacted laws to free themselves from slavery — some of them by the immediate and others by the gradual system. *

---

* Dates of Emancipation in the United States:
    Pennsylvania, on March 1, 1780, by Act of Legislature.
    Massachusetts, on March 2, 1780, by Court.
    Connecticut, on March 1, 1784, by Legislature.
    Rhode Island, on March 1, 1784, by Legislature.

The earlier legislation of the Churches occurred in connection with these schemes of State emancipation. In the measures adopted by the ecclesiastical courts, generally, they only aimed at a friendly coöperation with the civil authorities. But while this was substantially the case, they, at the same time, used language of general application, guarding it, however, by exceptions as to the States which had not passed emancipation laws.

The clergymen of the South readily acquiesced in the measures proposed. As ambassadors of Christ, they were to proclaim his Gospel to fallen men. Where no hindrance existed to the performance of their duties, they were not concerned about the repeal or modification of civil laws. As they were not required by their northern brethren to unchurch believing slaveholders, or to make war upon the institutions of the Southern States, they were perfectly willing to allow northern clergymen, in turn, the fullest latitude in their experiments upon the negro at the North. So long as they of the South were exempted from the rules adopted on slavery, they cared not what terms of church fellowship were imposed at the North. *

It was a great problem that was about to be solved. Could the negro population be rendered more accessible to the Gospel by freedom, or would the restraints of slavery, properly regulated, afford equal advantages in laboring for their conversion. The test, so far as it had been made in the West Indies, where the planters opposed the missionaries, had been unfavorable to the theory that slavery might not be adverse to the work of the Gospel among the blacks; but this did not discourage efforts at the South, where the masters acknowledged their Christian obligations, and were willing to have the precepts of religion taught to their slaves.

Practically, the question at issue between the ecclesiastics of the North and the South was this: Can the negro be evangelized while in slavery? Southern clergymen accepted the challenge,

New Hampshire, on Feb. 8, 1792, by Legislature.
Vermont, on July 4, 1793, by Constitution.
New York, on July 4, 1799, by Legislature.
New Jersey, on July 4, 1804, by Legislature.
* See the Rules of the Methodist Church, on a subsequent page.

and, to test this question, proceeded to enlarge their fields of operation for the conversion of the slaves. They did this the more confidently, because they were not about to enter upon an untried experiment. Already had the Gospel made considerable progress among the blacks. The Methodists, in 1793, report 16,227 colored members in their churches, while, in 1787, they had but 1,890 — such had been their rapid increase. From some cause, perhaps the working of the emancipation laws, the membership was reduced, in 1795, to 12,170.*

From other denominations we have no regular statistics for this period. In the history of the Presbyterians, however, it is stated that the work of the religious instruction of the blacks had been commenced as early as 1747, in Virginia, with very encouraging success. In one congregation in that State, in 1755, about 500 colored members are reported, and about an equal number in another congregation. In a third congregation, some time later, 200 are reported, for the care of whom black men had been ordained as elders. It is further stated, that multitudes of the colored people, in different places, were willingly and eagerly desirous to be instructed in religion.†

2. *Opinions of Revolutionary Statesmen upon the subject of Negro Slavery, and the propriety and prospects of Emancipation.*

Before proceeding to contrast the results of the efforts, North and South, in behalf of the blacks, it may be well to notice, more at large, the opinions entertained, in relation to the negro race and the propriety of emancipation, by some of our statesmen, subsequent to the Revolution.

---

* See Minutes of Conferences of the Methodist Episcopal Church. The statistics of the Methodist Episcopal Church, as presented in the published Minutes of that denomination, first separate the colored from the white members in 1787. From this date to 1795, the returns are given by congregations, as follows:

In 1787,	- -	1,890 members.	In 1792,	- -	13,871 members.
" 1788,	- - -	6,545 "	" 1793,	- - -	16,227 "
" 1789,	- -	8,243 "	" 1794,	- -	13,814 "
" 1790,	- - -	11,682 "	" 1795,	- - -	12,170 "
" 1791,	- -	12,884 "			

† Hand Book of the Slavery Question, by Rev. John Robinson.

On the question of negro equality, by emancipation, and the social and civil commingling of the two races, black and white, Mr. Jefferson took negative ground. He was inclined to consider the African inferior "in the endowments both of body and mind" to the European; and, while expressing his hostility to slavery earnestly, vehemently, he avowed the opinion that it was impossible for the two races to live equally free in the same government — that "nature, habit, opinion, had drawn indelible lines of distinction between them" — that accordingly, emancipation and "deportation" (colonization) should go hand in hand — and that these processes should be gradual enough to make proper provisions for the blacks in a new country, and fill their places in this with free white laborers. *

That Mr. Jefferson was considered as having no settled plans or views in relation to the disposal of the blacks, and that he was disinclined to risk the disturbance of the harmony of the country for the sake of the negro, appears evident from the opinions entertained of him and his schemes by John Quincy Adams. After speaking of the zeal of Mr. Jefferson, and the strong manner in which, at times, he had spoken against slavery, Mr. Adams says: "But Jefferson had not the spirit of martyrdom. He would have introduced a flaming denunciation of slavery into the Declaration of Independence, but the discretion of his colleagues struck it out. He did insert a most eloquent and impassioned argument against it in his Notes on Virginia; but, on that very account, the book was published almost against his will. He projected a plan of general emancipation, in his revision of the Virginia laws, but finally presented a plan leaving slavery precisely where it was; and, in his Memoir, he leaves a posthumous warning to the planters that they must, at no distant day, emancipate their slaves, or that worse will follow; but he withheld the publication of his prophecy till he should himself be in the grave." †

Mr. Jefferson was not alone in his views of the difficulties attending emancipation. Dr. Franklin, in 1789, as President of

---

* Randall's Life of Jefferson, vol. I, page 370.
† Life of John Quincy Adams, pages 177, 178.

the PENNSYLVANIA ABOLITION SOCIETY, issued an appeal for aid to enable his society to form a plan for the promotion of industry, intelligence, and morality among the free blacks, and he zealously urged the measure on public attention, as essential to their well-being, and indispensable to the safety of society. He expressed his belief, that such is the debasing influence of slavery on human nature, that its very extirpation, if not performed with care, may sometimes open a source of serious evils; and that so far as emancipation should be promoted by the society, it was a duty incumbent on its members to instruct, to advise, to qualify those restored to freedom, for the exercise and enjoyment of civil liberty.

The state of public sentiment, at this period, on the subject of emancipation, was stated by Mr. Jefferson, January 24, 1786, in his answers to questions propounded by M. de Meuisner:

" I conjecture there are 650,000 negroes in the five Southern States, and not over 50,000 in the rest. In most of these latter, effectual measures have been taken for their future emancipation. In the former, nothing is done toward that. The disposition to emancipate them is strongest in Virginia. Those who desire it, form, as yet, the minority of the whole State, but it bears a respectable portion of the whole in numbers and weight of character, and it is continually re-cruiting by the addition of nearly the whole of the young men as fast as they come into public life. I flatter myself it will take place there at some period of time not very distant. In Maryland and North Carolina a very few are disposed to emancipation. In South Carolina and Georgia, not the smallest symptom of it, but, on the contrary, these two States, and North Carolina, continue importations of slaves. These have long been prohibited in all the other States." *

These statements of Mr. Jefferson, made the year preceding the founding of Sierra Leone, contradict the claims set up in modern times, that the sentiments of the fathers of the Republic, were almost unanimously in favor of emancipation. Dr. Franklin, too, as above quoted, while favoring emancipation, was convinced that many difficulties and dangers surrounded that policy, both to the negroes themselves and to society, unless the means of instruction should accompany their admission to freedom.

* Jefferson's Complete Works, vol. IX, page 290.

Time has shown that the views of Dr. Franklin were the most rational of all those who wrote upon the subject of emancipation.

3. *Effects of Freedom upon the Negroes of the United States, previous to West India Emancipation.*

The tone of the ecclesiastical legislation, up to 1830, will be seen by reference to the chapters on that subject. It was conservative in its character, generally, and in some instances agreed with the opinions expressed by Franklin. But it partook of the foreign type, strongly indicating that the disposition of clergymen to interfere in civil affairs, would be the same here, in this free government, that it had been in Europe for centuries past. Yet, notwithstanding this zeal for emancipation, the moral culture of the free colored people, may be said to have been almost totally neglected; and their degradation, throughout the North, had become so much a matter of public notoriety, as to lead to the adoption of Colonization, as the only hope of their elevation. Their separation from the whites was considered essential to their moral redemption. This had become the prevalent sentiment from 1816 to 1830. Why had this opinion been adopted? Why had not the moral progress of the blacks kept pace with their advancement in personal freedom? Leaving these questions to the reader, we shall proceed to the statement of the results which followed the emancipation of the blacks :

"How far Franklin's influence failed to promote the humane object he had in view, may be inferred from the fact that, forty-seven years after Pennsylvania passed her act of emancipation, and thirty-eight after he issued his appeal, *one-third* of the convicts in her penitentiary were colored men ; though the preceding census showed that her slave population had almost wholly disappeared—there being but *two hundred and eleven* of them remaining, while her free colored people had increased in number to more than *thirty thousand*. Few of the other free States were more fortunate, and some of them were even in a worse condition—*one-half* of the convicts in the penitentiary of New Jersey being colored men.

"But this is not the whole of the sad tale that must be recorded. Gloomy as was the picture of crime among the colored people of New Jersey, that of Massachusetts was vastly worse. For though the number of her colored convicts, as compared with the whites, was as *one to six*, yet the proportion of her colored population in the penitentiary was *one* out of *one hundred and forty*, while the proportion in New Jersey was but *one* out of *eight hundred and thirty-three*. Thus, in Massachusetts, where emancipation had, in 1780, been *immediate* and unconditional, there was, in 1826, among her colored people, about six times as much crime as existed among those of New Jersey, where *gradual* emancipation had not been provided for until 1804." *

The moral condition of the colored people in the free States, generally, at the period we are considering, may be understood, more clearly, from the opinions expressed, at the time, by the *Boston Prison Discipline Society.* This benevolent association included among its members, Rev. Francis Wayland, Rev. Justin Edwards, Rev. Leonard Woods, Rev. William Jenks, Rev. B. B. Wisner, Rev. Edward Beecher, Lewis Tappan, Esq., John Tappan, Esq., Hon. George Bliss, and Hon. Samuel M. Hopkins.

The first annual report of this Association was made in 1826, the second in 1827. In discussing the progress of crime, with the causes of it, they give the first place to the degraded character of the colored population; and, from the facts stated, derive an argument in favor of their education. They mention, also, as a remarkable fact, that about *one-fourth* part of all the expense incurred, by the several States mentioned, is for the colored convicts; and argue, that, if their character can not be raised, where they are, a powerful argument is thereby afforded in favor of colonization. The statistics presented by the society, enable us to state the proportion of the whole population sent to the penitentiary, with the proportion of the colored population imprisoned therein, for 1826, in the five States named below, and the proportion of the colored to the white convicts:

	Proportion of the Population sent to Prison.	*Proportion of the Colored Popu'on sent to Prison.*	*Proportion of Color'd to white conv'ts.*
In Massachusetts, - -	1 out of 1665	1 out of 140	1 to 6
In Connecticut, - -	1 out of 2350	1 out of 205	1 to 3
In New York, - -	1 out of 2153	1 out of 253	1 to 4
In New Jersey, - -	1 out of 3743	1 out of 833	1 to 3
In Pennsylvania, - -	1 out of 2191	1 out of 181	1 to 3

* Cotton is King, page 37.

The second report shows that, in New Jersey, the proportion of the colored convicts to the white convicts was *one* to *two*, while the proportion of the colored population to the white was *one to thirteen*. In Massachusetts the proportion of the colored population to the white was 1 to 74, in Connecticut 1 to 34, in New York 1 to 35, and in Pennsylvania 1 to 34.

To the testimony of the Boston Prison Discipline Society, may be added that of the General Assembly Presbyterian Church, on the degraded condition of the free colored population. In 1819, the question of encouraging the American Colonization Society being overtured to the Assembly, they adopted, along with an approval of that Society, the following language :

" The situation of the people of color in this country, has frequently attracted the attention of this Assembly. In the distinctive and indelible marks of their color, and the prejudices of the people, an insuperable obstacle has been placed to the execution of any plan for elevating their character, and placing them on a footing with their brethren of the same common family."

The Assembly, after thus acknowledging that the free colored people are placed in a position in which insuperable obstacles exist to their elevation, proceed to express the hope that their removal to Africa may not only favor their elevation, but be the means of introducing the Gospel to the benighted nations of that continent. Again, in 1825, the Assembly recur to the subject, in connection with colonization, and say:

" The General Assembly having witnessed with high gratification the progress of the American Colonization Society, in a great work of humanity and religion, and believing that the temporal prosperity and moral interests of an extensive section of our country, of a numerous, degraded and miserable class of men in the midst of us, and the vast continent of Africa, now uncivilized and unchristian, are intimately connected with the success of this institution, therefore, resolved," &c.

The resolution recommends the churches, under the care of the Assembly, to make contributions to this object on the 4th of July.

That the common conviction of the community, at this period, was nearly uniform, as to the degraded condition of the free blacks, and the undesirableness of having them as neighbors, is still more apparent from the action of the Indiana Yearly Meeting of Friends, in 1826. The following we extract from their published minutes:

"The committee charged with the concerns of the people of color, made the following satisfactory report: ...... We having received a communication from the Trustees of the North Carolina Yearly Meeting describing the difficult and perilous situation of a number of persons of color under the care of Friends, and informing, that some of them inclined to remove to the States north of the Ohio river, and requesting our attention to them. After solidly deliberating on the subject, and having our minds clothed with feelings which breathe ' good will to men,' we have come to the conclusion to inform Friends, that we are free to extend such assistance to those who may be found among us, as our means will permit; and, although *it is desirable to avoid an accession of this class of population as neighbors,* we are concerned to impress it on the minds of all, that our prejudices should yield when the interest and happiness of our fellow-beings are at stake; and that we exert no influence that would deprive them of the rights of free agents, in removing to any part of the world congenial to them; and that Friends everywhere render them such assistance, in procuring them employment, and promoting a correct deportment among them, as occasion may require."

The testimony in relation to the degraded condition of the free colored people, at the period under consideration, might be greatly multiplied, as the facts were very fully brought out by the discussions on Colonization; but we care not to dwell upon this melancholy topic. As, in England, the negroes, declared free by Lord Mansfield's decision, became a nuisance requiring government aid for its abatement; so, in the United States, the free colored people became a burden too heavy to bear, and demanding the aids of Colonization to remedy the evil. Thus, in both cases, the efforts for Africa's redemption were produced by the evils falling upon society, as a necessary consequence of emancipation.

Nearly a half century had now elapsed, since the Northern States had commenced the work of emancipation, and since the first acts of ecclesiastical legislation, favoring that object, had been spread out before the Christian world. The free blacks, as a body, had made no progress, morally, beyond that of their condition in slavery; but remained overshadowed by all the moral gloom which had darkened their souls under African barbarism. The facts show that northern Christians, busied with their own cares, either had grossly neglected their duty; or the freedom of the colored man, while commingled with a superior race, was unfavorable to his evangelization.

But the history of the times proves more than this. It is a fact, the truth of which cannot be controverted, that the clergy, at the period under consideration, much more willingly engaged in efforts to control the civil legislation of the country, in reference to slavery, than in projecting and sustaining measures for the elevation of the free colored men, at their doors, to the position in morality and intelligence which a patient course of Christian instruction was calculated to effect.

Here, now, is an accurate picture of the moral condition of the free colored population of the North, at the period approaching the time of the West India Emancipation, and of the inauguration of modern abolitionism in the United States. The difference in the moral condition of the free colored people at the North, as contrasted with that of the slave population at the South, will be understood on the examination of the facts given in the next chapter. It was at the close of the period we have been considering, that the British theories on slavery began to be urged on this country, and universal emancipation claimed to be indispensable, both to the economical prosperity of the South, and to the evangelization of the blacks.

4. *Contrast of the results of freeing the blacks in the North, with the continuation of them in slavery at the South.*

Under the preceding head, we have seen the discouraging condition into which the free colored people were thrown, at the North, by the systems of emancipation adopted. We shall now proceed to give the main facts, in reference to the moral progress of the slaves at the South, so that the legitimate results of the two systems may be brought into fair contrast: the North giving freedom, and withholding the means of moral elevation; the South subjecting to restraint, but supplying the means of moral progress.

The American clergymen who accepted the British theory —
that slavery and African evangelization are incompatible — must
have taken but little care to understand the question, or else they
must have willingly closed their eyes to the most important facts.
British Colonial slavery furnished them the data upon which they
based their opinions; but they failed to perceive, that the hin-
drances to the Gospel, in the West Indies, arose, not essentially
from slavery, but from the hostility of the slaveholders. They
were blind, as only a fanatical spirit can render men blind. They
had before them not only the facts which demonstrated that the
blacks had made progress under American slavery; but they had
the additional fact, that the free colored people of the North had
made less progress, as a body, than the slaves of the South. The
reason of this difference in results is obvious. At the North, the
negro, while a slave, was considered a burden, to be cast off at all
hazards; and when he was driven into freedom, no one felt any
responsibility for his moral culture. Thrown upon society in a
state of destitution, what could the poor colored man do, but —
as he did in London, under the decision of Lord Mansfield — fall,
as a helpless child, into neglect and degradation — filling the
jails and workhouses, instead of taking the proud stand which
freemen should maintain. But it was not so in the South, so far
as the progress in crime was concerned. This was due, doubtless, to two causes: the restraints of slavery, and the increasing
attention paid to their religious instruction. Many Christian
masters felt their responsibility, before God, for the welfare of
the souls of their slaves. Under the influence of this obligation,
they either gave instruction themselves to their blacks, or allowed
the ministry to teach them. With fixed homes, and the rigid
restraints of slavery, controlling their movements, the religious
teacher was certain, from Sabbath to Sabbath, of finding the
same slaves meeting him for moral training. If this had not been
the case, how could such results have followed, as are found to
have occurred. Let us examine them:

All the religious denominations can tell of the fruits of their
labors, in this field of toil, and can point to the evidences of their
success. But the Methodists were not only eminently successful
in the work, but have preserved accurate statistics of the results.

From the minutes of that denomination, therefore, we shall cull
out the evidences to disprove, triumphantly, the British theory
on slavery, as applicable to slaves in America; and to show, conclusively, that the northern ecclesiastics were in error in supposing that slavery necessarily prevents the evangelization of the
blacks. They overlooked the great truth, that God, in his Providential care of the world, never places men in conditions where
the blessed Gospel of his Son is not adapted to their circumstances. Had this truth been felt, in its legitimate power, by
northern Christian hearts, the free colored people would not have
been so strangely neglected, as though they had no interest in
the Great Salvation!

But we must proceed with the proof of these assertions. The
minutes of the Methodist Episcopal Church, from 1796 to 1801,
was given by States, and presents the following as its colored
membership:

STATES.	1796	1797	1798	1799	1800	1801
Vermont	....	.....	1	1	1	6
New Hampshire						3
Maine						
Massachusetts	2	8	11	11	6	12
Rhode Island	—	2	1	1	3	3
Connecticut	8	15	22	17	25	24
New York	218	238	245	276	223	284
New Jersey	105	127	163	167	173	172
Pennsylvania	380	198	224	309	300	507
Delaware	811	832	939	900	867	1,447
Maryland	4,910	5,106	4,950	5,079	5,497	6,815
Virginia	2,458	2,490	2,432	2,312	2,531	2,578
North Carolina	1,288	2,071	1,810	1,659	2,109	2,092
South Carolina	825	890	1,179	1,169	1,283	1,360
Georgia	146	148	222	216	252	202
Tennessee	43	42	49	51	62	62
Kentucky	84	57	51	65	115	115
North West Territory	.....	.....	....	.....	2	2
Upper Canada	2	3	3	3	3	4
Total	11,280	12,218	12,302	12,236	13,452	15,688

The dotted lines (......) indicate that the Church had not yet been organized. The dash, (——)
that the Church had been organized, but had no colored members of that date.

Here, at the very time when it was doubtful whether a missionary could maintain a foothold in the West Indies, the Methodists
in the United States had a colored membership exceeding 15,600,
of whom more than 14,000 were in the States which had passed

no emancipation laws — New York having passed hers in 1799, and New Jersey in 1804.

To understand the point illustrated by the foregoing statistics — the degree of success attending the labors of the Methodists among the colored population — it is necessary to show the rate of progress among the whites also; and to give the number of free blacks and slaves in the several States. They stood as follows:

STATES.	WHITE MEMBERS. 1796	WHITE MEMBERS. 1800	FREE COL'R'D POPULATION. 1800	SLAVE POPULATION. 1800
Maine	357	1,197	818	
New Hampshire	68	171	856	8
Vermont	....	1,095	557	
Massachusetts	822	1,571	6,452	
Rhode Island	220	224	3,304	381
Connecticut	1,042	1,546	5,330	951
New York	3,826	6,141	10,374	20,343
New Jersey	2,246	2,857	4,402	12,422
Pennsylvania	2,631	2,887	14,561	1,706
Delaware	1,417	1,626	8,268	6,153
Maryland	7,506	6,549	19,587	105,635
Virginia	11,321	10,859	20,124	345,796
North Carolina	7,425	6,363	7,043	133,296
South Carolina	2,834	3,399	3,185	146,151
Georgia	1,028	1,403	1,019	59,404
Tennessee	503	681	309	13,584
Kentucky	1,666	1,626	741	40,343
Total	44,912	50,226	106,930	886,173

The dotted lines (......) indicate that the Church had not yet been organized.

Continuing these statistics to 1811, during which time the missions at Sierra Leone had made no progress, and the slaves of the West Indies were still, mainly, in the darkness of barbarism, we find that the colored membership of the Methodists had increased to more than 35,700. The statistics are given by Conferences. It will be noticed that the greater number, by far, are in the slave States:

CONFERENCES.	1803	1804	1805	1806	1807	1808	1809	1810	1811
Western..................	464	518	736	630	621	795	1,117	1,144	1,467
South Carolina.......	2,815	3,446	3,831	4,389	4,432	5,111	6,284	8,202	9,129
Virginia	3,794	3,757	3,573	4,548	5,668	5,834	5,739	6,150	6,232
Baltimore...............	6,414	6,877	6,805	7,221	7,453	7,143	7,200	7,452	7,438
Philadelphia..........	8,561	8,442	8,914	9,782	10,899	10,524	10,534	10,714	10,354
New England.........	14	59	56	62	56	64	73	69	73
New York..............	391	432	401	625	734	837	937	942	986
Genessee	....	....	....	....	....	....	....	51	53
Total............	22,453	23,531	24,316	27,257	29,863	30,308	31,884	34,724	35,732

The dotted lines (......) indicate that the Church had not yet been organized.

Passing by an interval of several years, during which the Conferences were multiplied, and the colored members greatly increased, we next select the nine years ending with 1834. This is an important epoch, as it was in this year that the British Emancipation Act went into operation in the West Indies, and the slaves were all placed in the relation of apprentices to their old masters. The returns are given by the Conferences:

CONFERENCES.	1826	1827	1828	1829	1830	1831	1832	1833	1834
Pittsburgh	194	206	201	176	163	175	187	261	285
Ohio.	184	195	208	193	268	274	344	321	502
Kentucky	2,821	2,812	3,650	3,682	4,884	5,284	4,594	4,651	5,709
Illinois	64	125	124	116	172	276	204	61	72
Indiana	....	....	....	....	....	....	....	182	273
Missouri.................	339	356	335	350	414	451	*451	756	996
Holston..................	1,485	1,620	1,864	2,012	2,182	2,362	2,319	2,316	2,593
Tennessee	2,112	2,075	2,257	2,499	3,248	3,733	3,624	3,805	4,674
Mississippi.............	2,494	2,724	3,283	3,576	4,247	*4,247	5,185	2,645	2,622
Alabama.................								2,770	3,163
South Carolina........	15,708	16,555	18,460	21,276	24,538	19,144	20,197	22,326	22,788
Georgia....................						6,167	7,330	7,946	7,421
Virginia	7,847	8,567	9,090	9,756	9,967	9,194	8,210	7,447	8,083
Baltimore	9,406	9,507	10,402	10,302	10,454	10,905	11,566	12,732	13,851
Philadelphia..........	7,650	8,043	8,354	8,159	8,169	8,549	8,516	8,960	9,025
New York..............	378	371	428	371	281	418	615	586	516
New England.........	250	248	252	220	245	261	289	304	320
Maine....................	6	6	1	3	10	8	8	8	8
Genessee	110	120	135	39	45	69	56	49	109
Canada	36	12	12	10					
Troy......................	....	....	....	....	....	....	....	50	69
Oneida...................	....	....	....	74	88	111	111	111	69
New Hampshire and Vermont..............	....	....	....	....	8	11	11	6	8
Total	51,084	53,542	59,056	62,814	69,383	71,589	73,817	78,293	83,156

The dotted lines (......) indicate that the Church had not yet been organized. The dash, (——) that the Church had been organized, but had no colored members of that date.

* The last year's report.

Here, at the very moment of British emancipation, and when the British theories were considered as demonstrated, the Methodist Church in the United States had more than 83,000 colored members, only 2,231 of whom were outside of the slave States and the Philadelphia Conference. This Conference covers considerable territory in the slave States. The total converts among the colored people, in all the religious denominations in the United States, at this date, could not have fallen far short of 160,000.* It is worthy of note, that the colored membership of the Methodist Church, in the six New England States, was less than 330; while in seven of the slave States it was more than 65,000. The New England States at this date, 1834, had a free colored population of 21,331. Nothing, therefore, is plainer, than that the spiritual welfare of the colored people was better promoted in the South, under restraint, and with the means of moral progress, than it was in the North, under freedom, but without the means of moral elevation.

5. *Deductions from the facts stated.*

The moral condition of the free colored people in the United States, at the period under consideration, can now be understood. The founders of the American Republic had not erred in opinion, in reference to the burden which the African race might lay upon the shoulders of the people. Franklin, with the forecast of a philosopher and statesman, foresaw that emancipation, without education, would be fruitless of good to the negroes, and might open up a series of evils to themselves and society. The reports of the Boston Prison Discipline Society, the declarations of the Presbyterian General Assembly, and other authorities quoted, in relation to their degraded condition, are ample proofs that the early opinions entertained were founded in sound views of the negro character, in his then barbarous condition. The Prison Discipline Society's Report shows, that, in Massachusetts, after nearly fifty years of freedom had prevailed, *one* out of every *one hundred and forty* of the free colored population of that State

---

* This estimate is based on the fact, that the Methodist Church, at present, has less than one-half of the colored members in the slave States.

were in the penitentiary; while the Presbyterian General Assembly asserts, that "in the distinctive and indelible marks of their color, and the prejudices of the people, an insuperable obstacle has been placed to the execution of any plan for elevating their character, and placing them on a footing with their brethren of the same common family." And, again, the Assembly speaks of them as "a numerous, degraded, and miserable class of men in the midst of us."

In contrast with this deplorable picture of the moral degradation of the free colored people of the United States at the date of West India emancipation, we have the encouraging fact, that the religious progress of the slave population had not fallen behind that of the whites, as to the rate of increase in church members, in any part of the Union. Of the 83,000 colored members in the Methodist Church at that date, not less, probably, than 75,000 were in the slave States, and were either slaves or dwelling in the midst of slavery. The other denominations, doubtless, had an equal number, making the total membership, among the colored people in the slave States, about 150,000. As the total slave population of the preceding census, was over 2,000,000, it appears that nearly *one* out of every *thirteen* was a church member. *

Thus, then, about the same time that *one* out of every *one hundred and forty* of the free colored people of Massachusetts was in the Penitentiary; about *one* out of every *thirteen* of the colored population in the slave States was in the Christian church — a happy difference of condition, truly, and supplying a forcible example of the difference in the effects of the northern and southern systems of policy upon the negro race.

But we have a double contrast to make. In comparing the missionary results in the West Indies, during the existence of slavery, with those in the United States, among the slave population, during the same period, it does not appear that there was any difference in the degrees of success attained. Their missions were frequently broken up; ours went on without interruption.

---

* This estimate is only intended as an approximation. It does not include the free colored people in the slave States.

Their religious teachers had to be supplied from Great Britain, and were fewer in number than ours; the teachers of our colored population were more numerous, and lived among them, preaching to them, mostly in connection with their white parishioners. At the time of final emancipation, in 1838, they must have had near 80,000 African converts; in 1834, we had not less than 166,000, including slaves and colored freemen.

The conclusion, then, to which we are forced is, that the British theory under consideration — that slavery presents an insuperable barrier to the evangelization of the Africans subjected to its control — is not sustained by the results which happened up to the date of emancipation; and that, therefore, the American ministers, who adopted it as true, have been laboring under a delusion — a delusion that has been fatal to the peace of the Church; fatal to the welfare of the African race; fatal to our beloved country!

CHAPTER III.

EXAMINATION OF THE ERRORS IN THE BRITISH THEORIES AS AP-
PLIED TO AMERICAN SLAVERY AFTER WEST INDIA EMANCIPA-
TION.

SECTION I.—THE CIRCUMSTANCES UNDER WHICH ABOLITIONISM
TOOK ITS RISE IN THE UNITED STATES.

THE preceding chapters bring the history of the movements
in behalf of the African race, down to the period of the final
action of Great Britain on her Colonial Slavery. It was this important measure that gave the impulse to the abolition movement
in the United States. The American people had been looking to
Colonization, for the previous seventeen years, as a means of
relief from the burdens imposed by emancipation. But the system of Colonization worked tardily. The Society had been unable
to remove a tithe of the increase of the colored population. It
was too slow in its operations to satisfy those who had been accustomed to look forward to the total extinction of slavery. They
had become excited by the passage of the British Emancipation
Act; and demanded, for the American bondmen, a more speedy
redemption than that promised by Colonization. But Colonization had many supporters, who had full faith in its beneficent
results, and who would not abandon the enterprise. Its continuance was considered, by many anti-slavery men, as an obstacle
to the success of emancipation. The South, becoming jealous of
the Society, denounced Colonization as an abolition scheme in
disguise. The Society, in self-defense, had to define its position,
as having reference only to the removal of the free colored people, and that it had no design of interfering with slavery. For

this reason, " the Anti-Slavery Society began with a declaration of war against the Colonization Society." * The doctrine of " immediate, not gradual abolition," had been announced in England as the creed of the friends of the African race. Emancipation, they contended, was indispensable to the success of the Gospel among the blacks. Under various degrees of modification, this view was adopted by the anti-slavery men of the United States. In 1831, the first abolition society, of the modern type, was organized in Rhode Island. In 1832, the anti-slavery movement was begun in Boston; and, in 1833, a national organization, under the name of THE AMERICAN ANTI-SLAVERY SOCIETY, † was founded in Philadelphia. This body boldly took the ground that nothing short of *immediate* and unconditional emancipation, could satisfy the demands of justice, and fulfill the righteous law of God — that as slaveholding, in every form in which it prevailed, was sinful, it was the duty of all engaged in it to cease immediately, and that there could be nothing to fear from the consequences of so doing. ‡

The North now everywhere resounded with the cry of " immediate abolition : " but while this motto was borrowed from the English abolitionists, their American imitators had no disposition to act upon the magnanimous principles adopted by the British government, in giving a liberal compensation to the masters. The South were required to sacrifice all their wealth upon the altar of northern philanthropy : and British eloquence, in the person of Mr. George Thompson, was employed to give an impulse to the fanatical scheme.

The year 1837 found the abolitionists numbering 1,015 societies, having 70 agents in the field, and an income, for the year, of $36,000. || The Colonization Society, on the other hand, was greatly embarrassed. Its income, in 1838, was reduced to $10,000; it was deeply in debt ; the parent society did not send a single emigrant that year to Liberia ; and its enemies pronounced it bankrupt and dead. §

The doctrine previously held by the few — that slavery is ne-

* Gerritt Smith, 1835.   † This may be best designated by the term *Abolition*.
‡ History of the Separation in Indiana Yearly Meeting of Friends.
|| Life of Benjamin Lundy.   § Cotton is King, p. 52.

cessarily sinful — and which lies at the foundation of all abolition action, now became the doctrine of the many. It demanded the exclusion of all slaveholders from the communion of the Church. This element in the controversy on slavery — so unlike anything taught by the Saviour and his Apostles, while laboring in the midst of slaveholders — can be dimly traced throughout the early ecclesiastical legislation of the North. In general, slavery was declared to be a moral evil; but the idea connected with this phrase was the same as that attached to monarchical and despotic forms of government. According to the notions of right and wrong then prevailing, all laws which limited the personal freedom of men, were pronounced moral evils, to be removed as speedily as possible, so that the whole world, ultimately, might become democratic. The idea of sinfulness was not generally attached to the phrase, in the sense that slavery, as a moral evil, was to be classified with blasphemy, robbery, or murder. In the churches legislating on the subject, this view was long held, and all efforts were directed to the reform of abuses; while, at the same time, they gave a hearty coöperation to the civil authorities in the promotion of emancipation, wherever that policy was agreed upon.

At length, however, the doctrine that slaveholding is a sin began to prevail, and was introduced into church legislation. In some churches it soon gained the ascendency, in others it was held in check by more conservative principles. There was this difference between the aims of the churches and those of the Abolitionists. The ecclesiastical legislation, avowedly, aimed only at freeing the Church from slavery; while the abolition action demanded, imperatively, that the government also should free itself from the crime of human bondage, by immediate emancipation. Thus it was, that there seemed to be a wide distinction between these two parties; but it was a distinction without a difference. Both parties aimed at accomplishing the same object: the one by church legislation, the other by political action — both expecting their efforts to be crowned with the abolition of slavery.

SECTION II.—WHAT THE EARLY ANTI-SLAVERY WRITERS TAUGHT IN RELATION TO THE BIBLE AND SLAVERY.

We must go back a little, in order to examine the opinions advocated by the earlier anti-slavery writers, who inaugurated the scheme of excluding slaveholders from the communion of the Church. This is the more necessary, as the clergymen to whom we refer, gave the impulse to the abolition movement, while undertaking only the task of purging the Church from slavery.

We open Volume 1st of the *Christian Intelligencer*, published at Hamilton, Ohio, and edited by Rev. DAVID McDILL, * assisted by two other neighboring ministers of the Gospel. This periodical was started at the time that the ASSOCIATE REFORMED SYNOD OF THE WEST had under consideration the question of making slavery a term of communion — that is, the casting of slaveholders out of the Church. As this was a novel doctrine, it required novel means to bring the people of that Church to assent to the proposition. On page 6th, we find this statement, as embracing the condition of the slavery question at that early day. The date is January, 1829:

" The question of slavery is, at the present time, agitated in several branches of the Church : but its character is much changed from what it once was. Formerly, as a practice which had long prevailed, and had rarely been called in question, it was supposed to be probably lawful ; † (1) and what was necessary to be done was to prove its immorality ; (2) and by depicting its horrors, and showing its contrariety to the ' holy, just, and good law,' endeavor to awaken the public mind to a sense of its moral turpitude. (3) This ground is nearly won : and the object of the present and future efforts on the subject, must be, for the most part, to shew, that being a heinous sin, a system most contrary to the spirit of the Gospel, it ought not to be connived at in the Church. And so very different are these questions — so generally are Christian men now convinced, it would seem, that slavery is a moral evil of no small magnitude, that all reasonings from its moral character

---

* Now Rev. David McDill, D. D., of Illinois.

† The reader on subsequent pages, will find remarks on the points here noted by numerals.

are pronounced inapplicable to the question at issue, *i. e.* whether the obstinate, irreclaimable holder of slaves should be excluded from the communion of the Church. If this be so — if so great a change has already been wrought on the public mind, that proving the immorality of slavery is only proving what no one denies, there is encouragement to hope that what remains will also in due time be accomplished : — that it will soon be conceded, that a system which is so bad, that no person can have a word to say in its direct vindication, ought to be speedily banished from the pale of the Church ; (4) and that we ought, all of us, to cease, and cease at once, from holding a language, which slaveholders *do view* as a special pleading for their practice."

After referring to several Churches — the General Assembly Presbyterians, and his own, among the number — which had not yet taken decided action, the editor continues :

" When we consider what has been done, and is still being done by the Quakers, Methodists, &c., if these bodies of professing Christians which have been mentioned as having the subject under consideration, would only disenthral themselves from all human schemes of policy and prudence, and stand forth on scriptural grounds, the decided advocates of justice, humanity, and equal rights and privileges to all God's rational creatures, in that system of things with which we are connected, what happy results to the family of man might not be anticipated, from their harmonious and well-directed efforts. If, instead of folding up their hands and saying, we cannot touch the subject of slavery— the evils admit of no remedy, at least till the millenium — the laws lay an embargo on the cause of emancipation ; — they would only consider that public opinion is superior to the laws, so that tyrannical and oppressive laws cannot stand it out against correct and enlightened public opinion — that, if any of our fellow Christians are withheld from doing their duty, by laws which are an usurpation on the rights of men, and an enormity under the government of God, it is because public opinion has become corrupt through the apathy and supineness of those who ought to have been exerting themselves to keep it in a pure and healthy state ; and if every man who possesses a particle of influence, either direct or indirect, on the common weal, would rise up, and come forward, and bring with him all the aid in his power, to correct the stream of human blessing in its fountain head ; — we should soon find laws relaxing from their rigor, customs melting down into goodness, and the obstacles which obstruct the current of emancipation giving way, (5) sooner than many who make goodly professions would be willing to see them." *

The men who first commenced the anti-slavery agitation, are not to be charged with evil intentions ; but they are liable to the imputation of having been influenced by a spirit of fanaticism that blinded their judgments — that led them to overlook the progress made in the conversion of the slaves in the United States, and to greatly exaggerate the cruelties practiced upon them by their masters. The plan of action they adopted to revolutionize public sentiment, we have said, was a novel one. At that day, free discussion was not considered the best means of establishing a theory ; as, to allow it, might defeat the object of the reformer. Here is the language employed by the editor of the *Christian Intelligencer*, to announce the principles upon which the controversy was to be conducted :

" As slavery is a plain practical question, claiming the attention of every one who has any part to act in the affairs of the day, it is difficult to see how any one can be without an opinion on the subject. Our object, so far as this question is concerned, was, from the first, to *show our opinion :* and those who wish to meet and refute our views, or to see them met and refuted, must apply elsewhere. *We* can have no hand, either directly or indirectly, in perpetuating an evil so repugnant to the laws of God, and so afflictive to the family of man ; nor are we under the influence of so much of that *neutral feeling,* which is necessary to the *more perfect examples of prudence,* that we can obtain our own consent to labor in balancing the scale of argument, for the pleasure of leaving it in a state of equipoise." † (6)

It may be well to explain, that the question of excluding the slaveholder from the Church, had been brought before the Synod, some two or three years before the *Christian Intelligencer* had been started ; and that one chief object of its publication was to advocate that measure, and free the Associate Reformed Church from all connection with slavery. A communication in opposition to the policy had been sent to the editor, and, on publishing it,

---

* Christian Intelligencer, January, 1829, p. 7.
† Ibid., June, 1829, p. 180. The italics are the editor's.

the foregoing announcement was made.   Having thus secured himself against all assailants, the way was open for the circulation, among the people of the Church, of any opinions which the editor and his associates might choose to utter.   Some of these opinions we shall present to the reader, that he may learn how the public became tinctured so readily with abolition sentiments. Appearing, as they did, from the pens of men who could quote Hebrew, Greek, and Latin, the statements made were received by their readers as true ; and no contradiction being allowed, their demonstration was reckoned complete.   With the reasonings employed, we need have nothing to do, at this late day.   The conclusions at which the writers arrived, are all that it is necessary to notice.   The object they had in view, it must be remembered, was to secure the passage of an act, by their Church, excluding slaveholders from its communion.

But before proceeding to make additional quotations, it will be well to analyze the programme of action adopted : *

1. It is admitted by the editor that slaveholding, formerly, was supposed to be probably lawful.   This was the opinion held by the British Churches, in reference to the Christian master, Mr. GILBERT, who first introduced the Gospel into Antigua ; and in reference, also, to the masters, in the other islands, who built chapels on their estates, or aided in building them in their neighborhoods, for the benefit of the slaves.   In all these cases the Christian slaveholder was treated as a brother beloved.   The same sentiments long prevailed in the United States ; and only those slaveholders who refused to allow their slaves the benefits of the Gospel, were ranked as unchristian in heart and conduct.

2. Such being the fixed opinion of Christians, generally, it was found necessary, before a revolution of sentiment could be produced, to prove the immorality of slavery itself.   To have labored for the conversion of the masters, and by that means to have secured their coöperation in the work of evangelizing the slaves, was not in accordance with the designs of the movers in the anti-slavery reform.   This policy might have led to the conversion of both masters and slaves ; but then, such a result, leaving

---

* The reader will observe that the several points noticed are indicated by numerals, and refer to corresponding figures in the quotations from the editor.

Christians contented with these fruits of their labors, would have tended to perpetuate slavery. Indeed, where masters were engaged in the religious instruction of the bond-men, the act was looked upon with suspicion, by Northern men, as not being prompted by any care for the spiritual welfare of the colored population; but only as a means of satisfying public opinion, and perpetuating the legal claim to their slaves. On this subject the SYNOD OF INDIANA, in a memorial to THE GENERAL ASSEMBLY OF THE PRESBYTERIAN CHURCH IN THE UNITED STATES, in 1829, uses the following language:

" In fine, believing that the encouragement of Sabbath school instruction, and other religious exercises, are too often resorted to by slaveholders merely as a compromise with public opinion, and to soothe the clamors of conscience, without any intention to ' let the oppressed go free,' so soon as by those means they may be prepared for the enjoyment of civil liberty — we do most earnestly, yet most respectfully, entreat your venerable body to take the subject into consideration, and to adopt such measures as in your wisdom may appear best calculated to effect a speedy and entire abolition of slavery within the bounds of the Presbyterian Church." *

3. The next step taken, according to the programme, was to depict the horrors of slavery, and show its contrariety to the Divine Law, so as to awaken the public mind to a sense of its moral turpitude. In their discussions of this topic, no reference was made to the success attending the labors of other denominations among the slaves; none to the fact, that the Methodists, alone, in that same year, 1829, reported their colored membership, in the United States, at 62,814, most of whom were slaves; none to

---

* Christian Intelligencer, Hamilton, Ohio, May, 1829, p. 145.

NOTE.—Even as late as 1844, this feeling was still entertained, and received its expression in the Fraternal Letter of the SYNOD OF NORTHERN INDIANA, in the following language:

"That many masters strive to avert these evils from their slaves does not alter the general effect; and their example, by presenting the fairest aspect of slavery, quiets the conscience of the holder; and it may be said, without exaggeration, that the better a limited portion of the slaves are made, the worse it is for the whole, since the good of the few becomes a palliation for the evil of the many."— See Robinson's "Hand-Book of the Slavery Controversy."

the fact, that the several missions in the West India Islands had at least 80,000 converts among the slaves ; and none to the fact, that the denominations which had become most zealous in the anti-slavery movement, had, themselves, a very meager member-ship of whites, and had done little or nothing among the blacks. *

4. The horrors of slavery being depicted, and the public mind awakened to its moral turpitude, the future mode of action was to show that, being a heinous sin, slaveholding ought not to be connived at in the church.

5. The churches having taken their stand in denouncing slav-ery as a sin, and being firm in the discharge of duty in the ex-clusion of slaveholders from the church, their moral influence, it was believed, would be such as to bring the people to mould the legislation of the country, so as to prepare the way for emanci-pation.

6. Emancipation, then, being the object at which the anti-slavery men aimed, the next step to be taken was the closing of the columns of their organ against all free discussion. The church was the agent to be employed in producing the proposed revolution. The exclusion of the slaveholder from its communion, was the means to be used in awakening public attention to the subject. But the ministry could not act without the concurrence of the people. The members of the church, therefore, were the tribunal to whom the decision had to be referred; but only the advocates on one side of the case were permitted to plead, and only the testimony that would sustain their claims was allowed to be offered. These things seem strange at this day. Men having confidence in the justice of their measures, and intending to ad-here strictly to truth in their discussions, would blush, now, to ask such advantages in controversy. And yet, these gentlemen, doubtless, intended to act in strict conformity with duty. Their fault was that of the age in which they lived. There was more or less of a disposition among certain clergymen of that day, to distrust the judgment of the people upon moral and religious questions. This was especially the case with those of the smaller

---

* The Associate Synod only reported 10,141 members, and the Associate Re-formed Synod of the West had a less number; the two combined not having over one-third as many members as the Methodists had of colored converts.

denominations, who were taking the lead in attempts to purge the church from the sin of slaveholding. Take an example or two. The Associate Synod had a rule prohibiting its people from hearing aught but the sermons of its own ministers. To listen to a sermon from any one else, was to incur the censures of the church; and if the offender manifested no sorrow for his sin, he was cast out until brought to repentance and reformation. The Reformed Presbyterian Church had a different rule, but it operated with equal efficiency in keeping its people from worshiping with those of other religious bodies. Its members were not censured, like the Associate Synod's people, for "occasional hearing," but were required to meet in "Society," on their silent Sabbaths, and always to be present when their own minister preached. The rules of both these denominations were carried out, at the period under consideration, with a great degree of strictness, and tended to foster and intensify the prejudices of their people against all other denominations. The Associate Reformed Church was more liberal in its rules, and allowed its people to exercise their own judgments as to listening to sermons from other ministers than their own. The editor, from whom we have quoted, was a minister in this church; but while he was liberal in church discipline, he was unwilling to trust the people with a free discussion of the slavery question. To have permitted this in his periodical, he tells us, might have left the minds of his readers in "equipoise," and led them to reject the proposed reform in the discipline of the church. But his fault, and that of his associates, as we have said, was that of the age in which they acted. Men of education had not all learned to reason on the inductive system, but indulged in conjectures after the manner of the wise men of olden times. They were not careful to note all the facts and principles involved in the questions considered, but, indulging much in speculation, they ran into hasty generalizations, like tyroes in science, and, consequently, fell into egregious errors. In this fact is to be found the source of nearly all the conflicting theories in relation to the negro race. At best, all that had then been done for the colored people was mere experiment, and results, such as we have now, were unknown. It is not surprising, therefore, that what was then held as orthodox, should now be scouted as fanatical.

The aim of the writers for the *Christian Intelligencer*, in undertaking the agitation of the question of slavery, in connection with ecclesiastical legislation, can now be understood. They found public sentiment endorsing the doctrine of the probable lawfulness of slavery, and only condemning its abuses. To accomplish their object, they must change this public sentiment; and this they proposed to do, by proving the immorality of slavery itself, separate and apart from its abuses. This they expected to effect, by depicting its horrors, showing its contrariety to the Divine law, and thus proving its great moral turpitude. When this should be accomplished, and the practice of slavery proved to be a most heinous sin, the Church would be easily persuaded that she must no longer tolerate the system. This point gained, it was believed that the influence of the Church, expressed through her judicial acts, and thereby enforced upon her people, could control civil legislation and thus secure the emancipation of the slaves. *

This, then, is the scheme they proposed; and we may now proceed to show how it was carried out. To depict the horrors and show the moral turpitude of slavery were the first steps to be taken. The world had unanimously pronounced the slave trade a crime of the deepest dye. To show the moral turpitude of slaveholding, the editor thus classifies it with the slave trade:

" The Africans *were stolen* from their country ; no man will do himself any credit by denying it : and that the actual holder of property which is known to be stolen, is as criminal as the thief, is both *logic and law*." †

Again the editor says :

" The *principle* of slavery is unrighteous — this is its condemnation. The *practice* can not be spared, and so regulated as to make it *on the*

---

* It will be seen, by reference to Chapter VII., that a few years later, the Associate Church attempted to carry out this policy, by interdicting freedom of opinion in her members in relation to voting.

† Christian Intelligencer, Hamilton, Ohio, June, 1829, page 184.

whole a blessing to any part of the human family — more than any other sinful practice." *

From the editor, we turn to one of his assistants, who undertakes to show the horrible character of American slavery, as compared with all other systems which ever had an existence. He comes to the following conclusions:

"The slavery which existed in the Roman Empire in the Apostles' time, was by no means so debasing, hopeless, and oppressive, as negro slavery in our country." . . . . . "No one . . . . . can escape the conclusion, that slavery in modern times exists in its mildest form in countries where the Roman Catholic religion is the established religion, and where the government is despotic or *purely* monarchical, as in the Spanish and Portuguese colonies — that it becomes more ferocious and oppressive in Protestant countries, where the government is a mixed monarchy, as in the British colonies — and that it is most debasing of all in countries, where the religion is purely Protestant, and the government free and republican, as *our own*." †

This wholesale denunciation of American slavery, as the most ferocious, oppressive, and degrading system that ever existed, ‡ and this unqualified condemnation of his own government, as sanctioning cruelties unheard of in the history of the world, may have been necessary to maintain the positions assumed in the anti-slavery programme; but it was all based upon the sheerest conjecture as to Roman slavery, and was wholly destitute of any support from existing facts, so far as concerned American slavery as compared with that of the Portuguese, Spanish and British slave colonies. The reader will find these assertions fully sustained, by the opinions and facts elsewhere stated in this work.

In the farther prosecution of the efforts to show that American slavery was contrary to the Divine law, and thus to influence Church legislation, it was necessary to refer to what the Apostles — the founders of the Church — had said and done in reference to Roman slavery. Here, however, was complete silence.

---

* Christian Intelligencer, Hamilton, Ohio, February, 1829, page 64.

† Ibid., August, 1829, page 230.

‡ The writer, in his discussions, refers to slavery, generally, as well as to that of Rome.

They found precepts to regulate the relation, but not a word of condemnation. This silence proved an exceedingly embarrassing difficulty. But it had to be met, and one of the assistant editors makes the attempt to dispose of it as follows:

"Now, considering all these things, is it not, on the supposition that the Apostles did tolerate slavery, most unfair to reason from what the Apostles, in their circumstances, did, to what we, in our circumstances, should do, in regard to the toleration of this acknowledged evil? May not much more be expected of us, and may we not attempt much more in its abolition? And now let the reader take into the account not only our more favorable civil relations, but also the superior knowledge of the age and nation, and the fact that in many important respects, the slavery which our opponents wish us, amidst all the circumstances of the times, to tolerate from Apostolic example, is far more hopeless and debasing than that which, they say, the Apostles tolerated." *

Again, he says:

" I defy the world to prove that slavery *was* tolerated by the Apostles, and that it is in harmony with the spirit of the Christian religion." †

And, again:

"Slavery is contrary to the general principles of the Word of God, and to the spirit of the religion of the meek and lowly Jesus, our compassionate Redeemer. As might be expected of such a system, it gets no support from the Apostles. There is no evidence that they tolerated, in the Church, the slavery which existed in the Roman Empire; and, even if they did, there is evidence, that the slavery of the Romans, bad as it was, did not possess many of the most cruel, degrading, and hopeless properties of negro slavery, with which we have to do." ‡

But what does all this amount to? The writer says, that even supposing the Apostles did tolerate Roman slavery, that is no reason why we should tolerate American slavery — the latter, in

---

* Christian Intelligencer, Hamilton, Ohio, August, 1829, page 242.

† Ibid., August, 1829, page 229.

‡ Ibid., September, 1829, page 266.

his opinion, being so much the more unrighteous of the two. But laying aside his hypothetical case, he becomes more bold, and defies the world to prove that slavery was tolerated by the Apostles. Then, again, as if doubtful of this point, he comes back to the first supposition, and avers, that even if Roman slavery was tolerated by them, there is no evidence that it was as bad as our slavery. Here we are still upon the old platform—that the Church is only required to deal with the abuses of slavery. If Roman slavery had been as bad as American slavery, then, according to this writer, the Apostles could not have remained silent, but must have spoken out in its condemnation.

A step beyond this had to be taken, therefore, so that something more convincing than hypothesis and assertion might be afforded. Another assistant editor, coming to the rescue, thus attempts to meet the difficulty :

"Again it is said, slavery was practiced in the visible church while the Apostles were yet living; and that instead of testifying against slavery, they put it under regulation, giving directions to masters and servants; which fact, it is thought, gives us a warrant to tolerate it now. . . . . . I deny that they taught the lawfulness of such slavery as this : or that they tolerated such an evil without testifying against it. They could not do every thing at once, although they were inspired men. I think any person who will take a view of the history of God's Church throughout the former dispensation must see, that idolatry and other abominations were practiced in the church while she had inspired teachers : reader, look into the writings of the prophets, and see if this were not the case. Why did not the inspired men keep out all visible immorality ? Yea, there were inspired men who practiced polygamy. Now, if it be no reflection upon these inspired men to purge out certain evils which they did not keep out, neither is it any reflection upon the Apostles to endeavor to purge out what, according to some, they did not purge out." *

Here, again, is a denial that Roman slavery was as bad as ours, or that the Apostles tolerated it, without testifying against it. And, as an apology for their seeming neglect, in not making it a prominent object of discipline, as they did idolatry, he supposes

* Christian Intelligencer, Hamilton, Ohio, March, 1830, page 65.

they found it impracticable to do every thing at once; and then goes on to say, that idolatry, and other abominations, were practiced in the Church of God, under the former dispensation, while she had inspired teachers; and that, if it be no reflection upon them that they did not keep idolatry out of the Jewish Church, neither is it any reflection upon the Apostles that they did not purge out slavery from the Christian Church, which they were founding. The writer, however, neglects to remind the reader, that all the inspired teachers were loud in their denunciations of idolatry, and did extirpate it whenever they had the power, as the priests of Baal found to their dismay and ruin; but that the Apostles, in no instance, denounced slavery, or ever attempted to make such an example of any slaveholder, that all should be deterred from the practice by the dread of the judgments of Heaven. But we must hear this writer some farther:

"I will go a step farther and state, that if the Apostles did not perceive that such slavery as existed among *us* is contrary to the law of God, it does not follow that it is sanctioned by that law. Bishop Butler compares the sacred penmen to the collector of certain memoirs written by others. He who wrote the memoirs is supposed to understand fully what he intended in his own writing, and what he intended is the true sense. The compiler, however, may not always see the whole of what was intended: so God always understands all the proper applications of his word, though the penman, perhaps, in many instances did not see the whole of its intention. . . . . . The prophets had to study their own writings: the Apostles we may suppose had to do the same. What they wrote we likewise have to study as the Providence of God directs." *

Now, what have we here, but a denial that the Apostles comprehended, with certainty, the Divine mind, as to the plainest moral duties. Why should such a startling and unscriptural doctrine as this be advocated by these writers? The reference is not to prophecies relating to future events, such as were recorded by the Old Testament prophets, but to moral duties relating to the conduct of the members of the Christian Church. The answer is at hand. The writers had been met by the startling fact, that

---

* Christian Intelligencer, Hamilton, Ohio, March, 1830, page 65.

the Saviour and his Apostles adopted no rule to exclude slave-holders from the Church. Idolatry, blasphemy, murder, adultery, robbery, bearing false witness, covetousness, were all broadly condemned as inconsistent with the Christian character. But slavery was nowhere specifically forbidden. On the contrary, the relative duties of parent and child, husband and wife, magistrates and people, master and servant, were all clearly pointed out. The logical inference from this fact, was, that all these relations were, in themselves, lawful, and that abuses of authority, only, were to be condemned.

But our reformers had demonstrated, to their own satisfaction, that American slaveholding was a heinous sin — a sin as heaven-daring as the slave trade — which could not be tolerated by the modern churches. How to reconcile their doctrines with the action of the Apostles, presented a difficulty of no small magnitude. Resolute men, however, do not stop at difficulties; it is their province to overcome them. With military men, what can not be accomplished by fair combat, is to be carried by strategy. Surely, ministers, in warring with the Prince of Darkness, may profit by the example — being careful, however, that they are not manning a masked battery of the enemy of souls. Having silenced the opposition, by refusing free discussion in their columns, these writers could utter any charges they chose against the system of slavery, or against their own government for continuing to give it support.

But the silence of the Apostles on the subject of slavery, seems to have given the editor quite as much trouble as it did his associates. He had pronounced slaveholding as equally criminal with slave trading. That was surely to stamp the character of the master as so blackened with crime, as to make him a fit associate only for demons; and, hence, he must be cast out of the church, and delivered over to Satan. In accomplishing this work, the task would have been easy, but for the want of scriptural precept or example. The silence of the Apostles on the subject, therefore, was an exceedingly vexatious fact that had to be disposed of in some plausible manner. The assistant editors had been unable to demonstrate the sinfulness of slavery, in the abstract, from either the acts or the writings of the Apostles; and, unless this could be done, the people could not be induced to abandon their old theory — that slavery, like prevailing forms of despotic governments, was not necessarily sinful, but became so only by abuses of the power possessed. The editor also lent his aid, to give greater certainty to the work.

In replying to strictures made upon views which he had previously expressed,* he said that he had taught that idolatry was "a system incorporated with the civil institutions of the Romans, and diametrically opposed to the doctrines of the Gospel;" and that slavery was "a system incorporated with the civil institutions of the Romans, and contrary to the spirit of the Gospel indeed, but yet not so diametrically opposed to the Gospel but that the two might coëxist for a time : and hence reasoned, that though the Apostles *may have* pursued a different course in relation to the one from that pursued in relation to the other, the church may, notwithstanding, under her present circumstances treat them both as *really* if not *equally* deserving her censure." †

This is still an admission, that Roman slavery could not have been considered, by the Apostles, as *sin per se*, like idolatry, otherwise it must have been denounced as equally sinful with idol worship; and, yet, the editor, without informing us how the transformation was effected, assures us that slavery should now be considered as being really as censurable an offense as idolatry. But how does he reason himself into this belief? Simply, by denying that the Apostles were enabled to decide a question of this kind, as they had been in reference to the subject of idolatry. In effect, he says, of the Divine teachings, that slavery in despotic relations will be slurred over; but in connection with republican governments it is condemned. Look at it now, and it is wicked; but look at it in a given former period, and its immorality is too doubtful to admit of attention. The Gospel is only a remedy for a part of human ills; of some it can take no notice at all. When evils are complicated in civil relations, the sacred Scriptures will speak of them; but in such a way as can only be understood after the lapse of ages and the change of nations. Evils and immor-

---

* The Overture on Slavery, addressed to the Churches, is here referred to, which was prepared by the editor.

† Christian Intelligencer, Hamilton, Ohio, February, 1829, page 34.

alities, interwoven in civil relations, they will make a league with; but when the civil relations are dissolved, they will attack them. Their moral tone is clear, and their utterance decided; but we must wait, in order to find this out, when the needed changes take place. But the editor continues:

"In the details of their office — in the application of the 'law and the testimony' to many particular cases, they [the Apostles] had only that *kind* of gracious assistance which may be ordinarily expected by the ministers of the Gospel; and had to consult, deliberate, and determine, as we have to do, according to the wisdom given them, before they acted." * "No man can — an Apostle could not, do every thing at once. . . . . . And be it remembered, the church was not completely organized — or if you will, the whole system of doctrines and duties, was not delivered to the Church, till the last Apostle had written his last Epistle. As these Epistles were scattered among the churches to which they were written, there is not the least reason to believe, that any one individual, or any one church, had ever seen all the inspired books of the New Testament, till long after the last Apostle had gone to be 'present with the Lord.' To suppose, then, that any one of the churches could have that knowledge, on any article of faith or duty, which lay ever so little out of the Apostle's common track of preaching, which we may have, by comparing all the scriptures one with another, is supposing a perfection among the Christians of that day, which we have no reason to suppose existed. The conclusion, therefore, almost forces itself on us, that practices and omissions of duty, might have existed among them, which ought not to be tolerated in the Church now." †

This is a picture of the primitive church, which few will be willing to recognize as true in fact. The Apostles, before the crucifixion, had been assured by the Saviour, that the Comforter, which is the Holy Ghost, should teach them in all things, and bring all things to their remembrance, whatsoever he had said unto them. ‡ And, again, he assured them, that when He, the Spirit of truth, should come, he would guide them into all truth. § This gave the Apostles the most positive assurance, that they should

* Christian Intelligencer, Hamilton, Ohio, February, 1829, page 35.
† Ibid., February, 1829, page 36.
‡ John's Gospel, xiv: 26.　　　§ John, xvi: 13.

have the Holy Spirit to guide them into all truth, and to bring to their remembrance whatsoever the Saviour had said to them. Now, is it possible, as the editor would have us believe, that the Saviour left his disciples to grope their way in the dark, on a question affecting the personal rights of one-half the population of the Roman Empire? Is it possible that the Holy Spirit would withhold all knowledge of the Divine will from them, on so important a question? And, is it possible, that the Apostles would be contented to remain in uncertainty, during all their lives, as to what duty required in relation to sixty millions* of bondmen, without once asking for Divine direction? Most assuredly, they could not have thus acted, or been thus ignorant on the subject. The Saviour had informed them, most particularly, that their prayers should be heard. His language is incapable of misinterpretation: "And whatsoever ye shall ask in my name, that will I do, that the Father may be glorified in the Son. If ye shall ask anything in my name, I will do it." † Now, according to the editor, the Saviour could never have instructed the Apostles as to slavery, the Holy Spirit could never have revealed to them the truth on the subject, nor did the Apostles ever ask for Divine direction to guide them in duty as to the slaves! For, if any one of these things had occurred, the Apostles could not have been ignorant on so grave a question.

But the editor had a theory to sustain, and an object to accomplish. His object could not be effected, unless he could establish his theory. He must prove that slavery in the abstract was sinful — that was the task he had undertaken — or the church would not cast out the slaveholder. He, therefore, attempts to convince his readers, that the Apostles had been silent on the subject — not because slavery was not sinful, but because they

---

* Rev. Albert Barnes, in his work on Slavery, quotes and adopts, from the *Biblical Repository*, the following statement in reference to the number of slaves in the Roman Empire in the Apostles' day: "It is unnecessary to enter into proof that slavery abounded in the Roman Empire, or that the conditions of servitude were very severe and oppressive. This is conceded on all hands." . . . . . "Of course, according to this, the number of slaves could not have been less than sixty millions in the Roman Empire, at about the time when the Apostles went forth to preach the Gospel."

† John, xiv: 13, 14.

had so much else to do that it had to be overlooked — the Holy
Spirit seeing proper to give them, individually, no special revelation on slavery, but leaving the whole question to be determined
by the church, in after years, from the careful study of the completed revelation.   And there it stood, without notice, from age
to age, until the *Christian Intelligencer*, more than eighteen hundred years afterwards, began 'to shed its light upon the subject!

Reader, can you suppose that slaveholding is sinful, and yet,
that the Apostles never could find five minutes to say so; or
·never had any Divine directions how to deal with the slaveholder!
To say that the Apostles could not do everything at once, will
in no wise account for the difference in the clearness of the sacred Scriptures on idolatry and slavery.   If they could not do
everything at once, in regard to slavery, neither could they in
regard to idolatry; and the excuse that they did not declare in
regard to slavery, because they could not do everything at once,
implies that their action in regard to idolatry was not inspired,
but because it was in their power to attend to it at once.

The editor continues :

" As to the general subject of slavery, there was a reason why the
Apostles might regard it as lying *out of their way*, which does not exist
with us.   If there is any such thing as a historical verity, the Christians to whom they wrote, lived under a military despotism — a government most remote in its character from a Representative Republic.
The people had no influence on the making or administration of the
laws, more than our slaves.   But we, the people, make our laws ; and
from us, all our civil institutions take their character.   In the sins of
the government under which they lived, they had comparatively no
share : and hence slavery, an evil growing out of their civil institutions, was a thing for which they were not accountable, as we are.
The Apostles *could not* direct ' those whom they reformed ' to set immediately about the ' work of reforming the social system.'   They
could only watch unto prayer, and wait in faith and hope till ' the
greatness of the Kingdom ' should be on the side of righteousness.

" The attention of the Apostles might not have been particularly
turned to the subject for another reason.   The condition of a slave
was but little different from that of his master.   The great mass of the
population were rude and ignorant — human rights were not under-

stood — were little regarded — for any practical purpose, it was a matter of comparatively small importance, whether an individual enjoyed his inalienable rights or not." *

Truly, the silence of the Apostles, on the question of slavery, must have been a great puzzle to the editor. This is an additional conjecture, as to the reason why they may have passed slavery unnoticed, as well as failed to require emancipation as a condition of receiving the slaveholder into the Church. Let us examine it: the Roman government was despotic, the great mass of the population rude and ignorant, human rights not understood nor regarded, and, for all practical purposes, it was a matter of comparatively small importance, whether an individual enjoyed his inalienable rights or not. Here are the reasons, offered by the editor, why the Apostles did not urge emancipation. Can he tell us, if freedom would have been of no importance to an ignorant Roman slave in the first century, of what value it would be to a still more degraded African slave in the nineteenth century? But ignorance and degradation were not universal in Rome. Art, science, literature, flourished in a high degree. Even slaves were often men of letters and of science, though subjected to the rigid rule of their masters. Surely, liberty would have been of value to them; and yet the Apostles took no measures for their relief. If, then, the Apostles attached so little importance to human rights, as compared with the salvation of men, that they gave no directions for freeing the social system from slavery, why should the ministers of the Gospel now consider it necessary to make that topic one of leading interest in their ecclesiastical councils? Again: if the Apostles found it necessary to occupy themselves so constantly in preaching the Gospel, that they found no time to attend to civil affairs, how is it that ministers can now turn aside to dabble in politics, without being chargeable with treason to their Divine Master, whose kingdom is not of this world? And, again: if slaveholding be necessarily sinful, why was it not so under despotic Rome, as well as under Republican America?

---

* Christian Intelligencer, Hamilton, Ohio, April, 1829, page 109.

We must here repeat one of the editor's strongest propositions:

" The Africans *were stolen* from their country; no man will do him-self any credit by denying it: and that the actual holder of property which is known to be stolen, is as criminal as the thief, is both *logic and law*."

Failing to prove slaveholding a *sin per se*, by either Scripture precept or example, the editor, to accomplish his purpose, be-takes himself to logic and law.   He maintains, that the crimi-nality of the slaveholder grows out of the principle in law which makes the receiver of stolen property equally criminal with the thief.   This is a novel mode, certainly, of settling the question of the sinfulness of slaveholding.   But it is one that the Apos-tles seem not to have recognized as correct, in their intercourse with the Roman people.   The slaves then in the Empire numbered sixty millions of souls, and consisted, perhaps universally, of captives taken in war or their descendants.   The wars in which the captives were taken, had been waged for the aggrandizement of the reigning tyrants, who, from generation to generation, had ruthlessly deluged the earth in blood, to gratify an unhallowed ambition.   These were the slave traders of old, from whom the Roman masters, from reign to reign, had obtained their slaves. The slaveholders in the Apostles' day, very generally, must have been the inheritors only of slaves who were the descendants of the original captives; just as, in 1829, the slaveholders in the United States, very generally, were only inheritors of slaves, and had no complicity with the African slave traders, who had ceased their vocation in 1808. *   Were the Roman masters, in the Apostles' day, equally criminal with the remorseless conquerors who brought their captives to Rome to be sold into bondage?   The logic of the editor says they were; but the practice of the Apostles says they were not.   The Apostles set an example which the editor and the churches may well imitate.   They recognized the gov-ernment of Rome as the ordinance of God for the execution of his purposes toward a world sunk in sin; and they gladly recog-nized the Divine hand in the movements which had brought, from

* Only about 400,000 slaves had been imported between 1620 and 1808, while at the latter date, the whole number of slaves was 893,041.

the uttermost parts of the earth, the slaves who stood before
them.   Instead of demanding emancipation as a condition of
preaching the Gospel, the Great Salvation was everywhere offered to both masters and slaves.

But not only is the editor's logic at fault here; his theology
is equally as defective, and much more pernicious.   The doctrines taught by him and his associates, if true, would place the
church in a deplorable attitude, as it would leave her no sure
foundation of faith.   According to this view, the example of the
early Christians is not to be our guide; and the declarations of
the Apostles are to be no rule of action to us.   They could not
comprehend the Divine mind, as revealed to them, with as much
certainty as we can ourselves, now that we have a full revelation.
Here is a masked battery of Satan, erected by the professed disciples of Christ, and afterwards used with effect by the infidel
wing of the abolition army.   Look well at this point.   If the
Apostles did not understand the Divine will as to slavery, what
assurance is there that they comprehended it in relation to any
revealed duty?   Such doctrines are not in accordance with those
of the Christian church.   Prophecies of future events, for potent
reasons, were not always understood by their writers; but moral
duties were of present obligation, and, when revealed, must have
been fully comprehended by the Apostles.   Any other view is
infidel in its tendency, and could only have been uttered by orthodox men, under the blinding influence of a fanatical zeal for
a theory that could not otherwise be sustained.   We repeat, if
the Apostles were not competent judges of the morality or immorality of Roman slavery, they cannot be safe guides on any
other doctrine or rule of duty : so that, if this be true, there remains no certainty that any thing they enjoined is binding on the
conscience, but all is left to human reason, and nothing to the
word of God, as interpreted by the Apostles.

The force of these general objections to the grounds of the
Christian Intelligencer's position on the subject of slavery, will be
strengthened by an examination of the particulars of their position in detail.   1. We are told, that the Apostles might do, "in
their circumstances," what we may not do "in our circumstances;"
which amounts to nothing more than an endeavor to protect us

against the pernicious influence of their example, if they failed to condemn slavery. The contrary of this doctrine, is that which is expressly taught by inspiration : Phil. iii : 17 ; 2 Thes. iii : 9. In these passages the authority of apostolic example is directly enforced.

2. In justification of this position, and in farther carrying of it out, we are told, that "there were inspired men who practiced polygamy," and if it was "no reflection upon these inspired men" that they did not "purge out certain evils," "neither is it any reflection upon the Apostles," that they did not, and that they permitted slavery to go uncondemned. The Apostles did not tolerate "such an evil without testifying against it :" or, if they did, it is nothing more nor less than was in correspondence with the practice of even inspired men, some of whom were polygamists. The Apostle Peter spoke reverently of inspired men, and called them "holy men of God ;" [2 Pet. i : 21,] but as their course did not suit the editors, they account for the fact by classing them with polygamists.

3 But there is still "a step farther" that may be taken. "If the Apostles did not perceive that such slavery as existed among *us* is not sanctioned by the law of God, it does not follow that it *is* sanctioned by that law." The Apostles did not "understand fully" what was intended in their own writings. This is indeed "a step farther." Slavery *is* condemned in the Bible, but the inspired penmen themselves were ignorant of the fact. Their course in regard to the institution is not to be insisted upon, for, such is the possibility, they themselves might have condemned it in their own writings, and yet not have known it. If this is true, it is easy, in any given case, to get the Apostles out of the way, and whenever they are troublesome to be wholly rid of them, on the simple ground that they did not know their own sayings. In this "step farther," there is, moreover, an intimation that there is a directing Providence, as well as an inspired word, and this, that is apart from the word, is so essential that we "have to study as the Providence of God directs." Now as the Apostles "had" to study just as all other men, and all men are at liberty to judge for themselves as to how Providence directs, it is clear that this Providence may direct them, in their own estimation, to views in

the widest possible degree differing from those of the Apostles, and so these ancient worthies be effectually and entirely disposed of.

Turning from these views of the Apostles, we may next direct attention to the estimate placed upon the sacred writings, and the notions entertained respecting the first Christians. If they were not understood to condemn slavery, in the times of the Apostles, it was because they were not all written at the same time, and all put in circulation together. Those who had them, had them in various portions, and not as a connected whole— "the whole system of doctrines and duties,"— as we now have them. In the first place, there had all along been scriptures among the Jews, and these were continually referred to, as when our Saviour said: "search the scriptures;" [John v : 39;] and, in the second place, there was no such contrariety in the Old and New Testament scriptures, as that the rules of morality and of holy living, only, were known, as some portions of the New Testament had been happily obtained. Paul addressed Timothy [2 Tim. iii : 15] saying, that "from a child" he had "known the Holy Scriptures," and they were such scriptures as "were able to make" "wise," and he who had this wisdom would be saved. "Long" *before* "the last Apostle had gone to be 'present with the Lord'" the pen of inspiration had declared [2 Tim. iii : 17] that through the then existing scriptures, the *man of God* (a beautiful epithet,) might be "thoroughly furnished," and that "unto *all good works.*" Our editors say, not quite "all;" we have no reason to suppose that they equaled ourselves. So far from being "thoroughly furnished," they were not up to our standard in "any article of faith or duty which lay ever so little out of the Apostle's common track of preaching." Who does not see that this representing of the primitive church as without any scriptures, except to a meager extent, is contrary to the representation of the Apostles, who maintained that they not only possessed them, but that they were "profitable" to the ends for which they had been inspired, and urged home upon all the obligation to be "thoroughly furnished" by means of them? Who can fail to observe, also, that this position makes the commendation of the Bereans, [Acts xvii : 11,] for their study of the Scriptures, to convey the false impression, that the Church had suitable and sufficient scriptures for their guidance and instruction when they had not? Besides all which, it leaves the Apostles to the task of founding the Christian church, without the aid of a written literature that was fully available, until after the last of their number had gone to be "present with the Lord" — a position which could not be maintained, as is further evident, because it is contrary to all the analogy of God's providence; which, from the beginning, has made a written literature to be indispensably connected with the establishment of the true religion, and to that end first gave language, and then the first records, in language, that were ever known to the human family. It is not strange, therefore, that this theory of the editors brings them into direct conflict with the declaration of the inspired penmen in such passages as these: [2 Peter i: 9 :] "WE HAVE," (not there will be, after the last of us has gone to be "present with the Lord") "also, a *more sure word of prophecy* (or instruction,) to which we *do well to take heed*, as unto a light that shineth in a dark place." Again, [Col. iii: 16,] "Let the word of Christ dwell in you *richly*, in ALL wisdom, teaching," &c.

This representation of the earlier Christians, by the editors, as being without the Scriptures, is with a view to establish two points : 1. The clearness of the Scriptures as possessed by us, makes the overthrow of slavery to be obligatory upon us, while it was not upon them. 2. It takes away all the force of the example of primitive and Apostolic times, as they were in part without the Scriptures. "Practices and omissions of duty might have existed among them, which ought not to be tolerated in the church now." He therefore strenuously objects to "supposing a perfection among the Christians of that day" equal to what is attained by those of our day.

The plausibility of this position is attempted to be sustained by the farther suggestion of its reasonableness. "No man can — an Apostle could not do everything at once." Again, "they could not do every thing at once, although they were inspired men." It is unreasonable to suppose, according to this view, that the primitive church could have been framed so as to afford a suitable example. There was too much to be done, and, therefore, if we find anything to condemn which it did not condemn,

such as slavery, it need be no matter of surprise. Having found
an easy way to dispose of the Apostles, it was easy to dispose
of that which was built upon their "foundation." [Eph. ii : 20.]

To what straits will not men be driven by a theory! The
character of the Apostles, inspired as teachers in the primitive
church, and clothed with power of working miracles to establish
their authority and to confirm their mission; the fullness, the
sufficiency, the clearness, and the purity of the inspired Scriptures
of truth, no less remarkable in the manner of God's preserving
them, than in the fact of his having given them; the church that
was established with "Jesus Christ himself" as "the chief corner
stone;" all these are assailed with surmises, and innuendoes, and
suppositions, and for what? Why, that seventeen centuries after
the last of the Apostles had gone to be "present with the Lord,"
it might be possible, through a directing Providence, to make
room for new light on the subject of slavery!

One topic alluded to in the *Christian Intelligencer*, yet unnoticed by us, remains to be briefly handled, and we have done. It
is in an article from the pen of an assistant editor, and will be understood from the title which is at its head: "*The Emancipation
of the Slaves practicable — their Mental and Moral Culture impracticable.*" * This production was, substantially, an endorse-
ment of the British theory — that slavery and African evangelization are incompatible. The writer, in support of his theory,
quoted certain laws, in the slave States, which prohibit the education of slaves, but altogether avoided any mention of the success
that had attended the missionaries in the West Indies, where slavery then prevailed; and, with equal care, neglected to notice the
results of the labors of the Methodists, and others, among the
slaves in the United States. He theorized entirely, offering no
facts to sustain his proposition; or, rather, he avoided any notice
of existing facts, that would be in opposition to his theory. †

The course adopted by this writer, in his pertinacious adher-
ence to his theory, while facts enough existed around him to dis-

---

* Christian Intelligencer, March, 1829, page 65.

† In justice to the editor, it must be said, that he corrects the writer so far
as to say, that very few of the laws referred to absolutely prohibit the mental
instruction of the slaves.

prove its correctness, reminds us of an anecdote told in relation to an eminent Geologist, who had a fashion of never yielding a favorite theory, however much newly developed facts might make against him.

In a certain mountain district, an excitement had long prevailed in relation to the discovery of copper ores. Several very valuable mines had been found and opened. The Geologist was attracted to the spot, and, before leaving, received an invitation to a locality a few miles distant, where some new excavations, in a different class of rocks, had been made. Examining the pile of rocks around the mouth of the shaft, he at once pronounced their labor as lost — stating, that the slate rocks in which they were digging, had long been familiar to him, in various sections of the country, and were uniformly barren of all metallic ores. The miners listened patiently, until he closed his remarks, and then politely invited him to descend the shaft, and see the strata of rocks in a side-drift which they had run out from the bottom. He readily complied, remarking, that sections of newly cut rocks were always interesting to Geologists. Down they went, lamps in hand, and, on reaching the spot, a magnificent vein of copper ore met his astonished vision ! Fact exploded theory.

Reader, descend the shaft excavated into the strata of the history of negro instruction, by the preceding chapters, and behold the West Indies, at the time the writer quoted prepared his argument, with over 90,000 Christian converts among the slaves, and the United States with about 120,000 ; and, then, never again rely upon any theory that is based upon speculation instead of ascertained facts.

The arguments on slavery, by which the revolution in church discipline was effected, are now before the reader. They contain the germs of nearly all the arguments afterward employed by the abolitionists, in their fiery assaults upon the system, and upon those who sustained it. Even the infidel abolitionist found his warrant therein for assailing the Bible, and the semi-infidel for demanding "an anti-slavery Constitution, and anti-slavery Bible, and an anti-slavery God." * Garrison, too, could point to more

---

* Anson Burlingame.

than one assertion in justification of his declaration, that the "United States Constitution is a covenant with death and an agreement with hell." *

Such was the office performed by the writers in the *Christian Intelligencer*, for the Church and for the country. †

The progress of ecclesiastical legislation, from the terms of the old platform to the new, may be seen by reference to the chapters on that subject. The churches, generally, which had pronounced slavery a moral evil, to be speedily remedied, were not able at once to carry out the new rule proposed, in its literal meaning, because of the opposition of conservative men. Exceptions to the rule were made, in some cases, in relation to those of their members who resided in States disallowing emancipation. One denomination proposed that a *moral emancipation* might be substituted for a legal manumission — the master still holding his legal title to the slave, not as property, but as guardian — thus freeing the slaveholder from all guilt by this fictitious change of relation. ‡ But this rule, in the view of anti-slavery men, would be liable to great abuses, as under it every slaveholder might take refuge, and the abolition of slavery never be effected. The broader doc-

---

* Garrison's *Liberator*.

† NOTE.—It may be doubted, that preaching from the pulpit on the subject of slavery, was authorized and required by any ecclesiastical legislation on the subject; but such doubts must yield to the facts in the case. The editor, and associate editors, of the *Christian Intelligencer*, belonged to the First Presbytery of Ohio, in connection with the Associate Reformed Synod of the West. They drew up the Reports, and managed the Slavery Question, it is understood, when it was under consideration in that Synod. At the meeting of this Presbytery, in September, 1833, the subject of the action of the Synod was brought forward, considered, reported on, and the following resolution, among others, was adopted, as the principles which should thereafter regulate the Presbytery and the churches under its care:

"*Resolved* 1. Ministers should not fail, by the pulpit, and, so far as practicable, by the press, to show, in a faithful and temperate manner, from the Word of God, the iniquity and ruinous consequences of this sin. The truth on this subject is always important, but it derives very great *present* importance from the prevalence of slavery in our country, and from the interest which the subject excites in the public mind."—*Christian Intelligencer*, Hamilton, Ohio, July, 1834.

‡ See Chapter VII.

trine of the *Christian Intelligencer*, and its disciples, the abolitionists, that slaveholding is *malum in se* — in itself a sin — under all circumstances, was, therefore, urged upon public attention with great zeal, and no small amount of success.   A practical application of this doctrine, by a few of the religious denominations, soon resulted in the withdrawal of their ministry, as heretofore stated, from the whole of the slave States — thus leaving both master and slave in total destitution of the ordinances of religion.*

SECTION III.—HOW THE ABOLITIONISTS WERE MET BY ARGUMENTS AGAINST THEIR BIBLE THEORIES.

We have said, that, in the outset of the abolition movement, the conservative element predominated in some of the churches, so as to hold in check the fanatical spirit every where manifesting itself.   This was so fully the case, in the PROTESTANT EPISCOPAL CHURCH, that the subject of slavery was never agitated in its councils, so as to lead to legislation on the subject.   The same thing is true of the CHRISTIAN CHURCH, (otherwise called Campbellites.)

The METHODIST EPISCOPAL CHURCH, as well as the GENERAL ASSEMBLY PRESBYTERIANS, both had a long struggle on this question.   The discussions in the former body, in attempting to keep the Church from taking ultra ground, were very ably conducted; and the Church was saved from the evils of abolitionism for many years.   In this controversy, their ablest men were engaged; and the conclusions at which they arrived, were very different, indeed, from those of the writers in the *Christian Intelligencer*.   Rev. Dr. BANGS, in 1834, thus wrote:

" At the time he (Christ) made his appearance in our world, slavery existed all over the Roman Empire, not excepting even the highly favored land of Judea, to such an extent that it has been estimated

---

* A striking example of this kind is recorded by the *British Friend*, of 1854, as having occurred in Virginia.   The agitation of the subject of slavery began among the Society of Friends, at an early day, in the district to which it refers.   "There were, at the time," says the *Friend*, "seven meetings of Friends in that part of Virginia, but they have all long since been deserted, and the country literally desolated."

that about one-half of the population of that vast empire were in a state of civil bondage. . . . . . When Jesus Christ sent out his Apostles to preach, did he give them a command to denounce those masters because they held slaves? and to tell them that unless they let those oppressed go free, they could not repent and enter the kingdom of heaven? *Nothing of this.* We do not recollect a *single instance* of his having uttered a word on this subject." *

Bishops EMERY and HEDDING, in an address of September, 1835, say, that "within the Roman Empire, slaves were both more numerous, and their legalized condition worse, than the legalized condition of the same class in any portion of our own country."

Rev. Dr. FISK, and others, in the " Counter Appeal," say, that "Christianity spread in a land where slavery existed as cruel and licentious as ever existed in this country." And in referring to Ephesians vi: 5–9, they assert, that "it places it beyond debate or a doubt, that the Apostle did permit slaveholders in the Christian Church." And, again, in commenting on Colossians iii: 22, they say:

" We say, then, that this text proves *to a demonstration*, that, in the primitive Christian Church at Colosse, under the Apostolic eye, and with the Apostolic sanction, *the relation of master and slave was permitted to subsist.* The slave is addressed as continuing a slave, the master as permanently a master; the former is exhorted to obedience, the latter to justice and equity in *the exercise* of his authority. Who can assert, in the face of this text, that no slave-master is 'truly awakened,' nor can be endured in a Christian Church?"

Rev. Dr. BOND, thus wrote:

"Slaveholding itself is no where in terms forbidden in Scripture, though the practice was general in the time of our Lord and his Apostles; yet there is no express prohibition to Christians to hold slaves, though there are express exhortations to slaves to obey their masters, and to make this a matter of conscience." †

---

* Christian Advocate and Journal, December 5, 1834.

† As quoted by Rev. Dr. Elliott, in his "Great Secession" page 260.

Professor STUART, of Andover, having been addressed on the subject by Rev. Dr. FISK, who asked for historical information, thus wrote:

"Every one knows, who is acquainted with Greek and Latin antiquities, that slavery among heathen nations has ever been more unqualified, and at looser ends, than among Christian nations. Slaves were *property* in Greece and Rome. That decides all question about their *relation*. Their treatment depended, as it does now, on the temper of their masters. The power of the master over the slave was, for a long time, that of life and death. Horrible cruelties, at length, mitigated it. In the Apostles' day, it was, at least, as great as among us."
. . . . . "1 Tim. vi: 2, expresses the sentiment that slaves who are Christians, and have Christian masters, are not, on that account, and because as Christians they are brethren, to forego the reverence due to them as masters. That is, the relation of master and slave is not, as a matter of course, abrogated between all Christians. Nay, servants should, in such case, *a fortiori*, do their duty cheerfully. This sentiment lies on the very face of the verse." . . . . . "The precepts of the New Testament respecting the demeanor of slaves, and of their masters, beyond all question *recognize* the existence of slavery. The masters are *believing masters*, so that a precept to them how they are to behave *as masters*, *recognizes* that the relation may still exist, *salva fide et salva ecclesia* — without violating the Christian faith of the Church. Otherwise Paul had nothing to do but to cut the bond asunder at once. He could not lawfully and properly temporize with a *malum in se* — that is, itself a sin. If any one doubts, let him take the case of Paul's sending Onesimus [*a slave*] back to Philemon [*his master*,] with apology for his running away, and sending him back to be his servant for life. The relation did exist, may exist. The *abuse* of it is the essential, fundamental wrong." *

Rev. Dr. CLARKE, (Comment. 1 Tim. vi: 1,) says:

"The word δουλοι ('servants,') here means *slaves* converted to the Christian faith; and the ζυγοσ, or yoke, is the *state of slavery*."

* These quotations, as well as the others in reference to the Methodist Episcopal Church, are taken from the pamphlet of Rev. Nathan Scarlet, of the Kansas Conference.

Again, he says, (Tit. ii : 9) :

" The Apostle refers to those who were *slaves*, the *property* of their masters."

Again, (Col. iv : 1,) he says :

" The condition of slaves among the Greeks and Romans was wretched in the extreme ; they could appeal to no law ; and they could neither expect justice nor equity."

Again, (Comment. 1 Tim. vi : 3) :

" With political questions, or questions relative to private *rights*, our Lord scarcely ever meddled ; he taught all men to *love one another ;* to respect each other's rights ; to submit to each other ; to show all fidelity ; to be obedient, humble, and meek ; and to know that his kingdom was not of this world."

Again, (Comment. 1 Cor. vii : 24) :

" It is very likely that some of the slaves at Corinth, who had been converted to Christianity, had been led to think that their Christian privileges absolved them from the necessity of continuing slaves, or, at least, brought them on a level with their Christian masters. A spirit of this kind might have soon led to confusion and insubordination, and brought scandals into the Church. It was, therefore, a very proper subject for the Apostle to interfere in ; and to his authority the persons concerned would doubtless respectfully bow."

Again, (on 1 Cor. vii : — end of the chapter) :

" The *conversion* which the Scripture requires, though it makes a most essential change in our *souls* in reference to God, and in our *works* in reference both to God and man, makes none in our *civil state,* even if a man is *called, i. e.,* converted, in a state of slavery, he does not gain his manumission in consequence of his conversion ; he stands in the same relation both to the *state* and to his fellows that he stood in *before ;* and is not to assume any *civil* rights or privileges in consequence of the conversion of his soul to God. The Apostle decides the matter in this chapter, and orders that every man should abide in the calling wherein he is called."

Again, (on Phil. — end of the chapter,) he says:

"Christianity makes no change in men's civil affairs; even a slave did not become a freeman by Christian baptism."

And, again, in remarking on another passage, he says:

"The Apostle, therefore, informs the proprietors of these slaves that they should act toward them both according to *justice* and *equity;* for God, their Master, required this of them, and would at last call them to account for their conduct in this respect."

Rev. Dr. FISK, in the "Counter Appeal," says:

"'Servants, be obedient to them that are your masters according to the flesh, with fear and trembling, in singleness of heart as unto Christ; not with eye-service as men-pleasers, but as servants of Christ doing the will of God from the heart; with good-will doing service, as to the Lord, and not to men; knowing that whatsoever good thing any man doeth, the same shall he receive of the Lord, whether he be bond or free. And, ye masters, do the same thing unto them, forbearing threatening; knowing that your Master also is in heaven; neither is there respect to persons with him.' On this text we remark: 1. It places beyond debate or doubt, that *the Apostle did permit slaveholders in the Christian Church.* There were already such in the Church of Ephesus, or he would not have addressed them by the term master, as a legitimate and continuous title; without one word of emancipation, he directly enjoins upon them the mild exercise of that authority, 'forbearing threatening.' 2. He exhibits the difference between slave-holding in the hands of a Christian master, and a tyrannical and heathen master. While the former might exercise the proper duties of the station, the latter would, no doubt, be guilty of all the cruelties and abominations of which Greek and Roman slavery was preëminently full. Yet the enormity of its abuses did not, in his opinion, require the immediate abolition of the relation itself. 3. The New Testament, here and elsewhere, enjoins obedience upon the slave as an obligation *due* to a present *rightful* authority. They are to be 'obedient,' not deceitfully, but with 'singleness of heart,' and 'to please them in all things, not answering again, not purloining, but showing all good fidelity.'—Titus ii: 9. It is perfectly ludicrous to pretend that this injunction is parallel with the command to be passive under inflictions for righteousness' sake. It is perfectly irrelevant for our brethren to

challenge any man in the world to show how, by our rules of interpretation, the command to pray for persecutors does not justify persecution.   To say nothing of the fact that we find no persecutors
holding an acknowledged standing in the primitive Christian Church;
that we find no injunctions to persecutors to discharge their duties
with moderation, 'forbearing threatening;' that we find no successive
addresses to Christians persecuted, and Christian persecutors, mutually
to perform toward each other the correlative duties of those respective
characters.   'We challenge any man in the world to show,' if the case
of the slave and the persecuted Christian be parallel, how the former
is not justified in 'gainsaying,' in refuting, in 'answering again,' and
in fleeing from one city to another.   What command obliged the persecuted Christian to please his persecutor 'in all things,' with 'singleness of heart,' and 'with all good fidelity?'   These are exhortations
that sound like injunctions to perform duties of at least a present
rightful relation.   If that relation be invariably sinful, how, indeed,
can any slave be justified in perpetuating the oppressive system upon
others by submission to it himself?   How could the Apostle be justified in thus obliging them to aid in that oppression by even forbidding
a breach of 'fidelity?' and how are abolitionists justified — who repel
the charge of preaching insubordination or escape — in conniving, by
their silence, at the slave's ignorance of his rights, and thus combin-
ing with their oppressors in perpetuating the yoke?''

Rev. Dr. ELLIOTT, in his '' Great Secession,'' page 818, says:

''And those few churches in recent times, which have made or attempted to make absolute non-slaveholding a term of membership,
have done little or nothing religiously to benefit slave or master; or
they have shut themselves out entirely from the field of labor.   The
reason is, they have adopted a mere arbitrary theory in the place of
the Gospel panacea, of enlightenment, regeneration, and sanctification,
and therefore could not succeed.   This is history, and can not be met
except by dogmatism and self-sufficiency, and with some mixture of
fanaticism and narrow sectarianism.''

The BOARD OF BISHOPS, in their address, in 1840, say:

'' We are fully persuaded that, as a body of Christian ministers, we
shall accomplish the greatest good by directing our individual and
united efforts, in the spirit of the first teachers of Christianity, to

bring both master and servant under the sanctifying influence of the principles of that Gospel which teaches the duties of every relation, and enforces the faithful discharge of them by the strongest conceivable motives. Do we aim at the amelioration of the condition of the slave? How can we so effectually accomplish this in our calling as ministers of the Gospel of Christ, as by employing our whole influence to bring both him and his master to a saving knowledge of the grace of God, and to a practical observance of those relative duties so clearly prescribed in the writings of the inspired Apostles. Permit us to add, that, although we enter not into the political contentions of the day, neither interfere with civil legislation, nor with the administration of the laws, we can not but feel a deep interest in whatever affects the peace, prosperity, and happiness of our beloved country. The Union of these States, the perpetuity of the bonds of our National Confederation, the reciprocal confidence of the different members of the great civil compact — in a word, the *well-being* of the community of which we are members, should never cease to lay near our hearts, and for which we should offer up our sincere and most ardent prayers to the Almighty Ruler of the Universe. But can we, as ministers of the Gospel, and servants of a Master 'whose kingdom is not of this world,' promote these important objects in any way so truly and permanently, as by pursuing the course just pointed out? Can we, at this eventful crisis, render a better service to our country than by *laying aside all interference with relations authorized and established by the civil laws*, and applying ourselves wholly and faithfully to what specially appertains to our 'high and holy calling;' to teach and enforce the moral obligations of the Gospel, in application to all the duties growing out of the different relations in society."

It is not necessary to trace these discussions any farther. The controversy extended itself to all the religious denominations, but, as before stated, a few of them managed to prevent its introduction into their legislative councils. The debates were often of the most exciting character, and the press, availing itself of its rights in a free country, gave an interest to their columns by reporting the speeches. The reproach which this was calculated to bring upon a fanatical ministry soon became obvious, and, in certain quarters, the offending editors were rebuked with severity. We find the following in the *Christian Intelligencer*, for February, 1836:

" *Religious Papers.* — We are, moreover, of opinion that, however valuable and popular the *New York Observer* may be, it does more mischief than all our religious newspapers put together; and the editors are acquiring popularity at a fearful expense to our church and the reputation of her ministry.   To attend our judicatories in times of excitement, and publish all the angry words and half-inch speeches, which good men utter, may gratify a morbid curiosity; but exposes our church and her ministry, in the very worst attitude in which they can be placed before the public eye.   Their virtue and devoted and active piety are thrown in the shade, and the moment of excitement is seized to draw their likeness and place it in bold relief before a censorious and scoffing world." — *Pittsburgh Christian Herald.**

Upon this the editor of the *Intelligencer* thus remarks:

" This is a great truth.   Mr. Baird deserves the thanks of the Christian community for daring to utter it,   Such is the desire of many editors of ' religious papers' to swell their subscription list, that they will gratify this ' morbid curiosity,' and furnish ' views' to suit all kinds of readers at all hazards; and, unless it is checked, the time must soon come, when no church will be permitted to keep its business in its own hands.   Not a measure will be taken up, or even mentioned in an ecclesiastical judicatory, but it will be reported in the newspapers, and placed before the public mind in some false attitude — the prejudices of some will be excited, and the passions of others inflamed, so as entirely to preclude the possibility of cool and rational reflection."

This shrinking from the scrutiny of the public press, comes with an ill-grace from parties who were clamorous for free discussion: and, the more especially is it so, when the whole of the church enactments on slavery were put to vote, and carried, under the highest state of excitement.   But, with them, free discussion must have been like submission to church authority by William Tennent, and his fellow Protesters, in 1741, when re-

---

* The complaint of the editor of the *Herald* may have had reference to the trial of Rev. Lyman Beecher, D. D., for heresy, which had taken place some time before the date of the above remarks, and which had been reported for the *New York Observer*, but it will apply with equal force to the slavery controversy, then rife in the churches.

quired to submit to the decisions of the Presbyterian Synod. In effect they asserted: " If we were the majority, it would be binding on you to obey the rules; but, seeing you sightless and Christless ones are in the majority, the rules are null, and, like yourselves, fit only to be despised." *

It would be easy to make a volume of extracts, from abolition documents and speeches, of the period between 1830 and 1840, showing the vehement spirit animating those who conducted the crusade against slavery, and the fanatical spirit by which they were animated; but we shall allow Rev. Dr. CHANNING to draw their portrait. In 1836, in one of his works, he says:

"The abolitionists have done wrong, I believe; nor is their wrong to be winked at because done fanatically or with good intentions; for how much mischief may be wrought with good designs! They have fallen into the common error of enthusiasts, that of exaggerating their object, of feeling as if no evil existed but that which they opposed, and as if no guilt could be compared with that of countenancing and upholding it. The tone of their newspapers, so far as I have seen them, has often been fierce and abusive. They have sent forth orators, some of them transported with fiery zeal, to sound the alarm against slavery through the land, to gather together young and old, pupils from schools, females hardly arrived at the years of discretion, the ignorant, the excitable, the impetuous, and to organize these into associations for the battle against oppression. Very unhappily they preached their doctrine to the colored people, and collected them into societies. To this mixed and excitable multitude, minute heart-rending descriptions of slavery were given in piercing tones of passion; and slaveholders were held up as monsters of cruelty and crime. The abolitionist, indeed, proposed to convert slaveholders; and for this end he approached them with vituperation and exhausted on them the vocabulary of abuse. And he has reaped as he sowed."

The tendencies of the abolition movement, did not escape the attention of discerning men. It was foreseen, and predicted, that its ultimate results would be the dissolution of the Union, as a necessary consequence of the alienation of feeling which it engendered between the North and the South. Two or three years

---

* Webster's History of the Presbyterian Church in America, p. 164.

after Dr. Channing uttered his views of abolition, the *Princeton Review* made this prophetic declaration:

" The opinion that slaveholding is itself a crime must operate to produce the disunion of the States and the division of all ecclesiastical societies in the country. Just so far as this opinion operates it will lead those who entertain it to submit to any sacrifices to carry it out, and give it effect. We shall become two nations in feeling, which must soon render us two nations in fact."

To check the tendencies to this result, many of the most pious and intelligent men in the church, as well as in the state, set their faces, as steel, against the abolition movement. The same year that Dr. Channing expressed his opinion of the abolitionists, the General Conference of the Methodist Episcopal Church, holding its session in Cincinnati, passed a series of resolutions in reprobation of abolitionism, by an overwhelming majority. *

But we must leave this part of our field of discussion, to present a class of facts which are indispensable to a proper understanding of the question of the best mode of promoting African Evangelization. We shall, however, resume the discussion, in another chapter, of the abolition movements, in their connection with the ecclesiastical legislation at the North, so as to show that they were the natural outgrowth of that legislation.

SECTION IV.—INQUIRIES INTO THE DIFFERENCE IN THE DEGREES OF SUCCESS ATTENDING THE ATTEMPTS TO EVANGELIZE THE AFRICAN RACE THROUGHOUT THE WORLD.

Among an unthinking people, writers and orators may frame acceptable theories, based only on the speculations of their own imaginations; but he who would secure attention from an intelligent public, must found his theories upon facts. In no field of investigation is an appeal to facts so imperiously demanded, at this moment, as in that of the slavery question. False theories on the subject have done their fatal work upon our country. A writer has recently observed, that " It is in the arena of politics

* See Chapter VIII., session of 1836.

that every moral and theological short-coming reaches maturity, and meets its final penalty." This has been strikingly true in reference to the United States. The pulpit began the crusade against slavery, and the press brought it to maturity upon the arena of party politics : the nation is now meeting the penalty. *

But I am met with the assertion, that certain evils are so inimical to the interests of humanity, that an exemption from them is cheaply purchased by war. This may all be true ; but, then, if the evils complained of cannot be remedied by war, a terrible responsibility rests upon those who provoke it. How is it in the present case? The evil complained of, is the degradation of the negro, under slavery, in the Southern States. His moral elevation, it is contended, can be effected only by emancipation, as a means of making him accessible to the Gospel. This has been the burden of the cry of the abolitionists from the beginning. It is well, therefore, to ascertain whether the moral elevation of the negro will necessarily follow emancipation. This cannot be determined by theorizing about the natural equality of men, but only by an examination of the facts connected with the history of the African race. And if it should appear, under all the varied circumstances in which the Providence of God has placed the colored man, that his condition in the United States, under slavery, has been the most favorable to his evangelization, then there can be no longer any reason for Christian men to wage war upon the system, so as to endanger the peace of the country.

In prosecuting this inquiry, attention is asked to the principal

---

* Near the close of 1838, in the midst of the abolition excitement, the *Vermont Chronicle,* in commenting upon GUIZOT'S HISTORY OF CIVILIZATION, and applying some of the teachings of history to the condition of slavery in the United States, made the following sensible remark:

"Whatever of religious influence there is, therefore, among slaveholders and slaves, ought to be fervently rejoiced in, and sedulously cherished. To denounce all religious effort in slaveholding countries, is not only unchristian and injurious conduct toward the population of those countries, but treason against religion itself. The history of the progress of liberty, under any other than religious auspices, is not such, surely, as to encourage Christian men in relying on any other than Christian principles for " breaking every yoke."

facts connected with the various Christian missions among the Africans throughout the world, whether in bondage or in freedom:

1. *The obstacles to African Evangelization in South Africa.*

In this investigation, we must avail ourselves of former labors,* to some extent; and before commencing the missionary history of South Africa, a brief reference must be had to its civil history:

The Dutch took possession of the Cape in 1650, and this occupancy was followed by an extensive emigration of that people to Cape Town and its vicinity. The encroachments of the emigrants upon the Hottentots, soon gave rise to wars, which resulted in the enslavement of this feeble race. The English captured Cape Town in 1795, ceded it back in 1801, retook it in 1808, and still hold it in possession.

The climate of South Africa being favorable to the health of Europeans, an English emigration to the Cape commenced soon after it became a British province. This led to further encroachments upon the native tribes, and to much disaffection upon the part of the Dutch, who were designated by the term *Boers.* † They remained in the Colony, however, until 1834, when the emancipation act of the British Parliament, set the Hottentots free. This so enraged the Boers, that they emigrated in large bodies beyond the limits of Cape Colony. In seeking new homes, they came in contact with the Zulus, as already stated, and aided in the subjugation of that powerful people. Driven by the English from the Zulu country, the Boers passed on to the north-west, far into the interior, where we shall soon hear from them again.

The English, in extending their settlements to the north-east of Cape Town, soon came into collision with the Caffres; who, being a powerful and warlike race, made a vigorous resistance to their advances. The Caffres stole the cattle of the whites, and the whites retaliated on the Caffres. These depredations often resulted in wars, each of which gave the English government a pretext to add a portion of the Caffre territory to its own. As war followed on war, the Caffres improved in the art, acquired something of the skill of their enemies, and learned the use of European weapons. Thus every Caffre war became more formidable, requiring more troops, costing more money, and, of course, demanding more territory. In consequence of these

---

* See " Ethiopia," for full particulars.   † The German term for farmers.

various annexations from the Caffres, Zulus, and others, the English possessions in South Africa now cover a space of 282,000 square miles; 105,000 of which have been added since 1847.

The Missionary History of South Africa, though of great interest, must also be very brief.

A Moravian mission, begun in 1736, among the Hottentots, was broken up at the end of six years, by the Dutch authorities, and its renewal prevented for 49 years. Having been resumed in 1792, it was again interrupted in 1795, but soon afterward restored under British authority. Here, the hostility of the Dutch government to Christian Missions excluded the Gospel from South Africa during a period of half a century.

A mission to the Caffres, begun in 1799, by Dr. Vanderkemp, was abandoned in a year, on account of the jealousies of that people toward the whites, and their plots to take his life. The other missions, of various denominations, begun from time to time, in South Africa, have also been interrupted and retarded by the wars of the natives with each other, and more especially with the whites.

The pecuniary loss to the English, by the war of 1835, was $1,200,000 ; and by that of 1846–7, $3,425,000. This, however, was a matter of little importance, compared with the moral bearings of these conflicts. The missions suffered more or less in all the wars, either by interruptions of their labors, or in having their people pressed into the army. In that of 1846–7, the London Society had its four stations in the Caffre country entirely ruined, and its missionaries and people were compelled to seek refuge in the Colony.

But the most disastrous of all these conflicts, and that which has cast the deepest gloom over the South African Missions, was the Caffre war of 1851–2–3. These missions, with the exception of that to the Zulus, were under the care of ten missionary societies, all of which were European. They had recovered from the shocks of the former wars, and were in an encouraging state, when, in December, 1850, the Caffre war broke out. In consequence of that war, many of the missions were reduced to a most deplorable condition ; affording a sad commentary on the doctrine that the white and black races, in the present moral condition of the world, can dwell together in harmony.

The missions of the Scotch Free Church were in the very seat of war, the buildings of two of them destroyed, and the missionaries forced to flee for their lives; while the third was only saved by being fortified.

The Berlin Missionary Society had its missionaries driven from two of its stations, during the progress of the war.

The Mission of the United Presbyterian Synod of Scotland, which consisted of three stations, was all involved in ruin. The war laid waste the mission stations, scattered the missionaries and converts, suspended entirely the work of instruction, and did an amount of evil which can scarcely be exaggerated. The Report for 1853 declared that the mission could not be resumed on its old basis, as the Caffres around their stations were to be driven away; and though the native converts, numbering 100, might be collected at one of the stations, it was deemed better that a delegation visit South Africa, and report to the Board a plan of future operations.

The London Missionary Society also suffered greatly, and some of their missionaries were stript of every thing they possessed. The Report for 1853, says: "This deadly conflict has at length terminated, and terminated, as might have been foreseen, by the triumph of British arms. The principal Caffre chiefs, with their people, have been driven out of their country; and their lands have been allotted to British soldiers and colonists. And on the widely extended frontier, there will be established military posts, from which the troops and the settlers are to guard the colony against the return of the exiled natives."

Such, indeed, was the hostility of the whites toward the missionaries themselves, at one of the Churches in the white settlements, that *bullets* were not unfrequently dropped into the collection plates.*

Both Moravian and Wesleyan Missions have been destroyed. In one instance, 250 Hottentots perished by the hands of English soldiers, in the same Church where they had listened to the word of God from the Moravian missionaries; not because they were enemies, but in an attempt to disarm a peaceful population. Such were the cruelties incident to this war!

The Paris Missionary Society had thirteen stations in South Africa. Its Report, for 1853, complained of the interruptions and injuries which its missions had suffered, in consequence of the military commotions which had prevailed in the fields occupied by its missionaries. In alluding to the obstacles to the Gospel which every where existed, Dr. Grandpierre, the Director of the Society, said: "But how are these obstacles multiplied, when the missionary is obliged to encounter, in the lives of nominal Christians, that which gives the

---

* Missionary Mag. and Chron., Oct., 1853.

lie to his teachings. Irritated by the measures which are employed against them, may not the aborigines rightfully say to the whites, with more truth than ever, 'You call yourself the children of the God of peace; and yet you make war upon us. You teach justice; but you are guilty of injustice. You preach the love of God; and you take away our liberty and our property.' "

One of the Scotch Societies, near the close of the Caffre war, when summing up the effects it had produced, draws this melancholy picture:

"All missionary operations have been suspended; the converts are either scattered or compelled, by their hostile countrymen, to take part in the revolt; the missionaries have been obliged to leave the scenes of their benevolent labors; hostile feelings have been excited between the black and white races, which it will require a long period to soothe down; and the prospects of evangelizing Caffreland have been rendered dark and distant."

We turn now to another class of missions, and, for the brief synopsis presented, are indebted to the *Missionary Magazine*, the organ of the AMERICAN BAPTIST MISSIONARY UNION, which copies from the *London Missionary Chronicle* — the paragraphs descriptive of the Bushmen being from the *London Quarterly Review*.

The first mission of the London Missionary Society, in South Africa, was begun in 1799, among the BUSHMEN. The station selected was 400 miles from Cape Town, on the Zak River. This station was abandoned in 1805, owing to the quarrels of the native tribes, the difficulty of obtaining the means of subsistence, &c. The next effort among the Bushmen was made in 1814, at Thornberg, and two years afterward, a removal effected to a point nearer the Great Orange River, which they called Hepzibah. In this place some success followed their efforts; but, through the influence of the Boers, the British authorities peremptorily ordered the missionaries within the colony, on the plea that " these institutions were detrimental to the colony." Though the Society has never since been able to form a mission to the Bushmen, nevertheless, in connection with the Griquas, the Hottentots at Kat River, and among the Namaquas and the Bechuanas, out stations have been formed for Bushmen, among whom some deeply affecting instances of spiritual good have been witnessed.* The following account of the Bushmen will interest the reader. It is from a late number of the *London Quarterly Review:*

"On the banks and in the valleys of the Snowberg or Snowy Mountains, which form the northern boundary of the Cape, humanity is found in the very lowest state of degradation in which it has ever been exhibited. The Bosjesmans, or Bushmen, two or three specimens of which race were brought to this country a few years ago, present an exaggeration even of the hideous form which characterizes the Hottentot. Hunger, and cold, and nakedness, and every description of privation and distress, have so dwarfed their forms and depraved their minds, that they present a spectacle painful to look upon. The stature of these pigmy inhabitants of the desert rarely exceeds four feet, or four feet two inches. Thieves by profession, cruel and treacherous, without a fixed habitation, without society, without any sort of common interest or government, and living only from day to day, and from hand to mouth, they were objects of loathing to neighboring tribes, even before Europeans had approached their country. The more civilized of the Hottentots and Caffres waged a deadly war against them; and the sight of one of these diminutive savages is said to rouse the passions of that race to an unaccountable fury. Many years since, a Caffre saw in the Government House at Cape Town, among the other domestics, a Bushman eleven years of age. With the impulse of a beast of prey he darted upon him, and transfixed him with his aggesai.

"The little intelligence which the Bushmen possess is displayed chiefly in robbery and the chase. Rivaling the antelope in fleetness and the monkey in agility, they accompany their wild, half-famished, savage dogs until they come within bowshot of their game, or run down the objects of their pursuit. Arrayed generally with a bow, a quiver full of arrows, a hat and a belt, leather sandals, a sheep's fleece, a gourd, or the shell of an ostrich's egg, to carry water, these puny creatures wander over their parched and desolate plains, supported by a food which, unless when occasionally varied by the luxuries of the chase, consists entirely of roots, berries, ant-eggs, grasshoppers, mice, toads, lizards, and snakes. They smear the arrows which they use for hunting, and in war, with a poison which, extracted from a bulb, and mingled with a venom drawn from the jaws of the

---

* Missionary Magazine, Jan., 1861 — copied from London Miss. Chron.

yellow serpent, forms a compound of the most noxious character, for no creature was ever pierced by a dart prepared with this deadly virus, and lived. They have another poison more fearful in its effects, which is extracted from a caterpillar. The agony produced by it, Dr. Livingstone says, is so intense, that the person wounded cuts himself with knives, and flies from human habitation a raving maniac. The effect upon the lion is equally terrible. He is heard moaning in distress, becomes furious, and bites trees and the ground in his rage.

"They are said to be totally void of natural affection; 'and there are instances,' adds a missionary, (Mr. Kicherer) who lived for some time in the neighborhood, 'of parents throwing their tender offspring to the hungry lion who stood roaring before their cavern, refusing to depart until some peace-offering was made to him. They shun the face of strangers, concealing themselves amongst the rocks and bushes, and even throwing themselves over precipices rather than fall into the hands of their enemies. But they have been known, when escape has been cut off, to fight with the most determined resolution. Religion they have none. They regard the thunder as the voice of an angry demon, and they reply to it with curses and imprecations. Their language is inarticulate to all but themselves; and there appears to be scarcely even a possibility of either civilizing or converting them. In the north-east of Natal, where the Bushmen appear in their lowest type, they reside in holes of the earth scraped out with their nails, or rather with their claws. 'They will not receive kindness,' says a close observer of their character; 'or if they do, they only make a return of treachery, robbery, and murder. No presents of cattle or corn, no inducements to locate and settle, can prevail upon them to relinquish their wild life, or to make any approach toward civilization.' The only satisfactory thought connected with them is the belief of their gradual extinction. They exist, in the meantime, an awful proof of the degradation to which humanity, in its gradual deterioration, can fall, and an instance of physical and moral degeneracy probably unparalleled in the world."

How are the principles of the Declaration of Independence to be applied to this people? Suppose they were in the United States, would the abolitionist claim for the Bushmen a political equality with the intelligent white man? *

---

* THE LOWEST TYPE OF HUMANITY.—The following extract is from an Article on "Barbarism and Civilization, in the *Atlantic Monthly*, 1861:

Intimately connected with the mission to the Bushmen, was that to the NAMAQUAS and CORANNAS, living north and west of Cape Colony, and chiefly beyond the Orange River. It was, like that to the Bushmen, attended with great privation and extreme peril, and, by the Divine favor, with instances of marvelous success. " It is difficult to imagine the arid, desolate, barren, rocky surface, which this part of Africa presents. The migratory tribes that removed from fountain to fountain to find grass for their cattle were as ignorant and spiritually necessitous as the Bushmen." In 1805 they set out for the mission, and in 1807 baptized their first converts. In 1810 the missionaries fled to the colony to escape from the sword of Africaner, a noted robber chief, who destroyed the mission, reducing the buildings to ashes after having secured the plunder. In 1812 the mission was renewed at a point south of the Orange River. Africaner, having had the missionaries commended to his care, welcomed one of them to his village, and afterwards became, himself, a truly converted man. In 1818 Mr. Moffatt reached Africaner's kraal, and, under his instructions, the former man of blood became a preacher of righteousness. He died in 1823, cheered to his latest hours by the hopes of the Gospel of Christ. In 1830 the Gospels, which had been translated into the Namaqua tongue, were printed and welcomed by the people. *

The mission among the GRIQUAS was commenced in 1801. " This people were numerous, at this time, and comparatively rich in cattle, more intelligent, and by the possession of fire-arms,

---

"On the island of Borneo there has been found a certain race of wild creatures, of which kindred varieties have been discovered in the Philippine Islands, in Terra del Fuego, and in South Africa. They walk, usually, almost erect, on two legs, and, in that attitude, measure about four feet in hight; they are dark, wrinkled, and hairy; they construct no habitations, form no families, scarcely associate together; sleep in caves or trees; feed on snakes and vermin, on ant-eggs, on mice, and on each other; they cannot be tamed nor forced to any labor; and are hunted and shot among the trees like the great gorillas, of which they are a stunted copy. When they are captured alive, one finds to his surprise that their uncouth jabbering sounds like articulate language; they turn up a human face to gaze at their captor, and females show instincts of modesty; and, in fine, these wretched beings are men."

* Missionary Magazine, January, 1861; taken from London Missionary Chronicle.

more powerful than the tribes among them; but in morals and social condition, little, if at all, superior to the Bushmen. They were indolent and improvident, wandering from place to place, as they found pasturage for their herds. The missionaries followed their movements, and endured all the discomfort and privation of such a mode of life, in order to induce them to receive their message." Finally, a part of the Griquas were induced to settle down to agriculture, under the care of one of the missionaries, while the other missionary accompanied those who went with the cattle. This was the commencement of a settled habitation among them. The headstrong perverseness of the people, the want of suitable and sufficient food, the exposure to attacks from bands of marauding Caffres, and long continued and alarming illness, greatly depressed the missionaries during the earlier years of their labors; but they kept their great object — the salvation of the souls of the people — steadily in view; and, after six years' labor, administered baptism to twelve individuals, and, before the close of the year, a church of converted natives was organized, and the ordinance of the Lord's Supper celebrated. A few years later the mission was disturbed by an order from the government, at Cape Town, demanding twenty men to serve in the Cape regiment, and the appointment, subsequently, of an agent to reside at the town. Suspecting that the missionary had favored this measure, the people lost confidence in him; and a portion of them, rather than submit to the imposition, withdrew from the settlement to a mountainous part of the country, where they determined to resist any attempt of the government to enslave them, and to oppose that portion of their own people who were even favorable to the presence of a government agent among them. These evils were increased by other incidents, and for the space of fifteen years after the peace of the settlement had been destroyed by the demand of the government for men, the mission suffered a series of fearful calamities. The missionary never recovered the confidence of the people, but, broken in spirit, retired in 1820. The seceding party, maddened and reckless, committed fearful ravages and murders among the defenceless tribes, attacked and burned part of Griqua Town itself, and were only induced to retire by the persuasions of the missionary, who went to their intrenchments, prayed with them, and exhorted them to desist. The Church was reduced from 200 to less than 30, and the mission brought to the verge of ruin. In 1830, the mission began to revive, and the other stations which had been commenced in the meantime, began to bear fruits, so that, in 1840, the congregations at the several stations averaged between 3,000 and 4,000; the communicants were 630, and 900 were taught in the schools. Causes altogether beyond the control of the missionaries or people, had, however, been some time in operation, which threatened ultimately to drive both from the country. The Boers removed, in 1845 and 1846, in large numbers and settled among the Griquas and neighboring tribes. They soon made war upon the Griquas, and when the British government interfered in 1848, they rose in rebellion, but were defeated. By the treaty which followed, the country was surrendered to the Boers in 1854, and the Griquas left in their power. Additions have been every year made to the communicants, which amount to 400; but the evils and disturbances created by the conflict between the Boers and the natives, and their political difficulties, are forcing them — after the people have occupied the country for the best part of a century, and the Society has labored among them for sixty years — to seek in some distant region another, and, as they hope, a more peaceful home. Though the district connected with Griqua Town has been exempt from disturbance by the Boers, the people have been impoverished and dispersed by severe drouths, sometimes continued through six or seven successive years. Among those who remain, religious observances are maintained, at the several stations, where from 1,200 to 2,000 assemble for worship every Lord's day. An attempt was making, at a point thirty miles distant, to irrigate the lands with waters from the Vaal river, and on the success of this effort the continuance of the mission in its present locality seems to depend. Lekatlong, another mission, has been itself but slightly troubled, though assaults in other stations have increased the numbers, amounting to 13,000, now depending on its efforts, of whom 690 are united in Christian fellowship. *

We turn next to the mission among the BECHUANAS. This tribe

---

* Missionary Magazine, April, 1861, copied from London Miss. Chronicle.

lives in the country east of the Namaquas and north of the Griquas. It may be said to be composed of numerous tribes all bearing the name of Bechuanas. In 1813, the proposition was made to the chief to receive Christian teachers. "Send them, and I will be a father to them," was the reply. In 1817, the missionary removed from the station first occupied, with the people, to the Kuruman, where, in 1821, he was joined by Rev. Mr. MOFFATT, the well-known historian of South African Missions. In 1823, a horde of 40,000 fierce Mantatees, who had desolated every country over which they had passed, approached the Kuruman, but were arrested through the vigilance of Mr. MOFFATT, who secured the aid of the Griquas; and the mission station, as well as the adjacent portions of the colony, were saved from ruin. After twelve years' severe and patient toil, the missionaries welcomed to their Christian brotherhood, their first convert. He was soon afterward followed by six others; a Christian church was then organized, and the first communion celebrated in the same year, 1829. The Psalms and the New Testament were translated into the language of the natives, and brought to the mission in 1843. The work was then prosecuted with great vigor and success. At the principal station, civilization and social improvement advanced rapidly, the schools received a new impetus, and the church numbered 400 communicants. In 1851, the station at Mamusa was broken up by a conflict between the natives and the Boers, who had taken possession of the country beyond the Vaal river. A treaty with the British secured the country to the Boers and left the natives exposed to their tyranny, without the means of defence, as the British were bound not to sell the natives any arms or ammunition. The Boers soon manifested their intentions toward the natives and the missions; Mabotsa and Matebe were broken up, and the people dispersed; Kolobeng was attacked and burned, numbers of the people killed, and Dr. Livingstone's house plundered of its contents, while two other missionaries were required to leave the country in fourteen days, and Mr. Moffatt and the Kuruman threatened. But the Governor of the Cape interfered, and that mission is yet safe. The labors of Dr. Livingstone, as an explorer, opened up new fields for missions, and the Christians of Britain are supplying them with missionaries as rapidly as possible. "Thus while the Society has abundant reason to acknowledge the Divine goodness in the work which the devoted brethren, who have labored during the last sixty years in Southern Africa, have been enabled to accomplish, it is deeply impressed with the urgent necessity for increased effort and more constant prayer in relation to the extended and important fields to which Divine Providence now invites its labors." *

Again, we must turn to former labors for the principal facts in relation to the only remaining mission which we shall notice — that to the Zulus of South Africa: †

The Mission of the American Board to the Zulus, in South Africa, was begun in 1835. One station was commenced among the maritime Zulus, under king Dingaan, who resided on the east side of the Cape, some seventy miles from Port Natal; and the other among the interior Zulus, under king Mosilikatsi. ‡ This station was broken up in 1837, by a war between the Zulus and the Boers, who were then emigrating from the Cape. The missionaries were forced to leave, and join their brethren at Natal; but, in doing this, they were compelled to perform a journey of 1,300 miles, in a circuitous route, 1,000 of which was in ox wagons, through the wilderness, while they were greatly enfeebled by disease, and disheartened by the death of the wife of one of their party.

The missionaries to the maritime Zulus, when their brethren from the interior joined them, had succeeded in establishing one station among king Dingaan's people, and another at Port Natal, where a mixed population, from various tribes, had collected among the Dutch Boers, then settling in and around that place. In 1838 a war occurred between Dingaan and the Boers, which broke up the missions and compelled the missionaries to seek refuge on board some vessels, providentially at Natal, in which some of them sailed to the United States and others to the Cape.

Peace being made in 1839, a part of the missionaries returned to Natal and resumed their labors. But a revolt of one-half the Zulus in 1840, under Umpandi, led to another war, in which the new chief and the Boers succeeded in overthrowing Dingaan. His death by the hand of an old enemy, into whose territory he fled, left the Zulus

* Missionary Magazine, June, 1861, from London Miss. Chronicle.
† See "Ethiopia," for full particulars.
‡ See Moffatt's South African Missions.

under the rule of Umpandi. This chief allowed the mission in his territory to be renewed in 1841. But, in 1842, a war broke out between the Boers, at Natal, and the British; who, to prevent the Boers from organizing an independent government, had taken possession of that place. In this contest, the Boers were forced to submit to British authority, and British law was extended to the population around Natal. This led to large desertions of the Zulus to Natal, to escape from the cruelties of Umpandi; and he, becoming jealous of the missionary, attacked the mission and butchered three of the principal families engaged in its support. Thus, a second time, was this mission broken up and the mission family forced to retreat to Natal.

Here, then, at the opening of 1843, nearly eight years after the missionaries reached Africa, they had not a single station in the Zulu country, to which they had been sent; and they were directed, by the Board, to abandon the field. From this they were prevented, by the timely remonstrances of the Rev. Dr. Philip, of the English mission at the Cape.

A crisis, however, had now arisen, by which the conflicting elements hitherto obstructing the Gospel, were rendered powerless or reduced to order, by the strong arm of Great Britain. The fierce Boers had destroyed the power of both Mosilikatsi and Dingaan, and taught the Zulu people that they could safely leave the standard of their chiefs; while the Boers, in turn, had been subjected to British authority, along with the Zulus whom they had designed to enslave. The basis of a colony, under the protection of British law, was thus laid at Natal, which afforded security to the missionaries, and enabled them to establish themselves on a permanent basis. An attempt was also made to renew the mission in the Zulu territory, but Umpandi refused his assent, and the strength of the mission was concentrated within the Natal Colony.

Owing to the continued cruelties of Umpandi, the desertions of his people to Natal increased, until the Colony included a native population, mostly Zulus, of nearly 100,000.

No serious interruptions have occurred, since the British occupied Natal; and opportunities have been afforded for studying the Zulu character, and the remaining obstacles to missionary success among that people. Time has shown, that the tyranny of the chiefs, and the wars of the tribes with each other, or with the whites, are not the most obstinate difficulties to be overcome.

From the Report of the Board for 1850, we learn, that though there were then, in this field, 12 missionaries, 14 assistants, 6 native helpers,

18 places of preaching, and 8 schools; there were but 78 church members and 185 pupils. The report attributes the slow progress made, to the extreme moral degradation of the population; and, in mentioning particulars, names polygamy as the most prominent. As among the native Africans generally, so is it here, superstition and sensuality are the great barriers to the progress of the Gospel.

But these difficulties do not deter the American Board from persevering in their great work of converting Africa. The men composing the Board know, full well, that the evils existing in all mission fields can only be removed by God's appointed means, the Gospel; and, that to withdraw it from Africa, would be to render its evils perpetual. Hence, as obstacles rise, they multiply their agencies for good; and, in view of the consistent conduct and piety of the native converts, the Report of 1850, recommends the establishment of a Theological school for training a native ministry for that field. The Reports for 1851 and 1852 are more encouraging, and show an increase of 86 church members, 16 children baptized, and 15 Christian marriages solemnized. The Report for 1853 is less encouraging. The whole number of church members is now 141, of whom only 8 were received during the year. Family schools are sustained at all the stations; *but none of the heathen send their children.* Three day-schools are taught by native converts, in which the children of those residing at the stations, where they are located, receive instruction. One girls' school, consisting of about 20 pupils, is taught by Mrs. Adams. * The Christian Zulus are advancing in civilization and in material prosperity; but the heathen population are manifesting more and more of stupid indifference or bitter hostility to the Gospel. This is more particularly indicated in their refusal to send their children to school.

The passage of this mission from the class beyond the protection of the Colonies, to that of those deriving security from them, released it from the annoyances occasioned by native wars, and left it to contend with the obstacles, only, which are inherent in heathenish barbarism. It had, consequently, begun to progress encouragingly. But a new element of disturbance has recently been introduced, which threatens to be no less hurtful than the old causes of interruption and insecurity. We refer to the immigration of the English into the Natal Colony, and their efforts to dispossess the Zulus of their lands. Before taking any further notice of this threatening evil, we must

---

* Missionary Herald, for December, 1853, and January, 1854

call particular attention to another point, the importance of which has, perhaps, been too much overlooked. In January, 1853, the Rev. Mr. Tyler thus wrote :

"I have many thoughts, of late, concerning the great obstacle which lies in the way of elevating the Zulus. It seems to me that it is *their deep ignorance.* We find it exceedingly difficult to throw even one ray of light into minds so darkened and perverted by sin. . . . . Of the great mass who attend our services on the Sabbath, but few, probably, have any clear knowledge of the plan of salvation through faith in Christ. Especially is this true of the female sex, whose condition, both temporal and spiritual, seems almost beyond the reach of improvement."

Mr. Tyler proceeds to show, that the Zulus, in their *religious belief,* their *worship,* and their blind submission to the *witch-doctors,* evince the most deep, gross, and stupid ignorance imaginable ; but he presents nothing as belonging to that people, which is not common to the African tribes generally. Without, at present, remarking on the relation which the *ignorance of barbarism* bears to the progress of missions, we shall recur to the effects of the immigration of the whites into the Colony of Natal.

When the Zulus deserted their king and took refuge at Natal, there were but few whites present to be affected by the movement, and allotments of lands were readily obtained for them. Soon afterward, however, an emigration from Great Britain began to fill up the country. The main object of the whites was agriculture, and the best unoccupied lands were soon appropriated. The new immigrants then commenced settling on the possessions of the Zulus. The designs of the whites soon manifested itself so openly, that the missionaries have been obliged to interpose for the protection of the natives. Accordingly, a committee of their number was deputed to wait upon the Lieutenant-Governor, to learn his intentions on the subject. The report of the interview, as made to the American Board, read as follows:

"He plainly gave us to understand, that instead of collecting the natives in bodies, as has hitherto been the policy, it was his purpose to disperse them among the colonists, and the colonists among them. The natural result will be, to deteriorate our fields of labor, by diminishing the native population, and by introducing a foreign element, which, as all missionary experience proves, conflicts with christianizing interests. Nor did he assure us that even our stations would not be infringed by foreign settlers; but our buildings and their bare sites, he encouraged us to expect, would at all events remain to us undisturbed.   But lest this statement convey an impression which is too discouraging, we would say, that many of our fields embrace tracts of country so broken, as not to be eligible as farms for the immigrants; and, hence, no motive would exist for dispossessing the native occupants, unless it would be to transfer them to the more immediate vicinity of the white population, in order to facilitate their obtaining servants; which at present is so difficult as to be considered one of the crying evils of the Colony.   So deep is the feeling on this subject, that many and strenuous are those who advocate a resort to some system of actual imprisonment.   This seems a strange doctrine to be held by the sons of Britain!"

Then, after expressing an opinion that the obstacles in the way of this measure may prevent its execution for some years to come, the report concludes:

"Yet it is more than probable, that some of our stations will experience the disadvantages of the too great proximity of white settlers. The evils of such a proximity are aggravated by the prejudices which exist against missionaries and their operations.   And perhaps we should say, that, as American missionaries, we are regarded with still greater jealousy.   We fear it will require years to live down these prejudices.   Public opinion is more or less fashioned by the influence of unprincipled speculators, alike ignorant of missionaries, their labors, or the native people.   Such men, greedy of the soil of the original proprietors, are naturally jealous and envious of those who, they suppose, would befriend the natives in maintaining their rights. If we speak at all, of course we must say what we think to be justice and truth.   If we remain silent, as we have hitherto done, we are misrepresented, and our motives are impugned.   So that whichever course we take, we can not expect to act in perfect harmony with all the interests of all the men who, within the last few years, have come to the Colony."*

Passing on to 1861, we find the annual report of the Board stating the strength of this mission thus: stations 12, out-stations 6, missionaries 14, female assistant-missionaries 14, native helpers 2, members 283.

---

* Missionary Herald, February, 1853.

The government now takes an interest in the mission, and has given titles to the land upon which the buildings of the several stations are situated.   The report says, in relation to the success of the mission :

"To the ten churches established by our brethren among the Zulus, there have been received, in all, 283 members, who, for the most part, have exhibited a consistent Christian deportment, certainly to as great extent as could have been expected, when we take into view their former lives and the circumstances in which they are placed.   It is not surprising that there have been cases of defection.   Twenty-six were added to the churches during the last year."

This closes what is necessary to understand the condition of the South African missions, and the relation they sustain to the missions elsewhere established for the benefit of the African race. These missions, in 1858, stood as follows, as estimated in the Encyclopædia of Missions.   Ten Missionary Societies occupied the field, and their number of converts, as far as reported, was 14,258 — three of the smaller societies not reporting any members.

The missionaries among the American slaves have rested upon downy pillows, as compared with the hardships endured by those of South Africa.

2. *The obstacles to African Evangelization in West Africa.*

The missions at Sierra Leone have been noticed in Chapter I., and the reader will take note of the facts in this connection.   No progress whatever was made so long as the slave trade prevailed ; but from the date of its suppression the work began to prosper. The Episcopal mission, established in Sierra Leone, in 1808, has been continued without interruption, except what necessarily arose from the great mortality among the missionaries.   A college and several schools were established at an early day, in which orphan and destitute children were boarded and instructed. Besides teaching the schools, the missionaries preached to the adults, a few of whom embraced the Gospel ; but no very encouraging progress was made for many years.   In 1817, however, the labors expended began to unfold their effects, and the mission to make encouraging advances ; so that, by 1832. it had

638 communicants and 294 candidates in its churches, 684 Sabbath-scool scholars, and 1,388 pupils in its day-schools.

Thus, in forty-five years after the founding of Sierra Leone, and twenty-four after the abolition of the slave trade, was the basis of this mission broadly and securely laid. Since that period it has been extended eastward to Badagry, Abbeokuta, and Lagos. In connection with all these missions, but chiefly in Sierra Leone, the Episcopal Church, in 1850, had 54 seminaries and schools, 6,600 pupils, 2,183 communicants, and 7,500 attendants on public worship. Of the teachers in the schools at Sierra Leone, it is worthy of remark, that only *five* were Europeans, while *fifty-six* were native Africans.

The mission of the English Wesleyans, in 1831 — *twenty years* after its commencement — included 2 missionaries, 294 church members, and about 160 pupils in its schools. This mission, like the Episcopal, progressed slowly at first; but as it collected the elements of progress within its bosom, it, also, began to expand, and is now advancing prosperously. Its stations have been extended westward to the Gambia, and eastward to various points, including Cape Coast Castle, Badagry, Abbeokuta, and Kumasi. In connection with these missions, the Wesleyan Methodists, in 1850, had 44 chapels, 13 out-stations, 42 day-schools, 97 teachers, 4,500 pupils, including those in the Sabbath-schools, 6,000 communicants, on trial 560, and 14,600 attendants on public worship.

The missions of both these Societies, established to the eastward of Sierra Leone, have encountered many difficulties from the wars of the natives, provoked, mainly, by the influence of the slave traders.

The strength of these missions, in 1860, stood as follows : *

DENOMINATIONS.	MISSIONARIES.	TEACHERS.	SCHOLARS.	MEMBERS.
Episcopal Church............	120	200	6,000	3,000
Methodist Church............	20	160	5,000	18,000
Total....................	140	360	11,000	21,000

The missions connected with Liberia are also of great interest

* Scotch Record, as quoted by the Missionary Magazine.

in connection with the subject under consideration. Details of their history, at length, need not be given, as the results of the establishment of the colony are familiar to all.

The METHODIST EPISCOPAL CHURCH IN THE UNITED STATES has one of its principal missions in Liberia. The nucleus of this mission consisted of several members, and one or two local preachers, of the Methodist Church, who went out, in 1820, with the first emigrants. In March, 1833, Rev. Melville B. Cox, the first ordained missionary, landed in Monrovia. In 1853, this mission embraced 1,301 members, of whom 116 were natives, and there were 115 probationers. The mission had 15 Sunday-schools, with 839 pupils, of whom 50 were natives; and 20 week-day-schools, with 513 scholars. There were also 7 schools among the natives, with 127 pupils.

According to the Report for 1861, this mission embraces 1,392 Americo-Liberian members, 89 probationers, 72 native members, 600 scholars in week-day-schools, and 930 in Sabbath-schools.

On contrasting these results, with those of a few years back, it would appear that the progress of this mission, among the natives, has not been very encouraging. There have been adequate causes for this — causes which the Christian world, and especially the American abolitionist, should calmly consider. Their nature may be inferred from what has been reported on the subject by Bishop SCOTT, who made an official visit to Liberia — leaving at the close of 1852, and returning in April, 1853, having spent seventy days in the Colony. He represents the spiritual condition of the mission, as generally healthy and prosperous; and the work as going steadily onward. In relation to the civil and social condition of the Colony, the Bishop bears the following testimony:

"The government of the Republic of Liberia, which is formed on the model of our own, and is wholly in the hands of colored men, seems to be exceedingly well administered. I never saw so orderly a people. I saw but one intoxicated colonist while in the country, and I heard not one profane word. The Sabbath is kept with singular strictness, and the churches crowded with attentive and orderly worshipers."

But, as regards the missions among the natives, the Bishop says,

very little indeed has been done — much less than the friends of the
mission seem to have good reason to expect — much less than he himself expected.   The result of his inquiries is by no means flattering,
and he felt, and feared that the Board would feel, disappointed.
These results, however, he says, are not due to any want of faithfulness on the part of the missionaries; as other denominations have
not been more successful — perhaps not quite so much so — but are
the result of the peculiar condition of the native population.

The first difficulty, says the Bishop, which meets the missionary,
on going to this people is an unknown tongue; a tongue, too, which
varies so much, as he passes from one tribe to another, within the
space of only a few miles, that it often amounts to a different language.
The nature of this obstacle will be so easily comprehended, that the
details given by the Bishop, need not be quoted.   He thus proceeds:

"But now another difficulty assails him — one which his knowledge
of men in other parts of the world had given him no reason to anticipate.   Though he may in some way get over the difficulty presented
in a rude foreign tongue, yet he now finds, to his utter surprise, that
he can not gain access to this people unless he *dash* them, (that is,
make them presents,) and only as he dashes them.   When, where, or
how this wretched custom arose I can not tell, but it is found to prevail over most parts of Africa, and, so far as I know, no where else.
But what shall our missionary now do?   Will he dash them?   Will
he dash them 'much plenty?'   Then they will hear him — they will
flock around him — nay, he may do with them almost as he wists,
and a nation may be born in a day.   But let him not be deceived, for
all is not gold, here especially, that glitters.   So soon as he withholds
his dashes, ten to one they are all *as they were*.   But is he poor and
can not dash them? — or able, but on principle will not?   Then, as a
general fact, he may go home.   They will not hear him at all, nor
treat him with the least respect.   Indeed, they will probably say,
'He no good man,' — and it will be well for him if they do not get
up a palaver against him and expel him from their coasts.   This
dashing is a most mischievous custom — dreadfully in the way of missionary labor, and I know not how it is to be controlled.   I am sick
of the very sound of the word.   The Lord help poor Africa!

"But the difficulties multiply.   Now a hydra-headed monster gapes
upon our missionary, of most frightful aspect, and as tenacious of life
as that fabled monster of the ancient poets.   It is *polygamy*.   He
finds to his grief and surprise, that every man has as many wives as

he can find money to buy. He must give them all up but one, if he would be a Christian. But will he give them up? Not easily. He will give up almost any thing before he will give up his wives. They are his slaves, in fact; they constitute his wealth. And then it is difficult, not to say impossible, to persuade him that it is not somehow morally wrong to put them away. ' Me send woman away? — where she. go to? — what she do?' This I consider the hugest difficulty with which Christianity has to contend in the conversion of this people, and makes me think that she must look mainly to the rising generation.

"But here, too, a difficulty arises. The female children are contracted away — are sold, in fact — by their parents while they are yet very young, often while they are infants; and if the missionary would procure them for his schools, he must pay the dower — some fifteen or twenty dollars.

"But our missionary finds that the whole social and domestic organization of these people is opposed to the pure, chaste, and comely spirit of the Gospel, and that, to succeed in this holy work, it must not only be changed, but revolutionized — upturned from the very foundation. Is there no difficulty here? Are habits and customs, so long established and so deeply rooted, to be given up without a struggle? The native people, both men and women, go almost stark naked, and they love to go so — and are not abashed in the presence of people better dressed; they eat with their hands, and dip, and pull, and tear, with as little ceremony and as little decency as monkeys, and they love to eat so; they sleep on the bare ground, or on mats spread on the ground, and they love to sleep so; the men hunt or fish, or lounge about their huts, and smoke their pipes, and chat, and sleep, while their wives, *alias* their slaves, tend and cut and house their rice — cut and carry home their wood — make their fires, fetch their water, get out their rice, and prepare their 'chop' — and all, even the women, love to have it so. And to all the remonstrances of the missionary, they oppose this simple and all-settling reply : ' This be countryman's fash.' They seem incapable of conceiving that your fash is better than theirs, or that theirs is at all defective. Your fash, they will admit, may be better for you, but theirs is better for them. So the natives of Cape Palmas have lived, in the very midst of the colonists, for some twenty years, and they are the same people still, with almost no visible change."

The Bishop next notices their superstitions and idolatries, and the evils connected with their belief in witchcraft; and says, that though, by the influence of the colony and missions, their confidence is, in some places, being shaken in some of them; they generally even yet think you a fool, and pity you, if you venture to hint that there is nothing in them. But we must not quote him farther than to include his closing remarks:

"But what! Do you then think that there is no hope for these heathen, or that we should give up all hopes directed to that end? Not I, indeed. Very far from it. I would rather reiterate the noble saying of the sainted Cox: 'Though a thousand fall even, in this attempt, yet let not Africa be given up.' I mention these things to show, that there are solid reasons why our brethren in Africa have accomplished so little; and also to show, that the Churches at home must, in this work particularly, exercise the patience of faith and the labor of love. We must still pound the rock, even though it is hard, and our mallets be but of wood. It will break one day."*

The other missions, established in Liberia, are under the control of the following denominations: AMERICAN PROTESTANT EPISCOPAL CHURCH, THE PRESBYTERIAN BOARD OF MISSIONS, (O. S.,)

---

* It will be proper, here, to add some testimony from another source, in reference to the terrible moral degradation of the inhabitants of Africa, where civilized men have not yet extended their sway. Within the jurisdiction of Sierra Leone and Liberia, the cruelties of African superstitions can no longer be practiced with impunity. This result, alone, will amply repay the toil and treasure expended upon these colonies.

The *New York Observer*, of September 5, 1861, has the following article:

"HEATHENDOM AT THE PRESENT HOUR.—Du Chaillu, in his new and popular book on Africa, as well as in his lectures, has brought prominently before the Christian public the horrible effects of a belief in witchcraft among the tribes in the interior of Africa. Other writers have testified to the same state of things, and we refer to a recent letter written by a missionary of the United Presbyterian Church of Scotland, for the purpose of citing a few facts to exhibit the condition of society at the present moment within sixty days' travel of our church doors:

"'His death was the occasion of a painful display of the evil passions that are nurtured by the superstitions of heathenism. All Africans believe that certain persons know how to make charms that are potent to destroy human life. It was alleged that an uncle of the deceased, named Egbo Eyo, had thus destroyed his nephew. There was also a feud between this man and the slaves of his brother, old King Eyo; he regarded them with scorn, and they cherished toward him a fierce hatred.

"'The body was buried on the day after the decease, in the manner usual

THE FOREIGN MISSIONARY BOARD OF THE SOUTHERN BAPTIST CONVENTION, and THE AMERICAN BAPTIST MISSIONARY UNION. In addition to these missions in Liberia, there are others, among the native Africans, in Western Africa, which deserve a notice. These are the missions of the AMERICAN BOARD, on the Gaboon, and the mission of the AMERICAN MISSIONARY ASSOCIATION, at Mendi, with a few others.

---

among the Efik people. Many valuables, and a large amount of goods, were put into the grave, along with certain parts of a cow, slaughtered for the purpose. On that day, the news having spread, many of the slaves gathered into the town. Egbo Eyo, along with the other freemen of the town, busied himself in the funeral ceremony. It would appear that the slaves began to regard him with an evil eye, either from having heard the report already mentioned or under the influence of the hatred which they bore to him, or both; and early next morning they made an attack on his place, fired into it, and shot one of his women. Seeing escape hopeless, the poor man surrendered; and the infuriated mob dragged him to the market-place, slashing him with their cutlasses, and beating him with sticks and the butt end of their guns. The poor man was no craven; he behaved with the greatest courage; coolly and sharply answered the taunts of the armed mob; and neither tried to flee nor stooped to beg. The probability is that they would have killed him outright at once, but for the interference of the Europeans who happened to be at Creek Town that morning. The missionary at that place being on a sick bed, and unable to be on the scene, the teacher, Mr. Timson, exerted himself on the poor man's behalf, which his knowledge of the language enabled him the better to do. But their united efforts could not save the victim — the people were determined that he should die; but they agreed to talk over the matter, in regular Efik form, with the freemen of the town, and with a deputation who came from Duke Town. The greater part of the day was spent in this palaver; but nothing that was said produced the slighest effect on the minds of the people. There was no power in the country to take the man out of their hands; and, at length, after he had lain in his blood in the sand all day, they hung him on a tree, he himself helping to put the rope round his neck.

" 'The same evening they hung a slave, who was believed to have made the charm for Egbo Eyo, by means of which King Eyo had died. One of his women also was dragged out by a band of women, and, after being severely beaten, was mercilessly hung. Some days afterward, a slave of Egbo Eyo's, who was accused of having been art and part with his master, was caught and hung.

" 'But a more painful illustration of heathen wickedness remains to be told. Between two of the daughters of old King Eyo, by different mothers, an old and growing hatred existed. One of these, Ansa, who was a sister of the late King by the same mother, came forward to accuse her half sister, Inyang, of having killed their brother by a secret power called *ifot*, and also of having by the same means destroyed the reason of a younger brother, who appears to be in a state of hopeless idiocy. She alleged that this had been revealed by

The present condition of all these missions — and, also, of the English missions at Sierra Leone, and their out-stations — appears from the following statistics, which we find in the *Missionary Magazine,* June, 1861, which copies them from the *Scotch Record*:

RELIGIOUS DENOMINATIONS.	MISSIONAR'S.	TEACHERS.	MEMBERS.	SCHOLARS.
Wesleyan Methodist, (*English*)......	* 20	160	18,000	5,000
Church Mission, (*English*)............	† 120	200	3,000	6,000
Methodist Episcopal, (*American*)...	23	22	1,400	850
Baptist Mission, (*American*).........	23	20	700	500
Presbyterian Mission, (*American*).	25		150	200
Episcopal Mission, (*American*)......	13	27	369	550
English Baptist Mission...............	6	15	130	300
Basle Society, (*Lutheran*)............	3		40	400
American Missionary Association, (*Mendi Mission*)......	17		‡ 307	150
Scotch Presbyterian, (*United Secession*)................	15			
Total...............	265	444	24,096	13,950

several abudiong whom she had consulted; and she demanded that Inyang Eyo should be tried by the ordeal of the *esere*. The *esere* is a bean of a very poisonous nature; and it is believed that if a person who has *ifot* eat this bean he is sure to die, while if he have it not he will certainly vomit all up. Inyang defended herself, admitting that she had had many a quarrel with their deceased brother about their father's property, but declaring that they had been reconciled, and denying that she had ever done anything against the life of their brother. She refused to take the *esere* by herself, but if her accuser were made to take it along with her, she would consent. But the malice of the other was not to be thus baulked. She distributed new muskets among some of the people, pledging them to shoot Inyang, if she did not die by the *esere*. At length the poor woman gave in, was conveyed into one of the yards of her father's place, took the ordeal, and died.'

"The people among whom such atrocities are perpetrated to-day, are accessible to the arts and appliances of civilized life, and if there was any power in education or trade, to rescue them from the degradation and misery of such a state of society as is here disclosed, it would be the dictate of common humanity to attempt to save them. But Christians believe there is power in the Gospel to transform such superstitious and cruel beings, into kind, humane, and happy people. The Gospel has done it for others, and may do the same for them. Yet there is not enough practical christianity in the whole world to enlighten the interior of Africa with the knowledge of salvation, and it is probable that the present generation, if not the next, will pass away before anything effectual will be done to dispel the darkness of those habitations of cruelty."

* In addition, there are 75 local preachers.
† This includes native assistants, many of whom are ordained
‡ These figures are from the American Christian Record, 1860.

The obstacles to missionary success in Africa, referred to by Bishop Scott, are not the only ones operating in that field. The unhealthiness of the climate has been very fatal to the health and lives of the white missionaries. The extent of this mortality may be inferred from the fact, that—

Of the *white* missionaries who entered the field in Liberia, during the first thirty years of its existence, but two or three remained at the close of that period—all the others having died or been disabled by the loss of health. Take, as an example, the Episcopal Mission. *Twenty* white laborers, male and female, entered that mission, up to 1849, of whom only the Rev. Mr. Payne and his wife, and Dr. Perkins, remained. All the others had fallen at their posts or been forced to retreat. Take that of the Presbyterian Board also : Of *nineteen* white missionaries, male and female, sent out, up to May, 1851, *nine* had died, *seven* returned, and *three* remained ; while of *fourteen* colored missionaries, male and female, employed, but *four* have died, and *one* returned on account of ill health. Take the Methodists likewise : Of the *thirteen* white missionaries sent out, *six* had died, *six* returned, and one remained, in 1848; while of *thirty-one* colored missionaries employed by this church, only *seven* had died natural deaths, and *fourteen* remained in active service. The extent of this mortality among the white missionaries will be comprehended, when it is stated, that their average period of life, up to nearly the last-named date, has been only two years. The mission work in Liberia, therefore, has necessarily fallen into the hands of colored men ; and, thus, the Providence of God has afforded to that race an opportunity to display their powers, and to show to the world what, under favorable circumstances, they are capable of achieving.*

A more striking illustration of the dangerous character of these mission fields, to white missionaries, will be afforded by giving the details of one of them—the Baptists'. This mission was begun, in 1822, under the care of Lot Carey and Collin Teage. On the death of Mr. Carey, the mission had to be supplied from the United States ; and the following are the results :

In December, 1830, Rev. B. Skinner, a white man, with his wife

---

* See "Ethiopia."

and two children, reached Monrovia, to take charge of the mission. They were all seized with the African fever, soon after landing, and Mrs. Skinner and the children died. Mr. S. so far recovered as to embark for home, in July following, but died the twentieth day of the passage.

In 1834, Dr. Skinner, the father of the missionary, went out as a physician, and was afterward appointed governor of the colony. Soon after his arrival, he recommended the Baptist Board to establish their mission, for the benefit of the natives, among the Bassa tribe.

In 1835, two other white men, Rev. G. W. Crocker and Rev. Mr. Mylne, were sent out to the Bassas. Mrs. Mylne, who had accompanied her husband, died in a month, and Mr. M., after laboring nearly three years, was forced, by ill health, to return to the United States. Mr. Crocker continued his labors, and was married, in 1840, to Miss Warren, who had gone out as a teacher. She died soon afterward, and the declining health of Mr. Crocker compelled him to leave for the United States.

In 1838, two years before Mr. Crocker left, he had been joined by Rev. Ivory Clarke and wife, whites, who continued to occupy the station, and labored with great success for several years.

In December, 1840, Messrs. Constantine and Fielding, with their wives, all whites, reached the Bassa mission. Mr. and Mrs. F. both died in six weeks; and Mr. and Mrs. C. were so much debilitated by the fever that they were compelled to return home in 1842.

In 1844, the health of Mr. Crocker had become so far restored, that he resolved to return to Africa; and, having been united in marriage to Miss Chadbourne, he sailed for Liberia, but died two days after landing. "Thus fell, in the midst of high raised hopes, and at an unexpected moment, a missionary of no common zeal and devotion to the cause."*

On the death of Mr. Crocker, his widow attached herself to the mission, and labored for its advancement for two years; when the wreck of her constitution, under the influence of the climate, compelled her to abandon the work, in 1846, and return home.

In 1848, Mr. Clarke and his wife found their constitutions so completely shattered, and their strength so nearly exhausted, that they left the mission to return to the United States. But he had tarried at his post too long; death overtook him on the passage, and the sea supplied him a grave.

---

* Gammel's History of the American Baptist Missions.

Thus, after thirteen years' labor, and the sacrifice of a noble band of martyrs to the cause of African redemption, was the Bassa mission left without a head, except so far as it could be supplied by the native converts. Among them, there was one preacher and four teachers, who kept up the organization of the little church, and continued the schools.

It was not until 1852, that the Board had any offers of missionaries for Bassa, to supply the place of those who had fallen or retreated. In that year, however, Rev. J. S. Goodman and Rev. W. B. Shermer, and their wives, offered themselves to the Board, and were accepted. They set sail November 27, 1852, and were accompanied by Mrs. Crocker, who longed to return to the mission and devote her life to the service of her Lord and Master.

This Mission family was permitted to reach its field of labor in safety; but recent information brings the painful intelligence of the death of Mrs. Crocker and Mrs. Shermer; and that Mr. Shermer himself, had also been very ill, and had left Africa to return home by way of England. In writing from London, under date of January 13, 1854, he says: "That during the past twelve months, six missionaries of different denominations have died, and eight have been and are obliged to return to America; all of whom had gone to Africa within the last year. This is indeed a fearful mortality among African missionaries. Yet God has a people there, and if the white man can not live to evangelize them, he can and will raise up other agencies. Educated colored men, in all probability, must and will be the only instrumentality employed in the conversion of Africa." *

THE EPISCOPAL MISSION IN LIBERIA has its principal seat at Cape Palmas. Rev. Mr. Payne, long at its head, was appointed a Missionary Bishop for Africa, in 1850.

In speaking of the necessity of extended effort in the Republic of Liberia, the Bishop makes this important statement: "It is now very generally admitted, that Africa must be evangelized chiefly by her own children. It should be our object to prepare them, so far as we may, for their great work. And since colonists afford the most advanced materiel for raising up the needed instruments, it becomes us, in wise co-operation with Providence, to direct our efforts in the most judicious manner to them. To do this, the most

---

* Baptist Missionary Magazine, March, 1851.

important points should be occupied, to become in due time radiating centers of Christian influence to Colonists and Natives."*

The missionaries and teachers in Liberia are nearly all colored men, and citizens of the Republic, who yield a cordial support to its laws, and enjoy ample protection under its government. These missionaries have the control of the schools and churches; and, consequently, they possess the entire direction of the intellectual, moral, and religious training of the youth. Liberia, therefore, may be denominated a *Missionary Republic.* And such is the influence the colony has exerted over the natives, that their heathenish customs and superstitions are fast disappearing before the advancing Christian civilization. In the county of Messurado, including the seat of government, there no longer exists a single temple of heathen worship. †

The GABOON MISSION is under the care of the American Board of Commissioners for Foreign Missions. Its statistics are not included in the preceding table, but will be found in the tabular statement of the converts in the missions of the Board. Its first missionaries landed in Africa in 1834, and commenced their labors under the protection of the Colony at Cape Palmas. Believing they could succeed better in an independent position, they removed, in 1842, to the mouth of the Gaboon river, 1,200 miles eastward from Liberia. They took with them a few converts from Cape Palmas. The missionaries have labored devotedly, but have suffered many interruptions, both from sickness, and the interference of the slave traders. The coolie traffic, also, conducted by the French, has likewise presented obstacles to success. In speaking of the obstacles in general, one of the missionaries, a few years since, remarked, that here, as elsewhere, the habit of taking many wives, or rather concubines, operates as a great hindrance to the Gospel; and that, "demoralizing as this state of things is, the people are, nevertheless, firmly attached to it, and will continue to be so, until they are inspired with better and purer feelings by the Holy Ghost." This mission, in 1850, consisted of one church of 22 members; but the report for 1859, instead of showing any increase, states that there was a reduc-

---

* Report of Bishop Payne, June 6, 1853.
† Officer of U. S. Navy, in Mr. Gurley's Report, 1858.

tion of the membership to 12. The annual report of the Board, for that year, 1859, thus speaks of the discouraging prospects of this mission :

" The Gaboon mission is attended with more difficulty. The climate is unhealthy; the tribes of people reached by the mission are small, scattered, and changing in their locality, and often warring on each other. After a series of exhausting labors, continued for many years, during which about half of our missionary force, on an average, have been obliged to be absent from the field, for the recruiting of health, but one church, now consisting of twelve members, is reported. Our work is one of faith ; we would wait the returns of harvest; still, in a range of labors so extended and varied as those of this Board, that particular localities and missions should be surrendered for others of less discouragement, and greater prospect of success, is a matter to be expected. Some change respecting the Gaboon mission seems to be demanded. The committee have grave doubts respecting the wisdom of continuing it as at present constituted, and while they are not ready to recommend its abrupt termination, they highly appreciate a suggestion in the Prudential Committee's Report, that efforts be made to obtain native preachers and helpers from Sierra Leone and other places, and train them for the work."

The Report for 1861, contains the suggestion, from one of the missionaries who had investigated the subject, that the discouragements at the Gaboon are not peculiar to that place; and that no change of locality would give a more hopeful field. It is also stated that a more decided religious interest had prevailed during the last year than for a long period before. The members, as given in the " Memorial Volume," number 15.

The MENDI MISSION is one of peculiar interest, and will be referred to in connection with the West India Missions. The results of this mission, as well as that at the Gaboon, serve a good purpose, as illustrating the mistaken views of the abolitionists, in their estimate of the character of the African race in its barbarous state.

3. *The obstacles to African Evangelization in Brazil.*

The blacks transported from Africa to Brazil have been subjected to influences as unfavorable to moral improvement as those taken to any other country. Unfortunately for Brazil, its early settlers from Europe failed to secure to themselves any degree of liberty of conscience in the exercise of their religious principles; but, in accordance with the spirit of the times, the most rigid and extreme measures were adopted to preserve unity of faith. Two ministers and fourteen students, sent out to Brazil by the Protestant Church of Geneva, were prevented, by the sanguinary fanaticism of the adherents of the established religion, from introducing a Bible Christianity. The leading men of the party of Huguenots, who fled to Brazil in 1555 from persecution in France, were thrown into prison; and, after eight years' confinement, John Boles, the most prominent of the prisoners, was martyred, at Rio de Janeiro, "for the sake of terrifying his countrymen, if any of them should be lurking in those parts." The Methodist Episcopal Church of the United States, a few years since, attempted to enter Brazil as a missionary field, but the effort, proving unsuccessful, was abandoned.

Without the Bible as a moral instructor of youth, and without the presence of the advocates of religious liberty, as rivals to stimulate and liberalize the state religion, it is not a matter of wonder that the Brazilians should have sunk in the scale of moral being. The population of Brazil, in 1850, included but 1,500,000 whites, while there were 3,000,000 slaves, and 2,500,000 Indians and free negroes. The rising generations of whites, coming more or less under the influence of the native heathenism, could not attain as high a standard of intelligence and morals as those which had preceded them. It was to be expected, therefore, that the costly church edifices, erected by the pious zeal and profuse liberality of the early Portuguese emigrants, should often be perverted from the use to which they were originally consecrated; and, as is asserted in KIDDER'S BRAZIL, that the preaching of the Gospel should not be known among the weekly services of the church; and, also, as declared by SOUTHEY, that its practices should be those of polytheism and idolatry. Such were the evil tendencies of the religious system of Brazil, that, in 1843, the minister of justice and ecclesiastical affairs, addressed the Imperial Legislature on the subject, and called for reform. Among many other things he said:

"The state of retrogression into which the clergy are falling is notorious. . . . . . . It may be observed, that the numerical ratio of those priests who die, or become incompetent through age and infirmity, is two to one of those who receive ordination. . . . . . . This is not the place to investigate the causes of such a state of things, but certain it is, that no persons of standing devote their sons to the priesthood. . . . . . . In the province of Para, there are parishes which, for twelve years and upward, have had no pastor. The district of the river Negro, containing some fourteen settlements, has but one priest; while that of the river Solemoens is in similar circumstances. In the three comarcas of Belem, and Upper and Lower Amazon, there are thirty-six vacant parishes. In Maranham, twenty-five churches have, at different times, been advertised as open for applications, without securing the offer of a single candidate. The Bishop of St. Paulo affirms the same thing respecting vacant churches in his diocese, and it is no uncommon experience elsewhere. In the diocese of Cuyaba, not a single church is provided with a settled curate, and those priests who officiate as stated supplies, treat the Bishop's efforts to instruct and improve them with great indifference. In the Bishopric of Rio de Janeiro, most of the churches are supplied with pastors, but a great number of them only temporarily. This diocese embraces four provinces, but during nine years past not more than five or six priests have been ordained per year."

Among this general dearth of religious instruction among the Brazilians, it will of course be expected that the moral training of the poor slave has been totally neglected, and that he yet remains in all the darkness and degradation of barbarism. An American in Brazil, writing to the *Boston Advocate*, from Rio, in 1849, says :

"Every one, on his first landing at Rio, will be forced to the conclusion that all classes indiscriminately mingle together; all appearing on terms of the utmost equality. If there be any distinction, it is perceptible only between freedom and slavery. There are many blacks here quite wealthy and respectable, who amalgamate with the white families, and are received on a footing of perfect equality. The mechanical arts are at least half a century behind those of our own. The churches, some fifty in number, are falling to decay, which gives to the city a look of dilapidation; few are still observant of its ceremonies; but little or no attention is paid to the Sabbath. The stores

do business, and the workshops are open, the same as on other days.
A few may be seen going to worship on the Sabbath, but a greater
number resort to billiard tables in the afternoon, and to theaters at
night.   The slave population is estimated at three times the number
of that of the whites.   They are allowed to go almost naked, the
upper part of the body of both male and female entirely so."

4. *The Obstacles to African Evangelization in Cuba.*

In relation to Cuba, the tale is soon told.   According to M'Queen,
its slave population, some years ago, was four hundred and twenty-five
thousand, of whom one hundred and fifty thousand were females, and
two hundred and seventy-five thousand were males.   This disproportion of the sexes will sufficiently indicate the social evils growing out
of such a condition of things.   Since that period, the slave trade has
received a great stimulus, by the opening of the English markets to
slave-grown sugar; and the continued importation of slaves into Cuba,
gives her at present six hundred thousand.   She has also one hundred
thousand free colored persons, and six hundred and ten thousand
whites.

A report read before the London Anti-Slavery Society, 1843, represents the plantation slaves of Cuba as never receiving the least
moral or religious instruction.   "Most of them are baptized, because
the curate's certificate of baptism serves as a title deed in the civil
courts of the island.   They live, in general, in a state of concubinage.
They have not the most distant idea of Christianity.   The annual
decrease by deaths over births is, among the plantation slaves, from
ten to twelve per cent., and among the others from four to six per
cent.   The births exceed the deaths among the free colored population, from five to six per cent." *

5. *The Obstacles to African Evangelization in Hayti.*

Hayti has not been passed unnoticed by the Christian world
As early as 1816, the English Wesleyans commenced a mission
in the Island, but in 1819 the missionary had to leave on account
of persecution from the adherents of the prevailing religion.
Religious freedom was not allowed.   The missionaries found
ignorance and immorality predominant at this period, and, in
one or more instances, had sufficient evidence afforded to prove

* See "Ethiopia" for full particulars.

that idolatry was practiced in the island. In the outset, President Boyer manifested the greatest readiness to encourage and promote the plans of the missionaries; and, on their departure, not only expressed himself as highly satisfied with their conduct, but transmitted a donation of £500 to the Society. After the missionaries took their leave, the small congregation they had gathered could only meet by stealth; and, on one occasion, a number of them were seized by the police, and carried to prison. On trial, they were prohibited, in the name of the President, from meeting together; still, however, a few remained faithful, and in 1834, another missionary arrived, followed afterwards by others, so that, in 1853, the mission had 429 converts in its connection. In 1860, the Society report, that the new government look with favor on the mission, and is as liberal as they can desire. The attendance on preaching is encouraging.

In 1835, the American Baptist Missionary Society made an attempt to establish a mission in the island, which at first promised success, but was abandoned in 1837.

"About twenty years ago, a society of Wesleyan Methodists established a mission in the town of Porto Plata. The Church still lives, and is, by foreigners, comparatively well attended; but they have not converted a single Catholic, by preaching, from that day to this. The reason is, the Catholics will not go to hear them. Yet, for the benefits of an education, about one hundred and fifty children were sent regularly to school, and there, by the 'infidel' teaching of the Wesleyans, they soon learned to distrust the ceremonies of the mother Church. Unfortunately, about two years since, this school was discontinued, and, having succeeded in weaning the people from positive Catholicism, without yet embracing the Protestant religion, it seems to have left them with a general belief in every thing, which is, as I take it, the nearest point to a belief in nothing." *

Of this mission, the Wesleyan Missionary Society, in 1860, thus speaks: "The missions in St. Domingo have not recovered from the confusion and difficulty created by political changes."

Between 1820 and 1829, a brisk emigration from the United

---

* Summer on the Caribbeean, by Mr. Harris, an intelligent colored man, and Emigration Agent.

States to Hayti was conducted, transferring 8,000 free colored persons to that island, the expenses of 6,000 of whom were paid by the Haytien government.*   This emigration scheme was undertaken by those who distrusted the Colonization Society; but failing to send missionaries and teachers along with the emigrants, they never were able to reap any fruits from their sowing.   This incident in the history of the black man affords another lesson of instruction: standing alone, the uneducated negro was as helpless in Hayti in 1830, as he was in London in 1787.

The social and moral condition of the island, at the time Boyer was overthrown, may be inferred from the fact, that a leader of the revolution entered into correspondence with Christian men in the United States, in relation to the introduction of missionaries.   One of the letters from the Haytien, dated in 1843, says:

" You have exactly hit on the essential points in recommending the establishment of individual families by marriages, to serve as a basis of the great social family, the establishment of institutions for the diffusion of moral and religious instruction," etc.

In 1849, one of the editors of the *Christian Reflector* visited the island, and in reporting on its condition, socially and morally, he said:

" The Sabbath is the great business day of the week to the middle and lower classes, while the rich employ it as a holiday.   It is the day especially devoted to military parade and marketing.   The public squares are crowded with buyers and sellers, and all the shops are thronged with customers as on no other day of the week.   The marriage relation is, for the most part, sustained without a marriage contract, and divorce and polygamy are too common to excite attention.   The faithful husband of a wife is a character so rare as to be a marked exception to the general rule. . . . . . In a word, the institutions of the Sabbath and of marriage are alike prostrate.   Both have a name; but the Divine object of neither is secured, with a vast majority of the population.   As a legitimate consequence, profane-

---

* Life of Benjamin Lundy.

ness, intemperance, and vulgarity extensively characterize all classes of society."

In 1860, Mr. Harris, before quoted, in speaking of the Haytien end of the island, and the policy of President Geffard, says:

" Under Protestant influences, also, several large schools, in which hundreds of young girls and boys are being educated, promise in due time to present to the world a virtuous female offspring of these heroic revolutionists, adorned by all the graces attending the use of both the French and English languages, and a body of youths skilled at once in commerce, and in the sciences of government, the sword, the anvil, and the plow."

In speaking of an emigrant settlement of colored Americans, not far from Porto Plata, the same writer remarks:

" How happy will be the effect of such an enterprise on a non-progressive people, you have probably anticipated from what I have previously observed;" and, then, as an evidence of the indolence of the population, he elsewhere adds, " there is but one saw-mill on the Spanish end of the island, near St. Domingo city, and that not now in operation."

These facts indicate, very clearly, that African Evangelization has made but little progress in Hayti. Now that Spain has taken possession of the Spanish part of the island, it remains doubtful whether Protestant missions will be tolerated therein; and should France reclaim the other portion, the whole island may become closed to the Protestant missionary.

6. *The Obstacles to African Evangelization in the British West India Islands.*

While it was believed that the Christianization of the blacks was impracticable under slavery, there were good reasons why British Christians should use all lawful means to have that hindrance to the Gospel removed. This was a moral duty which the British subject, as a Christian, could not overlook. Under this view of the question, emancipation became a necessity. But the view was founded in a misconception. Time has shown, that it was not the condition of servitude which hindered the Gospel among the blacks in the West Indies. Indeed, as in the case of the Wesleyan mission in Jamaica, emancipation was not everywhere followed by a corresponding efficiency in the mission work; but, on the contrary, in a few years grievous backslidings occurred, and the population became less inclined than before to yield themselves to religious control.*

The rise of the mission work in these islands, and its progress during the period of slavery, is noticed quite fully in Chapter I. Some references are made to the results down to the present date; but the main facts occurring since emancipation were left to be used in this contrast. To that task we now proceed.

More information has come into our possession, relative to missionary operations in the West Indies, from American than from British sources. The American testimony is all from anti-slavery authorities, and may, therefore, be considered as reliable in reference to the questions it is brought to sustain. The details are more extensive than we could wish, but they better represent the facts than if more condensed. In adopting this plan, we are able to employ the language of the Associations quoted, and can thus avoid the charge of not being sufficiently full in the particulars.

First, we shall notice the mission of the ASSOCIATE SYNOD in Trinidad. This mission is the more interesting, because it was attempted by the Church which first pronounced slaveholding a sin. This term, *sin*, was used as early as 1808, in reference to slaveholding, by one of the Presbyteries which constituted this Synod.†

The ASSOCIATE SYNOD, at its meeting in Philadelphia, 1843, appointed missionaries to Trinidad, who soon after set sail for that island. The incipient steps towards establishing this mission had been taken in 1841. They chose Savanne Grande as the place of their operations, where they erected a church and a dwelling-house, and the mission was for some time in successful operation. The death of one of the missionaries, the year following, required the appointment of another to supply his place. He, however, remained but a short time in the field, having felt

---

* See Chapter I.   † See Chapter VII.

it to be his duty to return. The other missionary returned with him, leaving the mission vacant; but he was reäppointed, and resumed his labors. In 1847, a gentleman and his wife were added to the mission, as teachers. In 1848, the missionary again presented himself before the Synod, a vote approving his labors was passed, and he once more returned to his work. The Synod had resolved to increase the mission, but the mission board were unsuccessful in obtaining the services of another missionary. In the mean time, the teachers returned, leaving the devoted missionary alone upon the field, who, in consequence of ill-health, obtained leave to return, after the expiration of six months. No missionaries being obtained to succeed him, he left the field, committing his charge to the care of a Scotch missionary, residing seven miles distant. It was not until June, 1851, that another missionary set sail for Trinidad, accompanied by his wife, and a female assistant, as a teacher; but he returned in the same year, leaving the mission, as before, under the care of the Scotch missionary. In 1853, the Synod placed the mission under the care of this Scotch brother, who labored in it until sometime the next year, when he came to the United States, after placing the mission under the oversight of another Scotch missionary, who could only render it occasional services. The mission being thus left entirely destitute, with the exception of the little attention the Scotch missionary could render, the Synod, in 1855, transferred the mission to the Free Church of Scotland, with a donation of four hundred dollars, annexing, as a condition, that it might be resumed again, by Synod, at any future time. It was not, however, until November, 1856, that a missionary could be obtained; when one was sent out, but who, after laboring with encouragement until near the close of the last year, was compelled, from failure of health, to leave his field of labor. *

"This mission has been an exceedingly expensive one to the Associate Synod. It has met with many reverses, and experienced severe trials, but it is believed to have exerted a most happy influence, and has not been without special tokens of the Divine favor." †

* The facts, in this last case, are taken from the *Christian Instructor*, May 15, 1861.

† This statement with the exception referred to in the last footnote, is con-

It was the privilege of the author to listen to the explanations of some of the missionaries who returned from Trinidad. The greatest obstacle to success, which they had to encounter, was the unsettled state of the population. Emancipation left the people without fixed homes, or any certainty of constant employment in the same situation. The hearers of a sermon on one Sabbath, were often out of the reach of the preacher on the next. Congregations of listeners could be readily gathered, but could not be retained together. The low wages offered for labor, by the planters, had little fascination for the new-born freeman, who rioted in his liberty to run where he listed. What was true of the efforts to sustain congregations, was true, also, of the attempt to establish schools. But this unstable condition of things, seems likely to terminate in a few years. The necessities of existence inevitably force population into positions where bread can be made most secure. Where the soil, and not the chase, yields the means of subsistence, people must find fixed homes as soon as they become crowded. This has long been true as to Barbadoes and Antigua.* The large influx of coolies, imported into Trinidad, to supply the deficiency of labor resulting from emancipation, is fast tending to concentrate the colored people of that island also, by lessening their chances to squat at will over the island. Thus far the mission of the Associate Church, in Trinidad, has accomplished but little, except to prove the error of that Church as to the advantages of emancipation in promoting the conversion of the negroes

It was most fortunate that this denomination undertook a mission in the West Indies. Its ministry and people are of the best in the Christian Church. Their family discipline is rigid, and religious instruction made imperative. At an early day, the Synod took decided action against slavery, and, ultimately, disengaged itself from all connection with slaveholders. In common with the prevailing American sentiment, its people placed a high estimate upon human freedom; and, falling in with the

---

densed from the CHURCH MEMORIAL, 1858, a volume published under the patronage of the United Presbyterian Church, into which the Associate Synod is now merged.

* See Chapter V., for full particulars.

British theories — or importing them, rather, as the ministers were mostly from Scotland and Ireland — they considered slavery as antagonistic to the progress of the Gospel. Having placed themselves, by their ecclesiastical legislation, in a position which rendered it impossible for them any longer to approach the colored man in slavery, they resolved to reach him where he reveled in freedom. But the Trinidad mission brought them into contact with the negro, as a barbarian. Wrenched by force from the midst of African barbarism, he had made but little advancement under British slavery, except to learn the English language. One generation had succeeded another, without the lights of civilization having penetrated their darkened understandings. The missionaries, therefore, found the barbarism of the population a much more stubborn element to subdue than had been anticipated. It was the first foreign mission that this Church had attempted; and, consequently, its missionaries had but little experience in relation to the difficulties connected with attempts to control the wills of savage men. The mission was projected only three years after the emancipation of the slaves, and the work was begun exactly at the moment when the Jamaica missionaries found the population most difficult to control.

This mission has done but little toward African evangelization. It is at present, (October, 1861,) destitute of a missionary.

The AMERICAN MISSIONARY ASSOCIATION have a mission in Jamaica. The mission is occupied mainly with labor in behalf of the emancipated colored people of that island. It was commenced by five Congregational ministers, who sailed from New York in the fall of 1839 — the year following the final emancipation of the blacks. They went to Jamaica with the expectation of receiving a moderate support from the emancipated people themselves; but in this they were disappointed, and as there was then no missionary society in the United States that could undertake the support of a mission there, they were reduced to circumstances of distressing privation. They, too, had formed no just conception of the work before them. A committee was organized of gentlemen residing in New York and New England, called the WEST INDIA MISSIONARY COMMITTEE, who received and forwarded contributions for this mission, but without undertaking its support.

In 1847, the mission was transferred to the AMERICAN MISSIONARY ASSOCIATION, under whose care it remains. In 1843, the missionaries formed a Congregational Association, under the name of the JAMAICA CONGREGATIONAL ASSOCIATION; and the mission is now known in the island, as the AMERICAN CONGREGATIONAL MISSION. *

This mission, in 1858, is represented as embracing 12 stations, 7 missionaries, 2 male assistants, 13 female assistants, 4 native assistants, 8 churches, 433 members, and 716 scholars. The full details can be found in the Encyclopædia of Missions, from which we quote.

Turning from the statements in the Encyclopædia, to the reports of the AMERICAN MISSIONARY ASSOCIATION itself, † much light is derived in relation to the moral condition of the people of Jamaica. In its seventh Annual Report, 1853, page 30, it is said:

"One of our missionaries, in giving a description of the moral condition of the people of Jamaica, after speaking of the licentiousness which they received as a legacy from those who denied them the pure joys of holy wedlock, and trampled upon and scourged chastity, as if it were a fiend to be driven out from among men — that enduring legacy, which, with its foul, pestilential influence, still blights, like the mildew of death, every thing in society that should be lovely, virtuous, and of good report; and alluding to their intemperance, in which they have followed the example set by the governor in his palace, the bishop in his robes, statesmen and judges, lawyers and doctors, planters and overseers, and even professedly Christian ministers; and the deceit and falsehood which oppression and wrong always engender, says: 'It must not be forgotten that we are following in the wake of the accursed system of *slavery* — a system that *unmakes man*, by warring upon his conscience, and crushing his spirit, leaving naught but the shattered wrecks of humanity behind it. If we may but gather up some of these floating fragments, from which the image of God is well nigh effaced, and pilot them safely into that better land, we shall not have labored in vain. But we may *hope to do more*. The chief fruit of our labors is to be sought in the *future*, rather than in the *present*.' It should be remembered, too, (continues the Report,) that there is but a small part of the population yet brought within the reach of the influence of enlightened Christian teachers,

---

* Encyclopædia of Missions, 1858, page 773.
† This Association is strictly an Abolition Institution.

while the great mass by whom' they are surrounded are but little removed from actual heathenism." Another missionary, page 33, says, it is the opinion of all intelligent Christian men, that "nothing save the furnishing of the people with ample means of education and religious instruction will save them from relapsing into a state of barbarism." And another, page 36, in speaking of certain cases of discipline, for the highest form of crime, under the seventh commandment, says; "There is *nothing* in public sentiment to save the youth of Jamaica in this respect."

The Report, near its close, says:

" For most of the adult population of Jamaica, the unhappy victims of long years of oppression and degradation, our missionaries have great fear. Yet for even these there may be hope, even though with trembling. But it is around the youth of the island that their brightest hopes and anticipations cluster; from them they expect to gather their principal sheaves for the great Lord of the harvest."

The *American Missionary*, a monthly paper, and organ of this Association, for July, 1855, has the following quotation from the letters of the missionaries, recently received, in further confirmation of the moral condition of the colored people of Jamaica:

" From the number of churches and chapels in the island, Jamaica ought certainly to be called a Christian land. The people may be called a church-going people. There are chapels and places of worship enough, at least in this part of the island, to supply the people if every station of our mission were given up. And there is no lack of ministers and preachers. As far as I am acquainted, almost the entire adult population profess to have a hope of eternal life, and I think the larger part are connected with churches. In view of such facts, some have been led to say, ' The spiritual condition of the population is very satisfactory.' But there is another class of facts that is perfectly astounding. With all this array of the externals of religion, one broad, deep wave of moral death rolls over the land. A man may be a drunkard, a liar, a Sabbath-breaker, a profane man, a fornicator, an adulterer, and such like — and be known to be such — and go to chapel, and hold up his head there, and feel no disgrace from these things, because they are so common as to create a public sentiment in his favor. He may go to the communion table, and cherish a hope of heaven, and not have his hope disturbed. I might tell of persons guilty of some, if not all, these things, ministering in holy things."

Coming down to a later date, we find the report of the Association, for 1858, giving the membership of its West India Missions as 308, in the four principal stations — the other three stations not being reported. Again, in 1860, the membership, in all the stations, one excepted, is given as 404, and the whole number of scholars in the week-day schools, one out-station excepted, as 450.

The report of 1858, in noticing the progress of the missions, in two of the stations, says that the advices from the missionary affirms, " that no satisfactory advance has been made during the past year, either in educational or spiritual things ; " and then quotes from him as follows :

" We trust there is a remnant here, a church within the church, through and by whom God can work. *The few* yet left of those who during the darkness of slavery received and followed the truth as they understood it, and who follow it still as the light shines clearer; *the few* who were truly converted in the great ingatherings into the Church at and just after emancipation ; and a few of those who from time to time have been admitted of late years — these are the hopes of Jamaica. They are the salt of the land, notwithstanding their light, it may be, is dim, their strength but feeble, and much dross may be mixed with the gold."

Another quotation is made, from the missionary at a third station, as follows :

" A few weeks ago I commenced having inquiry meetings, and the number that attend has gradually increased, until this week twenty-six were present. . . . . In the little meetings which we hold among the people, the truth seems to take effect. . . . . We see some indications of the Holy Spirit among the people. . . . . Only a few of the Church members appear to understand the part Christians have to do in gathering souls into the kingdom of God. . . . . I am often made to feel that the masses will go down to eternal death. We are stimulated to labor and do what we can, and we find promises in the

Word of God that cause us to hope that our labors will be blessed in saving souls."

From the fourth and fifth stations, another writes :

" The statistical table shows, that in these two churches the past has been a *dry* year. Happily the other churches of the mission have been more blessed, although throughout Jamaica generally, spiritual deadness seems to prevail in as marked a manner as at present spiritual activity in the churches of our native land. With a grade of moral culture so vastly below that of the churches of America, I do not believe that we could reasonably expect a movement like that; but the Spirit of God knows how to move on all hearts, barbarian and civilized, and I would fain hope that our brethren at home rejoice in this favored time, and will not forget to pray that the good work may spread into other lands. The progress of the people in outward prosperity has been quite encouraging during the past year."

The Report of 1860 mentions several encouraging features connected with these missions, and some, also, that are discouraging. A quotation from one of the missionaries shows, that correct views are forcing themselves upon his mind. He says :

" Whatever may be true in other places, I am convinced that it is the sheerest folly to think of upholding missionary operations here, without giving an active support, in one way or another, to religiously-conducted schools. The government ought to care for this, and, very meagerly it does so; but what it leaves undone must be supplied by Christian zeal, here and abroad, except so far as the people can be persuaded to do it themselves ; and they do not now value education sufficiently to lay any very heavy tax upon themselves in support of it."

From another station, during this year, 1860, comes this language, as contained in the report :

" From what we observe in our neighborhood, and from what we hear from other parts, I do think we may say the day dawneth. There are some unmistakable signs of improvement. Very much that is lamentable and reproachful still remains, but no candid, thorough observer can speak of Jamaica now otherwise than hopeful."

The report on the Jamaiça mission closes with this paragraph, explanatory of the relative condition of the crowded and productive population of Barbadoes and the squatter farmers of Jamaica :

"Some extracts have been published in the *American Missionary*, from the communications of the correspondent of the *Times*, forming a perfect vindication of the people of Jamaica, from the slanderous charges that have been brought against them, and proving that the emancipated people and their descendants in Jamaica do work as diligently as those of Barbadoes; but for themselves, on their own freeholds, instead of for the planter on his estate. Wisdom is justified of her children. In Jamaica, as elsewhere, God has demonstrated that it is safe, even for man's pecuniary interest, to obey God, and refrain from injustice."

It must be remembered, that the whole of the preceding quotations come from the same body of men, writing at different dates, and having different objects to accomplish, at the different times their pens were employed. It is no part of our duty to reconcile any seeming discrepancies. But, as in accord with what they have said, and as indicating one of the sources of " the slanderous charges " referred to, it may be well to give, in connection with what has been quoted above, a few extracts from the Annual Report of the AMERICAN AND FOREIGN ANTI-SLAVERY SOCIETY, for 1853, which discoursed thus, in its own language, and in quotations which it endorsed.* It is the language of American Abolitionists, going out under the sanction of their annual reports :

"The friends of emancipation in the United States have been disappointed in some respects at the results in the West Indies, because they expected too much. A nation of slaves can not at once be converted into a nation of intelligent, industrious, and moral freemen."
. . . . . . "It is not too much, even now, to say of the people of Jamaica, ... their condition is exceedingly degraded, their morals woefully corrupt. But this must, by no means, be understood to be of universal application. With respect to those who have been brought under a healthful educational and religious influence, *it is*

* Page 170.

not true. But as respects the great mass, whose humanity has been ground out of them by cruel oppression — whom no good Samaritan hand has yet reached — how could it be otherwise? We wish to turn the tables; to supplant oppression by righteousness, insult by compassion and brotherly kindness, hatred and contempt by love and winning meekness, until we allure these wretched ones to the hope and enjoyment of manhood and virtue." * . . . . . . " The means of education and religious instruction are better enjoyed, although but little appreciated and improved by the great mass of the people. It is also true, that the moral sense of the people is becoming somewhat enlightened. . . . . . But while this is true, yet their moral condition is very far from being what it ought to be. . . . . . It is exceedingly dark and distressing. Licentiousness prevails to a most alarming extent among the people. . . . . The almost universal prevalence of intemperance is another prolific source of the moral darkness and degradation of the people. The great mass, among all classes of the inhabitants, from the governor in his palace to the peasant in his hut — from the bishop in his gown to the beggar in his rags — are all slaves to their cups." †

This is truly a dark picture of the moral degradation of the West India black population. But it comes from the pens of Abolitionists, who expect the Christian world to accept their assertions as true. Being themselves the prime promoters of abolition, they, of course, must be allowed to announce the results of their own policy. Such declarations, however, as to the moral gloom overshadowing the West Indies, should be taken with some allowance, on account of the peculiar position occupied by the missionaries who make the reports. Their honesty of intention, and devotion to their work, none will doubt; but they belong to an organization preëminently partizan in its character, and distinguished for the strength of its zeal in behalf of abolition theories. This association was based, by its founders, upon the assumption, that all existing denominations tolerated sin — tolerated the use of tobacco, intoxicating drinks, slavery, caste, and polygamy — and that a pure Church was necessary to the universal success of the Gospel. The element of Christian charity,

---

* Extract from the report of a missionary, quoted in the Report, page 172.

† Extract from the report of another missionary, page 171, of the Report.

in its exercise toward other professors of religion, exists in that body in a much less degree, it is feared, than the spirit of hatred of all who will not accept their claims to preëminent holiness, and their divine commission to dictate laws to the civil as well as the ecclesiastical world.*

But notwithstanding the high pretensions of the American Missionary Association, they have not succeeded any better than other missionary societies, in lifting the heathen out of their barbaric darkness. The Holy Spirit has not descended in any greater power upon their missions than upon others; and they apologize to the world for their failures, by assigning, as a reason for their want of success, that slavery is accountable for the results — that the Gospel is powerless where the black man has been reduced to a "chattel" by the white man. Now, if this has been the true cause of their impotency among the African race, where slavery to the whites has prevailed; all they have to do, to insure success, is to transfer their labors to Africa, where barbarism, in its uncorruptedness, holds undisputed sway.

This experiment, fortunately, they have tried, and the results in Africa, where the white man, to use a favorite abolition phrase, has not "reduced the negro to the condition of a chattel," can now be compared with those in the West Indies. And what does this comparison show? Have patience, reader, and you shall see.

The American Missionary Association established a mission, in connection with the return of the Amistad Africans, at Kaw-Mendi, in Africa, in 1842; only four years after emancipation in the West Indies, and three years later than the origin of their mission in Jamaica. The reports of the earlier years of the Mendi Mission, are details of trials, sufferings, and deaths, among the missionaries; arising from the fatality of the climate, the untutored savageism of the natives, and the frequency of the wars of the hostile tribes. Encouraging seasons often sprung up, succeeded by disappointments calculated to sadden the hearts of the truly zealous missionaries. The Report of the Association for 1858 gives the extent of the mission as embracing three stations and seven out-stations; but neither that report nor the one

---

* See the resolutions of the Chicago clergymen, Chapter XI., for a specimen of the claims set up by abolition clergymen.

for 1860,* present any statistics, in tabular form, of the membership of their churches. Some details, however, are given in the extracts from the letters of the missionaries, which are of great interest, when taken in connection with similar facts in the missions of other denominations in Africa. It seems to be a settled question, in missionary operations among the blacks, that little success, in their moral elevation, can be hoped for, excepting where the children are separated from their parents, and taken into the families of the missionaries. Where this is impracticable, the natives may dwell along-side of the missions, or the civilized colonists, and still retain all their heathenism of mind and soul. "So the natives of Cape Palmas have lived, in the very midst of the colonists, for some twenty years, and they are the same people still, with almost no visible change." † The controlling influence of the superior race seems essential to the inferior, to impart the moral courage necessary to resist surrounding temptations. Unrestrained by the white man, the black falls an easy prey to the vices of his heathenish neighbors. The proximity of the barbarous man to the civilized, without proper moral control, results in the former copying the vices of the latter, rather than his virtues. It is for reasons such as these, that African missions seem to progress so slowly; and that some, hitherto hopeful as to African evangelization, are now almost despairing of the possibility of subjecting the population of Africa to the laws of Christian morality.

The American Missionary Association have been operating in Africa almost twenty years. A reference to the statistics of its West India mission, which was begun twenty-two years since, shows, that its church members, and the pupils in its schools, in that field of labor, are so few in number as to prove a great source of discouragement to the missionaries. Indeed, setting out with the high pretensions made by the Association, the results may be considered as almost a failure — attributed, by them, as we have seen, to the preëxistence of slavery upon the ground. But the results in Africa have been still more discouraging. How is this

---

* We have not that of 1859 at hand.

† Report of Bishop Scott, of the Methodist Episcopal Church of the United States, in relation to his visit to the missions of Liberia.

to be accounted for? Is the difficulty inherent in the African race, sunk as it has been, for thousands of years, in the darkest barbarism? Or can it be, that the Association, with its missionaries, hold opinions so much at variance with the Gospel — employ themselves so much with side issues about human rights, to the neglect of the salvation of human souls — that the Great Head of the Church refuses to make them the honored instruments in the evangelization of the African race?

But let us examine the results of the African missions of the Asssociation. From Good Hope station, in 1858, the missionary wrote:

"Twenty-five children live under my roof, and receive daily school instruction. . . . . . . Our out-school is taught in the chapel by a man from Sierra Leone, and numbers over twenty scholars. . . . . . . Our sabbath-school for a long time was attended only by the children in the mission family, but now we have about fifty scholars, and three-quarters of them can read in the Bible, and they understand English quite well. . . . . . . Our congregation numbers about one hundred and fifty. . . . . . . Our prayer-meetings are pretty well attended, and we have a few people with us, who are, we think, true Christians. . . . . . . Though we do not see the people flocking to Christ, and are not able to report a great ingathering of converts, still the truth is doing its work, and is like leaven, affecting the whole community."

The station at Kaw-Mendi, says the Report for 1858, is less encouraging. The missionary, above quoted, thus writes in relalation to this station:

"I removed Mr. Jowett, our native teacher at Kaw-Mendi, to this place, (Good Hope,) some six months since, because I had no teacher for the out-school here. He met with very little encouragement there. For a long time after I returned from America, he had but ten scholars. Afterward it increased to thirteen. Seven of these were supported by the mission. The people there manifested a great deal of indifference about the school. . . . . . . Father Johnson is as suitable a person to have charge of the meetings at Kaw-Mendi, and watch over the few church members, as any one we could find. There are not more than five or six persons there whom Father Johnson and Mr. Jowett think give evidence of conversion."

From Boom Falls station, the only remaining one under the care of the Association, the missionary thus writes, as copied in the Report:

"Some of the boys are, to all appearances, loving the Lord!
. . . . . . Eight of them are now anxious about their souls. . . . . . .
The family at Mo-Tappan house has been increased during the year.
We have now fourteen boys and four girls. . . . . . . Our family is a very pleasant one, and for it I entertain high hopes. Some of its members are hopefully pious."

The Board closes its Report on its African missions, characteristically, by speaking in strong terms of reprobation against the colonization of Africa from the United States — thus still exhibiting their hostility to the American Colonization Society.

The Report for 1860, in speaking of Good Hope station, says:

" The formation of the Church at Good Hope was reported last year. At its close it numbered eighteen members.   Two new members had been added in April. Our Sabbath-school is gradually increasing in numbers.   We now have between sixty and seventy."

In May six new members were added to the Church, two by letter, and four on profession of their faith, from the mission school. The mission school numbers twenty-five scholars, all of whom are wholly under the care of the mission.

" Their proficiency in ordinary studies has been all that could have been reasonably expected, and their acquaintance with the Bible and its precious truths, is such as might well put to shame thousands brought up in a Christian land with the advantages of Sabbath-school and sanctuary privileges. . . . . . . The out-school now numbers over thirty scholars."

A new station established, had been attacked by a war party and robbed of its movable effects.

The report for 1860, thus speaks of the Boom Falls station:

" The church at Mo-Tappan, that numbered fourteen at our last report, numbered twenty-four the first of January, six having been baptized and added to it at the last preceding communion. . . . . . .

Regular Sabbath services, generally preaching, were held in eight different places. A school was taught during the week at the station, and three small out-schools, under the care of native teachers, in as many different towns."

The missionary, and three of his native assistants, were constantly engaged in itinerant missionary labor, each in turn leaving the mission on Monday morning, and returning on Saturday evening A small school has been commenced at another station. The missionaries consider the country as fully opened to missionary labor, and plead most urgently to their friends at home to send forth more laborers into that part of the moral vineyard of the Lord.

But while the missionaries express themselves as very hopeful as to the future, it is apparent, from the facts given in the Report of the Association, that the African mission has been even less successful than the one in Jamaica; and that, therefore, slavery can not be fairly chargeable with the failures in the West Indies. On the contrary, West India slavery, like that of the United States, had prepared the blacks for the more ready acceptance of the Gospel, by having trained them in the use of the English language — the want of which, in Africa, being a great obstacle to missionary success.

The truth is, the American Missionary Association has had much to learn in relation to the real condition of the barbarous inhabitants of Africa.   They set out with false notions, and have had to reap the fruits of their errors.   Cherishing bitter prejudices against the slaveholder, they could not say too many extravagant things in reprobation of slavery. Ignoring the Providence of God in that great movement which transferred millions of barbarians into contact with civilized men, they could only see, in the movement, the cruelties and oppressions of the agents who were permitted to perform the work. Like professional philanthropists, in general, they based their action on a single idea, and repudiated with indignation every fact that would not sustain their theory. Expecting that their claims to superior sanctity would be endorsed in heaven, they felt confident that the Holy Spirit, in Pentecostal abundance, would be out-poured upon their labors, so that, soon, the heathen would be given to them for an inheritance, and the uttermost parts of the earth for a possession. Are their pretensions and expectations over-estimated? Listen to the language of their Report for 1858—remembering that they have charged, by implication at least, all other ecclesiastical organizations with tolerating sin :

"The Gospel is to be taught and preached; the *whole* Gospel—not an emasculated Gospel; not such portions only of the true Gospel as men are willing to receive. The Gospel is to be inculcated upon 'all nations' — the accessible part of every nation ; not a selected nation, or selected portions of a nation merely, where it is easy, convenient, and safe. Not alone in China, in Hindostan, in the islands of the sea, in the free States of the American Union, but in all countries ; in the slave States as well as in the free States ; among the Indian tribes, not omitting the Choctaw and Cherokee nations. They also are to have a full, unadulterated, free Gospel preached to them.

"Among the slaves and the .slaveholders, the Gospel, as it came from its divine founder, is to be preached without concealment or compromise. Wherever God opens the way, it is to be preached, and preached faithfully, whether human enactments authorize or forbid it. 'The field is the world.' It belongs to Christ, and his word is not bound. His followers are to remember that his commands constitute the 'higher law;' that they are to be obeyed at all hazards, and if human enactments come in conflict with the divine statutes, human enactments are to be trampled under feet. They are not to be resisted by force of arms, but simply *disobeyed*. . . . . . Nothing is to be taught as the Gospel which is not a part of it. . . . . The Christian teacher, be he a minister, Sabbath-school teacher, missionary, colporteur, editor, or private Christian, is to go forth in the name of the Great Captain of his salvation, among his fellow-men, among gainsayers, opposers, enemies of truth, and 'lower law' men, wherever he has opportunity, as a soldier of the cross, faithful to his marching orders : 'Thou shalt say unto them, Thus saith the Lord God : Be not afraid of them, neither be afraid of their words, though briars and thorns be with thee and thou dost dwell among scorpions ; be not afraid of their words, nor be dismayed at their looks, though they be a rebellious house. And thou shalt speak my words unto them, whether they will hear, or whether they will forbear ' . . . . . 'speaking the truth in love.'

"It was in view of these truths, and under a full persuasion that they had been grievously overlooked, that the American Missionary

Association was organized. Its founders deeply felt the necessity of a new missionary organization; one that would aim to bring about the development of the mind and heart of Christ in the Church, in missionary societies, in the religious institutions of the country, and would send forth missionaries at home and abroad, to preach a free, an evangelical, an anti-slavery Gospel; a Gospel that made no compromise with sin; that had no complicity with caste, polygamy, or slaveholding; that would fearlessly and perseveringly, in the name and spirit of Jesus Christ, proclaim freedom, peace, temperance, holiness, the equality of man before the law, and the impartial love of God.

"Believing that they were led by the Great Head of the Church, and recognizing the unmistakable hand of Providence in their earliest movements, they formed the Association, promulgated their principles, solicited funds, appointed missionaries, and embarked in the great undertaking of publishing in this and other lands what they understood to be the true Gospel, and carrying out its holy and evangelical principles, as God should give them ability, the means, and opportunity. . . . . . On all fit occasions, without considering the Association an anti-slavery society, we have not hesitated to proclaim, as became a missionary institution, the anti-slavery character of the Association, and its agreement with an anti-slavery Gospel. We are anti-slavery, because we deem slaveholding a great obstruction to the conversion of the world."

This will serve to convey a clear idea of the pretensions and expectations of this Association. The results of their missionary efforts, assuredly, do not meet their anticipations. Their experiments, however, have a very important bearing, as the effects resulting therefrom cast much light upon a very important question. Acknowledging the want of success among the adult population of Jamaica, the missionaries assume that slavery so thoroughly "unmakes man," that the Gospel can not prevail in its "wake." Passing over to Africa itself, no better success attends their labors. Why, then, do they not acknowledge their error, and attribute the inefficiency of their missions to the true cause—the deep mental and moral degradation of the African race, where they are not subjected to proper restraints and carefully instructed by a civilized people.

It has already been remarked, that some allowance, perhaps,

should be made in considering the testimony borne by the American Missionary Association, in relation to the missions of the other denominations in Jamaica, on account of the peculiar views held by that society. The use of spirituous liquors and tobacco are viewed as sinful, or at least so inconsistent with Christianity, that those who use them are considered unfit to assume the offices of religious teachers, and none such are commissioned by the Executive Committee of the Association.* In speaking so disparagingly of their neighbor missionaries, in the West Indies, this society, of course, include, among the sins tolerated by others, the use of tobacco and rum — thus undertaking to decide a question properly belonging to the medical profession, whether narcotics and stimulants may not be essential to health in tropical climates. Making allowance, then, for whatever of prejudice may have influenced the judgments of the missionaries, in reporting on the present moral condition of the mission churches in the West Indies, belonging to other denominations, we are to remember that, as they are men of truth, there may be some foundation for the charges made. But if the charges do approximate the truth, then the emancipation of the blacks has not produced the favorable moral advancement which was expected to follow that measure.

This point demands careful examination. By referring to Chapter I., it will be seen that, during slavery, where no opposition prevailed, very encouraging success accompanied the labors of the missionaries of all denominations, in both the English and Danish islands; and yet, notwithstanding this, we are now asked to believe that the colored population of these islands, since emancipation, are almost wholly inaccessible to the Gospel. If this be true, the logical inference from the fact is, that a state of freedom is less favorable to the evangelization of the African race than a state of slavery. Are the American Missionary Association not aware, that their testimony very strongly corroborates the testimony of Southern slaveholders — that the moral advancement of the negro progresses much more rapidly under slavery than under freedom ? The falling off in the number of

* See 14th Annual Report, 1860, p. 62.

church members, in the West India missions, heretofore noticed,
which occurred a few years after emancipation, may also be cited
as sustaining the views held by the missionaries of the Association — that the present condition of the freedmen of the West
Indies is exceedingly unfavorable to the success of the Gospel.
But as the missions conducted during slavery, when undisturbed,
were very successful, the present want of success can not be a
consequence of the preexistence of slavery, but must be attributed, as heretofore suggested, to another cause — the want of
proper moral control over the negroes.

If nothing more, then, has been done, by this attempt of the
American Missionary Association, to propagate an anti-slavery
Gospel, this, at least, has been determined: that circumstances
have existed, under which slavery was more conducive to African evangelization than freedom. This is an important fact;
and the slave may well rejoice at the result, as, hereafter, it must
not be claimed that emancipation shall precede all efforts for his
conversion, and he be left without the means of salvation until
his freedom is secured.

But to return to the West Indies. An examination, a little
more in detail, of the results of missionary labors in the West
Indies, before and after emancipation, will be useful in forming
a judgment upon this question — the effects of slavery upon the
African race, in reference to their conversion to Christianity.

It will be observed, in the preceding pages, that the membership in the Moravian missions, in the Danish islands, during the
ninety years ending in 1832 — that is, the number of persons
baptized during that period — was 37,000; in Antigua, during the
fifty years preceding 1823, the number of converts, young and
old, was 16,099; in Jamaica, in 1804, the number that had been
baptized was 938; and in St. Kitts, in 1800, the converts were
estimated at 2,000 — making a total of 56,000. This is an unusual mode of presenting statistics, but they are not accessible in
any other form; nor could they be obtained for later dates, so
as to exhibit the results of the Moravian missions up to the
period of emancipation.

The statistics of the English Wesleyan missions, in the West
Indies, have not been obtained to any important extent, for the

period preceding emancipation; but six years afterward, 1844, their membership was, in Jamaica alone, 26,585; and in St. Vincent, in 1794, it was over 1,000. From the other islands we have no returns for this slavery period. This 26,585, in Jamaica, may be taken as representing the whole membership.

The Baptist missions, in Jamaica alone, had a memb̈ership, in 1831, of 10,838, and in 1841, of 27,706.

These statistics do not include all the missions, and yet they foot up 94,400, as the probable number of converts, under slavery, within the islands named. *

Here, now, was the basis upon which the missions, after emancipation, had to operate. It was a very different foundation, indeed, from that upon which the first missionaries to these islands had to build. They began with a population who had never heard the Gospel, and many of whom were new imports from Africa — the slave trade being then in full activity. In addition to this, the planters, mostly, were opposed to the missions, and frequently broke them up. The present missions may all be said to have had their origin since emancipation, as the circumstances, by which they have been surrounded, are entirely different from those in which the first missionaries were placed. The planters have made no opposition to the missionaries; and they have had the advantage — if advantage it be — of laboring among a population of freemen. Such is the difference in the condition of the two classes of missions — the one operating before emancipation and the other after the abolition of slavery.

Let us examine the results: The WESLEYAN METHODIST MISSION, in Jamaica, which, six years after emancipation, numbered 26,585, was reduced, in 1853, to 19,478 — a loss of over 7,000, being a decrease of *twenty-seven* per cent. during *eleven* years of freedom!

Later information, in reference to these missions, is contained in the proceedings of the English Wesleyan Missionary Society, at its anniversary for 1860, but no statistics are given. † They speak of Antigua as having improved financially. The St. Vin-

---

* See Chapter I., for full particulars.

† Wesleyan Methodist Magazine, June, 1860.

cent and Demarara district, is represented as containing "eleven circuits, in only one of which any increase has taken place during the year; the numbers in all the rest being somewhat reduced." Of Jamaica they say:

"Its condition presents at least one hopeful feature, in the steady and successful efforts made to reduce the chapel debts, and thus to place the financial affairs of the several circuits in a more satisfactory position. The members in society do not increase."

This will be a matter of astonishment to American anti-slavery men, of all grades — the members in society, of the zealous Methodist missionaries, in Jamaica, do not increase! Already, they had been reduced, in 1853, under eleven years of freedom to the extent of *twenty-seven* per cent.; and still they do not increase!

The ENGLISH BAPTISTS, it will be remembered, were actively engaged in the mission work, in Jamaica, during the period of slavery, and suffered greatly from the persecution of the planters. The *Missionary Magazine*, March, 1861, embraces a synopsis of the report of a deputation which had visited the Baptist churches of Jamaica. The *Magazine* copies from the *London Missionary Herald*. There are several points made in the Report, a few of which we shall notice:

1. "The prompt, vigorous, and searching discipline usually maintained throughout the churches, whether under the pastorate of European or native brethren, and the respect paid to the decisions of the church on all matters relating to the spiritual well-being of the fellowship. If the number of exclusions is a source of deep regret, yet are they clear evidence of the attachment of the churches to righteousness and purity. If, in our judgments, the discipline on some points is too severe, yet the general effect on the moral tone of the community at large, in the repression of superstition, in the respect shown to the ordinance of marriage, (which, indeed, yet re quires further elevation, in the general estimation of the outside population,) has been most valuable."

2. This point has reference to the tender interest manifested by the church, toward those who have been excluded from fellowship.

3. The delegation express themselves as greatly pleased with the devotedness of the deacons and elders, in their care of the spiritual interests of the people.

The membership of the churches, in 1859, as stated by the delegation, was 19,360, in the Island of Jamaica. After giving some statistics on the subject, it is remarked:

"It thus appears that while there has been a continuous diminution in the number of the churches, there has also been a small but steady decrease in the sums contributed to the pastors. At the same time the *general* contributions of those in membership do not appear to have become less, but to have increased since 1849. . . . . . The pastors have suffered rather from the diminution in the number of their members, than from a decline in their liberality. These facts certainly prove that their appeals for assistance are not without a real foundation."

The membership of the Baptists, in 1841, was 27,706. * In 1859, as above stated, it was 19,360 — a decrease of 8,346 in eighteen years, being a loss of *thirty* per cent. All this decrease has occurred under freedom, as the final emancipation took place only three years before the year 1841, when the church census was taken. In that year, it will be remembered, the churches declared themselves independent of the parent society, and became self-supporting; now, they have to appeal to the society for aid, and thus manifest their conviction that the Jamaica negroes must still be cared for by the white race.

"The history of the LONDON MISSIONARY SOCIETY's operations in Jamaica is brief, extending over little more than twenty-five years. By the Act of Emancipation, in 1834, eight hundred thousand of our fellow-creatures passed from a state of abject and cruel slavery to one of comparative freedom, called 'apprenticeship.' This happy change afforded greatly increased facilities for usefulness among the agricultural laborers in the West Indies; and of these advantages the directors promptly availed themselves, anxious to take a part in preparing them for the still greater change which would, in a few years, take place in their social condition, when they would be put into the full possession of their rights and privileges as freemen."

See Chapter I.

Thus discourses the *Missionary Magazine,* of August, 1861 The views presented are in accordance with the British theory Let us see, then, how the results stand, as compared with missionary operations among the American slaves. The society sent out six missionaries, with their wives, to Jamaica. They had no difficulty in finding locations; and they so selected their positions as to form centers from which to operate by means of out-stations. Some of the out-stations soon became of sufficient importance to induce the directors to send out additional missionaries to occupy them; and the work has progressed, so that, in 1860, the mission stands thus: European missionaries 6, native pastors 3, native candidates for the ministry 3, native catechists and schoolmasters 11, Sabbath-school scholars 2,243, day scholars 1,346, church members 1,691 — a very small increase, indeed, as compared with the accessions of colored members, during the same period, to the churches South.

The Report of the BOARD OF FOREIGN MISSIONS OF THE MORA- VIANS, at the triennial meeting of the Provincial Synod at Beth- lehem, Pennsylvania, June; 1858, presents the condition of its missions in the West Indies. In eight of these islands — five British and three Danish — the Moravians have 38 stations, 104 missionaries, and 36,441 converts. This does not include the missionaries and converts in Tobago, the returns of which are not given. *

Contrasting the present condition of the missions of this church, in the West Indies, with what it was during the period of slavery, and it is found that they have not held their ground. During slavery, their converts could not have been less than 50,000; † and now they are reduced to 36,441 — a decline, under freedom, of 13,559! A reported revival during last year has afforded some encouragement of better prospects in the future; but, thus far, freedom has done nothing for the greater increase of converts among the blacks under the direction of the Moravians.

Taking, then, the total number of church members, in all the missions in the West Indies, as indicated by the reports quoted, and the contrast between Slavery and Freedom stands as follows:

---

* American Christian Record, 1860.　　† See Chapter I.

Under Slavery, the various missionary societies, commencing their labors among the barbarous blacks, gathered more than 94,400 converts.

Under Freedom, eight missionary societies, commencing their labors with 94,400 converts as a basis, and with freedom upon which to progress in their work, have increased the converts to 112,807 * — being an actual addition of only 18,407.

The results of the mission-work in the West Indies, under slavery and under freedom, respectively, are now before the reader. The statistics for the first period are not complete. They are sufficiently full, however, to show that the mere condition of slavery was no barrier to African evangelization; but that the checks it received, arose only from the hostility of the masters. In the estimates for this period, it must be observed, that the four years of apprenticeship are included, from 1834 to 1838. This is done from necessity, as the statistics are only accessible for the dates used; and, besides, these two periods are properly classified together, as the apprenticeship was a system of rigid constraint — more so, even, than the slavery which preceded it — the only difference being, that the missionaries had uninterrupted access to the population. In every other respect, the bondage of the negro was as complete as while he was in slavery. Three years of freedom are included in the statistics of the Baptists, and six years in those of the Methodists. But as an offset to this, the missions, under freedom, have had the advantage of all the membership gained during slavery. Taking into account, then, all the circum-

---

* These Missionary Associations, with their membership, are as follows:

DENOMINATIONS.	MEMBERS.
Wesleyans,	48,000
English Baptists,	19,360
Church of England,	696
London Missionary Society,	4,000
Moravians,	36,441
Scotch Presbyterians,	3,900
American Missionary Association,	404
United Presbyterian Church, U. S.,	6
Total,	112,807

A portion of these statistics are from the Encyclopædia of Missions.

stances, it is apparent that the success has been greatest during the period of servitude. None of the missions have even maintained the ground gained under slavery. This result disproves the theory of the American Missionary Association, that the present inaccessibility of the population to the Gospel is due to the preëxistence of slavery; because, if the missionaries were successful in christianizing the blacks while in bondage, the want of success under emancipation must be due to some other cause than slavery.

The history of missions in the West Indies affords a useful lesson to those who have been struggling for the extension of human rights, to the neglect of the use of the means appointed to promote the salvation of the souls of men — to those who have been careful to tithe the mint, anise, and cummin (tobacco, whisky, and rum,) to the neglect of the weightier matters of the law. The results are the more startling, when it is considered that there has been a large increase of missionaries in this field, and that no interruption of their labors has occurred, from the planters or others. Freedom, full and absolute, was granted to a barbarous people — barbarous, except to the extent to which the mission-work had progressed — and the results have been nothing more than should have been expected. In disposition and knowledge, the African race, with few exceptions, are but children, as compared with the white race; and when thrown upon their own resources, like neglected children, of any color, they must necessarily run to ruin.

7. *The Obstacles to African Evangelization in the French West India Islands.*

The moral condition of the negro population of Hayti, before emancipation, may be taken as the type of that of the blacks of the other French islands. We find that the question of their moral condition, under slavery, was a subject of investigation in 1839.

"Some time ago, a commission was appointed to examine the question of the abolition of slavery in the French colonies. The following extract is taken from a summary of the report presented by M. DE TOCQUEVILLE, in the name of the commission:" *

---

* Christian Intelligencer, Hamilton, Ohio, December, 1839.

"The report passes lightly and contemptuously over the arguments in favor of slavery, and takes for granted the conviction, in every mind, that it ought to be done away with. It passes immediately to the question of its being necessary to prepare the slave for emancipation, previous to liberating him. M. de Tocqueville, in the name of the commission, asserts that all attempts to improve, enlighten, and prepare the slave, as long as he is a slave, are impossible. . . . . The commission, therefore, abandons the idea of preparing the slave for freedom by any regulations of his treatment while a slave. Emancipation, it adds, can not be deferred. The prospect of it, the idea of its necessity, of its necessary arrival at no distant time, render the slave incapable of tranquil obedience and good conduct as a slave. He is in a false position. The master can no longer retain him, especially at night."

It was not until 1848 that emancipation was declared in the French West India Islands, by a decree of the Republic. Their population, including free persons and slaves, we find stated as follows : *

COLONIES.	FREE.	SLAVES.
Martinique........................(1846)........................	47,352	75,330
Gaudaloupe ....(do)........................	40,428	89,349
Bourbon......................... (do)........................	45,512	62,154
Nossi Be and Nossi Cumba.........(do). }		
Nossi Falli and Nossi Mitsou....(do). }	14,512	7,698
St. Mary Magdalene.................(do)........................	3,465	2,415
Senegal........................(1845)........................	8,427	10,113
Algiers, (estimate)........................		10,000
Total........................	159,696	257,059

A fact or two will illustrate the effects of emancipation upon the economical interests of these islands. When M. de Tocqueville made his report, the production of cane sugar, in the whole of the islands, was 161,500,000 lbs.† per annum. In the first *nine* months of 1847, the exports to France were 168,884,177 lbs. This shows that the production of the islands was on the increase, previous to emancipation. But the abolition of slavery, in 1848, at once arrested cultivation, so that, in the first *nine* months of

* Anti-Slavery Reporter.
† This was the crop of 1840.

1849, the exports were reduced to 96,929,336 lbs. * — being a reduction, during the second year of freedom, of more than *fifty-seven* per cent. This sudden falling off in the production of the colonies soon led to the supply of a laboring population, to supplant the idle free negroes, by the adoption of the " immigration " system. The imported laborers were brought from Africa, and their procurement, as will be remembered, produced some trouble between the French and the authorities of Liberia. It also greatly interrupted the American Board's missions on the Gaboon river.

We find in M. de Tocqueville a zealous disciple of the English theories — that the moral elevation of the blacks can not be secured under slavery. Time has shown that this gentleman, as well as the English theorists, were extremely short-sighted in reference to the effects of emancipation. They can now see, that freedom to a barbarous population is not necessarily followed by the intellectual and moral elevation of the people set at liberty.

No Protestant missions have been established in these islands. The planters are no longer responsible for the slaves of which they were robbed; and, in the midst of continuous importations of barbarians from Africa, they can not improve.

8. *The Obstacles to African Evangelization among the Free Colored people of the United States and Canada.*

It may be well, in the outset of this investigation, to refer again to the moral condition of the free colored population at the North, as indicated by the statistics of crime. The preceding chapter shows what it was, up to 1826 and 1827; it is only necessary, therefore, to direct attention to their moral condition since that period. The results will enable us to determine whether the anti-slavery zeal of the North, for the good of the African race, has spent as much of its force for the elevation of those already free, and at their doors, as has been expended by them in efforts for the emancipation of the slaves at the South. The statistics below are from the COMPENDIUM OF THE CENSUS OF THE UNITED STATES for 1850 — those of 1860 not being out:

---

* See "Ethiopia," page 136.

" *Tabular Statement of the number of the native and foreign white population, the colored population, the number of each class in the Penitentiaries, the proportion of the convicts to the whole number of each class, the proportion of colored convicts over the foreign and also over the native whites, in the four States named, for the year 1850:*

CLASSES, ETC.	MASS.	N. YORK.	PENN.	OHIO.
NATIVE WHITES...............................	819,044	2,388,830	1,953,276	1,732,698
In the Penitentiary..................	264	835	205	291
Being 1 out of.........................	3,102	2,860	9,528	5,954
FOREIGN WHITES	163,598	655,224	303,105	218,099
In the Penitentiary..................	125	545	123	71
Being 1 out of.........................	1,308	1,202	2,464	3,077
COLORED POPULATION	9,064	49,069	53,626	25,279
In the Penitentiary..................	47	257	109	44
Being 1 out of......................	192	190	492	574
Colored convicts over foreign........	6.8 times	6.3 times	5 times	5.3 times
Colored convicts over native whites..................................	16.1 times	15 times	19.3 times	10.3 times

" It appears from these figures, that the amount of crime among the colored people of Massachusetts, in 1850, was $6\frac{8}{10}$ times greater than the amount among the foreign-born population of that State, and that the amount, in the four States named, among the free colored people, averages *five-and-three-quarters* times more, in proportion to their numbers, than it does among the foreign population, and over *fifteen* times more than it does among the native whites. It will be instructive, also, to note the *moral condition* of the free colored people in Massachusetts, the great center of abolitionism, where they have enjoyed equal rights ever since 1780. Strange to say, there is nearly three times as much crime among them, in that State, as exists among those of Ohio! More than this will be useful to note, as it regards the direction of the *emigration* of the free colored people. Massachusetts, in 1850, had but 2,687 colored persons born out of the State, while Ohio had 12,662 born out of her limits. Take another fact: the increase *per cent.*, of the colored population, in the whole New England States, was, during the ten years from 1840 to 1850, but $1\frac{71}{100}$, while in Ohio, it was, during that time, $45\frac{76}{100}$.

" There is another point worthy of notice. Though the New England abolition States have offered equal political rights to the colored man, it has afforded him little temptation to emigrate into their bounds. On the contrary, several of these States have been diminishing their free colored population, for many years past, and none of them can have had accessions of colored immigrants; as is abundantly proved by the fact, that their additions, of this class of persons, have not exceeded the natural increase of the resident colored population."*

A useful lesson is here taught, in relation to the great problem of the progress of the African, in civilization, side by side with the Caucasian.

But we must not pass over an important fact, embraced in the question of the moral condition of the free colored population. Look again at their condition in Massachusetts, as compared with Ohio. In the former, in 1850, one out of every 192 were in the Penitentiary, and in the latter, only one out of every 574. Why should the colored people be so much better in Ohio than in Massachusetts? In Ohio, more than half the number were born out of the State. On coming to Ohio, where did they emigrate from? Massachusetts? Scarcely a man of them. The immigration of the free colored people, into the Western free States, is nearly all from the slave States. This is a significant fact, showing that, even under slavery, the colored man makes more progress in morality and industry, than he can do under the shade of abolition philanthropy in Massachusetts!

From the testimony afforded by statistics, we turn to that furnished by abolitionists themselves; so as to learn whether, in their opinion, the free colored people have made any advance within the last thirty years. Listen to that well-known abolitionist, Hon. GERRITT SMITH, who, in addressing Governor HUNT of New York, in 1852, said:

"Suppose, moreover, that during all these fifteen years, they had been quitting the cities, *where the mass of them rot, both physically and morally,* and had gone into the country to become farmers and mechanics — suppose, I say, all this — and who would have the hardihood to affirm that the Colonization Society lives upon the malignity of the whites — but it is true that it lives upon *the voluntary degradation of the blacks.* I do not say that the colored people are more debased than the white people would be if persecuted,

---

* See Cotton is King, for full details.

oppressed and outraged as are the colored people. But I do say that they are debased, deeply debased; and that to recover themselves they must become heroes, self-denying heroes, capable of achieving a great moral victory — a two-fold victory — a victory over themselves and a victory over their enemies."

In referring to the action of the free colored people of New York, in 1855, to secure to themselves the right of suffrage, the *New York Tribune* said:

"It is not logical conviction of the justice of their claims that is needed, but a prevalent belief that they would form a wholesome and desirable element of the body politic. Their color exposes them to much unjust and damaging prejudice; but if their degradation were but skin-deep, they might easily overcome it. . . . . . . Of course, we understand that the evil we contemplate is complex and retroactive — that the political degradation of the blacks is a cause as well as a consequence of their moral debasement. Had they never been enslaved, they would not now be so abject in soul; had they not been so abject, they could not have been enslaved. Our aborigines might have been crushed into slavery by overwhelming force; but they could never have been made to live in it. The black man who feels insulted in that he is called a 'nigger,' therein attests the degradation of his race more forcibly than does the blackguard at whom he takes offense; for negro is no further a term of opprobrium than the character of the blacks has made it so."

Rev. H. W. Beecher, in referring to the degraded condition of the free colored people at the North, in his sermon in reference to the Harper's Ferry affair, said:

"How are the free colored people treated at the North? They are almost without education, with but little sympathy for their ignorance. They are refused the common rights of citizenship which the whites enjoy. They can not even ride in the cars of our city railroads. They are snuffed at in the house of God, or tolerated with ill-disguised disgust. Can the black man be a mason in New York? Let him be employed as a journeyman, and every Irish lover of liberty that carries the hod or trowel, would leave at once, or compel him to leave! Can the black man be a carpenter? There is scarcely a carpenter's shop in New York in which a journeyman would continue to work, if a black man was employed in it. Can the black man engage in the common industries of life? There is scarcely one in which he can engage. He is crowded down, down, down through the most menial callings, to the bottom of society. We tax them and then refuse to allow their children to go to our public schools. We tax them and then refuse to sit by them in God's house. We heap upon them moral obloquy more atrocious than ,that which the master heaps upon the slave. And notwithstanding all this, we lift ourselves up to talk to the Southern people about the rights and liberties of the human soul, and especially the African soul! . . . . . The degradation of the free colored men in the North will fortify slavery in the South!"

Mr. Beecher never uttered anything nearer the truth, than the last sentence quoted. The failure of the abolitionists of the North, to enable its free colored people to profit by freedom, has effectually barred all farther State emancipation at the South.

From such facts as the preceding, it appears that emancipation, as heretofore conducted, has left the colored man unprotected and unsupported, to fall, ultimately, as a helpless burden upon the whites, or to sink down again toward his original barbarism. Lord Mansfield's decision had this effect upon the colored people of England; and the burden was only, removed, by their transfer to Africa. The results of emancipation in the British islands have been of a similar character, producing wide-spread ruin, generally, in the economical interests of the islands, which has only.been arrested where large importations of coolies have been made to carry on the cultivation, or where the density of the population has compelled the blacks to labor or starve. * No better results have followed the freedom of the negroes in Hayti; and, now, it is likely to be wholly blotted out as a republic, and restored to its former productiveness, under the control of a superior race. The same results, substantially, followed the liberation of a portion of the slaves, at an early day, in the United States — leading to colonization as a means of relief from the presence of a helpless class of freemen.

After the abolition movement had been fairly inaugurated, the subject of the helpless condition of the free colored people was a frequent topic of discussion; and it became a popular argument

---

* See what Mr. Sewell says, in Chapter V. of this volume.

against farther emancipations, as useless, because valueless to the colored people themselves.   It was urged by the abolitionists, in reply, that the elevation of those who had been liberated, could not be hoped for, so long as any of the race remained in bondage. This was, practically, to say : we of the North find it impossible to elevate the few thousands whom we have humanely set free ; therefore, you of the South must emancipate the several millions which you own; so that the whole of the African race, among us, may be improved, in their moral condition, by one grand movement embracing the whole country.   This position of the abolitionists, was in direct opposition to the opinions which had been held at the North, in relation to the benefits of emancipation; and was, in fact, an admission, substantially, that the South had been right in its views of the inefficiency of mere personal freedom, as a means of advancement to the negro race. *

That there had been gross neglect of the colored men in the North, is abundantly apparent from what has been stated; but it will appear still more apparent, from the additional statistics of the Methodist Episcopal Church, from 1836 to 1845, including the period of the disruption of this Church.

---

* That a determination existed to force emancipation upon the South, regardless of consequences, and without consulting the history of past experiments, is apparent from the fact, that, as early as 1831, fifteen petitions were presented in Congress from Pennsylvania, praying the abolition of slavery in the District of Columbia, and the abolition of the slave trade therein.   Mr. Adams, in presenting these petitions, very frankly gave it as his opinion, that the abolition of slavery in the District was improper, and he would not support any such measure; but as the existence of the traffic in slaves within the District might be a proper subject of Congressional inquiry, he would move the reference of the petitions to the committee having charge of its interests. Whatever his opinion of slavery in the abstract, or of slavery in the District of Columbia might be, he said he hoped the subject might not be discussed in the House.   He would say that the most salutary medicine unduly administered, was the most deadly poison.   It might have been well for the peace of the country, if Mr. Adams had ever afterward maintained the ground here taken on the slavery question.

The petitions were referred to the committee on the District of Columbia, of which Mr. Doddridge, of Virginia, was chairman, who afterward made a report asking to be discharged from the farther consideration of so much of said petitions as asked the abolition of slavery in the District.   In 1817, several petitions were presented against the slave trade between the Middle and Southern States, which were read and referred.—[See *Polit. Text-Book*, by M. W. Cluskey

Colored membership of the Methodist Episcopal Church, from 1836 *to* 1845, *the year* 1840 *being omitted as imperfect in its returns:*

CONFERENCES.	1836	1837	1838	1839	1841	1842	1843	1844	1845
New England..	395	381	393	235	235	—	139	—	—
Maine	3	—	—	—	—	—	—	—	—
N. Hampshire.	15	18	12	—	—	—	—	—	—
New York	434	434	538	452	405	419	440	424	380
Troy	61	61	105	105	78	89	84	149	92
Providence	......	......	......	......	......	104	93	—	
Oneida & Black River	90	87	95	96	92	26	113	119	119
Genessee	75	56	73	63	50	88	60	78	74
New Jersey	......	502	478	496	542	643	769	817	763
Pittsburgh	318	298	295	427	474	487	532	495	405
Erie	......	34	33	46	50	52	61	72	86
Ohio	465	564	537	613	662	606	611	640	523
North Ohio	......	......	......	...,.	91	89	128	65	40
Michigan	......	40	59	......	12	14	5	20	10
Indiana	240	335	308	327	407	235	245	257	159
North Indiana.	......	......	......	......	......	......	......	......	47
Illinois	68	66	109	182	80	44	54	73	71
Rock River	......	......	......	......	21	18	20	36	23
Iowa	......	......	......	......	......	......	......	......	12
Missouri	1,189	940	812	906	1,224	1,399	1,874	2,388	2,530
Kentucky	5,321	4,951	4,770	5,854	6,321	6,761	8,544	9,951	9,362
Tennessee	4,693	3,901	4,598	5,190	4,405	4,234	4,336	6,478	6,859
Holston	2,189	1,997	2,129	1,820	2,420	2,832	3,805	4,001	4,001
Memphis	......	......	......	......	1,995	2,289	3,535	4,451	4,843
Arkansas	......	599	592	683	725	828	1,091	1,804	1,775
Texas	......	......	......	......	230	407	536	856	1,005
Florida	......	......	......	......	......	......	......	......	2,653
Alabama	3,463	2,884	2,830	3,530	5,821	7,505	9,373	12,061	13,537
Mississippi	2,531	1,841	1,587	3,905	4,178	4,089	6,048	7,087	7,799
Georgia	7,204	6,664	7,126	8,358	9,989	11,457	14,056	15,346	13,994
South Carolina.	23,643	23,166	23,498	24,822	30,481	30,860	33,375	37,952	39,495
North Carolina	......	......	3,896	4,315	4,480	4,733	5,163	6,226	6,390
Virginia	7,081	6,117	2,950	2,951	3,086	3,558	3,777	4,799	4,949
Baltimore	13,867	13,527	13,301	13,544	13,904	13,526	17,995	16,973	16,412
Philadelphia...	8,951	7,777	8,112	8,304	8,778	9,086	10,712	10,917	10,742
Total	82,296	76,240	79,236	87,197	101,236	106,478	127,574	144,535	149,150

The dotted lines (.....) indicate that the Church had not yet been organized. The dash, (——) that the Church had been organized, but had no colored members of that date.

But did the disruption of the Methodist Church, and the disconnection of the Northern ministers from those of the South, give them any more power over the free colored people? Let the statistics of the succeeding years answer that question; it being remarked, that the border States, to some extent, remained with the Church North; and that the Philadelphia Conference includes the State of Delaware and a part of Maryland.

Colored membership of the Methodist Episcopal Church North, from the disruption until the Annual Conferences ceased to distinguish the colored from the white members:

CONFERENCES.	1846	1847	1848	1849	1850
Baltimore *	17,315	16,387	16,156	15,759	15,802
Philadelphia..............................	9,537	9,992	9,612	9,306	8,938
Providence.......................................					
New Jersey..................................	748	699	718	676	641
New England.....................................					
New York......................................	393	379	381	268	257
New York East	......	......	.....		
Troy..	89	97	84	——	——
New Hampshire	——	——			
Vermont......................................			——		
Black River..................................	23	20	——		
Pittsburgh........................	391	345	533	170	118
Western Virginia............................	......	......	......	378	382
Oneida	86	86		——	—.—
Wisconsin....................................	......	......	11	10	6
Erie...	61	58	57	48	53
Rock River..................................	19	27	14	14	19
North Ohio..................................	31	55	28	24	27
Genessee....................................	58	58	16	——	——
East Genessee...............................	......	......	43	33	——
Maine.......................................	——	——		.	
East Maine..................................	......	......			
Ohio..	680	514	345	402	346
Missouri	......	......	10	226	197
Iowa..	8	32	26	30	15
Illinois....................................	47	60	73	36	27
North Indiana...............................	42	50	21	32	17
Michigan	33	8	——		
Indiana.....................................	164	174	161	144	177
Total	29,725	29,041	28,289	27,526	27,022

The dotted lines (......) indicate that the Church had not yet been organized.   The dash, (——) that the Church had been organized, but had no colored members of that date.

It was with such returns as these before them, of the failure of the Methodist ministry to benefit the free colored people, that the Bishops, in the General Conference of 1844, New York City, felt constrained to give the subject their most serious consideration. We quote but a few sentences, referring the reader to their Letter at large: †

"We can not but view it as a matter of deep regret, that the spirit-

* The figures for the year 1849 and 1850, in the Baltimore Conference, include members and probationers.   † See Chapter VIII., session of 1856.

ual interests of the people of color, in these United States, have been
so long and so greatly neglected by the Christian churches. And it
is greatly to be feared that we are not innocent in this thing. . . . . .
Let *facts* give the answer. From an examination of official records,
it appears that there are four annual conferences, in which there is
not a single colored member in the church. Eight others have an
aggregate number of four hundred and sixty-three, averaging less
than sixty. And taking fifteen, about one-half of the conferences in
the connection, and some of them among the largest, both in the
ministry and membership, and the whole number of colored members
is but one thousand three hundred and nine, giving an average of less
than ninety. It is well known that in many of these conferences
there are a numerous population, and in each of them a considerable
number. It is presumed that the freedom of the people of color,
within the bounds of these conferences, will not be urged as the
cause of their not being brought under religious influence, and gathered into the fold of Christ. We are certainly not prepared to admit
that a state of servitude is more favorable to the success of the Gospel, in its experimental and practical effects, than a state of freedom."

The force of the remarks of the Bishops, and the pungency
of the rebuke they administered, will be understood, when it is
stated, that the conferences which had done the least for the free
colored people were those which, as a general thing, had been
the most zealous in forwarding abolition memorials to the General Conference.

This question will be well understood by a careful examination
of the preceding statistical tables. From 1836 to 1845 the colored membership increased from 82,296 to 149,150, nearly the
whole of which increase was in the slave States. Exclusive of
the Philadelphia Conference, there was an increase of only 640
in the free States, during these nine years!

This Church resolved to divide in 1844, but the statistics were
not taken separately until after 1845. From this date, then, the
conferences at the North are no longer trammeled by an alliance
with the South — some of the border churches and conferences,
only, remaining with the Church North. What, then, are the
results? The statistics from 1846 to 1850, inclusive, show a decrease of the colored membership, in these four years, of 2,703 —
2,102 of which decrease was in the border conferences of Balti-

more and Philadelphia, and 601 of the decrease in the other twenty-seven conferences.   Truly, the disruption of the Methodist Church has been disastrous to the cause of African evangelization, so far as the Methodist ministry are concerned, not only in the border slave States, but throughout the free States generally.   The language employed, in reference to the churches among the freedmen of Jamaica, applies with equal force to the conferences in the Northern States, so far as relates to their colored converts: "The members in society do not increase !"

The Methodist Church was not alone in having lost her influence with the free colored people of the North, as a consequence of the abolition controversy.   Very few of the churches of the whites had any considerable number of colored people in their communion ; and where they had, they were rarely able long to retain them.   The abolition controversy was so conducted as to awaken the most bitter prejudices in the minds of the colored professors against the whites.   They were taught to believe that no slaveholder could be a Christian, and that the churches, whose jurisdiction extended into the slave States, were not Christian churches.   We must not be understood, here, as attributing these ultra views as coming, in this form, from any ecclesiastical body of respectable standing, but mainly from the abolitionists and their lecturers, who traversed the country to propagate abolition doctrines. *   They were further taught, that the Almighty pos-

---

* Gerritt Smith, on August 5, 1857, in addressing the editor of the *New York Tribune*, used the following language, from which it will be seen that he urged the colored people to abjure all churches which spared slavery — all, of course, who did not occupy abolition ground :

"Our colored people complain of your treatment of them.   I think myself that it is sometimes too rigorous, though, in the main, I candidly approve it. You are their friend in demanding that they shall, by their own good conduct, redeem themselves from their deep debasement.   You deal but justly with them, when you declare that their own bad influence goes further than the arts of the worst slaveholders to uphold slavery.

"So far from making their wrongs and outrages an excuse for their continued degradation, the free colored people should, in view of these wrongs and outrages, arouse themselves to the irresistible determination to equal and surpass their persecutors in all that honors manhood.   They should swear that they will be Pariahs and lepers no longer.   To this end, they should quit the towns, in which they are wont to congregate, and where they are but servants,

sessed no attribute which could tolerate or sanction the principle of slavery, or the holding of "property in man." This doctrine, advocated by the *Christian Intelligencer*, was copied into the abolition papers, and proclaimed throughout the North.

And what was the consequence of this teaching? Among the educated young colored men were some who had a little knowledge of logic. More than once the author has heard them discuss this point, of "the right of property in man," and dispose of it thus: "The Almighty can neither sanction nor tolerate the holding of property in man: the Bible sanctions the holding of property in man: therefore the Bible is not the word of God." They relied upon Exodus xxi: 20, 21, to sustain them in their position: "And if a man smite his servant, or his maid, with a rod, and he die under his hand, he shall be surely punished. Notwithstanding, if he continue a day or two, he shall not be punished; for he is his money." They insisted that the last clause of this quotation clearly taught, that the slave is the property of his master — "for he is his money." These young infidels are men now advanced in life, but they have never embraced the Bible as the word of God. Who is responsible for misleading them?

Fortunately, the entire mass of the colored professors of religion were influenced more by their piety than they were by the logic employed against the Bible. And, though their alienation of affection for the white churches became complete, they still adhered to their profession of religion, and went into the organization of African churches. This task was the more easily performed, because churches of this class had been established in the country at an early day. A brief notice of these organizations will be necessary to a proper understanding of the position of the colored professors of religion in the North.

AFRICAN METHODIST CHURCH. — This body had its origin in

---

and should scatter themselves over the country in the capacity of farmers and mechanics. They should cease from the habit of wasting their earnings in periodical balls. They should never wet their lips with intoxicating drinks nor defile them with tobacco. They should never so war upon their self-respect as to join a Church which spares slavery, or join a political party which knows law for slavery."

the city of Philadelphia, in 1787, owing to difficulties growing out of the colored people and the whites meeting together for public worship. Bishop White of the Episcopal Church, sympathizing with the colored people, ordained one of their own number as pastor. In 1793, their numbers had so increased that a meeting-house was erected for them, and dedicated by Bishop Asbury, of the Methodist Episcopal Church, under the name of Bethel — the members giving a preference for the Methodist Church. Various difficulties beset them, in their relations with the Methodist Church, when, in 1816, a convention was called in Philadelphia, for the purpose of organizing on a broader basis, so as to include the colored professors in Baltimore and elsewhere. An organization was formed under the name of the African Methodist Episcopal Church. The first annual conference was held at Baltimore, April, 1818; "since when, the Church has been making quiet but steady progress. It has a Book Concern and a Missionary Society." *

ZION AFRICAN METHODIST EPISCOPAL CHURCH. — The rise of this society was also due to disagreements between the whites and colored people. It had its origin in New York city, and its first church was built in 1800. In 1820, the society erected itself into a distinct and independent body. It received into connection with it several other Churches, and, in 1821, held an annual conference in New York city. Twenty-two ministers were in attendance, and the number of church members reported was 1,426. At the annual conference, in 1838, the society elected its first superintendent.

The estimated membership of the Bethel and the Zion Methodist Episcopal Churches is 26,746; the traveling preachers 193; the local 444. †

We have before us the Report of the Twelfth General Conference of this AFRICAN METHODIST EPISCOPAL CHURCH, held in Pittsburgh, Pennsylvania, in 1860. The conference was presided over by Bishops Quinn, Nazrey, and Payne, all colored men. Seven conferences were represented, besides that of Canada, from which a delegate was present.

---

* American Christian Record, 1860, pages 141, 142.   † Ibid., p. 143.

In the course of the proceedings relating to Canada, it was decided to be expedient that the conference in that province should be separated from the General Conference of the United States; and the following very sensible reason was assigned in its favor:

"Because all societies, in their organization, in order to receive protection from civil law, must be subject to the government, and recognize the authority that exists. In the present state of things this can not be done by the Canadian Conference, while they use our form of Discipline.

The conference also passed resolutions in recognition of the Liberia Methodist Episcopal Church. This is a movement in the right direction, and shows that the bitter hostility once existing against Liberia is yielding under the progress of intelligence in this body.

But the most important portion of the proceedings is the argument of Bishop Payne, defending himself against the decision of a committee who had disapproved his action in a case where he had rejected an applicant for deacon's orders, on the ground that he was not a member of the annual conference, and to ordain him, therefore, would be a violation of Discipline. The Bishop took an appeal from the decision of the committee, and was sustained by the conference.

We refer to this case, to make a short quotation from the argument of the Bishop. It is a fair example of the advantages of a little common sense, in dealing with questions which, in its absence, have led men's minds into inextricable confusion. The applicability of the Bishop's argument to the abolition interpretations of the Constitution of the United States will be at once apparent. Had his strong common sense, as applied to a question respecting constitutional church polity, been exercised in relation to the National Constitution, we should never have had the troubles that are now upon us. But let us hear the Bishop, at the same time keeping in mind that what he says is designed to be applied by us to the subjects discussed in the chapter on Political Abolitionism:

"In every well-organized government, which has continued for any length of time, say a single generation, there will be found three different kinds of laws:

"1. Constitutional law.

"2. Statute law.

"3. Common, or unwritten law.

"The Constitutional is that which enters into the structure of the government, whether it be civil or ecclesiastical, and is sometimes called the organic law. It is, therefore, fundamental and *supreme*. Being supreme, it controls both the statute and common law.

"Statute laws are legislative enactments, made for the purpose of accomplishing some end expressed or implied in the constitutional, and, therefore, *must* always be subordinate to the constitutional; never subversive of it.

"Whenever a statute law is subversive of the constitutional, it becomes *null* and *void — a mere dead letter*.

"The common, or unwritten, law derives its authority from custom or usage. In the State it is always called *the common law;* in the Church it is always called *usage*. The common law, or usage, like the statute, must always be subordinate to the constitutional. If subversive of the constitutional, it must be set aside, and trampled under foot.

"Now, the verdict of the committee is based upon a statute law of the American Methodist Episcopal Church, to which they refer in Discipline of 1856.

"But the venerable committee seem to have forgotten that there is a higher law than the one to which they refer, for they make no allusion to it; I mean, the constitutional. . . . . .

"It is also maintained that it is the usage of our Church to ordain local preachers who are not members of the annual conference. But what is *usage*, in the presence of constitutional law? Why *nothing more than chaff before the wind*. That man who suffers statutes or usages to subvert the constitutional law, is not a good governor, but a bad one. To do this *is to be guilty of misrule*. . . . . .

"Men! brethren! fathers! I call upon you to sustain the government!

"Remember that the privilege is not to be given till the obedience is yielded; nor. the right secured and enjoyed till the duty is performed.

"Brother Michum requests a privilege before he yields the required obedience — he demands a right before the duty is performed. Will you do this? Nay! You will not; — you can not.

"Men! brethren! fathers! I call on you to preserve the statute in harmony with the constitution; and both in obedience to the law of God."

The details of the condition of the conferences of this Church are not in our possession. One only, the Report of the Cincinnati Conference, has come within our reach. Its session of 1860 reported, as under its care, 16 stations in principal cities and towns; 70 circuits; 3,902 members and 283 probationers. This conference seems to cover the territory of Ohio and Western Pennsylvania.

In relation to the colored BAPTIST Churches, we have been unable to obtain full information. We have before us, however, the Minutes of the SEVENTEENTH ANNUAL MEETING OF THE UNION ANTI-SLAVERY BAPTIST ASSOCIATION, which met in Pike county, Ohio, 1857. Two preceding reports are also before us. The report of 1857 embraces 27 churches, which had received, by baptism, during the year past, 161 members, and they had a total membership of 1,423 — four of the congregations not reporting, but which had previously reported 144 members, making a probable total, in 1857, of 1,567. The report for 1856 gives an increase for the year, by baptisms, of 135, and a total membership of 1,282 — the statistics being full, and 22 churches represented. The report for 1855 gives an increase, by baptisms, for the year, of 83, and a total membership of 1,430 — there being three congregations not represented, two of which, in the report of 1856, give a membership of 107, thus giving a total of more than 1,537.

It appears from these statistics, that no very encouraging progress has been made by these colored Baptist churches, if we compare them with the success of the Baptists South among the colored people.

We have also before us the MINUTES OF THE TWENTY-FIFTH ANNIVERSARY OF THE PROVIDENCE ANTI-SLAVERY BAPTIST ASSOCIATION, held in Jackson county, Ohio, 1859. Delegates to the number of 40 were present. Several churches were not represented. The total membership reported is 980, there being three congregations which made no returns. This organization seems to be limited to Ohio. It issued a most excellent Circular Letter, which breathes the true spirit of Christian piety, humility, and devotion. But on the very next page, we have a fair illustration of the injurious effects of clergymen interfering in civil affairs. In referring to the arrest and imprisonment of the colored men who rescued a fugitive slave from the United States marshal, and were then suffering the penalty of their violation of law, the Association passed the following resolutions:

"16th Item. *Resolved*, That C. H. Langston and his worthy associates, who, in defiance of the Fugitive Slave Law, rescued the man John from his claimants, gave a practical illustration of Christianity in that act, which needs to be often repeated, if we would save Christianity from the sneer of the infidel; for, that Christianity which expends itself in distributing tracts, in making long prayers, in erecting splendid church edifices, and reclining upon richly cushioned seats, listening to invectives against crinoline, chewing tobacco and dancing, while it opens not its ears to the piteous groans of the bleeding slave, as they issue from the *hell* of slavery, and through fear of imprisonment and bonds, loss of reputation and money, will permit the poor slave, as he flees, all trembling, broken-hearted and bleeding, to be clutched by his blood-hound pursuers, and dragged back into the *hell* of slavery, is certainly not the religion of the holy Jesus, but a lie, and they who preach and practice it, are hypocrites.

" *Resolved*, That in rescuing John, despite the rigors of the Fugitive Slave Law and the insolence of governmental officials, which they knew would be mercilessly exercised over them, Langston and his associates rendered themselves illustrious as practical, Christian philanthropists.

" *Resolved*, That our brethren every where emulate each other in striving to show who can do the most to relieve those men from their pecuniary embarrassments, occasioned by that noble act.

" The reading of these resolutions brought pretty much the whole Association to their feet, all of whom, as they could get opportunity, warmly advocated their adoption.

"Unanimously adopted."

These councils, coming from professed ministers of the Gospel, are not calculated to give the impression that such men are well prepared to act their part as safe members of civil society. It is such a spirit as this, in the free colored men, that determines all sober-thoughted citizens to resist the emancipation of a race

who never have, while standing alone, been able to maintain civil
institutions; and who, in connection with the superior races, have
always, to a greater or less extent, been a disturbing element in
civilized communities.   Encouraging resistance to law, under the
guise of religion, is no palliation of the crime, come from whence
it may.   But the colored ministers, in extenuation of their offense,
can plead the example of white ministers of the Gospel.   This,
however, is only an additional evidence of their want of a sound
judgment, and of the ease with which they yield to their passions and prejudices when under the influence of bad men.

The obstacles to the moral progress of the free colored people
in the North have been very great.   A moment's attention to this
point is necessary to a correct understanding of their true position.   As in the South so in the North, there had been colored
men admitted into the ministry upon whom the Gospel had exerted its influence; and who were laboring not only to keep themselves unspotted from the world, but to bring others, also, into
the practice of Gospel purity.   Aware of the advantages of education to preachers of the Gospel, the effort was made, by leading colored men, to establish institutions of learning for the education of colored youth.   Without adequate wealth of their own,
they appealed to the whites for aid, but, generally, without any
great degree of success.   Nor did the leaders of abolitionism
seem to take much interest in direct efforts for the elevation of
the colored men already free; but, on the contrary, these applications for assistance were often viewed as great annoyances.
In speaking of them, the *New York Tribune*, on one occasion,
said:

"At present white men dread to be known as friendly to the black,
because of the never-ending, still-beginning importunities to help
this or that object of negro charity or philanthropy to which such a
reputation inevitably subjects them."

To give money for the publication of incendiary documents —
for the aid of escaping fugitive slaves — for Sharpe's rifles to
shoot pro-slavery men in Kansas — for anything that would in-
jure or annoy the slaveholder — were objects liberally supported
by donations from abolitionists: but to contribute to the estab-

lishment of colleges and seminaries, for the education of the free colored people, were enterprises that could not enlist their sympathies, so as to open their purse-strings. To applications of this kind we know the reply, in substance, has often been:

" We, abolitionists, are laboring for the destruction of slavery, and, at present, can do nothing for you. Until that evil is removed, the free colored people can not rise into respectability, or be relieved from the prejudice which now bears them down. Universal emancipation, therefore, is the first object to be gained; as, after that, prejudice will disappear, and the best schools and colleges in the land be thrown open to the colored man."

Thus repelled, but self-reliant, the colored men, to whom we have alluded, toiled on, almost unaided, in the work of Christian instruction and moral reform. Their field of labor has been beset with many difficulties. Concentrated mostly in large cities and towns, the colored population are subjected to many temptations, thus rendering the task of their elevation the more difficult of accomplishment. The preachers, in many cases, have to pursue some occupation to aid in making a support, and have thus less time for study. That they are able to sustain their churches, in the midst of so many obstacles to success, argues well for their faithfulness as ministers of the Gospel.

By reference to the statistics of the Methodist Episcopal Church (whites) in the preceding pages, it will be seen that the Pittsburgh and Ohio Conferences, which covered the ground now occupied by the colored conference, had a colored membership, in 1834, of 921; in 1843, of 1,143; in 1845, of 968; and in 1850, of only 491. The withdrawal of the colored membership, from the old to the new organization, will explain this decrease; and these statistics also show, that the African Methodist Church have made an increase, on the former membership in the old church, extending from 1,143, in 1843, to 4,185, including probationers, in 1860 — an increase of nearly fourfold.

CANADA has long been the promised land of the colored man; it, therefore, demands a somewhat more extended notice. In the outset it must be remembered, that the colored population of Canada are mainly fugitive slaves. The original colored settlers were mostly from Cincinnati, and embraced some men of excellence and piety. The AMERICAN MISSIONARY ASSOCIATION attempted to take the religious oversight of these people, and, at first, with promises of success; but, after a time, the teachers and missionaries lost their influence, and had, in a good degree, to abandon the field. Out of four stations, at the opening of 1853, but one school remained at its close. All the others had been abandoned, and all the missionaries had asked to be released. * Early in the year, one of the missionaries wrote to the association, saying — " that the opposition to white missionaries, manifested by the colored people of Canada, had so greatly increased, by the interested misrepresentations of ignorant colored men pretending to be ministers of the Gospel, that he thought his own and his wife's labors, and the funds of the association, could be better employed elsewhere."

In 1857, the association report but one missionary in Canada, and he had been mobbed by the colored people, and, at one time, his life was thought to be in danger. In June, his church was burned down; and, in August following, another building which he had secured shared the same fate — both being the work of incendiaries. " This field," says the Eleventh Annual Report, " is emphatically a hard one, and requires much faith and patience from those who labor there."

In 1858, the missionary wrote : " My wife's school is in a prosperous condition. She has nearly forty scholars, and they learn well. There are numbers who can not come to school for want of suitable clothing. They are nearly naked." † On another occasion it is said, " the missionaries find it extremely difficult to win the confidence of the colored people of Canada." ‡

The report of 1859 shows that several Sunday-schools and two churches had been formed among the colored population of the Canada mission; and that Mr. Hotchkiss had added eighteen converts to the churches under his care in a little more than a year.

But we have an example of a different kind to report, and one that confirms what we have heretofore said — that it is only

---

* Seventh Annual Report of American Missionary Association.
† American Missionary, October, 1858.
‡ African Repository, January, 1858.

where proper moral control is exercised, that any real progress can be made by the blacks :

"Some years ago, the Rev. William King, a slave owner in Louisiana, manumitted his slaves and removed them to Canada.   They now, with others, occupy a tract of land at Buxton and the vicinity, called the 'Elgin Block,' where Mr. King is stationed as a Presbyterian missionary.

"A recent general meeting there was attended by Lord Althorp, son of Earl Spencer, and J. W. Probyn, Esq., both members of the British Parliament, who made addresses.   The whole educational and moral machinery is worked by the presiding genius of the Rev. W. King, to whom the entire settlement are under felt and acknowledged obligations.   He teaches them agriculture and industry.   He superintends their education, and preaches on the Lord's day.   He regards the experiment as highly successful." *

The records of crime in Canada, as in Massachusetts, will furnish the best index to the moral condition of the great mass of the colored population.   Aside from the favorable operations of Mr. King, among his own people, and over whom he exerts about as much control as he did in Louisiana, we can not learn that any considerable progress is being made, by the free negroes, in Canada.   A few points, collated from an extended investigation of this subject, will set the question in its true light.

On the 27th of April, 1841, the Assistant Secretary to Government addressed Colonel ROBERT LACHLAN, Chairman of the Quarter Sessions for the Western District, Canada, requesting information relating to the colored immigrants in that quarter.   From Colonel LACHLAN'S reply, we make a few quotations : †

---

* African Repository, January, 1858.

† "Colonel Lachlan entered the public service of the British Government in 1805, and was connected with the army in India for twenty years. Having retired from that service, he settled in Canada in 1835, with the intention of devoting himself to agriculture; but he was again called into public life, as sheriff, magistrate, colonel of militia, Chairman of the Quarter Sessions, and Associate Judge of the Assizes.   In 1857, he removed to Cincinnati, where he now resides. A true Briton, he is an enemy of the system of slavery; but having been a close observer of the workings of society, under various circumstances, systems of law, degrees of intelligence, and moral conditions, he is opposed to placing two races, so widely diverse as the blacks and whites, upon

"The first time that I had occasion to express myself thus strongly on the subject, in an official way, was more than three years after my arrival in the District, while holding the office of sheriff — when, in corresponding with Mr. Secretary Joseph, during the troubles in January, 1838, I, in a postscript to a letter in which I expressed unwillingness to call in aid from other quarters, while our own population were allowed to remain inactive, was led to add the following remarkable words : 'My vote has been equally decided against employing the colored people, except on a similar emergency ; in fact, though a cordial friend to the emancipation of the poor African, I regard the rapidly increasing population rising round us, as destined to be a bitter curse to the District ; and do not think our employing them as our *defenders* at all likely to retard the progress of such an event ;' an opinion which all my subsequent observation and experience, whether as a private individual, as Sheriff of the District, as a local Magistrate, as Chairman of the Quarter Sessions, or as an anxious friend to pure British immigration, have only the more strongly confirmed. . . . . . .

"That place may now be regarded as the Western rendezvous of the colored race — being the point to which all the idle and worthless, as well as the well disposed, first direct their steps, before dispersing over other parts of the District — a distinction of which it unfortunately bears too evident marks in the great number of petty crimes committed by or brought home to these people — to the great trouble of the investigating local magistrates, and the still greater annoyance of the inhabitants generally — arising from the constant nightly depredations committed on their orchards, barns, granaries, sheepfolds, fowl-yards, and even cellars. . . . . . . In Gosfield, I am given to understand their general character is rather above par ; . . . . . . while in the next adjoining township of Mersea, so much are they disliked by the inhabitants, that they are, in a manner, proscribed by general consent — a colored man being there scarcely suffered to travel along the high roads unmolested.

---

terms of legal equality ; not that he is opposed to the elevation of the colored man, but because he is convinced that, in his present state of ignorance and degradation, the two races can not dwell together in peace and harmony. This opinion, it will be seen, was the outgrowth of his experience and observation in Canada, and not the result of a prejudice against the African race. The Western District, the field of his official labors, is the main point toward which nearly all the emigration from the States is directed ; and the Col. had, thus, the best opportunities for studying this question."—["Cotton is King," p. 177.

"The first thing that forcibly struck me, in these people, was a total absence of that modest and unpresuming demeanor which I had been somehow led to expect, and the assumption, instead, of a 'free and easy' independence of manner as well as language toward all white inhabitants, except their immediate employers; together with an apparent utter indifference to being hired on reasonable average wages, though, as already stated, seemingly without any visible means of a livelihood; and their also, at all times, estimating the value of their labor on a par with, if not above that of the white man.   And I had scarcely recovered from surprise, at such conduct, as a private individual, when, as a magistrate, I was still more astonished at the great amount of not only petty offenses, but of crime of the most atrocious dye, perpetrated by so small a body of strangers compared with the great bulk of the white population : and such still continuing to be the unabating case, Session after Session, Assize after Assize, it at length became so appalling to my feelings, that on being placed in the chair of the Quarter Sessions, I could not refrain from more than once pointing to it in strong language in my charges to the Grand Juries.   In July last year, for instance, I was led, in connection with a particular case of larceny, to observe. . . . . . .   'The case itself will, I trust, involve no difficulty so far as the Grand Jury is concerned; but it affords the magistrates another opportunity of lamenting that there should so speedily be furnished no less than five additional instances of the rapid increase of crime in this (hitherto in that respect highly fortunate) District, arising solely from the recent great influx of colored people into it from the neighboring United States — and who unfortunately not only furnish the major part of the crime perpetrated in the District, but also thereby a very great portion of its rapidly increasing debt — from the expense attending their maintenance in jail before trial, as well as after conviction !' . . . . . .

"In spite of these solemn admonitions, a large proportion of the criminals tried at the ensuing September Assizes were colored people ; and among them were two aggravated cases of rape and arson ; the former wantonly perpetrated on a respectable farmer's wife, in this township, to whom the wretch was a perfect stranger ; the latter recklessly committed at a merchant's store in the vicinity of Sandwich, for the mere purpose of opening a hole through which to convey away his plunder.   And, notwithstanding 'the general jail delivery' that then took place, the greater part of the crimes brought before the following month's Quarter Sessions (chiefly larceny and assaults) were furnished by the same people ! — a circumstance of so alarming and distressing a character, that I was again led to comment upon it in my charge to the Grand Jury in the following terms: 'Having disposed of the law relating to these offenses, I arrive at a very painful part of my observations, in once more calling the particular attention of the Grand Jury, as well as the public at large, to the remarkable and appalling circumstance that among a population of near 20,000 souls, inhabiting this District, the greater portion of the crime perpetrated therein should be committed by less than 2,000 refugees from a life of *abject slavery*, to a land of *liberty, protection, and comfort* — and from whom, therefore, if there be such generous feelings as thankfulness and gratitude, a far different line of conduct might reasonably be expected. I allude to the alarming increase of crime still perpetrated by the colored settlers, and who, in spite of the late numerous, harrowing, *convicted examples*, unhappily furnish *the whole of the offenses now likely to be brought before you!*' . . . . . .

"But, sir, the wide-spreading current of crime among this unfortunate race was not to be easily arrested; and I had long become so persuaded that it must sooner or later force itself upon the notice of the Legislature, that on feeling it my duty to draw the attention of my brother magistrates to the embarrassed state of the District finances, and to the greater portion of its expenses arising from this disreputable source, I was led, in framing the report of a special committee (of which I was chairman) appointed to investigate our pecuniary difficulties, to advert once more to the great undue proportion of our expenses arising from crime committed by so small a number of colored people, compared with the great body of the inhabitants, in the following strong but indisputable language: 'It is with pain and regret that your committee, in conclusion, feel bound to recur to the great additional burthen thrown upon the District, as well as the undeserved stigma cast upon the general character of its population, whether native or immigrant British, by the late great influx of colored people of the worst description from the neighboring States — a great portion of whom appear to have no visible means of gaining a livelihood — and who, therefore, not only furnish a large proportion of the basest crimes perpetrated in the country, such as murder, rape, arson, burglary, and larceny, besides every other description of minor offense — untraceable to the *color* of the perpetrators in a miscellaneous published calendar; but also, besides the constant trouble they entail upon magistrates who happen to reside in their neighborhood, produce a large portion of the debt incurred by the District, from the great number committed to and subsisted in prison, etc.; and they would, with all respect for the liberty of the subject, and the sincerest good will toward their African brethren generally — whom they would wish to regard with every kindly feeling, venture to suggest, for the consideration of Government, whether any legislative check can possibly be placed upon the rapid importation of the most worthless of this unfortunate race, such, as the good among themselves candidly lament, as has of late inundated this devoted section of the Province, to the great detriment of the claims of the poor emigrant from the mother country upon our consideration, the great additional and almost uncontrollable increase of crime, and the proportionate demoralization of principle among the inhabitants of the country.' . . . . . .

" Notwithstanding all these strenuous endeavors, added to the most serious and impressive admonitions to various criminals after conviction and sentence, no apparent change for the better occurred; for at the Quarter Sessions of last January, the usual preponderance of negro crime struck me so forcibly as again to draw from me, in my charge to the Grand Jury, the following observations : 'I am extremely sorry to be unable to congratulate you or the country on a light calendar, the matters to be brought before you embracing no less than three cases of larceny, and one of enticing soldiers to desert, besides several arising from that ever prolific source, assaults, etc. I can not, however, pass the former by altogether without once more emphatically remarking, that it is as much to the disgrace of the free colored settlers in our District, as it is creditable to the rest of our population, that the greater part of the culprits to be brought before us are still men of color : and I lament this the more, as I was somewhat in hopes that the earnest admonitions that I had more than once felt it my duty to address to that race, would have been attended with some good effect.' . . . . . .

" In spite of all these reiterated, anxious endeavors, the amount of crime exhibited in the calendar of the following Quarter Sessions, in April last, consisted solely (I think,) of five cases of larceny, perpetrated by negroes ; and at the late Assizes, held on the 20th instant, out of five criminal cases, one of enticing soldiers to desert, and two of theft, were, as usual, committed by men of color !!!

" Having thus completed a painful retrospect of the appalling amount of crime committed by the colored population in the District at large, compared with the general mass of the white population, I now consider it my duty to advert more particularly to what has been passing more immediately under my own observation in the township of Colchester."

The record from which we quote, has, under this head, the statement of the township collector, as to the moral and social condition of the colored people of the township, in which he says, " that, in addition to the black women there were fourteen yellow ones, and fifteen *white* ones — that they run together like beasts, and that he did not suppose one-third of them were married; and further, that they would be a curse to this part of Canada, unless there is something done to put a stop to their settling among the white people."

The Report of Col. Lachlan is very extensive, and embraces many topics connected with the question of negro immigration into Canada. His response to Government led to further investigation, and to some legislative action in the Canadian Parliament. The latest recorded communications upon the subject, from his pen, are dated November 9th, 1849, and June 4th, 1850, from which it appears that up to that date there had been no abatement of the hostile feeling of the whites toward the blacks, nor any improvement in the social and moral condition of the blacks themselves.

In 1849, the Elgin Association went into operation. Its object was to concentrate the colored people at one point, and thus have them in a more favorable position for intellectual and moral culture. A large body of land was purchased in the Township of Raleigh, and offered for sale in small lots to colored settlers. The measure was strongly opposed, and called out expressions of sentiment adverse to it, from the people at large. A public meeting, held in Chatham, August 18th, 1849, thus expressed itself:

" The Imperial Parliament of Great Britain has forever banished slavery from the Empire. In common with all good men, we rejoice at the consummation of this immortal act; and we hope that all other nations may follow the example. Every member of the human family is entitled to certain rights and privileges, and no where on earth are they better secured, enjoyed, or more highly valued, than in Canada. Nature, however, has divided the same great family into distinct species, for good and wise purposes, and it is no less our interest, than it is our duty, to follow her dictates and obey her laws. Believing this to be a sound and correct principle, as well as a moral and a Christian duty, it is with alarm we witness the fast increasing emigration and settlement among us of the African race; and with pain and regret do we view the establishment of an association, the avowed object of which is to encourage the settlement in old, well-established communities, of a race of people which is destined by

nature to be distinct and separate from us. It is also with a feeling
of deep resentment that we look upon the selection of the Township
of Raleigh, in this District, as the first portion of our beloved country, which is to be cursed with a systematic organization for setting
the laws of nature at defiance. Do communities in other portions
of Canada feel that the presence of the negro among them is an annoyance? Do they feel that the increase of the colored people among
them, and amalgamation, its necessary and hideous attendant, are
evils which require to be checked? With what a feeling of horror
would the people of any of the old settled townships of the eastern
portion of this Province, look upon a measure which had for its
avowed object the effect of introducing several hundreds of Africans
into the very heart of their neighborhood, their families interspers-
ing themselves among them, upon every vacant lot of land, their
children mingling in their schools, and all claiming to be admitted
not only to political, but to social privileges? and when we reflect,
too, that many of them must, from necessity, be the very worst species of that neglected race — the fugitives from justice — how much
more revolting must the scheme appear? How then can you adopt
such a measure? We beseech our fellow-subjects to pause before
they embark in such an enterprise, and ask themselves, ' whether
they are doing by us as they would wish us to do unto them.' . . . .
Surely our natural position is irksome enough, without submitting to
a measure which not only holds out a premium for filling up our
district with a race of people upon whom we can not look without a
feeling of repulsion, and who, having been brought up in a state of
bondage and servility, are totally ignorant both of their social and
political duties; but at the same time makes it the common receptacle
into which all other portions of the Province are to void the devotees.
of misery and crime. Look at your prisons and your penitentiary.
and behold the fearful preponderance of their black over their white
inmates in proportion to the population of each. . . . . . We have no
desire to show hostility toward the colored people, no desire to banish
them from the Province. On the contrary, we are willing to assist in
any well-devised scheme for their moral and social advancement. Our
only desire is, that they shall be separated from the whites, and that
no encouragement shall hereafter be given to the migration of the
colored man from the United States, or any where else. The idea
that we have brought the curse upon ourselves, through the establishment of slavery by our ancestors, is false. As Canadians, we have

yet to learn that we ought to be made a vicarious atonement for European sins.

"Canadians: The hour has arrived when we should arouse from our lethargy; when we should gather ourselves together in our might, and resist the onward progress of an evil which threatens to entail upon future generations a thousand curses. Now is the day. A few short years will put it beyond our power. Thousands and tens of thousands of American negroes, with the aid of the abolition societies in the States, and with the countenance given them by our philanthropic institutions, will continue to pour into Canada, if resistance is not offered. Many of you who live at a distance from this frontier, have no conception either of the number or the character of these emigrants, or of their poisonous effect upon the moral and social habits of a community. You listen with active sympathy to every thing narrated of the sufferings of the poor African; your feelings are enlisted, and your purse strings unloosed, and this often by the hypocritical declamation of some self-styled philanthropist. Under such influences many of you, in our large cities and towns, form yourselves into societies, and, without reflection, you supply funds for the support of schemes prejudicial to the best interests of our country. Against such proceedings, and especially against any and every attempt to settle any township in this District with negroes, we solemnly protest, and we call upon our countrymen, in all parts of the Province, to assist in our opposition.

"Fellow Christians: Let us forever maintain the sacred dogma, that all men have equal, natural, and inalienable rights. Let us do every thing in our power, consistent with international polity and justice, to abolish the accursed system of slavery in the neighboring Republic. But let us not, through a mistaken zeal to abate the evil of another land, entail upon ourselves a misery which every enlightened lover of his country must mourn. Let the slaves of the United States be free, but let it be in their own country. Let us not countenance their further introduction among us; in a word, let the people of the United States bear the burthen of their own sins.

"What has already been done, can not now be avoided; but it is not too late to do justice to ourselves, and retrieve the errors of the past. Let a suitable place be provided by the Government, to which the colored people may be removed, and separated from the whites, and in this scheme we will cordially join. We owe it to them, but how much more do we owe it to ourselves? But we implore you that you will not, either by your counsel or your pecuniary aid, assist those who have projected the association for the settlement of a horde of ignorant slaves in the town of Raleigh.   It is one of the oldest and most densely-settled townships, in the very center of our new and promising District of Kent, and we feel that this scheme, if carried into operation, will have the effect of hanging like a dead weight upon our rising prosperity.   What is our case to-day, to-morrow may be yours ; join us, then, in endeavoring to put a stop to what is not only a general evil, but in this case an act of unwarrantable injustice ; and when the time may come when you shall be similarly situated to us, we have no doubt that, like us, you will cry out, and your appeal shall not be in vain."

On the 3d of September, 1849, the colored people of Toronto, Canada, held a meeting, in which they responded at length to the foregoing address.   The spirit of the meeting can be divined from the following resolutions, which were unanimously passed :

" 1st. *Resolved*, That we, as a portion of the inhabitants of Canada, conceive it to be our imperative duty to give an expression of sentiment in reference to the proceedings of the late meeting held at Chatham, denying the right of the colored people to settle where they please.

" 2d. *Resolved*, That we spurn with contempt and burning indignation, any attempt, on the part of any person, or persons, to thrust us from the general bulk of society, and place us in a separate and distinct classification, such as is expressly implied in an address issued from the late meeting above alluded to.

3d. *Resolved*, That the principle of selfishness, as exemplified in the originators of the resolutions and address, we detest, as we do similar ones emanating from a similar source ; and we can clearly see the workings of a corrupt and depraved heart, arrayed in hostility to the heaven-born principle of *liberty*, in its broadest and most unrestricted sense."

These resolutions indicate that the colored people of Canada had been well instructed in the dogmas of Abolitionism.

On the 9th of October, 1849, the Municipal Council of the Western District adopted a Memorial to His Excellency, the Governor General, protesting against the proposed Elgin Association, in which the following language occurs :

. . . . . . " Clandestine petitions have been got up, principally, if not wholly, signed by colored people, in order to mislead Government

and the Elgin Association.   These petitions do not embody the sentiments or feelings of the respectable, intelligent, and industrious yeo-
manry of the Western District.   We can assure your Excellency that
any such statement is false, that there is but one feeling, and that is
of disgust and hatred, that they, the negroes, should be allowed to
settle in any township where there is a white settlement.   Our language is strong; but when we look at the expressions used at a late
meeting held by the colored people of Toronto, openly avowing the
propriety of amalgamation, and stating that it must, and will, and
shall continue, we can not avoid so doing. . . . . . The increased immigration of foreign negroes into this part of the Province is truly
alarming.   We can not omit mentioning some facts for the corrobora-
tion of what we have stated.   The negroes, who form. at least one-
third of the inhabitants of the township of Colchester, attended the
township meeting for the election of parish and township officers, and
insisted upon their right to vote, which was denied them by every
individual white man at the meeting.   The consequence was, that the
Chairman of the meeting was prosecuted and thrown into heavy costs,
which costs were paid by subscription from white inhabitants.   In
the same township of Colchester, as well as in many others, the inhabitants have not been able to get schools in many school sections, in
consequence of the negroes insisting on their right of sending their
children to such schools.   No white man will ever act with them in
any public capacity; this fact is so glaring, that no sheriff in this
Province would dare to summons colored men to do jury duty.   That
such things have been done in other quarters of the British domin-
ions we are well aware of, but we are convinced that the Canadians
will never tolerate such conduct."

But here we have testimony of a later date.   Hon. Colonel
PRINCE, member of the Canadian Parliament in 1857, had resided
among the colored people of the Western District; and, like other
humane men, had sympathized with them, at the outset, and shown
them many favors.   Time and observation changed his views, and,
in the course of his parliamentary duties, we find him taking a stand
adverse to the further increase of the negro population in Canada.
Hear him, as reported at the time:

"On the order of the day for the third reading of the emigrants'
law amendment bill being called, Hon. Col. Prince said he was wish-
ful to move a rider to the measure.   The black people who infested
the land were the greatest curse to the Province.   The lives of the

people of the West were made wretched by the inundation of these animals, and many of the largest farmers in the county of Kent have been compelled to leave their beautiful farms, because of the pestilential swarthy swarms. What were these wretches fit for? Nothing. They cooked our victuals and shampooned us; but who would not rather that these duties should be performed by white men? The blacks were a worthless, useless, thriftless set of beings — they were too indolent, lazy, and ignorant to work, too proud to be taught; and not only that, if the criminal calendar of the country was examined, it would be found that they were a majority of the criminals. They were so detestable that unless some method were adopted of preventing their influx into this country by the 'underground railroad,' the people of the West would be obliged to drive them out by open violence. The bill before the House imposed a capitation tax upon emigrants from Europe, and the object of his motion was to levy a similar tax upon blacks who came hither from the States. He now moved, seconded by Mr. Patton, that a capitation tax of 5s for adults, 3s 9d for children above one year and under fourteen years of age, be levied on persons of color emigrating to Canada from any foreign country.

" Ought not the Western men to be protected from the rascalities and villainies of the black wretches? He found these men with fire and food and lodging, when they were in need; and he would be bound to say that the black men of the county of Essex would speak well of him in this respect. But he could not admit them as being equal to white men; and, after a long and close observation of human nature, he had come to the conclusion that the black man was born to and intended for slavery, and that he was fit for nothing else. [Sensation.] Honorable gentlemen might try to groan him down, but he was not to be moved by mawkish sentiment, and he was persuaded that they might as well try to change the spots of the leopard as to make the black a good citizen. He had told black men so, and the lazy rascals had shrugged their shoulders and wished they had never run away from their 'good old massa' in Kentucky. If there was anything unchristian in what he had proposed, he could not see it, and he feared that he was not born a Christian."

The *Windsor Herald*, of July 3d, 1857, contains the proceedings of an indignation meeting, held by the colored people of Toronto, at which they denounced Colonel Prince in unmeasured terms of reproach. The same paper contains the reply of the Colonel, copied from the *Toronto Colonist;* and it is given entire, as a specimen of the spicy times they have, in Canada, over the negro question. The editor remarks, in relation to the reply of Colonel Prince, that it has given general satisfaction in his neighborhood. It is as follows:

"DEAR SIR:—Your valuable paper of yesterday has afforded me a rich treat and not a little fun in the report of an indignation meeting of 'the colored citizens' of Toronto, held for the purpose of censuring me. Perhaps I ought not to notice their proceedings—perhaps it would be more becoming in me to allow them to pass at once into the oblivion which awaits them; but as it is the fashion in this country not unfrequently to assume that to be true which appears in print against an individual, unless he flatly denies the accusation, I shall, at least, for once, condescend to notice these absurd proceedings. They deal in generalities, and so shall I. Of the colored citizens of Toronto I know little or nothing; no doubt, some are respectable enough in their way, and perform the inferior duties belonging to their station tolerably well. Here they are kept in order—in their proper place—but their 'proceedings' are evidence of their natural conceit, their vanity, and their ignorance; and in them the cloven foot appears, and evinces what they would do, if they could. I believe that in this city, as in some others of our Province, they are looked upon as necessary evils, and only submitted to because white servants are so scarce. But I now deal with these fellows as a body, and I pronounce them to be, as such, the *greatest curse* ever inflicted upon the two magnificent western counties which I have the honor to represent in the Legislative Council of this Province! and few men have had the experience of them that I have. Among the many *estimable* qualities they possess, a systematic habit of *lying* is not the least prominent; and the 'colored citizens' aforesaid seem to partake of that quality in an eminent degree, because in their famous *Resolutions* they roundly assert that during the Rebellion 'I walked arm and arm with colored men'—that 'I owe my election to the votes of colored men'—and that I have 'accumulated much earthly gains,' as a lawyer, among 'colored clients.' All Lies! Lies! Lies! from beginning to end. I admit that one company of blacks did belong to my contingent battallion, but they made the very worst of soldiers, and were, comparatively speaking, unsusceptible of drill or discipline, and were conspicuous for one act only—a stupid sentry shot the son of one of our oldest colonels, under a mistaken notion that he was thereby doing his duty. But I certainly never did myself the honor of 'walking arm-in-arm' with any of the colored gentlemen of that distinguished corps. Then, as to my election. Few, very few blacks voted for me. *I never canvassed them*, and hence, I suppose, they supported, as a body, my opponent. They took compassion upon '*a monument of injured innocence*,' and they sustained the monument for a while, upon the pedestal their influence erected. But the monument fell, and the fall proved that such influence was merely ephemeral, and it sank into insignificant nothingness, as it should, and I hope ever will, do; or God help this noble land! Poor Blackies! Be not so bold or so conceited or so insolent, hereafter, I do beseech you.

"Then how rich I have become among my 'colored clients!' I assert, without the fear of contradiction, that I have been the friend, the steady friend of our western 'Darkies' for more than twenty years; and amidst difficulties and troubles innumerable, (for they are a litigious race,) I have been their adviser, and I never made twenty pounds out of them in that long period! The fact is that the poor creatures had never the ability to pay a lawyer's fee.

"It has been my misfortune, and the misfortune of my family, to live among those blacks, (and they have lived *upon* us,) for twenty-four years. I have employed *hundreds* of them, and, with the exception of one, (named Richard Hunter,) not one has ever done for us a week's honest labor. I have taken them into my service, have fed and clothed them, year after year, on their arrival from the States; and in return I have generally found them rogues and thieves, and a graceless, worthless, thriftless, lying set of vagabonds. That is my very plain and very simple description of the darkies as a body, and it would be indorsed by all the western white men with very few exceptions.

"I have had scores of their George Washingtons, Thomas Jeffersons, James Madisons, as well as their Dinahs, and Gleniras, and Lavinias, in my service, and I understand them thoroughly; and I include the whole batch (old Richard Hunter excepted) in the category above described. To conclude: You 'gentlemen of color,' East and West, and especially you 'colored citizens of Toronto,' I thank you for having given me an opportunity to publish my opinion of your race. Call another indignation meeting, and there make greater fools of yourselves than you did at the last, and then 'to supper with what appetite you may.'"*

---

* See "Cotton is King," for full details, pp. 177 to 196.

What was true of the colored population of the Western District of Canada, in 1841, while Colonel Lachlan filled the chair of the Quarter Sessions, seems to be equally true in 1859. The *Essex Advocate* contains the following extract from the Presentment of the Grand Jury, at the Essex Assizes, November 17, 1859, in reference to the Jail:

" We are sorry to state to your Lordship the great prevalence of the colored race among its occupants, and beg to call attention to an accompanying document from the municipal Council and inhabitants of the township of Anderdon, which we recommend to your Lordship's serious consideration:

" ' *To the Grand Jury of the County of Essex, in Inquest assembled:* We, the undersigned inhabitants of the Township of Anderdon, respectfully wish to call the attention of the Grand Inquest of the county of Essex to the fearful state of crime in our township. That there exists organized bands of thieves, too lazy to work, who nightly plunder our property! That nearly all of us, more or less, have suffered losses; and that for the last two years the stealing of sheep has been most alarming, one individual having had nine stolen within that period. We likewise beg to call your attention to the fact, that seven colored persons are committed to stand trial at the present Assizes on the charge of sheep stealing, and that the warrant is out against the eighth, all from the town of Anderdon. We beg distinctly to be understood, that though we are aware that nine-tenths of the crimes committed in the County of Essex, according to the population, are so committed by the colored people, yet we willingly extend the hand of fellowship and kindness to the emancipated slave, whom Great Britain has granted an asylum to in Canada. We, therefore, hope the Grand Jury of the County of Essex will lay the statement of our case before his Lordship, the Judge, at the present Assizes, that some measure may be taken by the Government to protect us and our property, or persons of capital will be driven from the country.' "

The Judge, in afterward alluding to this Presentment, remarked that —

" He was not surprised at finding prejudice existing against them (the negroes) among the respectable portion of the people, for they were indolent, shiftless, and dishonest, and unworthy of the sympathy that some mistaken parties extended to them; they would not work when opportunity was presented, but preferred subsisting by thieving from respectable farmers, and begging from those benevolently inclined."

Here, now, are the results of the experiments made in the Northern States and in Canada for the elevation of the colored people who had gained their freedom. The testimony relating to their condition in Canada is all taken from the official action of its public officers, or the declarations of its public men. All these witnesses are decided abolitionists. The testimony in relation to their condition in the United States is also taken from official sources, or the declarations of abolitionists.

We have included the free States and Canada under one head, because of the sameness of origin of their colored population; and because the evangelization of the Africans, thus thrown upon the care of British and American abolitionists, has been the last thing they seem disposed to undertake.

It must be apparent to the most superficial observer, when taking into account the condition of the free colored people, in both Canada and the free States, that their conduct has rendered the prospects of the African race, at large, tenfold more dark and gloomy than it was thirty years ago. And when the results here are coupled with those in the West Indies, generally, it must be obvious to all, that what has been attempted for the colored race is wholly impracticable; and that, in its present low state of advancement from barbarism, the attainment of civil and social equality with the enlightened white races, is utterly impossible. The means employed have been wholly inadequate to the ends proposed to be attained.

But then, on the other hand, we find such evidences of religious progress among the colored people, as to afford ample reasons for believing that their moral elevation is practicable; but practicable, not by their neglect, as hitherto prevailing, but only by their careful training under the control of enlightened teachers who will subject them to proper moral restraints. How long it will take to elevate the black race, by such agencies, we shall not venture to say; but of this we feel assured: that the neglect to which those already free have been subjected, in the midst of

their professed friends, English and American, if continued, will
forever leave them a degraded people.

9. *The Obstacles to African Evangelization in connection with
American Slavery.*

We come, now, to the examination of the progress of the Gospel in the midst of American slavery. The results have been
partially stated in the course of the preceding investigations.
But no accurate statistics, excepting of the Methodist Episcopal
Church, were available for the earlier periods of slavery; and,
indeed, we have none from other churches, stating their colored
membership, until of late years. It now appears that the Methodists and Baptists have been most successful among the colored
people. In 1859, the number of colored converts in the South
were stated to be 453,000, of which the Methodists had 203,000
and the Baptists 175,000 — all the other denominations having
but 75,000. The membership of the Methodist Church, among
the colored people, may, therefore, be estimated as equaling considerably less than one-half of the total colored converts in the
slave States. These converts, however, are not all to be taken
as slaves, as, doubtless, the free colored people in the slave
States afford some church members; but the whole number are
within the jurisdiction of slavery, and all afford evidence that
Christianity is not inoperative in the midst of that institution.

The references made, in the course of our investigations, to the
work of African evangelization have not been so full and general
as to convey a true idea of the character and present condition
of that work in the United States. It may be remarked, in proceeding to the execution of the task of giving more extended
details, that the Reports from the South, for 1861, were expected,
but have not reached us, on account of the stoppage of the mails.
This, however, will not materially affect the interest of our pages,
as the older Reports embrace all that is necessary to understand
the nature and extent of the missionary work in that field.

The *New York Evangelist,* 1858, says:

" The South Carolina Methodist Conference have a missionary
committee devoted entirely to promoting the religious instruction of
the slave population, which has been in existence twenty-six years.

The Report of the last year shows a greater degree of activity than is generally known. They have twenty-six missionary stations in which thirty-two missionaries are employed. The Report affirms that public opinion in South Carolina is decidedly in favor of the religious instruction of slaves, and that it has become far more general and systematic than formerly. It also claims a great degree of success to have attended the labors of the missionaries."

The Report of the Missionary Board, of the Louisiana Conference, of the Methodist Episcopal Church, 1855, says:

" It is stated upon good authority, that the number of colored members in the Church South, exceeds that of the entire membership of all the Protestant missions in the world. What an enterprise is this committed to our care ! The position we, of the Methodist Church South, have taken for the African, has, to a great extent, cut us off from the sympathy of the Christian Church throughout the world; and it behooves us to make good this position in the sight of God, of angels, of men, of churches, and to our own consciences, by presenting before the throne of His glory multitudes of the souls of these benighted ones abandoned to our care, as the seals of our ministry. Already Louisiana promises to be one vast plantation. Let us — we must — gird ourselves for this Heaven-born enterprise of supplying the pure Gospel to the slave. The great question is, How can the greatest number be preached to ? The building roadside chapels is as yet the best solution of it. In some cases planters build so as to accommodate adjoining plantations, and by this means the preacher addresses three hundred or more slaves, instead of one hundred or less. Economy of this kind is absolutely essential where the labor of the missionary is so much needed and demanded.

" On the Lafourche and Bayou Black Mission-work, several chapels are in process of erection, upon a plan which enables the slave, as his master, to make an offering toward building a house of God. Instead of money, the hands subscribe labor. Timber is plenty ; many of the servants are carpenters. Upon many of the plantations are saw mills. Here is much material ; what hindereth that we should build a church on every tenth plantation ? Let us maintain our policy steadily. Time and diligence are required to effect substantial good, especially in this department of labor. Let us continue to ask for buildings adapted to the worship of God, and set apart ; to urge, when practicable, the preaching to blacks in the presence of their masters, their overseers, and the neighbors generally." *

" One of the effects of the great revival among colored people has been the establishment of a regular system of prayer-meetings for their benefit. Meetings are held every night during the week at the tobacco factories, the proprietors of which have been kind enough to place those edifices at the disposal of the colored brethren. The owners of the several factories preside over these meetings, and the most absolute good conduct is exhibited." †

" In Newbern, North Carolina, the slaves have a large church of their own, which is well attended. They pay a salary of $500 per annum to their white minister. They have likewise a negro preacher in their employ, whom they purchased from his master. ‡ "

And Newbern in this respect is not isolated. For in nearly every town of any size in the Southern States, the colored people have their churches, and, what is more than is always known at the North, *they sustain their churches and pay their ministers.* §

The Synod of Virginia, in 1858, passed the following resolution :

" *Resolved*, That the religious instruction of our *colored population* be affectionately and earnestly commended to the ministry and eldership of our churches generally, as opening to us a field of most obligatory and interesting Christian effort, in which we are called to labor more faithfully and fully, by our regard for our social interests, as well as by the higher considerations of duty to God and the souls of our fellow men. ||

The following extracts are copied from the *New York Observer* of 1859 :

The Presbytery of Roanoke, Virginia, (O. S.,) has addressed a Pastoral letter, on the instruction of the colored people, to the churches under its care, and ordered the same to be read in all the churches of the Presbytery, in those that are vacant, as well as where there are pastors or stated supplies. It commences by saying : " Among the important interests of the kingdom of our Lord Jesus

---

* New York Observer, 1856.
† Lynchburgh (Va.) Courier, quoted by African Repository, January, 1858.
‡ Southern Monitor, quoted by African Repository, January, 1858.
§ Express, quoted by African Repository, January, 1858.
|| African Repository.

Christ, which have claimed our special attention since the organization of the Presbytery in April last — that the work of the Lord may be vigorously and efficiently carried forward within our bounds — *the religious instruction of the colored people* is hardly to be placed second to any other."

After speaking of the obstacles and encouragements to the work, it gives the following statistics:

"In the Presbytery of Charleston, South Carolina, 1,637 out of 2,889 members, or considerably over one-half, are colored. In the whole Synod of South Carolina, 5,009 out of 13,074 are colored members. The Presbyteries of Mississippi and Central Mississippi, of Tuscaloosa and South Alabama, of Georgia, of Concord and Fayetteville, also show many churches with large proportions of colored communicants, from one-third to one-seventh of the whole. Our own Presbytery reports 276 out of 1,737 members. In the whole of the above-mentioned bodies, there are 9,076 colored out of 33,667 communicants. Among the churches of these Presbyteries, we find twenty with an aggregate colored membership of 3,600, or an average of 130 each. We find also such large figures as these, 260, 333, 356, 525! These facts speak for themselves, and forbid discouragement."

Speaking of the obligations to instruct this class, the letter says:

"But these people are *among* us, at our doors, in our fields, and around our firesides! If they need instruction, then the command of our Lord, and every obligation of benevolence, call us to the work of teaching them, with all industry, the doctrines of Christ. The *first and kindest* outgoings of our Christian compassion should be toward them. They are not only near us, but are also entirely dependent upon us. As to all means of securing religious privileges for themselves, and as to energy and self-directing power, they are but children, forced to look to their masters for every supply. From this arises an obligation, at once imperative and of most solemn and momentous significance to us, to make thorough provision for their religious instruction, to the full extent that we are able to provide it for ourselves. This obligation acquires great additional force when it is further considered, that besides proximity and dependence, they are indeed *members of our 'households.'* As the three hundred and eighteen 'trained servants' of Abraham were 'born in his own house;' *i. e.*, were born and bred as members of his *household*, so are our servants. Of course, no argument is needed to show that every man is bound by high and sacred obligations, for the discharge of which he must give account, to provide his *family* suitably, or to the extent of his ability, with the means of grace and salvation."

After dwelling on the duties of the ministry, the letter goes on:

" But the work of Christianizing our colored population can never be accomplished by the labors of the ministry alone, unaided by the hearty co-operation of families, by carrying on a system of *home instruction. We must begin with the children.* For if the children of our servants be left to themselves during their early years, this neglect must of necessity beget two enormous evils. Evil habits will be rapidly acquired and strengthened; since if children are not learning good, they will be learning what is bad. And having thus grown up both ignorant and vicious, they will have no inclination to go to the Lord's house; or if they should go, their minds will be found so dark, so entirely unacquainted with the rudimental language and truths of the Gospel, that much of the preaching must at first prove unintelligible, unprofitable at the time, and so uninteresting as to discourage further attendance. In every· regard, therefore, masters are bound to see that religious instruction is provided at home for their people, especially for the young.

" If there be no other to undertake the work, (the mistress, or the children of the family,) the master is bound to deny himself and discharge the duty. It is for him to see that the thing is properly done; for the whole responsibility rests on him at last. It usually, however, devolves upon the mistress, or upon the younger members of the family, where there are children qualified for it, to perform this service. Some of our young men, and, *to their praise be it spoken*, still more of our young women, have willingly given themselves to this self-denying labor; in aid of their parents, or as a duty which they themselves owe to Christ their Redeemer, and to their fellow-creatures. We take this occasion, gladly, to bid all these ' God speed ' in their work of love. Co-workers together with us, we praise you for this. We bid you take courage. Let no dullness, indifference, or neglect, weary out your patience. You are laboring for Christ, and for precious souls. You are doing a work the importance of which *eternity* will fully reveal. You will be blessed, too, in your deed even now. This labor will prove to you an important means of grace. You will have something to pray for, and will enjoy the pleasing consciousness that you are not idlers in the Lord's vineyard. You will be winning stars for your crowns of rejoicing through eternity. Grant that it will cost you much self-denial. Can you, not-withstanding, consent to see these immortal beings growing up in ignorance and vice, at your very doors ?

" The methods of carrying on the home instruction are various, and we are abundantly supplied with the needful facilities. We need not name the reading of the Bible ; and judiciously selected sermons, to be read to the adults when they can not attend preaching, should not be omitted. Catechetical instruction, by means of such excellent aids as our own ' Catechism for young children,' and ' Jones' Catechism of Scripture doctrine and practice,' will of course be resorted to ; together with teaching them *hymns* and *singing with them.* The reading to them, for variety, such engaging and instructive stories as are found in the ' Children's column ' of some of our best religious papers ; and suitable Sabbath-school, or other juvenile books, such as, ' The Peep of Day,' ' Line upon Line,' etc., will, in many cases, prove an excellent aid, in imbuing their minds with religious truth. *Masters should not spare expense or trouble,* to provide liberally these various helps to those who take this work in hand, to aid and encourage them to the utmost in their self-denying toil.

" Brethren, the time is propitious to urge your attention to this important duty. A deep and constantly increasing interest in the work, is felt throughout the South. Just at this time, also, extensively throughout portions of our territory, an unusual awakening has been showing itself among the colored people. It becomes us, and it is of vital importance on every account, by judicious instruction, both to guide the movement, and to improve the opportunity.

" We commend this whole great interest to the Divine blessing ; and, under God, to your conscientious reflection, to devise the proper ways ; and to your faithful Christian zeal, to accomplish whatever your wisdom may devise and approve."

The *Mobile Daily Tribune*, in referring to the religious training of the slaves, says : *

" Few persons are aware of the efforts that are continually in progress, in a quiet way, in the various Southern States, for the moral and religious improvement of the negroes ; of the number of clergy-men, of good families, accomplished education, and often of a high degree of talent, who devote their whole time and energies to this work ; or of the many laymen — almost invariably slaveholders them-

---

* Quoted in African Repository, April, 1858.

selves — who sustain them by their purses and by their assistance as catechists, Sunday-school teachers, and the like. These men do not make platform speeches, or talk in public on the subject of their 'mission,' or theorize about the 'planes' on which they stand : they are too busy for this, but they work on quietly in labor and self-denial, looking for a sort of reward very different from the applause bestowed upon stump agitators. Their work is a much less noisy one, but its results will be far more momentous.

"We have very limited information on this subject, for the very reasons just mentioned, but enough to give some idea of the zeal with which these labors are prosecuted by the various Christian denominations. Thus, among the Old School Presbyterians it is stated that about one hundred ministers are engaged in the religious instruction of the negroes exclusively. In South Carolina alone there are forty-five churches or chapels of the Episcopal Church, appropriated exclusively to negroes; thirteen clergymen devote to them their whole time, and twenty-seven a portion of it; and one hundred and fifty persons of the same faith are engaged in imparting to them catechetical instruction. There are other States which would furnish similar statistics if they could be obtained.

"It is in view of such facts as these, that one of our cotemporaries, (the *Philadelphia Inquirer*,) though not free from a certain degree of anti-slavery proclivity, makes the following candid admission :

"'The introduction of African slavery into the colonies of North America, though doubtless brought about by wicked means, may in the end accomplish great good to Africa; a good, perhaps, to be effected in no other way. Hundreds and thousands have already been saved, temporally and spiritually, who otherwise must have perished. Through these and their descendants it is, that civilization and Christianity have been sent back to the perishing millions of Africa.' "

The Fourteenth Annual Report of the Missionary Society of the Methodist Episcopal Church South, 1859, says :

"In our colored missions great good has been accomplished by the labors of the self-sacrificing and zealous missionaries.

"This seems to be at home our most appropriate field of labor. By our position we have direct access to those for whom these missions are established. Our duty and obligation in regard to them are evident. Increased facilities are afforded us, and open doors invite our entrance and full occupancy. The real value of these missions is often overlooked or forgotten by *Church census-takers* and statistic-reporters of our benevolent associations. We can but repeat that this field, which seems almost, by common consent, to be left for our occupancy, is one of the most important and promising in the history of missions. At home even its very humility obscures, and abroad a mistaken philanthropy repudiates its claims. But still the fact exists; and when we look at the large number of faithful, pious, and self-sacrificing missionaries engaged in the work, the wide field of their labors, and the happy thousands who have been savingly converted to God through their instrumentality, we can but perceive the propriety and justice of assigning to these missions the prominence we have. Indeed, the subject assumes an importance beyond the conception even of those more directly engaged in this great work, when it is remembered that these missions absolutely number more converts to Christianity, according to statistics given, than all the members of all other missionary societies combined."

The Tennessee Conference of the Methodist Episcopal Church South, in their Report for 1859, say:

"It is gratifying that so much has been done for the evangelization of this people. In addition to the missions presented in our report, thousands of this people are served by preachers in charge of circuits and stations. But still a great work remains to be accomplished among the negroes within your limits. New missions are needed, and increased attention to the work in this department generally demanded. Heaven devolves an immense responsibility upon us with reference to these sable sons of Ham. Providence has thrown them in our midst, not merely to be our household and agricultural servants, but to be served by us with the blessed Gospel of the Son of God. Let us then, in the name of Him who made it a special sign of his Messiahship that the poor had the Gospel preached unto them—let us in his name go forth, bearing the bread of life to these poor among us, and opening to them all the sources of consolation and encouragement afforded by the religion of Jesus."

The Texas Conference of the Methodist Episcopal Church South, in their Report for 1859, say:

"At the last Conference, Gideon W. Cottingham and David W. Fly were appointed Conference African missionaries, whose duties were to travel throughout the Conference, visit the planters in person, and organize missions in regions unsupplied. They report an extensive field open, and truly white unto the harvest, and have succeeded in organizing several important missions. All the planters, questioned upon the subject, were willing to give the missionary access to their servants, to preach and catechize, not only on the Sabbath, but during the week. And this willingness was not confined to the professors alone, but the deepest interest was displayed by many who make no pretensions to religion whatever. An interest shown not merely by giving the missionary access to their servants, but by their pledging their prompt support. The servants themselves receive the word with the utmost eagerness. They are hungering for the bread of life; our tables are loaded. Shall not these starving souls be fed? Cases of appalling destitution are found: numbers who heard for the first time the word of life, listened eagerly to the wonders it unfolded. The Greeks are truly at our doors, heathens growing up in our midst, revival fire flames around them, a polar frost within their hearts. God help the Church to take care of these perishing souls! Our anniversaries are usually scenes of unmingled joy. With our sheaves in our hands, we come from the harvest field, and though sad that so little has been done, yet rejoicing that we have the privilege of laying any pledge of devotion upon the altar."

The Mississippi Conference of the Methodist Episcopal Church, in their Report for 1859, say:

"We are cheered to see a growing interest among our planters and slave-owners in our *domestic missions*. Still that interest is not what the importance of the subject demands. While few are willing to bar their servants all Gospel privileges, there is a great want in many places of suitable houses for public worship. Too many masters think that to permit the missionary to come on the plantation, and preach in the gin, or mill, or elsewhere, as circumstances may dictate, is their only duty, especially if the missionary gets his bread. None of the attendant circumstances of a neat church, and suitable Sunday apparel, etc., to cheer and gladden the heart on the holy Sabbath, and cause its grateful thanksgiving to go up as clouds of incense before Him, are thought necessary by many masters.

"Notwithstanding, we are cheered by a brightening prospect. — Christian masters are building churches for their servants. Owners in many places are adopting the wise policy of erecting their churches so as to bring two, three, or more plantations together for preaching. This plan is so consonant with the Gospel economy, and so advantageous every way, that it must become the uniform practice of all our missionary operations among the slaves. Our late Conference wisely adopted a resolution, encouraging the building of churches for the accommodation of several plantations together, wherever it can be done."

The South Carolina Conference of the Methodist Episcopal Church, in their Report for 1859, say:

" Meanwhile the increasing claims of the destitute colored population must not be ignored. New fields are opening before us, the claims of which are pressed with an earnestness which nothing but deeply-felt necessity could dictate. And the question is pressed upon us, What shall we do? Must not the contributions of the Church be more liberal and more systematic? Must not the friends of the enterprise become more zealous? Will not the wealthy patrons of our society, whose people are served, contribute a sum equal in the aggregate to the salary of the missionaries who serve their people? This done, and every claim urged upon your Board shall be honored.

" This is wondrous work! God loves it, honors it, blesses it! He has crowned it with success. The old negro has abandoned his legendary rites, and has sought and found favor with God through Jesus Christ. The catechumens have received into their hearts the gracious instructions given by the missionary, and scores of them are converted annually, and become worthy members of the Church. Here lies the most inviting field of labor. To instruct these children of Ham in the plan of salvation, to pre-occupy their minds with " the truth as it is in Jesus," to see them renounce the superstitions of their forefathers, and embrace salvation's plan, would make an angel's heart rejoice."

In referring to the missionary work in the South, and the success attending the labors of the Methodist missionaries, the Rev. Dr. ELLIOTT, in his book, " The Great Secession," 1854, says:

" The Methodist Episcopal Church, South, since their secession, has carried on the missionary work among the slaves and colored people with great energy and success. At the present time they have about 150,000 colored members, or about the same number that was in the Methodist Episcopal Church before the secession in 1845. There are many missionaries laboring solely among the colored people, with great success, preaching the Gospel, instructing catechetically the children, visiting the families pastorally, and benefiting their charges effectually.

"They pursue and carry out the same modes of instruction employed by the Wesleyans in the West Indies, and by the Methodist Episcopal Church in her missions. They are doing a great practical work. And whatever exceptions we or others may take to some of the principles and measures of the Methodist Episcopal Church, South, their missionary labors among the slaves of the South have no parallel in the world at this day. While they are denounced without stint by Northern and some British abolitionists of the recent school, they are doing more good, practically and Scripturally, for the enlightenment, reformation, elevation, and future advantageous emancipation of the slaves, than all their censurers are. . . . . . Another thing we feel bound to mention here. We mean the warm and cordial reception and support which our Southern brethren give to the leading institutions and usages of the Methodist Episcopal Church. Whatever exceptions we may take to some of their positions, they are ardently attached to all the fundamentals and peculiarities of Methodism, the instance of slavery excepted. They are less disposed to innovation than the North is, and hold most tenaciously to the leading parts of pure and original Methodism."

Take, also, a short extract from Dr. Bond, as quoted by Dr. Elliott, (Great Secession, p. 261). He says:

"The Southern ministers are not excelled in piety, zeal, talents, and usefulness. Men of rare talents have spent years among the slaves on the rice plantations, exposed to all the ordinary privations of missionary labor, with the additional danger to health and life of the deadly malaria from the swamps, acted on by the intense heat of a Southern sun."

These descriptions of the character and ability of the missionaries, among the Southern slaves, are but just tributes to the moral worth and eminent usefulness of these brethren. The present missionary force, independent of the regular ministry, is 136.* The results of their labors show, conclusively, that the eulogy passed upon them is nothing more than what is merited by them. When Dr. Elliott wrote, the slave converts in the Methodist Church South were 150,000; now they are over 200,000! A vast work has been accomplished here!

* American Christian Record, 1860.

SECTION V.—INTERESTING FACTS IN RELATION TO THE METHO-
DIST EPISCOPAL CHURCH AND ITS RULE ON SLAVERY.

The prominent position occupied by the Methodists, in the
great work of African Evangelization, awakens an interest in all
their movements much beyond that of any of the other denominations; for, although the Baptists have also done a great work,
and are not very far behind the Methodists, yet, in consequence
of the independent character of their churches, the progress they
have made can not be so easily traced. Before closing these
investigations, therefore, some additional particulars, in reference
to the Methodist Church, must be given. Its legislation on
slavery will be found, in detail, in Chapter. VIII. The churches
which had been gathered, previous to 1784, were, in that year,
organized into annual conferences, and the General Conference·
was permanently created in 1796. At this date the entire colored membership, as given by States, stood as follows:

Delaware	811	Pennsylvania	380
Maryland	4,910	New Jersey	105
Virginia	2,458	New York	218
North Carolina	1,288	Connecticut	8
South Carolina	825	Massachusetts	2
Georgia	146	Rhode Island	none
Tennessee	43	Maine	none
Kentucky	84	New Hampshire & Vermont	none

These figures will serve as a starting point, in estimating the
progress of the Gospel among the African population of the
United States; and they are especially interesting when considered in connection with the civil legislation of that period. Pennsylvania had adopted a system of gradual emancipation in 1780,
and was still a slaveholding State in 1796; New York remained
slaveholding until 1799, and New Jersey until 1804 — both
adopting the same system that Pennsylvania had introduced.
The six New England States, in 1796, were all free,* and had
only *ten* converts, from the colored people, in the communion of
the Methodist Church; while the States remaining slaveholding,

---

* See foot note in Chapter II.

exclusive of Pennsylvania, had a colored membership in that Church of 10,878.

It was not until a few years after 1784, that two or three missionaries were sent into South Carolina and Georgia, and the very name of Methodism had not reached them previous to that date. From South Carolina, the first missionary was sent into Mississippi in 1802, and into Alabama in 1808. As for New England, in 1784, the bright morning of the birth of Methodism in that field had not yet dawned. There were no Methodists there.* And even in 1796, the white membership in Massachusetts was but 822; and, in all the New England States, but 2,509.† New England, therefore, at the date of the organization of the Generel Conference was in no very favorable condition to dictate laws to the Church at large, with its 40,000 white members in the slave States; nor did she make any attempt of the kind, as she was then in her childhood, as to strength, when compared with the Churches in the other States. Even as late as 1808, the New England States had but 64 colored members in the Methodist Church; while, at the same time, there were 28,612 colored members in the slave States, including the Philadelphia Conference. The New England States, in the early days of Methodism, were without influence in that body.

The point to which we wish to call attention, here, is the prevalent opinion, that the history of the legislation of the Methodist Church presents a constant concession from the North to the South. That this opinion is not founded in fact, is rendered certain, because Methodism had made but little progress in the free States, until after the whole question in relation to the Rule on slavery had been finally settled. The history of this matter may be briefly stated:

In 1780, the existing societies had disapproved the holding of slaves and advised their liberation. The organization of the conferences was effected in 1784, when all private members were required to liberate their slaves in the States where the laws allowed emancipation. But in six months the Rule was suspended. In 1796 it came up again, in 1804 again, and in 1808 all that

---

* Speech of Rev. Dr. Capers, in the case of Bishop Andrews, 1844.
† See statistics of white members, Chapter II.

related to holding slaves among *private members* was stricken out, and no Rule on the subject has existed since. *

Now, all this legislation, in reference to slaveholding, occurred, mainly, among the slaveholders themselves — the non-slaveholders being a very small minority — and the question was finally adjusted in accordance with the practice of Mr. Wesley himself. This is apparent from two leading facts: 1. The case that has been mentioned in reference to the introduction of the Gospel into Antigua. † In that case, two of the slaves of the planter, Mr. GILBERT, who had accompanied him to England, were converted under the preaching of Mr. Wesley, and baptized by him. Afterward Mr. Gilbert himself was also converted, and on his return to Antigua, under the sanction of Mr. Wesley, he became a preacher, and proceeded to organize the first Society in that island. Mr. Wesley did not exclude Mr. Gilbert from the ministry, although he was a slaveholder. 2. But this is not the only instance in which Mr. Wesley made no distinction between the slaveholder and the non-slaveholder, in the admission of members to the communion of the Church. This rule was general throughout the West Indies, as appears from the testimony of Bishop Hedding. The Bishop, in 1837, presided at the Oneida and Genessee Conferences, in New York, when some resolutions of an abolition stamp were offered, which he was unwilling to put to vote. In his address to them he said:

"Methodist Societies were formed in the West Indies several years before the death of Mr. Wesley. They were under his superintendence, and, from the best information I have been able to obtain, slave-owners were admitted into those Societies; and, in perfect accordance with the above views, that practice was continued up to the time slavery was abolished in those islands by the British Government."

"Let it be further remarked, that for several years before the organization of our Church, many of our preachers and people in the South owned slaves; but they were permitted to do it only under our Saviour's rule. But who permitted those preachers and members to own slaves? You will be astonished when I tell you, it was Mr. Wesley. By his permitting it, I mean he did not hinder it when he

---

* Speech of Rev. Dr. Durbin, on the case of Bishop Andrew, 1844.
† See Chapter I.

had the power to do so. The preachers, in this country, acted under his direction; and under that direction the preachers had the sole power of receiving and expelling members. Had Mr. Wesley then said to his preachers, 'Receive no slave-owner;' or, 'expel the slave-owners,' it would have been done, as he commanded. But it was not done; therefore Mr. Wesley never commanded it. . . . . . . Mr. Wesley's views on this subject have been misunderstood and misrepresented. For, after all he said against the slave trade, against the system of slavery as established by the British Government, and against men's holding slaves where the laws were such that they could put them away to the advantage of the slaves, he never said one word, that I can find, against the Christian man's holding his slave in circumstances where he could not put him away without injuring him. And the fact of his allowing some of his preachers and members in this country to hold slaves for several years before our Church was organized, is sufficient evidence, to my mind, that he saw that nothing better could be done for the slaves, circumstanced as those owners were, than to hold, feed, protect, and govern them. While this state of things continued, Mr. Wesley ordained a Bishop and two Elders, for this country, sending them over to organize his preachers and societies into an Episcopal Church, at the same time appointing Mr. Asbury joint superintendent with Dr. Coke, when he must have known that many, both of his preachers and members in this country, held slaves. Yet I have been severely condemned for expressing an unwillingness to put a resolution to vote in an *Annual Conference* tending to censure our brethren in the South for doing the same thing which Mr. Wesley allowed their fathers to do when in connection with him, and when also he possessed full power to prevent their doing so, or to expel them."

In addition to this testimony, Rev. Dr. Elliott says, in his "Great Secession," page 107 : "The Wesleyans had slaveholders in their communion, in the West Indies, without rebuke, up to the very day on which emancipation took place."

The true spirit of the Methodist Church, in the early years of its existence, was to labor for the propagation of the Gospel, and to avoid all conflicts with the civil laws. This is proved to be the fact, from the character of the instructions given, by the English Wesleyans, to their missionaries in the West Indies. The following is an extract from the instructions adopted in 1817, being sixteen years before the emancipation act was passed:

" We can not omit, without neglecting our duty, to warn you against meddling with political parties, or secular disputes. You are teachers of religion, and that alone should be kept in view. It is, however, a part of your duty, as ministers, to enforce, by precept and example, a cheerful obedience to lawful authority. . . . . . . As, in the colonies in which you are called to labor, a great proportion of the inhabitants are in a state of slavery, the Committee most strongly call to your recollection what was so fully stated to you, when you were accepted as a missionary to the West Indies, that your only business is to promote the moral and religious improvement of the slaves to whom you may have access, without, in the least degree, in public or private, interfering with their civil condition. On all persons, in the state of slaves, you are diligently and explicitly to enforce the same exhortations which the Apostles of our Lord administered to the slaves of ancient nations, when, by their ministry, they embraced Christianity."

The stringent Rule on slavery, first adopted at the North, seems to have been the work of Dr. Coke, one of Mr. Wesley's superintendents. The character of these regulations can be seen in Chapter VIII. It will also be seen, that the regulations were modified, as follows, in 1804, so as to leave the South in the position it occupied, on the first organization of the Church, in that section of the United States :

" Nevertheless, the members of our societies in the States of North Carolina, South Carolina, and Georgia, shall be exempted from the operation of the above rules."

This was passed by the General Conference in 1804. In 1816, it was found that much confusion prevailed throughout the Conferences, as to the manner of executing the rules, and it was deemed necessary to embody the whole requirements of the Church in a single article, as follows :

" Therefore, no slaveholder shall be eligible to any official station in our Church hereafter, when the laws of the State in which he lives will admit of emancipation and permit the liberated slave to enjoy freedom."

But this article, though quieting discussion for a time, did not entirely satisfy the ministry in the North. It allowed considerable latitude of interpretation. But few of the States positively prohibited emancipation; yet none of them allowed the free negro the same enjoyment of freedom which the whites possessed. To secure this to the emancipated man of color, it was necessary that he should be removed to a free state. This measure was not required by the Rule; and, in most of the slave States, therefore, the official members could retain their slaves. By the Rule, too, the private members of the church were left in the full possession of their slaves; thus placing the terms of communion, as to private members, on the same basis that the English Wesleyans adopted for the West Indies, and Bishop Asbury imposed upon South Carolina.

Thus stood the question, as to slaveholding in the Methodist Church, when abolitionism arose in the United States. The rise and progress of the warfare waged by the anti-slavery ministers, against this Rule of 1816, will be found in Chapter VIII., and must greatly interest the reader. In 1844, the antagonist parties were brought face to face, for a trial of strength, on the case of Bishop ANDREW — the South contending that the Rule should remain unaltered, and the North that it should be abolitionized. Technically, this was not the ground upon which the prosecution was based, but, substantially, it embraced this principle. * The North, here, was the aggressor: the South, being satisfied with the position she had so long occupied, and which was fully in accordance with the practice of Mr. Wesley. The disruption of the Church left some of the border Conferences in connection with the North, and this has tended to renew the efforts to alter the Rule — a measure that would have been easily accomplished after the division of the Church, but for the membership in the border slave States.

The relation which the Methodist Church sustained toward the cause of African evangelization, at the moment of the trial of Bishop Andrew, is a matter of the greatest possible interest. The ministers in both the North and the South, doubtless, were equally zealous in their desires to promote the spiritual welfare of the colored people. But the measures of the two parties were

* See Chapter VIII,

as opposite in principle as day is to night. One or the other must have been laboring under a spirit of fanaticism. We have seen that the ministers in the North were almost wholly unsuccessful with the colored people. Let us see how it had been with those of the South:

Membership, in the Methodist Episcopal Church, of colored persons, at the several dates given below.

CONFERENCES.	1826	1830	1834	1838	1842	1845
Philadelphia *	7,650	8,169	9,025	8,112	9,086	10,742
Baltimore	9,406	10,454	13,851	13,301	13,526	16,412
Virginia	7,847	9,967	8,083	2,950	3,558	4,494
North Carolina				3,896	4,733	6,390
South Carolina	15,708	24,538	22,788	23,498	30,840	39,495
Georgia			7,421	7,126	11,457	13,994
Alabama			3,163	2,830	7,505	13,537
Mississippi	2,494	4,247	2,622	1,587	4,089	7,799
Arkansas				592	828	1,775
Texas					407	1,005
Tennessee †	3,597	5,430	7,167	6,727	9,355	15,703
Kentucky	2,821	4,884	5,709	4,770	6,761	9,362
Missouri	339	414	996	812	1,399	2,530
Total	49,862	68,103	80,825	76,201	103,544	143,238

It will be noticed, that the colored membership of the Methodist Church, in Virginia, was reduced more than 7,000, between 1830 and 1838. This reduction, doubtless, was caused by the "Nat. Turner insurrection," and supplies a fair example of the effects of such movements upon the religious interests of the colored people. The masters, having full confidence in the missionaries, allow them free access to the slaves; but, losing confidence in the honesty of their purposes, the slaves are forbidden to hear them; and the results are disastrous to the progress of religion. It was in view of this fact, that Rev. Dr. CAPERS, in his speech on the

---

* Reference has frequently been made to the Philadelphia Conference, as including portions of the territory of Maryland and Delaware. The Report for 1857, gives a colored membership in this Conference, of 8,304, and probationers 848. Of this number there are only 138 members in the North Philadelphia District, 80 in the South Philadelphia District, and 19 in the Reading District, being in all only 239; and of probationers in the whole of these Districts there were but 39 — the remainder being in the slave States.

† The three Conferences of Tennessee are added together.

case of Bishop Andrew, made such a powerful appeal to the
Northern members of Conference, to desist from pressing their
anti-slavery measures upon the attention of that body.   Already
the missionaries could show, as seals of their ministry, nearly
150,000 converts among the slaves.   It was all-important that
this great work should progress without interruption.   This it
could not do, excepting the anti-slavery crusade against slaveholders should be checked in its progress.   In attempting to effect
this object, Dr. Capers said:

"I beseech brethren to allow due weight to the considerations
which have been so kindly and ably urged by others on this branch
of the subject.   I contemplate it, I confess, with a bleeding heart.
Never, never have I suffered as in view of the evil which this measure
threatens against the South.   The agitation has already begun there;
and I tell you that though our hearts were to be torn out of our
bodies, it could avail nothing, when once you have awakened the feeling that we can not be trusted among the slaves.   Once you have
done this thing, you have effectually destroyed us.   I could wish to
die sooner than to live to see such a day.   As sure as you live, brethren, there are tens of thousands, nay, hundreds of thousands, whose
destiny may be periled by your decision on this case.   When we tell you
that we preach to a hundred thousand slaves in our missionary field,
we only announce the beginning of our work — the beginning of the
openings of the door of access to the most numerous masses of slaves
in the South.   When we add, that there are two hundred thousand
now within our reach who have no Gospel unless we give it to them,
it is still but the same announcement of the beginnings of the opening of that wide and effectual door, which was so long closed, and so
lately has begun to be opened, for the preaching of the Gospel, by our
ministry, to a numerous and destitute portion of the people.   O, close
not this door !   Shut us not out from this great work, to which we
have been so signally called of God.   Consider our position., I pray
you, I beseech you by every sacred consideration, pause in this matter., Do not talk about concessions to the South.   We ask for no
concessions — no compromises.   Do with us as you please, but spare
the souls for whom Jesus died.   If you deem our toils too light, and
that after all there is more of rhetoric than cross-bearing in our
labors, come down and take a part with us.   Let this be the compromise, if we have any.   I could almost promise my vote to make the
elder a bishop who should give such a proof as this of his devotion

to, — I will not say the emancipation of the negro race, but what is better — what is more constitutional and more Christian, — the salvation of the souls of the negroes on our great Southern plantations. Concessions! We ask for none. So far from it, we are ready to make any in our power to you. We come to you not for ourselves, but for perishing souls; and we entreat you, for Christ's sake, not to take away from them the bread of life which we are just now beginning to carry them. We beg for this — I must repeat it — with bleeding hearts. Yes, I feel intensely on this subject. The stone of stumbling and rock of offence of former times, when George Daugherty, a Southern man, and a Southern minister, and one of the wisest and best that ever graced our ministry, was dragged to the pump in Charleston, and his life rescued by a sword in a woman's hand, — the offence of the anti-slavery measures of that day has but lately begun to subside. I can not, I say, forget past times, and the evil of them, when in those parts of my own State of South Carolina, where slaves are most numerous, there was little more charity for Methodist preachers than if they had been Mormons, and their access to the negroes was looked upon as dangerous to the public peace. Bring not back upon us the evil of those bitter days. . . . . .

" I said, sir, that we ask for no concessions. We ask nothing for ourselves. We fear nothing for ourselves. But we ask, and we demand, that you embarrass not the Gospel by the measure now proposed. Throw us back, if you will, to those evil times. But we demand that when you shall have caused us to be esteemed a sort of land pirates, and we have to preach again at such places as Riddlespurger's and Rantoule swamp, you see to it that we find there the souls who are now confided to our care as pastors of the flock of Christ. Yes, throw us back again to those evil times; but see that you make them evil to none but ourselves. Throw us back, but make it possible for us to fulfill our calling; and by the grace of God we will endure and overcome, and still ask no concessions of you. But if you can not do this; if you can not vex us without scattering the sheep, and making them a prey to the wolf of hell, then do we sternly forbid the deed. You may not, and you dare not do it. I say again, if by this measure the evil to be done were only to involve the ministry, without harm or peril to the souls we serve, we might bow to the stroke without despair, if not in submissive silence. We know the work as a cross-bearing service; and as such we love to accomplish it. It pleased God to take the life of the first missionary sent to the negroes, but his successor was instantly at hand. And in the name of the men who are now in the work, or ready to enter it, I pledge for a brave and unflinching perseverance. This is not braggardism. No, it is an honest expression of a most honest feeling. Life or death, we will never desert that Christian work to which we know that God has called us. We ask to be spared no trial; but that the way of trials may be kept open for us. We ask to be spared no labor; but that we may be permitted to labor on, and still more abundantly. Add, if you please, to the amount of our toils. Pile labor on labor more and more. Demand of us still more brick; or even the full tale of brick without straw or stubble; but cut us not off from the clay also. Cut us not off from access to the slaves of the south, when (to say nothing of "concessions to the South") you shall have finished the measure of your demands for the North."

These appeals were all in vain, and the only means by which the Southern ministers could maintain themselves in the South, and continue their labors among the blacks, was to withdraw from the Northern conferences, and organise the Southern conferences on the principles originally adopted by Bishop Asbury, of dropping the Rule on slavery.

Section VI.—Interesting Facts connected with the Congregational and Baptist Churches, of the United States, in their relations to Slavery.

Thus far, no reference has been made to the Congregational Churches of the United States, in the relation they sustain to slavery. Their church polity does not bring such questions before their conferences, in a formal manner, with the view of deciding any principle relating to terms of Christian fellowship. All such questions are decided by the congregations separately. Upon the great question of slavery, we are informed that they are very harmonious in their sentiments, not only in New England, but throughout the country. At their General Conference, some eight or ten years since, a deliverance on the subject of slavery was given. It was decidedly anti-slavery in its tone, and may be reckoned as maintaining the abolition ground. The "three thousand and fifty clergymen of New England," who addressed Congress, in 1854, in a protest against the Kansas-Nebraska Bill, included a large number of Congregational ministers. Their views may be inferred from the tone of that document, which the reader will find in a subsequent Chapter, together with the debates in Congress, to which it gave rise. The memorial on the same subject, from the clergymen of Chicago and the North West, and the reply of Mr. Douglass to the same, will also be found in that chapter. A large portion of its signers, likewise, were Congregationalists.

A notice of this denomination is quite in place in this connection. They were the first to occupy New England, and, for many years, had little or no rivalry from other denominations. They have had many men of great intelligence and piety in their ministry, and would seem to have had but few obstacles, indeed, to their success in the propagation of the Gospel. In reference to slavery, they, in general, held the British theory — that it was incompatible with the progress of the Gospel. In Massachusetts, especially, Congregationalism has had a fair field, and should have made rapid progress, according to their abolition theory, as compared with the advancement of the Gospel in the slave States. And how do the results compare?

During September, 1861, the GENERAL CONFERENCE OF THE CONGREGATIONAL CHURCHES OF MASSACHUSETTS held its session at Newburyport.

"At the meeting last year, in Springfield, the following resolution was passed :*

"*Resolved*, That in view of the spiritual desolations, which are known to exist in this Commonwealth, and the fact that so large a portion of our population are not reached at present by the ordinary means of grace, a committee of five be appointed by this Conference to consider and report next year what can be done to reach more effectually these masses, and more thoroughly evangelize every portion of our Commonwealth.

"The committee appointed in pursuance of this resolution, presented at the late meeting of the Conference a carefully-prepared Report, intended to answer briefly the question, " What can be done " by the Congregationalists as a denomination in this matter. Inasmuch as this was the first time that such a question was ever pro-

---

* We copy from the New York Observer's report of the proceedings.

pounded to the representatives of these churches in council, and, as it was expected that ' *Home Evangelization* ' would constitute hereafter a prominent object of this General Conference, the Committee were led to inquire into the *adaptation* of the Congregational polity and the agencies in its employ for this work. And in order to present a full view of the subject, an historical sketch of Congregationalism in Massachusetts was given, together with a notice of the rise and progress of the other Evangelical denominations. It was found, on instituting a comparison, that all these denominations had gained very much upon the Congregationalists. From the landing of the Pilgrims to 1790, the latter had almost the entire possession of the ground. At that period there were no Methodists, only one or two Episcopal, and a small number of Baptist churches in the State. From the year 1800 all these denominations increased rapidly, but no accurate statistics were collected till 1820, or afterwards, so that a comparison of relative growth can be made. The Committee obtained, after much research, the exact number of ministers, churches, and communicants belonging to the Evangelical denominations in Massachusetts at each decade of years, from 1820 to 1860; and, taking the church membership as the most correct standard of comparison, it was found that from 1830 to 1860, the gain of the Congregationalists had been 101 per cent.; that of the Baptists, 129 per cent.; that of the Methodists, 199 per cent.; and that of the Episcopalians, 408 per cent. And that from 1850 to 1860, the gain of the Congregationalists had been much less than any previous decade of years. In fact, the additions to the Congregational churches in Massachusetts, for the last ten years, have scarcely made good the loss by deaths and removals from the State. Whereas, the Episcopalian, the Methodist, and the Baptist churches have, in the same time, received large additions. The exact number of churches and members of these denominations in 1860 was as follows: The Congregationalists had 488 churches, with 76,371 members; the Methodists, 260 churches, with 27,788 members; the Baptists, 268 churches, and 36,250 members; the Episcopalians, 73 churches, and 7,744 members. According to these facts and figures, it seems that the Congregational denomination has not, for some causes, relatively increased equal to the others here mentioned. These causes this Committee endeavored carefully to analyze, showing what agencies and influences have been operating in past years to build up certain denominations more rapidly than our own. While some of these agencies lie beyond the range of any religious body, the most efficient are directly under the control of every denomination. In comparing and analyzing these agencies of church action and aggression, the object of the Committee was to inquire *wherein* the Congregationalists have failed or erred in the use of such means as both propriety and duty might naturally impose upon any religious organization."

It is not necessary to copy the apologies offered by the Committee, for the want of success in the Congregational churches. That the New England ministry have failed, as well as that of all the other denominations, in coming up to the perfect standard of the Gospel minister, according to the example of Paul, is lamentably apparent, from the results attending their labors. Contrast their preaching on the question of slavery, with the preaching of the Apostle Paul, as described by himself: "For I determined not to know anything among you, save Jesus Christ and him crucified." * The burden of Paul's preaching, both to the Jews and also to the Greeks, he assures us, "was repentance toward God, and faith toward our Lord Jesus Christ." † Felix never would have trembled before Paul, except with rage, had the Apostle employed his eloquence in depicting the horrors of slavery throughout the Roman Empire, and the duty of granting equal rights to all mankind.

It will be seen that the membership of the Congregational churches, in Massachusetts, with all the advantages of an early monopoly of the ground, is now only 76,371, while the membership among the colored people, in the slave States, is 465,000! Had the Gospel been faithfully preached in Massachusetts, would the Head of the Church have left its ministers with so few seals to their ministry?

The BAPTIST CHURCH, in the United States, is also Congregational in its Church polity. It divided, several years since, on the slavery question. The division grew out of the disagreements in relation to the mode of conducting their foreign missionary operations; and they have now two Boards — one North and the other South. In Section VII., the results of the efforts of these two Boards are given — the one laboring among freemen, in heathendom, and the other among slaves in the Southern

---

* 1 Corinthians ii : 2.   † Acts xx : 21.

slave States. That Section embraces the whole of the results of all the mission-work of the American churches, throughout the world.

The condition of the Baptist Church North, as to numbers, at present, as compared with its condition before separating from the South, we have no means of determining; but one of the organs of the Church,* in referring to the spiritual condition of the congregations, at large, reviews the Associational year as follows:

" It has been a year of general spiritual dearth. The Presidential election, with the great issues involved, absorbed the attention of all good citizens in the last autumn, and activity in the ordinary religious channels was lessened. The exciting events which have followed, culminating in a disastrous civil war, have not been favorable to calm meditation, or deep religious feeling. The newspaper has been read more than the Bible, the armory has exerted a stronger magnetism than the conference-room; and even on the Sabbath, solicitude for the country has usurped time consecrated to the Lord. Ministers have found it a hard year to preach, from the double difficulty of arresting the attention of the people, and keeping themselves zealously at work in the study. Superintendents have found a truant disposition gaining ground among scholars and teachers. Faithful attendants at social meetings have had occasion to regret that the zeal of some of their weaker brethren has grown cold.

" We anticipate, therefore, barren reports from the churches. Few baptisms will be reported, and little spiritual life. The letters will glow with patriotism, but will say little of growth in godliness."

The Witness, the Baptist paper of Indiana, has a similar sad tale to relate. It says, in a notice of a recent Association in that State:

" The letters from the churches indicated great barrenness of spiritual life and power, and hence a decline of numbers. There seem few, if any, marks of progress in any of our Associations, except downward, and there certainly seems very little effort to turn the current. The brethren seem unwilling to allow themselves time to even make reckoning with themselves. Very few seem to be ' weeping between the porch and the altar;' very few are ready to cry, ' Watchman, what of the night ? ' and very few watchmen offer any response. To our mind the rapid decline of our churches is inevitable. There ap-

---

* Watchman and Reflector, Boston, September, 1861.

pear to be no great objects brought before them, and pressed upon their hearts. There seem to be no laymen or ministers, impressed enough with the barren state of things to bring forward any great issue."

These remarks are copied, to call attention to the closing sentences of the last article. There is no one "to bring forward any great issue;" and, alas! the progress of the Church is downwards. Here is the true secret, we fear, of the spiritual declension of the churches. During the last half century, the ministry have brought forward several "great issues" before the people. Among these issues, slavery has been preëminent; but it can no longer serve as a rallying cry, to rouse up the zeal of lax professors. Some new issue, therefore, is demanded. And has it come to this, that, in a world of fallen men, who are resting under the wrath and curse of an offended Deity, the very ministry appointed to reconcile them to God through the Gospel of his Son, have to lament that they can find no "great issue," of sufficient interest to attract their perishing fellow-men to the Saviour! Surely, the editor was not conscious of the import of his language. He could not have intended to convey the idea, that the love of Jesus has no longer any attractions. No issue! when men are sinking to perdition! Why, man, there is no theme, no issue, like that of perdition on the one hand, and salvation on the other. Drop, then, all your old stale issues; seek no new-fangled ones, the novelty of which will attract men to your standard; but, like Paul, resolve to preach Christ and him crucified; but above all things, never again paralyze the piety of the Church by political preaching.

In immediate connection with these remarks, a quotation from the pen of the former editor of the *Christian Intelligencer*, written in 1861, will be appropriate. It will be seen that the editor of 1829 has changed his views, in a considerable degree, in 1861. With age comes wisdom. He thus announces his present views:

"There may be too much of a good thing. It may well be doubted, whether, just at this time, many ministers of the Gospel are not in danger of keeping the subject of slavery too much before their own minds, and the minds of their hearers, as the source, and the only source, of our national troubles. A minister may preach long and

loud against slavery, or any other sin, and yet not bring one soul to
Christ. In the present crisis, when the question is soon to be tested,
whether, as a people, we have enough of that 'virtue and intelligence'
which is the basis of free government, to save us from bringing ruin
on ourselves, a minister will serve his country best by teaching his
hearers to 'fear God, and keep his commandments.' " *

SECTION VII. — RESULTS OF THE FOREIGN MISSIONARY WORK OF
THE AMERICAN CHURCHES, AS COMPARED WITH THE RESULTS OF
THEIR DOMESTIC MISSIONS AMONG THE SLAVES OF THE UNITED
STATES.

1. THE METHODIST EPISCOPAL CHURCH. — This religious denomination had become deeply enlisted in the work of foreign missions before its division into two bodies. The Church North is
still prosecuting the foreign work with great zeal. The Forty-
second Annual Report of its Missionary Society, 1861, presents
the following tabular statement of its foreign missions. We add
to it, from the domestic missions, the statistics of its Indian mission — the whole presenting the following results :

MISSIONS.	MISSIONARIES.	ASSISTANTS.	NATIVE MEMBERS.	AMERICAN MEMBERS.
Africa........................	27	25	72	1,481
China........................	5	13	54	8
India.........................	10	22	67	76
Bulgaria.....................	3	4		
Germany.....................	15	17	1,637	
Scandinavia	6	13	663	
South America...............	1	1		79
Indian Missions..............	21	19	1,171	
Total................	88	124	3,664	1,644

The American members in the African mission, are the colonists from the United States. The same class of members in the
China, India, and South American missions, are white residents
in those countries. The missions in Germany and Scandinavia,
being in Christian countries, are not to be classed with heathen
missions. The expenditures, in 1860, for the China mission, were
$25,567; the foreign German mission, $25,664; the India mis-

---

* Christian Instructor and Western United Presbyterian.

sion, $30,642; the Liberia mission, $20,937; the Norway and Sweden mission, $6,093; the Bulgarian mission, $2,682; and the Buenos Ayres mission, $146. Total, $111,731.

The first introduction of Methodism into Liberia, occurred in connection with the colonists, about forty years since; but the mission was not formally organized until 1832. Something more than a half million of dollars has been expended on this mission. From causes assigned by Bishop Scott, and quoted elsewhere, the success of the missionaries among the natives has not been very encouraging — there being at present only *seventy-two* converts. Deducting the German and Scandinavian converts from the number of the native converts, and adding thereto the American colonists in Liberia, and the whole number of church members which should be estimated in this connection is 2,845.

The Methodist Church South, including the members in the border Conferences, can offset this by showing a colored membership of over 215,000!

2. The AMERICAN BAPTIST MISSIONARY UNION is the agency of the Baptist Churches North, for conducting their missionary operations in the foreign field. The missions of this Board, according to the Annual Report for 1861, stand as follows:

WHERE LOCATED.	MISSIONS.	STATIONS.	OUT-STATIONS	MISSIONARIES	FEMALE ASSISTANTS.	NATIVE PREACHERS AND ASSISTANTS	CHURCHES.	NUMBER MEMBERS.
Asia	14	17	311	36	37	387	288	16,174
N. American Indians...	2	7	9	5	7	5	15	1,600
Europe	2	71	861			141	79	9,239
Total	18	95	1,181	41	44	633	382	27,013

The Baptist missionaries, sent to Asia, were the first who left the United States for a heathen country. They set sail in 1812. Nearly fifty years have elapsed since that date, and their missions in Asia now number 16,174 converts. Those among the North American Indians, commenced at a later day, have 1,600; making a total membership, in the Baptist mission churches, in their heathen fields, of 17,774.

The SOUTHERN BAPTIST BOARD OF MISSIONS, have their fields of labor in Africa, and in the Southern States. In the latter field alone, the number of converts, in 1859, was 175,000! This, however, includes the whole membership in all the Baptist congregations, missionary as well as anti-missionary. In Africa, they have had no better success than other churches.

The missions of the Baptist Churches North, were established among a people called free. Those in Asia had to encounter the difficulties attending the mission work among an idolatrous population, speaking a foreign language; while those among the Indians were not more favorably situated. The Northern Board, in conducting its missions, had the advantage of being supported by a more numerous people, who could greatly exceed the South in the amount of their contributions. It had the further advantage, also, of having the aid of the South for many years, or until the Northern and Southern churches divided on the question of slavery. Its heathen missions, alone, are noticed in this contrast, those in Europe being among a civilized people.

The Southern Board had to send its missionaries among a slave population, where the world at large averred the Gospel could make no progress. But in this belief the world was mistaken. The colored people, under slavery, had never formed any attachments to the religion of their fathers; and they had acquired the use of the English language. This was a progress vastly beyond the condition of the population of Asia; and the results show a corresponding success — the converts in the missions of the Northern Board being 17,774, and of the Southern Board, 175,000!

There is a point of great interest here, and at the risk of some repetition of what is elsewhere said, we call attention to it in this connection. The slow progress of the mission-work in the foreign fields, so far as natural causes operate, are the results of the deeply-seated systems of idolatry which prevail, and the social practices that are their natural out-growth: all of which are wholly antagonistic to the pure principles of the Gospel. These have to be uprooted before Christianity can succeed. The American slaves born among a people acknowledging Christianity, are unaffected by false idolatrous systems of religion, and are, therefore, more accessible to Christian instruction.

3. THE PRESBYTERIAN BOARD OF FOREIGN MISSIONS. — This Board is the agency appointed by the General Assembly Presbyterians, O. S., for conducting their missions in the foreign field. Its Report for 1861, gives the extent of its missions, with the results as follows:

WHERE LOCATED.	MISSIONS.	STATIONS.	AMER. MINISTERS.	NATIVE MINISTERS.	AMER. TEACHERS, ETC.	NATIVE'CH. ERS, ETC.	SCHOLARS.	CHURCH MEMBERS.
Indian Tribes..............	7	13	15	3	62	8	708	2,179
Africa	3	9	12		12	6	242	250
India	2	17	23	3	23	48	3,475	259
Siam..........................	1	1	6		5	1	31	8
China.........·..............	4	5	13		18	17	188	161
Japan	1	1	1		3			
South America............	1	2	4		3		20	
Total *	19	48	74	6	126	80	4,664	2,857

These missions are efficiently sustained by the contributions from the congregations of this denomination. No Christian people in the world more regularly, zealously, and conscientiously sustain their religious enterprises. In this respect the Old School Presbyterians are educated up to a commendable degree of liberality, it being no longer necessary to employ agents for the collection of funds.

The success of the missions of this Church abroad, has not been equal to the success of its less systematic efforts at home. The foreign field, in 1861, gives but 2,857 converts among the heathen; while the home field, in 1859, gave 12,000 converts among the slaves.

4. THE AMERICAN BOARD OF COMMISSIONERS FOR FOREIGN MISSIONS. — This Board derives its support, mainly, from the Congregationalists and New School General Assembly Presbyterians. It has been in existence fifty years, and has just issued a *Memorial Volume*, for 1860, in celebration of its Jubilee Meeting. The total expenditure of the Board, from its organization to the date

---

* The mission to the Jews in New York, of one minister, and that to Papal Europe, are omitted, as not being Pagan, and as not reporting any members.

of the issuing of this volume, or in the first fifty years of its operations, has been $8,633,381. The expenditure for 1860 was $361,958; and, for the four years preceding, an average of $217,680 per annum. This Missionary Association is probably the best supported and most efficient Board in the country, and may be considered the model institution of its class.

The following tabular view of the missions of the Board, including the number of churches established, the number of converts received in the congregations during the year, the present number of the members in the several churches, and the number of converts from the beginning, will afford a true idea of the success attending the efforts of the Association:

MISSIONS.	CHURCHES.	RECEIVED THE LAST YEAR.	PRESENT NUMBER.	NUMBER FROM THE BEGINNING.
Gaboon Mission..........	1	6	15	38
Zulu Mission...............	7		186	
Armenians	40	226	1,277	1,450
Syria Mission.............	3	19	119	157
Mosul.......................	1		19	
Nestorian Mission		51	385	401
Mahratta Mission.......	13	69	396	466
Madras Mission...........	2	11	74	
Arcot Mission, (1857)...	5		126	
Madura Mission..........	28	78	1,012	1,278
Ceylon Mission...........	9	46	457	
Three China Missions.	3	13	28	35
Amoy Mission, (1857)..	5		126	130
Sandwich Islands........	23	573	14,413	43,758
Micronesia Mission.....	1		4	4
Cherokee, (1859).........	5		248	
Choctaws, (1859).........	12	132	1,362	
Dakotas & Ojibwas......	2	5	91	
Senecas & Tuscaroras..	3	27	283	
Total................			20,621	

The number of ordained missionaries and assistant missionaries sent forth from the beginning has been 1,258 — ordained missionaries 415, physicians not ordained 24, assistants 819; males 567, females 691.

5. The BOARD OF MISSIONS OF THE PROTESTANT EPISCOPAL CHURCH IN NORTH AMERICA held its twenty-fourth annual and eighth triennial meeting in Richmond, Virginia, October, 1859. The Report, in relation to the foreign fields, exhibits an expenditure of money, in the several missions, which indicates a great

degree of liberality, on the part of the people of this church, in the support of Gospel ordinances in the heathen world. The several amounts stood thus: The mission in Greece, $3,300; China, $19,902; Africa, $41,321; South America, $100; Japan, $1,832. Total, $66,455 — fractions omitted.

"Very marked changes are going on in large portions of the continent of Africa. Exploration has done much to bring to light that which was before unknown, and to exhibit features in the condition of the country and its inhabitants, encouraging more intimate relations with those engaged in business and commercial pursuits, and inviting to largely-increased benevolent and missionary operations." *

In relation to the African mission under the charge of Bishop Payne, this devoted missionary writes, in October, 1861, that the mission stands thus: communicants, foreign and colonist, 211; native, 158: total, 369. Boarding scholars, colonist, 37; native, 103: total, 140. Day scholars, colonist, 133; native, 250: total, 383. Sunday-school scholars, colonist, 334; native, 150: total, 484. †

The China mission is comparatively of recent origin, but presents encouraging aspects. It consists of a bishop, 3 presbyters, 6 deacons, 2 native deacons, 3 candidates for orders, (2 foreign, 1 native,) 12 female missionaries: total, 27. Baptisms, 12; communicants, about 70. As there have been but 12 baptisms, it is inferred that the greater number of these communicants are foreigners, residing in China.

The Board, in reference to Japan, take pleasure in announcing that, in point of time, their mission was the first one actually established in that empire.

The mission in South America is also in its infancy.

The statistics of the Greek mission are not given in the work from which we quote the foregoing particulars. ‡ From the small amount appropriated for its support, it is inferred that it is an infant mission.

6. The *American Christian Record*, for 1860, has the following

---

* American Christian Record, 1860.
† Report of Bishop Payne, African Repository.
‡ American Christian Record, 1860.

notice of the AMERICAN MISSIONARY ASSOCIATION. It refers to
the report of 1859 :

" The missionaries have been instructed to labor for the overthrow
of slavery, as of any other sin, and they do not receive slaveholders
into the church, nor invite them to communion.

" The number of foreign missions was 8; stations and out-stations
29; and 9 out-preaching places. Number of laborers in the foreign
field, including those about to sail, 69. . . . The Jamaica mission had
7 stations, 3 out-stations, and 24 missionary laborers, including 4 native
assistants. The reports exhibit a less favorable condition than in
former years. . . . The Ojibue mission being unpromising, the committee recommended its relinquishment. The Ojibue and Ottowa
mission had had 7 additions to the church membership in the preceding eight months. . . . . Sixty had been added to the church at the
Sandwich Islands. Several Sunday-schools and two churches had
been formed among the colored population of the Canada mission.
Mr. Hotchkiss had added 18 to the churches under his care, in a little
more than a year. The Siam mission was at length beginning to present cheering indications. . . . . The Coptic mission had made no
progress during the year, in consequence of the illness of Mr. Martin, who had asked and obtained permission to retire."

Of the African mission little more is said, in the work from which
we quote, than what has been already stated. No statistics of
membership are given, so that we are left without satisfactory
data from which to judge of the progress of the foreign missionary work of this Board. It must be remarked, however, that
with the exception of the West India, the African, and the Canada mission, the fields entered upon have not been long occupied.
The membership in the West Indies is elsewhere stated at 400,
and that of Africa at 300. Total, 700.

7. The REFORMED PROTESTANT DUTCH CHURCH has three foreign missions under its care — the Amoy, the Arcot, and the
Japanese. The Amoy mission was founded in 1842, and, in
1859, was composed of 5 missionaries, and 3 assistant female
missionaries, with 8 native helpers, making 16 in all. There
were, in 1859, under the care of the mission, 185 communicants, 3
parochial schools, and 4 theological students under its patronage.
The Arcot mission has 5 churches, with an aggregate of 146

members, 29 of whom were received during the year. The mission is composed of 7 missionaries, 5 of whom belong to the Scudder family, so eminent for their devotion to the cause of their Divine Master; and 6 female assistant missionaries and 1 male assistant — in all 14. Total communicants in these two missions, 331.

The Japanese mission is composed of 3 missionaries and 4 assistant missionaries. This mission is of recent origin.

The MORAVIANS of the United States act in concert with their brethren throughout Europe. Their missions are, therefore, omitted in this statement of the operations of the American churches, but are included in another section, referring to the missions of Protestant Christendom.

We are now prepared to contrast the missions of the American churches among the heathen, with those which have been conducted among the slaves of the United States. They stand as follows :

DENOMINATIONS.	HEATHEN MISSIONS.	DENOMINATIONS.	MISSIONS IN SLAVE STATES.
Methodists, (North)........	2,845	Methodists, (South)*......	215,000
Baptists, (North)............	17,774	Baptists, (South)............	175,000
Presbyterians, (O. S.)......	2,857	Presbyterians, (O. S.)......	12,000
American Board.............	20,621	Presbyterians, (N. S.).....	6,000
Protestant Episcopal Ch..	439	Protestant Episcopal Ch., (estimated,)................	7,000
American Missionary Association...................	700	Christian Church..........	10,000
Reformed Protestant Dutch Church.............	331	Cumberland Presbyterians	20,000
Mr. King's, and others, Canada......................	300	Other Denominations......	20,000
Total..................	45,867	Total...................	465,000

If we deduct from the converts in the missions of the American Board, the church members in the Sandwich Islands, the remainder, belonging to all the other missions of the Board, will be 6,208, or only about the same number that the New School Presbyterians lost to their Assembly, among the blacks of the South, by the agitation of the subject of slavery.

---

* This includes all the colored membership in the border Conferences of the Church North, within the slave States, along with those in the Church South.

Comments upon the above figures are not required, to convince the intelligent reader that American Slavery presents no such obstacles to the progress of the Gospel as are found in the pagan world.

SECTION VIII. — GENERAL RESULTS OF THE MISSIONARY EFFORTS AMONG THE AFRICAN RACE, IN FREEDOM AND IN SLAVERY, PLACED IN CONTRAST.

We are now prepared to look at results, in another direction, and to contrast the success of the Gospel among the slaves of the United States, with the progress it has made in all the other portions of the world, where the missionary has extended his aid to the African race.

The work of missions, for the benefit of the negro race, may be considered as having been fairly commenced, only a short time before the beginning of the present century. The Moravian missions had their origin at an earlier day; but those of the other denominations, in South Africa, the West Indies, and the United States, had then been in operation only a little more than a dozen years. The missions in West Africa are of a different type from all the others, as slavery has not prevailed in either Sierra Leone or Liberia. The British emancipation act gave freedom to both South Africa and the West Indies. The South African missions have had their own peculiar obstacles to overcome, and many of them are yet in a very embarrassing position. The contrast for the West Indies has already been drawn, between the periods of slavery and freedom; and the facts show that, with the advantages of all the previous missionary labor in the islands, upon which to found their free churches, and with double the number of societies actively at work, the colored membership, in these islands, is now but little advanced beyond what it was before emancipation; and the general testimony, contained in the missionary reports, is, that the membership does not increase.

This result is very different, indeed, from what was expected by British Christians, while laboring for West India emancipation, and supplies a striking example of the lack of foresight governing their actions.

The missions in the WEST INDIES, in 1858, embraced a membership of 92,494, belonging to the several Missionary Associations, as follows : *

SOCIETIES.	MISSIONARIES.	MEMBERS.	SCHOLARS.
Wesleyans...................................	79	48,589	18,247
English Baptists............................	7	† 18,009	753
Church of England.........................	36	696	384
London Missionary Society...............	19	4,000	3,000
Moravians....................................	87	‡ 36,441	
Scotch Presbyterians......................	23	3,900	3,000
American Missionary Association........	6	300	513
Total.................................	256	111,935	25,861

The missions in SOUTH AFRICA, in 1858, embraced a membership of 14,258, belonging to the several missionary societies operating in that field, as follows : §

SOCIETIES.	MISSIONARIES.	MEMBERS.	SCHOLARS.
Moravians	29	1,882	
London Missionary Society...............	32	4,301	3,483
Scotch Missions............................	8	109	
French Protestant Missions...............	14	1,183	310
American Board.............................	12	166	188
Wesleyan Society...........................	39	4,970	7,479
Gospel Propagation Society	50		
Rhenish Missionary Society...............	21	1,647	
Norwegian Missionary Society............	6		
Berlin Missionary Society..................	14		418
Total.................................	225	14,258	11,878

In addition to the missionary force here stated, there were 10 European or American assistants, and 154 native missionaries, and 672 native assistants.

According to the Scotch Record, for 1861, these missions must have a less number of members now, than in 1850, before the Caffir war of 1851, '52, '53, as it places the number of scholars, for 1861, below that of Baird's Retrospect, for 1850, by 5,000.

---

* Encyclopædia of Missions, 1858, page 775.

† Includes the churches not now aided by the Society.

‡ These are later statistics, from American Christian Record, 1860.   This includes the Danish islands as well as the British.

§ Encyclopædia of Missions, 1858, page 58.

The mission of the London Missionary Society, in the AFRICAN ISLANDS, reports a membership of 1,170.

The missions in WEST AFRICA include those of Sierra Leone and Liberia, and have a membership of 23,770. *

In Canada, the mission of Rev. Mr. King, in 1859, had a membership of 70, and an attendance of 200 to 300. † We have no other statistics from Canada, as to the colored churches, but have seen a newspaper statement that the membership is about 300.

The progress of African evangelization, then, among the free colored people outside of the United States, will stand as follows:

	MEMBERS.
West Indies	111,935
South Africa	14,258
African Islands, †	1,170
West Africa	23,770
Canada, (estimated,)	300
Total outside of the United States	151,433
Total converts in the Slave States of the United States	465,000
Difference in favor of missions in the United States	203,567

The result of this contrast must forever silence the advocates of the British theory — that slavery presents an insuperable barrier to African evangelization. But these contrasts would be incomplete, were we to stop here. The Christian world feels encouraged to proceed with the missions in heathen countries. Look, then, at the following section, and see how their results compare with the results among our slaves.

SECTION IX. — CONTRAST OF THE RESULTS OF ALL THE MISSIONARY FORCE EMPLOYED BY PROTESTANT CHRISTENDOM, WITH THE RESULTS OF THE MISSIONS IN THE SLAVE STATES OF THE UNITED STATES.

This is one of the most interesting points in the whole of our contrasts. The Protestant missions, among heathen nations, are prosecuted by the Protestant Christian denominations throughout Europe and America. These missions have been extended to Asia, Africa, Pacific Islands, West Indies, and North American

* Scotch Record, 1861.

† Address of Rev. Mr. King, in Glasgow, Scotland, December, 1859.

Indians. NEWCOMB'S ENCYCLOPÆDIA OF MISSIONS, for 1858, gives the whole number of converts, in all these missions, at 211,389; but more recent estimates make the number, at present, approximate 250,000.

The converts in the slave States are 465,000, and exceed the whole of the converts throughout heathendom by 215,000!

Thus, while the larger number of religious men, throughout Christendom, have been denouncing American slavery as incompatible with African evangelization; a handful of pious men, in the slave States, regardless of the reproaches cast upon them, have labored for the salvation of the slave, with a success nearly double that attending the efforts of all the other missionaries throughout the heathen world.

The Rev. Dr. Elliott, in his "Great Secession," on this point uses the following language; in speaking of the success of the missionaries of the Methodist Church South, among the slaves:

"Their missionary labors among the slaves of the South have no parallel in the world at this day. While they are denounced without stint by Northern and some British abolitionists of the recent school, they are doing more good, practically and Scripturally, for the enlightenment, reformation, elevation, and future advantageous emancipation of the slaves, than all their censurers are."

SECTION X. — CONTRAST OF THE SUCCESS OF THE SCOTTISH AMERICAN PRESBYTERIAN CHURCHES, WITH THAT OF THE MISSIONARIES IN THE SOUTHERN SLAVE STATES.

Another contrast, here, will be useful. From causes known only to God himself, many of the religious denominations, besides those noticed in Section VI. of this Chapter, have made no such rapid progress as might have been expected from the numbers, the learning, and the zeal of their ministry. The Scotch Presbyterian Churches were the first to engage, successfully, in the work of discarding all slaveholders from their communion. * They once had a stronghold in the slave States, but had to withdraw to the free States, on account of the rigidness of the rules they

---

* See Chapter VII. It is true that the Methodists, at the North, attempted the same thing, at an earlier day, but soon gave it up.

adopted against slaveholding, when they embarked in the anti-slavery crusade. We have not been able to obtain the early statistics of these denominations; but in 1829, the Associate Church had 10,141 members; the Associate Reformed Synod of the West, probably not so many; and the Reformed Presbyterian Church, then undivided, a much less number. The aggregate membership was about 25,000, certainly not more than that number. In the year following, the number of Africans in the Christian Church, in the United States, was about 140,000. It was under these circumstances, that the Scotch Presbyterian Churches began their anti-slavery excitement, in which it was contended that the Gospel could not prevail among the slave population, while they remained in bondage.

The years 1860 and 1861 bring out results that should lead the clergymen of these denominations, who have heretofore taken such high anti-slavery ground, to pause and reflect on the results of their conduct. In 1859, the number of ministers was 525. Their labors have been devoted to the white population, in the free States. Beginning before the American Revolution, they have had a fair field of labor — not an obstacle existing except of their own creation. Here are the results of their labors on the one hand, and that of the missionaries among the colored people, in the slave States, on the other hand:

	MEMBERS.
United Presbyterian Church, 1861	58,781
Reformed Presbyterian Church, (O. S.,) 1861	8,000
Reformed Presbyterian Church, (N. S.,) 1861	10,000
Total membership in Scotch Presbyterian Churches, *	76,781
Total colored converts in slave States	465,000
Excess of colored members over Scotch Presbyterians	388,219

On which side, now — Scotch Presbyterianism or slavery — do we find the Gospel most fatally hindered in its progress? On the side of the former, the converts have been raised, in thirty years, from about 25,000 to 76,700: on that of the latter, from 140,000 to 465,000!

And, notwithstanding these results, the whole of these denom-

* Presbyterian Historical Almanac, 1861.

inations are still pressing their old theories upon public attention, with as much zeal as though the Gospel had been utterly excluded from the slave States, and not a child of Africa had been brought to a knowledge of the Saviour!

SECTION XI. — CONTRAST OF THE SUCCESS OF THE GENERAL ASSEMBLY PRESBYTERIANS, WITH THAT OF THE MISSIONARIES IN THE SOUTHERN SLAVE STATES.

The preceding section presents very strange results, indeed, as compared with what the Northern actors in the abolition drama expected to accomplish. The General Assembly Presbyterian Church was also much agitated by the abolition movement. Those who troubled her held the prevailing abolition theory, that slavery and the Gospel are incompatible; and continued to press the question upon the attention of both General Assemblies, even up to 1861.

In 1830, this Church was undivided, and had a membership of 173,329, as against 140,000 colored church members in the slave States. In 1859, when the Church was divided into two General Assemblies, the two bodies had a membership of 417,589, as against 453,000 colored members in the Churches in the slave States! But, in this membership of the General Assemblies there is included, as elsewhere stated, a colored membership of 18,000; leaving the white membership of these two bodies somewhat less than 400,000, while the whole colored church members in the South were, at that date, more than 450,000!

CONCLUDING SECTION.—THE CHRISTIAN CHARACTER OF THE CONVERTS IN THE MISSIONS AMONG THE HEATHEN, CONTRASTED WITH THAT OF THE CONVERTED SLAVES IN THE UNITED STATES.

In the earlier periods of African slavery in America, the utmost latitude of opinion was allowable, in speculating about the moral elevation of the slaves. But little was then known of the character of the negro race, and 'still less of the laws governing the progress of Christian missions among barbarous populations. The deep moral degradation of the African, throughout the world, was calculated to enlist the sympathies of Christian men. In projecting schemes for his relief, speculation had to supply the office of fact; and all Church legislation was merely a random venture toward a proper discharge of what was felt to be a moral duty—the Christian instruction of the colored people. In relation to all that was done, up to 1820, no man could then tell whether any other measures, than those projected, were more likely to promote the moral progress of the African race. As time rolled on, however, light began to break in upon the darkness, and at the moment when the abolition excitement began, say 1830, the developments of Providence clearly indicated, to unprejudiced minds, the proper policy to be pursued. Many parts of the North had become crowded with free negroes, whose deep degradation had united the public in an effort to transfer them to Africa. Freedom, without the means of moral culture, had proved itself of no value to the colored man; while, on the contrary, slavery, accompanied by religious instruction, had given the Methodist Church, alone, in 1830, a colored membership of nearly 70,000. Of these Christian converts, only 1,280 were in the free States, outside of the Philadelphia Conference. Thus, the Gospel had begun, fairly, to show its power over the slave, and to demand of Christians a united effort for their conversion. But, instead of obeying this unequivocal call of Divine Providence, the Churches, almost with one accord, suffered themselves to be led onward in efforts to secure equal civil rights for the slaves, instead of engaging in the more practical and useful work of preaching to them the Gospel, as a means of their moral elevation.

As an apology for declining to coöperate in missions among the slaves, it has been denied that the slave converts are entitled to be considered as Christian, either in their intelligence, morality, or piety. In replying to this, it is only necessary to say, that if the colored members of the Church in the South are not to be classified with Christian men, then the converts in our heathen missions must also be denied a place in the Christian Church, as the standard of Christian morality is fully as high in the former as in the latter. It has been alleged, also, that the converts reported in the Southern Churches have been gathered, largely, by negro preachers, who, on getting up excitements, proceeded to enroll all who offered, regardless of their having any just appreciation of the nature of the step they were taking. But this is not the mode in which the work has been accomplished. The laws, in perhaps all the slave States, prohibit negro preaching, excepting in some rare cases. The mission work is performed by white ministers, and the same rules are observed in the admission of members, and in their after subjection to discipline, that prevail among the white congregations of the respective denominations to which the missionaries belong. Quite a large proportion of the colored members, it must also be stated, belong to regularly organized Churches of white people; and are, in every respect, subjected to the same rules which regulate the conduct of their white fellow-professors. That they are inferior in general intelligence to the white church members, will readily be admitted. But that they stand fair as to piety and purity of moral character, we have testimony from a source which is entitled to the confidence of every abolitionist. The *Anti-Slavery Standard*, of a late date, has the following in reference to this question :

"Mr. Edward L. Pierce, one of the Massachusetts soldiers who served in the three months' campaign under Gen. Butler, contributes to the November number of the *Atlantic Monthly* an interesting article on the 'Contrabands at Fortress Monroe.' Mr. Pierce was assigned to the exclusive control and supervision of the negroes, directing the hours of their labor and their rest, without interference from any one ; and hence enjoyed peculiar facilities for observing their habits and arriving at just conclusions in regard to their condition. He shows us that the slaves are not imbruted savages, but an intelligent and docile race, 'quite equal,' he says, 'to the mass of the Southern population,' if not so thrifty and practical as the Yankees. We copy a few passages from Mr. Pierce's excellent narrative :

"'There was one striking feature in the contrabands which must not be omitted. I did not hear a profane or vulgar word spoken by them during my superintendence, a remark which it will be difficult to make of any sixty-four white men taken together anywhere in our army. Indeed, the greatest discomfort of a soldier, who desires to remain a gentleman in the camp, is the perpetual reiteration of language which no decent lips would utter in a sister's presence. But the negroes, so dogmatically pronounced unfit for freedom, were in this respect models for those who make high boasts of civility of manners and Christian culture. Out of the sixty-four who worked for us, all but half a dozen were members of the Church, generally the Baptist. Although without a pastor, they held religious meetings on the Sabbaths which we passed in Hampton, which were attended by about sixty colored persons and three hundred soldiers. The devotions were decorously conducted, bating some loud shouting by one or two excitable brethren, which the better sense of the rest could not suppress. Their prayers and exhortations were fervent, and marked by a simplicity which is not unfrequently the richest eloquence. The soldiers behaved with entire propriety, and two exhorted them with pious unction, as children of one Father, ransomed by the same Redeemer.' "

On perusing these statements, an anti-slavery clergyman remarked, exultingly, that, if the negroes had made such progress as this, they should be free. His view of the subject is of a piece with much of the hasty generalization prevalent in reference to slavery. But it by no means follows that because a people, rising from barbarism, have become sober, orderly, and pious, under slavery, that they are, therefore, prepared for the enjoyment of independence. On this subject, the American Board is a competent witness. Hear what it says in reference to its most prominent mission :

" The Board can not be said to have completed the work of any one of its missions, if this involve the idea of a native Christian community able to stand alone. Yet several of the heathen communities in which it has labored have been Christianized, in the popular acceptation of that term. The Sandwich Islands have been thus Christianized. . . . . The nation was composed of thieves, drunkards, and debauches. The land was owned by the king and his chiefs, and the people were slaves. Constitutions, laws, courts of justice, there were none, and no conception of such things in the native mind. Property, life, every thing was in the hands of arbitrary, irresponsible chiefs, who filled the land with discord and oppression. But that people has become a Christian nation; not civilized, in the modern acceptation of the term ; not able, perhaps, to sustain itself unaided in any one great department of national existence. Laws, institutions, civilization, the great compact of social and political life, are of slower growth than Christianity. A nation may be Christian, while its intellect is but partially developed, and its municipal and civil institutions are in their infancy. In this sense, the Hawaiian nation is a Christian nation, and will abide the severest scrutiny by every appropriate test."

. . . . . "But, so much, indeed, was the blood of the nation polluted by an impure commerce with the world, before our Christian mission, that the people have a strong remaining tendency to licentiousness, which the Gospel will scarcely remove till a more general necessity exists for industry and remaining at home. The weakness of the nation is here."*

Nations are composed of individuals. As a " nation may be Christian, while its intellect is but partially developed, and its civil institutions are in their infancy:" so an individual may be Christian, without possessing the necessary intelligence to make him a safe member of civil society — a proper judge of the laws necessary to its protection and progress. This, in the opinion of the whites at the South, is precisely the condition of the Christian converts among the blacks; and constitutes a reason why they will not assent to emancipation.

In comparing the condition of the converts gathered into the mission churches of the American Board, with the moral stand- ard prevailing among Church members in Christian countries, it says :

"The fact undoubtedly is, that visible irregularities and disorders, and even certain immoralities, are more to be expected in churches gath- ered from among the heathen, than in the churches of Christendom ; and they are, at the same time, more consistent with grace in the Church, than in countries that have long enjoyed the light and influ- ence of the Gospel. . . . . The popular sentiment at home is believed to have required too much of the missions. A standard has been pre- scribed for their ultimate success, which renders their satisfactory ter- mination quite impossible, or at best throws it into the far, uncertain future. The Christian religion has been identified, in the popular conception of it, with a general diffusion of education, industry, civil liberty, family government, and social order, and with the means of a respectable livelihood and a well-ordered community. Hence our idea of piety in native converts has generally involved the acquisition and possession, to a great extent, of these blessings; and our idea of the propagation of the Gospel by means of missions is, to an equal extent, the creation among heathen tribes and nations of a state of

---

* "Memorial Volume," pages 253, 254, to which the reader is referred for details.

society such as we enjoy. And for this vast intellectual, moral, social transformation we allow but a short time. We have expected the first generation of converts, even among savages, to come pretty fully into our fundamental ideas of morals, manners, political economy, social organization, justice, equity, — although many of these are ideas which old Christian communities have been ages in acquiring. If we have discovered that converts under the torrid zone go half clothed, are idle on a soil where a small amount of labor supplies their wants, sometimes forget the apostle's cautions to his converts, 'not to lie one to another,' and 'to steal no more,' in communities where the grossest vice scarcely affects the reputation, and are slow to adopt our ideas of the rights of man, we at once doubt the genuineness of their conversion, and the faithfulness of their missionary instructors."*

What are we to infer from all this, but that the standard among the converts from heathenism, in the mission churches of the American Board, is, in some respects, lower than we find it among Church members at home; and that it is not to be expected that converts from heathenism should, in a single generation, attain a position, in every respect, equal to that which the Churches in Christian countries have gained after centuries of religious training. But this admission of the Board is not intended to create the impression that the converts in their missions are not true Christians; nor is the admission that the slave converts are not, in some respects, the equals of the white professors of religion, intended as an admission that they are not true disciples of Christ.

The further admission of the Board is as important as it is true: that laws, institutions, civilization, the great compact of social and political life, are of slower growth than Christianity; and that, notwithstanding the Christian character of some of their missions, the intellectual development made by the population is not in proportion to their religious progress; and that, therefore, they are not prepared to stand alone, unsupported by the counsel and control of a superior race. This is exactly the view entertained, of the negro population of the South, by all considerate men. As a race, not only in the South, but throughout the world, the blacks have made no such advances beyond their original barbarism, as

* Memorial Volume, pages 250, 251.

to be able to sustain civilized institutions without the direction and control of the superior races. It is so in the West Indies and Sierra Leone, where all civil affairs are under the control of the British; it is so in Liberia, where the American Colonization Society still lends its friendly aid; it is so everywhere; and why should the opposite rule be demanded for the United States? We thank the American Board for its timely testimony in relation to the workings of Christian missions among the barbarous races. It gives encouragement to believe that our slave converts are not behind their fellow-converts in heathen lands.

But it is urged, as an argument for emancipation, that the means of religious progress are not adequately supplied to the slave population of the South. The preaching of the Gospel, and oral instruction in the Sabbath-schools — including the memorizing of the Catechism and portions of Scripture — embrace about all the means of instruction now publicly afforded to the slaves. Is this plan of teaching sufficient to enlighten a people born in the midst of a Christian civilization, where they have been uninfluenced by pagan superstitions and idolatry? Let us again refer to the American Board for the results of their experience on this point:

" There has been a growth of experience and skill in the conduct of missions during the past half century. It is indeed true that our fathers, at the outset, gave the preëminence to the preaching of the Gospel, in their theory of missions, as really as do their successors. Thus they wrote as far back as the year 1813, and nothing stronger can be said now: 'Important as the distribution of the Scriptures among the heathen, in their own language, is held to be by us and by the Christian public generally, it should never be forgotten that the *preaching of the Gospel*, in every part of the earth, is indispensable to the general conversion of mankind. Though the Scriptures alone have, in many individual cases, been made the instrument of regeneration, yet we have no account of any very extensive diffusion of Christianity except where the truths of the Scriptures have been preached. Were the heathen generally anxious to receive the Scriptures and to learn divine truth, they would, like the Ethiopian eunuch, apply for instruction to those who had been previously acquainted with the same Scriptures, and, when asked if they understood what they had read, would reply, 'How can we, except some man should guide us?' The distribution of the Bible excites inquiry, and often leads those who receive that precious book to attend public worship in the sanctuary. But the preaching of the Gospel is, after all, the grand means appointed by Infinite Wisdom for the conversion and salvation of men. Without this, the Scriptures, however liberally distributed, will have comparatively little effect among any people, whether Pagan or nominally Christian.' And again, in 1817: 'The translation and dispersion of the Scriptures, and schools for the instruction of the young, are parts, and necessary parts, of the great design. But it must never be forgotten, or overlooked, that the command is, to 'preach the Gospel to every creature,' and that the preaching of the word, however foolish it may seem to men, is the grand mean appointed by the wisdom of God for the saving conversion of the nations.'

"From this practical view of the work, taken by the Board at the opening of its career, there has been no intentional departure, either by the Prudential Committee or by the missions. Schools and the press have always been regarded as subordinate to preaching. When agriculture and the mechanic arts have also been taught, as in the Indian missions, and at first on the Sandwich Islands, it has been as a subordinate means. At the same time, there has been a tendency in the more important of the auxiliary influences to transcend their proper limits. Book-making has sometimes acquired an undue prominence, especially in the early periods, when some brethren may have found it easier to translate the Scriptures than to preach in a foreign tongue, and when preaching yielded little apparent fruit, and schools were easily multiplied, and tracts and books could be circulated to any extent. In the chapter on the difficulties in obtaining the Board's charter, it was seen how translating and circulating the Scriptures then preponderated, in the public mind, over preaching as a means of converting the heathen.

"The subordinate agencies have been gradually falling into their places, and it is reasonable to expect, under the lead of the Great Captain, that the progress of the Gospel will be more rapid in the second half-century than it has been in the first."

The remarks of the Board on this topic are quoted entire. The preaching of the Gospel, in its opinion, is the grand means appointed by Infinite Wisdom for the conversion and salvation of men. Schools, the press, agriculture, mechanic arts, circulating the Scriptures, are viewed as subordinate means. According to this view — and its accuracy will not be denied — the slave population are in the enjoyment of the grand means appointed for the conversion and salvation of men. They have the Gospel preached to them; they also enjoy the subordinate means to a limited extent; and are in constant training in the pursuits of agriculture or the mechanic arts — a training essential to progress in civilization. Upon the whole, their means of improvement are fully equal to those possessed by the people of the primitive churches, or their successors, down to the time of the discovery of the art of printing, and the general diffusion of education by common schools. If, then, the slaves enjoy as great privileges as the primitive Christians, and have supplied to them the grand means necessary to success in modern missions, why should it be thought a strange thing that they, also, should have accepted the offered salvation, and been transformed, in the spirit of their minds, into the divine image of Jesus, in knowledge, righteousness, and true holiness. *

---

* Among the various arguments employed to prove the necessity of abolishing slavery, there is one, remaining unnoticed, to which attention must be called. The seeming slow progress of the Gospel, in heathen lands, is accounted for on the principle that the missionaries belong to a country tolerating slavery; and that, before success can be expected, slavery must be abolished in our country. A speaker in a religious convention states the case as follows:

"We have a pure Gospel to send, but we disgrace it. If our Christianity was in pure hands, it would be effective. But we have in our land covetousness, drunkenness and slavery. They to whom we would send the Gospel hear of these things, and they mock us." *

During the same meeting another speaker said:

"There are three millions of human beings in bondage in this land to whom the word of God can not be preached. Our fearful complicity in this giant wrong is one great reason why God has made the heavens as iron and the earth as brass." †

Strange, that these reverend gentlemen should be so illy informed, or rather that they should allow their prejudices to mislead them so egregiously. What! Slavery now an obstacle to foreign missions, when it presented no barrier in the days of the Apostles and their successors! The ministers of the Gospel at this day, must not be allowed to shield their own inefficiency by any such plea. Rome had sixty millions of slaves at the dawn of the Christian Era; and yet the Gospel spread abroad with great rapidity. It is not the

* Address of Rev. J. B. Johnson, before the Convention of the Scottish American Presbyterian Churches, Xenia, Ohio, March, 1857.
† Rev. R. A. Brown.

That the standard of Christian character among the converted slaves, is as high as that of the converts in the foreign missions, can not be doubted when the circumstances are considered in which the two classes are placed — the one growing up amidst the elevating maxims of Christian civilization, the other under the debasing customs of heathenism. The reasons offered for ignoring the missionary labors among the slaves at the South, on account of any existing imperfections among the Christian converts, will apply with equal force to missions among the heathen. If the one should be abandoned on account of inefficiency, the other should no longer be prosecuted, for the reason of their more limited success. But if both have been successful, as is true beyond all doubt, then the prayers and contributions of Christians should not be withheld in behalf of the one any more than of the other.

A word as to the difference in the success of the Gospel among our slave population, as compared with the heathen populations addressed by our foreign missionaries. Isaac Taylor, as previously quoted, states, that—

"Christianity at first went wherever a preparation had been made for its reception by the scattering and settlement of the Jewish race, and by the preëxistent diffusion of the Scriptures of the Old Testament, in the Greek language. Within *these* limits the Gospel seated itself, and there it held its position with more or less of continuity; and beyond the same limits it was, indeed, carried forth, and it won its triumphs; but soon it lost its hold; soon it retreated, and disappeared, leaving only some scattered and scarcely appreciable fragments on its spots, to denote the course it had taken." *

It is a point of great interest to know why it was that Chris-

---

abolition of slavery that is so much needed, as a ministry imbued with the spirit of the Apostles — a ministry that will give heed to teaching the Word, instead of preaching politics. But the assertion that slavery is a barrier to the progress of the Gospel in heathen countries, is not more strange than the declaration that the Gospel can not be preached to the three millions of slaves in the Southern States! We scarcely know how to view such declarations as we have here quoted. These speakers did not intend to tell untruths, or present false deductions from historical facts; and, yet, that they did so, is abundantly evident from the testimony that has been produced. It is from such careless, such criminal conduct, that the public have been misled.

* Isaac Taylor's Wesley and Methodism, page 293.

tianity failed in establishing itself permanently, excepting where the Jews and the translations of the Hebrew Scriptures had imparted to the population some knowledge of the true God. An editorial in a religious paper, under charge of the professors in an eminent theological seminary, says, that one-half of the converts in the Roman Empire were slaves;* and this statement coincides with the opinions of the historian Gibbon. Many of these slaves, doubtless, had been brought from the surrounding nations, where Christianity afterward failed to maintain a foothold. † Why was it that those who were captives in Rome, so much more readily received the Gospel, than those of their countrymen who had not been enslaved? It can only be accounted for on the principle, that their residence in Rome was a means of bringing them under the influence of the teachings which had prepared both Jews and Romans for the reception of the Gospel. In this result we have a very significant fact; and one that is applicable to the slave population of the United States. It enables us to answer, intelligibly, the question, why there should have been nearly double the number of converts in the slave States, from the ranks of the African race, that there are in all the missions of Protestant Christendom established throughout the heathen world. The Africans under American slavery, like the captives in Rome, have had a preparation for the reception of the Gospel, in consequence of their contact with a people possessing a knowledge of the true God, and of the way of salvation through faith in his Son.

But this lesson from Roman history, confirmed by the results under American slavery, has a still more important bearing, as affecting the question of the conversion of the world. Our mis-

---

* Christian Herald and Presbyterian Recorder, Cincinnati and Chicago.

† We have recently seen a statement, made on the floor of Congress, that Christianity entered Africa only where the Roman arms controlled the population; that there it greatly flourished as long as the Roman power prevailed; but that, when Rome declined, and her power was no longer maintained in Africa, Christianity also declined, and finally disappeared. Rev. J. L. Wilson, long a missionary in Africa, on the Gaboon, has expressed the opinion that the great want of Africa, to render it accessible to the Gospel, is the establishment of civil government. It would seem then that God puts honor on his own ordinances — civil government and the Church.

sionary systems are doing for idolatrous nations a preparatory work far more important than the Jews did for Rome. The sacred Scriptures, now complete, are being translated into the languages of every nation under the sun; and the day seems dawning when the kingdom of Christ shall have universal dominion in the earth.

A comprehensive view of the agencies at work in the propagation of Christianity, and the certainty of the results which must follow the general circulation of the Scriptures and the preaching of the Gospel, makes the heart of the Christian swell with emotions too great for utterance, and should lead the man who would raise a finger to obstruct its progress among any class of men, slave or free, to doubt whether the love of Christ pervades his soul.

CHAPTER IV.

AFRICAN SLAVERY AND AFRICAN EMANCIPATION, IN THEIR EFFECTS, RESPECTIVELY, UPON THE NATIONAL WELFARE OF THE CAUCASIANS.

Thus far, mainly, the investigations have had reference to the moral and religious effects produced upon the African race, in their connection with the Caucasian, whether as bondmen or freedmen. The object in view would be imperfectly accomplished, without an examination of the effects which the blacks, under slavery, and emancipation, respectively, have had upon the economical and political welfare of the countries into which they have been introduced. When this is done, it will afford a useful lesson on the dangers of premature emancipation, and the hasty enfranchisement of uncivilized men, upon the progress of civil liberty and the safety of civil government.

SECTION I.— EFFECTS OF EMANCIPATION IN BRAZIL, MEXICO, AND THE SOUTH AMERICAN REPUBLICS.

At the time of the prohibition of the slave trade by England and the United States, Brazil belonged to Portugal, and the remaining South American provinces and Mexico to Spain. The most active period of the slave trade, as already shown, was that which succeeded its prohibition, and that which followed West India Emancipation. All the slaves exported westward from Africa, during this epoch, were taken to the Spanish, Portuguese, and French colonies of South America and the West India islands. This gave them a very considerable African population — the slaves of Brazil, in 1850, being equal in number to those of the United States, and the number in the Spanish islands falling but little short of one-third of that number. The French colonies, at the

(255)

time of emancipation, in 1848, had a colored population of 416,755, of whom 257,009 were slaves.

Now, what have been the results with these our neighbors? Brazil has never emancipated her slaves. She remains a stable, progressive, and prosperous government, as compared with the countries by which she is surrounded, although her slave population is double that of the white citizens.

Cuba, still belonging to Spain, has never emancipated its slaves, but continues to augment their numbers by means of the slave trade. Its productiveness is regularly on the increase, and its economical prosperity unsurpassed by any equal extent of territory in the world.

Mexico, in 1813, threw off the yoke of Spain, and declared herself a Republic. But the attempt of Iturbide to restore a despotism, raising up a race of military chieftains for his overthrow, afterwards produced a struggle for power, resulting, in 1824, in the prohibition of the slave trade, and the adoption of a Constitution declaring *free* all born after that date. Pedraza being elected President, Santa Anna, at the head of the military, interposed, and placed in the presidential chair the defeated candidate, Guerrero, who — to strengthen himself, and the better to resist an invasion from Spain, then in process of execution — issued a decree, September, 1829, emancipating all slaves.

Thus was liberty and equality at once secured to the blacks of Mexico, and, under the law, the African, in a moment, made the equal of the descendants of the proud Castillians who had conquered Montezuma ; * and thus, also, was another instance of emancipation effected under circumstances where it was required by a political necessity, just as, in England, it was demanded by a conjectural economical necessity. But in neither case was the good of the black man the principal motive urged to give to him his freedom — it being in the one case to secure troops to sustain a usurper, in the other with the belief that free labor would be more profitable than slave labor.

And what have been the results of the Mexican expedient to gain a political advantage, by placing the African on terms of

---

* See " Ethiopia," page 102.

equality, side by side with the Caucasian? Happily, the consequences have been depicted by a master hand, in the abolition ranks. We refer to the late Judge Jay, who thus drew the picture of Mexico to the life, in 1846:

" The republic of Mexico had long been the prey of military chieftains, who, in their struggle for power, and the perpetual revolutions they had excited, had exhausted the resources of the country. Without money, without credit, without a single frigate, without commerce, without union, and with a feeble population of seven or eight millions, composed chiefly of Indians and mixed breeds, scattered over immense regions, and for the most part sunk in ignorance and sloth, Mexico was certainly not a very formidable enemy to the United States." *

In addition, Judge Jay states that the exports from Mexico, in 1842, were, exclusive of gold and silver, only one million and a half of dollars. It has increased but little since that period, owing to its being torn and distracted by almost constant wars, and because it has none of the elements of progress in its present state of society.

Here, now, we have the results of the practical application, by the Mexicans, of the doctrine that all men are created free and equal! Indians, negroes, whites, were all declared equal at the ballot-box; and scarcely a single President, elected by the popular vote since that event occurred, has ever been able, for any considerable time, to maintain himself in his seat. Such has been Mexican emancipation, and such its results!

The condition of the South American Republics is so nearly like that of Mexico, that details in relation to the results of their emancipation schemes may be spared. The portrait of Mexico, with some slight modifications, may stand for the whole group; and its state of society may be inferred from the character of its population. Mr. Jay states it as follows:

Whites	1,000,000
Mixed Breeds	2,009,509
Negroes	6,000
Indians	4,000,000
Total	7,015,509

* Jay's Review of the Mexican War.

The wisdom and foresight of the Fathers of the Republic of the United States, averted such evils as have afflicted Mexico, by not committing the folly of commingling barbarism and civilization, on equal terms, in the Constitution. Had they emancipated the negroes, and, like Mexico, admitted both negroes and Indians to citizenship, the United States, to-day, might have been little better, in its moral and civil condition, than Mexico has been for years. By the course which we adopted, the emigrants from Europe, with their labor, skill, capital, and intelligence, flocked to our shores, instead of to the milder climates of Mexico and South America. Thus we were strengthened while they remained weak and distracted — the ignorance and degradation of their barbarous population rendering it a suitable instrument, in the hands of ambitious military adventurers, for the disturbance of the public peace. Had the course of Mexico, toward her uncivilized population, been productive of the greatest good to the cause of humanity, it would afford a justification of her action. But no one familiar with the facts will, for a moment, deny that the great body of our slaves are better provided for, and have made more rapid advances in civilization, than the mongrel breeds of Mexico; and yet, the Indians, mixed breeds, and negroes, have long been in the possession of the privileges of citizenship in that Republic — have long had all the rights which abolitionists claim for the slave, without any of the blessings which, they insist, will necessarily follow in the wake of emancipation.

Another remark or two may be useful here, in reference to the subject of emancipation. Human freedom is the richest of blessings, where men are prepared for it; but it may be productive of serious evils when prematurely conferred. Take an example, in another relation of life : the inheritance of wealth is a boon that may bring lasting happiness ; but the law wisely forbids its transfer to the heir, until he has attained an age when it is supposed he must be capable of using it prudently. The negro and Indian races are to be considered as minors in their relations to the freedom guarantied in civilized society, and the great mass of them, at present, and most likely for ages to come, as wholly incapable of using it safely. The time may come when it will be otherwise ; but, till then, the prudent Christian will not be in haste to disturb existing relations. Dr. Livingstone, who has enjoyed the very best opportunities for studying the condition of African society, recommends this course of policy to the British nation, in its efforts to promote cotton culture in Africa. Slavery there is general, and must be let alone, if increased cultivation be desired. * The people of Britain, after immense sacrifices in the cause of African freedom, are now forced to acquiesce in this policy. This point will be referred to again.

Section II.—Effects of Emancipation in the Island of Hayti.

In Hayti, the negroes found themselves freemen, before they were prepared to profit by the change. It is not claimed that they would have been better in slavery. Their masters had done nothing for their moral advancement; and a thousand years, under such treatment as they had endured, would have still found them savage. But freedom to savage Africans, like the freedom of the savage Indians, does not, necessarily, become an element of progress in civilization. We have a proof of this in the economical results of Haytien emancipation. We are aware, however, that too much importance may be attached to the production of wealth, as indicating an increasing civilization; and, yet, it is the best evidence the world can have on that subject. Abolitionists readily avail themselves of it as an argument for emancipation, when the statistics are supposed to be on their side. But while increasing production certainly shows that intelligence guides cultivation, the subordinate operatives may be acquiring intelligence in no greater degree than the mules they drive. Such was, in general, the slavery of the British West Indies; and such is now, specially, the slavery of Cuba and Brazil. The truth is, that increasing ability to export the products of slave labor, is no proof that the slaves, themselves, are advancing in civilization. It only shows that the ruling class, by judicious management, are making slave labor a profitable system. On the other hand, where a free people, who are the owners of the soil, are, from year to year, aug-

---

* The Doctor suggests that to make labor effective, the present condition of society must be left undisturbed.

menting the amount of their exports and imports, or increasing
their manufacturing as well as their agricultural industry, it is
proof positive that they are advancing in civilization.   But where
a community of free people, for a long series of years, fail to increase the amount of their exports, and do not manufacture their
own fabrics and implements, it is evident that they lack ordinary
industry and energy and can not be progressing in civilization.
And further : where a country has once shown itself as possessing
extensive sources of wealth, and then suddenly loses nearly all its
capacity for production, without any diminution in the fertility
of its soil, the cause of the decline must be sought for in the
changed condition of the people.

Hayti furnishes an illustration of the correctness of the preceding observations.   That island was exceedingly productive
before emancipation ; but its productions were the fruits of com-
pulsory labor, under the control of superior intelligence.   Its exports, then, were very large — being equal to *three-fifths* of the
produce of all the French West India colonies.   They amounted,
in value, to more than $50,000,000; and the island, in return,
consumed, of French manufactures, more than $49,430,000. *
This statement has reference, only, to the French part of the
island, which, in 1789, had a population of 30,826 whites, 27,548
free colored persons, † and 480,000 slaves employed in agriculture.
The Spanish part of the island employed only 15,000 slaves in
agriculture. ‡

"The political troubles of Hayti began in 1790, between the mulattoes and whites, the slaves remaining industrious, quiet, and orderly.
But in August, 1792, the slaves joined in the rebellion, and the massacre of the whites commenced.   The most dreadful scenes of cruelty
and bloodshed continued to be enacted until 1801, when a constitution
was adopted, and the island, under the name of Hayti, formally proclaimed an independent neutral power. §   At the close of this year,
Bonaparte made an effort to reconquer the island, and, in order to

* Blackwood's Magazine, 1848, page 6.
† Westminster Review, 1850, page 261.
‡ Macgregor, page 1152.
§ St. Domingo was the the name by which the island was known previous to
this date.

succeed, the French General, Le Clerc, first attempted to restore the planters to their former authority over the negroes, many of whom, in the preceding struggles, had been granted their freedom; but, failing in this, he was forced, as a last resort, on the 25th of April, 1802, to 'proclaim liberty and equality to all the inhabitants, without regard to color.' The Haytien chieftains, Touissant, Dessalines, Christophe, etc., being immediately deserted by the blacks, were forced to submit, and the French sovereignty was again recognized throughout Hayti. As a first step to deprive the people of their efficient leaders, Le Clerc seized Touissant and his family, in the night, about the middle of May, and hurried them on board a vessel, which sailed immediately for France. * This act of perfidy at once aroused the population to resistance; and the French, after a loss of 40,000 men by disease and war, and being menaced by a British fleet, were compelled to capitulate, November, 1803, and, with a remnant of the army, of only 8,000 men, beg leave to depart from the island. Dessalines now assumed the authority, and a general massacre of the remaining French inhabitants took place." †

The intellect of the island had disappeared amidst the savage butcheries that occurred, and with it the capacity of the population for productive industry. ‡   Look at the facts as presented in

---

* Confined to a loathsome dungeon, he died the next year.

† See Life of Benjamin Lundy, and also Macgregor, as condensed in "Ethiopia."

‡ The loss of Hayti to France subjected Napoleon to the necessity of furnishing a supply of sugar for the nation. The cultivation of the beet-root was encouraged, and by this means, together with the increased production of cane sugar in the other French islands, the supply was kept up. In 1848, the consumption of sugar in France, of all kinds, was 290,000,000 lbs.; of which 140,000,-000 lbs. were of beet-root sugar produced at home. The emancipation of the slaves in the French islands took place in 1848. In 1840, they produced of cane sugar, 161,500,000 lbs. For the first nine months of 1847, the year preceding emancipation, they supplied 168,884,177 lbs., showing a continuous increase under slavery; but no sooner had emancipation fairly been inaugurated, than, as was the case in the British West India islands, a decrease of cultivation followed, so that for the first nine months of 1849, they supplied only 96,929,336 lbs., being a falling off to the extent of 71,854,841 lbs. in the first nine months of freedom. These results have thrown the French people more and more upon the consumption of beet-root sugar, so that, with a heavy duty on foreign sugars, they at present consume but very little slave-grown sugar.

the relative amounts of the exports, before and after the freedom of the island was secured : *

YEARS.	SUGAR, LBS.	COFFEE, LBS.	COTTON, LBS.	REMARKS.
1789............	141,089,931	76,835,219	7,004,274	Island tranquil.
1790............	163,318,810	68,151,180	6,286,126	Whites & mulatto's at war.
1801............	18,534,112	43,420,270	2,480,340	Slaves freed in 1793.
1818............	5,443,765	26,065,200	474,118	Boyer in power.
1819............	3,790,300	29,240,919	216,103	
1820............	2,517,289	35,137,759	346,839	
1821............	600,934	29,925,951	820,563	
1822............	200,451	24,235,372	592,368	
1823............	14,920	33,802,837	332,256	
1824............	5,106	44,269,084	1,028,045	
1825............	2,020	36,034,300	815,697	
1826............	32,864	32,189,784	620,972	
1835............	1,097	48,352,371	1,649,717	Exports for whole Island.
1836............	16,199	37,662,672	1,072,555	
1837............		30,845,400	1,013,171	
1838............		49,820,241		
1839............		7,889,092	1,635,420	
1840............	741	46,126,272	922,575	Republic declared.
1841............	1,363	34,114,717	1,591,454	
1848............		† 33,600,000		

The independence of Hayti dates from the year 1803. Its population at this time was 348,000, ‡ being 132,000 less than the slave population in 1789. The preceding statistical table exhibits the effects of the freedom of the negroes upon the economical interests of the island in a very suggestive form. The soil, after the revolution, was owned by the blacks themselves, and it had lost none of its fertility; and, yet, the exports soon ran down, in all the articles requiring constant labor, to nearly nothing. Even coffee § which grows almost unaided, suffered an enormous

---

* Macgregor, London Edition, 1847. † Campbell Arnott & Co.

‡ Macgregor, page 1152. The history is given more at large in "Ethiopia."

§ In remarking on the productions of Dominicana, Mr. Harris, in his "Summer on the borders of the Carribeean Sea," explains why it is that the article of Coffee is still exported to a considerable extent, while all other productions have been almost entirely discontinued. "There is some Coffee, which grows wild in abundance through the island and on the mountains, and is collected and shipped. After the abandonment of the Coffee plantations, the trees continued to grow thick on them, and finally spread into the woods and on to the mountains, where they now grow wild in great quantities. Lacking the proper culture, its quality is not the best, but the climate and soil is capable of producing it unexcelled by any in Porto Rico or any of the West Indies or Brazil. The writer is informed, however, that there are a few Coffee plantations under culture about St Domingo City."

diminution. The subsequent history of Hayti is interesting, as illustrating the instability of its government:

" The reign of the first emperor, Dessalines, was short and turbulent, and his designs against the mulattoes cost him his life. After the death of Dessalines, 1807, General Christophe was made chief magistrate, and, in 1811, crowned himself King Henry I. Meanwhile the mulattoes, having cause to distrust him also, elected General Petion to preside in the southwest, which he did to the entire satisfaction of his constituents, by many of whom he is still affectionately remembered. He died in 1818. Christophe shot himself in 1820. In 1822, Boyer, who had been elected President in 1818, united the whole island under his government."

The revolution of 1842, which caused Boyer to flee, placed Reviere in the Presidency. Two years after, the Dominicans overpowered Reviere, and in February, 1844, reëstablished their government, or rather the present government of Dominicana. In 1849, Solouque, the President of Hayti, undertook to reconquer Dominicana, but was defeated by General Santana, its President.* The subsequent history of Hayti is familiar to the intelligent reader. After passing through the farcical scene, under Solouque, of calling itself an empire, with an emperor wearing a royal crown of a half million's value, it is once more revolutionized, and declared a republic, under Geffard. The other portion of the island, Dominicana, has recently been threatened by the Spanish government, and may be permanently reännexed to that crown.

Between 1820 and 1829, a brisk emigration from the United States to Hayti, was conducted, which transferred 8,000 free colored persons to that island; but no good came of it, the moral condition of the population being such, that the emigrants, unsustained by the whites who sent them, soon sunk to the level of the natives.

The standard of morals and intelligence is very low, indeed, in Hayti and Dominicana; but we shall omit the details of facts, here, as not necessary to our purpose. In referring to the ignorance and degradation of the population, we mean no disparage-

---

* These historical statements are mainly derived from a small work, by Mr. J. Dennis Harris, Emigration Agent for Hayti, entitled " A Summer on the borders of the Carribeean Sea," 1860. The author is a respectable colored man.

ment of the African race, in the sense that the Haytiens are to be censured for their ignorance. In Africa the race is barbarous. Under the slavery of St. Domingo, no adequate provision existed for their elevation. Freedom brought with it no institutions of learning for the population in general. Their rulers have been military despots — necessarily so ; — and the youth, like their fathers, have risen into manhood under circumstances that precluded the possibility of progress.

From the best information possessed, it is safe to affirm, that the slaves of the United States are greatly in advance, morally and intellectually, of the free negro population of Hayti. * This assertion will not be disputed; and the fact is not stated to afford an argument in behalf of slavery, but only to illustrate the truth of the position taken by Franklin, that mere emancipation does not necessarily elevate the negro in the scale of humanity. Slavery and freedom are both alike in this respect, where no means of intellectual and moral culture are provided. Consequently, there may be progress under slavery, while the intellect may be at a dead stand-still under freedom. It is in this respect, mainly, that the colored race in the United States have differed so widely from their fellows in all other countries. Limited as the means of improvement may be, which are afforded to the American slave, they are very greatly superior to the advantages enjoyed by an equal number of the blacks in any other portions of the world.

A word of explanation is needed in relation to the present economical interests of Hayti. The amount of its exports, down to 1848, are given on a preceding page. Its total foreign exports, at present, are not accessible, but its traffic with the United States, which is understood to be its principal market, for the year ending June 30, 1860, was as follows : The total value of imports into the United States, from Hayti, was $2,062,723, of which $1,679,657, was for 15,621,751 lbs. of coffee; while the exports to Hayti, from the United States, were, in value, $2,441,905, chiefly provisions. The exports to Dominicana were only $156,054, and the imports from it, $283,098.

* The term "Hayti," is used here to designate the whole Island of St. Domingo.

The effects of emancipation upon Mexico, the South American Republics, and Hayti, in retarding their progress, interrupting their peace, and destroying their prosperity, can now be readily understood by intelligent men.   On this question there is no longer any difference of opinion.

SECTION III. — EFFECTS OF EMANCIPATION IN THE BRITISH WEST INDIA ISLANDS.

As regards the British West Indies, there is, however, considerable difference of opinion, both in Europe and the United States, in relation to the effects of emancipation, and many contradictory statements have appeared.   Generally, the subject has been argued in reference to the economical interests involved — some insisting that emancipation has been an economical failure; others, that it has been an economical success.   The truth can only be discovered by a careful examination of the leading facts, in the history of the British West Indies, under both slavery and freedom.   This we shall proceed to do.

The subject necessarily divides itself into four parts : the productiveness of the islands previous to the suppression of the slave trade in 1808; their productiveness from that date to the passage of the emancipation act in 1833; their productiveness under the apprenticeship system from 1834 to 1838; and their productiveness under freedom from 1839 to the present date, as indicated by the exports.

The statistics can not be obtained for the whole of the British islands, for each one of these periods; for this reason, and because it best represents the results of emancipation, the island of Jamaica is taken.   It is, by far, the largest of the whole group, and has been unaffected by great density of population, or the introduction of coolie labor.   Sugar being the principal production of the island, the exports of that commodity alone are given.   The same degree of reduction occurred as to rum also, which has always been an important article of export.   To save space, the average exports for several years together, in most cases, are presented; but in no instance are the figures so collated, as to give an erroneous impression.   The few years given separately were extraordinary ones, being either above or below the general average:

Exports of Sugar from the Island of Jamaica. *

YEARS.	POUNDS.	YEARS.	POUNDS.
1772 to 1775	123,979,700	1811 alone	218,874,600
1788 to 1791	143,794,837	1812 to 1821	183,706,280
1793 to 1798	145,598,850	1822 to 1832	153,760,431
1799 to 1803	193,781,140	1833 to 1835	131,129,100
1804 alone	177,436,750	1836 alone	75,990,950
1805 alone	237,751,150	1839 to 1843	67,924,800
1806 alone	231,656,650	1846 to 1848	67,539,200
1807 to 1808	197,963,825	1856 to 1858	46,456,592
1809 to 1810	180,963,825	1859 to 1860	

To comprehend the bearing of the foregoing statistics, it must be borne in mind that the slave trade was prohibited in 1808, and all supplies of labor from Africa suspended; that in 1833 the emancipation act was passed, leaving the negroes, after August 1st, 1834, in the condition of apprentices: and, finally, that emancipation was fully effected in 1838, since which the cultivation of the island has depended upon the labor of the negroes alone — no coolies, to any effective extent, having been imported into Jamaica by the planters. The island has thus been dependent upon the emancipated blacks for its cultivation, and has been losing its ability to export, from year to year, until, in the three years ending with 1858, its sugar exportation was reduced to an annual average of 46,456,000 pounds, or more than 191,000,000 pounds less than what it was in 1805. The effect upon the production of cotton was equally disastrous — the exports of that article in 1800 being 17,000,000 pounds, and in 1840 but 427,000 pounds.

Recently, however, a certain class of writers — while admitting that the prosperity of the West India islands had been greatly reduced for some time after emancipation — have represented them as rapidly recovering from their depressed condition; and that they are now exporting a greater amount of products than they had done while slavery prevailed. The AMERICAN MISSION-

---

* These statistics, up to 1836, are taken from a table in Martin's British Colonies, a work of great research, the facts of which are derived from official sources. The exports for 1839 to 1843, and 1846 to 1848, are from the letters of Mr. Bigelow, of the N. Y. Evening Post, in Littell's Living Age, 1850, No. 309, p. 125; and those from 1856 to 1858 are from the London Economist, July 16, 1859.

ARY ASSOCIATION, in its report for 1857, gives currency to the assertion that " they yield more produce than they ever did during the existence of slavery." Mr. C. Buxton, in the *Edinburgh Review*, April, 1859, insists that —

Existing facts "show that slavery was bearing our colonies down to ruin with awful speed; that had it lasted but another half century, they must have sunk beyond recovery.   On the other hand, that now, under freedom and free trade, they are growing day by day more rich and prosperous; with spreading trade, with improving agriculture, with a more educated, industrious, and virtuous people; while the comfort of the quondam slaves is increased beyond the power of words to portray.

" Now all this seems very encouraging; but how such language can be used, without its being considered as flatly contradicting well-known facts, and what the American Missionary Association, Mr. Bigelow, and others, have heretofore said, will seem very mysterious to the reader.   And yet, the assertions quoted would seem to be proved, by taking the aggregate production of the whole British West India islands and Mauritius, * as the index to their commercial prosperity. But if the islands be taken separately, and all the facts considered, a widely different conclusion will be formed, by every candid man, than that the improvement is due to the increased industry of the negroes. On this subject the facts can be drawn from authorities which would scorn to conceal the truth with the design of sustaining a theory of the philanthropist.   This question is placed in its true light by the *London Economist*, July 16, 1859, in which it is shown that the apparent industrial advancement of the islands is due to the importation of immigrants from India, China, and Africa by the ' coolie traffic,' and not to the improved industry of the emancipated negroes.   Says the *Economist*:

" ' We find one of the Emigration Commissioners, Mr. Murdock, † in an interesting memorandum on this subject, giving us the following comparison between the islands which have been recently supplied with immigrants, and those which have

---

* Mauritius is not in the West Indies, as the maps will show, but in the Indian Ocean.

† The statement was made at a meeting which met to consider the evils of the Chinese and coolie system of immigration into the West Indies and Mauritius.

ISLANDS.	NUMBER OF IM-MIGRANTS.	SUGAR, POUNDS. THE 3 YEARS BEFORE IMMI-GRATION.	SUGAR, POUNDS. THE LAST 3 YEARS.
Mauritius............................	209,490	217,200,256	469,812,784
British Guiana..........................	24,946	173,626,208	250,715,584
Trinidad	11,981	91,110,768	150,579,072

"'With these are contrasted the results in Jamaica, where there has been very little immigration. In the three years after apprenticeship, Jamaica produced 202,973,568 pounds of sugar, while in the last three years corresponding to the last column of the above table, the production of sugar was only 139,369,776 pounds.'

"Here, now, is presented the key to the mystery overhanging the British West Indies. Men, high in station, have asserted that West India emancipation has been an economic success; while others, equally honorable, have maintained the opposite view. Both have presented figures, averred to be true, that seemed to sustain their declarations. This apparent contradiction is thus explained. The first take the aggregate production in the whole of the islands, which, they say, exceeds that during the existence of slavery; * the second take the production in Jamaica alone, as representing the whole; and thus the startling fact appears, that the sugar crop of the last three years in Jamaica, has fallen 63,603,000 pounds below what it was during the first three years of freedom. This argues badly for the free negroes; but it must be the legitimate fruits of emancipation, as no exterior force has been brought into that island to interfere, materially, with its workings. In Mauritius, Trinidad, and British Guiana, it will be seen that the production has greatly increased; but from a very different cause than any improvement in the industry of the blacks who had received their freedom — the increase in Mauritius having been more than double what it had been when the production depended upon them. The sugar crop, in this island, for the three years preceding the introduction of immigrant labor, was but 217,200,000 pounds; while, during the last three years, by the aid of 210,000 immigrants, it has been run up to 469,812,000 pounds.

"Taking all these facts into consideration, it is apparent that West India emancipation has been a failure, economically considered. The production in Jamaica, where it has depended upon the labor of the

---

* They must refer to slavery in its later years, after the suppression of the slave trade. Previous to that event, the production of Jamaica was more than 75 per cent. greater than at present.

free blacks alone, has materially declined since the abandonment of slavery, and is not so great now as it was during the first years of freedom ; and, so far is it from being equal to what it was while slavery prevailed, and especially while the slave trade was continued, that it now falls short of the production of that period by an immense amount. In no way, therefore, can it be claimed, that the cultivation of the British West India islands is on the increase, except by resorting to the pious fraud of crediting the produçts of the immigrant labor to the account of emancipation — a resort to which no conscientious Christian man will have recourse, even to sustain a philanthropic theory."

In confirmation of the statements here given, in relation to the falling off in the productions of Jamaica, it is only necessary that the declaration of the Colonial Minister should be given, as it appeared in the *New York Tribune*, and was thence transferred to the *American Missionary*, February, 1859 :

"The Colonial Minister says : ' Jamaica is now the only important sugar-producing colony which exports a considerably smaller quantity of sugar than was exported in the time of slavery, while some such colonies, since the passage of the emancipation act, have largely increased their product.' "

But it is claimed that an exception exists in the island of Barbadoes, the exports of which having been considerably increased without the aid of coolie labor.   As we shall elsewher, refer to this point, it need only be remarked here, that that island is a small one — 22 miles in length by 14 in breadth — and has been very densely populated for the last hundred years.   Its population now numbers about 800 to the square mile. *   When emancipation came, the negroes had no waste land, like their brethren in Jamaica, upon which to squat; but had to remain on the plantations, as the only means of earning their bread. †

These investigations need not be prosecuted any further.   Men of intelligence will no longer claim that any miracle has occurred in the British West Indies, to demonstrate the moral duty and economical advantages of emancipation.   A people degraded like the

* "Cotton is King" gives full particulars on this point.
† London Economist.

blacks of these islands were when liberated, never have become
producers, in agriculture, to an extent much beyond the supply of
their absolute necessities.   They have not done it in the United
States, in Canada, in Mexico, the South American Republics, or
Hayti.   They never will do it as long as the world stands.   They
must be educated before they can rise to the dignity of enlightened
freemen, capable, from their own voluntary industry, of supplying
a large surplus of products to commerce.   Indeed, the apology
offered for the abolition of West India slavery, by prominent
British writers, is no longer based upon the economical benefits
resulting from that measure.   The downward tendency of the productiveness of the islands, where negro labor alone is employed,
is fully admitted ; but the advantages of emancipation, it is now
claimed, exist in the fact that *free labor* can, at present, be introduced to an extent equaling the demands of the owners of estates
— a policy that was impracticable as long as slavery existed.   The
free labor referred to, it is scarcely necessary to add, consists of
imported coolies !   As long as slavery prevailed, say these writers,
free labor could not be introduced, because freemen could not labor
by the side of slaves — the control of the two classes requiring
widely different systems of management.

We repeat a previous remark.   The domestic exports of a country are not always to be taken as a true measure of the personal
comforts or moral progress of its population.   This proposition
has been claimed as having an illustration in the West Indies.
While admitting the diminution of exports, it is asserted that the
comforts of a population are greatly enhanced by the consumption
of an increased amount of their own productions.   On this question, however, some dispute has arisen.   As the utmost fairness is
the author's aim, no other testimony, to any considerable extent,
than that of anti-slavery men, will be used on this point, nor shall
even that be extensively paraded.

Mr. BIGELOW, of the *New York Evening Post*, spent a winter in
Jamaica, and became well acquainted with its condition and prospects.   Since his return, he has still watched the progress of
events in the island with anxious solicitude.   In reviewing the
returns published by the Jamaica House of Assembly, in 1853, in
reference to the ruinous decline in the agriculture of the island,

and stating the enormous quantity of lands thrown out of cultivation, since 1848, the *Post* said :

" This decline has been going on from year to year, daily becoming more alarming, until at length the island has reached what would appear to be the last profound of distress and misery, ... when thousands of people do not know, when they rise in the morning, whence or in what manner they are to procure bread for the day."

The *London Times*, of about the same date, in speaking of the results of emancipation in Jamaica, says :

" The negro has not acquired, with his freedom, any habits of industry or morality.   His independence is but little better than that of an uncaptured brute.   Having accepted few of the restraints of civilization, he is amenable to few of its necessities ; and the wants of his nature are so easily satisfied, that at the current rate of wages, he is called upon for nothing but fitful or desultory exertion.   The blacks, therefore, instead of becoming intelligent husbandmen, have become vagrants and squatters, and it is now apprehended that with the failure of cultivation in the island will come the failure of its resources for instructing or controlling its population.   So imminent does this consummation appear, that memorials have been signed by classes of colonial society hitherto standing aloof from politics, and not only the bench and the bar, but the bishop, clergy, and ministers of all denominations in the island, without exception, have recorded their conviction, that, in the absence of timely relief, the religious and educational institutions of the island must be abandoned, and the masses of the population retrogade to barbarism."

The remedy for the existing evils, as proposed by prominent British writers, is to force the free colored people into habits of greater industry by the introduction of coolie labor.   The *London Economist* recently said :

" We have always been warm advocates of the coolie immigration into the West Indies.   We are convinced that by no other plan can the population of these fertile islands be increased up to the high-pressure point at which alone Africans can be induced to labor hard. Barbadoes is the only highly successful island among our West India colonies, because Barbadoes is so fully peopled that the negroes are compelled to work for their subsistence, and to work hard.   We can not lay too great stress, as Mr. Buxton wisely said, on the duty of aiding the overflowing population of China and India to fill up the vacuum in our West India colonies. We know now this can be done without inhumanity and with the greatest advantage to both the coolie and the English planter. And it is the part of common sense and good judgment to do it as effectually as we have already done it in the Mauritius, and as speedily as possible."*

This, then, is the remedy proposed for saving the British islands from the effects of emancipation. The negro will not work voluntarily. The whip must no longer be applied to compel him to do so; but work he must, or British trade and commerce and British revenues will suffer. Experience has suggested the remedy. The negroes of Barbadoes "work hard," because where 800 men have to gain a subsistence from the space of 640 acres of land, they must work in earnest or *starve ;* and they must labor, too, according to some efficient system, devised by intelligence, or, even then, a subsistence can not be gained from the soil. The proposition is, that the other islands shall be rendered productive, as Barbadoes was during the prevalence of the slave trade, by crowding them with laborers. It is proposed that they, too, shall be over-populated, so as to keep the inhabitants constantly at the starvation point; and thus instead of prompting them to action, as under slavery, by the "beneficent whip," to force them into industry, as freemen, by the philanthropic application of *hunger !*

Such are the measures deemed necessary, by British writers, to remedy the evils growing out of the benevolence of Great Britain toward the African race ! She resolved that the negroes should no longer be coerced into industrious habits, and now she is compelled to starve them to it, otherwise her own people at home must be brought to suffering for want of the productions which they can supply.

The injurious effects of African emancipation, upon the national prosperity of the Caucasians, can now be comprehended.

---

* London Economist, 1861.

CHAPTER V.

SECTION I.—GENERAL CONDITION OF THE BRITISH WEST INDIA ISLANDS AT THIS MOMENT.

SINCE the completion of the foregoing chapters, the work of WILLIAM G. SEWELL, ESQ.,—"The Ordeal of Free Labor in the West Indies,"—has been laid before us.* There had long been much of mystery overhanging the free labor systems of the British West Indies. Mr. Sewell has turned aside the vail more fully than any other writer consulted, and has given the public a candid statement of facts which came under his own observation. But he looks at everything from the "free soil" and "free labor" point of view; so that, though he finds ruin overwhelming the planters, and many grievous evils existing among the blacks, he yet claims that they are not the results of emancipation, or if they are, that even death is preferable to slavery.

Beginning with BARBADOES, he says: "It must be borne in mind, that, protected by her small area, and dense population— a population larger to the square mile than that of China—Barbadoes, since emancipation, has not suffered for the want of labor like other colonies. To this cause more, perhaps, than to any other, she owes her present wonderful prosperity."†

In another paragraph, the author explains the mode by which the planters secure the labor of the free negroes:

"At the time of emancipation the slaves were left in possession of their houses and allotment lands, which they continued to occupy after

---

* Mr. Sewell traveled in the West Indies as correspondent for the *New York Times.*   † Sewell, page 31.

their term of apprenticeship had expired. In Barbadoes the tenant
worked for the landlord at twenty per cent. below the common market
rate, and his service was taken as an equivalent for rent. But the
practice produced endless difficulties and disagreements; the law did
not bear out the planter, and another system was introduced. Under
the new practice, still in force, a laborer has a house and land allotment on an estate for which he pays a stipulated rent; but he is under
an engagement besides, *as a condition of renting*, to give to the estate
a certain number of days' labor, at certain stipulated wages, varying
from one-sixth to one-third less than the market price. The rate of
wages for field labor, in Barbadoes, is about twenty-four cents per day;
but the laborer, fettered by the system of tenancy-at-will, is compelled
to work for his landlord at twenty cents per day. *He is, therefore, virtually a slave;* for if he resists the conditions of his bond, he is ejected by
summary process, and loses the profit he hoped to reap on his little stock."[*]

But why should freemen submit to such exactions? The reason
is explained in a subsequent paragraph:

"I must again repeat that Barbadoes offers a solitary exception to
the general argument. The population here, as I have said, is extremely
dense, averaging eight hundred persons to the square mile, and partly
from an aversion of the negro to leave his home, partly from his fear,
still easily excited, of being sold into slavery, no material emigration
from the island has ever taken place. In Barbadoes, therefore, labor
has been always abundant, and the island, which out of 106,000 acres
has 100,000 under cultivation, presents the appearance of a perfect
garden. Land, as I shall hereafter show, averages $500 an acre; and
when it is added that the land which brings such a price is purchased
for agricultural purposes only, we have, in the fact, conclusive evidence
of most remarkable prosperity. All this, practically considered, is
owing, in a greater degree, to an adequate laboring population, than to
the special benefits of abolition, as illustrated in an anti-slavery society's
annual report. But no credit is due to the Barbadian plantocracy for
retaining that adequate laboring population in their employ. *To the
latter it was the option of work at low wages, and on most illiberal
terms, or starvation.*"[†]

Again, on this point, Mr. Sewell says: "Barbadoes is so thickly
inhabited that work or *starvation* is the only choice."[‡]   And again,

---

* Sewell, page 31.   † Ibid., page 33.   ‡ Ibid., page 106.

in contrasting the free negroes of Jamaica with those of Barbadoes, he says : " I do maintain, without any hesitation, that the creole of Jamaica works as diligently as the creole of Barbadoes; but with this difference—that the former works for himself, while the latter works only for a master—that the work of the one is more profitable because it is well-directed and economized, while the work of the other is less profitable because it is ill-directed and wasted."*

From these statements, there is no escaping the conclusion, that emancipation, while giving a nominal freedom to the blacks, has really left the population almost as much in the power of the planter as it was under slavery. And, yet, after saying all that has been quoted, when, in another place, the author comes to compare Cuba, Jamaica, and Barbadoes, he says :

" Barbadoes offers the most perfect example of free labor, and of the capacity and willingness of the African to work under a free system."†
. . . . " Now Barbadoes is a living proof that the negroes do work under a free system."‡ . . . " The doctrine of emancipation, that free labor is cheaper than slave labor, is proved to demonstration."§

ANTIGUA, with 70,000 acres of land, of which 58,000 acres are owned by large proprietors, was found by emancipation in a similar position, as regards density of population, with Barbadoes. The planters in Antigua dictate the terms of labor, like those of Barbadoes, and pay even less wages than those of the former island. " In Antigua, a field laborer scarcely earns, on an average, twenty cents per diem ; in Barbadoes, he earns from twenty-two to twenty-five cents ; and in Trinidad, he earns thirty cents."||

The present population of Barbadoes is estimated at 140,000.¶ Sugar is the principal production. Its exports, for a series of years, are given thus :**

1720 to 1800, annual average	....	....	23,000 hhds.
1800 to 1830,	"	"	.... 20,000 "
1835 to 1850,	"	"	.... 26,000 "
1851 to 1858,	"	"	.... 43,000 "

* Sewell, page 273. † Ibid., p. 272. ‡ Ibid., p. 273.
§ Ibid., p. 273. || Ibid., page 146. ¶ Ibid., p. 60.
** Ibid., pp. 62–3. *Note.*—From 1826 to 1830, the average weight of a hogshead was 12 cwt.; from 1830 to 1850, 14 cwt.; and is now from 15 to 16, and even 17 cwt.

In 1858, alone, the exports were 50,778 hhds., being the largest crop ever produced in the island, and more than twice as much as the annual average exports from 1800 to 1830, during most of which time the slave trade was forbidden and hence, no supply of labor obtained from that source. From 1720 to 1808, the slave trade prevailed, and the exports, consequently, were larger. This was the result in all the islands—a diminution of production following the suppression of the slave trade. In Barbadoes and Antigua, alone, has any increased production, to any considerable extent, followed emancipation. In these islands only, the overcrowded state of the population leaves the laborers under the necessity of submitting to starvation or engaging in work for the planters. For this reason these two islands are naturally grouped together in these investigations. Barbadoes being the larger island, and its crowded condition having enabled it to export more sugar under freedom than under slavery, it has been cited as a triumphant proof that free labor is more productive than slave labor; and many, without examination, have accepted the fact as the grandest truth of the nineteenth century.

But let us see what will become of this boasting about the superiority of free labor, by contrasting its productiveness with that of the slave labor in the United States. The exports of Barbadoes, given above, begin with 1720 and end with 1858. Sugar is the principal article of growth in Barbadoes, and cotton in the United States. The home consumption of each may be left out of view, and the exports alone given in contrast. Cotton, however, was not an article of regular export until 1791.

We must commence, therefore, with that date, and take it at regular intervals of ten years to the present date—except as to additions of a year or two as explanatory. The amounts are given in pounds:

YEAR.		YEAR.	
1791	189,316	1840	743,941,061
1800	17,789,803	1849	1,026,602,269
1810	93,900,000	1850	* 635,381,604
1820	127,800,000	1859	1,372,755,006
1830	298,459,102	1860	1,767,686,339

* The crop of 1850 was a short one.

The contrast between the rate of increase here and in the sugar statistics of Barbadoes, must put an end to all boasting. Here the reader sees what can be done by a slave population, well fed, well housed, and with proper medical attendance. The slave trade furnishes no aid here, nor has Coolie labor lent a hand, and yet the increase is enormous. It will not do any longer to attempt to impose upon an intelligent public the oft-repeated tale — as applicable to the negro race — that free labor is more productive than slave labor. The negro question can not at present be argued on that principle; and it never should have been placed upon that ground.

From the industrial we turn to the moral condition of the island. On this subject, Mr. Sewell presents a horrible picture of degradation:

"I can not speak as highly of the morality of the laboring population of Barbadoes as I can of their industry. The clergy may publish church and school statistics, which, I admit, go to show that scholars and churchmen multiply. But statistics on such subjects are not of much importance when they run counter to common every-day experience. To prove that the vicious put on a religious demeanor with their Sunday coat, and will listen patiently to a tedious, incomprehensible sermon, only makes the case worse. It is shown that since emancipation the higher crimes are less frequently committed than they were before. Crimes of violence are almost unknown, and in the streets, thanks to efficient police regulations, the most perfect order is preserved; but crimes of calculation, thieving, swindling, and the minor vices, have apparently increased. I speak from prison statistics; and it must be borne in mind that over a large number, if not all, of these offenses the planter formerly had exclusive jurisdiction, and they were never known beyond the precincts of his own estate. It is, therefore, unfair to make any deductions from the criminal records of the present day, and compare them with those of the past, when no just comparison can be instituted. But I have seen exhibitions of unrestrained passion, of cruelty, and of vice, to which, in a state of slavery, the negro would never be permitted to give vent. I have seen parents beat their children in such an inhuman manner as to make me feel that liberty to them was a curse to all over whom they were allowed to exercise any authority or control. I am speaking now of what is the rule rather than the exception among the lowest class of the negro population. Among their other vices, immorality and promiscuous intercourse of the sexes are almost universal. From the last census, it appears that more than half of the children born in Barbadoes are illegitimate.[*]

"Against the middle class—as a class—the imputation of unfaithfulness to the marriage vow could not be maintained; but among the laboring people, morality, not now through ignorance and compulsion, but from choice, remains at the lowest ebb. I leave the reader to draw what inference he pleases from such a state of things. I simply report facts. But it seems to me that the moral grounds of the abolitionist for removing the restrictions of slavery, are, in Barbadoes, at least, the very worst that could be selected. Morality has not kept pace with material progress. Making every allowance for the influence of climate, there is still no palliation for such a superabundance of vice."[†]

On the subject of education, it is remarked: "Education in Barbadoes is confined to those who have the means to pay for the luxury of knowledge; and though statistics show a marked progress since the date of emancipation, it is rather the progress of a class than of the whole population. . . . . But all the schools are under church influence, and are necessarily imbued with church prejudices; and were education on such a system much more extended than it really is, one would scarcely look for any wholesome diffusion of popular instruction."[‡]

In relation to social customs, it is said: "The distinctions of caste are more strictly observed in Barbadoes than in any other British West India colony. No person, male or female, with the slightest taint of African blood, is admitted to white society. No matter what the standing of a father, his influence can not secure for his colored offspring the social *status* that he himself occupies; and the rule is more rigidly carried out among women than it is among men. The amalgamation of the two races is, nevertheless, very general, and illicit intercourse is sanctioned, or at least winked at, by a society which utterly condemns and abhors a marriage between two people of different colors. . . . . The amalgamation of the African and Anglo-Saxon, and the exclusiveness of the latter, have thus combined to build up the half-castes, and make them somewhat of a distinct people—a people neither African nor European, but more properly West Indian. This class—the middle

---

[*] Sewell, p. 41.   [†] Ibid., p. 42.   [‡] Ibid., 42.

class—is already very large and intelligent, and is rapidly increasing. It is composed of small landed proprietors, of business men, clerks in public and private establishments, editors, tradesmen, and mechanics."*

In addition to the exports of sugar from Barbadoes and Antigua, it is claimed that many minor productions are now exported which were not cultivated during slavery; and that, therefore, the foreign goods consumed in the islands is a better index to the actual prosperity and comfort of the population. Judged by this rule, the following results are presented: "Turning now to the imports of Barbadoes, I find that their average annual value, from 1822 to 1832, was about £600,000 sterling. In 1845, the imports amounted in value to £682,358 sterling; and in 1856, to £840,000, of which about £640,000 were consumed in the islands."†

As no intimation is given of any re-exports having been made in 1822 to 1832, of the foreign imported articles, we are at a loss to know whether the whole of the importations of that date were consumed in the islands; if so, then the present consumption is an increase of only £40,000 on that of the former period.

In Antigua, from 1822 to 1832, the average annual value of imports was £130,000 sterling; and in 1858, £266,364—being more than double its former imports. ‡

The educational progress of Antigua has been more favorable than in Barbadoes. "It further appears that education has raised the standard of morality in Antigua. Marriages are much more frequent than they used to be, and concubinage is discountenanced. The number of illegitimate births averages 53 per cent. In some other islands, it exceeds 100 per cent." §

The middle and lower classes, in Antigua, are entirely excluded from the polls by a high property qualification, thus leaving all legislation exclusively in the hands of the whites.‖ The population of this island equals three hundred and eighteen to the square mile.¶ The black population, for twenty years past, has diminished at the rate of a half per cent. per annum, although

---

* Sewell, p. 68.   † Ibid., p. 63.   ‡ Ibid., p. 145.
§ Sewell, p. 143.   ‖ Ibid., p. 150.   ¶ Ibid., p. 152.

the island is remarkably healthy. The mortality is greater now than in the days of slavery; and the mortality is less on estates, at present, than it is in the villages where the laborers reside on their own lands.* In Barbadoes, the census returns are not very satisfactory, but no material increase has taken place there since emancipation;† so, then, it would appear, that a decrease of population is the law of freedom in the West Indies—the other islands, mainly, as it will be seen, having also suffered a diminution of population. This result, we are told, has arisen from the fact, that "the life of a field laborer has been made so distasteful to the peasant that the possession of half an acre, or the most meager subsistence and independence, seem to him, in comparison with estate service, the very acme of luxurious enjoyment."‡

One fact must be noted here. The plantation labor required of these blacks is, with a slight difference in wages, exactly what the Coolie, in other islands, accepts as a munificent inheritance; and what Mr. Sewell, as we shall see, considers one of the most beneficent schemes for the civilization of the Pagans of the East Indies who may be transferred to the West Indies.

From all the facts before us, we must conclude, that emancipation, in Barbadoes and Antigua, has utterly failed in producing the favorable results anticipated from that measure by the English philanthropists. They never conceived it possible that, under the freedom they were conferring, the black population of these islands would be forced to labor for the planters or starve, and that their condition, instead of being improved, would be virtually that of slaves. Much less did they look to emancipation as resulting in a decrease of population, threatening the ultimate extinction of the African race in the islands, and creating a demand for the transfer of other laborers from abroad, to prevent the estates from being rendered useless. Nothing at all of this was anticipated, as will be evident by a perusal of the book of the good Mr. Gurney, describing what he saw in the West India Islands soon after emancipation. With the light of time cast in full blaze upon the British scheme of abolition, no

---

* Sewell, pp. 154, 156. † Ibid., pp. 60, 61. ‡ Ibid., p. 154

one can now read the book of Mr. Gurney without marveling how one so good could be so credulous.

But we must pass on to the other islands, and see how far they meet, or fail in meeting, British expectation, as to the results of emancipation. And first, of the smaller British West India Islands. In noticing this class of islands, the references will be limited to the points of importance in the investigation on hand.

ST. VINCENT and her GRENADINE dependencies, which, before emancipation, exported, on an average, 25,000,000 lbs. sugar, now export only 16,000,000 or 17,000,000 lbs.* The population of St. Vincent, in 1831, amounted to 27,000, and now stands at 30,000.† This estimate is for 1859, so that, in twenty-eight years, there has been an increase of population amounting to only 3,000, or a little over one hundred per annum; whereas, if the increase had been equal to that of the slaves in the United States, it would have been more than seven hundred a year, and the population now have been doubled. "There are now encouraging prospects that, even in the cultivation of sugar, St. Vincent will soon be restored to its former prosperity. The island has already made preparations for the importation of Coolie labor."‡ The cultivation and export of minor products has increased; but the imports of foreign products, as indicating increasing comforts in living, are not given. "Out of a population of 30,000, there is an average church-attendance of 8,000. There is little provision for educational purposes, and no effort was made to enlighten the people until 1857, when the legislature established a board of education. In that year, the school-attendance was about 2,000."§

GRENADA, which exported 22,000,000 lbs. of sugar before emancipation, now exports something less than half that amount.|| The decline, in Grenada, commenced as far back as 1776. "The total population of Grenada is now about 33,000, an increase of three or four thousand over the population of 1827."¶ "Grenada has taken the lead of St. Vincent in the importation of Coolie la-

---

* Sewell, p. 75.   † Ibid., p. 79.   ‡ Ibid., p. 82.
§ Sewell, p. 81. || Ibid., p. 75.   ¶ Ibid., p. 86.

borers."* In 1857, the imports amounted to £109,000,† against
£78,000, £73,000, and £77,000, during the years immediately
preceding emancipation.‡ "The average church-attendance
throughout the island was, in 1857, over 8,000, against 7,000
before emancipation; but the school-attendance is comparatively
small, being only 1,600. Education, among the creoles of Grenada, has been, up to this time, at a very low ebb, for it has been
looked upon with jealousy and distrust."§ . . . .

TOBAGO, in 1819, had 15,470 registered slaves; in 1832, there
were but 12,091, while the number, including non-effectives, for
whom compensation was claimed by Tobago proprietors, was only
10,500. The present estimated population is 15,674, of which
one hundred and sixty are whites. The production of sugar, in
this island, is now from three to four thousand hogsheads, against
seven thousand some twenty-five years ago.|| The average
church-attendance, in Tobago, is large, being forty-one per cent.
of the entire population. There is an average school-attendance
of 1,600.¶

ST. LUCIA, in 1816, had 16,285 registered slaves, and in 1836,
the number was reduced to 13,291. The population is now 25,-
307, of whom nine hundred and fifty-eight are whites. The sugar
exports of St. Lucia, in 1857, amounted to 6,261,875 lbs. against
an average yearly export of from three to five millions before
emancipation. The *Metairée* system prevails in this island, and
is productive of favorable results—the profits of the production
being divided with the laborer, and tenancy-at-will being dis-
pensed with.**

DOMINICA, prior to emancipation, had a population of 18,650,
and in 1844, the last census, it had 22,220—there being included
in the number eight hundred and fifty whites. In 1858, this isl-
and exported 6,262,841 lbs. sugar, against an annual average of
6,000,000 lbs. before emancipation. The total imports, in 1858,
were valued at £84,906, against an average of £62,000 for five

* Sewell, p. 89.
† Mr. Sewell's book has it marked $, which must be an error.
‡ Sewell, p. 89.   § Ibid., p. 87. || Ibid., p. 90.
¶ Ibid., p. 91.   ** Ibid., pp. 92, 93.

years preceding emancipation. About 2,600 children, on an average, receive instruction in the different schools.*

NEVIS, in 1830, had a population of 9,250, and has now 9,570. In 1858, this island exported 4,400,000 lbs. of sugar, against an annual average of 5,000,000 lbs. before emancipation. More than two-thirds of the population, between the ages of five and fifteen, are receiving instruction.†

MONTSERRAT, at present, has a population of 7,033, being a decrease of some 300 on the population of 1828. The exports of sugar from this island, in 1858, were 1,308,720 lbs., against an annual average of 1,840,000 lbs. prior to emancipation. "The value of imports, in 1858, was £17,844; and between this figure and the average value of imports before emancipation, there appears to be no marked variance." ‡

ST. KITTS, according to the census of 1858, has a population of 20,741; and seems to have decreased nearly 3,000 since 1830. In 1858, this island exported 9,853,309 lbs. of sugar, against an annual average of 12,000,000 lbs. before emancipation. There are 2,704 scholars receiving instruction in the schools. §

The British VIRGIN ISLANDS have a population of 5,053 persons; but the statistics of their former numbers are not given. Most of them are rocky islets, unsuited to cultivation. Tortola is their capital. The islands annually export stock, sheep and goats, lime, charcoal, salt, vegetables, some five or six thousand pounds of cotton, and about two hundred thousand pounds of sugar. The vessels that visit these islands are of inferior tonnage, and their principal trade is with St. Thomas.

The foregoing statements include the number of the population, the amount of exports, and the amount of imports, as far as given, for the several islands named, together with the church and school-attendance, wherever it is given by Mr. Sewell. The following tabular statement of the exports and the population of the several islands, before and after emancipation, places the figures in contrast, and affords a true idea of the facts. The highest estimates of Mr. Sewell are taken, and the islands only included which are complete in their statistics :

* Sewell, p. 161. † Ibid., p. 162. ‡ Ibid., pp. 162, 163. § Ibid., p. 163.

ISLANDS.	EXP'TS BEFORE EMANCIPATION.	PRESENT EXPORTS.	POPULATION BEFORE EMANC.	PRESENT POPULATION.
St. Vincents, etc............lbs.	25,000,000	17,000,000	27,000	30,000
Grenada ....lbs.	22,000,000	11,000,000	29,000	33,000
St. Lucia ....lbs.	5,000,000	6,261,875	....	....
Dominica...................lbs.	6,000,000	6,262,841	18,650	22,220
Nevis.......................lbs.	5,000,000	4,400,000	9,250	9,570
Montserrat.................lbs.	1,840,000	1,308,720	7,333	7,033
St. Kitts ....lbs.	12,000,000	9,883,309	23,700	20,741
	76,840,000	56,116,745	114,933	122,564

Another point needs examination here. The increased consumption of foreign imported goods is given by Mr. Sewell, as indicating, in dollars and cents, the increased comfort of the free population at present, as compared with the deprivation to which, while in slavery, it was subjected. The islands only are given for which the statistics are complete. The recent imports are for 1857 and 1858:

ISLANDS.	IMPORTS BEFORE EMANCIP.	POPULAT'N BEFORE EMANCIP.	IMPORTED COMFORTS PER HEAD.	IMPORTS AT PRESENT.	POPULA-TION AT PRESENT.	IMPORTED COMFORTS PER HEAD.
Grenada, average 3 yrs...	$380,000	29,000	$13.10	$545,000	33,000	$16.51
Dominica, " 5 " ...	300,000	18,650	16.08	422,530	22,220	19.01
Nevis, " 10 " ...	142,500	9,250	15.40	183,505	9,570	19.06
Montserrat.................	89,220	10,000	8.92	89,220	7,033	12.68

Here, now, are the facts. The foreign imports into these islands, immediately preceding emancipation — that is, during the last years of slavery — equaled in value an average of $13.37 per head, for the whole population, white and black; now, under freedom and free labor, the imports have risen to $16.81 — being an increase of barely $3.44 per head. That is to say, emancipation has brought to each individual, providing an equal division be made, the means of increasing his comforts yearly, beyond what he enjoyed under slavery, to the extent of less than *three and a half dollars!*

But, even this, small as it is, would be very encouraging as a beginning, were it not for certain other existing facts. By referring to the table of figures immediately preceding the last one, it will be seen that there has been a decrease in the population of two of them, and a very small increase in a third, while the other three have fallen very far short of the ordinary rate of increase in populations comfortably fed and housed.   Taking this tendency to decrease in the black population, and their probable consequent extinction in the future, into account, and adding thereto the wretchedly meager increase of their means of procuring comforts under freedom, it is impossible to come to the conclusion that emancipation, in these smaller islands, has been a success at all approximating what was expected by the British people.

Mr. Sewell, however, comes to a different conclusion, viewing the matter from his stand-point; and to this theory of his we shall refer again.   In the meantime, we shall proceed to another of the British islands.

TRINIDAD, says Mr. Sewell,

" Has been surnamed the Indian Paradise, and as far as external beauty may entitle it to pre-eminence, it is magnificently pre-eminent in this Western Archipelago.   In point of size — containing over 2,000 square miles — Trinidad is the largest British West India island after Jamaica; and, in positional importance, from its proximity to the Venezuelan coast, it is only second to Cuba. . . . . The whole island, in its physical character, is one of the most beautiful that it is possible to imagine. . . . . With only a present population of 70,000 or 80,000 souls, Trinidad can sustain a million.*   Its soil is of exceeding richness, and of the million and a quarter acres which cover its surface, twenty-nine thirtieths are fit for cultivation.   Its resources are immense.   Every product of the tropics, and many fruits and vegetables of the temperate regions, can be grown here; and a laboring population is only wanted to develop the wealth that lies hidden in forests tenanted still by some scattered representatives of the ancient Carib.   The island, as I shall hereafter show, is fast receiving that laboring population; and, since the immigration of Indian coolies commenced, it has sprung from a condition of hopeless lethargy into one of activity and life — an example and a guide to the other colonies. Within the last few years, the extension of sugar cultivation has been very great, and the improvement still goes on." †

It seems, then, that Trinidad, notwithstanding its great natural

---

* Some estimates place the population at 100,000.   † Sewell, p. 101.

advantages, had sunk into a condition of " hopeless lethargy,"
under emancipation, and that it was only aroused into "activity
and life " by the introduction of coolie labor.   But Mr. Sewell
must be allowed to describe its condition more fully :

"Cotton, coffee, and tobacco can all be cultivated in Trinidad ; but
the first two could not, by any possibility, be made as profitable to the
planter as sugar, and the cultivation of the last is not encouraged."*
"There have been imported into the colony, during the last thirteen
years, about 18,000 Eastern laborers — principally coolies — a population which is fast giving to the island its only want, a laboring class.†
. . . . Trinidad, even under slavery, never had anything like an
adequate laboring population.   Barbadoes is so thickly inhabited that
work or starvation is the laborer's only choice.   In Trinidad, land is
exceedingly rich, plentiful, and cheap, while labor is scarce and extrav-
agantly high ;‡ in Barbadoes, land is dear, and labor is comparatively
cheap.   So that it is impossible to make the case of Barbadoes applicable, in any one particular, to Trinidad, or *vice versâ*.   The only similarity between the two islands is, that sugar forms the staple production of both ; and that both have been successful, though from very
different causes, under a free-labor system."

That is to say, Barbadoes secures to itself a plentiful supply
of labor, by making work or starvation the laborer's only choice ;
Trinidad secures to itself an increase of labor, not from the free
negroes of the island, but by the importation of coolies.

The island of Trinidad was originally settled by the Spanish,
and came into the possession of the English, by conquest, in 1797.

"The majority of the people of Trinidad are negroes and half-castes.
They include creoles of this and other islands, brought here in the days
of slavery and since ; native Africans imported as free laborers from
Sierra Leone ; Africans taken from captured slavers ; and a few hundred liberated slaves, who emigrated to this island, about sixteen years
ago, from the United States.   Many of these people are nearly, and
some are perfectly white, and the census, probably from the fear of
giving offense, does not classify the population according to color.   For
convenience sake, I shall speak of all the colored inhabitants of the

---

* Sewell, p. 101   † Ibid. 106.   ‡ The wages are 30 cents per day.

island as creoles of African descent. Their number, according to the best information I can obtain, is in the neighborhood of 50,000. On looking back to the period immediately preceding emancipation, we find the total number of slaves to have been 21,000, and the free colored about 16,000. Of the former class not more than 11,000 were field laborers. To-day, the number of Trinidadian creoles, attached to sugar and cacao estates, is not more than 5,000."*

To remedy this defect in labor, and extricate themselves from their difficulties, the planters encouraged inter-colonial immigration, by giving bounties for every laborer brought by captains of vessels to Trinidad. Immigrants were also obtained from the United States and Africa. The total importation of negroes, (including creoles from other islands,) Africans, and Americans, amounts to 20,000; and if they could have been retained, says Mr. Sewell, "they, with the creole laborers of Trinidad, would have sufficed at least for immediate want. But many of them returned home; others bought land for themselves, or engaged in trade, or as domestics; and the remnant of this immigration, and of the native Trinidad laboring force, now working on the sugar and cacao properties, does not exceed 13,000 estate and day laborers."†

Here we get some light to explain the causes operating to produce an increase of exports from Trinidad. Under slavery, there were not more than 11,000 slaves employed as field laborers. The coolies imported, during the last thirteen years, amount to 18,000. Add these to the 13,000 Trinidad laboring forces of all classes, and it gives 31,000 at present, against 11,000 previous to emancipation — an increased laboring force of nearly two-thirds!

With all this additional labor, the results are as follows: "Statistics show conclusively that the increase is principally, if not wholly, due to the importation of foreign labor, for it is only since the importation was commenced in earnest that the improvement is to be noticed."‡ The exports, before and after the introduction of coolies, stood thus, as given by Mr. Sewell:

---

* Sewell, pp. 107, 108.　　† Ibid., pp. 117, 118, 119.　　‡ Ibid., p. 138.

YEARS.	BEFORE IMMIGRATION.	hhds.	YEARS.	AFTER IMMIGRATION.	hhds.
1842		20,506	1854		27,987
1843		24,088	1855		31,693
1844		21,800	1856		34,411
1845		25,399	1857		35,523
			1858		37,000

" The highest average exportation before emancipation, during the same number of years, was 25,000 hhds. of very inferior weight, not equal to 20,000 hhds. of the present day."*

The island, it must be remembered, only came into the possession of England eleven years before the prohibition of the slave trade. In 1783, fourteen years previous to its capture by Great Britain, it had a population of only 2,763, of whom 2,032 were Indians. In 1793, the population had increased to 17,718, of whom 10,009 were slaves.† Trinidad, unlike the other British West Indian islands, had not a sufficient slave-labor force to give any great productiveness to the island before 1808, when the prohibition of the slave trade prevented any further supply. This will account for the inferiority of the exports of the island under slavery, as compared with the other islands.

The necessity for continuous labor, in Trinidad, is thus accounted for by Mr. Sewell:

" Perhaps in no island was impending ruin, consequent upon emancipation, so glaring, so palpable, so apparently certain, as it was in Trinidad after the liberation of the slaves. Unlike other Carribean Islands, the seasons in Trinidad are purely tropical, divided into rainy and dry. The latter only lasts five months, and if the planter has not completed his crop operations by the 1st of June, his loss is certain and irremediable. For this reason, steady labor in Trinidad, during crop season, was and is of paramount importance, and the planters had every reason to be alarmed that, in this island, above all others, the effect of emancipation would be to deprive them of that continuous labor with which they were so scantily supplied. . . . The laborers, as soon as they were free, asked, and for a time received, higher wages than the planters, incumbered as their property was by debt,

---

* Sewell, pp. 138, 139.   † Ibid., p. 105.

could afford to pay; and when this rate of wages was subsequently reduced, the majority of the emancipated deserted the estates to better their condition, and to seek a more independent livelihood. . . . . Instead of endeavoring to promote a good understanding between themselves and their laborers, the planters adopted, and still retain, in Trinidad, the odious system of tenancy-at-will. The laborer who lives on an estate is compelled to work for that estate, and no other, on peril of summary ejection, with consequent loss of the crop which he has raised on his little allotment. He is still in a position of *virtual slavery*, and it is a matter which can excite no surprise that, after emancipation, those who had the means to purchase parcels of ground, should have preferred to leave the estates.* . . . They accordingly did leave the estates; and, in a few years after abolition, the majority of the entire laboring force—itself always inadequate to the wants of the large and rapidly developing colony — were lost to the proprietary. Several estates, for want of necessary labor, were deserted, and, at one time, it seemed probable that sugar cultivation, in Trinidad, would be altogether abandoned."†

About 4,000 of the liberated creoles remained on the cacao estates, but very few of them on the sugar plantations. The 7,000 who left the estates, Mr. Sewell believes, have very materially improved their condition—five-sixths of them having become proprietors of from one to ten acres, which they now own, and which they grow in provisions for themselves and families. To supply their other wants, they give casual labor to the estates, especially in crop time.‡ Those who forsook the field for trade, Mr. S. says, by joining themselves to the free creoles of the island, have formed an extensive class engaged in mercantile and mechanical pursuits—from keeping a store down to selling a sixpence worth of mangoes in the streets—and, by bringing up their children to these callings, have given an excess of traders and mechanics to the island. In several instances, great success has attended their efforts at money-making.§

Throughout all his remarks, Mr. Sewell is disposed to apolo-

---

* In another place, where a fuller statement is made, Mr. Sewell says that a portion of the liberated slaves squatted on the public lands belonging to the crown.

† Sewell, p. 110.   ‡ Ibid., p. 111.   § Ibid., p. 113.

gize for the free negro, and to defend him from the charge of
indolence—attributing the ruin of the island to the mismanagement of the planters, and not to emancipation. Here, however,
he makes a statement, explanatory, which relieves the planter
from the charge of being a hard task-master: " It is true that
the Trinidad planter exacts no rent from the laborer on his
estate, and supplies him with medical attendance; but the laborer, in return, is compelled to work for the estate alone, and
for five cents a day less than the current rate of wages. It may
be urged, with truth, that house-rent and medical attendance are
worth more than five cents a day; but for these privileges the
laborer is required to give up his independence, and I do not
think it natural that even the negro should, of his own free
choice, prefer the exchange."*

The industrious and intelligent laborer never imagines he has
lost his independence because his employer requires the fulfillment of his contracts. It is only the indolent who are restless
under voluntary engagements, and are disposed to break away
from regular industry to lead lives of desultory labor, for the
sake of independence. Judged by this rule, the negroes can not
take the first rank as laborers.

But, with their emancipation—with their release from the
shackles of slavery—with the liberty of going hither and thither
at will—with the enjoyment of the most unbounded freedom—
have the Trinidad negroes made any moral progress? This is,
after all, the great question, and the one by which all human
measures must be tried. Liberty is of no value, if it secures not
the moral elevation of those upon whom it is conferred. On this
subject, Mr. Sewell says:

" The moral condition of the people whom I have thus briefly endeavored to trace from the time of slavery down to the present day, has
not kept pace with their material prosperity; and all I have said of Barbadians, in a former chapter, under this particular head, may, with still
greater force, be applied to Trinidadians. The amalgamation of the
European and African races is even more general in Trinidad than in

* Sewell, p. 119.

Barbadoes; and though marriage between whites and people of color is not opposed here with anything like the feeling it meets with in Barbadian society, yet I find, on examination, that, in Port-of-Spain, the ratio of births is 100 legitimate to 136 illegitimate — an exhibition of morality considerably below that of Havana. . . . . Taking up the matter of crime, I find that the annual average of convicted offenders, for the last five years, is, for felony, 63; for misdemeanor, 865; and for debt, 230; against a much lower average before emancipation. . . . . Trinidad, like all the other islands, is lamentably behind the age in educational science; and there is ample room to hope that when knowledge becomes more general, crime will decrease. Educational statistics do not show that there is any great eagerness, on the part of the creole population, to learn, or, on the part of their rulers, to place the means of instruction within their reach. Before emancipation, the number of children attending public and private schools was above a thousand; last year, the average of children attending all the schools and seminaries was considerably under three thousand, accounting for little more than the natural increase of the population. : . . . In regard to church statistics, I have no means of ascertaining the number of persons who attend places of Divine worship in this island; but were they in my possession, I should not have much faith in them as an evidence of the moral· or religious tone of the community. To judge from appearances, the creole inhabitants of Port-of-Spain are even fonder than Barbadians of showing off their Sunday garments." *

Section II.—Some interesting Facts and Speculations in reference to the Introduction of Coolies into the West Indies.

But another subject demands attention, in connection with the history of emancipation, and its disastrous results in Trinidad. The workings of the coolie system of labor has been involved in much obscurity, and contradictory accounts of its nature and effects have prevailed. Mr. Sewell is very full on this question, and offers arguments in favor of the system quite in harmony with the reasons presented by American slaveholders for the renewal of the slave-trade — its benefits as a civilizing agency.

---

* Sewell, pp. 114, 115, 116.

The reader will, doubtless, be interested in seeing what can be said in favor of this system:

"The first ship with Chinese immigrants arrived in the harbor of the Port-of-Spain in 1845. But the importation of Indian coolies was soon substituted for that of China. The experiment remained for some time doubtful. . . . . But now that it has been fairly and fully tested, the advantages to the colony of this importation of Indian labor are so thoroughly established that no one who visits Trinidad in 1859, after having seen her in 1846, can hesitate to believe that, not only has the island been saved from impending ruin, but a prospect of future prosperity has been opened to her such as no British island in these seas ever before enjoyed under any system, slave or free."[*]

It appears, from this statement, that the coolie system, in the opinion of Mr. Sewell, is much more effective than either negro free labor, or negro slave labor, and he expresses the hope that it will be continued as a measure alike beneficial to the laborer and his employer, and that the outcry against coolie immigration will not be allowed to prevail;[†] and why should it, as "it is merely the removing of British subjects from one portion of the empire to another, and where the prospects of the laborer are infinitely better and brighter?"[‡] These coolies "are perfectly free men and women, and, at their own option, leave the squalid filth and misery in which they have been accustomed to live, on a promise, guaranteed by government, of a free passage to the West Indies, certain employment, and fair remuneration for their services. . . . They live on the estates, rent free, in comfortable cottages; if sick, they receive medical attendance without charge; and their wages are five times more than they could earn at home."[§] . . . "The coolie works, on an average, nineteen and a half days during the month, and receives $5.35."[||] . . . . . "I heard of a coolie, the other day, who returned, after a residence in the island of ten or twelve years, with $9,000;"[¶] as this is more than six times the amount of his wages, even at the highest rates, it would be interesting to know how so much money came into his possession.

---

[*] Sewell, p. 120.   [†] Ibid., p. 121.   [‡] Ibid., p. 122.
[§] Ibid., p. 123.   [||] Ibid., p. 127.   [¶] Ibid., p. 125.

The terms upon which the coolies are employed may be learned from the legislative enactments upon the subject.

"By a colonial ordinance, passed in 1854, the Indian immigrants who have arrived subsequent to that period are only entitled to a free return after a residence of ten years. . . . The 'indenture,' of which I have spoken, is the contract of service into which the immigrant enters with his employer, and may be general or specific in its obligations, according to option. The immigrant is indentured for three years. As soon as that period has expired, he can release himself from any subsequent indenture, by paying $1.20 to the agent-general for every month that may be wanting to complete his term. After the immigrants have fulfilled the obligations to which they bound themselves, they receive a certificate of what is called 'industrial residence,' which empowers them to act as independently as they choose for the future. . . . After they have fulfilled their terms of service, many voluntarily renew their contracts." *

Mr. Sewell continues :

"The blessing of giving labor and life to the colony is scarcely equal to the blessing that this immigration scheme has conferred upon the coolie himself." . . . "A poor pagan, he is brought in contact with civilization, and soon forgets and abandons the gross superstitions in which he was wont to put his faith. Under this system of immigration more might be done toward Christianizing and civilizing the people of India in one year than has been done by all the missionaries that ever emigrated to the East under the influence of the most enthusiastic zeal. The coolies who go back after an industrial residence, go back to spread abroad the seeds of civilization and Christianity, and, on this ground, the free return, granted by the government, may be advocated with some show of reason." †

This is truly an encouraging picture of the coolie system in its moral bearings, and commends itself to the consideration of the Foreign Missionary Societies of all nations. To accomplish more in one year than has been done by the whole of them for the last fourscore years, would be worth the effort! But Mr. Sewell fails in explaining one thing, and this may prevent the

---

* Sewell, pp. 125, 126.   † Ibid., p. 128

Christian world from profiting by his suggestion. He has failed to explain why it is, if the potency of Trinidad, as a school of morals and civilization, is so great, that it has manifested so little of its power upon its own negro population!

But the advantages to the island are so great, that Mr. Sewell seems never tired of referring to them:

"The coolies have saved the island from ruin, but, so far, they have not nearly supplied its wants."*   .   .   .   "I do not hesitate to say, and no one in this island will express a contrary opinion, that immigration has been the salvation of Trinidad. It is a blessing both to the employer and the employé . This is no vague assertion; it can be demonstrated; first, by an exhibition of the improved and improving condition of the laborer; secondly, by the increased demand for his services; thirdly, by the extension of sugar cultivation on the island; and fourthly, by the augmentation of its trade."†   .   .   .   "It seems to have been decreed in the Providence of God that these fair and fertile islands should ultimately become an asylum for millions of wanderers from heathenesse; and the scheme of immigration, instead of being condemned, should be upheld, defended, and perfected by philanthropists, above all others, as a plan most happily devised for the elevation of a degraded people, and for the restoration to prosperity of a splendid inheritance."‡

Mr. Sewell shows, by figures which he presents, that the cost of slave labor, in former years in the British islands, and at this moment in Cuba, is much greater than the present coolie free labor, and thus demonstrates, to his entire satisfaction, that free labor is more economical than slave labor.§ He might extend the comparison between the two systems still farther, and, in addition to the favorable moral bearings of the coolie system upon the immigrants, there might be added other reasons in its favor, of equal force, in relation to its advantages over slavery to the planters themselves. Under slavery the industrial life of the imported slave lasted only about five years; the period of coolie labor extends to about ten years. Under slavery the planter

---

* Sewell, p. 130.   † Ibid., p. 135.
‡ Ibid., p. 134.   § Ibid., pp. 55 and 279.

had to support the aged and infirm; under the coolie system his obligations terminate with his contract, and the laborer then shifts for himself. Under slavery the planter had to support the children born on the plantation, a measure more expensive than to purchase full-grown laborers from the slave-traders; under the coolie system the parents maintain their own children, and, at the same time, labor for a less sum of money than it cost the planter to purchase and support his slaves. By this mode of reasoning it would appear that the coolie system, in an economical point of view, has a vast advantage over the old system of slavery, both to the planter and the coolie himself! The American planter, therefore, may take a lesson from Mr. Sewell, and, no longer insisting upon the renewal of the slave trade as a means of increasing his labor forces, proceed to introduce immigrants from Africa, as ten-year laborers, returning them to their native homes after the termination of their "industrial residence."

The failure of emancipation in Trinidad is fully conceded by Mr. Sewell, and its restoration to prosperity from a condition of "hopeless lethargy," is attributed entirely to the introduction of coolie labor.

But is this the successful termination to the scheme of emancipation which was expected to follow the destruction of slavery? Certainly not. Here we have a change of the whole issue made in the original controversy upon emancipation. Its success is placed upon new grounds, never mentioned when the freedom of the slave was proposed and executed. Then it was contended that free labor would be more productive than slave labor, and that emancipation, therefore, would be an economic success. But the freeman whose labor was to be doubly productive over that of the slave, was that self-same slave elevated to the condition of a freeman. As a freeman, however, he is almost worthless in the department of labor; and the utter ruin of the island had been prevented only by the substitution of the labor of a people of a different race, who can be stimulated to industry by the offer of wages.

SECTION III.—THE SOCIAL, MORAL, AND INDUSTRIAL CONDI-
TION OF JAMAICA, AS ILLUSTRATING THE EFFECTS OF EMANCIPA-
TION WHERE IT IS UNACCOMPANIED BY ADEQUATE MEANS OF
MORAL PROGRESS.

JAMAICA is the most important of the whole of the British
West India Islands. It is much the largest in size, has the
greatest amount of uncultivated land, and hence affords the best
possible example of the results of negro emancipation. Unlike
Barbadoes, there is no overcrowding of the population. The
planters can not compel the negroes to work, but they are left
free to roam as they please. Whatever of energy or intelligence
may have been possessed by the blacks, ample room for its display has been afforded in Jamaica. Whatever of indolence may
be inherent in them as a race, there has been nothing here to
prevent its broadest development.

Mr. Sewell's book has let in a flood of light upon the industrial, social, and moral condition of Jamaica. In the examination of his researches into its condition, the rule adopted in
scientific investigations—that of classifying the facts—will best
serve to elicit truth, and establish a correct theory as to the
results of emancipation. His book supplies much that is inval-
uable on the negro question—much that can not be found elsewhere—and, aside from his eagerness to shield the Jamaica
negro from the charge of indolence, and to prove that emancipation has been an undoubted success, he gives an abundance of
facts to enable reflecting men to form their own opinions.
Hitherto, writers of his school had kept back the facts relating
to the prosperous condition of the West Indies, as long as the
planters had a regular supply of laborers through the agency of
the slave trade, and had commenced their investigations with the
suppression of that traffic. It was thus very easy to show—as
will be seen from the statistical table on a preceding page—that
the decline of the exports from Jamaica had commenced nearly
thirty years before the final emancipation of the negroes was
effected; and that other causes, therefore, than emancipation,
must have been at work in producing the gradual ruin of the
island. Mr. Sewell, however, enters upon the whole field of

inquiry, and admits the prosperity of the island, and of the West Indies generally, as long as the slave trade continued.* Disbelieving the theory that emancipation can have wrought any ill to Jamaica, and admitting that ruin—wide-spread and desolating ruin—has overtaken the island, he seeks other causes for the destruction which wrecked its prosperity. But we must defer further remarks here, and proceed with our quotations :

"I do not think it can be disputed, if history and statistics are to be believed, that, since the abolition of the slave trade, fifty-two years ago, Jamaica has never for a moment paused in her downward career. I do not think it can be disputed, if actual observation is to be relied upon, that she has not even yet reached the lowest point of possible depression. Lower still she can sink—lower still she must sink, if her people are not imbued with a more pregnant patriotism, if the governing classes are not stimulated to more energetic action, and are not guided by more unselfish counsels. I know of no country in the world where prosperity, wealth, and a commanding position have been so strangely subverted and destroyed as they have been in Jamaica, within the brief space of sixty years.† . . . . No other English island has the natural advantages that Jamaica possesses ; no other English island exhibits the same, or anything like the same, destitution ; yet all have passed through the same experience—all have undergone the same trial.‡ . . . . If the city of Kingston be taken as an illustration of the prosperity of Jamaica, the visitor will arrive at more deplorable conclusions than those pointed out by commercial statistics. It seems like a romance to read, to-day, in the capital of Jamaica, the account of that capital's former splendor. Its ' magnificent churches,' now time-worn and decayed, are scarcely superior to the stables of some Fifth-avenue magnate. There is not a house in the city in decent repair ; not one that looks as though it could withstand a respectable breeze ; not a wharf in good order ; not a street that can exhibit a square yard of pavement ; no side-walks ; no drainage ; scanty water ; no light. The same picture of neglect and apathy greets one everywhere. . . . . . The streets are filthy, the beach-lots more so, and the commonest laws of health are totally disregarded. Wreck

---

* The author of the present volume had executed this task several years since, in both his "Ethiopia" and "Cotton is King."

† Sewell, p. 169.   ‡ Ibid., p. 170.

and ruin, destitution and neglect! There is nothing new in Kingston. The people, like their horses, their houses, and all that belongs to them, look old and worn. There are no improvements to be noted; not a device, ornament, or conceit of any kind, to indicate the presence of taste or refinement. The inhabitants, taken *en masse*, are steeped to the eyelids in immorality; promiscuous intercourse of the sexes is the rule; the population shows an unnatural decrease; illegitimacy exceeds legitimacy; abortion and infanticide are not unknown. . . . . The marks of a helpless poverty are upon the faces of the people whom you meet, in their dress, in their very gait. . . . . Have I described a God-forsaken place, in which no one seems to take an interest, without life and without energy, old and dilapidated, sickly and filthy, cast away from the anchorage of sound morality, of reason, and common sense? Then, verily, have I described Kingston in 1860. Yet this wretched hulk is the capital of an island the most fertile in the world; it is blessed with a climate most glorious; it lies rotting in the shadow of mountains that can be cultivated from summit to base, with every product of temperate and tropical regions; it is mistress of a harbor where a thousand line-of-battle ships can safely ride at anchor. The once brimming cup of Kingston's prosperity has indeed been emptied to the dregs."*

Having, in a preceding page, given the exports of sugar from Jamaica, during a long series of years, quotations from Mr. Sewell, on this subject, need not be given here. They very fully sustain all he says in reference to the ruin which has fallen upon the island. One sentence only need be quoted, as it includes one year later than our statistics:

"A comparison of Jamaican exports in 1805, her year of greatest prosperity, with her exports in 1859, must appear odious to her inhabitants. In the former year, the island exported over 150,000 hhds. of sugar, and in the latter year she exported 28,000 hhds. The exports of rum and coffee exhibit the same proportionate decrease." †

But who are the sufferers by this enormous decline in the agricultural prosperity of the island?

"The large landed proprietors and merchant potentates of the island, these are the men who have fallen from their high estate. The slaves

---

* Sewell, pp. 173, 174, 175. † Ibid., p. 173.

of other days, the poor, the peasantry, these are the men who have progressed, if not in morality, at least in material prosperity."*

Let us, then, see what is the condition of this population of freedmen, whose progress has been promoted by the ruin of the class who "controlled the elements of civilization."

"The people of Jamaica are not cared for ; they perish miserably, in country districts, for want of medical aid ; they are not instructed ; they have no opportunities to improve themselves in agriculture or mechanics ; every effort is made to check a spirit of independence, which, in the African, is counted a heinous crime, but in all other people is regarded as a lofty virtue, and the germ of national courage, enterprise, and progress. Emancipation has not been wholly successful because the experiment has not been wholly tried. But the success is none the less emphatic and decided."†

"Jamaica, even now, has a larger number of inhabitants to the square mile than any State in the Union, except Connecticut, Massachusetts, New York, and Rhode Island. But she stands in need of immigration more than any State in the Union, *because a working man in America does as much as ten men in Jamaica.*"‡

"I do not mean to say, for a moment, that the estates have anything like a sufficiency of labor ; they are entirely without that continuous labor required, not merely for bare cultivation, but for extension and improvement. In the remarks I have here made, I wish merely to give point-blank denial to a very general impression prevailing abroad, that the Jamaica negro will not work at all. I wish to show that he gives as much labor, even to the sugar estate, as he consistently can, and that it is no fault of his if he can not give enough."§

"The latest Blue-book returns give the number of males and females engaged in agriculture at 187,000—more than one half of the population of the island—tending in itself to disprove the assertion that the people are averse to the tillage of the soil ; but when the further fact appears, that out of this number 50,000 men, with their families, have elevated themselves to a proprietary rank, it speaks volumes, not merely in their own favor, but in favor of general intelligence and a wholesome progress. These small proprietors can not be said to live comfortably, in our sense of the word. Their huts are usually made

---

* Sewell, p. 172.
‡ Ibid., p. 279. The italics are ours.
† Ibid., p. 178.
§ Ibid., p. 202.

of bamboo sticks, thatched with cocoanut leaves. Most of them prefer the floor to sleep upon, and few understand the enjoyment of a regular meal. They eat when they are hungry, and will sometimes take enough in the morning to last them the entire day." *

"The apprenticeship was, in a moment of bitter excitement, cut short by the planters themselves, and 320,000 slaves—an undisciplined, degraded, half-savage crowd—were, without any preparation or training, left to their own devices. The free colored creoles numbered 60,000, and the total black and colored population of the period consisted, therefore, of 380,000 souls. By the census of 1844, the last taken, the total black and colored population was only 361,657; and if the estimate of mortality by cholera and small-pox within a few years past be correct, I do not believe, after making every allowance for a proper increase by birth, that the black and colored population of Jamaica exceeds, at the present day, 350,000. It will be remarked, and possibly with surprise, that the population of Jamaica, between 1834 and 1844, must have annually decreased at the rate of nearly a half per cent. This decrease, it is true, is nothing like the decrease that went on prior to emancipation,† but it is sufficiently serious to demonstrate the existence of some very aggravating causes of mortality among a people of temperate habits, and in a climate of unquestioned salubrity. In the absence of statistics on the subject, it is impossible to arrive at exact conclusions; indeed, official neglect, in all matters statistical, is so conspicuous, that I am not disposed to place implicit faith in the returns of the census itself. But supposing a decline, undoubted as I believe it to be, fully established, I do not think it difficult to assign more than one reason. Within a quarter of a century, some 15,000 whites have withdrawn from the island, and the increase of half-castes has been, in consequence, greatly checked. Another important cause of the decrease of population, particularly among the blacks, is the lack of medical practitioners in remote country districts. The mortality among children, for want of proper attention, is frightful. Nor, unfortunately, is this the only evil that deprives Jamaica of a legitimate increase in her population, and of the wealth that such an increase would, of necessity, bring. Many of the vices engendered by slavery remain a heavy burden and curse upon society, and, among them, immorality of the grossest kind pervades all classes, tainting alike the

---

* Sewell, p. 248.

† This greater mortality, at that period, we have elsewhere assigned to the disparity of the sexes, due to imports of an excess of males.

civilization of towns, and the unchecked intercourse of laborers in the cane-fields. The natural growth of the population has thus been arrested, and some of the most detestable crimes known to society are, even now, of frequent occurrence."*

" But Jamaica, with all her faults of omission and commission, offers, I believe, the best examples that can be produced of the emancipated negro; her inhabitants are more independent and better off than the inhabitants of other islands, in which over-crowded labor, or a less productive soil, has kept the masses in the same position that they occupied as slaves. Here the masses have made a great step forward." †

" Of the 320,000 slaves that were liberated, only the tradesmen and head people, numbering not more than 45,000, had ever picked up the merest waifs of knowledge. The others—field laborers and domestics— were almost as savage and untutored as their fathers were when they were dragged from their homes on the African coast. The change they have undergone within twenty-two years is, assuredly, no sign of incapacity, no proof of indolence, no indication of unconquerable vice."‡

" When Government fails, as it fails in Jamaica, to care for human life, and to see, with unaccountable apathy, the country destitute of medical aid, it is not surprising that the population should exhibit an annual decrease. When Government fails, as it fails in Jamaica, to give any consideration to popular education, it is not surprising that vice and immorality should alarmingly prevail. [The appropriations for education are "less than a shilling for the instruction of each child during a space of twelve months."] Under a rule of such pernicious neglect, it is not surprising that the Governor, in proroguing the Legislative session of 1858, should say that, 'in many of the country districts, the people are abandoned to the spells and debasing superstitions of the working Obeah§ and Myalism, and to the scarcely less injurious practices of other ignorant empirics of the lowest grade.' "‖

" I think that the position of the Jamaica peasant, in 1860, is a standing rebuke to those who, wittingly or unwittingly, encourage the vulgar lie that the African can not possibly be elevated. . . . I think the creoles of Jamaica have disproved, by their own acts, the calumny of a hostile interest, that they do not work. The most ignorant work whenever they can get work. There are fully 20,000, of both sexes,

---

* Sewell, pp. 245, 246.   † Ibid., p. 246.   ‡ Ibid., p. 247.
§ A species of witchcraft practiced among the African negroes.
‖ Sewell, p. 257.

who work for the estates, and who may still be regarded as a laboring class. There are, probably, 10,000 who work as domestics. There are 3,000 at work upon the roads, where scarcity and idleness of laborers are made no grounds of complaint. The small proprietors work on their own lands and on the estates, also, whenever they can."* . . . "But in all they grow, they may be held to waste five times as much as they reap."† . . . "No friendly settler from abroad has ever appeared among them, to stimulate their exertions by showing them what science has accomplished in other lands."‡

"I estimate the laboring force on the estates at 20,000—about equal to the number of acres in cane cultivation. This would give some sixty or seventy laborers to each estate. . . . . But it must not be imagined that these are steady laborers, working on the same estate from year's end to year's end. Many of them are perpetually on the move; others only work on estates for a month or two out of the twelve; some offer their services when they are least wanted; some have provision-grounds of their own, which require their attention when the estates are most hardly pressed for labor; nearly all, if they chose, might be independent of the planter for their daily bread. Jamaica labor is essentially of this uncertain character."§

"Want of money is certainly epidemic in Jamaica. No creole seems to possess the commodity; and strangers who are believed to possess it, are made to pay for the general deficiency." ‖ . . . . "I dislike excessively the sea-port towns of Jamaica. . . . . All the worst fellows in the island collect in them, and give to foreigners a most mistaken idea of the country people. . . . . I do not doubt that many proprietors really suffer from the partiality of young men to towns; but, at the same time, I do not doubt that many of these young men prefer, and very naturally prefer, the greater certainty of regular payment that town business offers." ¶

"A stranger in Jamaica, and especially an American, who knew nothing of its past history or present wants, would never dream that labor was the great desideratum. He finds, on arriving at Kingston, a dozen boatmen eager to convey him ashore—a dozen porters ready to carry his luggage—a dozen messengers quarreling to run his errands. He is pestered with able-bodied men, and their offers of assistance for a paltry remuneration. He sees as many attendants in a petty Kings-

---

* Sewell, p. 254.   † Ibid., p. 252.   ‡ Ibid., p. 253.
§ Sewell, p. 264.   ‖ Ibid., p. 205.   ¶ Ibid., pp. 205, 206, 207.

ton shop as in a Broadway store, and a government clerk with as many servants as a foreign embassador. Servants must have under-servants, and agents, sub-agents. If he travel through the country, he finds half-a-dozen men watching a herd of cattle, and as many more looking after a team of oxen. He *sees* labor everywhere—on the roads, the streets, the wharves ; and it is only upon the plantations that he *hears* any complaint. . . . . He will infer, of course, that the labor market is overstocked rather than understocked, and his inference will neither be wholly wrong, nor yet wholly right. It will be nearer the truth to say that the actual labor force of the island is frittered away. The laboring classes of Jamaica—I mean the men and women who live by labor for daily wages—dislike plantation-work, and prefer to earn their livelihood, whenever they can, by any other kind of toil. They disliked it at first, because it was the badge of a slavery still fresh in their remembrance."*

"No sum of money would tempt a mulatto to work in the field. It is the province of the blacks alone. It ceases to be their province as soon as they buy the acre of land and the independence after which their souls yearn. It was the badge of slavery ; and it is no matter of surprise that there should be a prejudice against the emblem long after the reality has passed forever away." †

"I admit that Montego Bay quite charmed me with its clean streets, neat little patches of garden, and utter quietude, with its air of by-gone respectability, and the cool complacency of its people, who did not know or care how they lived from day to day. 'Well, massa, we do best we can in dese times,' was all the answer I got to repeated inquiries for a solution of the mystery of life in Montego Bay." ‡

"Lucea is an unclean, ragged-looking village, without two houses conjoined, and without one house in decent repair. . . . . The people on the route look as wild as the aspect of the country. They run away from a stranger, or glare at him, half in terror, half in curiosity, from behind a bush." §

"It was Christmas-eve—a season at which the West Indian negro goes wild with excitement. . . . . No negro will work for love or money during this carnival time. He is literally demented, and can hardly give a sane answer to the most ordinary questions. All night long, and for eight successive nights, an infernal din—a concert of cracked drums, shrill voices, and fire-crackers — is maintained.

---

* Sewell, p. 284.   † Ibid., p. 288.   ‡ Ibid., p. 211.   § Ibid., p. 213.

Those poor devils who can not enjoy this species of amusement suffer
the most exquisite torture." *

The transportation to market and the sale of the products of
the independent farmers are thus described :

"The road lies through a wooded and rather swampy district, and,
if it be a Saturday morning, the traveler will encounter, for several miles,
a continuous stream of sturdy, good-looking wenches, carrying, on their
heads, to the Spanish-Town market, most marvelous loads of fruit and
vegetables. A few of them, more fortunate than their fellows, have
donkeys, with well-filled panniers, but they do not, on this account,
neglect the inevitable head-load. Considering the distance they come,
the heat of the weather, the size of their burdens, and the paltry
remuneration they get at market, the performance is highly creditable
to the enterprise, energy, and activity of Jamaica negro women. I
doubt whether our laboring *men* could execute the same task; they
certainly would not undertake it for the same consideration." † . . . .
"Commend me to a West Indian market as a fit illustration of Babel
after the confusion of tongues. These people are quite as anxious to
sell as the progeny of Noah were to build. The sum of their ambition
is to get rid of the little lot of yams and oranges that they have brought
many a weary mile. They get a shilling or two for their produce, and
return as happy as though they were millionaires." ‡

Here the quotations in reference to the condition of the colored
population of Jamaica may be closed. Before making any comments, the position and policy of the planters, and the embarrassments by which they have been surrounded, as a consequence of
emancipation, must be briefly noticed.

SECTION IV.—THE CIVIL POSITION OF THE PLANTERS UNDER
EMANCIPATION, AND THE CAUSES CONTRIBUTING TO THEIR RUIN.

"The planters of Jamaica constitute no longer the overruling oligarchy, or 'plantocracy,' that they once actually were, and are still
somewhat insolently designated in the bitterness of party spirit.
Poverty may not have humbled their pride, nor changed their belief

---

* Sewell, p. 184.   † Ibid., p. 184.   ‡ Ibid., p. 187.

in the 'divine right' of the white man to enslave the black; for, in their own homes, and on their own estates, and in public, whenever an opportunity offers, they wage, under different guises, the old war against free labor. But, as a political body, with power to control the destinies of the island, they no longer live. One after another, the relics of the system of coercion to which they clung are being swept away. Their complaints have been disregarded—their petitions have been rejected—until, in despair and disgust, they have almost altogether retired from the contest, and left the field open to their undisguised and uncompromising opponents." *

But we must go outside of Mr. Sewell's book to do justice to the planters, by more fully stating the causes that have led to their ruin; and, in so doing, the discussions will be extended beyond the island of Jamaica.

The first sample of West India sugar was manufactured in Jamaica, in 1673. In 1713, Great Britain, having secured the monopoly of the slave trade, at the treaty of Utrecht, proceeded vigorously in the development of her West Indian cultivation.. By the commencement of the present century, the whole of her West Indian Islands were exporting 636,000,000 lbs. of sugar, 31,600,000 lbs. of coffee, 17,000,000 lbs. of cotton, and other products in proportion—Jamaica alone, in 1805, supplying over 237,000,000 lbs. of sugar.† The slave trade having been prohibited in 1808, the consequent decrease of population so affected the production of Jamaica, that from 1807 to 1831, its exports of sugar fell off 38.38 per cent., and its coffee 33.8-10 per cent. The exports of sugar from the whole of the islands, in 1831, was reduced to 459,600,000 lbs. This amount seems to have been sufficient for the home-consumption of the English people, as the importation of 65,320,000 lbs. of foreign sugars, that year, was for *re-export* alone.‡ Up to 1844, all foreign sugars were excluded from the British markets, so as to secure a practical monopoly to the West India planter. The duty on foreign sugar was sixty-three shillings per cwt.; on sugar, the growth of her East India possessions and Mauritius, thirty-seven shillings per

---

* Sewell, p. 230.   † See statistical table, preceding chapter.
‡ London Quarterly Review, 1850, p. 97.

cwt.; and on her West India colonies only twenty-seven shillings per cwt.—being a difference of ten shillings per cwt. in favor of the West Indies as against the other British colonies, and of thirty-six shillings as against all foreign sugars.*

In 1844, however, the first inroad was made on the West India monopoly, by the passage of an act allowing foreign *free labor* sugar to be imported for consumption at a lower duty.† This measure was demanded by the British people as a public necessity—the West Indian colonies being no longer able to supply the demand for sugar. In Jamaica alone, its exports were reduced from 237,700,000 lbs. in 1805, to 67,900,000 lbs. in 1843.‡ The other islands were nearly all in the same depressed condition.

At this date, the English Government found its commerce greatly lessened, and its home-supply of tropical products falling below the actual wants of her own people. This diminution rendered her unable to furnish any surplus for the markets of those of her colonies and other countries which she formerly supplied; and they were thus left open to the competition of slave-grown products, and became sources of additional encouragement to slavery and the slave trade.

This was another of the effects of West Indian emancipation not foreseen by the projectors of that movement. Emancipation had not only broken down England's own colonies, but it was followed by results which tended to encourage directly, in other countries, both the slave trade and slavery. Here we have an exhibition of its workings in relation to the slave trade: In 1788, the exports of slaves, westward, from Africa, were estimated at 100,000 annually; from 1798 to 1810, at 85,000; from 1810 to 1815, at 93,000; from 1815 to 1819, at 106,000; from 1819 to 1825, at 103,000; from 1825 to 1830, at 125,000; from 1830 to 1835, at 78,500; and from 1835 to 1840, at 135,800.§

These were alarming facts, and called loudly for energetic

---

* Westminster Review, 1850, p. 276.   † London Economist, 1850, p. 85
‡ This is the average of five years.
§ Report of Select Committee of House of Commons, quoted in Westminster Review, 1850, p. 263.

action. The ablest men in the kingdom came forward to aid in averting the impending dangers. They did not enter into discussions to prove that slavery had been, from the beginning, tending to the ruin of the colonies. It was quite otherwise in their judgment. Such theories were left for the philanthropists of a later day. While Great Britain had possessed the monopoly of tropical production, she had been able to retain her national ascendency. She was now threatened with a diminution of her prosperity. To regain her former leading control, she must recover the monopoly of tropical cultivation; and this she could do only by embarrassing those who had gained an advantage over her in this golden field of enterprise.

That slavery, sustained by the slave trade, was an immensely efficient system for the promotion of tropical cultivation, was abundantly proved by reference to Cuba and Brazil. In 1832, the exports of sugar from Cuba were only about 100,000,000 lbs., while, by 1848, they had increased to near 600,000,000 lbs. During the same period, Brazil and the Spanish West Indies, (excluding Cuba,) increased their exports of coffee from 94,080,-000 lbs. to 313,600,000 lbs. This enormous increase was all effected in sixteen years, as a consequence of having a full supply of labor which could be controlled and multiplied to any desired extent; and because England's prohibition of the slave trade, and her emancipation scheme had left open to their products a vast range of markets previously supplied from the British West Indies.

But long before 1848, and while these developments were progressing, Englishmen took the alarm, and began to consider how the impending evils were to be averted. Hear what McQueen, the able British statistician, said, in 1844, when urging upon his government the necessity of securing to itself the control of the labor and the productions of tropical Africa. The importance of the measure he proposed was thus urged, by showing what the West Indies had formerly done for the support of the British throne :

" During the fearful struggle of a quarter of a century, for her existence, as a nation, against the power and resources of Europe, directed by the most intelligent but remorseless military ambition against her, *the command of the productions of the torrid zone,* and the advantageous commerce which that afforded, gave to Great Britain the power and the resources which enabled her to meet, to combat, and to overcome her numerous and reckless enemies in every battle-field, whether by sea or land, throughout the world. In her the world saw realized the fabled giant of antiquity. With her hundred hands she grasped her foes in every region under heaven, and crushed them with resistless energy."

Now, if the possession and control of tropical production gave to England such immense resources, and secured to her such superiority and such power in the last century, then she would not yield them in the present but in a death-struggle for their maintenance. That struggle had commenced when Mr. McQueen came forward with his appeals to the nation to resort to Africa for the remedy. Mr. George Thompson had made a similar appeal, in behalf of India, a few years previous, and the British people had responded, most heartily, to both these gentlemen.*

English philanthropy had long been engaged in efforts for the elevation of the African race. The slave trade and slavery had both disappeared from English soil. The year 1844 demonstrated the futility of the schémes pursued. British tropical cultivation, and the commerce it sustained, both lay in ruins, while the slave trade and slavery laughed them to scorn. English statesmanship was now demanded to consider how the nation was to be compensated for the losses sustained by emancipation. The country was found in a position so disadvantageous, arising from the progress of other nations in tropical cultivation, that one principal means of her extrication, they believed, was in organizing an extended system of tropical industry in Africa. The alarm which prevailed was well-founded, and its causes were thus stated by Mr. McQueen:

"The increased cultivation and prosperity of foreign tropical possessions is become so great, and is advancing so rapidly the power and resources of *other nations*, that these are embarrassing this country

---

* See Chapter XI.

(England) in all her commercial relations, in her pecuniary resources, and in all her political relations and negotiations."

In proof of his assertions, Mr. M. presented the following facts, contrasting the condition of Great Britain with only a few other countries, in the production of three articles alone of tropical produce:

SUGAR — 1842.

BRITISH POSSESSIONS.	CWTS.	FOREIGN COUNTRIES.	CWTS.
West Indies	2,508,552	Cuba	5,800,000
East Indies	940,452	Brazil	2,400,000
Mauritius	544,767	Java	1,105,757
		Louisiana	1,400,000
Total	3,993,771		
		Total	10,705,757

COFFEE — 1842.

	POUNDS.		POUNDS.
West Indies	9,186,555	Java	134,842,715
East Indies	18,206,448	Brazils	135,000,800
		Cuba	33,589,325
Total	27,393,003	Venezuela	34,000,000
		Total	337,432,840

COTTON — 1840.

	POUNDS.		POUNDS.
West Indies	427,529	United States	790,479,275
East Indies	77,015,917	Java	165,504,800
To China, from East Indies	60,000,000	Brazil	25,222,828
Total	137,443,446	Total	981,206,903

This exhibition of facts will be full of meaning to the intelligent reader, when it is stated that nearly three-fourths of this slave-grown produce, according to Mr. McQueen, had been created within thirty years preceding the date of his calling attention to the subject. Java and Venezuela alone were free-labor countries, and all the others, Louisiana excepted, were dependent upon the slave-trade for the increase of their cultivation. * England, therefore, must either regain her advantages in tropical countries and tropical products, or she must be shorn of a part of her power and greatness; and, more than this, if she could not effect that object, then the slave-trade and slavery must advance, notwithstanding the immense sacrifices she had made for their extinction.   On this point, Mr. McQueen declares:

* See " Ethiopia " for full details.

"If the foreign slave trade be not extinguished, and the cultivation of the tropical territories of other powers opposed and checked by British tropical cultivation, then the interests and the power of such states will rise into a preponderance over those of Great Britain, and the power and the influence of the latter will cease to be felt, feared, and respected amongst the civilized and powerful nations of the world."

Another aspect of this subject may be considered. The measures adopted by Great Britain for the benefit of the black race resulted so disastrously to her own islands, and so favorably to the interests of those countries employing slave labor, by enlarging the markets for slave-grown products, that the difficulty of inducing them to cease from it was increased a hundred fold. Nor did the expedients to which she resorted prove successful in extricating her from the difficulties in which she was involved. A duty of thirty-nine shillings, afterward raised to forty-one shillings the cwt., or four and a half pence the pound, was levied on *slave-grown* sugar. This was done with the design of prohibiting its importation into England, and of securing the monopoly of her markets to the West India planter. This *bonus* upon West India *free-labor* sugar was to be used in stimulating the negro to labor, so as to restore the islands to their former prosperity. But it failed to do this, as we have already seen, and resulted only in taxing the English people by the increase of prices consequent upon a diminution of the supply, in a single year, to the enormous amount of $25,000,000 more than the inhabitants of other countries paid for the same amount of sugar.* This enormous tax accrued, during 1840, from the protective duty, but was greatly above that of any other year during its continuance. The whole amount of the bounty to the planter thus drawn from the pockets of the English people and placed in those of the West India negro laborer in excessive high wages, in the course of six or seven years, amounted to $50,000,000.†

To relieve the English people from the onerous tax of the sugar duties, and, at the same time, in obedience to the dictates of public

---

* Porter, in his "Progress of Nations."   † McQueen, 1844.

opinion, which required the exclusion of *slave-grown* products from the British markets, sugar, the product of *free labor*, as previously noticed, was admitted at a duty of ten shillings the cwt. This act, passed in 1844, at once brought in an increased supply of that commodity. But these imports of free-labor sugar came chiefly from Java and Manilla—possessions of Holland and Spain. It was soon discovered that the Dutch and Spaniards, outwitting the English for once, were compensating themselves for the amount of ordinary supplies thus diverted to a profitable market, by sending to Cuba and Brazil for a sufficient quantity of their cheaper slave-labor sugar to make up the deficiency. By this curious but very natural turn in trade, the great object of the English was defeated. Slavery, instead of having received a check, by the exclusion of its products from the British markets, was securing to itself the most active encouragement from the very measures intended to promote its destruction.

Another course of policy was immediately adopted. The act admitting *free-labor* sugar was passed in 1844. In 1845, a general reduction of the sugar duties was made, which reduced the protection against foreign slave-grown sugars one-half, and, in 1846, the final act was passed, admitting all foreign sugars on advantageous terms. This act made a progressive reduction of the duties on foreign sugar, so that it should come in on equal terms with that of the colonies in 1849.* The conditions of the act being afterwards extended to 1854, the planters had a slight protection up to that date.

The immense falling off in the exports of the British West India colonies, which had taken place after emancipation, and the impossibility of her Eastern possessions supplying the deficiency, left the government of Great Britain no other alternative but a reduction of the sugar duties, and the admission of *slave-grown* sugar. A struggle to stimulate the West India negroes to greater industry, and to advance them in civilization, had been continued unavailingly throughout thirteen years, from 1833 to 1846, resulting only in taxing the English people, by protective duties, to the extent of $150,000,000 more than the

* Blackwood's Mag., 1849, p. 85.

consumers of other countries had paid for an equal quantity of sugar. The blacks had passed through a period equaling one generation of freedom, and the second generation seemed less efficient than the first. English philanthropy despaired of African barbarism, and the efforts to sustain the planters had to be abandoned. By this result, the whole field of the foreign markets, formerly supplied with English sugar, was left open for that of slave-labor origin.

One point needs a word of explanation. There was a marked decrease in the number of slaves exported from Africa between the years 1830 and 1835, and an unusual increase again from 1835 to 1839. The impulse given, among other nations, to the slave-trade, when it was abandoned by the United States and Great Britain, received no material check, until 1830, when a reduction of the price of sugar from forty-four shillings and six pence the cwt. to twenty-four shillings and eight pence, diminished the export of slaves from Africa thirty-seven per cent., or from an annual average of 125,000 the preceding five years, to 78,500 the succeeding five years.* But this depression in the slave trade lasted only during the time that the price of sugar remained at that reduced rate. In 1836, sugar again rose to twenty-nine shillings and three pence the cwt., and gave an impulse to that traffic. that increased the exports of slaves from Africa seventy-three per cent., or to 135,800 per annum, from that time till the close of 1839. †

Such was the condition of the slave trade at the time the West India emancipation law went into operation. Its subsequent history is very interesting, but can not be given in this connection.

Ten years later, when the emancipation scheme was manifesting its tendency, the measure underwent the most rigid scrutiny. The low state of civilization in the West India Islands, it was found, had left the population with few wants. The blacks, for the most part, could not be induced to labor on the estates of the planters for more than three or four days in the week, and from five to seven hours in the day. So few, indeed, were their

---

* See preceding pages in present chapter.   † London Times, 1849.

wants, that they had no adequate stimulant to perform a regular amount of labor.* This condition of things put it out of the power of the planters to produce sugar for less than £20 per ton, on the average, while the cost, in slave countries, was only £12 per ton.† This discloses the fact that the planters of Cuba, employing *slave labor*, could manufacture sugar for £8 the ton less than those of Jamaica could produce it by *free labor*. As one of the immediate results of this condition of things, it was asserted, in 1848, that "the great influx of slave-grown produce into the English markets has, in the short space of six months, reduced the value of sugar from £26 to £14 per ton; while, under ordinary circumstances of soil and season, the cost to us, of placing it in the market, is not less than £20 per ton."‡ This subjected the planter to a direct loss of £6 per ton. But that was not all of the obstacles with which the planter had to contend. The duties on foreign sugar, after 1846, afforded no real protection to him, and for this reason:

"The slave sugars are all so much better manufactured, which the great command of labor enables them to do, that, to the refiner, they are intrinsically worth more than ours. In short, they prepare their sugars, whereas we can not do so, and we pay duty at the same rate on an article which contains a quantity of molasses. So that, if the duties were equalized, there would virtually be a bonus on the importation of foreign sugar. The refiners estimate the value of Havana, in comparison with West India free sugar, as from three to five shillings per cwt. better in point of color and strength. The reason is, that these sugars are partially refined or *clayed*."§

The question in relation to the decline of cultivation in the British West India Islands, previous to the prohibition of the slave trade, may now be dismissed with the remark, that the modern theory—that slavery was precipitating the colonies to ruin even before 1808—is not sustained by the facts in the case, or by the opinions of the ablest British writers. Look at the statistics of the exports from Jamaica, for a long series of years

---

* Blackwood's Mag., 1848, p. 227.   † Ibid., p. 230.
‡ Ibid., p. 230; from Resolutions of a meeting at St. David's Jamaica
§ Ibid., May 1848, p. 230.

before the prohibition of the slave trade. They show that there had been, up to that date, a regular increase in the production of the island, affected only by peace or war, or the influence of the seasons. The deterioration in the exports of the island did not begin until after the act of 1808 had cut off all supplies of labor. Individual instances of misfortune, mismanagement, or bankruptcy did not affect the general prosperity any more than occasional failures, in large cities, retard the general success of business men. Why should the British islands alone have begun to decline under a system that supplied an adequate labor force, when it is notorious that the production of Cuba and Brazil has increased immensely under slavery, while sustained by the slave trade—the increase of Brazil, in sixteen years, having been nearly *three hundred and fifty per cent.*, and that of Cuba, in the same period, *six hundred per cent.*

With all these facts before us, it is apparent that the causes leading to the ruin of Jamaica and the other English West India Islands had their origin subsequently to the prohibition of the slave trade, and that their nature was such that emancipation could not remove them.

Before considering this point, however, we must again turn to Mr. Sewell's book, and conclude our investigations in relation to Jamaica.

" British emancipation may have been unwise; regarded as a great social revolution, the manner in which the scheme was executed must be utterly condemned; private rights were violated; their sacredness was dimmed by the splendor of an act which gave freedom to a people who did not know what freedom meant; but the ruin attributed to it is, in Jamaica, too broad and too deep to be set down any longer as the effect of that one solitary cause. No other English island has the natural advantages that Jamaica possesses; no other English island exhibits the same, or anything like the same destitution; yet all have passed through the same experience—all have undergone the same trial."*

" If the change could be traced solely to emancipation, I should be loth to justify emancipation, believing, as I do, that it would be wholly

* Sewell, p. 170.

inconsistent with morality or the dictates of a sound policy to degrade that portion of the population which controlled the elements of civilization, in order to enrich an ignorant and undisciplined people. But the decline of Jamaica has been so stupendous as of itself to create a doubt whether it can be laid, in whole, or even in part, to the emancipation of the slaves."*

The aim of Mr. Sewell is to prove that other causes than emancipation have produced the pecuniary ruin of Jamaica. Contrasting the exports preceding the prohibition of the slave trade with those of the present day, he fully proves his assertions as to the ruin which has fallen upon the island. He thus states the question :

" It will be found, upon examination, that the most prosperous epoch in Jamaican commerce was that embraced in the seven years immediately preceding the abolition of the slave trade. Yet it is a notorious fact, to be proved by parliamentary blue-books, that even then over one hundred estates on the island had been abandoned for debt. During the seven years indicated, that is, from 1801 to 1807, the sugar exports of Jamaica amounted annually to an average of 133,000 hhds. During the seven years succeeding the year in which the slave trade was abolished, from 1807 to 1814, the annual exports fell off to an average of 118,000 hhds. During the next seven years, from 1814 to 1821, the annual average was about 110,000 hhds.; and from 1828 to 1835, it was 90,000 hhds.; thus showing a steady decline, not so alarming, it is true, as the decline of subsequent years (for the whole sugar exportation of Jamaica is now only 30,000 hhds.,) but sufficiently serious to demonstrate that Jamaica had reached its maximum prosperity under slavery, and had commenced to deteriorate nearly thirty years before the emancipation act was passed, and many years before the design of such a measure was elaborated, or Mr. Canning's note of warning was sounded in West Indian ears. A comparison of Jamaican exports in 1805, her year of greatest prosperity, with her exports in 1859, must appear odious to her inhabitants. In the former year, the island exported over 150,000 hhds. of sugar, and in the latter, she exported 28,000 hhds. The exports of rum and coffee exhibit the same proportionate decrease." †

---

* Sewell, p. 172.   † Ibid., pp. 172, 17

Lest any one should imagine that this immense falling off in the productions of Jamaica is in consequence of the impoverishment of the soil, Mr. Sewell must be permitted to speak on this point also:

"The island, unlike others that can be mentioned, is in no exhausted condition, but is fresh and fair, and abundantly fertile as ever, with every variety of climate, and capable of yielding every variety of product. Up in these tremendous hills you may enjoy the luxury of a frosty night; down upon the plains you may bask in the warmth of a fiery sun. There you can raise potatoes, here you can raise sugar-cane. There you will find interminable forests of wild pimento, here interminable acres of abandoned properties—a mass of jungle and luxuriant vegetation choking up the deserted mansions of Jamaica's ancient aristocracy. Scenes most wonderfully fair, most picturesque, but most melancholy to look upon; scenes that a limner might love to paint, but from which an American planter would turn in disgust and contempt."*

"The Jamaica question is prolific of controversy, and I can not hope that my allegations and inferences will pass unchallenged. I shall, for this reason, confine myself as much as possible to statements of facts. . . . I hope to be able to show to others as plainly as the conviction has come home to myself, that disaster and misfortune have followed—not emancipation—but the failure to observe those great principles of liberty and justice upon which the foundations of emancipation were solidly laid."† . . . "I admit, and shall prove, that want of labor has been one cause of the island's depreciation; but if it were the sole cause, or even the preponderating cause, it would be only reasonable to expect that those parishes most sparsely populated would be the first to abandon the cultivation of cane. The reverse, however, happens to be the case."‡

"This want of capital—quite irrespective of a want of labor, which I admit to exist—has been a fruitful cause of the abandonment of sugar cultivation. The most hasty tour through the island will convince any one that *contract* or *permanent* labor—wholly independent of the valuable but *transient* work of the negroes, who have their own properties to look after—is absolutely needed before the cultivation of the cane, in Jamaica, can be largely extended, or real estate command its positive

---

* Sewell, p. 176.   † Ibid., p. 177.   ‡ Ibid., p. 189.

value. I do not believe that the absence of this contract labor explains the present great depression of Jamaican commerce. My belief is, that the contract or permanent labor of coolies is needed, as a supplementary labor to that of the creole, alike on the richest and the poorest estates. There is sufficient labor in Jamaica now for the bare wants of its reduced cultivation, if the planter had means enough to pay his laborers, fairly and punctually, the wages they earn. Those wages are not too high, for they are scarcely one-fourth of what a day-laborer can command in America. This I state unhesitatingly. But, at the same time, I state with equal confidence that, in Jamaica, permanent labor, that is, daily labor throughout the year—that kind of labor which will enable the planter to improve his property and extend his cultivation— is wholly wanting, and, it seems to me that, without it, neither capital nor confidence will ever fully return to the island. The point I make is this: Jamaica wants labor, but that want is not the preponderating cause of her decline."* . . . "In a precarious business like sugar-cultivation, where the loss of an entire crop must, now and then, be expected, there is no salvation for the Jamaican planter who can command neither capital nor credit when an unfavorable season overtakes him."†

"An intelligent resident of Green Island, himself a proprietor, informed me that he knew of no estate in Hanover whose owner, possessed of capital, or even out of debt, had been compelled, from mere want of labor, to abandon sugar cultivation. When I have put the same question to any respectable landholder in any part of the island, I have, in nine cases out of ten, received the same answer. The want of continued or contract labor is greatly deplored as a great evil ; but it is wrong to suppose that that want alone has ever compelled resident proprietors to abandon their estates to ruin."‡

"But the fact remains that the island is nearly destitute of labor ; that, partly through want of labor, sugar cultivation has been abandoned; and by an adequate supply of labor can it only be revived. Covering an area of over 4,000,000 of acres, Jamaica has a population of 378,000, white, black, and mulatto. This makes about eleven acres to each person. In the flourishing island of Barbadoes the proportion is nearly one and a half persons to each acre. If Jamaica were as thickly populated as Barbadoes, it would contain over 5,000,000 of souls, and would export a million hogsheads. Till its population has

---

* Sewell, pp. 226, 227.   † Ibid., p. 226.   ‡ Ibid., p. 214.

been doubled and trebled, no material improvement can be looked for. But where is the money—where are the vigor and the energy necessary to obtain this population? Whose fault is it that these are wanting, and that Jamaica, with far greater advantages than Trinidad or Guiana, has failed to follow the footsteps of their success? Is this also the result of emancipation?"*

"During all this time the prosperity of Jamaica was on the decline. The exportation of sugar had gradually decreased from 150,000 hhds., in 1805, to 85,000 hhds., in 1833. It was not emancipation, or the thought of emancipation, that dragged down the island suddenly from the pinnacle of prosperity. The deterioration progressed slowly. Between the years 1814 and 1832, the coffee crop was also reduced one half; and during the fifty years that preceded emancipation, it is estimated that two hundred sugar estates were abandoned. The planters say that the fear of impending abolition induced them to withdraw capital from their estates; but abolition was not dreamed of when the decline of Jamaica set in. While the slave trade was yet in operation, over one hundred properties had been deserted—deserted, too, for the same cause that compelled their desertion in later years—debt and want of capital."†

"Sugar cultivation, it is hardly necessary to say, to be carried on with profit to the proprietor, and with ordinary chances of ultimate success, requires an enormous capital, not only at the outset, but to provide against the losses that unfavorable seasons very frequently entail."‡

"Hypothecation, rendered necessary by the expenses of the slave system and the extravagance of the planters, increased so fast that nine out of ten estates, at the time of emancipation, were mortgaged far beyond their value. Their creditors were English merchants, who vainly tried to keep up the cultivation of the property that reverted to them. How could they do so? Estates that yielded an average annual income of seven per cent., with the proprietor resident, could not, with the proprietor absent, pay attorneys and overseers, and still be worked at a profit. Many proprietors tried the impossible experiment, and failed, while the agents and overseers made money, or ultimately bought in the estate at a nominal cost."§

"Since emancipation, this want of capital has been the chief cause

---

* Sewell, p. 117.   † Ibid., p. 232.
‡ Sewell, p. 233.   § Ibid., p. 236.

of an unceasing depression. The sum received by the planter for his slaves was insufficient to pay off his mortgages; he had no money to improve his estate, or even sustain a naked cultivation; he had no money to keep roads in repair, or build trainways; he had no money to pay for labor; he had no money to meet misfortune. His mortgages were foreclosed; he reduced his cultivation; he sold small lots to settlers to meet pressing wants; the roads were so bad that the transportation of sugar to the shipping port became one of his heaviest items of expenditure; the laborers, whom he neglected to pay, went elsewhere; the day of misfortune came and overwhelmed him with ruin. He was bankrupt before emancipation; but it was emancipation that tore down the vail which concealed his poverty."*

"It was their misfortune, that, between 1815 and 1825, the price of their great staple fell twenty-five per cent.; that between 1825 and 1835, it fell another twenty-five per cent.; and that between 1835 and 1850, it fell twenty-five per cent. yet again. It was their misfortune that the British nation would no longer consent to be taxed to support them, and that the protective tariff upon West India sugars should have been abolished. It was their misfortune to have been disturbed at home and abroad, and to have been the victims of a jealousy that refused, for years, to Jamaica alone, of all the West Indies, the privileges and the advantages of a wholesome immigration." †

"It was their fault that they listened to no warning—that they heeded not the signs of the times — that they opposed all schemes for gradual emancipation, and even for ameliorating the condition of the slaves, until the crushing weight of public opinion broke the chain of slavery asunder, and threw suddenly upon their own resources an ignorant and undisciplined people. Theirs were the faults of policy and government that drove the creoles from plantations, that kept the population in ignorance, that discouraged education, and left morality at the lowest ebb. It is their fault that, under a system of freedom from which there is no relapse, they have made no brave attempt to redeem past errors and retrieve past misfortunes, but have been content to bemoan their fate in passive complaint, and to saddle the negro with a ruin for which they themselves are only responsible." ‡

"This was the old plantocracy—the generous, hospitable, improvident, domineering plantocracy of Jamaica. Their power no longer

---

* Sewell, p. 238.   † Ibid., p. 240.   ‡ Ibid., p. 241.

predominates. They command no credit, and no respect; and they obtain little sympathy in their misfortune. Even from domestic legislation they have sullenly retired, and their places are being fast filled by the people whom they have so long and so vainly tried to keep down." *

Mr. Bigelow, already quoted, when speaking of the legislation of the island, says:

" The center of legislative control is in London, and the members of the colonial legislature are mere shadows, destitute of the vital functions of legislators. The veto power of the Governor, who is appointed by the Queen, enables him practically to control all legislation."

Is it any wonder, then, that the planters should have retired in disgust from all legislation, when they were neither permitted to control the free labor of the island, nor secure a sufficient amount of labor by coolie immigration? By the earlier laws, the enormous property qualification required to make a man eligible to a seat in the legislature, excluded from that body all but the landholders.† This placed the legislation within the control of the intelligence of the island, and measures would have been adopted, but for the anti-slavery influence in England, that would have restored confidence, and secured advances of capital to the owners of the estates. Such has been the policy in several of the British colonies, and the planters are not only prospering, but have paid off the mortgages upon their estates. Jamaica, unfortunately, has had to bear the brunt of the anti-slavery attack; ‡ and all the legislation of the planters, for their own relief, has been rendered a nullity by that influence. It has not only succeeded in this, but as effected a change in the qualifications for membership, which, has Mr. Sewell says, has swept away the power of the planters forever. Let us hear what he has to say in relation to this change:

" If I were asked to describe, in as few words as possible, the effect of emancipation on Jamaica, I should say—the creation of a middle

---

* Sewell, p. 242.   † Bigelow.   ‡ Sewell, p. 230.

class. There was no middle class under slavery, and could be none. Master and servant made up the population. . . . . But one most beneficial result stands out to-day, so prominently, and in such bulky proportions, that the most prejudiced can not close their eyes to its presence. Emancipation has created a middle class—a class who are born in Jamaica, and will die in Jamaica—a class of proprietors, tax-payers, and voters, whose property, patriotism, happiness, and comfort are bound up in the island's prosperity." *

"At the lowest estimate that I have heard given, there are now in the island of Jamaica fifty thousand small proprietors, owning, on an average, three acres of land."† . . . . "The small proprietors work on their own lands, and on the estates, also, whenever they can. Very large numbers work as merchants, mechanics, and tradesmen, and not a few of the ex-slaves of Jamaica, or their children, are members of the legislature, and fill responsible offices under government. In the Assembly alone there are seventeen black and colored members out of a total of forty-seven."‡ . . . . "Both houses were in session when I passed through Spanish-Town; but as I shall hereafter have occasion to explain the franchise, and the effects of recent legislation in the island, I lay up these matters for further experience. Nor will I do unto others as I was done by, and victimize the reader with the debates of the Jamaican Assembly. The ability of members, with one or two exceptions, did not seem to me to reach even a provincial standard of mediocrity, and the subjects discussed were, of course, most uninteresting to a stranger."§ . . . . "The election law now in force, and passed in 1858, is a decided improvement on previous enactments of a similar nature. Under its provisions, a voter must possess a freehold of a clear rental of £6 sterling a year, or he must pay £20 rent, or have an annual income, derivable from business, of £50 a year, or, finally, he must pay taxes to the extent of £2 per annum. There are, probably, 50,000 freeholders in Jamaica with a clear income of £6 a year, but the number of actual voters does not exceed 3,000. A tax of ten shillings, *per capita*, for registration, explains the discrepancy. The negro does not care so much about voting as to be willing to pay government ten shillings for the privilege. . . . · But it must not be supposed that Jamaica legislation is perfect now, because it is no longer the exclusive prerogative of the plantocracy.

---

* Sewell, p. 244.   † Ibid., p. 247.
‡ Sewell, p. 254.   § Ibid., p. 182.

It is, in fact, most wretchedly imperfect. Planters, too, of the right
sort, are much needed in both houses. The island depends—no one
can doubt the fact—upon the extension of sugar cultivation for a revival
of prosperity. . . . . In Barbadoes, the plantocracy are still able to
rule as they please; in Jamaica, they have been borne down by an
independent middle class, who would not be denied their rights, or
defrauded of their privileges."* . . . . "I think a majority of the
small proprietors and settlers are intelligent enough to exercise the
right of voting to their own advantage, and to the advantage of this
great dependency of the English crown ; but it is an experiment, which,
if carried out, will entirely remove the government of the island from
the control of the planters—a control that, for some time, they have
seemed utterly indifferent about possessing. The plantocracy of Jamaica is a thing of the past, and, in its stead, democracy is lifting up
its head." †

"I have already explained the system of immigration that obtains
in other colonies, and shall only observe here the peculiarities of the
Jamaica law, which came into force in 1858. By the provisions of this
act, the immigrant laborer is entitled, free of all charges, to a certificate
of 'industrial residence,' after he has worked five years under indenture.
He can shorten this term of service, and receive his certificate, by paying a commutation fee of $20 at the end of the third year, or of $10 at
the end of the fourth year. At the end of the *second year*, and of each
subsequent year, he can, at his own election, change his employer, and
give his service to whomsoever he pleases."‡ . . . . "It only
remains to add that, under the Jamaica law of 1858, the entire expense
of immigration is imposed upon the planting interest."§ . . . "The
present scheme of immigration is, in fact, a victory of the anti-slavery
party of Jamaica, whose views the planters have been compelled to
adopt. A few years ago, the proprietors scouted any plan that did not
indenture the laborers for ten years. They are now content that the
indenture shall not exceed two or three years—sufficient to guarantee
the planter a return for his outlay, and to give the laborer a necessary
industrial training. The Jamaica law of 1858 was opposed in England,
very unwisely, as I think, and much more strenuously than it was
opposed even by ultraists within the colony. It can not, under any
circumstances, be considered a triumph of the planting interest; it is

---

* Sewell, pp. 258, 259.   † Ibid., p. 183.
‡ Sewell, p. 299.   § Ibid., p. 301.

rather a fair expression of the liberal public sentiment of the island on a much debated question of the highest importance." *

Under this act, the planters are authorized to import 50,000 coolies within a year. But such are its provisions, that it seems doubtful if they will act under it. The coolie needs industrial training, and, from the intimation above given, it appears that two or three years are necessary to accomplish this object. The coolie may leave the planter at the end of two years, or about as soon as he is prepared to become a useful laborer—the planter being thus deprived of all advantage from the care he has taken in his instruction. The whole bill is the result of the efforts of the " middle class," under English anti-slavery dictation, to render the planters powerless for oppression. The planters, broken down pecuniarily by British legislation in behalf of the negro race,—hurled from the proud position assigned them as chief supporters of the crown,†—are now in the humiliating position of being controlled by the " middle class,"— the " democracy which is lifting up its head,"—whose legislators, in ability, do not " reach even a provincial standard of mediocrity." ‡

And why have the planters been thus embarrassed by the legislation of the island, as well as by that of the British parliament? Why have they not been allowed a full supply of coolie labor, enabling them, like the other islands who adopted the system, to recover from the ruin which followed emancipation? These questions are readily answered. The English abolitionists fear the result of the experiment. They have a theory to maintain, in reference to the capacity of the African race for civilization. Jamaica affords the best field for their operations. The introduction of a coolie population, to the extent of the wants of the planters, would displace the blacks, and leave them to their own resources—to ultimate extinction. To save the theory, and prevent this calamity, the coolie system was long opposed as a means of relief to Jamaica; and when, at length, a law authorizing the employment of imported labor in the island was passed by the

* Sewell, pp. 304, 305.   † See **McQueen**, on a preceding page.
‡ Sewell, p. 282.

colonial legislature, its provisions rendered it of little practical importance to the planter. The reason of its inefficiency is easily explained. The legislation of the Imperial Parliament had long since rendered the planter bankrupt. The colonial law, authorizing the importation of coolies, throws the cost of their transportation upon the planter alone. He has no money to meet that expense. But he could obtain advances from British capitalists, if there was an absolute certainty that the coolies employed could be retained long enough to enable him to repay his loan. The provisions of the law give him but two years of initiatory labor, at the end of which he may be again without the means of cultivating his estate, and paying his debt. The law, therefore, amounts to nothing, as a means of permanent relief to any of the planters, excepting such as have capital of their own on hand—a class which are not numerous.

But another point must be noticed, before this subject is further discussed. The opinions of the planters have been quoted, showing that free labor could not compete with slave labor—that the free negroes of Jamaica could not be induced to work like the slaves of Cuba, in the production of sugar, and that the decrease in its price, consequent upon the great increase of slave labor, had led to ruinous consequences. But Mr. Sewell presents a different view of this question. He shows, as he thinks, that, at the present rate of wages, free labor can compete with slave labor, providing the free labor can be secured. His remarks on this point are worthy of consideration on account of the admissions made:

" The superior economy of free labor, as compared with slave labor, can be demonstrated even from the imperfections and shortcomings of Jamaica. The planter, who complains the loudest against the parent government for admitting slave-grown sugars on a par with free-grown sugars, does not deny that free labor is the cheaper of the two. He attributes his misfortunes to the abolition of one system without a corresponding introduction of the other. He offers to compete with slave labor, provided he can command a sufficient supply of free labor. . . With its present force of 20,000 uncertain laborers engaged in sugar cultivation, and utterly destitute of capital, Jamaica can not be considered the rival of Cuba, nor ought any conclusion unfavorable to free labor be deduced from the depression of the one, and the high prosperity of the other. It is not a competition between slave and free labor, but, practically, between slave labor and no labor at all. And herein we find a state of things for which the Imperial Government is, in a measure, responsible. It was not that they committed the dazzling mistake of a too sudden emancipation; it was not that they withdrew protection from the infant system, and left it, unaided, to fight out the battle, but that they cut off the reinforcements which, in a sparsely-settled country, free labor imperatively demands; they refused supplies of labor, more needed in Jamaica than in northern colonies, and without which even the most enduring energy would have been compelled to halt in the race for empire. It is folly to dream over the mistakes of British emancipation, if we fail to read in them a practical lesson; and such a lesson as will benefit Jamaica at the eleventh hour, is yet to be learned. By the light of experience we are able now to see that if a free immigration had been poured into the island *before* abolition—if free labor had been introduced to fight slave labor on its own ground—slave labor must have been defeated in the contest; and no violent revolution would have marked its extinction. If free immigration had been poured into Jamaica *after* abolition, there can not be a reasonable doubt that the island would have been redeemed from bankruptcy, and from other burdens laid upon it by a slave system, and the peculiar aristocracy that it fostered. Other colonies have thus regained their lost position. Other colonies established, beyond a peradventure, the superior economy of free labor, and even Jamaica, with its ruined proprietary and scanty population—desolate, deserted, degraded Jamaica, points feebly to the same result." *

What have we here, but the acknowledgement that the only hope for the restoration of "desolate, deserted, degraded Jamaica" to her original prosperity is—not in the improving industry of the blacks, but—in the introduction of coolies? And what is this, but to admit that the expectations of the British people, in reference to the moral and industrial progress of the negroes, under freedom, have been wholly disappointed?

Mr. Sewell must be consulted a little further. He presents estimates, showing the difference in the cost, per pound, of the production of sugar under slavery and under freedom, in Cuba,

* Sewell, pp. 260, 261, 262.

Jamaica, Trinidad, and Barbadoes. For the general statements upon which his conclusions are based, the reader is referred to the book itself. The estimates for Cuba are for 1852, and though the crop and the labor force, under the influence of the slave trade, have increased one hundred per cent. within the last eight years, yet Mr. Sewell thinks they are as applicable now as then.* His statement is as follows :

ISLANDS.	POUNDS OF SUGAR PRODUCED.	LABOR FORCE.	AV. OF LBS. PER LAB'RER	COST OF EACH LAB. PER ANN.	COST OF SUGAR PER POUND.
Cuba, (slave)......	577,200,000	120,000	4,810	$144,30	3 cts.
Jamaica, (slave).	160,000,000	70,000	2,286	100,00	4 37-100 cts.
Jamaica, (free)...	50,000,000	20,000	2,500	50,00	2 cts.
Trinidad, (free)..	65,000,000	17,000	3,823	66,00	1 72-100 cts.
Barbadoes, (free)	68,000,000	22,000	3,090	44,00	1 2-5 cts.

Now, let us understand this matter, and not intermix classes of facts which should be kept separate. The prohibition of the slave trade had been followed by a large decrease in the slave population, and a corresponding diminution in the amount of exports. This decrease was mainly due to the fact, notorious to all, that the slave trader, obeying the demand in the slave market, imported a large excess of males, and that the mortality among this class of laborers was always very rapid. Great embarrassments had fallen upon the planters, in consequence of these results of the prohibition of the slave trade. British commerce was also suffering in a proportionate degree. Two objects were proposed to be accomplished by emancipation. It was to restore the material prosperity of the planters, and advance the physical and moral improvement of the negroes. These results, it was urged, would surely follow the abolition of slavery, because one freeman, laboring under the stimulus of wages, would be more than equal to two slaves, toiling beneath the lash ; and then the negro, desirous of acquiring a position of social equality with the white man, would eagerly prosecute an education for his intellectual elevation, and avoid every vice that would add a stain to his moral character. It was expected that these objects would be accomplished by the harmonious action and co-operation of the parties interested—the planters and the negroes. But if these

* Sewell, p. 270.

objects failed in the accomplishment, then emancipation would be a failure; and not only would the planters and negroes be the sufferers, but British commerce would also receive injury, and the nation fail to maintain its ascendant position.

Well, the co-operation of the planters and the negroes has proved to be wholly impracticable. In no one thing have the negroes imitated the whites, except in avoiding continuous labor. As a necessary consequence of this unforeseen result, the planters have been ruined. It is undeniable, then, that emancipation, in its expected results, as a measure for the restoration of the economical prosperity of Jamaica, is an utter failure.

But some further examination of this point is needed. It is useless to contend that free labor is less expensive than slave labor; nay, it is mockery to do so, when the free labor cannot be had. Am I not right in this assertion? What are the facts? Jamaica has lost none of her black population by emigration. The former slaves, or their descendants, are still upon the island. The only difference is, that they are now freemen. In the best days of slavery, when the planters controlled the blacks, they exported, during the three years preceding the prohibition of the slave trade—1805 to 1808—an annual average of nearly 222,-500,000 lbs. of sugar. With that same population, or its descendants, as freemen, the planters now export less than 50,000,000 lbs. We are told that the cost of the production of this free-labor sugar is only 2 cents per lb.; whereas, the former cost of production, under slavery, was 4 37-100 cents per lb. Be it so; but which system—freedom or slavery—yields the greatest aggregate profit? The sugar of both kinds sold at, say 7 cents per lb.; or a profit of 5 cents per lb. on the free-labor product, and 2 63-100 cents per lb. on the slave-labor product. The net profits to the planters on the 50,000,000 lbs. of free-labor sugar is, therefore, $2,500,000, while on the 222,500,000 lbs. of slave-labor sugar it was $5,851,750—a difference of $2,351,000 per annum in favor of slavery. Or, taking the last years of slavery, from 1822 to 1832, when the average annual exports were reduced to 153,760,-000 lbs., and still slavery receives $4,043,000 for its sugar—being an advantage over free labor of. $1,543,000.

This, then, to the planter of Jamaica, is the result of emancipation; and this its effects upon British commerce. The prohibition of the slave trade reduced the exports from 222,000,000 lbs. to 153,000,000 lbs.; and emancipation, still more disastrous, reduced it to less than 50,000,000 lbs. Never was there a greater failure in any human expectations than has followed the abolition of slavery in Jamaica, so far as relates to the economical interests involved.

In justice to Mr. Sewell, however, it must be observed, that he makes the comparison of the relative cost of the production of sugar under slavery and freedom as an argument for the introduction of coolie laborers—a few ten thousands of whom, as in Mauritius and Trinidad, would, in his opinion, soon restore the prosperity of Jamaica.

With these remarks in relation to the economical results of emancipation in Jamaica, we may proceed to the consideration of its moral effects upon the negro population of that island—referring, in passing, to the others also.

In a preceding chapter, the history of missions in the West India Islands, together with the opposition of the planters to the religious instruction of the slaves, has been very fully presented. It may be remarked here, that little had been accomplished in the West Indies by the missionaries until near the time of the prohibition of the slave trade. The foreign missionary work was then in its infancy, and but few stations had been established in heathendom. Encouraging success attended the efforts made among the slaves, and their moral progress, under instruction, was fully equal to that of any other barbarous people where missions had been introduced. Any tardiness occurring in the progress of the work was caused more by the hostility of the planters than by any indisposition on the part of the slaves to attend upon religious instruction. Placed under restraints that confined them within the limits of the estates to which they belonged, they gladly listened to the Gospel as the first exhibition of human sympathy ever made in their behalf. Unable to wander from their homes, their instruction had a regularity that gave it efficiency. Had this system of instruction and restraint been continued without interruption, the moral progress of the negroes might have been greatly promoted; but the instruction was interrupted by the planters, and the restraint wholly removed by emancipation. As a necessary consequence of the unstable character of the blacks, this freedom from restraint greatly embarrassed the missionaries. Such was the serious nature of the reverses experienced, as a legitimate result of the abolition of slavery, and such the diminution in the number of converts, that the greatly increased missionary force since employed, has scarcely been able to bring up the missions to the condition in which emancipation found them.

To the question, whether emancipation was necessary as a means of moral progress to the blacks, but one answer can be returned. The planters, especially in Jamaica, continued their hostility to the religious instruction of their slaves up to the last moment. There is no reason to suppose that this hostility would have abated, had they been left to follow their own inclinations. So far, then, as the planters were concerned, no progress could have been made by the slaves while the authority of the masters was continued. Emancipation, or a change in the policy of the masters, was necessary, therefore, under the circumstances, to the moral progress of the blacks.

But the end to be attained was the moral elevation of the negroes, and emancipation was only urged as a measure essential to the accomplishment of that object. Had the masters all exerted themselves for the spread of the Gospel among their slaves, or had they even permitted the missionaries to have free access to them, British Christians would not have urged emancipation as necessary to the Christianization of the blacks. This is apparent from the fact that the few planters who introduced the Gospel into some of the islands were viewed as men of extraordinary piety and moral worth, and their deaths lamented as an irreparable loss to the Church.

The object, then, to be attained, was not emancipation for the sake of the measure itself, but emancipation as the only means by which the slaves could be placed in a position favorable to moral progress. If that progress could have been attained without emancipation, and the welfare of the negro had been the only question involved, there is no reason to suppose that the British people would have insisted upon the abolition of slavery. But, at that moment, there appeared to be no hope for the negro except in freedom; and freedom was accordingly conferred upon him. This, also, was the more cheerfully done, as the advancement of the black man was expected to secure a proportionate increase in the economical prosperity of the islands.

SECTION V.—EFFECTS OF EMANCIPATION UPON THE MORAL AND PHYSICAL CONDITION OF THE NEGROES IN THE BRITISH WEST INDIA ISLANDS, AS COMPARED WITH THAT OF SLAVERY UPON THE SAME RACE IN THE UNITED STATES.

The point of greatest interest in our investigations is just here, and the whole subject, so far as it relates to the colored people, involves itself in a single question — Has the progress of the West India negroes, under freedom, been such as was expected by the British people, or at all proportionate to the sacrifices made for their advancement? If it has not, then emancipation has been not only an economical failure, but it has been of so little benefit to the negroes, that if religious instruction, under slavery, could have been secured, as is the case in the United States, then their moral progress and physical welfare would both have been better promoted while in bondage than it has been under freedom.

Up to the date of West India emancipation, the physical welfare of the slaves of the United States had been so well secured that their increase was equal to that of any other people in the world. Their moral progress, too, was quite favorable, as is indicated by the numbers who had become converts to Christianity. Very different, indeed, was the condition of the slaves of the United States, in these respects, as compared with the freemen of the West Indies at this moment. Am I not justifiable in making this assertion?

Taking the testimony of Mr. Sewell, in connection with what is contained in some of the preceding chapters, as a fair exhibition of facts, no one can doubt that the colored people of the whole of the islands have utterly failed in meeting public expectation. They have failed in the progress anticipated, both physically and morally. I do not say that they would have improved under slavery, had emancipation not been adopted. I believe they could not have made much progress under the system of West India slavery, because the planters refused to allow them the means of moral progress. But the Gospel, which was then refused to them by the planters, is now voluntarily rejected by themselves. The means of moral elevation, which the despotism of their masters withheld from them, as slaves, is now repelled with equal force by their own unbridled licentiousness, as freemen. What says Mr. Sewell as to their condition, both physically and morally? "Immorality of the grossest kind pervades all classes, tainting alike the civilization of towns and the unchecked intercourse of the laborers in the cane-fields. The natural growth of the population has thus been arrested, and some of the most detestable crimes known to society are, even now, of frequent occurrence." In the capital of Jamaica, "the inhabitants, taken *en masse*, are steeped to the eyelids in immorality;" while "they perish miserably in country districts for want of medical aid." This rural population "are not instructed;" and "they have no opportunities to improve themselves in agriculture;" so that "in all they grow they may be held to waste five times as much as they reap;" and, besides, "a working-man, in America, does as much as ten men in Jamaica." "In many of the country districts the people are abandoned to the spells and debasing superstitions of the working Obeah and Myalism," a species of African witchcraft. In Barbadoes, "among their other vices, immorality and promiscuous intercourse of the sexes are almost universal. From the last census it appears that more than half of the children born in Barbadoes are illegitimate." In Antigua, "the number of illegitimate births averages fifty-three per cent. In some other islands it exceeds one hundred per cent." In Kingston, Jamaica, "promiscuous intercourse of the sexes is the rule; the population shows an unnatural decrease; illegitimacy exceeds legitimacy." In Antigua, "the agricultural population, for twenty years past, has diminished at the rate of a half per cent. per annum, although the island is remarkably healthy. The mortality is greater now than it was in the days of slavery; and the mortality is less on estates, at present, than it is in the villages where the laborers reside on their own lands." In Jamaica, "the mortality among the children, from want of proper attention, is frightful. Nor, unfortunately, is this the only evil that deprives Jamaica of a legitimate increase in her population." Among the squatters and small proprietors, "few understand the enjoyment of a regular meal. They eat when they are hungry, and will sometimes take enough in the morning to last the entire day."

Upon this array of facts, from the pages of Mr. Sewell, which are elsewhere presented in a more extended form, many will be surprised at the conclusions drawn by that gentleman. But there is nothing unusual in men drawing false conclusions from the facts before them. Nothing is more common in the field of the natural sciences—the branch of geology, for example—than for the most successful collectors of facts to prove themselves very often the poorest in generalization—the least capable of comprehending the true relations of the materials they have accumulated. The case of the *Plutonists* and *Neptunists*, in the early history of geology, is one in point. Every fact discovered among the rocky strata of the earth's crust proved to the Plutonists that the world had its origin from *fire;* while the same kind of researches, by the Neptunists, led them to contend that all such things had their origin from *water.*

So is it of the class of men to whom Mr. Sewell belongs. They have theories in relation to slavery and emancipation:—that only evil can come of the one, and only good of the other; so that all facts and results which do not accord with these theories make so little impression upon their minds as to receive no attention in arriving at their conclusions. Hence it is, that all facts which would show any good results from slavery, or any ill results from freedom, are instinctively rejected by this class of philanthropists.

With this solution of the process by which the mental action of Mr. Sewell is controlled, the reader may solve many seeming mysteries in the statements of that gentleman, quoted at large, in the present chapter. A few only of the prominent defects in his reasonings need be noted here.

The enjoyment of perfect freedom of action, by the negro, is held, by Mr. Sewell, to be paramount to all other considerations. This is a fair inference from much of the language he employs; and yet, no doubt, he would deny that he advocates any such an absurdity. But what are the facts? He commends the negro for refusing to assent to the abridgement of his liberties, required by the system of tenancy-at-will. Rather than submit to this regulation, which demands continuous labor, Mr. Sewell justifies him in taking up his residence beyond the reach of schools, churches, physicians, and every means of civilization, and almost every personal comfort—sleeping upon the floor of his bamboo hut, eating his one meal a day, and leaving his wife to carry to market, upon her head, the crop of vegetables they produce!

According to Mr. Sewell, the negro endures all these disadvantages most heroically, not to avoid slavery — for the question is no longer between liberty and slavery—but merely from an inveterate aversion to engaging, upon the sugar plantations, in regular contract labor. This aversion to continuous industry is considered by Mr. Sewell as the natural outgrowth of emancipation: because all the ideas of slavery that ever entered the mind of the negro were associated with sugar culture; and all the dreams of liberty that ever agitated his thoughts included the hope of entire exemption from that kind of work. His master was a gentleman, but his master never engaged in working at sugar cultivation; therefore, argued the negro, to be a gentleman, he must not work at that employment.

Such sentiments in the negro, Mr. Sewell believes, go very far in demonstrating that he has made vast progress toward a higher and nobler manhood; and yet, the terms of the contract made with the coolie, and so highly commended in his book, for its Christianizing and civilizing tendencies, is essentially the same, in all its provisions, with the tenancy-at-will required of the negro, and which he rejects with disdain as so insulting to his dignity!

But this point needs no further comment, except to say that no one who will carefully study the traits of character attributed by Mr. Sewell to the West India negroes, and fairly contrast them with the well-known habits of the native Africans, can come to any other conclusion than that the inherent barbarism of the race is fast resuming its sway over the great majority of the blacks in the West Indies!

Nor is this result, under the circumstances, a strange one. On the contrary, it is just what should have been anticipated. The slave trade found the negroes barbarous: slavery, with a few exceptions, left them barbarous; and, destitute as they have been of the means of moral elevation, they, of course, could make no moral progress.

But who was in fault in producing these melancholy results? Not the negro, but the system adopted for his liberation from bondage. He had been kept, while in slavery, in utter ignorance and degradation; and emancipation, making no provision for his education, "delivered him bound hand and foot by his own ignorance, incapacity, and vice, to a miserable destruction." *

Is this language too strong? Then, look again at what is said in relation to the destructive vices prevailing in all these islands, and the influence which the demoralization of the population has had in diminishing their inhabitants. This is a dreadful fact, and, though it has been often referred to in the course of our investigations, it yet demands a more minute examination in this new aspect of the emancipation question.

To judge accurately in relation to the effects of emancipation upon the increase or decrease of the African population in the British West Indies, some suitable standard of reference must be taken, which will show the ordinary rate of increase of the race under favorable circumstances. Africa has no statistics. Mexico and the South American Republics are equally unsatisfactory. The United States affords the only standard that can be used; and of it the assertion has been made, that "the slavery which existed in the Roman Empire, in the apostles' time, was, by no means, so debasing, hopeless, and oppressive as negro slavery in

---

* Boston Courier, March 29, 1861.

our country."* This assertion was made in the early days of the anti-slavery movement, when the advocates of the abolition of slavery first began their employment of the press to influence ecclesiastical legislation, and secure the exclusion of the slave-holder from the communion of the Church.

But we must again hear the above writer. After referring to several authors, he says no one can escape the conclusion "that slavery, in modern times, exists in its mildest form in countries where the Roman Catholic religion is the established religion, and where the government is despotic or *purely* monarchical, as in the Spanish and Portuguese colonies — that it becomes more ferocious and oppressive in Protestant countries, where the government is a *mixed* monarchy, as in the British colonies — and that it is most debasing of all in countries where the religion is purely Protestant, and the government free and republican, as *our own*." †

The standard chosen with which to compare the West Indies, if we give credit to this writer, should give to these British colonies a decided advantage, inasmuch as the slavery of the United States, in his judgment, has been the most ferocious, oppressive, and debasing of all other countries—British, Spanish, Portuguese, Roman. But if it has been otherwise, then we have, in his language, a fair specimen of the unscrupulous character of the men who, by gross misrepresentation, misled the churches into measures destructive of their peace, and laid the foundation for that political agitation which precipitated the country into civil war.

Let us, then, look at the facts, remembering we are writing history, and not depending upon imagination for the basis of our conclusions. Already we have drawn the contrast between the facilities afforded in the West Indies and the United States for the religious instruction of the slaves. By turning to the history of that work, in a preceding chapter, and tracing it from the beginning up to 1830, it will be seen that the facts are altogether different from the representations of this writer of 1829. No reference, therefore, need be made here to anything but the effects of emancipation upon the increase or decrease of population.

---

* Christian Intelligencer, Hamilton, Ohio, August, 1829, p. 230.   † Ibid.

Taking the United States as the standard of comparison, it is found that, at the date of the Declaration of American Independence, the several colonies had an aggregate of about 500,000 slaves. This fact is stated in the *American Almanac*, and is based on satisfactory data.* The first census was taken in 1790, and from that period to the present, the ratio of annual increase has been fully ascertained. In the year 1800, the slaves of the United States had increased to 893,000, and in 1830, to 2,009,-043—being an average annual increase, from 1800 to 1830, of 3.10-100 per cent. The ratio of annual increase was slightly augmented from 1800 to 1810, by the addition of 39,000 blacks, on the admission of Louisiana; and was diminished, from 1820 to 1830, by the emancipation of the remnant of 10,000 slaves remaining in New York, in 1827. For all practical purposes, the ratio of increase of the slave population in the United States may be estimated at three per cent. per annum, though it is a fraction less.

But this statement does not do full justice to the question of the increase of the African race in the United States. In 1790, there were only 40,212 free colored persons; in 1830, they had increased to 319,599, being an increase at the average rate of nearly 5½ per cent. per annum, and making a total colored population, slave and free, in 1830, of 2,328,642. Nearly one-half of the increase of the free colored people must have been by emancipation.

---

* The estimates are as follows, for the several colonies:

Massachusetts,	3,000
Rhode Island,	4,370
Connecticut,	5,000
New Hampshire,	629
New York,	15,000
New Jersey,	7,600
Pennsylvania,	10,000
Delaware,	9,000
Maryland,	80,000
Virginia,	165,000
North Carolina,	76,000
South Carolina,	110,000
Georgia,	16,000
Total,	501,599

Turning to the British West Indies, we find, that when the slave trade ceased, in 1808, these islands had a slave population of 800,000—being nearly equal to the number in the United States in 1800. Did they increase as rapidly as the colored population of the United States? By no means. Instead of that, the census of 1835, taken under the emancipation act, shows a reduction of the slave population to 660,000. This number includes only the slave population, and not the free colored and the whites.

Had the increase of the blacks in the British West Indies, after the suppression of the slave trade, in 1808, been equal to the increase of the slaves in the United States, these islands would have numbered, at the time of emancipation, in 1838, nearly 2,000,000; but, from causes before explained, there was no increase during that period, but a falling off in their numbers to the extent of 140,000!

Here, then, is the contrast between the slavery of the United States and that of the West Indies, in its effects upon the increase or decrease of the slave population in the two cases, respectively, from the prohibition of the slave trade, by both countries, to the final abolition of slavery in the British colonies. The comparison is for an equal number of years, but not of even date—the United States beginning with 1800 and ending with 1830, the colonies beginning with 1808 and ending with 1838. The slave population of each, in the outset, was nearly equal—893,000 to 800,000—and the final result shows an *increase* for the United States, exclusive of emancipations, of 1,116,000, and a *decrease* for the British colonies, on the slave population alone, of 140,000! *

But let us proceed to the main point—the effect of emancipation upon the population of the British West Indies, as contrasted with that of slavery on the slave population of the United States:

---

* Exactness as to the United States cannot be had, from 1790 to 1808, because emancipation, on the one hand, was adding to the free colored population, and the slave trade, on the other, was increasing the number of the slaves. The ratio of increase of the former, from 1798 to 1800, was 8 22-100 per cent. per annum, and of the latter, 2 79-100. Again, from 1800 to 1810, the increase of the former was 7 20-100, and of the latter, including 39,000 from Louisiana, it was 3 34-100 per cent. per annum. The census for the British colonies was taken in 1835, but will represent 1838.

Beginning where we left off, the slave population of the United States, in 1830, was 2,009,043, which had increased, in 1860, to 3,950,343—an increase indicating a condition of physical comfort fully equal to that of the populations of the civilized world generally. Between 1830 and 1840, the cholera visited America, and the ratio of increase of the slaves was considerably reduced.

The West India Islands, in 1838, emancipated 660,000 slaves. Besides these liberated slaves, the islands had a considerable population of whites and free colored people—Jamaica, alone, having 60,000 of the latter.* All the other islands, probably, had about an equal number of free colored persons. From the best data before us, the conjecture is, that the whites of the whole islands may have been near 50,000. If so, then, the whole population, including all colors, was about 834,000.

Here, now, as to population, is the point from which the British West India colonies took their start in the career of freedom. The whole population was now upon an equality, and white, yellow, black, could compete, upon equal terms, under the civil law, for wealth and distinction. A generation nearly had passed away since any blacks had been imported from Africa. The sexes had become equalized, and the belief existed, that from the date of emancipation, and as a necessary consequence of that measure, the natural increase of the population would be such as to add rapidly to the labor force of the islands.

We have seen that the slave population of the United States has doubled since 1830. Has anything so favorable occurred to the free population of the West Indies? Alas, no! American slavery proves itself, as to its effects upon population, a perfect paradise of physical comfort and moral influence, as compared with the British West Indies.

Let us ascertain the facts, as far as practicable. Jamaica emancipated 320,000 slaves in 1838, and, at the same time, had 60,000 free colored people. This gave her a total colored population of 380,000, at the time of emancipation. The present population of Jamaica, exclusive of the whites, is 350,000 †—

---

* Sewell, p. 245.   † Sewell.

being a *decrease* of 30,000 in 22 years! Had there been an increase of the colored population of Jamaica under freedom, in the same ratio in which those of the United States have increased under slavery, that island, in 1860, would have numbered about 640,000 souls, instead of having had a decrease of 30,000!

The total population of Jamaica, whites, blacks and mulattoes, at present, is 378,000,* of which, according to the above statistics, 350,000 are mulattoes and blacks. The cholera in Jamaica, as well as in the United States, was severe among the colored population; but their scattered condition in Jamaica, placing them beyond the care of the whites, and leaving them without proper medical attention, may have caused a greater proportional mortality among them, in that island, than occurred in the United States. This, however, was one of the consequences of freedom.

In turning to the other British islands, we find that Barbadoes, Antigua, St. Vincent, St. Lucia, Dominica, Tobago, Trinidad, Grenada, Nevis, Montserrat, St. Kitts, and the Virgin Islands, embrace an aggregate population of about 395,000, including whites, blacks, and mulattoes. The first six of these islands include nearly 21,400 whites, at present, but the number of the whites and free colored persons, and the number of slaves emancipated, in 1838, are not given;† so that it is impossible to determine, with exactness, the extent of increase or decrease in their colored population. The last six of these islands seems to have afforded to Mr. Sewell—from whom the statistics are gathered—no means of determining their white population, either at present or before emancipation; nor has he given the number of free colored persons in them at the time of the abolition of slavery. One reason of the defect is, that, under freedom, many of the islands are careful to exclude all reference to color in the census returns.

By adding the present colored population of these islands — 373,600—to the present number of the colored people in Jamaica

---

* Sewell, p. 177.

† Their white population stands thus, according to Mr. Sewell: Barbadoes, 15,824; Antigua, 2,172; St. Vincent, 1,500; St. Lucia, 958; Dominica, 850; Tobago, 160.

—350,000 — the whole colored population of the British West India colonies, in 1860, is found to be 723,600. This, however, includes the whites in the last six islands enumerated, and emancipation has that advantage in these estimates.

The contrast between freedom and slavery, in its effects upon population, may be thus summed up :

Total slaves emancipated in 1838, ...		660,000
By Jamaica,..	320,000	
By the other islands,......................................	340,000	
		660,000
Add free colored population in 1838,		
In Jamaica,......................	60,000	
In the other islands,..	60,000	
		120,000
Total colored population in 1838,...		780,000
Total colored population in 1860,..		723,600
Decrease of colored population under freedom,..............		56,400

Here we have the effects of emancipation upon the increase of population — resulting, in the aggregate, in causing a decrease in the population of the islands, during freedom, of more than 56,000 souls out of a population of 660,000, or more than *eight* per cent. of a loss in twenty-five years !

In reference to the production of the islands, and the economical failure of emancipation, especially in Jamaica, the late reports to Parliament fully sustain the assertions of Mr. Sewell, and corroborate the testimony we have collected from other sources. The report of the Governor, says the *New York Independent,* " gives a good account of the happiness of the population, so far as a mere animal life of independence is concerned, but holds out little encouragement to those who would hope that labor may be attracted to any system of combined enterprise, such as the growth of cotton, or of any produce in which joint-stock capital might be embarked. The four great staples of export are still sugar, rum, coffee, and pimento ; but the quantities of sugar and coffee seem rather to diminish than increase. An export of sugar of about 30,000 tons, more or less, according to the nature of the seasons, is considered the best result that can be hoped for from the existing population. . . . The obvious remedy is considered to lie in efforts for obtaining contract laborers from India and elsewhere. In that manner the island may one day again become a valuable possession, and meanwhile it is gratifying to know that the negro population, although inefficient for co-operative purposes essential to raise a country to any commercial standing, are by no means retrograding to barbarism."*

From many other anti-slavery sources, from year to year, we have been assured that West India slavery had kept the negro population in the ignorance and degradation of their original barbarism. If the truth was then told, the Governor may safely say that the population is not now "retrograding;" and, if Mr. Sewell tells the truth, we cannot see how the great bulk of the people can sink to any lower depth of moral debasement than that in which he found them.

On the question of the economical failure of emancipation, there can no longer remain the shadow of a doubt upon the minds of candid men. It is admitted by the Governor of Jamaica; and his only hope of the ultimate recovery of the islands to a prosperous condition, is by substituting coolie labor for that of the negroes.

We can give no more appropriate conclusion to this chapter, than to copy, from the *London Times*, a few paragraphs in relation to emancipation and its effects in the West Indies:

"There is no blinking the truth, . . . and it must be spoken out loudly and energetically, despite the wild mockings of 'howling cant.' The freed West India slave will not till the soil for wages; the free son of the ex-slave is as obstinate as his sire. He will not cultivate lands which he has not bought for his own use. Yams, mangoes, and plantains; these satisfy *his* wants; he does not care for *yours*. Cotton, sugar, coffee, and tobacco—he cares but little for them. And what matters it to him that the Englishman has sunk his thousands and tens of thousands on mills, machinery, and plants, which now totter on the languishing estate, that for years has only returned beggary and debt? He eats his yams, and sniggers at 'buckra.'

"We know not why this should be, but it is so. The negro has been bought with a price—the price of English taxation and English toil. He has been redeemed from bondage by the sweat and travail of some

---

* New York Independent, September 19, 1861.

millions of hard-working Englishmen. Twenty millions of pounds sterling—one hundred millions of dollars—have been distilled from the brains and muscles of the free English laborer, of every degree, to fashion the West India negro into 'a free and independent laborer.' 'Free and independent' enough he has become, God knows; but laborer he is not; and, so far as we can see, never will be. He will sing hymns and quote texts; but honest, steady industry he not only detests, but despises. We wish heaven that some people in England—neither government people, nor parsons, nor clergymen, but some just-minded, honest-hearted, and clear-sighted men would go out to some of the islands, (say Jamaica, Dominica, or Antigua,) not for a month, or three months, but for a year—would watch the precious *protegé* of English philanthropy, the free negro, in his daily habits; would watch him as he lazily plants his little squatting; would see him as he proudly rejects agricultural domestic services, or accepts it only at wages ludicrously disproportionate to the value of his work. We wish, too, they would watch him, with a hide thicker than that of a hippopotamus, and a body to which fervid heat is a comfort rather than an annoyance, as he droningly lounges over the prescribed task on which the intrepid Englishman, uninured to the burning sun, consumes his impatient energy, and too often sacrifices his life. We wish they would go out and view the negro in all the blazonry of his idleness, his pride, his ingratitude, contemptuously sneering at the industry of that race which made him free, and then come home, and teach the memorable lesson of their experience to the fanatics who have perverted him into what he is."

Taking, then, the whole testimony on the subject—civil, social, moral, physical, economical,—and it is fully proved that West India emancipation, in its expected results, is a miserable failure.

CHAPTER VI.

THE GENERAL ASSEMBLY PRESBYTERIAN CHURCH AND SLAVERY.

SECTION I.—EARLY LEGISLATION ON THE SUBJECT OF SLAVERY.

1. IN 1787, THE GENERAL ASSEMBLY PRESBYTERIAN CHURCH IN NORTH AMERICA, while yet acting under the title of the SYNOD OF NEW YORK AND PHILADELPHIA, announced its views on slavery. Six years later, 1793, when the General Assembly had been fully organized, the action of 1787 was re-affirmed and made the rule of the Church upon the subject. It was as follows:

" 'The Creator of the world having made of one flesh all the children of men, it becomes them, as members of the same family, to consult and promote each others' happiness. It is more especially the duty of those who maintain the rights of humanity, and who acknowledge and teach the obligations of Christianity, to use such means as are in their power to extend the blessings of equal freedom to every part of the human race.' (1)

" 'From a full conviction of these truths, and sensible that the rights of human nature are too well understood to admit of debate, overtured, that the Synod of New York and Philadelphia recommend, in the warmest terms, to every member of their body, and to all the churches and families under their care, to do every thing in their power, consistent with the rights of civil society, to promote the abolition of slavery, and the instruction of negroes, whether bond or free.' (2)

"The Synod, taking into consideration the overture concerning slavery transmitted by the committee of Overtures last Saturday, came to the following judgment:—

" 'The Synod of New York and Philadelphia do highly approve of the general principles in favor of universal liberty that prevail in America, and the interest which many of the States have taken in promoting the abolition of slavery; yet, inasmuch as men introduced from a servile state to a participation of all the privileges of civil society, without a proper education and without previous habits of industry, may be in many respects dangerous to the community, therefore they earnestly recommend it to all the members belonging to their communion to give those persons, who are at present held in servitude, such good education as to prepare them for the better enjoyment of freedom: (3) and they moreover recommend that masters, wherever they find servants disposed to make a just improvement of the privilege, would give them a *peculium*, or grant them sufficient time, and sufficient means of procuring their own liberty at a moderate rate, that thereby they may be brought into society with those habits of industry that may render them useful citizens; and, finally, they recommend it to all their people to use the most prudent measures, consistent with the interest and state of civil society, in the counties where they live, to procure eventually the final abolition of slavery in America.'"—*Min.* 1787, pp. 539–540.

"The Assembly of 1815 declared 'that, although in some sections of our country, under certain circumstances, the transfer of slaves may be unavoidable, yet they consider the buying and selling of slaves by way of traffic, and all undue severity in the management of them, as inconsistent with the spirit of the gospel. And they recommend it to the Presbyteries and Sessions under their care to make use of all prudent measures to prevent such shameful and unrighteous conduct.'

"The Assembly of 1815 'expressed their regret that the slavery of the Africans and of their descendants still continues in so many places, and even among those within the pale of the Church,' and called particular attention to the action of 1795 with respect to the buying and selling of slaves.

"In 1818, the Assembly unanimously adopted a report on this subject, prepared by Dr. Green, of Philadelphia, Dr. Baxter, of Virginia, and Mr. Burgess, of Ohio, of which the following is a part:—

"'We consider the voluntary enslaving of one part of the human race by another as a gross violation of the most precious and sacred rights of human nature, as utterly inconsistent with the law of God, which requires us to love our neighbor as ourselves, and as totally irreconcilable with the spirit and principles of the Gospel of Christ, which enjoins that "all things whatsoever ye would that men should do to you, do ye even so to them." Slavery creates a paradox in the moral system: it exhibits rational, accountable and immortal beings in such circumstances as scarcely to leave them the power of moral action. It exhibits them as dependent on the will of others whether they shall receive religious instruction; whether they shall know and worship the true God; whether they shall enjoy the ordinances of the gospel; whether they shall perform the duties and cherish the endearments of husbands and wives, parents and children, neighbors and friends; whether they shall preserve their chastity and purity, or regard the dictates of justice and humanity. Such are some of the consequences of slavery,—consequences not imaginary, but which connect themselves with its very existence. The evils to which the slave is *always* exposed often take place in fact, and in their very worst degree and form; and, where all of them do not take place,—as we rejoice to say that in many instances, through the influence of the principles of humanity and religion on the minds of masters, they do not,—still, the slave is deprived of his natural right, degraded as a human being, and exposed to the danger of passing into the hands of a master who may inflict upon him all the hardships and injuries which inhumanity and avarice may suggest.

" From this view of the consequences resulting from the practice into which Christian people have most inconsistently fallen of enslaving a portion of their *brethren* of mankind,—for God hath made of one blood all nations of men to dwell on the face of the earth,—it is manifestly the duty of all Christians who enjoy the light of the present day, when the inconsistency of slavery both with the dictates of humanity and religion has been demonstrated and is generally seen and acknowledged, to use their honest, earnest and unwearied endeavors to correct the errors of former times, and as speedily as possible to efface this blot on our holy religion, and to obtain the complete abolition of slavery throughout Christendom, and, if possible, throughout the world.'

"The Assembly also recommended 'to all the members of our religious denomination, (not only to permit, but to facilitate and encourage, the instruction of their slaves in the principles and duties of the Christian religion;' and added, 'We enjoin it on all church sessions and Presbyteries under the care of this Assembly to discountenance, and, as far as possible, to prevent, all cruelty of whatever kind, in the treatment of slaves, especially the cruelty of separating husband and wife, parents and children, and that which consists in selling slaves to those who will either themselves deprive these unhappy people of the blessings of the Gospel, or who will transport them to places where the Gospel is not proclaimed or where it is forbidden to slaves to attend upon its institutions.' (4)

" The foregoing testimonials on the subject of slavery were universally acquiesced in by the Presbyterian Church up to the time of the division in 1838." *

SECTION II.—THE LEGISLATION OF THE GENERAL ASSEMBLY, (O. S.,) AFTER THE DIVISION OF THE CHURCH.

I. The following embraces the legislation of the O. S. General Assembly, after the division of the Church, in 1838, as published in the ASSEMBLY'S DIGEST, issued by the Presbyterian Board of Publication, 1846. The subject having been from time to time, for a series of years, urged upon the Assembly, it was taken up in 1845, and the following paper adopted:

" The committee to whom were referred the memorials on the subject of slavery, beg leave to submit the following report:

(a.) " The memorialists may be divided into three classes, viz:

" 1. Those who represent the system of slavery, as it exists in these United States, as a great evil, and pray this General Assembly to adopt measures for the amelioration of the condition of the slaves.

" 2. Those which ask the Assembly to receive memorials on the subject of slavery, to allow a full discussion of it, and to enjoin upon the members of our Church, residing in States whose laws forbid the slaves being taught to read, to seek, by all lawful means, the repeal of those laws.

" 3. Those which represent slavery as a moral evil, a heinous sin in the sight of God, calculated to bring upon the Church the curse of God, and calling for the exercise of discipline in the case of those who persist in maintaining or justifying the relation of master to slaves.

(b.) " The question which is now unhappily agitating and dividing other branches of the Church, and which is pressed upon the attention of the Assembly by one of the three classes of memorialists just named, is, whether the holding of slaves is, under all circumstances, a heinous sin, calling for the discipline of the Church.

---

* The synopsis of the proceedings of the General Assembly, from 1815 to 1818, are copied from the publication made by the N. S. General Assembly at Cleveland, Ohio, in 1857.

(c.) "The Church of Christ is a spiritual body, whose jurisdiction extends to the religious faith and moral conduct of her members. She can not legislate where Christ has not legislated, nor make terms of membership which he has not made. The question, therefore, which this Assembly is called to decide, is this: Do the Scriptures teach that the holding of slaves, without regard to circumstances, is a sin, the renunciation of which should be made a condition of membership in the Church of Christ? (5)

(d) "It is impossible to answer this question in the affirmative, without contradicting some of the plainest declarations of the Word of God. That slavery existed in the days of Christ and his apostles is an admitted fact. That they did not denounce the relation itself as sinful, as inconsistent with Christianity; that slaveholders were admitted to membership in the churches organized by the apostles; that while they were required to treat their slaves with kindness, and as rational, accountable, immortal beings, and, if Christians, as brethren in the Lord, they were not commanded to emancipate them; that slaves were required to be ʻobedient to their masters according to the flesh, with fear and trembling, with singleness of heart as unto Christ,' are facts which meet the eye of every reader of the New Testament. This Assembly can not, therefore, denounce the holding of slaves as necessarily a heinous and scandalous sin, calculated to bring upon the Church the curse of God, without charging the apostles of Christ with conniving at sin, introducing into the Church such sinners, and thus bringing upon them the curse of the Almighty.

(e) "In so saying, however, the Assembly are not to be understood as denying that there is evil connected with slavery. Much less do they approve those defective and oppressive laws by which, in some of the States, it is regulated. Nor would they by any means countenance the traffic in slaves for gain; the separation of husbands and wives, parents and children, for the sake of ʻfilthy lucre,' or for the convenience of the master; or cruel treatment of slaves, in any respect. Every Christian and philanthropist certainly should seek, by all peaceable and lawful means, the repeal of unjust and oppressive laws, and the amendment of such as are defective, so as to protect the slaves from cruel treatment by wicked men, and secure to them the right to receive religious instruction.

(f) "Nor is the Assembly to be understood as countenancing the idea that masters may régard their servants as mere property, and not as human beings, rational, accountable, immortal. The Scriptures prescribe not only the duties of servants, but masters also, warning the latter to discharge those duties, 'knowing that their Master is in heaven, neither is there respect of persons with him.'

(*g*) "The Assembly intend simply to say, that since Christ and his inspired apostles did not make the holding of slaves a bar to communion, we, as a court of Christ, have no authority to do so; since they did not attempt to remove it from the Church by legislation, we have no authority to legislate upon the subject. We feel further constrained to say, that however desirable it may be to ameliorate the condition of the slaves in the Southern and Western States, or to remove slavery from our country, these objects, we are fully persuaded, can never be secured by ecclesiastical legislation. Much less can they be attained by those indiscriminate denunciations against slaveholders, without regard to their character or circumstances, which have to so great an extent characterized the movements of modern abolitionists, which, so far from removing the evils complained of, tend only to perpetuate and aggravate them.

"The apostles of Christ sought to ameliorate the condition of slaves, not by denouncing and excommunicating their masters, but by teaching both masters and slaves the glorious doctrines of the Gospel, and enjoining upon each the discharge of their relative duties. Thus only can the Church of Christ, as such, now improve the condition of the slaves in our country.

(*h*) "As to the extent of the evils involved in slavery, and the best methods of removing them, various opinions prevail, and neither the Scriptures nor our Constitution authorize this body to prescribe any particular course to be pursued by the churches under our care. The Assembly can not but rejoice, however, to learn that the ministers and churches in the slaveholding States are awake to a deeper sense of their obligation to extend to the slave population generally the means of grace, and many slaveholders not professedly religious favor this object. We earnestly exhort them to abound more and more in this good work. We would exhort every believing master to remember that his Master is also in heaven, and in view of all the circumstances in which he is placed, to act in the spirit of the golden rule: 'Whatsoever, ye would that men should do to you, do ye even the same to them.'

"In view of the above-stated principles and facts,

"*Resolved*, 1. That the General Assembly of the Presbyterian Church in the United States was originally organized, and has since continued the bond of union in the Church, upon the conceded principle that the existence of domestic slavery, under the circumstances in which it is found in the southern portion of the country, is no bar to Christian communion.

"2. That the petitions that ask the Assembly to make the holding of slaves in itself a matter of discipline, do virtually require this judicatory to dissolve itself, and abandon the organization under which, by the Divine blessing, it has so long prospered. The tendency is evidently to separate the northern from the southern portion of the Church; a result which every good citizen must deplore, as tending to the dissolution of the Union of our beloved country, and which every enlightened Christian will oppose as bringing about a ruinous and unnecessary schism between brethren who maintain a common faith. (6)

"The yeas and nays being ordered, were—yeas, 168; nays, 13; excused, 4.—*Minutes*, 1845, page 16."

Some agitation of the question of slavery was subsequently produced, by petitions presented and by overtures from Presbyteries, but any additional legislation upon the subject has been deemed inexpedient by the Assembly.

2. At the meeting of the General Assembly, (Old School,) in 1861, after much excited discussion, the following resolutions were passed:

"Gratefully acknowledging the distinguished bounty and care of Almighty God toward this favored land, and also recognizing our obligation to submit to every ordinance of man for the Lord's sake, this General Assembly adopt the following resolutions:

"1. *Resolved*, That in view of the present agitated and unhappy condition of this country, the first day of July next is set apart as a day of prayer throughout our bounds, and that on this day ministers and people are called on humbly to confess and bewail their national sins, and to offer our thanks to the Father of lights for his abundant and undeserved goodness toward us as a nation, to seek his guidance and blessing upon our rulers and their counsels, as well as the assembled Congress of the United States, and to implore Him, in the name of Jesus Christ, the great High Priest of the Christian profession, to turn away His anger from us, and speedily restore to us the blessings of a safe and honorable peace.

"2. *Resolved*, That this General Assembly, in the spirit of that

Christian patriotism which the Scriptures enjoin, and which has always characterized this Church, do hereby acknowledge and declare our obligations to promote and perpetuate, so far as in us lies, the integrity of these United States, and to strengthen, uphold and encourage the Federal Government in the exercise of all its functions under our noble Constitution, and to this Constitution, in all its provisions, requirements, and principles, we profess our unabated loyalty. And to avoid all misconception, the Assembly declares that by the terms 'Federal Government,' as here used, is not meant any particular Administration, or the peculiar opinions of any political party, but that central Administration which being at any time appointed and inaugurated according to the terms prescribed in the Constitution of the United States, is the visible representative of our national existence."

As we shall offer no extended remarks upon the proceedings of 1861, by either of the General Assemblies, we append a response to that of the Old School Assembly by the Presbytery of Louisville, Kentucky:

"Regarding the deliverances of the General Assembly not as mere expressions of opinion of an advisory council, to be quietly ignored if judged erroneous, but, on the contrary, as our standards teach, in the light of solemn enactments in the name of Christ, to be received with reverence, when in conformity with God's Word, or to be distinctly impugned and rejected, when opposed thereto, the Presbytery of Louisville, after duly considering the act of the late General Assembly touching the political allegiance of ministers and members of the Church, as found on p. 329, and in answer to protests, pp. 341 and 344, feels called upon in this solemn manner to testify against the dangerous errors in doctrine involved in that action, and to repudiate the same as of no binding effect upon our ministers and churches. It appears, from the reports of Commissioners, and from the minutes, (compare p. 329 with p. 303), that this action was taken under constraint, directly in opposition to the Assembly's own free and uncontrolled judgment previously given against making any such deliverance; that the pressure from without, from popular clamor, constrained the Assembly to reverse its decisions. We feel, therefore, the less hesitancy in setting aside this deliverance on this account.

"The action of the General Assembly on this subject involves these essential errors.

"First, the assumption of power to determine questions of political allegiance, is directly contrary to the teachings of Christ and His Apostles, who uniformly enjoin obedience to Cæsar as a Christian duty; but abstain from determining as between the claims of rival Cæsars to the allegiance of Christians. It is notoriously contrary to the great distinctive doctrine of the Church of Scotland, as attested by Martyrs, General Assemblies, and Confessions, 'that the power and policie ecclesiastical is distinct in its own nature from the civil power,' and that 'the two jurisdictions confounded, which God hath divided, directly tendeth to the wreck of all true religion.' It is directly in conflict with the corresponding declaration of our own confession—'Synods and Councils are not to intermeddle with civil affairs,' etc. It is in disregard of the testimony of the fathers who formed the Constitution of the American Presbyterian Church, who taking the principle, secured for it recognition by the civil government in the law of Virginia and the Federal Constitution.

"Second. In the answer to the protest against the resolution of the Assembly there are interpretations of Scripture which this Presbytery hold to be gravely erroneous, and also propositions concerning the relation of the civil to the ecclesiastical power, which we regard as dangerous, though we deem it inexpedient to cite them in detail or make deliverance in regard to them separately from the resolution of the Assembly. This Presbytery, therefore, utters this testimony against these errors of doctrine and principle, and solemnly rejects the action of the Assembly in the premises as unconstitutional and of no binding force upon us.

"The Presbytery, believing that the kingdom of Christ is not to be limited by civil bounds, will cordially unite with all true and conservative men in our beloved Church, North or South, in defending and preserving the purity, unity and prosperity of the Presbyterian Church in the United States of America."

SECTION III.—LEGISLATION OF THE GENERAL ASSEMBLY, NEW SCHOOL, AFTER THE DIVISION OF THE CHURCH.

1. The following embraces the legislation of the New School General Assembly, after the division in 1838, as authorized to be published by the Assembly of 1857:

"In the year 1846, the General Assembly made a declaration on this subject, of which the following is the introductory paragraph:—

"'1. The system of slavery, as it exists in these United States, viewed either in the laws of the several States which sanction it, or in its actual operation and results in society, is intrinsically an unrighteous and oppressive system, and is opposed to the prescriptions of the law of God, to the spirit and precepts of the gospel, and to the best interests of humanity.'

"In 1849, the Assembly explicitly re-affirmed the sentiments expressed by the Assemblies of 1815, 1818, and 1846.   In the year 1850, the General Assembly made the following declaration:—'We exceedingly deplore the working of the whole system of slavery as it exists in our country and is interwoven with the political institutions of the slave-holding States, as fraught with many and great evils to the civil, political, and moral interests of those regions where it exists.

"'The holding of our fellow-men in the condition of slavery, except in those cases where it is unavoidable by the laws of the State, the obligations of guardianship, or the demands of humanity, is an offense in the proper import of that term as used in the Book of Discipline, chap. 1, sec. 3, and should be regarded and treated in the same manner as other offenses.'

"Occupying the position in relation to this subject which the framers of our Constitution held at the first, and which our Church has always held, it is with deep grief that we now discover that a portion of the Church at the South has so far departed from the established doctrine of the Church in relation to slavery as to maintain that 'it is an ordinance of God,' and that the system of slavery existing in these United States is scriptural and right.   Against this new doctrine we feel constrained to bear our solemn testimony.   It is at war with the whole spirit and tenor of the gospel of love and good will, as well as abhorrent to the conscience of the Christian world. We can have no sympathy or fellowship with it; and we exhort all our people to eschew it as serious and pernicious error.

"We are especially pained by the fact that the Presbytery of Lexington, South, have given official notice to us that a number of ministers and ruling elders, as well as many church-members, in their connection, hold slaves 'from principle' and 'of choice,' 'believing it to be according to the Bible right,' and have, without any qualifying explanation, assumed the responsibility of sustaining such ministers, elders, and church-members in their position.   We deem it our duty, in the exercise of our constitutional authority, 'to bear testimony against error in doctrine or immorality in practice in any Church, Presbytery, or Synod,' to disapprove and earnestly condemn the position which has been thus assumed by the Presbytery of Lexington, South, as one which is opposed to the established convictions of the Presbyterian Church, and must operate to mar its peace and seriously hinder its prosperity, as well as bring reproach on our holy religion ; and we do hereby call on that Presbytery to review and rectify their position. Such doctrines and practice can not be permanently tolerated in the Presbyterian Church.   May they speedily melt away under the illuminating and mellowing influence of the Gospel and grace of God our Saviour !

"We do not, indeed, pronounce a sentence of indiscriminate condemnation upon all our brethren who are unfortunately connected with the system of slavery.   We tenderly sympathize with all those who deplore the evil, and are honestly doing all in their power for the present well-being of their slaves and for their complete emancipation.   We would aid, and not embarrass, such brethren.   And yet, in the language of the General Assembly of 1818, we would 'earnestly warn them against unduly extending the plea of necessity,—against making it a cover for the love and practice of slavery, or a pretense for not using efforts that are lawful and practicable to extinguish this evil.' (7)

"In conclusion, the Assembly call the attention of the Publication Committee to this subject, and recommend the publication, in a convenient form, of the testimony of the Presbyterian Church touching this subject, at the earliest practicable period.

"The vote upon its adoption was by yeas and nays.

"Adopted : yeas, 169 ; nays, 26 ; *non liquet*, 2."—*Minutes* 1857, pp. 401–404."

The decisions of the General Assembly being so decidedly anti-slavery in their character, the southern ministers felt themselves constrained to withdraw from its jurisdiction, and that body now stands clear of all connection with slavery or slaveholders.

2. At the meeting of the General Assembly (New School,) at Syracuse, New York, in 1861, the following resolutions, in relation to the "state of the country," were passed unanimously:

"The Committee to whom it was referred to inquire what action, by resolution or otherwise, it is meet for the Assembly to take in view of the present condition of our country, beg leave to recommend the following resolutions:

"1. *Resolved*, That inasmuch as the Presbyterian Church, in her past history, has frequently lifted up her voice against oppression, has shown herself a champion of constitutional liberty, as against both despotism and anarchy, throughout the civilized world, we should be recreant to our high trust were we to withhold our earnest protest against all such unlawful and treasonable acts.

"2. *Resolved*, That this Assembly and the Churches which it represents, cherish an undiminished attachment to the great principles of civil and religious freedom on which our National Government is based; under the influence of which our fathers prayed, and fought, and bled; which issued in the establishment of our independence, and by the preservation of which we believe that the common interests of evangelical religion and civil liberty will be most effectively sustained.

"3. *Resolved*, That inasmuch as we believe, according to our *Form of Government*, that 'God, the Supreme Lord and King of all the world, hath ordained civil magistrates to be, under him, over the people, for his own glory and the public good, and to this end hath armed them with the power of the sword for the defense and encouragement of them that are good, and for the punishment of evil-doers,'—there is, in the judgment of the Assembly, no blood or treasure too precious to be devoted to the defense and perpetuity of the Government in all its constitutional authority.

"4. *Resolved*, That all those who are endeavoring to uphold the Constitution and maintain the Government of these United States in the exercise of its lawful prerogatives, are entitled to the sympathy and support of all Christians and law-abiding citizens.

"5. *Resolved*, That it be recommended to all our pastors and churches to be instant and fervent in prayer for the President of the United States, and all in authority under him, that wisdom and strength may be given them in the discharge of their arduous duties; for the Congress of the United States; for the Lieutenant-General commanding the army-in-chief, and all our soldiers, that God may shield them from danger in the hour of peril, and, by the outpouring of the Holy Spirit upon the army and navy, renew and sanctify them, so that whether living or dying, they may be servants of the Most High.

"6. *Resolved*, That in the countenance which many ministers of the Gospel, and other professing Christians, are now giving to treason and rebellion against the Government, we have great occasion to mourn·for the injury thus done to the kingdom of the Redeemer; and that, though we have nothing to add to our former significant and explicit testimonies on the subject of slavery, we yet recommend our people to pray more fervently than ever for the removal of this evil, and all others, both social and political, which lie at the foundation of our present national difficulties.

"7. *Resolved*, That a copy of these resolutions, signed by the officers of the General Assembly, be forwarded to His Excellency, Abraham Lincoln, President of the United States."

SECTION IV.—REMARKS ON THE ECCLESIASTICAL LEGISLATION OF THE GENERAL ASSEMBLY PRESBYTERIANS.

Attention is called to a few points in the legislation of the General Assembly Presbyterians.

(1) The Presbyterian ministers, at the time our republic was founded, had no belief that mere personal freedom possessed any great advantages to mankind. (2) This is apparent from the emphatic manner in which they urge the "instruction of the negroes, whether bond or free." And, besides, while their people were exhorted to do every thing in their power to promote the abolition of slavery, they were to act consistently with the rights of civil society. (3) While approving the general principles in favor of universal liberty, and the interest which many of the States had taken in promoting the abolition of slavery, they yet believed that men introduced from a servile state to a participation of all the privileges of civil society, without proper education, and without previous habits of industry, may be in many respects dangerous to the community; and they earnestly recommended, therefore, to all the members belonging to their communion to give those persons, who were held in servitude, such good education as would prepare them for the better enjoyment of freedom. Such was the position of the Presbyterian Church in 1787.

(4) While taking higher ground, in 1818, and more strongly urging the duty of promoting emancipation, the Assembly still

gave paramount importance to the question of securing to the colored people the blessings of the Gospel. The duty of immediate and unconditional emancipation was not urged.

(5) In 1845, the Assembly (Old School,) had to meet the question whether slaveholding, without regard to circumstances, is a sin? This was a test question, designed to determine whether the General Assembly Presbyterians should take abolition ground, or maintain their former conservative position. They decided to maintain their old ground, and thus gave a rebuke to the abolition members of the Church, who had kept up the agitation of the slavery question; at the same time, however, the Assembly expressed the opinion, that the abuses of the relation of master and slave were suitable subjects for discipline, and called for action on the part of their people in applying the proper remedy. The Assembly further expressed the opinion, that it is only by the influence of the Gospel upon both masters and slaves, and the proper discharge of the relative duties of each to the other, that the condition of the slaves can be improved.

(6) But there is here one important declaration that must not be overlooked. The Assembly give it as their deliberate judgment, that the tendency of the abolition movements, by agitating the slavery question in the Church, was to promote the dissolution of the Union. Alas, this fear was but too well founded!

(7) It will be seen, that the action of the Assembly, (New School) after the separation in 1838, was more anti-slavery in its character than that of the Old School. While, however, it has been considered at the South as bearing the abolition stamp, we believe the Assembly itself did not contemplate taking abolition grounds.

The legislation here presented affords no adequate idea of the excitements which preceded and accompanied it. The documents going out to the public after 1830, are only an embodiment of the conservative element existing within the bosom of the Church. We refer especially to the Old School Assembly. Had nothing else appeared but the resolutions agreed upon, there would have been no grounds for alarm at the South, that the Presbyterians North were determined upon the overthrow of slavery. But, unfortunately, the violent men found means and ways of putting into circulation their high-toned abolition sentiments; and conservative men, taking no steps to counteract the effects of such productions, allowed them full sway in creating a public opinion at the South that was wholly unsupported by the real facts in the case. In this matter conservative men greatly erred. They should never have yielded to the abolition storm; but have spoken out boldly in reprobation of the fanaticism that has worked out its ruinous consequences upon both Church and State. There has no good, but much ill, resulted from the ecclesiastical legislation of the Presbyterian General Assemblies on the subject of slavery. This must be the conclusion of every right-minded Christian.

CHAPTER VII.

THE SCOTTISH AMERICAN PRESBYTERIAN CHURCHES AND SLAVERY.

THE Churches classed under this head are the Reformed Presbyterian Synod, the Associate Synod, the Associate Reformed Synod of the West, and the United Presbyterian General Assembly.

SECTION I.—THE LEGISLATION OF THE ASSOCIATE SYNOD OF NORTH AMERICA ON SLAVERY.

This Church, originally, was an off-shoot of the Seceders in Scotland. The subject of slavery was agitated by the mother Church as early as 1788. One of the original Presbyteries of the Associate Church in the United States had its location in Kentucky, and, as early as the year 1808, sent up an address to the Presbytery of Pennsylvania, asking that a warning might be issued against the sin of slaveholding. With this request the Presbytery complied, and in their warning declare slaveholding to be a moral evil and unjustifiable. Another memorial, of a similar character, was sent to the Synod the same year, 1808, from Green County, Ohio, asking ecclesiastical action for the exclusion of slaveholders from the communion of the Church. This led, in the end, to the adoption of an act, in 1811, which reads as follows:

"1. That it is a moral evil to hold negroes or their children in perpetual slavery; or to claim the right of buying or selling them; or of bequeathing them as transferable property.

"2. That all persons belonging to our communion, having slaves in possession, be directed to set them at liberty, unless prohibited from doing so by the civil law; and that in those States where the

(358)

liberation of the slaves is rendered impracticable by the existing laws, it is the duty of holders of slaves to treat them with as much justice as if they were liberated; to give them suitable food and clothing; to have them taught to read, and instructed in the principles of religion; and, when their services justly deserve it, to give them additional compensation.

"3. That those slaveholders who refuse to renounce the above claim, and to treat their slaves in the manner now specified, are unworthy of being admitted into, or retained in, the fellowship of the Church of Christ.

"4. That it may be lawful for persons in our communion to purchase negroes from those who are holding them in absolute and perpetual slavery, with a view to retain them in their service until they are recompensed for the money laid out in the purchase of the said slaves; provided it be done with the consent of the negroes themselves, and that they be treated, in the meantime, according to the second of these regulations.

"5. That it is the duty of Sessions to see that the above regulations be faithfully observed; but that, before they be acted upon in any congregation where the application of them is requisite, care shall be taken to have the people of that congregation not only apprised of these regulations, but instructed concerning the moral evil of the slaveholding here condemned."

The Synod, at this period, was composed of Presbyteries whose jurisdictions extended over the States of Virginia, North Carolina, South Carolina, and Tennessee, as well as throughout the Northern States. The provisions of the act of 1811 not being complied with, the Synod, after having had the subject before them for a number of years, at another meeting, in 1831, passed a more stringent act, by which all slaveholders were forthwith excluded from her communion. The act of 1831 is as follows:

"*Resolved*, That as slavery is clearly condemned by the law of God, and has been long since judicially declared to be a moral evil by this Church, no member thereof shall, from and after this date, be allowed to hold a human being in the character or condition of a slave.

"*Resolved*, That this Synod do hereby order all its subordinate judicatories to proceed forthwith to carry into execution the intention of the foregoing resolution, by requiring those church-members under their immediate inspection, who may *be possessed of* slaves, to relinquish their unjust claims, and release those whom they may have heretofore considered as their property.

"*Resolved*, That if any member or members of this Church, in order to evade this act, shall sell any of their slaves, or make a transfer of them, so as to retain the proceeds of their services, or the price of their sale, or in any other way evade the provisions of this act, they shall be subject to the censures of the Church.

"*Resolved*, Further, that where an individual is found who has spent so much of his or her strength in the service of another as to be disqualified from providing for his or her own support, the master in such a case, is to be held responsible for the comfortable maintenance of said servants."

Then follows a list of directions which the Synod recommends to be observed in carrying out the foregoing resolutions. It may be remarked here, also, that a protest, signed by six members of the Synod, was offered, and answered by a committee appointed for that purpose.

A few years previous to the date of this act, as appears from the Minutes of the Synod for 1824, the Associate Presbyterian Church had under its care *ninety-one* congregations, settled and vacant, of which *twenty-eight* were in the slave States, and distributed as follows: South Carolina, *eleven*, North Carolina, *ten*, Tennessee, *two*, Virginia, *five*.

In 1840, the Synod addressed a letter to the people under their inspection in the Presbytery of the Carolinas, in which " some allowance was made for those who might not be able to effect the emancipation of their slaves, provided they would agree to what was called *a moral emancipation*. This letter, however, was so far from conciliating the feelings of Southern slaveholders, that a mob of them visited with Lynch-law the minister* who was appointed to be the bearer of it, and that, too, while he was engaged with a congregation in the public worship of God. The effect of these proceedings was to purge the Church of the sin of slaveholding, and, at the same time, entirely extinguishing the Associate Presbytery of the Carolinas."

---

* Rev. Mr. Kendall, now of Oregon.

"In 1845, in compliance with the purport of various memorials, the Synod addressed a pastoral letter warning their people against the sin of voting for immoral characters. The same subject was brought before the Synod again in 1853, and a report was adopted in which the great iniquity of voting for wicked men is pointed out, and ministers are particularly enjoined to instruct their people in reference to this matter, and to warn them against being partakers in other men's sins, by exalting vile men to high places. (1)

"The course pursued by the government for promoting the cause of slavery, and the outrages perpetrated by the friends of that system, were regarded by the Synod of 1856 as loudly calling for some action. A report was accordingly adopted, condemning, in very pointed terms, 1st. Slavery itself; 2d. The Fugitive Slave Law; 3d. The gross and brutal attack on Senator Sumner ; 4th. The outrages in Kansas. This report the clerk of Synod was directed to forward to the President of the United States, and to each House of Congress."

The Associate Synod no longer exists as a distinct body, but has become merged in the *United Presbyterian Church*, by a union with the *Associate Reformed Church*.

The foregoing facts are taken from the *Minutes of the Associate Synod*, and from the *Church Memorial*, a work recently issued, under the patronage of the United Presbyterian Church, and embracing an historical sketch of the two bodies which united in the formation of this Church.

SECTION II.—THE LEGISLATION OF THE ASSOCIATE REFORMED SYNOD OF THE WEST ON SLAVERY.

This Church, like the Associate Church, was, originally, the offspring of the Scotch Seceders. Its action on slavery is quoted mainly from the CHURCH MEMORIAL, and embraces, substantially, its proceedings down to the time of its being merged in the United Presbyterian Church. Its action, like that of its kindred churches, resulted in excluding it from all the slaveholding States, excepting a congregation in St. Louis. The legislation of this Church on slavery was as follows :

"At an early period in its history, anxious inquiry was made as to the course that should be pursued in regard to this system ; and extending, as the body then did, into slaveholding territories, it was a practical question of grave moment. At different meetings of the General Synod, the subject was discussed, and committees were appointed to prepare statements of the Synod's views, but from various causes, nothing was effectually done during the existence of that body.*

" At the meeting of the Synod of the West, at Chillicothe, Ohio, May, 1826, the subject came formally up, in a memorial from the congregation of Hopewell, in the first Presbytery of Ohio, and a series of discussions and acts were entered upon, which resulted in the adoption, at the meeting in Chillicothe again in 1830, of the following resolutions, which, with some modifications and explana tions that we shall append in foot-notes, contains the final action of that portion of the Church:

" 1. *Resolved*, That the religion of Jesus Christ requires that involuntary slavery should be removed from the Church as soon as opportunity in the providence of God is offered to slave-owners for the liberation of their slaves.

" 2. *Resolved*, That when there are no regulations of the State to prohibit it; when provision can be made for the support of the freedmen; when they can be placed in circumstances to support the rank, enjoy the rights, and discharge the duties of freemen, it shall be considered that such an opportunity is afforded in the providence of God.†

" 3. *Resolved*, That the Synod will, as it hereby does, recommend it to all its members to aid in placing the slaves which are within the jurisdiction of this Synod in the possession of their rights as freemen; and that it be recommended to them especially to take up annual collections to aid the funds of the American Society for colonizing the free people of color in the United States.‡

---

* This Church was originally composed of three subordinate Synods—the Synod of the South, of New York, and of the West—represented in a General Synod.

† At a meeting in 1838, the Synod passed the following in reference to this resolution:

" *Resolved*, that an opportunity in the providence of God shall be considered as afforded when the master can emancipate his slave, and place him in circumstances where he shall not be liable to be immediately sold into bondage."

‡ In consequence of a memorial from Robinson Run congregation, the Synod at its meeting in 1839, adopted the following in regard to this resolution:

"4. *Resolved*, That the practice of buying or selling slaves for gain, by any member of this Church, be disapproved; and that slave-owners under the jurisdiction of this Synod be, as they hereby are, forbidden all aggravations of the evils of slavery, by violating the ties of nature, the separation of husband and wife, parents and children, or by cruel or unkind treatment; and that they shall not only treat them well, but also instruct them in useful knowledge and the principles of the Christian religion, and in all respects treat them as enjoined upon masters toward their servants by the apostles of our Lord Jesus Christ.

"Two years afterward, in 1832, the Synod issued a Letter of Warning, or an Occasional Testimony, in which these resolutions were quoted, and the following extracts will show in what sense they were intended and understood as the law of the Church : ' Now, brethren, it is expected that the foregoing resolutions will not be as a dead letter, but be respected and reduced to practice. It is expected that Sessions and Presbyteries will see them enforced. It is expected that slave-owners in the Church will make conscience of seeking and improving opportunities, and the very first which offer, of liberating their slaves. It is expected that in the meantime they will give satisfactory evidence to their respective Sessions that they do consider slavery a moral evil, that they do truly desire to get rid of it as soon as they can, and that it is their intention to embrace the first opportunity which God in his providence shall give them for so doing. And it is expected of Sessions that they will require this of slave-owning church-members or applicants,' etc. (2)

"These acts of the Synod of the West remain unchanged. They were carried into the General Synod of the West, were recognized in the union with the Synod of New York, and are strikingly similar to the Testimony on this subject in the basis of union with the Associate Church in May last."

The Letter of Warning, referred to above, among the many

"As there are two conflicting Societies operating in the community—the Colonization and the Anti-Slavery Societies—and as this Synod has recommended the former to the patronage of the Churches under its care; and as it is desirable the Synod should keep clear of this excitement; and as the Church should not be involved by the operation of bodies over which it has no control, therefore,

"*Resolved*, That this Synod withdraws the recommendation formerly given to the Colonization Society."

topics discussed, embraced the following paragraph, in which the Synod undertakes to interpret the dispensations of Providence :

"God is visiting our land with one of his 'sore judgments'—the *pestilence* [Asiatic cholera]. This visitation is a call from the Supreme Ruler to our nation, to consider their ways and repent; and when such a call is given, it is the duty of the Church, whose business it is to sustain the cause of God and righteousness on earth, to point out those national sins for which the righteous Lord inflicts national judgments. Now, one prominent national sin, on account of which—as well as on account of Sabbath-breaking, intemperance, and evil-speaking—the Lord is visiting our country, is slavery."

SECTION III.—THE LEGISLATION OF THE REFORMED PRESBYTERIAN CHURCH ON SLAVERY.

1. The following statement of the course of policy pursued by this Church, was supplied to the author of the HAND-BOOK ON THE SLAVERY QUESTION, by a venerable father in the ministry of that Church. Its legislation on the question of slavery, as in the case of the two Churches before noticed, excluded its ministers almost entirely from all the slaveholding States — a few members only, for many years, still adhering to it, in two or three places South :

"This Church, while recognizing the legitimacy of the relation of master and servant, has always borne testimony against slavery, as defined in the slave laws of the States, and colonies before they were States, of our country. But until the latter part of the eighteenth century that testimony was not formally judicative. It was given in the usual course of the ministrations of the sanctuary. At that time, however, (the latter part of the last century,) the subject was judicially acted on, and slavery, as defined by the slave laws of slaveholding States and their courts, was formally condemned as a personal, domestic, political, and moral evil; and slaveholding, and the approbation of it, as thus defined, excluded from the sacramental fellowship of the Church. During the present century, no slaveholder, or advocate of slavery on the chattel principle, has been admitted to the *ecclesiastical* connection of this department of the Church. Such is the *position* and such the *conduct* of this portion of the Presbyterian family on this subject.

"It ought to be remarked, perhaps, that this body has never denounced, as immoral *per se*, the right of property by one person in another, nor yet involuntary service as wrong. These, under legitimate regulations, may belong to the nearest relations of life. These do not constitute the slavery of the slave laws of the country. To confound them with it may perplex, but can not enlighten.

"In reference to the influence of this measure upon the prosperity of the body, it may be stated, that, at the time, it generally secured the disapprobation of other religious bodies, as indiscreet, if not wrong. It occasioned the loss of those, as members, who refused to comply with that measure, they finding an open door for their reception in other ecclesiastical connections. Upon our organizations in the slave States it has not been propitious. While at no time, on the part of the public functionaries of the States, was there any disposition to bear hardly or unkindly on Reformed Presbyterians, they being uniformly recognized as ardent patriots and good citizens; yet the existence, maintenance, and general operation of the slave laws were, in many respects, unpleasant to them. Hence the great body of this denomination, with their ministers, were induced to seek a more eligible home in the free States. This step affected the locality rather than the number of professors.

"But to the picture there is another side, and of it the following may be said:

"The Church is free, and for nearly half a century has been free, from the malign influence that goes to degrade the moral and immortal being to the class of chattels, made legally incapable of personal relations and rights. The self-denial evinced, both in the North and the South, in the ready emancipation of slaves by those who entered into the views of the Church, had a happy influence upon others in many respects. Occasion was given to numbers of the consistent friends of rational freedom, upon examination, to enter into the fellowship of the Church. This department of Zion is now, and has long been, exempt from that unhappy state of agitation which at present so extensively disturbs the peace of others. With us it is not a novelty, but a long settled matter.

"It may not be out of place to remark, that while this was the department of the Presbyterian family that first took such ground and action on the subject of slavery, there was no rashness in the measure. The degrading and cruel chattel principle was repudiated, and made a subject of ecclesiastical, corrective discipline. The legitimate rela-

tion of master and servant remained untouched. Provision was made
that the aged, the infirm, and minors be taken care of; and, while the
relation of superior and subordinate remained, the subordinate was
secured in all personal rights which the condition of the individual
morally required or admitted. In this case there was no social con-
vulsion."

The division in this Church, some years since, into what the
public designated as *Old Side* and *New Side*, in no way affected
the views of the parties on the question of slavery.

2. In 1859, the O. S. Synod, at its meeting in Allegheny City,
Pennsylvania, gave the following deliverance:

"That slavery, the holding of men as property, to be bought and
sold as 'chattels personal,' is a *malum per se*, (an evil in itself,)
wholly at variance with the Divine word.

"That we are more firmly convinced that the Constitution of the
United States is the great stronghold and bulwark of this system of
violence and oppression, and that, therefore, we will continue to testify against it, refuse to swear the oath of allegiance to it, or obey its
unholy requirements. (3)

"That those who attempt to defend slavery from the Bible, to impose upon the community the enormous lie that God, by his word,
sanctions a sin so heinous, are guilty of one of the worst and most
dangerous forms of infidelity exhibited in this age and nation. That
we will labor and pray for the emancipation of the captive, the
coming of that day when God will break every yoke, undo the heavy
burden, and let the oppressed go free."

At the same meeting, the Committee on a Memorial to Congress, reported: "That they had prepared a petition which asks
Congress to make such alterations in the Constitution of the
United States, that it will acknowledge the being and authority
of God, an acknowledgment of submission to the authority of the
Church, (4) to recognize the paramount obligation of God's law,
and that it may be rendered, in all its principles and provisions,
adverse to any form of slavery within the national limits."

3. The General Synod of the Reformed Presbyterian Church,
(N. S.,) at its session of 1861, adopted the following propositions
on the "state of the country:"

"1. Whatever may be the incidental causes of the present war, there can be no doubt that the existence of slavery, and the desire to continue it, is the fundamental cause.

"2. Both the light of nature and the plain teachings of the revealed Word of God demonstrate that there are occasions in which war is not only lawful, but dutiful; and that we believe the present war is one which is justifiable in behalf of our National Government, and which every Christian and patriot should be willing to sustain.

"3. The great object of the Gospel of our Lord Jesus Christ is to promote glory to God in the highest, and on earth peace and good-will to man; the fruit of the Spirit is peace, the duty of every Christian to seek for the things which make for peace, and which will turn wars into peace.

"4. There is reason to believe that the people of the slaveholding States of our confederacy misapprehend the principles and views of the people of the non-slaveholding States. It is a mistake to suppose that there is any intention to interfere with slavery in the States where it exists, by any other means than such as the right of free discussion of any subject of interest in politics or religion, properly conducted, will sanction; to suppose that there is a desire that the slaves should rise up in insurrection, murder their owners, and devastate their homes; that there is any plan to degrade or subjugate the South, and deprive its inhabitants of the equal rights which the Constitution of our country secures to all. (5)

"5. Notwithstanding, it is to be distinctly understood that the people of the North, with few exceptions, regard slavery as a great moral and political evil, and do desire its peaceable extinction.

"6. Slavery is the volcanic element in our political system; were it removed, there is no reason to apprehend any dissolution of the brotherly covenant which has bound our sovereign States together; and the highest welfare of the nation requires that measures should be taken for its removal. The providence of God is now most solemnly and distinctly upon us as a nation to devise some plan for this object. (6)

"7. There are sins in regard to this, as well as other things, with us as well as our brethren of the South. We feel bound to bear with them the burden and loss which may be required in the emancipation of the slave. We believe there are many in the South who recognize the evil of slavery, and would willingly coöperate for its removal.

"8. It behooves Christians of every name, whether in the North or

the South, under the example of our Saviour and the guidance of his
Spirit and his Word, to unite for this purpose."

4. *Extracts from the proceedings of the Reformed Presbytery of*
Pittsburgh, (N. S.) on the State of the Country.

At a meeting of the Pittsburgh Presbytery of the Reformed
Presbyterian Church, held at Centreville, Butler Co., Pa., on
Wednesday, the 1st of October, 1861, the Rev. Dr. Douglas, of
Pittsburgh, offered the following resolutions on the "state of the
country," which, after speeches of the intensest patriotism by the
mover, Rev. John Nevin, the seconder, Revs. George Scott, John
M'Millan, and J. F. Hill, were *unanimously adopted:*

"WHEREAS, a number of states in the Southern part of our country
are now in a state of armed rebellion against the government of the
United States, menacing its independence and perpetuation, and thereby endangering our peace, happiness, and prosperity; and *whereas,*
it is proper for us as a Presbytery, when national affairs assume a
moral and religious aspect, to give a judicial declaration in regard to
them, for the guidance and information of the people committed to
our charge, therefore,

"*Resolved,* That whatever may be its present complications, NE-
GRO SLAVERY is the primary cause of the war which is now distracting our country—prostrating its commercial and every other
interest.

"*Resolved,* That this war is the infliction of the just punishment
of an offended God upon our country and our government, for their
aiding and abetting the nefarious sin of human bondage.

"*Resolved,* That American slavery is radically and essentially wrong,
and 'no possible contingency can ever make it right;' that it involves
the horrid crimes of robbery, oppression, concubinage, and murder,
and stands alike in antagonism to the laws of humanity and the laws
of God.

"*Resolved,* That we pledge our support to the government so long
as it conducts the present war on the principle of undying hostility
to slavery, believing, as we do, that as long as slavery exists we never
can have peace. . . . . .

"*Resolved,* That, in times of rebellion, military authority takes the
place of all municipal institutions—'*slavery among the rest.*' That
the President of the United States, taking advantage of the emergen-

cies of war, 'has power to order the universal emancipation of the
slaves' held by the rebels, and that in doing so he would be acting
for the 'general welfare,' in accordance with the provisions of the
Constitution; that military commanders possess the same power in
their respective districts, and that we deprecate any Executive or
official interference that would go to nullify any such proclamations
which have been, or yet may be made. (7)

SECTION IV.—THE LEGISLATION OF THE UNITED PRESBYTERIAN
CHURCH OF NORTH AMERICA ON SLAVERY.

1. This Church was organized in the year 1858, by the Union
of the Associate and the Associate Reformed Churches. This
Church, at its organization, made the following declaration of
principles on the subject of slavery :

" *We declare*, That slaveholding—that is, the holding of unoffending
human beings in involuntary bondage, and considering and treating
them as property, and subject to be bought and sold—is a violation
of the law of God, and contrary both to the letter and spirit of Christianity.

" ARGUMENT AND ILLUSTRATION.—This declaration is in accordance
with the Confession of Faith, chap. iv, sec. 2, Larger Catechism,
ques. 142.

" That slaveholding is, as we have declared it to be, a violation of
the law of God, will appear from the following considerations :

" 1. The Word of God represents the whole human family as possessing a common nature. The slave is a *man*—as really and truly a man
as the most gifted and illustrious of the human family. He is a child
of Adam, who was made in the image and after the likeness of God,
(Gen. i: 26.) He is of 'one blood' with him who holds him in bondage, (Acts xvii: 26.) This being the case, his natural rights must be
the same as those of any other. If man possesses, by the law of
his creation, any natural and inalienable right, that right must be inconsistent with the condition of a person who is considered and treated
as property, subject to be bought and sold. Slaveholding, then, is at
war with humanity.

" 2. The word of God, in the grant of dominion which it makes,
restrains the power of man thus to treat his fellow man. He has, by
the authority of God, his Creator, dominion over all the lower creatures, (Gen. i: 26.) The possession of such a dominion by a person

is, in its very nature, inconsistent with his condition as a slave—a person who is himself considered and treated as property. While therefore, he is held in this condition, the grant of his Creator is rendered a nullity. Nor is this all: while this grant of dominion secures to the slave his right to liberty, it interdicts, by the clearest implication, the assumption of that right which the slaveholder claims. The grant of his Creator gives him dominion *over the lower creatures.* These he may make his property; thus far his dominion as owner extends, but no farther. Slavery, however, assumes this power. It reduces to the condition of property him who, by divine right, is lord of all. (Ps. viii: 6.)

"3. The law of God recognizes the right of all men to use the powers of body and mind which their Creator has given them, in the pursuit of happiness. It sanctions labor with a view to their support, (Gen. ii: 15 ; iii: 23; 1 Thess. iv: 11; 2 Thess. iii: 10–12.) But slavery, while it dooms its victims to toil, lays its hand upon the fruits of that toil, and appropriates it to him who has not performed the labor. It thus takes away from man that incentive to labor which the Creator has given to him, by giving to him a right to its fruits The slave, being himself the *property* of another, can own nothing, and, of course, can acquire nothing.

"4. The law of God enjoins it upon masters to give to their servants 'that which is just and equal,' (Col. iv: 1.) The slaveholder gives nothing to his slave, *as a right acquired by labor.* What he gives *as a slaveholder*, has a reference merely to the support of his slave, that he may thereby be qualified to labor. The fruits of that labor he appropriates to himself. He therefore violates the law of *justice* enjoined upon the master, and exposes himself to the wo pronounced against him who 'useth his neighbor's services without *wages*, and giveth him not *for his work*,' (Jer. xxii: 13.) Neither does he give his servant that which is 'equal.' There is no proportion between the labor performed by the slave and what he receives from his master. The slave may be hired out to another, by whom he is fed and clothed; but the *owner* of the slave receives from the man to whom he is hired the wages. Nor is there any proportion between what the *slave* receives and what another receives who performs the same amount of work. He therefore violates the principle of *equality*, which he is bound by the law of God to observe.

"5. The law of God recognizes marriage as the right of all, (Heb. xiii: 4.) It requires the parties to dwell together, (1 Pet. iii: 7,) and makes the relation indissoluble by man, (Gen. ii : 24 ; Matt. xix : 6.) But the right which the slaveholder claims to his slave as his property, subject to be bought and sold, is in direct conflict with these divine requisitions.   He may, by the exercise of his right as a slaveholder, forbid his marriage, or place him in circumstances in which he cannot enjoy this divine right; or if married, he may, at will entirely and forever separate the parties.   The laws which govern and control property imply all this.

" 6. The law of God requires parents to bring up their children in the nurture and admonition of the Lord, (Eph. vi : 4.)   The slaveholder, in virtue of the relation which he sustains, and by the right of ownership which he claims, may not only interfere with the government of the parent over his children, but entirely and forever separate them from each other.

" 7. The law of God requires every man to search the Scriptures, (John v : 39.)   The right of the slaveholder interferes with this The laws which govern all property necessarily secure to him the right of prohibiting his slave from doing anything which may operate against the attainment of the end for which this species of property, in common with all others, is held—his own gain.

" 8. The law of God forbids man-stealing (Deut. xxiv : 7 ; 1 Tim, i : 9, 10.)   In this the alleged right of one man to make merchandize of his fellow-man must have originated.   As the fountain is corrupt the stream can not be pure.

" The foregoing considerations clearly show this relation to be, as we have declared it to be, in violation of the law of God.

" We have also declared it to be contrary both to the letter and spirit of Christianity.   What says the Author of Christianity ?   He says : 'All things whatsoever ye would that men should do to you, do ye even so to them," (Matt. vii : 12.)   There is no slaveholder who would not resist being made a slave, and who would not feel an irrepressible conviction that a wrong had been done him.   This being the case, he is bound, by this express precept of the Saviour, to break the yoke, and let the oppressed go free, (1 Cor. vii : 21 ; Isa. lviii : 6.) And what is the spirit of Christianity ?   It is surely love, (Rom. xiii : 10 ; 1 John iv : 20, 21 ; Luke x : 27–37.)   Is not, however, the reduction of a fellow-being (he may be a brother in Christ,) to the condition of a piece of property, liable to be bought and sold, in violation of this holy and divine principle ?   Who, that is not a stranger to the impulses of a Christian's heart, will deny it ?

"We have, therefore, in the law of God, and in the letter and spirit of Christianity, abundant reasons for testifying against slaveholding as a sin, and consequently a disqualification for membership in the Church of Christ. It is the relation itself which we have examined in the light of Scripture, and which we have found to be so inconsistent with it, and not the many cruel laws which blacken the statute books of the slaveholding States, and the many gross and fearful evils that result from this relation. A consideration, however, of these laws and evils, which everywhere attend it, can not fail to impress the mind with a sense of the inherent wickedness of the system." (8)

2. This body, at its meeting in May, 1861, adopted a report and resolutions, on the "state of the country," from which we extract the following:

"Our beloved country is in a very deplorable condition. War is upon us, fraternal war, attended generally with greater ferocity and destructiveness than other wars. But, in God's great mercy to us, we are united among ourselves; and, having able leaders and boundless resources, peace and prosperity will, ere long, be established on surer foundations. Nevertheless, great calamities are upon us. They are from the Lord, who worketh all things after the counsel of his own will; and so the question naturally arises, *What meaneth the heat of this great anger?* The reply to which must be this: *Because we have sinned against the Lord, and have not served him with joyfulness and with gladness of heart for the abundance of all things.* That covetousness, which is idolatry in the sight of God, and the source of numberless disorders, has prevailed in every section and corner of this wide-spread country. Very many are involved in all the guilt of intemperance and filthy debaucheries. But the sins that have in an especial manner provoked the eyes of the Holy One, seem to be these:—

"1. Pride and self-sufficiency; glorying in our supposed wisdom and greatness.

"2. Inordinate and excessive ambition.

"3. Contempt of the unspeakable grace of God in Christ, for which Bethsaida and Chorazin were doomed to woe, and Jerusalem was made an utter desolation.

"4. Sabbath desecration.

"5. Obstinacy and incorrigibleness under former Providential rebukes. We have been visited with drouth and partial famine—with pestilence and malignant diseases—but we have not heard the Rod. We have not returned to the Lord; and, therefore, his hand is laid more heavily upon us.

"6. Slaveholding, the great and immediate cause of the present trouble, though seldom thought of as an evil by those who are directly concerned in it. Slavery must be exceedingly flagrant in the sight of the Great Parent and Ruler of men. If it is murder, the blackest of crimes, to violate the image of God instamped on man, what is it to debase and trample on that image, and treat it as a brutal thing? To tear asunder the tender ties of nature and affection—what is it but horrible cruelty? To work a man, and give him no wages, or no sufficient wages, is nothing but robbery and oppression. To forbid the great God to speak to his own creatures, that they may be saved, is bidding defiance to the very heavens. To deprive a people of the ordinance and privileges of marriage, is to keep them in beastly concubinage. It should not be thought that we, in the free States, have nothing to do with this monstrous iniquity. Have we not countenanced those who practiced it? Have we not contributed to extend, and establish, and fortify it? Paul was guilty of the murder of Stephen, though he did not cast a single stone. With regard to the aboriginal inhabitants of the land, it is to be feared that they also have had cause to complain of injustice and cruel rapacity."

3. *Extract from the Minutes of the First United Presbyterian Synod of the West, held in the First U. P. Church, Allegheny, Pa., commencing October 1st, 1861.*

"The Select Committee appointed by Synod to consider so much of the Reports and Petitions of Presbyteries as refer to our national troubles and the judgments with which we are at present afflicted, would most respectfully submit to Synod the following, as the result of its deliberations:

"*Whereas*, The Declaration of our National Independence recognizes, in accordance with the Word of God, the unity of the human race, that all men are created equal, have a right to life, liberty, and the pursuit of happiness; and, ...

"*Whereas*, This nation is in the midst of a great and wicked rebellion, which threatens the very existence of our Government, and seeks to fasten permanently upon the nation the system of slavery—a system at war with the Word of God, with the interests of humanity, with the Declaration of our National Independence, and the best interests, in any sense, of the nation; and,

" *Whereas*, We, as a nation, have too much countenanced this institution and given it support, and believe that by *this* and *our other sins*, we have brought our liberties into jeopardy, and subjected ourselves to the judgments of God in civil war and in other forms; and,

" *Whereas*, We can not expect a removal of our afflictions, and our restoration to the favor of God, until we acknowledge our sins, and turn from them unto Him; therefore,

" *Resolved*, 1. That we will, in every way consistent with the law of God, defend and seek to hand down to posterity, unimpaired, the religious and civil liberty inherited from our fathers; and, that in order to do this, we will uphold our Federal authorities in the prosecution of our present war for the suppression of the existing rebellion.

" *Resolved*, 2. That while, as Christian men and patriots, we zealously and heartily support our National Government in the present war for the maintenance of its integrity, we are not blind to the defects of our institutions, to the defective administration of law, and our sins as a nation; that we trace our present national difficulties mainly to slavery and the evils growing out of slavery; that by this, and our other sins, we have offended God, and there is no hope for us but in repentance and return to Him; and that we recognize that our repentance can not be acceptable to God, unless we, as a nation, break off our sins, unless we acknowledge Him and His law and providence, and ceasing to countenance this wicked system of slavery, use all the means in our power to carry into effect the law of the Bible, ' to loose the bands of wickedness, undo the heavy burdens, to let the oppressed go free, and that ye break every yoke,' and remembering that ' righteousness exalteth a nation,' and that ' sin is a reproach to any people,' in accordance with the principles of the Declaration of our National Independence, seek to maintain every man in the enjoyment of his rights as a man.

" *Resolved*, 3. That the Slave Power, by inaugurating this wicked rebellion against the government, has forfeited all claim to any protection or toleration of its peculiar institution; and as the most speedy way of establishing justice, insuring domestic tranquillity, and suppressing the rebellion, we approve of the manumission, by military proclamation, of the slaves, and the confiscation of all the property of those found in arms against the government, in all the military districts in which our commanding officers now have, or may hereafter have, military jurisdiction." (9)

A committee of six were appointed to go on to Washington, for the purpose of pressing upon the attention of the President, etc., the views of Synod, and urging the "necessity of taking immediate steps to put away our national sins, that we may be restored to the favor of God."

The Synods of New York, of Illinois, and Iowa, passed similar resolutions to the foregoing:

Section V.—Opinions of British Churches on American Slavery.

1. In 1860, a deputation was sent to Scotland, from the United Presbyterian Church, to attend the Sessions of the United Presbyterian Church of Scotland. The subjoined extracts, from the proceedings of that body, on the presentation of the delegates, together with the reply of Rev. Dr. Kerr, so far as he alluded to the subject of slavery, will interest the reader, as being in keeping with the whole tenor of the policy of American Anti-Slavery men.

"The Clerk of Committee of Bills and Overtures said that he had been instructed to introduce to the Synod the Rev. Dr. David R. Kerr, delegate from the General Assembly of the United Presbyterian Church of North America. The credentials of Dr. Kerr having been read, together with the letter tabled by him from the Church he represented, the clerk explained that with one branch of the United Church the Synod had formerly held fraternal intercourse. The United Presbyterian Church in North America held principles in common with the Synod, and adhered to the same doctrines and form of government. This Church was also honorably distinguished by their testimony against slavery. They regarded the system of slavery, as it existed in America, as not merely an evil, but a sin, and treated it in the same way as any other sin. It was made by them a term of communion. This fact, along with the other claims they had on their regards, entitled this Church to their warmest sympathy and Christian affection. He (the Clerk) had the highest satisfaction, in the absence of the Rev. Henry Renton, who had undertaken the duty, but was prevented from being present, to introduce Dr. Kerr to the affectionate regards of the Synod. (Applause.)

"Dr. Kerr then said—'It is my happiness to appear before this venerable body to present the salutations of a Church of kindred origin, of like faith and order, and, with the exception of national designation, of the same name—the United Presbyterian Church of North America. . . . . . . We declare, in our testimony, "That slave-holding—that is, the holding of unoffending human beings in involuntary bondage, and considering and treating them as property, and subject to be bought and sold—is a violation of the law of God, and contrary both to the letter and spirit of Christianity." And we not only bear testimony, but we bring our discipline to bear against this great moral evil of our land. We make our declaration on the subject a term of communion. We deal with slavery just as with other sins which, after due instruction and admonition, are unrepented of. We believe this to be the great sin of the American nation and Church; of the latter even more than the former; for if the Church had dealt faithfully with this subject, if she had brought her testimony and dis-cipline to bear on it, as faithfulness to the law of her King, and to the claims, not of Christianity simply, but of suffering humanity, de-manded, we may believe that, ere this time, slavery would scarcely have had a habitation or a name among us. And we may be at a loss which the more to deplore—the great evil itself, or the feeling of indifference with which so many Christians in our land have allowed themselves to regard it. But I am not here to reproach others, but, in seeking your acquaintance, to let you know precisely what we are ourselves. And, for my own Church, it is no ordinary gratification to be able to say that, however other churches may feel at liberty to deal with this subject, we have felt it to be a duty to array against slavery an earnest and consistent testimony.' (Cheers.)"*

Not one word have we here, nor in any part of the address of Rev. Dr. Kerr, in relation to the question of African Evangeliza-tion, by the United Presbyterian Church of America. Four millions of Africans, nearly, were then in the United States, and nearly a half million of them were freemen; and yet the Rev. gentleman could cite no efforts of his Church for their spiritual welfare; nor did the Scotch brethren ask what their American

---

* *Christian Instructor*, Philadelphia, August 22d, 1860.

brethren had done for the Christianization of the colored people. They seemed to care only to know that persistent efforts for the overthrow of slavery were still continued in the United States; while, at the same time, they were careful not to inform the American deputation that the British government were preparing for the coming emancipation in America, by earnestly promoting cotton culture, by slave labor, in Africa.*

2. It may interest the reader to see the mode in which foreign Churches have been interfering with the subject of American slavery. As a fair specimen of this brotherly kindness, we give the following, which sufficiently explains itself:

" UNITED PRESBYTERIAN CHURCH OF SCOTLAND ON AMERICAN SLAVERY.

"*Resolutions of the Synod of the United Presbyterian Church respecting American Slavery and its faithful opponents in the United States at the present time.*

" At Edinburgh, and within the Synod Hall, Queen Street, on Wednesday, 22d May, 1861, 11 o'clock, A. M. }

" The Synod of the United Presbyterian Church met, and was constituted by the Rev. John Robson, D. D., Moderator, when the Minutes of last Sederunt were read.

" Transmitted and read Overture by the Presbytery of Kelso, in favor of the Synod's renewal of the condemnation of American slavery, the tenor whereof follows :—

" ' That the disruption of the United States of America by the element of slavery—issuing, as it has done, in a new Confederation of the Southern States, founded on the principle of slavery, while the remaining Union of the Northern and Western States retains all that was defective in the original Constitution of the United States on that principle, and all the obnoxious laws which have been passed to up-

---

* See Chapter XI, on the Cotton Question. See also the Statistics, *Section* ——, Chapter III, from which it appears that the membership of both the United Presbyterian Church of Scotland and Rev. Dr. Kerr's Church, of the same name, in the United States, is 265,717 less than the number of slave converts in the South.

hold it—call for much concern and vigilance on the part of all who are opposed to the monstrous iniquity of treating human beings as property, that in the close commercial relations subsisting between Great Britain and the American States, the public sentiment of this country may not be deteriorated, nor its hostility to slavery abated—and calls no less for earnest sympathy and moral support on behalf of all those in the American States who are withstanding that iniquity, and laboring for its overthrow; and, therefore, that the Synod should at this time renew its condemnation of slavery and its repudiation of fellowship with slaveholders, and testify its respect for and sympathy with, those Christian churches and ministers in the United States who are maintaining a faithful and intrepid testimony against slavery as sin, and who are consistently carrying out that testimony by refusing all fellowship with slaveholders.'

"The Presbytery of Kelso were heard in support of their Overture, when the Synod, after reasoning, adopted the following resolutions:

"1. That the Synod, in the different bodies of which it consisted before the union, as well as in its united state since, has ever regarded slavery with unanimous and unqualified condemnation.

"2. That the grounds on which this Synod condemns slavery are not merely that it is impolitic, unjust, inhuman, and subversive of what are accounted the natural rights of man—personal liberty, the disposal of his own labor, and the enjoyment of its fruits—but that it is flagrantly opposed to the revealed will of God, and is, therefore a heinous sin, when maintained by those who possess the Holy Scriptures, and profess submission to them as the supreme rule of faith and practice.

"3. That of all systems of oppression and legalized iniquity at present. known in the world, this Synod regards that of slavery in the United States of North America to be the most inexcusable and guilty, as upheld by a nation which proclaims that all men have equal rights to life, liberty, and the pursuit of happiness, and which enjoys a widely-preached Gospel, a free circulation of the Scriptures, a free press, and public schools for the education of all its children.

"4. That the same principles which led this Synod and the congregations under its care to seek the total and immediate abolition of slavery throughout the British colonies a quarter of a century ago, prompt and require its earnest sympathy with those in other lands who are laboring for a similar end, and especially with Christian brethren in the United States of America, who, in the present crisis of that country, are, amid great opposition and obloquy, contending for the abolition of slavery throughout its territories.

"5. That copies of these resolutions be sent to the Synods of the United Presbyterian and Reformed Presbyterian Churches in the United States, and to the representatives and organs of the Christian abolitionists of other denominations in that country.

Appointed the Rev. Henry Renton and George C. Hutton, with Mr. James Henderson, Edinburgh, a Committee to transmit the resolutions to the parties named therein—Mr. Renton, Convener.

Extracted from the Records of Synod by

DAVID CRAWFORD, *Synod Clerk.*

3. We append another extract, as breathing the true spirit of the liberal-minded Christian. The General Assembly of the Free Church of Scotland held its meeting in Edinburgh, May, 1861.

"On the motion of the retiring Moderator, seconded by the Earl of Dalhousie, Dr. Candlish was, by acclamation, called to the Moderator's chair. In the course of his remarks upon taking the chair, Dr. Candlish made an eloquent address upon the religious condition of Scotland and of the world, and alluded to the state of things in this country as follows:

"'I own I have felt, I would almost say amazement, at the manner in which the present portentous spectacle looming upon us from across the Atlantic has been contemplated on our side. I speak of religious men and religious associations, and I can not but express surprise and sorrow that, amid the endless comments and speculations of politicians, the voice of our common Christianity has been so little heard, either in prayers to our Father, or in pleading with our brethren, that this gigantic fratricide may be stayed, and some better way found for ridding the land of the crime and curse of slavery than the deluging of its fertile plains with fraternal blood. (Hear, hear). When war seemed imminent between that country and our own some few years ago, there was no such silence. It may be that silence—the silence of suspense and awe—is the most emphatic speech the British Churches and British Christians can, at this juncture, send over the ocean. It may be that, in presence of so ominous a thunder-cloud, they can do no more than behold and wonder, and wait and weep. It may, however, on the other hand, be matter for consideration in our Assembly of Scotland's Free Presbyterian Church, accustomed to respect the great Presbyterian community in the States, to recognize among her sons some of the noblest champions of the faith that God has raised up in our day, and to rejoice with thankfulness in many revivals within her borders, from of old till now, whether some duty may not lie upon us, in this solemn pause, when the scarce unsheathed sword seems to be trembling ere it strike the first fatal and irrevocable blow. If no cry of ours, appealing to ties of Christian fellowship as yet unbroken, binding still in one church-communion the stern combatants in both camps, may be likely to be heard amid the din of gathering battle, at least our cry can go up to heaven, that it may please Him who is Head over all things to this Church, and who, making the wrath of man to praise Him, mercifully restrains the remainder thereof—to shorten these terrible days, for the elects' sake, and to bring, ere long, out of all these troubles a glorious issue of liberty and peace.' "

Section VI.—Brief Remarks on the Foregoing Legislation.

(1) The interference of the Associate Synod with the rights of its members to vote as they chose, never amounted to any thing. Her people, generally, were an intelligent class of men, and considered themselves about as capable of judging in civil affairs as their ministers. They never bowed the neck to this yoke.

(2) The resolutions of the Associate Reformed Church were interpreted differently in different sections of the Synod—some considering them as excluding the slaveholder from the communion of the Church, and others giving them a different interpretation. The people of this Church at large never attached much importance to the slavery resolutions, and but few indeed of its ministers ever ranked themselves as abolitionists. Some of its ministers, however, were rigid in their rule of excluding all clergymen of their sister Church at the South from their pulpits.

(3) The repudiation of the Constitution of the United States is a distinctive feature in the principles of the Reformed Presbyterian Church. They declare, unequivocally, that slaveholding is sinful. In this view both branches agree; but the *New Side* do not set aside the Constitution as sinful, but will vote and hold office.

(4) The doctrine, that the civil government should acknowledge its submission to the authority of the Church, is a peculiarity of this religious body. Its practical application seems impossible in the present condition of the Christian Church, torn, as it is, into so many fragments. It would be somewhat difficult, we think, to select the particular Church which should have the control of the Government in questions pertaining to religion and morals. This view would seem to be a fiction of the olden times, such as made the Pope supreme over the nations.

(5) Here we have a solemn truth. The great mass of the Northern people never have sympathized with the abolitionists; and could the Southern people have known this fact, they never would have been induced to rebel against the Government, from the fear that the North were determined to let their slaves loose upon them.

(6) But, notwithstanding what is said above is true, yet we have had continuous repetitions of such language as is contained in the sixth proposition of the Reformed Presbyterian Church; and which it is impossible for any Southern man to interpret in any other way, than that it embodies the essential elements of abolitionism.

(7) This resolution embodies the extreme radical ground since taken by the abolition politicians. We have here a fair specimen of the tender mercies of fanatical clergymen. The successful declaration of emancipation, under present circumstances, would be the letting loose of four millions of slaves, to pillage, burn, destroy, and murder all before them. This result can not but be foreseen, and yet the Reformed Presbytery of Pittsburgh would look with complacency upon the rapine and murder that would follow in the wake of their scheme of settling our national difficulties.

(8) The United Presbyterian Church, it will be seen, has taken the broad ground that slaveholding is a sin.

(9) Here we have, again, the very Christian-like proposition of letting loose the slave population upon defenseless women and children! We recommend to the brethren of this Synod the

declarations of the Rev. Dr. Candlish, of the Free Church of Scotland, copied on a preceding page.

In taking a survey of the ecclesiastical legislation embodied in the present chapter, it would be impossible for any one, not otherwise informed, to come to any other conclusion than that these whole Scottish Churches are intensely abolitionized; and yet such is not the fact, as to many of the ministry, and the great majority of their people.

The people of these Churches are among the most orderly and law-abiding of any of the citizens of the Union. At no one time, within the period of the excitement upon the subject of slavery, could there have been one-third of them induced to vote for the emancipation of the slaves at the South, except with the free and full assent of the masters; and not one in a hundred could ever have been induced to assent to a dissolution of the Union, as a means of being disconnected from slavery. The fanaticism on this question has been limited to the few, and the many have acquiesced in what has been done for the sake of peace. The rabid opinions expressed by the Pittsburgh Synod of the United Presbyterian Church, and the Reformed Presbytery of Pittsburgh, are acts done under intense excitement, and will be subjects of regret hereafter. The declaration of emancipation by the Executive, or by any of the commanding generals under him, as recommended by these religious bodies, is a measure that has already received the seal of condemnation by the President, and will not be attempted again. Why a Church court should volunteer its judgment upon a political measure of such moment, is a question that its members must answer for themselves. The public will naturally inquire, whether the ministers, assuming to dictate to the Government, have themselves given such evidences of being imbued with wisdom from on high—have had such success in their own field of duties—as to warrant their assumption of the office of dictators in civil affairs.

CHAPTER VIII.

THE METHODIST EPISCOPAL CHURCH IN THE U. S. AND SLAVERY.

THE Discipline of the Methodist Episcopal Church in the United States, as organized under the direction of Mr. Wesley, had a rule on slavery which aimed at the extirpation of the slave trade, and the promotion of emancipation. In 1784, the organization of the Annual Conferences was effected, and all business conducted by them until 1792. In 1796, the organization of the General Conference may be considered as completed. Its session for this year was held in Baltimore, and it has met once in four years since that period.

The action of the General Conference, at the meeting of 1796, on the subject of slavery, was as follows:

"Question 12. What regulations shall be made for the extirpation of the crying evil of slavery?

"Answer 1. We declare that we are more than ever convinced of the great evil of the African slavery which still exists in these United States; and do most earnestly recommend to the yearly Conferences, quarterly meetings, and to those who have the oversight of the districts and circuits, to be exceedingly cautious what persons they admit to official stations in our Church; and, in the case of future admission to official stations, to require such security of those who hold slaves, for the emancipation of them, immediately or gradually, as the laws of the States respectively, and the circumstances of the case will admit. And we do fully authorize all the yearly Conferences to make whatever regulations they judge proper, in the present case, respecting the admission of persons to official stations in our Church.

"2. No slaveholder shall be received into society, till the preacher who has the oversight of the circuit has spoken to him freely and faithfully on the subject of slavery.

(383)

" 3. Every member of the Society who sells a slave, shall immediately, 'after full proof, be excluded the Society. And if any member of our Society purchase a slave, the ensuing quarterly meeting shall determine on the number of years in which the slave, so purchased, would work out the price of his purchase. And the person so purchasing shall, immediately after such determination, execute a legal instrument for the manumission of such slave, at the expiration of the term determined by the quarterly meeting. And in default of his executing such instrument of manumission, or on his refusal to submit his case to the judgment of the quarterly meeting, such member shall be excluded the Society. *Provided also*, that in the case of a female slave, it shall be inserted in the aforesaid instrument of manumission, that all her children which shall be born during the years of her servitude shall be free at the following times, namely : every female child at the age of twenty-one, and every male child at the age of twenty-five. *Nevertheless*, if the member of our Society, executing the said instrument of manumission judge proper, he may fix the times of manumission of the children of the female slave beforementioned, at an earlier age than that which is prescribed above.

" 4. The preachers and other members of our Society are requested to consider the subject of negro slavery with deep attention till the ensuing General Conference ; and that they impart to the General Conference, through the medium of the yearly conferences or otherwise, any important thoughts upon the subject, that the Conference may have full light, in order to take further steps toward the eradication of this enormous evil from that part of the Church of God to which they are united."

In the year 1800, the General Conference again met in Baltimore. During this session resolutions, varying in character, were presented, but only two of them adopted: the first, asking for the appointment of a committee to prepare an affectionate address to the Methodist Societies, stating the evils of the spirit and practice of slavery, and the necessity of doing away the evil as far as the laws of the respective States will allow ; the second, that traveling preachers, becoming the owners of slaves, by any means, shall forfeit their ministerial character, unless they execute, if it be practicable, a legal emancipation of such slave or slaves, agreeably to the laws of the State in which they live.

In the year 1804, the General Conference again held its session in Baltimore.

"*May* 16.—A variety of motions were proposed on the subject of slavery, and, after a long conversation, it was moved and carried, that the subject of slavery be left to the three bishops, to form a section to suit the Southern and Northern States, as they, in their wisdom, may think best, to be submitted to this Conference.

"*May* 17.—Read the report of the Committee on Slavery—which, with amendments, was adopted by Conference, and forms section nine, ' Of Slavery.' "

This document is substantially the same as that of 1796, except that it has, as its 2d and 5th articles, the following :

"2. When any traveling preacher becomes the owner of a slave, or slaves, by any means, he shall forfeit his ministerial character in our Church, unless he executes, if it be practicable, a legal emancipation of such slaves, conformably to the laws of the State in which he lives.

"5. Let our preachers, from time to time, as occasion serves, admonish and exhort all slaves to render due respect and obedience to the commands and interests of their respective masters."

In the close of article 4, this amendment is made : " Nevertheless, the members of our societies in the States of North Carolina, South Carolina, and Georgia, shall be exempted from the operation of the above rules." (1)

During the sessions of 1808 and 1812, nothing of importance was done on the question of slavery, excepting, at the latter session, to lay upon the table a memorial on the subject.

In 1816, the General Conference met in Baltimore. The Committee on Slavery presented their report, which was concurred in by the Conference :

" The committee to whom was referred the business of slavery, beg leave to report, that they have taken the subject into serious consideration, and, after mature deliberation, they are of opinion that, under the present existing circumstances in relation to slavery, little can be done to abolish a practice so contrary to the principles of moral justice. They are sorry to say that the evil appears to be past remedy ;

and they are led to deplore the destructive consequences which have already accrued, and are yet likely to result therefrom.

"Your committee find that in the South and West the civil authorities render emancipation impracticable, and, notwithstanding they are led to fear that some of our members are too easily contented with laws so unfriendly to freedom, yet, nevertheless, they are constrained to admit that to bring about such a change in the civil code as would favor the cause of liberty, is not in the power of the General Conference. Your committee have attentively read, and seriously considered, a memorial on the above subject, presented from several persons within the bounds of the Baltimore Annual Conference. They have also made inquiry into the regulations adopted and pursued by the different annual conferences in relation to this subject, and they find that some of them have made no efficient rules on the subject of slavery, thereby leaving our people to act as they please; while others have adopted rules, and pursued courses not a little different from each other, all pleading the authority given them by the General Conference, according to our present existing rule, as stated in our form of Discipline. Your committee conclude that, in order to be consistent and uniform, the rule should be express and definite; and, to bring about this uniformity, they beg leave to submit the following resolution:

"*Resolved*, by the delegates of the annual conferences in General Conference assembled, That all the recommendatory part of the second division, ninth section, and first answer of our form of Discipline, after the word 'slavery,' be stricken out, and the following words inserted: 'Therefore no slaveholder shall be eligible to any official station in our Church hereafter, where the laws of the State in which he lives will admit of emancipation, and permit the liberated slave to enjoy freedom.'

In 1820, the General Conference met at Baltimore. Certain documents from Tennessee were referred to the Committee on Slavery, which, together with the report of 1816, were acted upon by the committee, a substitute reported, one of its propositions adopted, the report recommitted, and the whole subject finally postponed indefinitely.

In 1824, the General Conference met at Baltimore. The Committee on Slavery, in compliance with the several memorials presented, asking provision to be made for the spiritual welfare of the colored population, free and slave, reported, and, after various modifications, the following resolutions were adopted :

"*Resolved*, 1. That all our preachers ought prudently to enforce upon our members the necessity of teaching their slaves to read the Word of God; and also that they give time to hear the Word of God preached on our regular days of divine service.

"*Resolved*, 2. That our colored preachers and official members have all the privileges, in the district and quarterly meeting conferences, which the usages of the country in different sections will justify: *Provided*, also, that the presiding elder may, when there is a sufficient number, hold for them a separate district conference.

"*Resolved*, 3. That any of the annual conferences may employ colored preachers to travel, where they judge their services may be necessary, provided they be recommended according to the form of Discipline. (2)

"*Resolved*, 4. That the above resolutions be made a part of the section in the Discipline on slavery."

In 1828, the General Conference met at Pittsburgh, Pa. A resolution against the bad treatment of slaves was offered, and subsequently withdrawn, and resolutions passed approving the course of the American Colonization Society.

In 1832, the General Conference met at Philadelphia. During this session, the subject of the religious rights and privileges of the colored people, and also what change should be made in the section on the subject of slavery, were brought forward by resolution, and referred to committees.

In 1836, the General Conference met in Cincinnati, Ohio. The following resolution was offered :

"*Resolved*, That the committee appointed to draft a pastoral letter to our preachers, members, and friends, be, and they are hereby instructed, to take notice of the subject of modern abolition, that has so seriously agitated the different parts of our country, and that they let our preachers, members, and friends know that the General Conference are opposed to the agitation of that subject, and will use all prudent means to put it down.

"On motion of S. G. Rozel, a preamble and resolutions on the case of two members, lecturing on the subject of abolition in this city, was taken up, which produced considerable excitement and discussion, until the time for adjournment had arrived."

The discussion on Mr. Rozel's motion was prolonged throughout three sittings, and the following preamble and resolutions were finally adopted by an overwhelming majority :

"The whole of the motion, as adopted, is as follows, viz. :

"*Whereas*, great excitement has prevailed in this country on the subject of modern abolitionism, which is reported to have been increased in this city recently by the unjustifiable conduct of two members of the General Conference, in lecturing upon and in favor of that agitating topic ; and *whereas*, such a course, on the part of any of its members, is calculated to bring upon this body the suspicions and distrust of the community, and misrepresent its sentiments in regard to the point at issue ; and *whereas*, in this aspect of the case, a due regard for its own character, as well as a just concern for the interests of the Church confided to its care, demand a full, decided, and unequivocal expression of the views of the General Conference in the premises, therefore,

"*Resolved*, by the delegates of the annual conferences in General Conference assembled, 1. That they disapprove, in the most unqualified sense, the conduct of two members of the General Conference, who are reported to have lectured in this city recently upon and in favor of modern abolitionism.

"*Resolved*, 2. That they are decidedly opposed to modern abolitionism, and wholly disclaim any right, wish, or intention to interfere in the civil and political relation existing between master and slave, as it exists in the slaveholding States of this Union. (3)

"*Resolved*, 3. That the foregoing preamble and resolutions be published in our periodicals."

During this session a number of memorials on the subject of slavery were presented, and a report made by the judiciary committee in relation to grievances complained of by the Baltimore Annual Conference, and others, in which it is said, "that the exceptions to the general rule in the Discipline clearly apply to official members of the Church in Virginia, according to the laws of the Commonwealth, and do, therefore, protect them against a forfeiture of their official standing, on account of said rule."

"The chairman of the committee on the subject of slavery presented a report, which was read and adopted, as follows:

"The committee to whom were referred sundry memorials from the North, praying that certain rules on the subject of slavery, which formerly existed in our Book of Discipline, should be restored, and that the General Conference take such measures as they may deem proper to free the Church from the evil of slavery, beg leave to report:

"That they have had the subject under serious consideration, and are of opinion that the prayers of the memorialists can not be granted, believing that it would be highly improper for the General Conference to take any action that would alter or change our rules on the subject of slavery. Your committee, therefore, respectfully submit the following resolution:

"*Resolved*, That it is inexpedient to make any change in our Book of Discipline respecting slavery, and that we deem it improper further to agitate the subject in the General Conference at present."

In 1840, the General Conference met in Baltimore. During this conference the petitions against slavery were very numerous, from almost all portions of the North. There was also a considerable number of memorials protesting against any action of the General Conference upon the subject. Majority and minority reports were made by the committee on the subject of slavery. The whole subject seems to have been left among the unfinished business, though considerable discussion was had upon the majority report. The Address of the Bishops, for this year, takes notice of the slavery agitation in a conciliatory, conservative, and Christian spirit. The following extract will be found interesting and important. It would seem that these pious men, in viewing the tendencies of the slavery agitation, saw, with almost prophetic vision, that its practical tendency was to endanger the safety of the Union of these United States:

"The experience of more than half a century, since the organization of our ecclesiastical body, will afford us many important lights and landmarks, pointing out what is the safest and most prudent policy to be pursued, in our onward course, as regards African slavery in these States; and especially in our own religious community. This very interesting period of our history is distinguished by several characteristic features having a special claim to our consideration at the present time, particularly in view of the unusual excitement which now prevails on the subject, not only in the different Christian Churches, but also in the civil body. And, first: our general rule on slavery, which forms a part of the Constitution of the Church, has stood, from the beginning, unchanged, as testamentary of our sentiments on the principle of slavery and the slave trade. And in this we differ in no respect from the sentiments of our venerable founder, or from those of the wisest and most distinguished statesmen and civilians of our own and other enlightened and Christian countries. Secondly: in all the enactments of the Church relating to slavery, a due and respectful regard has been had to the laws of the States, never requiring emancipation in contravention of the civil authority, or where the laws of the States would not allow the liberated slave to enjoy his freedom. Thirdly: the simply holding or owning of slaves, without regard to circumstances, has, at no period of the existence of the Church, subjected the master to excommunication. Fourthly: rules have been made, from time to time, regulating the sale, and purchase, and holding of slaves, with reference to the different laws of the States where slavery is tolerated; which, upon the experience of the great difficulties of administering them, and the unhappy consequences both to masters and servants, have been as often changed or repealed. These important facts, which form prominent features of our past history as a Church, may very properly lead us to inquire for that course of action, in future, which may be best calculated to preserve the peace and unity of the whole body, promote the general happiness of the slave population, and advance generally, in the slaveholding community of our country, the humane and hallowing influence of our holy religion. We can not withhold from you, at this eventful period, the solemn conviction of our minds, that no new ecclesiastical legislation on the subject of slavery, at this time, will have a tendency to accomplish these most desirable objects. And we are fully persuaded that, as a body of Christian ministers, we shall accomplish the greatest good by directing our individual and united efforts, in the spirit of the first teachers of Christianity, to bring both master and servant under the sanctifying influence of the principles of that Gospel which teaches the duties of every relation, and enforces the faithful discharge of them by the strongest conceivable motives. Do we aim at the amelioration of the condition of the slave? How can we so effectually accomplish this, in our calling as ministers of the Gospel of Christ, as by employing our whole influence to bring him and his master to a saving knowledge of the grace of God, and to a practical observance of those relative duties so clearly prescribed in the writings of the inspired apostles? Permit us to add, that, although we enter not into the political contentions of the day, neither interfere with civil legislation nor with the administration of the laws, we can not but feel a deep interest in whatever affects the peace, prosperity, and happiness of our beloved country. The Union of these States, the perpetuity of the bonds of our national confederation, the reciprocal confidence of the different members of the great civil compact,—in a word, the *well-being* of the community of which we are members, should never cease to lay near our hearts, and for which we should offer up our sincere and most ardent prayers to the Almighty Ruler of the universe. But can we, as ministers of the Gospel, and servants of a Master 'whose kingdom is not of this world,' promote those important objects in any way so truly and permanently as by pursuing the course just pointed out? Can we, at this eventful crisis, render a better service to our country, than by laying aside all interference with relations authorized and established by the civil laws, and applying ourselves wholly and faithfully to what especially appertains to our 'high and holy calling;' to teach and enforce the moral obligations of the Gospel, in application to all the duties growing out of the different relations in society? By a diligent devotion to this evangelical employment, with an humble and steadfast reliance upon the aid of divine influence, the number of 'believing masters' and servants may be constantly increased, the kindest sentiments and affections cultivated, domestic burdens lightened, mutual confidence cherished, and the peace and happiness of society promoted. While, on the other hand, if past history affords us any correct rules of judgment, there is much cause to fear that the influence of our sacred office, if employed in interference with the relation itself, and, consequently, with the civil institutions of the country, will rather tend to prevent than to accomplish these desirable ends." (4)

In 1844, the General Conference met, on the 1st of May, in New York. The petitions on the subject of slavery, this year, were very numerous.　On the 14th, the following preamble and resolution was introduced:

"In view of the distracting agitation which has so long prevailed on the subject of slavery and abolition, and especially the difficulties under which we labor in the present General Conference, on account of the relative position of our brethren North and South on this perplexing question; therefore,

"*Resolved*, That a committee of three from the North and three from the South be appointed to confer with the Bishops, and report, within two days, as to the possibility of adopting some plan, and what, for the permanent pacification of the Church."

After a slight amendment, the resolution was adopted.

Almost immediately thereafter, the following resolution was offered and adopted:—

"*Resolved*, That to-morrow be observed as a day of fasting and humiliation before God, and prayer for his blessing upon the committee of six, in conjunction with the Bishops, on the present difficulties; and that the hour from twelve to one o'clock be devoted to religious services in the Conference."

This resolution was devoutly complied with at the time appointed.

On the 18th, Bishop Soule, in behalf of the committee of six, reported, that

"The Committee of Conference have instructed me to report, that, after a calm and deliberate investigation of the subject submitted to their consideration, they are unable to agree upon any plan of compromise to reconcile the views of the Northern and Southern conferences."

The report was accepted, and the committee discharged.

On the 20th, a crisis was produced, in this contest, by the presentation of the following preamble and resolution:

"*Whereas*, it is currently reported, and generally understood, that one of the Bishops of the M. E. Church has become connected with slavery; and *whereas* it is due to this General Conference to have a proper understanding of the matter; therefore,

" *Resolved,* That the Committee on the Episcopacy be instructed to ascertain the facts in the case, and report the results of their investigation to this body to-morrow morning."

The person referred to was Bishop Andrew, who had become connected with slavery by marriage. The history of this case need not be presented here. It led to the disruption of the Church. " The Southern members contended that, as the laws of the State in which the Bishop lived would not permit emancipation, the General Conference should not interfere in the case. The majority of the delegates insisted that as a Bishop was required 'to travel through the connection at large, any connection with slavery would embarrass both him and the Church in the performance of his duties,' and declared their judgment to be that Bishop Andrew should cease from the exercise of episcopal functions until he could relieve himself of this impediment. Then followed that separation which has become one of the great facts of ecclesiastical history." *

On the 6th June, the Committee on Slavery, after stating that about 10,000 signatures appeared attached to the various memorials from the people, and that they find petitions from nine Annual conferences, say, that they deem it inexpedient to recommend any farther action, except that suggested in their first report; and then proceed to say that they " have also received a statement of the votes from several of the annual conferences upon the alterations proposed to be made in the General Rules upon the subject of slavery. No evidence, however, has as yet reached the committee that a constitutional number of votes in the annual conferences has been obtained to make any alterations in the General Rules upon the subject of slavery."

The Address of the Bishops, for this year, embraced some very important statements in reference to the progress of the Gospel among the slaves, and the very limited success of the Church among the colored people of the free States. It says :

" Although we have not been able to extend the missions among the people of color in the southern and southwestern States, according to

---

* See Minority Report on Slavery, 1860.

our ardent desires, and the providential openings before us, for want of pecuniary means, still we rejoice that we have not been compelled to abandon the fields which we have already under cultivation; and that we have been enabled to occupy some new and very promising grounds. It is a matter of gratulation to the friends of humanity and religion, and of devout thanksgiving to God, that the unhappy excitement which, for several years, spread a dark cloud over our prospects, and weakened our hands, and filled our hearts with grief, has died away, and almost ceased to blast our labors. Confidence in the integrity of our principles, and the purity of our motives, which, for a time, was shaken, is restored. New and extensive fields are opening before us, and inviting us to the harvest. The conviction of the duty and benefit of giving religious instruction to servants is constantly increasing. The self-sacrificing zeal of the missionaries is worthy of the cause in which they are engaged—the cause of humanity; the cause of the salvation of souls; the cause of God. Brethren, suffer us to beseech you, by the tender mercies of God, by the precious blood of Jesus, and by the crying spiritual wants of perishing thousands for whom he died, to strengthen the hands and encourage the hearts of your fellow-laborers, who are more directly engaged in this blessed work, by your ceaseless prayers to God for them.

"We can not but view it as a matter of deep regret, that the spiritual interests of the people of color in these United States have been so long and so greatly neglected by the Christian Churches. And it is greatly to be feared that we are not innocent in this thing. While we profess to sympathize with millions of the African race in this land, being children of the same common Father of mankind, 'who has made of one blood all nations of men, to dwell upon the face of the whole earth;' but who are deprived of equal civil rights and privileges with the white citizens, by the laws and institutions of the country, over which we have no control, have we not been negligent of their higher, even their eternal, interests, which we are at perfect liberty, and have the means, to promote? And, if so, is not this neglect, especially in their circumstances, a violation of the laws of our common nature, and the obligations founded in the relations we sustain to them, in a common brotherhood? There is, blessed be God, no bar in the laws of our country to prevent them from receiving religious instruction, or being gathered into the fold of God. Here, then, we have an open door. We may preach the Gospel of Christ to them, unite them in the communion of his Church, and introduce them to a participation of the blessings of her fellowship, and thus be the instruments of their preparation for the riches of the inheritance of the saints in glory.   This, as ministers of Christ, is our *work*, and should be our glory and joy.   This, by the grace of God helping us, we can do; but to raise them to equal civil rights and privileges is not within our power.   Let us not labor in vain, and spend our strength for naught.   In this cause we are debtors both to the bond and the free; yea, to all men.   But are we, as servants of a Master whose kingdom is not of this world, discharging our obligations to the utmost extent of our ability?   Have we neglected no means within our power to promote the present and eternal well-being of this numerous and needy class of our brethren?   Let *facts* give the answer. From an examination of official records, it appears that there are four annual conferences in which there is not a single colored member in the Church.   Eight others have an aggregate number of four hundred and sixty-three, averaging less than sixty.   And taking fifteen, almost one-half of the conferences in the connection, and some of them among the largest, both in the ministry and membership, and the whole number of colored members is but one thousand three hundred and nine, giving an average of less than ninety.   It is well known that, in many of these conferences, there is a numerous colored population, and in each of them a very considerable number.   It is presumed that the freedom of the people of color, within the bounds of these conferences, will not be urged as the cause of their not being brought under religious influence, and gathered into the fold of Christ.   We are certainly not prepared to admit that a state of servitude is more favorable to the success of the Gospel, in its experimental and practical effects, than a state of freedom.   Facts will clearly show that this is not the cause.   In the city of Baltimore alone, there are nearly four times the number of colored people in the Church that we find in the fifteen conferences referred to; and yet a vast majority of them are as free as they are in almost all the states embraced in these conferences. It may be well for us to examine this subject carefully, in connection with our high responsibility."* (5)

As necessary to a proper understanding of the position of the South, in relation to slavery, we present the following historical statement from the Protest of the Minority of the General Con-

---

* Journals of the General Conference, 1844.

ce, against the action of that body, in the case of Bishop
ew. From this view of the subject, it appears that there
been an "irrepressible conflict" between the North and the
South, almost ever since the organization of the Methodist Church
in this country:

"The law of the Church on slavery has always existed since 1785,
but especially since 1804, and in view of the adjustment of the whole
subject, in 1816, as a *virtual, though informal, contract of mutual concession and forbearance*, between the North and the South, then, as
now, known and existing as distinct parties, in relation to the vexed
questions of slavery and abolition. Those conferences found in States
where slavery prevailed constituting the Southern party, and those in
the non-slaveholding States the Northern, exceptions to the rule being
found in both. The rights of the legal owners of slaves, in all the
slaveholding States, are guaranteed by the Constitution of the United
States, and by the local constitutions of the States respectively, as the
supreme law of the land, to which every minister and member of the
Methodist Episcopal Church within the limits of the United States
government professes subjection, and pledges himself to submit, as
an article of Christian faith, in the common creed of the Church.
Domestic slavery, therefore, wherever it exists in this country, is a
civil regulation, existing under the highest sanctions of constitutional
and municipal law known to the tribunals of the country, and it has
always been assumed at the South, and relied upon as correct, that
the North or non-slaveholding States had no right, civil or moral, to
interfere with relations and interests thus secured to the people of
the South by all the graver forms of law and social order, and that
it cannot be done without an abuse of the constitutional rights of
citizenship. The people of the North, however, have claimed to think
differently, and have uniformly acted toward the South in accordance
with such opposition of opinion. Precisely in accordance, too, with
this state of things, as it regards the general population of the North
and South, respectively, the Methodist Episcopal Church has been
divided in opinion and feeling on the subject of slavery and abolition
since its organization, in 1784: two separate and distinct parties have
always existed. The Southern conferences, in agreeing to the main
principles of the compromise law in 1804 and 1816, conceded, by express stipulation, their right to resist Northern interference in any
form, upon the condition, pledged by the North, that while the *whole*

Church, by common consent, united in proper effort for the mitigation and final removal of the evil of slavery, the North was not to interfere, by excluding from membership or ministerial office in the Church, persons owning and holding slaves in States where emancipation is not practicable, and where the liberated slave is not permitted to enjoy freedom.   Such was the compact of 1804 and 1816, finally agreed to by the parties after a long and fearful struggle, and such is the compact now—the proof being derived from history and the testimony of living witnesses.   And is it possible to suppose that the original purpose and intended application of the law was not designed to embrace every member, minister, order, and officer of the Methodist Episcopal Church?   Is the idea of excepted cases allowable by fair construction of the law?   Do not the reasons and intendment of the law place it beyond doubt, that every conceivable case of alleged misconduct that can arise, connected with slavery or abolition, is to be subjected, by consent and contract of parties, to the jurisdiction of this great conservative arrangement?

    "Is there anything in the law or its reasons creating an exception in the instance of bishops?   Would the South have entered into the arrangement, or in any form consented to the law, had it been intimated by the North that bishops must be an exception to the rule?   Are the virtuous dead of the North to be slandered by the supposition that they intended to except bishops, and thus accomplish their purposes, in negotiation with the South, by a resort to deceptive and dishonorable means?   If bishops are not named, no more are presiding elders, agents, editors—or, indeed, any other officers of the Church, who are, nevertheless, included, although the same rule of construction would except them also.   The enactment was for an entire people, east, west, north, and south.   It was for the Church, and every member of it—for the common weal of the body—and is, therefore, universal and unrestricted in its application; and no possible case can be settled upon any other principles, without a direct violation of this law both in fact and form.   The law being what we have assumed, any violation of it, whatever may be its form or mode, is as certainly a breach of good faith as an infringement of law.   It must be seen, from the manner in which the compromise was effected, in the shape of a law, agreed to by equal contracting parties, 'the several annual conferences,' after long and formal negotiation, that it was not a mere legislative enactment, a simple decree of a General Conference, but partakes of the nature of a grave compact, and is invested with all the sacredness and sanctions of a solemn treaty, binding respectively the well-known parties to its terms and stipulations. If this be so,— and with the evidence accessible who can doubt it?—if this be so, will it prove a light matter for this General Conference to violate or disregard the obligation of this *legal compromise*, in the shape of public recognized law!"

In 1848, the General Conference met in Pittsburgh. But one petition on the subject of slavery was presented, and no committee on the subject was appointed.

In 1852, the General Conference met in Boston. No committee was appointed on the subject of slavery, and the few petitions received were referred to the Committee on Revisals.

In 1856, the General Conference met at Indianapolis, in the State of Indiana. A Committee on Slavery, consisting of one member from each annual conference, was appointed. The petitions on slavery were very numerous, and demanded, among other things, such an alteration of the Rule on slavery as would exclude slaveholders. This demand was resisted, on the ground that many of the border Churches had agreed to remain in connection with the Northern division, on the ground of pledges given that no attempt would be made to alter the Rule, or give to it an abolition interpretation.

The majority of the committee reported at length on the subject. The spirit of this report can be understood from the following extracts:

"That the reduction of a moral and responsible being to the condition of property is a violation of natural rights, is considered by most men an axiom in ethics; but whatever opinions may have obtained in general society, the Methodist Episcopal Church has ever maintained an unmistakable anti-slavery position. Affirmations that 'slavery is founded in the philosophy of civil society,' that it 'is the corner-stone of republican institutions,' or that it is sanctioned by the Bible,' have never met with an approving response in our Church; contrariwise, the Founder of Methodism denounced the system in unqualified terms of condemnation, and the fathers unwaveringly followed the example of the venerated Wesley. The Methodist Episcopal Church has, in good faith, in all periods of its history, proposed to itself the question, ' What shall be done for the extirpation of the evil of slavery ?' and it has never ceased, openly and before the world, to bear testimony against the sin, and to exercise its disciplinary powers, to the end that its members might be kept unspotted from criminal connection with the system, and that the evil itself be removed from among men.

" It is affirmed and believed that the Methodist Episcopal Church has done more to diffuse anti-slavery sentiments, to mitigate the evils of the system, and to-abolish the institution from civil society, than any other organization either political, social, or religious. It is also affirmed and believed that the administrators of discipline in our Church within the bounds of slave territory have faithfully done all that, under their circumstances, they have conscientiously judged to be in their power *to answer the ends of Discipline in exterminating this great evil.* (6)   .   .   .   .   .   .

" We now inquire whether the time has come when it becomes the duty of the Church, through its representatives assembled in its highest ecclesiastical court, to so revise the statutes of the Church as to make them express our real sentiments, and indicate our practice as it is. We answer, yes! first, because it is just and equal; it is right before God and all men, that in a subject involving directly the personal liberties of thousands, and indirectly of millions of our fellowmen, the position of the Church should be neither equivocal or doubtful. Secondly, because we can not answer it to our own consciences, nor to God, the judge of all, if we fail to do what is in our power to bear testimony against so great an evil. Thirdly, because it is solemnly demanded at our hands by a very large majority of those whom we represent; and, fourthly, because the signs of the times plainly indicate that it is the duty of all good men to rally for the relief of the oppressed, and for the defense of the liberties transmitted to us by our fathers.

" We are aware that it is objected, that in the present excited state of the public mind, to take any action on the subject will be to place a weapon in the hands of our enemies with which they may do us essential injury. We reply, that in all cases, to say one thing and mean another, is of doubtful morality We judge the rather that on all questions vital to morality and re. ᵧon, the honor of the Church is better sustained by an unqualified decl .ation of the truth.

" We come now to state what, as it seems to us, is, always has been, and ever should be, the true position of our Church in respect to slavery. We hold that the buying, selling, and, by inference, the holding of a human being as property, is a sin against God and man; that because of the social relations in which men may be placed by the civil codes of slaveholding communities, the legal relations of master to slave may, in some circumstances, subsist innocently; that connection with slavery is *prima facie* evidence of guilt; that in all cases of alleged criminality of this kind, the burden of proof should rest upon the accused, he always having secured to him the advantages of trial and appeal before impartial tribunals.

"In view of these facts and principles, the committee recommend the adoption of the following resolutions:

"1. *Resolved*, by the delegates of the several annual conferences, in General Conference assembled, that we recommend the several annual conferences so to amend our General Rule on slavery, as to read, 'The buying, selling, or holding a human being as property.'

"2. *Resolved*, by the delegates of the several annual conferences, in General Conference assembled, that the following be, and hereby is, substituted in the place of the present seventh chapter of our Book of Discipline." . . . . . .

The chapter proposed as a substitute was made to conform to the first resolution, as interpreted by the majority report.

The first resolution was put to vote, the result being 122 ayes and 66 nays. "As two thirds of the members did not favor the motion, it was lost, according to the rule of the discipline in such cases made and provided."

The second resolution was not called up.

The minority of the committee reported, also, upon this subject, setting forth the destructive tendencies of the alteration of the Rule upon the Churches in the border slave States.

In 1860, the General Conference met in Buffalo, N. Y. A committee of 47 was appointed on the subject of slavery. The memorials presented were very numerous. They stood thus:

Against a change of the Rule, 32 annual conferences, 137 memorials, signed by 3,999 persons, and from 47 quarterly meeting conferences.

Asking for a change of the Rule, from 33 annual conferences, 811 memorials, signed by 45,857 persons, and from 49 quarterly meeting conferences.

The General Conference met on the 1st of May, and on the 16th the majority report was presented:

MAJORITY REPORT ON SLAVERY.

THE Committee on Slavery offer the following report:

When He who spake as never man spake would comprehend the sum of all human duty as between man and man in one brief sentence, he embodied that sentence in the following memorable words: " All things whatsoever ye would that men should do unto you, do ye even so unto them; for this is the law and prophets." The same sublime epitome of human duty is expressed in the words, "Thou shalt love thy neighbor as thyself." These precepts form the moral mirror which God has hung up before all humanity. Into this mirror every man is bound to look and see his own conduct as others see it, and as he sees that of others. Or, to change the figure, these precepts form the moral scales in which every man is bound to weigh his own actions as he weighs the actions of other men. This Golden Law of God sheds its divine light upon all the relationships which subsist between man and his fellow; and that which we would have a right to desire from any human being with whom we have to do, if we were in his circumstances and he in ours, is the exact measure of our duty.

The enslavement from generation to generation of human beings guilty of no crime, is what no man has a right to desire for himself or his posterity, and what no man ever did or can desire. The constant liability of the forcible separation of husbands and wives, of parents and children, even in the mildest forms of slavery, is a state of things from which every enlightened mind desires to be free. The impediments which slavery interposes in the way of the observance of the conjugal and parental relations, depriving the parents from governing and educating their children, and the children from honoring and obeying their parents, as God has commanded, is a state of things condemned alike by the Bible and all enlightened consciences, and from which the heart's holiest aspirations struggle to be free. The sacredness and inviolability of the marriage covenant is one of the corner-stones of all Christian civilization. Slavery, as it exists in the United States, is fundamentally at war with this most ancient and sacred institution. What should we desire, and have a right to desire, if we were in the place of the injured party? This is the measure of our duty.

A system which converts a human being into merchandise, which denies a man the rights of property, of family, of "liberty and the pursuits of happiness," and generally of the power to read the record which God has given for the regulation of all human conduct, is a state of things in which no intelligent and right-minded person ever did or can desire to be placed. In reference to all these, and to all other conditions of human wrong, the solemn mandate comes down from Heaven: "All things whatsoever ye would that men should do unto you, do ye even so to them."

God has laid the foundation of religious education in the family relationships. His claims upon us find their readiest response where the honor and obedience due to parents are properly inculcated. The obligation to love God, because he first loved us, finds its strongest response where the tenderness and affection breathed upon childhood, by its divinely constituted guardians, prepare the young heart for this high duty.* The strongest terms by which the indissoluble affection subsisting between God and his Church are expressed in Scripture,

---

* All the arguments of this nature are unsound, because they are based upon a totally mistaken view of the question at issue. Were the negroes, as a class, sufficiently civilized to be capable of imparting instruction in morals and religion to their offspring, the argument would have some weight; but, rising slowly from the lowest barbarism, they possess no such qualifications for teaching as are required of those who have the care of offspring among professing Christians. To emancipate them, would be to leave them to sink back again into barbarism; and what does African barbarism do for offspring? Listen to the story of a Christian missionary on this subject:

"A SAD SCENE IN AFRICA.—It was said in one of the Psalms, many years ago, 'The dark places of the earth are full of the habitations of cruelty.' They are just as full of such habitations now as they were then, and this is one of the reasons why we should send missionaries to all the heathens. A short time ago a missionary in Africa left his home to preach the Gospel in some towns several miles away from the mission station. As he entered one town his attention was attracted by two women, whose conduct was very light and trifling, and who appeared to be watching some object under the eaves of the opposite house. What was that shapeless object they were looking at? He drew near to see. It was a poor little boy, about three years old, reduced almost to a skeleton, but still breathing. Every rib in his little body might be seen, while his back appeared to be broken. By his side there was a raw cassada, (a kind of root somewhat like a potato), and a little gourd, holding water, which, with his poor, thin hand, he was trying to lift to his mouth. But the strength of the little fellow was unequal to it, and his low wailings of distress were most piteous, and filled the heart of the missionary with distress. He pointed the laughing women to the sufferings of the poor child; but they laughed all the more at his concern. He then learned that the child was an orphan, and had become the charge of one of the women of the family. Either through her

are taken from the parental and conjugal relationship. The inimitable prayer, commencing, "Our Father which art in heaven," is a further recognition of the same thing.

What, then, must be the religious effect of an institution which tramples these sacred relationships in the dust?

In short, there is not, in our judgment, one distinctive attribute of chattel slavery which is not incompatible with the Golden Rule.

The foregoing considerations, as it seems to us, are sufficient to justify the opposition which from the beginning we have manifested toward slavery; for, be it remembered, this opposition is no new thing among us, but is coeval with our very existence as a Christian organization.

The opinions of our revered founder need not be recounted here. Imbibing in larger measure, than was common in his day, the spirit of Him whose sympathies gush forth as an everlasting fountain toward the poor and the oppressed, Mr. Wesley uttered a testimony against slavery immortal as his own name.

His genuine sons in the Gospel have followed his example. The Conference of 1780 declared "slavery to be contrary to the laws of God, man, and nature, and hurtful to society; contrary to the dictates of conscience and pure religion, and·doing that which we would not that others should do unto us."

The General Conference of 1784 declared the practice of slaveholding to be "contrary to the Golden Law of God, and contrary to the inalienable rights of mankind, as well as to every principle of the Revolution." The Conference say: "We think it our most bounden duty, therefore, to take immediately some effectual method to extirpate this abomination from among us, and for that purpose we add the following to the rules of our society."

Then followed a plan of emancipation, specifying the age at which every person held in slavery should be free, and declaring that no

---

neglect, or from disease, it had become this miserable object, only a trouble to her, and she had left it there to die while she went to her farm in the bush!

"Two or three native Christian young men were with the missionary, who proposed to take the child to a little out-station on the opposite side of the lake, and take care of it. What a contrast between the conduct of these young Christians and that of the women who had left that child to die, not caring what might become of it! And what made the difference? Only the blessed Gospel; the entrance into their hearts of the knowledge of Him whose name is love."—*Central Christian Advocate*, Feb., 1861.

person thereafter holding slaves should be admitted into the society or to the Lord's Supper till he had previously complied with these rules concerning slavery. A note followed these stringent measures, declaring that they were to affect the members no further than they were consistent with the laws of the States in which they resided; and also, in view of peculiar circumstances, giving the members in Virginia two years in which to comply with these regulations. As these measures were admitted to constitute a new term of membership, all persons were allowed to choose between voluntarily retiring and being expelled.

About six months after, it was thought best to suspend, for the time, the execution of these rules, and give the members a longer time before the minute should be enforced. The suspension proved to be indefinite, but immediately following the suspension is the declaration: "We do hold in the deepest abhorrence the practice of slavery, and shall not cease to seek its destruction by all wise and prudent means." In 1789, the General Rule read: "The buying and selling the bodies and souls of men, women, or children, with an intention to enslave them." In 1792, it read: "The buying or selling of men, women, or children, with an intention to enslave them." From 1808 until now, the rule has read as at present, no one knowing how the *or* came to be substituted by *and*.

For seventy-six years the question at the head of our present chapter on slavery has remained substantially what it now is: "What shall be done for the extirpation of the evil of slavery?" During all this period and more, there has no day intervened in which our Church has not testified against slavery as a great evil, and one whose extirpation is to be sought by all lawful and Christian means. Nor has our acknowledged anti-slavery position been unproductive of good fruit. There is a power in the truth, when faithfully uttered, to influence the conscience of mankind. The testimony which our Church has borne has done much toward the formation of a correct public opinion. Under its influence many thousands of slaves have been set free; and many thousands, who otherwise would have been slaveholders, have refrained; and many thousands more, who are still holding slaves, are doing so with consciences ill at ease. But for this testimony a number of western States, now free, and embracing a vast range of territory, would probably to-day be slave States.

These facts are our answer to the question: "What good has our church-action on the subject ever done?" Is it a small thing that thousands of immortal beings have been delivered from bondage; that thousands more have been restrained from oppressing their fellow-men; and that regions of country, by many times larger than some of the mightiest empires of the earth, have been secured to freedom?

To the charge that we are violating the laws of the land, a brief answer must suffice. If we choose to keep as free as we can from the evils of slavery, how do we thus violate the laws of the land? Do the laws of the land require the members of the Methodist Episcopal Church to hold slaves? How do we then violate the laws by declining to hold them? Must we practice every evil which the laws will permit, lest we be charged with violating them?

While we have no sympathy with, but, on the other hand, strongly condemn the mad projects of reckless and desperate men, who, in defiance of law, seek, by violent means, either to establish or destroy slavery, we earnestly pray that the time may soon come when, through the blessed principles of the Gospel of peace, slavery shall cease throughout the length and breadth of this fair land.

But why should we seek any change in our Discipline, if it has worked so well?

We answer, 1. Much of our present Chapter on Slavery has become obsolete by the changed circumstances since its introduction, and the chapter is now, in consequence, no sufficient answer to the question with which it commences. Owing to the present laws of many of the slave States, the Rule in the chapter can have no practical application where we have any considerable membership.

Again, the chapter, by making one rule for official and another for private members of the Church, fails, we think, to embody our real doctrine on the subject of which it treats. We do not see the propriety of having one rule for the class-leader and another for the members of his class; one rule for the trustee and another for the member sitting by his side; one rule for a steward and another for the person of whom he collects quarterage. Such discriminations, we presume, will be admitted to be without any sufficient foundation, and we believe they are practically disregarded.

2. Within a comparatively recent period differences of opinion have sprung up as to the bearing our present General Rule has on the subject of slaveholding. A few among us have contended that the Rule condemns only the African slave trade; others believe that it condemns both the foreign and domestic traffic; others, that while it con-

demns the traffic, it thereby legalizes the holding of slaves; others, and we think by far the larger portion, hold that while the Rule in express terms condemns the traffic for a certain purpose, it also, by fair implication, condemns the holding for the same purpose.

To this last view we ask a somewhat more particular attention. What is the specific thing which the terms of the General Rule forbid? Not the buying or selling of a human being simply, but the buying or selling *with an intention to enslave.* The buying or selling with an intention to free is not forbidden. What, then, is the meaning of the qualifying phrase, "*with the intention to enslave them?*" This question can admit of but one answer. The person has already been reduced to slavery before he can be either bought or sold. Even in the foreign slave trade the persons have been seized and reduced to slavery before they come into the hands of the trader; and in the domestic traffic the persons bought or sold are already in a state of slavery. What, then, we repeat, is the meaning of the phrase, "*with the intention to enslave them?*" The only answer that can be given is, it means with the intention to *continue* them in slavery, by continuing to hold and use them as slaves; or, as in the case of selling, putting it in the power of others to continue them in slavery.

What, then, is it which, in the eye of the Rule, gives criminality to the act of buying or selling? The only answer is, *it is the intention to enslave them;* that is, the intention to *continue their enslavement.* This is what clothes the act of buying or selling with moral turpitude. It is the *enslaving,* therefore, by the continued holding and using as slaves, which gives criminality to the buying and selling. The holding and using are the only stimulus to the guilty traffic. We conclude, therefore, that as the holding and using are the only stimulating causes for the traffic, and as the intention to continue their enslavement is the only sinful element, so far as the Rule condemns it, the spirit of the Rule must condemn the holding and the using, as well as the buying and selling. The intention which gives criminality to an act, and without which the act would not be criminal, must itself be criminal.

We do not affirm that the holding of a slave is, under all circumstances, sinful; nor is the buying or selling. Otherwise it would be wrong to purchase a slave, even to free him. And the moral right to purchase a slave to free him involves also the moral right to hold the legal relation of owner to that slave until the benevolent intention of freeing can be carried into execution. So when, owing to whatever circumstances the immediate sundering of the legal relation would be manifestly a greater injury to the slave than its temporary continuance; and when the evident intention is to give freedom at the earliest practical moment, such an act of holding is not only not wrong, but it may be a duty. It is something necessary to be done in order to confer permanent freedom upon the person so held. In such a case the holder is not released from the obligation to give unto the servant "that which is just and equal," and to guard with the most religious care the sacred and divine rights of the conjugal and parental relations, and to see by all means that such legal provisions as are practicable shall be made to prevent such persons and their posterity from passing into perpetual slavery.

From the foregoing considerations it appears to us that the General Rule should, in plain words, embody the honest doctrine of the Church, as well on the subject of *slaveholding* as on that of the slave traffic. If the traffic for mercenary and selfish purposes should be condemned, so also should the holding. And if, as is almost universally admitted among us, the *spirit* of the Rule condemns mercenary and selfish slaveholding, then why may we not clothe this *spirit* in a visible *body*, and insert the word *holding* in our present Rule, subject to the same discriminating clause as the buying and selling? Such a rule would read: "The buying, selling, or holding of men, women, or children, with an intention to enslave them." This, we think, is only embodying in plain language the true doctrine of our Church on the subject.

So long ago as the year 1840, our bishops, in their Episcopal Address, in view of the different interpretations put upon the General Rule, desired the General Conference, then in session in Baltimore, to give an official exposition of it. The following is their language:

"We think it proper to invite your attention in particular to one point intimately connected with it, [the subject of slavery,] and, as we conceive, of primary importance. It is in regard to the true import and application of the General Rule on Slavery. The different constructions to which it has been subjected, and the variety of views which have been entertained upon it, together with the conflicting acts of some of the annual conferences, North and South, seem to require that, a body having legitimate jurisdiction, should express a clear and definite opinion, as a uniform guide to those to whom the administration of the Discipline is committed." This address is signed by R. R. Roberts, Joshua Soule, Elijah Hedding, James O. Andrew, Beverly Waugh, and T. A. Morris.

Without expressing an opinion here, as to the constitutional right

of the General Conference to place an official and legal exposition of
the General Rule in the Discipline, without the concurrence of the
annual conferences, we judge it the more prudent course that the exposition should be embodied in the Rule itself, by a process which can
leave no doubt as to its constitutionality.

We therefore recommend for adoption the following resolutions:

Resolved, 1. By the delegates of the several annual conferences in
General Conference assembled, that we recommend the amendment of
the General Rule on Slavery, so that it shall read: "The buying, selling, or holding of men, women, or children, with an intention to enslave
them."

[This resolution required a vote of *two-thirds* to carry it. There were 138 votes
cast for it, and 74 against it, so it was lost. See Journal, pp. 244–246.—EDITOR.]

Resolved, 2. That we recommend the suspension of the 4th Restrict-
ive Rule, for the purpose set forth in the foregoing resolution.

[This resolution was laid on the table, inasmuch as the *first* resolution failed.
See Journal, page 262.—EDITOR.]

Resolved, 3. By the delegates of the several annual conferences in
General Conference assembled, that the following be, and hereby is,
substituted in the place of the seventh chapter on slavery:

Question. What shall be done for the extirpation of the evil of
slavery?

Answer. We declare that we are as much as ever convinced of the
great evil of slavery. We believe that the buying, selling, or holding
of human beings as chattels is contrary to the laws of God and nature,
inconsistent with the Golden Rule, and with that Rule in our Discipline
which requires all who desire to remain among us to "do no harm,
and to avoid evil of every kind." We, therefore, affectionately admonish all our preachers and people to keep themselves pure from
this great evil, and to seek its extirpation by all lawful and Christian
means. (7)

                                        C. KINGSLEY, *Chairman.*

B. F. CRARY, *Secretary.*

[For the action of the conference amending and adopting the third resolution,
and adopting the report as a whole and as amended, see Journal, pages 259,
262. EDITOR.]

MINORITY REPORT ON SLAVERY.

The Minority of the Committee on Slavery appointed by this General Conference to take into consideration the interests of the Church in relation to this grave and perplexing subject, and also its duty in the premises, being unable to agree with the majority of the Committee, and believing that the present occasion demands at our hands a full exposition of our principles, submit the following report:

In order to present our position on this question with entire clearness, we ask attention to the following

FACTS OF HISTORY.

Up to 1844 we remained an undivided Church, wonderfully owned of God, and eminently successful in spreading Scriptural holiness over these lands; our ministers went to and fro, and the knowledge of God was greatly increased; the people felt and acknowledged the power of our anti-slavery Gospel, and by thousands were converted and gathered into our Methodist fold. In no part of this country did our Church find more favor and meet with more success than in the slaveholding States. Firm in our convictions, and honest in our avowal of them, we placed our Discipline in the hands of the slaveholder, containing provisions which limited his authority over the slave, and made him in reality the slave's guardian, under the supervision of the Church. In short, we taught the converted slaveholder to look upon his slave as an immortal being, and to provide for his moral and religious cultivation, by "teaching him to read the Word of God, and allowing him time to attend public worship on our regular days of divine service." Under this Scriptural Discipline we were instrumental in converting both masters and slaves, besides breaking the yoke from the neck of thousands even in those States where emancipation was not possible by law, except under great difficulties.

This was our condition as a Church when the General Conference of 1844 held its session. An episcopacy till then untarnished by connection with slavery had become implicated in the great evil, in the person of one of our bishops. Then came the trial of our anti-slavery principles, and the Border was true to its trust. The South contended that as the laws of the State in which the bishop lived would not permit emancipation, the General Conference should not interfere in the case. The majority of the delegates insisted that as a bishop was required "to travel through the connection at large," "any connection with slavery would embarrass both him and the Church in the performance of his duties," and declared their judgment to be that Bishop Andrew should cease from the exercise of episcopal functions until he could relieve himself of this impediment. Then followed that separation which has become one of the great facts of ecclesiastical history. In this contest for anti-slavery principles no portion of the Church was more inflexibly true to our Discipline than that which is now the Border.

Returning to their homes, the Border delegates discerned (what has since proved to be a well-grounded apprehension) a new source of danger in the preponderance given to the North by this separation. Already had the spirit of ultraism begun to agitate portions of the Church, and fears were entertained that innovations, destructive to the peace of the Border conferences, would be proposed and effected. These fears were, to some extent, quieted by the assurance that our Northern churches were true to the interests of the Border, and would faithfully resist all attempts to destroy its power, or to change the Discipline. These assurances were corroborated by the sympathy expressed for the Border in the organs of the Church generally, and the decided action of at least one of the New England conferences. The *Christian Advocate and Journal* asked, about this very time, the direct question: "Does New England propose to contend for a Rule of Discipline which shall make the emancipation of slaves by those who hold them a condition of membership?" *Zion's Herald* replied: "Deeming it both unjust and impolitic, it is her intention to abide by the Constitution of the Church *as it now is*, and to use her constitutional powers for the *extirpation* of slavery as prudence, the best interests of the whole Church, and the Providence of God may demand."

New England sustained the *Herald* in this declaration, and the Providence Conference, to show its sincerity, and to quiet the fears of the Border brethren, at its session in 1847, passed the following, by a rising vote of 54 to 4:

"*Resolved*, That we are satisfied with the Discipline of the Church, as it is, on the subject of slavery; and as we have never proposed any alteration in it, so neither do we now; and that, in connection with our brethren of the other conferences, *we will ever abide by it.*"

This same conference, at a subsequent session, reaffirmed the pledge previously made, as follows: "We pledge ourselves to maintain the same conservative and true anti-slavery ground by which the Providence Conference has already become distinguished." The late President Olin, about the same time, addressed a letter to the East through its paper, *Zion's Herald*, declaring that, as the Methodist Episcopal Church, *South*, was now gone, the internal controversy should now be considered as closed, and the Church should turn its energies to its great interests, namely: missions, revivals, education, etc. This was not only the sentiment of New England, but of the whole Church, and was fully indorsed by its official action. In support of this, we call attention to the fact the General Conference of 1848 appointed no Committee on Slavery, and but one petition was presented on the subject. The same General Conference abolished the "plan of separation," and took under its care the scattered membership which had been cut off by that plan in Kentucky, Arkansas, and Missouri.

It created conferences there, and thousands have been converted and gathered into the Church in those States. The sentiment of the Church remained substantially the same during the four succeeding years.

At the General Conference of 1852 no committee was appointed on slavery, and only seventeen petitions were presented on the subject. These facts are not only significant, but they are conclusive. The General Conference *was* satisfied with the position of the Border churches, and the membership North gave these suffering brethren their most hearty support.

During the eight years immediately succeeding "the separation," the Church, in her official action and sympathy, was faithful to her pledge to abide by the Discipline as it is.

In 1850, the danger of future aggressions, on the part of the North and East, was distinctly foreshadowed; and between the sessions of the General Conference, in 1852 and 1856, this agitation on the question of slavery in the Church made its first real development. The papers in those portions of the Church began to denounce their brethren on the Border, and this so far influenced the popular opinion in the North as to shake its confidence in the ministry of these conferences. *Here was the origin of the outside pressure, which the North now pleads as the only reason why the Discipline should be changed on the subject.*

In the General Conference of 1856, the first official effort to change the Discipline was made by the ministry of the North, without the support of the membership. Out of 790,000 not quite 5,000 petitioned for a change, and most of these were obtained by the personal efforts of preachers. That this first act of aggression was made by the ministry was admitted in 1856. The reason assigned was that twenty-nine annual conferences out of thirty-eight had asked the General Conference to make a change in our Discipline on the subject of slavery. In obedience to this demand the first Committee on Slavery for eight years was appointed, and a report presented in accordance with their views. That report presented two propositions : one for a general rule by the constitutional process to prohibit " the buying, selling, or holding of a human being as property ;" the other for a new chapter making slaveholding *prima facie* evidence of guilt, and declaring the man, charged with this offense, to be guilty until he proved himself innocent. That chapter was laid on the table, and the new rule failed to receive the vote necessary to send it to the annual conferences. The failure of this first effort on the part of the ministry only redoubled their exertions. They have, during the four years past, employed both the pulpit and the press to the utmost extent in preparing the sentiment of the Church for action at the present Session.

This controversy has been marked by most peculiar features, and attended with the most deplorable results. Churches in the North have been torn and severed, new and independent societies have been organized, papers in opposition to official organs supported, the friendship of years destroyed, confidence and fraternal affection between the North and the Border lost, our preachers mobbed by lawless and proslavery men, and bitterness of feeling engendered, until it has become almost impossible for us to become a united people.

There are now two parties in the Church, the one contending for an alteration in our Discipline on the subject of slavery, and the other opposed. The question vital to the issue, therefore, is : Which one of these two parties has changed its position ? We answer most emphatically, *The Border has not.* The Border was truly anti-slavery in 1844 ; it is as truly so now. It resisted the encroachments of the South then ; it resists the encroachments of the South now. It has steadily resisted the South till this present moment, at fearful cost and constant conflict. It has resisted pro-slavery assaults in the pulpit, on the platform, and through the press. The Border has stood faithfully to the Discipline, under the charge of pro-slaveryism from the North, and of abolitionism from the South. It has never denied being anti-slavery ; it could not if it would, and would not if it could. The Border stands now where it has ever stood, and though pressed sorely by the friends it has never forsaken, and by the foes it has always resisted, its representatives come to this General

Conference, asking for no change in the Discipline, and willing to abide by it as it is. We have always taught, and still teach, that slaveholding, for mercenary and selfish purposes, is wrong; but we have never held that the relation of master to slave, when either necessary or merciful, is sinful. On this principle we have received the slaveholder into the Church, and by it we have regulated our administration. If in any case the administration has been defective, it has been the exception, and not the rule. While our brethren in the North and Northwest have yielded to the pressure of an ultra-ism which, by their own action, they have largely contributed to create, we still battle for old-fashioned, anti-slavery Methodism. No human administration can be perfect, and our Border brethren do not claim that theirs is any exception to this rule; but they do claim that integrity of purpose has characterized their action. With the laws of the State against emancipation, so far as to prevent the liberated slave from enjoying freedom without the liability of being arrested and expatriated, they have, by their moral influence and discipline, lifted the yoke of bondage from the necks of thousands, who, with their children, are now contented and happy. Of late, owing to the agitated state of the country, their influence has been, to some extent, limited, but for this the Church of the Border is not responsible. This is the position claimed for itself by the Border, and the claim is sustained by the testimony of others.

The bishops, in their Address to the General Conference of 1856, gave the results of their observation in regard to the position and moral influence of our churches on the Border. In the Episcopal Address of the present session, they reaffirm their statements, and refer the General Conference to the language used by them in 1856.

The following is the passage referred to, namely:

"In our administration in the territory where slavery exists, we have been careful not to transcend, in any instance or in any respect, what we understood to be the will and direction of the General Conference. That body having retained its jurisdiction over conferences previously existing in such territory, and having directed the organization of additional Conferences, it becomes our duty to arrange the districts, circuits, and stations, and to superintend them as an integral part of the Church. As the result, we have have six annual conferences which are wholly or in part slave territory. These conferences have a white church-membership, including probationers, of more than one hundred and thirty-six thousand, with the attendants upon our ministry, making a probable population of between five and six hundred thousand. They have a colored church-membership, including probationers, of about twenty-seven thousand, with the attendants upon our ministry, making a probable population of upward of one hundred thousand. A portion of this population are slaves. The others are mostly poor. They are generally strongly attached to the Church of their choice, and look to it confidingly for ministerial services, religious sympathy, and all the offices of Christian kindness. The white membership in these conferences, in respect to intelligence, piety, and attachment to Methodist discipline and economy, will compare favorably with other portions of the Church.

"In our judgment, the existence of these conferences and churches, under their present circumstances, does not tend to extend or perpetuate slavery. They are known to be organized under a Discipline which characterizes slavery as a great evil; which makes the slaveholder ineligible to any official station in the Church, where the laws of the State in which he lives will admit of emancipation, and permit the liberated slave to enjoy freedom; which disfranchises a traveling minister who by any means becomes the owner of a slave or slaves, unless he executes, if it be practicable, a legal emancipation of such slaves, conformably to the laws of the State wherein he lives; which makes it the duty of all the ministers to enforce upon all the members the necessity of teaching their slaves to read the Word of God, and allowing them time to attend upon the public worship of God on our regular days of divine service; which prohibits the buying and selling of men, women, and children, with an intention to enslave them, and inquires what shall be done for the extirpation of slavery?

"With this Discipline freely circulated among the people, or certainly within the reach of any who desire to examine it, and with other Churches existing in the same territory without these enactments, these societies and conferences have, either by elective affinity, adhered to, or from preference, associated with, the Methodist Episcopal Church. In a few instances their church-relations have exposed them to some peril, and in numerous cases to sacrifice. But such have been their moral worth, and Christian excellence, and prudent conduct, that generally they have been permitted to enjoy their religious immunities, and serve and worship God according to their consciences."

This testimony of the bishops, in 1856, was corroborated by the delegates from the Border, and the Committee on Slavery appointed at that session confirmed its truth by the following language, which forms part of their report, namely:

"It is also affirmed and believed that the administrators of Discipline within the bounds of slave territory have faithfully done all that in their circumstances they have conscientiously judged to be in their power, to answer the ends of the Discipline in exterminating that great evil."

Such is the position of the Church on the Border, and it is the position held by most of the members of this General Conference. Very few indeed of the members of this body believe or teach that slaveholding, except for mercenary or selfish purposes, ought to be made a test of membership. Our view of the subject is sustained by the Scriptures, and also by Mr. Wesley, who received slaveholders into his societies, and is in strict accordance with the instructions given by the Wesleyan Connection to their missionaries in Jamaica. These instructions are in the following words, namely:

"As in the colonies in which you are called to labor a great proportion of the inhabitants are in a state of slavery, the Committee must strongly call to your recollection what was so fully stated to you when you were accepted as missionaries to the West Indies, that your *only* business is to promote the moral and religious improvement of the slaves to whom you may have access, without, in the least degree, in public or private, interfering with their civil condition." Who, then, have changed position on this subject? *The Border preachers have NOT.* The change of ground is with those who ask for an altered Discipline, a new term of membership.

In conclusion, the minority respectfully submit, 1. That the action proposed in the report of the majority has been recommended without the proper consideration, in Committee, of the documents referred to them by the General Conference, which, in our judgment, the gravity and importance of the subject demand.

2. The minority further represent, that the desire of the Church at large for any important change in our rules on the subject of slavery is not sufficiently indicated in the petitions that have been referred to this Committee to demand such action as is set forth in the report of the majority. The whole number of petitioners is less than one in twenty of the entire membership, and in those Conferences that have spoken most largely, two-thirds of the entire membership have remained silent. (8)

3. The action of the Annual Conference, as expressed in their

recorded votes, does not indicate such a desire for a constitutional change as to call on this General Conference to inaugurate an attempt to secure it by sending down a new rule for their action. This will be evident if we consider that, taking the highest vote obtained in the several Annual Conferences by any single measure, it falls short, to the extent of over five hundred of the requisite number among those voting, and falls short more than three thousand of three-fourths of the whole number of the traveling preachers in the Methodist Episcopal Church.

4. The change in the General Rule proposed in the report of the majority is still further objected to, in that the action they recommend approaches nearest in form to the one coming from the Providence Conference, and would be likely to be understood by our people as embodying the spirit of that most objectionable of all the changes which had been previously proposed.

5. The form of the chapter proposed in the report of the majority, the minority confidently believe will not be considered by the Church as embodying sufficient advantages over the present chapter to warrant the risk incurred in making any change. Though being intended only as a *declaration of sentiment*, as it is placed in what is regarded as a book of ecclesiastical law, it may become a source of embarassment by being misunderstood by our people and misrepresented by our enemies.

6. The minority further represent, that the action proposed in the report of the majority will very greatly embarrass and cripple, if it does not altogether destroy our Church in the slaveholding States and along the border. It is especially calculated to do this in the present highly excited state of the public mind in that territory.

7. The minority still further believe that such a result would involve a loss of position and influence in slaveholding territory, by the most decidedly anti-slavery Church among the larger denominations of the land, which it might require many long years to regain. Such a surrender of advantages now possessed must be deprecated by every one who sincerely asks, "*What shall be done for the extirpation of the evil of slavery?*"

8. It is further objected to the action proposed, that it would operate most disastrously upon the interests of the enslaved. It would not only deprive them of ministrations by which thousands of them have been blessed and saved, but from those by whom their emancipation can only be secured it would withdraw the influence of that

Church, in regard to which the majority of the Committee on Slavery in 1856 say: "It is affirmed and believed that it has done more to diffuse anti-slavery sentiments, to mitigate the evils of the system, and to abolish the institution from civil society, than any other organization, either political, social, or religious."

9. The members of the minority representing conferences located in non-slaveholding territory also submit, that the action proposed in the report of the majority would, in its results, as admitted by the majority (in committee) themselves, expose our ministerial brethren and their families, in the Border work, to privations and perils which, while they ought not to be shrunk from, if necessary to maintain uprightness and truth, yet, if brought about without sufficient cause, might properly be considered an unbrotherly recklessness as to their condition, specially calculated to alienate them from us in spirit and affection.

10. The testimony of the representatives of the work on the Pacific coast in this Committee, impresses us with the conviction that the results of the action proposed in the report of the majority would be highly disastrous in that quarter, destroying much of the fruit of their past labor, and greatly retarding the work for many years to come.

11. The minority are still further impressed with the conviction that among the results of the action proposed in the majority report, one painfully probable is the enfeebling of the prestige and moral power of the whole Church by the strifes and divisions that may ensue, which will greatly incapacitate her for the performance of that grand work, both at home and abroad, to which God in his providence is now so evidently calling her, in this the opening of the second century of her history, and in which, if her resources and influence are properly husbanded and guarded, she may achieve so eminent and glorious a success.

12. The minority are not insensible to the fact that an embarrassing pressure, produced by misrepresentations of our anti-slavery position, is felt in some portions of our work in non-slaveholding territory; but they believe that this may be relieved by a distinct and emphatic testimony on the subject, in a mode which would not involve the disasters apprehended from the course to which they object. They, therefore, recommend the adoption of the following RESOLUTIONS:

Resolved, 1. That the Methodist Episcopal Church has, in good faith, in all the periods of its history, proposed to itself the question,

"What shall be done for the extirpation of the evil of slavery?" and it has never ceased, openly before the world, to bear its testimony against the sin, and to exercise its disciplinary powers to the end that its members might be kept unspotted from criminal connection with the system, and that the evil itself be removed from among us.

Resolved, 2. That any change of our Discipline upon the subject of slavery in the present highly-excited condition of the country would accomplish no good whatever, but, on the contrary, would seriously disturb the peace of our Church, and would be especially disastrous to our ministers and members in the slave States.

Resolved, 3. That the Committee on the Pastoral Address be instructed to state our position in relation to slavery, and to give such counsel to our churches as may be suited to the necessities of the case.

JOHN S. PORTER, Chairman.
P. COOMBE, Secretary.

BUFFALO, *May* 16, 1860.

REMARKS ON THE PRECEDING ECCLESIASTICAL ACTION.

(1) The attempt to enforce a rule of the Church, excluding slaveholders from its communion, having failed, and the necessity of dropping it altogether in the South, argues a very different state of public sentiment, in the days of early Methodism, in relation to slavery, from what has been supposed to have existed. The duty of emancipation could not have been a common sentiment, otherwise the Rule of the Church on slavery would have been easily enforced. That it had to be abandoned, in both the North and the South, is conclusive on this question. In this fact we find another ground for setting aside the abolition interpretation of the Constitution, which claims that it must be understood as anti-slavery, because the sentiment of the country was then opposed to the institution. No such general hostility to slavery prevailed throughout the country; and even in the States where emancipation was finally adopted, the feeling in its favor was by no means unanimous.

(2) It will be noted, that as early as 1824, the General Conference made provision for the distinct organization of churches of the colored people, and for employing colored men as traveling preachers.

(3) The resolutions of General Conference, in 1836, in condemnation of abolitionism, are very pointed, and afford unmistakable evidence of the wisdom of the bishops in laying a strong hand upon it as a dangerous movement both to Church and State.

(4) Here are considerations, weighty, indeed, presented by the bishops, in favor of a firm reliance upon the Gospel as the means of meliorating the condition of the slaves, and against clerical interference in civil affairs. Had these admonitions of 1840 been heeded by the Methodist ministry, that Church, as well as our beloved Union, might now have been a unit, instead of being broken into fragments.

(5) The remarks of the bishops, in 1844, upon the subject of abolition petitions, and the neglect of the negro population, are well worthy the most deliberate consideration.

(6) The declaration of the committee of the General Conference, at Indianapolis, 1856, that the Methodist Church "has done more to diffuse anti-slavery sentiments," "and to abolish the institution from civil society, than any other organization, either political, social, or religious," was a proud boast, and may have been a truth. But, if so, where was the necessity for such boasting? If it had affected the committee alone; if it had been confined to the North, all would have been well, perhaps; but it flew upon the wings of the lightning to the extreme South; and there, in consequence of the claims here set up, the Methodist Church was pronounced an abolition organization, having in view the promotion of the abolition of slavery wherever she set her foot. Had not the committee set up such high claims, before Conference, for the efficiency of Methodism as an instrument in the promotion of emancipation, the soil of Texas would not have drank up the blood of the humble Methodist minister who was martyred on the suspicion that he was an emissary of abolition.

(7) It will be seen that, in the General Conference of 1860, the alteration of the Rule on Slavery was not carried — there not being two-thirds of the members in its favor. The chapter on Slavery, however, was altered so as to conform to the aboli-

tion sentiment in the Church—it requiring only a majority vote for its adoption.

(8) This authoritative statement, coming from the Committee of Conference, that two-thirds of the entire membership of the Methodist Church have remained silent, while only one-third had signed the abolition memorials—confirms the opinions heretofore expressed, that the great majority of the members, in nearly all the churches which have legislated on the subject of slavery, have been opposed to the action of their ecclesiastical courts. In this fact, we are to look for the origin of all the evils to Church and State which have flowed from the ecclesiastical legislation on the subject of slavery. Conservative Christian men have remained silent, while their fanatical brethren have been allowed to occupy public attention, so as to create the impression that abolition sentiments were in the ascendancy at the North. Had the facts been clearly known — had conservative men come boldly forward to rebuke and repudiate the fanatics who were troubling the land — we should, at this day, have seen our churches undivided, our Union existing in harmony, and our people in the enjoyment of their wonted prosperity. The responsibility of the evils which have befallen us must rest upon the conservative men who, for the sake of peace, have neglected to lift up a standard against the errors of abolitionism.

CHAPTER IX.

CONGREGATIONAL CHURCHES AND SLAVERY.

SOME notice is taken of the Congregational Churches, in their relations to slavery, in Chapter III. To afford a more definite view of their position on the great question of the day—forcible emancipation—we here append some extracts from two documents, which may be taken as representing the opinions of Congregationalists in general.

So universally have this body occupied abolition ground, as we have been told by one of their most intelligent clergymen, that we have not considered it important to gather up in detail their Church action upon slavery. Their present position will be understood by what follows:

1. THE GENERAL ASSOCIATION OF NEW YORK held its twenty-eighth annual session at Binghamton last week.*

A committee upon the "state of the country," consisting of Rev. J. P. Thompson, D. D., J. Butler, and H. N. Dunning, reported a series of resolutions which, after debate and amendment, were adopted. There was a deep and strong feeling in the meeting that slavery, as the original cause and fountain of our national troubles—as the serpent of evil which has entered our garden of liberty, to beguile us into sin and ruin, should not be left untouched by the nation in this eventful crisis, (1) that the occasion which the providence of God has offered, ought to be seized, to inflict upon its head a final and fatal blow. Some hesitation, however, was felt in *insisting* upon any particular measures as means of its destruction, which might embarrass the Administration, though it was felt that the public mind ought to be prepared

---

* New York Independent, Oct. 17, 1861.

for this issue, and the Government urged forward to confront and decide it in every way possible.

The following are the resolutions as adopted:

"It having pleased the Great Ruler of nations in his righteous sovereignty to visit this nation with the calamity of intestine war, crippling our industry, disabling our commerce, desolating large portions of our territory, and bringing anxiety and sorrow to thousands of families;—therefore,

" *Resolved,* That we pledge to the Government our constant devotion and earnest support in its determination to suppress the iniquitous and formidable rebellion of the South, and to re-establish and enforce the authority of the Constitution over the whole Union, and

" *Whereas,* The immediate occasion of this rebellion and its fomenting spirit was the determination of its leaders to secure and perpetuate the system of slavery ; and *whereas,* there can be no guarantee of peace and prosperity in the Union while slavery exists ;—therefore,

" *Resolved,* That we rejoice in every act and declaration of the Government that brings freedom to any of the enslaved, and earnestly hope for some definite and reliable measure for the abolition of slavery as the conclusion of this great conflict for the support of the Government and the Union.

" *Whereas,* In his good providence, God has opened the way for the emancipation of the enslaved in this land, either by the instructions of the Government to military commanders to enfranchise all slaves within their several districts, or by general proclamation of the President, or by act of Congress under the state of war ;—therefore,

" *Resolved,* That it is our duty, as Christian patriots, in all proper ways to urge this measure upon the attention of the Government, and to pray for its consummation, lest the condemnation of those who knew their duty to the poor and oppressed, and did it not, should be visited upon the nation.

" *Resolved,* That whatever the issue of the war upon slavery, and whatever political phases the question of slavery may hereafter assume, this Association will adhere to the testimony it has so often borne against the wickedness of holding human beings as property, and against the compound and stupendous iniquity of the whole system of slavery ; and that as our Congregational ministry and churches have been so far faithful and persistent in the past, in testifying against slavery as sinful, so they should continue faithful and unremitting in their opposition to it, until the iniquity shall be done away."

2. TRIENNIAL CONVENTION OF CONGREGATIONAL CHURCHES IN THE NORTHWEST.*

The organic rules of the CHICAGO THEOLOGICAL SEMINARY provide that in every third year it shall be the duty of the Board of Directors to call a Convention, consisting of one delegate from each of the Congregational Churches in the Northwest, and the ministers of the same, which Convention has the appointment of trustees, and has a right of perpetual patronage as founders of the Seminary. The Convention met at Chicago, Oct. 8th, 1861, and was attended by upward of 130 ministers and delegates.

The "state of the country" also occupied the thoughts of the Convention. An able committee was early appointed, consisting of Prof. Joseph Haven, Hiram Foote, G. S. F. Savage, H. D. Kitchel, Asa Turner, H. L. Hammond, S. D. Cochran, S. Wolcott, H. H. Hitchcock, and the second evening allotted to the consideration of their report. Eloquent speeches were made by Rev. Asa Turner, of Iowa, Dr. Charles Jewett, of Wisconsin, etc.

"REPORT OF THE COMMITTEE.

"As lovers of our country and of the cause and kingdom of Christ, it is with the deepest sadness that we look upon the present state of this nation, once united and prosperous, now distracted and torn asunder by civil war—a war which we can not but regard as groundless—wicked in its origin, and of which the whole fearful responsibilities rest, and ever will rest, on those who, without provocation or any just cause, have conspired to overthrow the Government and subvert the Constitution under which we live. If we look about us for the source of the evils which now afflict us, we can find it only in the system of American slavery. Whatever other causes may have contributed to this result, they sink into comparative insignificance beside this prime source and prolific fountain of all our woes. It is this which has raised the standard of revolt; it is this which has armed brother against brother, and State against State; it is this which has crippled our industry, wasted our resources, devastated our towns and cities, dishonored our flag, made desolate our homes, and brought such wide-spread confusion and disaster upon the nation. If we seek a remedy for these evils, we can find it only in the eradi-

---

* New York Independent, October 17, 1861.

cation and utter subversion of that which has been their producing
cause. Nothing short of this can or will reach the difficulty. The
present wicked rebellion is purely a rebellion of the slaveholding
portion against the rule of the majority, and against the principles
which lie at the foundation of all purely democratic institutions. It
can be brought to an end only by earnest and well-directed blows at
that which is the real root of the evil. It is no time for compromises
or sedatives. The black and bloody hand of African servitude is
upon the throat of this nation, and we must break that arm, or it
will strangle us. There can be no compromise with this gigantic
wrong. There can be no peace, no division of territory, no safe and
permanent adjustment of any kind while this system continues. We
are one nation, one territory, and we ought and shall remain one
people, from Maine to the Gulf of Mexico—one from the Atlantic to
the Pacific. Such are our profound convictions, our deliberate opinions; and entertaining these sentiments, we can not, as a Convention
of pastors and delegates representing the Congregational Churches
of the several Northwestern States, consent to disperse without first
bearing our united testimony to the truths which we have uttered,
and which we more definitely express in the following resolutions:

"*Resolved*, That the fearful strife in which our Government is now
engaged with the armed traitors who have risen up against it, involving, as it does, the defense of all that is dear to us as citizens and
patriots, and of the principles that underlie all free institutions, is, in
our view, a just and righteous war; that we are bound, by every interest of Christian patriotism and civilization, to prosecute this contest
with vigor, and, as speedily as possible, bring it to a triumphant conclusion; and that, in the efficient prosecution of this war, the Government has our profoundest sympathy, our most cordial support, and
our most earnest prayers.

"*Resolved*, That the present rebellion is, in our view, the direct
and legitimate result of the system of American slavery, which is at
once the radical cause and the main strength of the whole evil; and
that, consequently, the conflict can never be brought to a successful
end till that system shall also forever terminate.

"*Resolved*, That we can not but view, in the present war, the hand
of Providence, that divine Arbiter and Ruler of nations, opening the
way for the termination of this accursed system, this gigantic wrong;
and we pray God that the heart of this great people and of this Government may be brought to the fixed determination that that which

has brought this war upon us, shall itself be brought to a perpetual end; (2) and that wherever our armies go, and our flag waves, under the whole heavens, there shall also go freedom and universal emancipation."

REMARKS ON THE PRECEDING ARTICLES.

(1) We have here a very apt illustration indeed. The framers of our Constitution found a barbarous people in their midst, totally unfitted for the rights of citizenship, and held in servitude under pre-existent customs and laws. Slavery, under the Constitution, was declared to be the "forbidden fruit," which was to remain untouched by the nation at large. The declaration, on this point, virtually was, "in the day thou eatest thereof, dying, thou shalt die." The serpent of abolition entered the "garden of liberty," at the Northern gate, and beguiled the inhabitants "into sin and ruin." From the day that abolitionism put forth its hand, from New England, in disobedience to the commands of the Constitution, to pluck the fruit of "the tree of the knowledge of good and evil;" from that day, briars and thorns have been springing up, wherever the serpent's trail has left its slime; and the ruin now resting upon our Eden is traceable, directly, to those who, adopting abolition sentiments, taught treason to the Constitution in reference to the institution of slavery.

(2) Abolitionism being at the foundation of our national troubles, every true patriot can unite in the sentiment expressed by the Chicago resolutions, in the prayer to God, "that the heart of this great people and of this Government may be brought to the fixed determination that that which has brought this war upon us, shall itself be brought to a perpetual end;" that abolitionism shall be crushed into non-existence, and secessionism forced to lay down its arms of rebellion, so that the Union may once more arise in its glory and its power; and that, under our beneficent Constitution, the dominant race may continue to rise upward, and progress onward in intelligence and civilization, and the lowly continue to advance in personal comfort and Christian knowledge, until the millennial day shall find the whole human race redeemed from its long years of degradation.

CHAPTER X.

WE have seen that the early clerical anti-slavery writers, in discussing the question of slavery, as it affected the moral standing of church-members, believed they could thereby transfer the agitation of the subject to the arena of politics, and thus array the legislation of the country against the institution. It is true, that this party, in its efforts at religious reform, professed to have only in view the purification of the Church; but the opinions propagated, and the measures adopted, served as a most efficient basis for the organization of the Abolition party. The example of the Apostles, in their teachings on slavery, had been pronounced an insufficient guide to the people of this age, and a doubt was thus thrown over the Scriptures as an infallible rule of moral conduct. A higher law than the Bible, as heretofore interpreted, was demanded for the exigencies of the times. As anticipated, the ecclesiastical legislation prepared publc sentiment for political action, by creating an intense anti-slavery feeling among a portion of the members of the Church, who were ready to be roused into energetic effort for the overthrow of slavery, whenever an opportunity offered. But for the votes that could be secured at the polls, from the ranks of the religious anti-slavery men, no political party would ever have made the slavery question a plank in its platform. In this fact is contained the demonstration of the proposition, that the Churches are responsible for the political agitation of this subject, and for much of its deplorable consequences.

It was from the action of the Churches, almost exclusively, that Southern statesmen originally took the alarm, in relation to

Northern interference with their institutions. But in organizing an opposition to this interference, they did not base their resistance upon the true grounds of their alarm—the fear of forcible emancipation. Other issues at first were made, so that an avowal of the real source of their fears could be avoided. This is apparent from the testimony of competent witnesses then residing in the slave States, one of whom we quote below.* No political

---

* The following interesting extracts, descriptive of the condition and tendencies of Abolitionism, at the period when it had fully manifested its general character, are from the pen of JEREMIAH HUBBARD, Clerk of the Yearly Meeting of Friends in North Carolina, to a Friend in England. We copy from the *Christian Intelligencer*, of June, 1834:

"But I need not dwell much on the subject of universal emancipation, in stating the best or worst, or most probable results of such a measure, because the Southern people have no more idea of the general emancipation of slaves, without colonizing them, than the Northern people have of admitting the few among *them* to equal rights and privileges. Not even the friends of humanity here think that a general emancipation, to remain here, would better their condition; and if they did, I believe that none of the slave States' laws admit of emancipation without sending them out of the State. And the ultra slaveholders are as much opposed to the Colonization Society as the Northern manumissionists are, and have, for several years past, been viewing its growing popularity, and the Northern policy in Congress, with great jealousy; which keeps them upon the ground of nullification and the verge of rebellion, though they have other pretexts for it, such as the tariff, etc. But it is evident that slavery, or rather the general anticipation of its being abolished, is the primary cause of their discontent.* . . . It is a little singular, that the hardened slaveholders and the Northern manumissionists are so decidedly and bitterly opposed to each other as to threaten a dangerous collision, and a political division of this government, and, at the same time, are offering and urging the same reasons for abolishing the Colonization Society. But here we will leave the slaveholders inclosed in their chariots of iron, with an iron grasp upon their slaves, bidding defiance to the denunciations and imprecations of the New England anti-slavites, and watching, with a jealous eye, the mild, gradually increasing influence of the Colonization Society, and take a view of the plan of the Colonizationist, and that of the Universal Manumissionist, without colonization, and see which of the two is likely to abolish slavery in America.

"The primary object of the latter appears to be that of producing such a revolution in public sentiment as to cause the national legislation to be brought to bear directly on the slaveholders, and compel them to emancipate their slaves. And in order to effect this, they have formed themselves into a society, that they

---

* We omit here his remarks in relation to Colonization, and the disposition of a few to meliorate the condition of the slaves by that means, etc.

organizations for the overthrow of slavery had been effected in the North, when the hostility to a Protective Tariff, and the advocacy of the Nullification doctrines were first heard of at the South. But the action there, to guard against the evils of emancipation, by arresting all tendencies toward its adoption, only served to stimulate the efforts at the North for the promotion of that object. The anti-slavery men claimed that they had a right to use moral means for the removal of so great an evil as human bondage; and that in so doing, either by Church action or indi-

---

call the New England Anti-slavery Society; where they write and print a great many things against the evils of slavery, and against slaveholders and the Colonization Society, in a style and manner that savors more of the spirit of those who would ask for fire to come down from heaven to consume their enemies, than of those that would feed them if they were hungry, and if they were thirsty, give them drink. Their principal intrenchment appears to be in Boston, from whence they issue their periodicals, which, I suppose, they circulate pretty generally through the free States; but whenever one of the papers called the *Liberator*, edited by W. L. Garrison, chances to alight in any of the slave States, it is counted incendiary, and immediately proscribed. Their orators travel and lecture in the free States; there they propagate their doctrines or opinions of universal emancipation, coercion, etc., with much zeal and fluency, and, no doubt, with sincerity on the part of many of them; but mark, my friend, they are too discreet, or too timid, to travel and attempt to propagate these views, and harangue in the slave States. The general course of their efforts, of late, puts me in mind of what Young says about working the ocean into a tempest, 'to waft a feather or to drown a fly.' . . . The plan of the Northern anti-slavites, instead of softening, appears to be hardening the slaveholders. . . . I would give thee a little specimen of Garrison's style and manner of writing; in his opinion of the Colonization Society, he says: 'The superstructure of the Colonization Society rests upon the following pillars: 1st. Persecution; 2d. Falsehood; 3d. Cowardice; 4th. Infidelity. If I do not prove the Colonization Society to be a creature without heart, without brains, eyeless, unnatural, hypocritical, relentless, unjust, then nothing is capable of demonstration!' His language to slaveholders, or of slaveholders, is, 'They are hypocrites, man-stealers; and such as hold offices in the United States,' he says, 'are guilty of corrupt perjury, and unless they repent, will have their part in the lake that burns with fire and brimstone.' This kind of language is not at all calculated to make good impressions on the minds of slaveholders, even on those of whom it may be true."

One thing worthy of note is said by this venerable Quaker. The primary cause of discontent in the South, in 1834, was the general anticipation that slavery would be forcibly abolished by Northern influence. What was true in 1834 was equally true in 1860.

vidual effort, they were not violating the Constitution. To the Southern people, however, it mattered not whether their enemies employed moral suasion or physical force—logic, law, or lead—in promoting abolition measures, as the result to them would be the same—the loss of their property without their assent.

When abolitionism became fairly ingrafted upon the church-anti-slavery stock, its votaries claimed the right to use both moral suasion and political means to effect the abolition of slavery. Their plans of operation, in the main, contemplated the aggregate action of the States in the production of this result, by an amendment of the Constitution; or, in the event of the failure of this measure, some of them were determined, as a last resort, to effect a dissolution of the Union. The northern States, in abolishing slavery, had done so by their own uncontrolled action, and had brought upon themselves the burden of a helpless free colored population. This result presented a barrier to the progress of abolition, as the South were well-informed as to the disastrous results of emancipation in the North; and farther manumissions by State action, even where the measure had once been favorably entertained, could not now be effected. This made it necessary to the success of abolition, that the united action of two-thirds of the States should be secured, in the mode prescribed by the Constitution, for such an alteration of that instrument as would secure general emancipation, without the assent of the minority of the States. But the South denied that such powers had been conferred by the Constitution as would allow of any change in its provisions on the subject of slavery; and held, that each State was sovereign and independent, in relation to all measures not provided for, in express terms, in the Constitution. The Nullification movement was designed, in part at least, to serve as an emphatic remonstrance, by the South, against any interference with her domestic institutions by the North.

The general character of the political action against slavery, in its varying aspects, will be best understood by presenting the opinions expressed by representative men, and the principles avowed in the party platforms. It is impracticable here to give the history of these movements in detail; but enough can be presented to afford a true idea of the objects that were expected to be accomplished.

It must be remembered, as necessary to the comprehension of certain movements of the Churches in 1861, that many of the ministers who had produced the agitation of this subject in the ecclesiastical courts, continued to participate in the struggle when it had been taken up by the politicians.

It must also be noted, that after the first whirl of excitement had passed away, and the disturbed elements had subsided a little, two classes of political abolitionists were found arrayed against Southern slavery. The principles held by each are thus described by Dr. Bailey:

" The Liberty party take the ground that, under the Constitution of the United States, and the Constitutions of the several States, powers, fully adequate to the complete extinction of slavery in this country, are lodged in the hands of the citizens, and that, in supporting the Constitution of the United States, and using the powers it confers, no one is necessarily involved in moral wrong.

" What is called the Garrison party among abolitionists, assumes that the Federal Constitution is ' a covenant with death and an agreement with hell ;' that no man can make oath or affirmation to support it, without committing an immoral act; and that, consequently, to seek disunion becomes the duty of the citizen."*

The Abolition party "first made its appearance in national politics in the Presidential contest of 1840, when its ticket, with James G. Birney, of Michigan, as its candidate for the Presidency, and Francis J. Lemoyne, of Pennsylvania, as its candidate for Vice-President, polled 7,000 votes. In 1844, with Mr. Birney again as its candidate. it polled 62,140 votes. In 1848, with Martin Van Buren as the Presidential candidate of the Buffalo Convention, and Gerrit Smith as that of the more ultra anti-slavery men, it polled 296,232 votes. In 1852, John P. Hale, its nominee, polled 157,296 votes. In 1856, the candidate of the Republican party, John C. Frémont, supported by the entire abolition party, polled 1,341,812 votes."†

---

* Cincinnati Morning Herald, July 12, 1845. Editorial.

† Political Text-Book, by M. W. Cluskey, Postmaster of the House of Representatives of the United States Congress.

On the 29th December, 1841, a State Convention met in Columbus, Ohio.   This meeting was called by S. P. Chase, S. Lewis, T. Morris, J. Jolliffe, and W. Keys.   Its object was to organize a separate political action, so as " to make the cause of Liberty triumphant at the ballot-box."*   An address, prepared by Mr. Chase, was issued, and a series of resolutions adopted.   The first resolution charges that the General Government, for fifty-three years, had pursued a course of policy exhibiting great partiality to the slave States; the second, that the negotiations with foreign governments had been so conducted as to secure an admission of Southern products into foreign markets upon favorable terms, while the productions of the North, in the same markets, were subject to the payment of high duties; (1) the third, fourth, fifth, sixth, seventh, and eighth were as follows:

" 3. That experience has clearly shown that the institution of slavery, which establishes within a State a larger amount of non-laboring population than the laborers can possibly support in the habits of extravagance which it generates, always impoverishes the State in which it exists, and thus creates a demand for the agricultural, mechanical, and manufactured products, and for the money and merchandise of the free States, far beyond the means of repayment, and is a drain upon the resources so inordinate as to operate as a serious check upon their prosperity.

" 4. That our fathers ordained the Constitution of the United States to establish justice, promote the general welfare, and secure the blessings of liberty; but the powers which it confers have been used to promote injustice, endanger the general welfare, and to perpetuate the evils of slavery.   It is the duty of the people to see that the Constitution fulfills the ends for which it was established.

" 5. That the exclusion of slavery from the Northwestern Territory by Congress, in 1787, and the history of that period, clearly show that it was the settled purpose of the Government, not to extend or nationalize, but to limit and localize slavery, and to this policy, which should never have been departed from, the Government ought immediately to return.

" 6. That the patronage and support hitherto extended to slavery by the General Government, ought to be withdrawn, and wherever the

---

* Life of Samuel Lewis, page 308.

General Government possess constitutional jurisdiction, slavery ought
to cease.

" 7. That we expressly disclaim, in behalf of the General Government, all right to interfere with slavery in the States where it exists ;
but we shall ever insist that the General Government may and ought
to interfere with slavery in the District of Columbia, in Florida, and
on the seas.

" 8.—That the freedom of speech and of the press, and the right of
petition, and the right of trial by jury, are sacred and inviolable ; and
that all rules, regulations, and laws, in derogation of either, are oppressive, unconstitutional, and not to be endured by a free people."*

The Address issued by this Convention embraced the views
of the Liberty party. A few extracts will show its tone :

"Against hope, we have persevered, in hope that deliverance to the
people of this country from the manifold evils which they suffer in
consequence of the ascendancy of slaveholding influence in all the
departments of our General Government, would arise from the action
of one or the other of the political parties which now claim to divide
the country. All such expectation, however, after having been repeatedly disappointed and repeatedly resumed, is now finally relin-
quished. . . . The Constitution found slavery, and left it, a State
institution — the creature and dependent of State law — local wholly
in its existence and character. It did not make it a national institution. It gave it no national character—no national existence. . .
We admit—we assert it is strictly a State institution, and that Congress has no control over it in the States. . . .

" No candid man, acquainted with the history of his country, will
deny that, at the formation of the Constitution, a general expectation
prevailed that slavery would soon cease in all the States in which it
actually existed. (2) . . . But very different are the facts of history. Encroachment has succeeded encroachment, and usurpation
has followed usurpation, and the influence of slavery runs through
the whole action of the Government, and is felt in the remotest corner
of the land. . . .

" Fifty-three years have elapsed since the adoption of the Constitution of the United States. . . . During the same period seven
slave States have been added to the Union, and slavery has been

* Cincinnati Gazette, January, 1843.

maintained by the authority of the General Government in the District of Columbia and in the Territories of Louisiana and Florida. We will say nothing of the admission of Kentucky, Tennessee, and Alabama into the Union as slave States. The fact that these were taken from the original slave States may be admitted as an apology, though not as a sufficient warrant for it. But the continuance of slavery in the District, and in the Territories purchased from France and Spain, and the admission of Louisiana, Mississippi, Arkansas, and Missouri into the Union as slave States, were in violation of the implied pledge contained in the Ordinance of 1787—in manifest disregard of the principles of the Constitution—and utterly at variance with the original policy of the country in respect to slavery. Thus has the slave power prevailed in the admission of new slave States, and in the extension of slavery beyond its original limits.

"For a considerable period after the organization of the Federal Government, wheat and flour, the products of free States, constituted our chief articles of export and our principal means of paying for supplies from foreign nations. After some years, however, cotton, the product of slave labor, became the great article of export, and has since continued to be so. Every energy of our government has been put in requisition to secure this result. . . . Similar exports have been made in behalf of tobacco and rice, also, for the most part, products of slave States. In the mean time wheat, flour, and pork, and the other products of free labor, have been gradually excluded from foreign markets, and our government has cared nothing and thought nothing about the matter. At length the surplus of these products has become immense, and the free laborer anxiously looks for a market, but finds almost all the ports of the world nearly or absolutely closed against him. Thus has the slave power protected the interests of slave labor, and sacrificed the interests of free labor, through its influence on our foreign negotiations. . . .

"We ask you, fellow citizens, to acquaint yourselves fully with the details and particulars belonging to the topics which we have briefly touched, and we do not doubt that you will concur with us in believing that THE HONOR, THE WELFARE, THE SAFETY, of our country imperiously require the *absolute and unqualified divorce of the Government from slavery!** . . .

"This is the great object of our efforts. We believe that our national Constitution affords no sanction to the doctrine that man

* The italics and small capitals are in the original.

can hold property in man. We believe that its only safe refuge, from universal disavowal and repudiation, is in the constitution of the separate States which admit and sanction it. We believe that neither the domestic nor foreign policy of the Government will be permanently settled so as to secure steady and adequate rewards to free labor, until slavery shall be confined within the limits of those States, and the General Government be delivered from the control of the slave power.

"We would, therefore, withdraw the support of national legislation and negotiation from the system of slavery.

"We would enforce the just and constitutional rule that slavery is the creature of local law, and cannot be extended beyond the limits of the State in which it exists. (3) . . .

"We would secure to every man a speedy and impartial trial by jury, in all cases where life and liberty shall be in question."*

The Abolition Convention, in New York, held shortly after this period, is thus noticed by the *Cincinnati Gazette*, February 2d, 1842:

"The Abolitionists of New York seem to be governed by the fiercest bigotry. The proceeding of this Convention, as reported in the *Tribune*, are ultra in spirit, and rash to madness. They have addressed the *slaves at the South*, recommending them to run away, and so far as may be essential to their escape, to *steal* horse, or boat, or food, or clothing, urging their friends at the South to furnish them with pocket compasses and *locofoco matches* for this purpose. . . .

"The Convention closed by adopting the following resolution by acclamation:

"*Resolved*, That we solemnly and deliberately proclaim to the nation, that no power on earth shall compel us to take up arms against the slaves, should they use violence in asserting their right to freedom."

In the course of the proceedings of the abolitionists in their arrangements for prosecuting the presidential campaign of 1844, the Hartford Committee addressed Mr. Birney, asking his opinions on the various questions of the day. In his reply, Mr. Birney, under date of August 15, 1843, said:

---

* Cincinnati Gazette, January 13 and 14, 1842.

"4. I am not in favor of creating a National Bank while slavery is continued in our country. Slave labor, on a large scale, can never support itself; or I should rather say, it can never support the indolence and the prodigality which it never fails to beget in those who lay claim to its fruits.

"5. My mind strongly inclines to the opinion that, if Congress can rightfully abolish slavery in time of war, it may abolish it in time of peace. A vicious and dangerous state of things existing in the community generally, may as *certainly*, if not as *suddenly*, become as destructive of the government as war. The *principle*, then, on which Congress might rightfully proceed to abolish slavery as a measure of relief and safety in war, might be equally applicable and imperative, on the same grounds, in time of peace. In both cases, the *instant* at which emancipation would be ordered to take place would depend on the sound judgment of the government. (4)

"As a people, we have undertaken, before God and the nations of the earth, to maintain in our political organization the principles of liberty asserted in the Declaration of Independence, and substantially incorporated into the Constitution. Thus have we voluntarily brought ourselves under a guarantee to purge our country from whatever is inconsistent with these principles. Nothing is more palpably so than slavery. We are under a pledge, then, to the world, and to one another, to abolish it; and, in so far as our government has permitted slavery to remain at ease—much more to enlarge and magnify itself— it has proved recreant to its solemn undertaking—has brought on us, as a people, the charge of hypocrisy, and dishonored us before the heavens and the earth.

"Persons of great experience and intelligence, as jurists, have satisfied themselves that the Constitution authorizes, in express terms, the fulfillment of this guarantee, by the Government. Congress, say they, has nothing to do with the relation of *master and slave*. Neither the relation itself, nor the parties between whom it exists, are anywhere mentioned in the Constitution, while, at the same time, (Amendment IV,) it declares that no 'person' shall be deprived of liberty without due process of law:—and this without the slightest reference to his being a native or foreigner—a citizen or an alien—black or white. Those who are called '*slaves*' at the South, are called '*persons*' in the Constitution. Are these persons deprived of their liberty? Yes. By due process of law? No. Then why, it may be asked, are they not entitled to the benefits of the Constitutional provision within the words and spirit of which they are so expressly brought?

" But should the Liberty party be brought into power, a proceeding wholly unobjectionable as to its constitutionality—as simple as it is constitutional, and one that would prove as effectual as it is simple, would, doubtless, be adopted for the abolition of slavery. It is to confine the appointments to office under the Government to such as are not slaveholders. The justness and propriety of such a course would be as unobjectionable as its other characteristics; for, surely, nothing could be more reasonable than to exclude from all share in the administration of the Government—from its offices and its honors—those whose whole lives are passed in open contempt of its fundamental principles! (5)

" 6. It is my opinion that Congress can stop the domestic slave-trade between the States, under that provision of the Constitution which gives it the power to regulate commerce among them. If it be said that Congress has no power to obstruct the transit or removal of persons from one of the States into another—it may be replied, that, if commerce lay her hands on ' persons,' and transmute them into things to deal in, she brings herself, by that act, and in relation to that matter, completely within the scope of the Constitutional provision."* (6)

Again, under date of September 2, 1844, in reply to the Hartford Committee, and of August 5, 1844, in reply to Mr. Errett, of Pittsburgh, Mr. Birney said:

" The sentiments I have expressed above [on the National Bank, the Tariff, etc.], would not, I know, meet with acceptance in many parts of the country. Many, even of the most faithful of the Liberty party, would probably dissent from them. I have not been forward to publish them, lest, by doing so, I might, in some degree, contribute to divert our friends from our paramount object, *the overthrow of the slave power;*—and because I felt well-assured, as I still do, that, if the Liberty party come into power, the whole country will soon be brought into the most favorable circumstances for harmonizing all its apparently discordant interests, and for settling, on their proper bases, all the important existing questions of national policy. *Now*, the labor of the country is made up of two hostile parts—slave and free.

---

* Cincinnati Weekly Herald, Sept. 24, 1844.

Irreconcilable in their nature, they can never be brought to operate harmoniously together under *one* system of legislation. Let no one, then, look for jarrings and dissensions to pass away from among us, till *slave* labor have passed away, or be seen to be passing away, with a certainty of its speedy and entire disappearance.

"The accession to power of the Liberty party implies, as I take it, the speedy extinction of slavery everywhere within our country; and, of course, the bringing of all its *labor* into a homogeneous state. Till our labor be brought into this state, all legislation for its b ɔnefit must necessarily be, in a great measure, unavailing; and this can be done only by the extinction of slavery.*

"But you are ready to ask, how could the Liberty party, if in power, extinguish slavery, seeing, as is admitted on all hands, that the General Government—except as a *war* measure, to save *itself*— has no Constitutional power over that institution in the *States?* I reply—all that is necessary to be done is for the *appointing power* of the General Government to bring into its offices and stations of honor, and trust, and profit, throughout the South, only such as are *not* ɛʹaveholders—only such as practically acknowledge that all men are created equal, and entitled to their lives and liberty. No objection can be made to the constitutionality of such a course. It is as simple, too, as it is constitutional, and it will be found as effective as it is simple. Its spirit and object would commend it to all, except the slaveholders themselves; for I have always found it true, that however slow a people may themselves be to put away *wrong* from among them, yet when once justice is boldly *done* on it by their rulers, the act never fails of receiving their heartiest sanction and approbation.

"The slaveholders would first huddle together for their mutual defense. But it would be unavailing. They could no more withstand the influence of public opinion, now purified by an illustrious act of justice, and flaming on them from every side, than the snow-drift of an April night can withstand the meridian rays of the next day's sun."†

From Mr. Birney we turn to Mr. Chase.

The *Cincinnati Morning Herald*, May 21, 1845, contains the great speech of Hon. SALMON P. CHASE, on the occasion of his re-

---

* Here is the first dawn of the "irrepressible conflict."
† Cincinnati Morning Herald, Sept. 23, 1844.

ception of a silver pitcher from the colored people of Cincinnati. A few extracts will show his positions on the negro question. He said:

"I embrace, with pleasure, this opportunity of declaring my disapprobation of that clause in the constitution which denies to a portion of the colored people the right of suffrage.* . . . I regard, therefore, the exclusion of the colored people, as a body, from the elective franchise as incompatible with free democratic principles. . . . The exclusion of colored children from the schools is, in my judgment, a clear infringement of the Constitution, and a palpable breach of trust. I arraign the whole policy of our legislation in relation to our colored population. I deny its justice; I deny its expediency.(7)

"Let me turn now, for a moment, to the condition of the enslaved. They number two millions and a half. I claim for these the rights which the Constitution and the law, rightly interpreted, secure to them. I claim that nowhere, unless within the limits of the original States, can a single person be enslaved, except in violation of the Constitution and the laws. (8) I maintain that the Declaration of Independence and the Constitution of the United States are the expressions of the anti-slavery sentiment of an anti-slavery people. In the former, these expressions assumed the form of a solemn proclamation of the National Creed, on the subject of human rights. In the latter, these expressions took the shape of permanent declarations of the National Will embodied as the fundamental law of the land. The Declaration assumed the natural equality of all men as the foundation principle of all just government. The Constitution, acting on things as it found them, established the National Government, with such powers and such limitations of power, as would, it was then thought, secure the final conformity of the actual condition of the people to the theory of the Declaration.

"In the case of Watson, of which, sir, you have so feelingly spoken, the constitutional limitations of slavery were fully discussed. In that case it was my part to re-state the positions and reiterate the reasonings of the able lawyers associated with me. I may be permitted, therefore, to say that, in my judgment, the positions were sound and the arguments unanswerable. The first of these positions, and that on which the whole argument hinged, was that the Constitution was not designed to uphold slavery, and conferred no power on Congress

---

* The Constitution of Ohio is here referred to.

to establish, continue, or sanction slaveholding anywhere. We also maintained that slaveholding could not be continued anywhere without the sanction and aid of positive law. . . . Slavery is an institution of force. If I claim to own you, sir, and require you to do some service for me, and you refuse, and the law puts forth the power of the community, in aid of mine, to compel you to submit to my disposal, and you are compelled to submit, then you are a slave. Congress is not authorized to exert any such power in behalf of the master. Congress is expressly prohibited from exerting any such power by the fifth amendment of the Constitution, which declares that no person shall be deprived of life, liberty, or property, without due process of law. How, then, could slavery continue in the territory of Louisiana, after its acquisition by the United States? There was— there could be no law in the Territory inconsistent with the Constitution, which forbade that any person should be deprived of liberty without due process of law. There was—there could be no law in the Territory which did not exist either through the adoption or by the enactment of Congress, or of the Territorial Legislature, which derived all its power from Congress. Congress could not adopt law which it could not enact, nor confer a power on the Territorial Legislature which it did not itself possess. Congress has no power to legalize the practice of slaveholding. The practice of slaveholding, therefore, in the Territory could not be legalized. Nor could it be legalized in any state created out of the Territory, unless it can be maintained that a part of the people of any one of the States in this Union can convert another part into property, if they can get possession of the Legislature and have physical force enough to enforce its detestable enactments.

"I have no doubt of the correctness of these positions, or of the soundness of the inevitable inference from them, that slaveholding in Arkansas is unconstitutional, and, consequently, that Watson, having been conveyed to Arkansas, by his Virginia master, was free. But I was aware that this doctrine was too little in accordance with the received pro-slavery theories of constitutional construction, to find much favor upon a first hearing, and was not disappointed that the judge did not acquiesce in it. I expect, however, to live to see it recognized in all courts as sound law. . . .

"For myself, I am ready to renew my pledge, and I will venture to speak also in behalf of my co-workers—that we will go straight on, without faltering or wavering, until every vestige of oppression shall be erased from the statute-book; until the sun in all his journey from the utmost eastern horizon, through the mid-heaven, till he sinks beyond the western mountains into his ocean bed, shall not behold, in all our broad and glorious land, the footprint of a single slave." (9)

The proceedings of the "Southern and Western Liberty Convention," which met in Cincinnati, June 11, 1845, were published in the *Cincinnati Morning Herald*. A few extracts from the proceedings will serve to show the aims it had in view.

JAMES G. BIRNEY, Esq., on the first day of the session, said: "We are not met to abolish the Union. I have no idolatrous veneration for the Union. If slavery could not be abolished without the dissolution of the Union, I, for one, would go for dissolution. (10) But it is not necessary. We should feel some charity for those who think that dissolution is the only way of eradicating the evil. They do not oppose the Union *as it ought* to have been; but as it is, with the usurpation of the slave power."*

JOHN M. WILLS, of Pittsburgh, during the evening session, said: "Our object must be to build up a power in the North, which shall be as much dreaded as the slave power of the South. And we can do it. In several States we have already the *balance* of political power in the free States. We can soon obtain the balance of power in all the free States, and when we have done that, one of the political parties must inscribe one fundamental doctrine of the Liberty party, to wit: the entire divorce of the General Government from all connection with slavery. The moment this is done, the necessity of a Liberty party ceases. All we wish is the accomplishment of our object, and the party which shall give us this, destroys the necessity of our longer existence. And it is thus equally the interest of both Whig and Democratic parties to raise the standard of emancipation."† (11)

JUDGE STEVENS, of Indiana, during the same session, said: "We are now a separate moral and political organization. We shall ever continue so. The other parties may come to us, but we can not go to them. They are destined to become one simple chemical substance, fused into one by the Liberty principle. . . . We are asked how slavery is to be abolished? Sir, I will tell you. We must reach the abolition of slavery over the dead bodies of both the old

---

* Morning Herald, June 12, 1845.   † Ibid., June 13, 1845.

political parties. . . . In the second place, we must reach the abolition of slavery through the doors of 20,000 churches. . . . . But we are told that our plan is seditious and factious . . . . that we shall divide the churches! Sir, division implies separation, and what shall we separate? Why the sin of slaveholding from Christianity. . . . We are told, too, that we shall divide the Union—that we are disunionists. Now, sir, I am for the Union—but I say, if the only Union we can have with the South, in Church and State, is to be, and must be, cemented by the blood of three millions of my brethren, I say, in God's name, let it go down." (12) . . . "Judge Steven's Address produced a profound impression, and was received with applause."*

The following resolutions, among others, were adopted by the Convention:

"3. *Resolved*, That we love the Union, and desire its perpetuity, and revere the Constitution, and are determined to maintain it; but the Union which we love must be a Union to establish justice, and secure the blessings of liberty; and the Constitution which we support, must be that which our fathers bequeathed to us, and not that which the constructions of slavery and servilism have substituted for it.

"4. *Resolved*, That, as a national party, our purpose and determination is to divorce the National Government from slavery; to prohibit slaveholding in all places of exclusive national jurisdiction; to abolish the domestic slave trade; to harmonize the administration of the Government in all its departments with the principles of the Declaration; (13) and, in all proper and constitutional modes to encourage, and discontinue the system of work without wages; but not to interfere, unconstitutionally, with the local legislation of particular States."†

In the Address of the Convention to the people of the United States, we find the following: "We are willing to take our stand upon propositions generally conceded:—that slaveholding is contrary to natural right and justice; (14) that it can subsist nowhere without the sanction and aid of positive legislation; that the Constitution expressly prohibits Congress from depriving any person of liberty without due process of law. From these propositions we deduce, by logical inference, the doctrines upon which we insist. . . . The question of

---

* Morning Herald, June 13, 1845.

† Ibid., June 16, 1845.

slavery is, and until it shall be settled, must be, the paramount moral and political question of the day. We, at least, so regard it; and so regarding it, must subordinate every other question to it."*

We defer additional quotations from other sources, in the present section, but, if space permits, may do so in a subsequent one.

REMARKS ON THE PRECEDING PRODUCTIONS.

(1) The complaint made by the Columbus Abolition Convention, in both its resolutions and address, that Northern products were excluded from foreign markets while Southern products were admitted on advantageous terms, was not founded in an intelligent view of that question. Foreign nations, generally, were able then, as now, to grow their own breadstuffs and provisions, but could not produce their cotton. Hence, while they retained a tariff of duties on such commodities as the North produced, they were interested in admitting the products of the South on the most favorable terms. The argument was offered, doubtless, for political effect merely, and to enlist the prejudices of Northern and Western agriculturists against the South.

(2) Here we have the first authoritative announcement of the theory, that, "at the formation of the Constitution, a general expectation prevailed that slavery would soon cease in all the States in which it actually existed." This view is proven to be false, not only by the letter of Mr. Jefferson to M. Muissner, but by the action of the Methodist Church in dropping its Rule on Slavery in the Southern States. This theory has been the most dangerous one entertained by the abolitionists. They did not claim that the Constitution itself repudiated slavery, but that it was the general expectation, at the time of the adoption of the Constitution, that slavery would soon die out. This expectation was limited to the North, and never had an existence at the South. Southern statesmen never understood the Constitution as contemplating a course of legislation, under its provisions, that would secure the abolition of slavery. They adopted it with the distinct understanding, that "the powers not delegated to the

---

* Morning Herald, June 20, 1845.

United States by the Constitution, nor prohibited by it to the States, are reserved to the States respectively, or to the people." Slavery was an existing institution, over which Congress had no constitutional power granted to it; that institution, therefore, was left wholly under the control of the States and of the people. To urge emancipation on the ground of a sectional opinion, and in opposition to the plain provisions of the Constitution, was a palpable violation of the principles of that instrument, and, necessarily, provoked resistance on the part of those to be affected by the new doctrine.

(3) "Slavery is the creature of local law." This has been an axiom with abolitionists ever since the decision of Lord Mansfield in the case of Somersett; but its accuracy has not been acquiesced in by later English judges. The discussion of this point came up in the Congress of the United States, January 30, 1861, when Hon. JOHN W. STEVENSON, of Kentucky, in reply to Hon. Mr. STANTON, of Ohio, said:

"It pained me to hear the gentleman from Ohio, (Mr. STANTON,) for whom I entertain the highest respect, both as a lawyer and a man, assert that slavery was never sanctioned by the common law, or law of nations, but was the creature of local law. Sir, I differ with him, *toto cœlo*. Where can he show me a statute, in any State, establishing slavery? Our ancestors brought the common law with them, and it is an admitted historical fact, that African slavery existed in the thirteen original States. Now, if the common law does not sanction slavery, and no statute can be found establishing it, how was it recognized, and how did it originally find a footing in the free States? Whence the necessity of statutes for its abolition? Why did not the pernicious thing perish in the pure atmosphere of Puritanism of New England, denounced by the common law, and unsupported by any statute? Yet it continued for years; and, strange to say, opposition to the abolition of the slave trade, insisted on by Southern men, came from the ancestors of Republicans who wish us now to become their pupils in the school of morals. Nay, more, Mr. Speaker: I doubt not, even at this day, in New England, that a note given in New Orleans for the price of a slave, and transferred to some Boston merchant, could be recovered before a Republican jury, with a plea impeaching its consideration as vicious. If so, then slavery is not contrary to the law of nature, or of morals, since, '*ex turpi causa, non oritur actio*,' and I would cite Republican action against Republican theory.

"Mr. Speaker, I deny that slavery is the creature of municipal law. It is one of the erroneous corollaries which has been deduced from a loose noxious *obiter dictum* of Lord Mansfield in Somersett's case ; and which, I regret to say, but frankly admit, has crept into the opinions of many able judges in our American courts. I may be pardoned for saying it is, nevertheless, a legal heresy. I cannot, however, forbear making England herself, well known to be no apologist for slavery, a witness against the position of the gentleman from Ohio, (Mr. STANTON,) on this point. He is, I know, familiar with the case of the slave Grace, decided by Lord Stowell, and reported in 2 *Hazzard's Reports*, page 94. The facts of that case were, that Mrs. Allen, of Antigua, came to England, in 1822, bringing her female slave Grace. She remained with her mistress until 1823, when she returned with her voluntarily to Antigua. She continued as a domestic slave with Mrs. Allen until 1825, when she was seized by the waiter of the customs at Antigua, as forfeited to the king, on having been illegally imported in 1823. The vice-admiralty court of Antigua decreed the slave to her owner, Mrs. Allen, from which an appeal was prayed.

"Lord Stowell affirmed the judgment, in a learned, lengthy, and able opinion. I commend it to the gentlemen from Ohio. In it, he reviews Lord Mansfield's opinion in the Somersett case, with a spice of ironical satire. Lord Stowell says :

"'The real and sole question which the case of Somersett brought before Lord Mansfield, was, whether a slave could be taken from this country in irons and carried back to the West Indies to be restored to the dominion of his master? And all the answer, perhaps, which that question required was, that the party, who was a slave, could not be sent out of England in such a manner and for such a purpose, stating the reasons of that illegality. It is certainly true that Lord Mansfield, in his final judgment, amplifies the subject largely. He extends his observations to the foundation of the whole system of the slavery code ; for, in one passage, he says ' that slavery is so odious that it cannot be established without positive law.'

"'Far be the presumption of questioning any *obiter dictum* that fell' from that great man on that occasion ; but I trust I do not depart from the modesty that belongs to my situation, and, I hope, to my character, when I observe that ancient custom is generally recognized as a just foundation for all law ; that villenage of both kinds, which is said by some to be the prototype of slavery, had no other origin than ancient custom; that a great part of the common law itself, in all its relations, has little other foundation than the same custom; and that the practice of slavery, as it exists in Antigua and several other of our colonies, though regulated by law, has been, in many instances, founded upon a similar authority.'

"Lord Stowell adds, in regard to the suggestion in the Somersett case, that the air of the island was too pure for slavery—

"'How far this air was used for the common purposes of respiration during the many centuries in which the two systems of villenage maintained their sway in this country, history has not recorded.'

"Again, he says, as to the revival of slavery in the colonies:

"'I have first to observe that it (slavery) returns upon the slave by same title by which it grew up originally. It never was, in Antigua, the creature of law, but of that *custom* which operates with the force of law; and when it is cried out, that *malus usus abolendus est*, it is first to be proved that, even in the consideration of England, the use of slavery is considered as a *malus usus* in the colonies.'

"Here is a direct authority as to the usage and common law of England in tolerating slavery, and from a most eminent English jurist. This opinion, if I am not mistaken, was commended by the late Justice Story.

"Allow me to read another short opinion by the same distinguished judge, in the case of Demarara and its dependencies. (6 *Admiralty Reports*.) The question arose as to the character of slaves in the arsenals and forts of Demarara, on the 31st September, 1803, when it surrendered to Great Britain:

"'The slaves are in number three hundred and ninety-nine, of whom two hundred are no longer the subject of contest, but are now admitted to have belonged to the estate on which they were employed as *glebæ adscriptitii*; they were attached to the soil as part and parcel of the realty, and, upon that account, the question with respect to them has very properly been given up by the captors.

*   *   *   *   *   *   *

"'The first question is, whether slaves are at all given to the captors by the prize act, that is, whether they pass by words "stores of war, goods, merchandise, or treasure," which, by the third section of the statute, are to be deemed prize, and to be apportioned by his majesty between the army and navy, when acting in conjunction. Now, the fact is, that slaves have generally been considered as personal property. The word *mancipia*, as it has been well observed, signifies *quœ manu capiunter*. This is unquestionably the meaning of the word according to the civil law. In our West India colonies, where slavery is continued, and is likely to continue longer than in any of the countries of Europe, slaves have been for some purposes considered as real property; but I apprehend that, where the contrary is not shown, the general character and description of them is, that they are personal property, and I see no reason, in the present case, for saying that they are not within the general rule, and, consequently, that they are not to be considered "as goods or merchandise." They are liable to be transferred by purchase and sale, and although the owner may choose to employ them on his own works, instead of transferring them for a valuable consideration, they are not, I apprehend, the less "goods and merchandise" on that account. The very same observation applies to all other cases of personal property, for all such property, if saleable, is merchandise, although the person in possession may not be a merchant, or mean to dispose of it by sale.'

"Once more: in the case of Le Louis (6 *Admiralty Reports*) Lord Stowell is still more emphatic on the subject of the recognition by the law of nations of the African slave trade, if recognized as lawful by the country whose bottoms are engaged in it. He says:

"'It (the Court) must look to the legal standard of morality; and upon a question of this nature, that standard must be found in the law of nations, as fixed and evidenced by general, and ancient, and admitted practice, by treaties, and by the general tenor of the laws and ordinances, and the formal transactions of civilized States; and looking to those authorities, I find a difficulty in maintaining that the traffic is legally criminal.

"'Let me not be misunderstood, or misapprehended, as a professed apologist for this practice, when I state facts which no man can deny, that personal slavery, arising out of forcible captivity, is coeval with the earliest periods of the history of mankind; that it is found existing—and, as far as appears, without animadversion—in the earliest and most authentic records of the human race; that it is recognized by the codes of the most polished nations of antiquity; that, under the light of Christianity itself, the possession of persons so acquired has been, in every civilized country, invested with the character of property, and secured as such by all the protections of law; that solemn treaties have been framed, and national monopolies eagerly sought, to facilitate and extend the commerce in this asserted prop erty; and all this, with all the sanctions of law, public and municipal, and without any opposition, except the protests of a few private moralists, little heard and less attended to, in every country, till within these very few years, in this particular country. If the matter rested here, I fear it would have been deemed a most extravagant assumption in any court of the law of nations to pronounce that this practice, the tolerated, the approved, the encouraged object of law ever since man became subject to law, was prohibited by that law, and was legally criminal. But the matter does not rest here. Within these few years a considerable change of opinion has taken place, particularly in this country. Formal declarations have been made, and laws enacted, in reprobation of this practice; and pains, ably and zealously conducted, have been taken to induce other countries to follow the example, but at present with insufficient effect; for there are nations which adhere to the practice under all the encouragement which their own laws can give it. What is the doctrine of our courts, of the law of nations, relative to them? Why, that their practice is to be respected; that their slaves, if taken, are to be restored to them; and, if not taken under innocent mistake, are to be restored with costs and damages. All this, surely, upon the ground that such conduct, on the part of any State, is no departure from the law of nations; because, if it were, no such respect could be allowed to it upon an exemption of its own making, for no nation can privilege itself to commit a crime against the law of nations by a mere municipal regulation of its own. And if our understanding and administration of the law of nations be, that every nation, independently of treaties, retains a legal right to carry on this traffic, and that the trade, carried on under that authority, is to be respected by all tribunals, foreign as well as domestic, it is not easy to find any consistent grounds on which to maintain that the traffic, according to our views of that law, is criminal.'—*English Admiralty Reports*, vol. 2.

"Need I refer to the case of the Antelope, in which the distinguished and lamented Chief Justice Marshall held that—

"'The African slave trade had been sanctioned, in modern times, by the laws of all nations who possess distant colonies, each of whom has engaged in it as a common commercial business which no other could rightfully interrupt. It has claimed all the sanction which could be derived from long usage and general acquiescence.'

"The gentleman from Ohio (Mr. STANTON) will surely not contend that these decisions sustain his position, that African slavery is a local institution, created exclusively by State laws, or that the common law did not recognize property in a person. Sir, upon what ground could we have ever obtained indemnity, as we have often done, for the loss of our slaves on the high seas, if this doctrine were true? The official correspondence of our ministers abroad abounds in claims of this character, and many have been successful; but if foreign nations had followed the doctrines of the Republican party, our claims, in every instance, would have been ignored."*

(4) We have here the extraordinary claim set up by Mr. Birney, the Liberty party candidate for President, that Congress, even in time of peace, may rightfully proceed to abolish slavery. Mr. Clay, about this time, in speaking of abolitionism as a political element in the nation, used the following prophetic language:

"Mr. President:—It is at this alarming stage of the proceedings of the ultra-abolitionists, that I would seriously invite every considerate man in the country solemnly to pause, and deliberately to reflect, not merely on our existing posture, but upon that dreadful precipice down which they would hurry us. It is because these ultra-abolitionists have ceased to employ the instruments of reason and persuasion, have made their cause political, and have appealed to the ballot-box, that I am induced upon this occasion to address you."†

Again, Mr. Clay, referring to the abolitionists, said: "To the agency of their powers of persuasion they now propose to substitute the power of the BALLOT-BOX; and he must be blind to what is passing before us, who does not perceive that the *inevitable tendency* of their proceedings is, if these should be found insufficient, to invoke, finally, the more potent powers of the bayonet."‡

(5) Mr. Birney here proposes a very simple process indeed, and as silly as it is simple. His scheme for administering the Government, and eradicating slavery, is to disfranchise the slaveholders—a measure more easily proposed than executed.

(6) The prohibition of the transit of slaves from one State to another, has long been a favorite measure with abolitionists. Its

---

* Speech of Hon. John W. Stevenson, of Kentucky, on the State of the Union, delivered in the House of Representatives, January 30, 1861.

† Senate speech, 1839, as quoted in Cincinnati Morning Herald, Oct. 9, 1844.

‡ Ibid.

practical bearing is readily understood. The natural increase of the slaves, if it were all kept within a State, would soon lead to over-population; and thus their labor would become profitless, and emancipation become a necessity.

(7) The claim set up here for negro suffrage, and the commingling of all colors in the same schools, is in accordance with the views of the abolitionists, but has never been acceptable to others.

(8) This interpretation of the Constitution is such an extreme departure from that put upon it by the framers of that instrument, that it is no wonder the South took the alarm when the writer of this Address was elected, by the Legislature of Ohio, to the United States Senate.

(9) And not only was this novel interpretation of the Constitution thrown broadcast over the land, but we have the declaration of the determination of these abolitionists to go straight on, without faltering or wavering, until there shall not be seen, "in all our broad and glorious land, the footprint of a single slave."

(10) Here we have a candidate for the Presidency, Mr. Birney, declaring that, if slavery could not be abolished without the dissolution of the Union, he, for one, would go for dissolution. This traitorous utterance was a fatal one. The sentiment became a part of the abolition creed, and was afterward repeated by a thousand tongues.

(11) The policy announced by the Southern and Western Liberty Convention, by means of which the abolition of slavery was to be accomplished, was to persevere in its agitation of the subject until the balance of political power should be secured, and one or the other of the political parties forced to inscribe upon its banner the fundamental doctrines of the abolitionists. In conformity with this scheme, the abolitionists kept up their organization, in one form or another, until they succeeded in "fusing" with the "Free Soil party," under Mr. Frémont, as the Presidential candidate.

(12) It is painful to put upon record the traitorous utterances against the Union which abounded in the public demonstrations of the abolitionists at this period. The declaration of Judge

Stevens, that if the only union we can have with the South, in Church and State, is to be, and must be, cemented by the slavery of three millions of his brethren, then, in God's name, let it go down, was received with applause instead of with execration, as it should have been.

(13) The idea of making the legislative, judicial, and executive action of the nation conform to the Declaration of Independence, instead of to the Constitution, is as absurd as to make our intercourse with foreign nations conform to the non-importation, non-exportation and non-consumption compact of the colonists previous to the Revolution.* The Declaration had its uses when announced, and has its uses still, as embodying the great leading doctrines of human rights—rights that were denied to the colonists by the mother country. But the Declaration was never so interpreted, by those who adopted it, as to include any of the barbarous races, in the sense of admitting them to civil equality; otherwise, as we have elsewhere shown, that equality would have been recognized in the Constitution.† The grand error of the abolitionists has been in the adoption of this fiction in relation to the Declaration, and their persistence in urging that the Constitution must be interpreted in conformity with their negro equality interpretation of the Declaration. The non-intercourse compact had its uses also; but it was temporary in its character. Its history, however, teaches an important lesson, and one that has been overlooked by the abolitionists. It prohibited all importation of British goods, and all importation of slaves from Africa; and, yet, notwithstanding the Declaration of Independence, no sooner had the Revolution triumphed than the importation of both British goods and slaves was resumed. This resumption of the slave trade was with the assent and co-operation of the northern States, and could never have occurred had the fathers of the Revolution interpreted the Declaration as including the negro race.

(14) The Address of the Convention includes the fiction of Lord Mansfield, in the Somersett case, that slavery being contrary to natural law, can have no existence except by positive statute;

---

* See Chapter II, page 51.

† See discussion of this matter in Chapter II, page 52.

when the well-known fact is, that slavery, though recognized as a legal relation by almost every civilized nation, never has been established by positive law, any more than any of the other relations among men which are recognized by the common law.

To afford the reader a clearer conception of this question, we copy, in addition to the decisions presented by Mr. Stevenson, the argument of Charles O'Connor, Esq., in the Lemmon case, New York City, as condensed in the *New York Reports*, volume 20, 1857 :

"(2) Negro slavery never was a part of the municipal law of England, and, consequently, it was not imported thence by the first colonists. Nor did they adopt any system of villenage or other permanent domestic slavery of any kind which had ever existed in England, or been known to, or regulated by, the laws or usages of that kingdom. They were a homogeneous race of the free white men ; and in a society of such persons, the slavery of its own members, endowed by nature with mental and physical equality, must ever be repugnant to an enlightened sense of justice. Of course the colonists abhorred it—saw that it was not suited to their condition, and left it behind them when they emigrated. (*Doctor and Student Dialogue*, 2 *ch.*, 18, 19; *Wheaton* v. *Donaldson*, 8 *Pet.*, 659; *Van Ness* v. *Pacard*, 2 *Pet.*, 444; 1 *Kent Com.*, 373; *Const. N. Y.*, art 1, § 17; *Neal* v. *Farmer*, 9 *Cobb's Geo. R.*, 562, 578.) (3) As neither the political-bondage nor the domestic slavery which the European by fraud and violence imposed upon his white brethren ever had a legal foothold in the territory now occupied by these States, the inflated speeches of French and British judges and orators touching the purity of the air and soil of their respective countries, whatever other purpose they may serve, are altogether irrelevant to the inquiry what was or is the law of any State in this Union on the subject of negro slavery. (*French Eloq.*, A. D. 1738, 20 *State Trials*, 11 *note; English Eloq.*, A. D. 1762, 2 *Eden*, 117, *Ld.* NORTHINGTON; *Id.*, 1771, 20 *State Trials*, 1 *Ld.* MANSFIELD; *Scotch Eloq.*, 1778, *id.*, *note; Irish Eloq.*, 1793, *Rowan's Trial, Curran; Judge McLean's criticism in Dred Scott*, 19 *How.*, 535; *Lord* STOWELL'S *criticism*, 2 *Hagg. Ad.*, 109.) (*a*) The only argument against negro slavery found in the English cases at all suitable for a judicial forum, rests on the historical fact that it was unknown to English law. Mr. Hargrave, in Somersett's case, showed that white Englishmen were alone subject to the municipal slave laws of that country at any time; that negro slavery was a new institution, which it required the legislative power to introduce. (20 *State Trials*, 55; *Com.* v. *Aves*, 18 *Pick.*, 214.) (*b*) Lord HOLT and Mr. Justice POWELL were Mr. Hargrave's high authority for the proposition that whilst the common law of England recognized white English slaves or villeins, and the right of property in them, yet it 'took no notice of a negro.'' That a white man might 'be a villein in England,' but 'that as soon as a negro comes into England he became free.' It was only negro liberty that the know-nothingism of English and French law established. English and French air had not its true enfranchising purity till drawn through the nostrils of a negro. White slaves had long respired it without their *status* being at all affected. (*Smith* v. *Brown*, 2 *Salk.*, 666; 20 *State Trials*, 55, *note*.) (*c*) Lord MANSFIELD said, in Somersett's case, 'The state of slavery is of such a nature that it is incapable of being introduced on any reason, moral or political, but only by positive law,' and negrophilism has been in raptures with him ever since. Nevertheless it was a bald, inconsequential truism. It might be equally well said of any other new thing not recognized in any known existing law. (*Per Ashhurst*, *J.*, 3 *J. R.*, 63.) . . . . 2. The judicial department has no right to declare negro slavery to be contrary to the law of nature, or immoral, or unjust, or to take any measures, or introduce any policy, for its suppression, founded on any such ideas. Courts are only authorized to administer the municipal law. Judges have no commission to promulgate or enforce their notions of general justice, natural right or morality, but only that which is the known law of the land. (*Kent's Com.*, 448; *Doctor and Student Dialogue*, 1 *ch.*, 18, 19; *per* MAULE, *J.*, 13 *Ad. and Ell.*, *N. S.* 387, *note*.) 3. In the forensic sense of the word law, there is no such thing as a law of nature bearing upon the lawfulness of slavery, or, indeed, upon any other question in jurisprudence. The law of nature is, in every juridical sense, a mere figure of speech. In a state of nature, if the existence of human beings in such a state may be supposed, there is no law. The prudential resolves of an individual for his own government do not come under the denomination of law. Law, in the forensic sense, is wholly of social origin. It is a restraint imposed by society upon itself and its members. (*Rutherforth's Inst.*, *B.* 1, *ch.* 1, § 6, 7; 1 *Bl. Com.*, 43; 1 *Kent*, 2; *Wheaton's Elements of Int. Law*, 2, 19; *Cooper's Justinian*, *notes*, 405; *Bower on Public Law*, 47, *and onward*.) (1) If there was any such thing as a law of nature, in the forensic sense of the word law, it must be of absolute and paramount obligation in all climes, ages, courts, and places. Inborn with the moral constitution of man, it must control him everywhere, and overrule, as vicious, corrupt, and void, every opposing decree or resolution of courts or legislatures. And, accordingly, BLACKSTONE, repeating the idle speech of others upon the subject, tells us that the law of nature is binding all over the globe; and that no human laws are of any validity, if contrary to it. (1 *Wendell's Blackstone*, 40, 41, 42, *and notes*.) Yet, as the judiciary of England have, at all times, acknowledged negro slavery to be a valid basis of legal rights, it follows either that such slavery, in the practical judgment of the common law, is not contrary to the law of nature, or, if it be, that such law of nature is of no force in any English court. (*Acc. Bouvier's Inst.*, § 9; *Brougham, Ed. Rev., Apl.* 1858, 235.) (2) The common law judges of England, while they broke the fetters of any negro slave who came into that country, held themselves bound to enforce contracts for the purchase and sale of such slaves, and to give redress for damages done to the right of property in them. This involves the proposition that there was no paramount law of nature which courts could act upon prohibiting negro slavery. (*Maldrazo* v. *Willes*, 3 *B. and Ald.*, 353; 18 *Pick.*, 215; *Smith* v. *Brown, Salk.*, 666; *Cases cited in note*, 20 *State Trials*, 51; *The slave Grace*, 2 *Hagg. Adm.*, 104.) (3) The highest courts of England and of this country having jurisdiction over questions of public or international law, have decided that holding negroes in bondage as slaves is not contrary to the law of nations. (*The Antelope*, 10 *Wheat.*, 66; 18 *Pick.*, 211; *The slave Grace*, 2 *Hagg. Adm.*, 104, 122.) (4) When Justinian says, in his Institutes, (*book* 1, *tit.* 2, § 2,) and elsewhere, that slavery is contrary to the law of nature, he means no more than that it does not exist by nature, but is introduced by human law, which is true of most, if not all, other rights and obligations. His definition of the law of nature (*book* 1, *tit.* 2,) *de jure naturali*, proves this; his full sanction of slavery in *book* 1, (*tit.* 3, § 2, *tit.* 8, § 1,) confirm it. (*Cushing's Domat.*, § 97; *Bowyer on Public Law*, 48.) (5) All perfect rights, cognizable or enforceable as such in judicial tribunals, exist only by virtue of the law of that state or country in which they are claimed or asserted. The whole idea of property arose from compact. It has no origin in any law of nature, as supposed in the court below. (5 *Sandf.*, 711; *Rutherforth's Inst.*, *book* 1, *ch.* 3, § 6, 7.) (6) The law of nature spoken of by law writers, if the phrase has any practical import, means that morality which its notions of policy leads each nation to recognize as of universal obligation, which it therefore observes itself, and so far as it may, enforces upon others. It cannot be pretended that there ever was in England, or that there now is in any State of this Union, a law, by any name, thus outlawing negro slavery. The common law of all these countries has always regarded it as the basis of individual rights; and statute laws, in all of them, recognized and enforced it. (*The slave Grace*, 2 *Hagg. Adm.*, 104; *Per* SHAW, *Ch. J.*, 18 *Pick.*, 215; 1 *Kent*, 2, 3; *id.*, 2; 2 *Wood's Civil Law*, 2.) (*a*) No civilized state on earth can maintain this absolute outlawry of negro slavery; for, in some of its forms, slavery has existed in all ages; and no lawgiver of paramount authority has ever condemned it. (*Cooper's Justinian, notes*, 410, *Inst., book* 1, *tit.* 3; *Per* BARTLEY, *Ch. J.*, 6 *Ohio N. S.*, 724; *Senator* BENJAMIN, 1858.) (*b*) It has never been determined by the judicial tribunals of any country, that any right, otherwise perfect, loses its claim to protection by the mere fact of its being founded on the ownership of a negro slave. (7) The proposition that freedom is the general rule and slavery the local exception, has no foundation in any just view of the law as a science. Equally groundless is the distinction taken by Judge PAINE between slave property and other movables. (*a*) Property in movables does not exist by nature, neither is there any common law of nations touching its acquisition or transfer. (*Bowyer on Universal Public Law*, 50.) Every title to movables must have an origin in some law. That origin is always in and by the municipal law of the place where it is acquired, and such law never has *per se* any extra territorial operation. (*c*) When the movables, with or without the presence of their owner, come within any other country than that under whose laws the title to them was acquired, it depends on the will of such latter State how far it will take notice of and recognize, *quoad* such property and its owner, the foreign law. (*Bank of Augusta* v. *Earle*, 13 *Pet.*, 589.) (*d*) It has become a universal practice among civilized nations to recognize such foreign law except so far as it may be specially proscribed. This usage amounts to an agreement between the nations, and hence the idea of property by the so-called law of nations. (*e*) Hence it will be seen that property in African negroes is not an exception to any general rule. Upon rational principles, it is no more local or peculiar than any other property. And there is so much of universality about it that in no civilized State or country could it be absolutely denied all legal protection. 4. In fact there is no violation of the principles of enlightened justice nor any departure from the dictates of pure benevolence in holding negroes in a state of slavery. (1) Men, whether black or white, can not exist with ordinary comfort and in reasonable safety otherwise than in the social state. (2) Negroes, alone and unaided by the guardianship of another race, cannot sustain a civilized social state. (*a*) This proposition does not require for its support an assertion or denial of the unity of the human race, the application of Noah's malediction, (9 *Geo.*, 582), or the possibility that time has changed, and may again change, the Ethiopian's physical and moral nature. (*b*) It is only necessary to view the negro as he is, and to credit the palpable and undeniable truth, that the latter phenomenon cannot happen within thousands of years. For all the ends of jurisprudence this is a perpetuity. (*Facciolati's Latin Lexicon Æthiops.*) (*c*) The negro never has sustained a civilized social organization, and that he never can, is sufficiently manifest from history. It is proven by the rapid, though gradual, retrogression of Hayti toward the profoundest depths of destitution, ignorance, and barbarism. (*McCullough's Geo., Hayti,* 693, 694; *De Bow's Rev., vol.* 24, 203.) (*d*) That, alone and unaided, he never can sustain a civilized social organization, is proven to all reasonable minds by the fact that one single member of his race has never attained proficiency in any art or science requiring the employment of high intellectual capacity. A mediocrity below the standard of qualification for the important duties of government, for guiding the affairs of society, or for progress in the abstract sciences, may be common in individuals of other races; but it is universal among the negroes. Not one single negro has ever risen above it. (*Malte Brun's Geo., book* 59, 8; *Gregoire's Literature of the Negroes; Biog. Univ. Supt., vol.* 56, 83, *Gregoire.*) (*e*) It follows, that in order to obtain the measure of reasonable personal enjoyment and of usefulness to himself and others for which he is adapted by nature, the negro must remain in a state of pupilage under the government of some other race. (*f*) He is a child of the sun. In cold climates he perishes; in the territories adapted to his labors, and in which alone his race can be perpetuated, he will not toil save on compulsion, and the white man can not; but each can perform his appointed task—the negro can labor, the white man can govern. . . . . (*c*) Who shall deny the claim of the intellectual white race to its compensation for the mental toil of governing and guiding the negro laborer? The learned and skillful statesman, soldier, physician, preacher, or other expert in any great department of human exertion where mind holds dominion over matter, is clothed with power, and surrounded with materials for the enjoyment of mental and physical luxuries, in proportion to the measure of his capacity and attainments. And all this is at the cost of the mechanical and agricultural laborer, to whom such enjoyments are denied. If the social order, founded in the different natural capacities of individuals in the same family, which produces these inequalities, is not unjust, who can rightfully say of the like inequality in condition between races differing in capacity, that it is contrary to the law of nature, or that the governing race who conform to it are guilty of fraud and rapine, or that they commit a violence to right reason which is forbidden by morality. (4) '*Honeste vivere, alterum non lœdere et suum cuique tribuere,*' are all the precepts of the moral law. The honorable slaveholder keeps them as perfectly as any other member of human society. (*Inst., book* 1, *tit.* 1, § 3; 1 *Bl. Com.,* 409; *Georgia,* 582.)" . . . .

Section II.—The Slavery Agitation in the Halls of Congress.

It is not our purpose to enter minutely into the history of the abolition controversy in Congress, as that itself would fill a volume; but to present such portions of the debates as will enable the reader to understand the character of the assaults made upon the South, and the spirit in which the assailants were met by the members from that section of the Union. We pass over the period of "Nullification," by South Carolina, and take up the *Congressional Globe* for the Session beginning December, 1835.

There had been no political organization of the abolitionists at this date, and the ecclesiastical action alone had preceded the prevailing excitements. This action had then nearly spent its force, and politicians were calculating how they could best turn its results to their own advantage. But while the clergymen and politicians had each their distinct aims to accomplish—the first to free the church and country from slavery, and the second to promote their own political advancement—there was another class, as we shall see, who attempted so to control the abolition element as to make it subservient to the promotion of sectional interests. New England was becoming largely interested in manufactures, and needed a tariff of protection; but this she could not secure permanently, so long as the South and West had the preponderance in Congress. Southern interests demanded free trade ; and therefore, so long as slavery continued to extend, New England could not feel secure in her control of the national legislation. Abolition thus became an essential adjunct of New England policy, because of its being the irreconcilable enemy of the South.

We do not intend to be understood as saying that every man engaged in advancing abolitionism was doing so to promote the economical interests of New England. By no means. Each abolitionist had his own purposes to subserve—some purely philanthropic, others partly or wholly selfish. Abolitionists, generally, were not far-seeing men—they never have been so—they never have been able to foresee the results of their own measures ; they have, therefore, been the more easily controlled by the designing men who undertook to make them an agency for building up the interests of New England, by overwhelming in ruin her great antagonist, the South. But we must proceed.

To such an extent had the abolition agitation affected the public mind, in 1835, that General Jackson, then President of the United States, felt himself constrained to notice the progress of abolitionism in his annual message. The following extract from that document, will serve to show the apprehensions of danger to the Union, from the abolition movement, which he entertained, and will be an appropriate introduction to the discussions in Congress which followed :

"In connection with these provisions in relation to the Post Office Department, I must also invite your attention to the painful excitement produced in the South, by attempts to circulate through the mails inflammatory appeals addressed to the passions of the slaves, in prints, and in various sorts of publications, calculated to stimulate them to insurrection, and to produce all the horrors of a servile war.

"There is, doubtless, no respectable portion of our countrymen who can be so far misled as to feel any other sentiment than that of indignant regret at conduct so destructive of the harmony and peace of the country, and so repugnant to the principles of our national compact, and to the dictates of humanity and religion. Our happiness and prosperity essentially depend upon peace within our borders; and peace depends upon the maintenance, in good faith, of those compromises of the Constitution upon which the Union is founded.

"It is fortunate for the country that the good sense, and generous feeling, and the deep-rooted attachment of the people of the non-slaveholding States to the Union, and to their fellow-citizens of the same blood in the South, have given so strong and impressive a tone to the sentiments entertained against the proceedings of the misguided persons who have engaged in these unconstitutional and wicked attempts, and especially against the emissaries from foreign parts, who have dared to interfere in this matter, as to authorize the hope that those attempts will no longer be persisted in. But if these expressions of the public will shall not be sufficient to effect so desirable a result, not a doubt can be entertained that the non-slaveholding States, so far from countenancing the slightest interference with the constitutional rights of the South, will be prompt to exercise their authority in suppressing, as far as in them lies, whatever is calculated to produce this evil.

"In leaving the care of other branches of this interesting subject to the State authorities, to whom they properly belong, it is, nevertheless, proper for Congress to take such measures as will prevent the Post Office Department, which was designed to foster an amicable intercourse and correspondence between all the members of the confederacy, from being used as an instrument of an opposite character. The General Government, to which the trust is confided of preserving inviolate the relations created among the States by the Constitution, is especially bound to avoid in its own action anything that may disturb them. I would, therefore, call the especial attention of Congress to the subject, and respectfully suggest the propriety of passing such a law as will prohibit, under severe penalties, the circulation, in the Southern States, through the mail, of incendiary publications intended to instigate the slaves to insurrection." *

On the 16th of December, 1835, petitions were presented to the House, praying for the abolition of slavery in the District of Columbia. On motion to lay on the table, they were thus disposed of by a vote of 180 to 31. On the 18th of the same month, similar petitions were again presented; and at various subsequent periods they continued to pour in upon both Senate and House.

---

* Congressional Globe, vol. 3d, page 10, 1835.

A few extracts from the speeches of the members will serve to show what was then the sentiment in relation to this Northern interference with Southern rights.

MR. HAMMOND, of South Carolina, moved

"That the petitions be not received. The large majority by which the House had rejected a similar petition a few days ago, had been very gratifying to him, and no doubt would be to the whole South. . . . He was not disposed to go into the discussion of the question involved in the petitions; though, should it be urged, he would not shrink from it a hair's breadth; but he did think it due to the House and the country, to give at once the most decisive evidence of the sentiments entertained here upon this subject. He wished to put an end to these petitions. He could not sit there and submit to their being brought forward until the House had become callous to their consequences. He could not sit there and see the rights of the Southern people assaulted, day after day, by the ignorant fanatics from whom these memorials proceed."*

Mr. PIERCE, of New Hampshire, said:

. . . . "He was unwilling that any imputation should rest upon the North, in consequence of the misguided and fanatical zeal of a few—comparatively very few—who, however honest might have been their purposes, he believed had done incalculable mischief, and whose movements he knew received no more sanction among the great mass of the people of the North, than they did at the South.

"For one, said Mr. Pierce, while he would be the last to infringe upon any of the sacred reserved rights of the people, he was prepared to stamp with disapprobation, in the most express and unequivocal terms, the whole movement upon this subject. . . . . He felt confidence in asserting that among the people of the State which he had the honor, in part, to represent, there was not one in a hundred who did not entertain the most sacred regard for the rights of their Southren brethren—nay, not one in five hundred who would not have those rights protected at any and every hazard. There was not the slightest disposition to interfere with any rights secured by the Constitution, which binds together, and which he humbly hoped ever would bind together, this great and glorious confederacy as one family."†

---

* Congressional Globe, Dec. 1835, page 27.   † Ibid., page 33

Mr. SLADE, of Vermont, said:

"One of the objections he had heard strongly insisted on, was that abolition had a tendency to disturb the balance of the Constitution. He contended that the balance was disturbed on the other side by the gradual increase of slavery. It would not be long before the representation of the slave-holding States would far outweigh the proportions settled under the Constitution. And this was not through the relative increase of the white, but the black population. In the State of Virginia, the increase of the whites had been eighty-four, while that of the blacks had been one hundred and thirty-six; and in South Carolina the increase of the whites had been forty-four and a fraction, while that of the blacks had been ninety-four and a half per cent. This fact, he contended, would show that the progress of abolition was necessary to preserve the balance of the Constitution, or rather to restore it, for it had been already disturbed by the purchase of Louisiana." * (1)

Mr. MANN, of New York, said:

"The Union and the Constitution, sir, were the result of concession and compromise. The subject under debate formed one of the points. We agreed—we entered into the compact with our Southern brethren; and the question now presented by them to us—the real question (when the argument is pushed to the full extent) propounded to us of the North, is whether we will live up to the bargain we have made—to the compact and union we have entered into? For myself, for my constituents and friends, I answer, without hesitation or mental reservation, that under all circumstances and in every vicissitude, good or evil, we will—we will, though the Heavens fall." †(2)

Mr. CALHOUN, of South Carolina, said:

"He saw, in these petitions, that eleven of the States of the Union were grossly slandered, and no man could put his hand on his heart and say otherwise. They had refused to receive petitions because they implicated members of that body, and were they to receive petitions in which eleven of the States were deeply, basely, and maliciously slandered? Were they to put more reprobation on the

---

* Congressional Globe, Dec. 1835, page 49.   † Ibid., page 46.

slander of an individual member than on the slander of sovereign States?

"He demanded the question, because these memorials aimed at a violation of the Constitution. We have not the power, said he, under the Constitution, to interfere with the subject of slavery. He and his constituents understood this question. This was a preliminary abolition movement. These abolitionists moved first upon the District of Columbia, which was the weakest point, in order to operate afterward on the States; and he would resist them as firmly in this movement, as he would on the direct question of emancipation. He demanded the preliminary question as to receiving these petitions, because he was averse to an agitation which would sunder this Union. Sir, said he, we fear not these incendiary pamphlets in the South. The South was too well aware of what is due to itself, to permit the circulation of those pamphlets. It was agitation here that they feared, because it would compel the Southern press to discuss the question in the very presence of the slaves, who were induced to believe that there was a powerful party at the North ready to assist them. He objected to receiving these petitions, because the country was deeply agitated by them; because they were sundering the bonds which held this Union together. As a lover of the Union, he objected to receiving them; nay, they must cease, or the Southern people never can be satisfied. And how (asked Mr. C.) will you put a stop to them? By receiving these petitions, and laying them on the table? No, no! The abolitionists understand this too well. Nothing would stop them but a stern refusal; by closing the doors to them, and refusing to receive them." *

Mr. PRESTON, of South Carolina, said:

"They of the South had a right, under the Constitution, to demand some other action than the Government had pursued. He referred to the meetings held by abolitionists—the apostles they had sent out to preach their doctrines—the circulation of publications of every species, and their exciting character. All of them had seen these things, and he felt called upon to keep the South informed of them. They were calculated to spread terror throughout the South. Men's minds had already been disturbed there. The Government had been called upon to act upon them. They could not sit by, and see the

* Congressional Globe, January, 1836, page 77.

character of their constituents aspersed by ignorant, blood-thirsty fanatics. They were bound to appeal to the Government. For one, he did not fear an interference in the rights of the South. You cannot, said he, interfere with them, either in politics, in religion, in morals, or physical means. They were bound to defend, by all the means the God of nature had put into their power, against these incendiary attempts to wrap their land in flames, and to deluge it in blood. Sir, said he, they are filling our houses, our fields, and our hearths, with implacable murderers, and robbing us of our thousands! Sir, we demand repose! We insist that the Government shall say to us, in intelligible language, that you cannot legislate upon this subject—that you cannot receive the petitions of these hot-headed and cold-hearted fanatics—these men, women,* and children, who are waging a war of extermination against us. In this free government, said Mr. P., it may be impossible for the government authorities to stop them entirely; but, said he, we ask that Congress will distinctly and positively interfere between us and these fanatics, and that the General Government will not directly or indirectly be an agent in this system of destruction. I fear, unless it stands as an impassable barrier between these people and us, that the consequences will be terrible. We, in the South, exist under a bond of necessity which cannot be broken—our lives and our property are the ligaments that bind us together. Civil war was terrible—to the ratiocinations of the mind, it was dreadful. Interference must be direct or indirect. The people of the South demanded such action of Congress on these petitions, as would leave no possible doubt between them and this exciting subject. It was a matter on which there could be no difference of opinion. He abhorred the idea of mixing up politics with it. Their sole object was to protect their property and their lives. In a political point of view, it was extremely important to prevent agitation on this subject. He spoke of its bearings upon different sections of the country, and, said he, the overwhelming vortex of politics sweeps everything before it." †

Mr. BUCHANAN, of Pennsylvania, said :

"If any one principle of Constitutional law can, at this day, be considered as settled, it is, that Congress have no right, no power,

---

* Several of the petitions were signed by women.

† Congressional Globe, Jan. 1836, page 78.

over the question of slavery in the States where it exists. The property of the master in his slave existed in full force before the Federal Constitution was adopted. It was a subject which then belonged, as it still belongs, to the exclusive jurisdiction of the several States. These States, by the adoption of the Constitution, never yielded to the General Government any right to interfere with the question. It remains where it was previous to the establishment of our confederacy.

"The Constitution has, in the clearest terms, recognized the right of property in slaves. It prohibits any State into which a slave may have fled from passing any law to discharge him from slavery, and declares that he shall be delivered up by the authorities of such State to his master. Nay, more, it makes the existence of slavery the foundation of political power, by giving to those States within which it exists representatives in Congress not only in proportion to the whole number of free persons, but also in proportion to three-fifths of the number of slaves.

"An occasion very fortunately arose in the first Congress to settle this question forever. The Society for the Abolition of Slavery in Pennsylvania brought it before that Congress by a memorial, which was presented on the 11th day of February, 1790. After the subject had been discussed for several days, and after solemn deliberation, the House of Representatives, in Committee of the Whole, on the 23d day of March, 1790, resolved, 'That Congress have no authority to interfere in the emancipation of slaves, or in the treatment of them within any of the States; it remaining with the several States alone to provide any regulations therein, which humanity and true policy may require.'

"I have thought it would be proper to present this decision, which was made about a half century ago, distinctly to the view of the American people. The language of the resolution is clear, precise, and definite. It leaves the question where the Constitution left it, and where, so far as I am concerned, it ever shall remain. The Constitution of the United States never would have been called into existence—instead of the innumerable blessings which have flowed from our happy Union, we should have had anarchy, jealousy, and civil war among the sister republics of which our confederacy is composed—had not the free States abandoned all control over this question. For one, whatever may be my opinions upon the abstract question of slavery, and I am free to confess they are those of the people of Pennsylvania, I shall never attempt to violate this compact. The Union will be dissolved, and incalculable evils will arise from its ashes, the moment any attempt is seriously made by the free States in Congress.

"What, then, are the circumstances under which these memorials are now presented? A number of fanatics, led on by foreign incendiaries, have been scattering 'arrows, firebrands, and death,' throughout the southern States. The natural tendency of their publications is to produce dissatisfaction and revolt among the slaves, and to incite their wild passions to vengeance. All history, as well as the present condition of the slaves, proves that there can be no danger of the final result of a servile war. But, in the meantime, what dreadful scenes may be enacted, before such an insurrection, which would spare neither age nor sex, could be suppressed! What agony of mind must be suffered, especially by the gentler sex, in consequence of these publications! Many a mother clasps her infant to her bosom, when she retires to rest, under the dreadful apprehensions that she may be aroused from her slumbers by the savage yells of the slaves by whom she is surrounded. These are the work of the abolitionists. That their motives may be honest, I do not doubt; but their zeal is without knowledge. The history of the human race presents numerous examples of ignorant enthusiasts, the purity of whose intentions cannot be doubted, who have spread devastation and bloodshed over the face of the earth." *

Mr. BENTON, of Missouri, said:

"With respect to the petitioners, and those with whom they acted, he had no doubt but many of them were good people, aiming at benevolent objects, and endeavoring to ameliorate the condition of one part of the human race, without inflicting calamities on another part; but they were mistaken in their mode of proceeding, and so far from accomplishing any part of their object, the whole effect of their interposition was to aggravate the condition of those in whose behalf they were interfering. But there was another part, and he meant to speak of the abolitionists generally, as the body containing the part of which he spoke—there was another part, whom he could not qualify as good people seeking benevolent ends by mistaken means, but as incendiaries and agitators, with diabolical objects in

* Congressional Globe, January, 1836, page 78.

view, to be accomplished by wicked and deplorable means. He did not go into the proofs now to establish the correctness of his opinion of this latter class, but he presumed it would be admitted that every attempt to work upon the passions of the slaves, and to excite them to murder their owners, was a wicked and diabolical attempt, and the work of a midnight incendiary. Pictures of slave degradation and misery, and of the white man's luxury and cruelty, were attempts of this kind; for they were appeals to the vengeance of slaves, and not to the intelligence or reason of those who legislated for them. He, Mr. Benton, had had many pictures of this kind, as well as many diabolical publications, sent to him at St. Louis, during the past summer, the whole of which he had cast into the fire, and should not have thought of referring to the circumstance at this time, as displaying the incendiary part of the abolitionists, had he not, within these few days past, and while abolition petitions were pouring into the other end of the capital, received one of these pictures, the design of which could be nothing but mischief of the blackest dye. It was a print from an engraving, (and Mr. Benton exhibited it, and handed it to senators near him,) representing a large and spreading tree of liberty, beneath whose ample shade a slave owner was at one time luxuriously reposing, with slaves fanning him; at another, carried forth in a palanquin to view the half-naked laborers in the cotton-field, whose drivers, with whips, were scourging to the task. The print was evidently from the abolition mint, and came to him by some other conveyance than that of the mail, for there was no post-mark, or mark of any kind, to identify its origin, and to indicate its line of march. For what purpose could such a picture be intended, unless to inflame the passions of the slaves? and why engrave it, except to multiply copies for extensive distribution? But it was not pictures alone that operated on the passions of the slaves, but speeches, publications, petitions presented to Congress, and the whole machinery of abolition societies. None of these things went to the understandings of the slaves, but to their passions, all imperfectly understood, and inspiring vague hopes, and stimulating abortive and fatal insurrections. *

"Societies especially were the foundation of the greatest mischiefs. Whatever might be their objects, the slaves never did, and never can, understand them but in one way; as allies organized for action, and ready to march to their aid on the first signal of insurrection! It was thus that the massacre of San Domingo was made. The Society in

---

* The Nat. Turner slave insurrection in Virginia had taken place in 1831.

30

Paris, *Les Amis des Nois*, Friends of the Blacks, with its affiliated societies throughout France, and in London, made that massacre· And who composed that society? In the beginning it comprised the extremes of virtue and vice; it contained the best and the basest of human kind! Lafayette, and the Abbé Gregoire, those purest of philanthropists, and Marat and Anacharsis Clootz, those imps of hell in human shape. In the end, for all such societies run the same career of degeneration, the good men, disgusted with their associates, retired from the scene, and the wicked ruled at pleasure. Declamations against slavery, publications in gazettes, pictures, petitions to the Constituent Assembly, were the mode of proceeding; and the fish-women of Paris—he said it with humiliation, because American females had signed the petitions now before us—the fish-women of Paris, the very *poissardes* from the quays of the Seine, became the obstreperous champions of West India emancipation. The effect upon the French Island is known to the world; but what is not known to the world, or not sufficiently known to it, is that the same societies which wrapt in flames, and drenched in blood, the beautiful island which was then a garden and now a wilderness, were the means of exciting an insurrection on our own continent—in Louisiana—where a French slave population existed, and where the language of *Les Amis des Noirs* could be understood, and where their emissaries could glide. The knowledge of this event, Mr. Benton said, ought to be better known, both to show the danger of these societies, however distant, and though oceans may roll between them and their victims, and the fate of the slaves who may be excited to insurrection by then on any part of the American continent. He would read the notice of the event from the work of Mr. Charles Guyarre, lately elected by his native State to a seat on this floor, and whose resignation of that honor he sincerely regretted, and particularly for the cause which occasioned it, and which abstracted talent from a station it would have adorned. Mr. Benton read from the work, ' *Essai Historique Sur la Louisiane :* ' ' The white population of Louisiana was not the only part of the population that was agitated by the French Revolution. The blacks, encouraged, without doubt, by the success which their race had obtained in San Domingo, dreamed of liberty, and sought to shake off the yoke. The insurrection was planned at Pointe Coupeé, which was then an isolated parish, and of which the number of slaves was considerable. The conspiracy took birth on the plantation of Mr. Julien Poydras, a rich planter, who was then traveling in the United States, and spread itself rapidly throughout the parish. The death of all the whites was resolved. Happily, the conspirators could not agree upon the day for the massacre, and from this disagreement resulted a quarrel, which led to the discovery of the plot. The militia of the parish immediately took up arms, and the Baron de Carondelet caused them to be supported by the troops of the line. It was resolved to arrest, and to punish the principal conspirators. The slaves opposed it; but they were quickly dispersed, with the loss of twenty of their number killed on the spot. Fifty of the insurgents were condemned to death. Sixteen were executed in different parts of the parish; the rest were put on board a galley, and hung, at intervals, all along the river, as far as New Orleans, (a distance of one hundred and fifty miles.) The severity of the chastisement intimidated the blacks, and all returned to perfect order.'

"Resuming his remarks, Mr. Benton said, he had read this passage to show that our white population had a right to dread, nay, were bound to dread, the mischievous influence of these societies, even when an ocean intervened, and, much more, when they stood upon the same hemisphere, and within the bosom of the same country. He also read it to show the miserable fate of their victims, and to warn all that were good and virtuous—all that were honest, but mistaken— in the *three hundred and fifty* affiliated societies vaunted by the individuals who style themselves their executive committee, and who date from the commercial emporium of this Union their high manifesto against the President—to warn them at once to secede from associations which, whatever may be their designs, can have no other effect than to revive in the southern States the tragedy, not of San Domingo, but of the Parish of Pointe Coupeé.

"Mr. Benton went on to say, that these societies had already perpetrated more mischief than the joint remainder of all their lives, spent in prayers of contrition, and in works of retribution, could ever atone for. They had thrown the state of the emancipation question fifty years back. They had subjected every traveler and every emigrant from the non-slaveholding States to be received with coldness, and viewed with suspicion and jealousy, in the slaveholding States. . .

"Having said thus much of the abolition societies in the non-slaveholding States, Mr. Benton turned with pride and exultation to a different theme—the conduct of the great body of the people in all these States. Before he saw that conduct, and while the black question, like a portentous cloud, was gathering and darkening on the

north-eastern horizon, he trembled, not for the South, but for the
Union.   He feared that he saw the fatal work of dissolution about to
begin, and the bonds of this glorious confederacy about to snap; but
the conduct of the great body of the people in all the non-slaveholding States quickly dispelled that fear, and in its place planted deep
the strongest assurance of harmony and indivisibility of the Union
which he had felt for many years.   Their conduct was above all
praise, above all thanks, above all gratitude.   They had chased off
the foreign emissaries, silenced the gabbling tongues of female dupes,
and dispersed the assemblages, whether fanatical, visionary, or incendiary, of all that congregated to preach against evils which afflicted
others, not them, and to propose remedies to aggravate the disease
which they pretended to cure.   They had acted with a noble spirit.
They had exerted a vigor beyond all law.   They· had obeyed the enactments, not of the statute-book, but of the heart; and while that
spirit was in the heart, he cared nothing for laws written in a book.
He would rely upon that spirit to complete the work it has begun—to
dry up these societies—to separate the mistaken philanthropist from
the reckless fanatic and the wicked incendiary, and put an end to publications and petitions which, whatever may be their design, can have
no other effect than to impede the object which they invoke, and to
aggravate the evil which they deplore.

"Turning to the immediate question before the Senate, that of the
rejection of the petition, Mr. Benton said his wish was to give that vote
which would have the greatest effect in putting down these societies." *

Mr. GRUNDY, of Tennessee, said:

"He thought he was not mistaken when he declared that the moment the citizens of the non-slaveholding States should, in violation
of the Constitution, lay their hands on the property of the slaveholding States, the citizens of the latter would instantly consider the Union
dissolved, and the Government at an end.   They could no longer con-
fide in a government which, instead of protecting, plundered them of
their property.   The right of property in slaves is guaranteed to the
citizens of the States where slavery exists by the Constitution as fully as
the right to any other species of property; and should the non-slaveholding States at any time violate these guarantees in so important a particular
as this, it would be such a departure from the great principles of the com-

---

* Congressional Globe, Jan. 1836, pages 79 and 80.

pact, that the injured party would at once be absolved from all the obligations it imposes on them. It would be impossible tamely to submit to it. The citizens of the slaveholding States, therefore, entreat those of the non-slaveholding States to step forward and put down this spirit of abolition, before it produces the ruin of this Government. . . . . These abolitionists reside among them. There they have to be met. There the battle has to be fought. They are beyond our reach. If a straggler comes among us propagating his insurrectionary and incendiary doctrines, he is sent away with an admonition which will prevent his return. This is done in defense of ourselves. No other way is known by which the mischief growing out of this plan of abolition can be prevented. Therefore, as we have no power to reach these abolitionists, as we can not prevent their incendiary publications, we ask our brethren of the North and East to persevere in their efforts in putting down the labors of these men, which must terminate, unless they are arrested, in the destruction of ourselves and families. If a man, whether madman, fanatic, or worse than either, shall be seen approaching a neighbor's house with a lighted torch, to consume it, ought not all good men to arrest him and prevent the mischief? It therefore seems, said Mr. Grundy, that too much is not asked, when we say to our friends at the North that it is their duty to adopt such means as will prevent the threatened danger.* (3)

Mr. PINCKNEY, of South Carolina, in reply to inquiries made of him as a member of the committee on the abolition petitions, said :

" That the whole number of memorials presented to Congress this session, amounted to 176; that they came from ten States, embracing an aggregate population of nearly 8,000,000; that the whole number of signatures was about 34,000 ; and that of those, more than two-fifths were females. He thought these facts ought to be known. The people of the South ought to know everything respecting these memorials. They could see the immense disproportion between the millions of freemen who are determined to maintain their constitutional obligations to their southern brethren, and the band of incendiary agitators who would trample on all laws, human and divine, in the relentless prosecution of their diabolical designs. He believed that there never was a healthier tone of sentiment in the non-slave-

* Congressional Globe, March, 1836, page 215.

holding States, in reference to the domestic institutions of the South, than at this moment. There was, unquestionably, abundant reason for vigilance and caution in relation to the fanatics; but there was also abundant reason to rely on the enlightened patriotism of the non-slaveholding States. There are great moral causes at work in favor of the South. We should trust their efficacy, and watch their progress. The people of the non-slaveholding States are alive to the dangers connected with this question, and they are generously fighting the battle of the South. They should be encouraged by confidence and gratitude, not repelled by vituperation and suspicion. . . The South had nothing now to fear, except from those who are determined to continue the agitation of slavery for the purpose of excitement. Abolitionism has attained its hight; it has begun to go down, and will soon disappear entirely, if we do not fan the flame ourselves, and will only allow our friends in the non-slaveholding States to fight the fanatics in their own way, and not trammel them in their operations by mixing up extraneous and unnecessary questions with the subject of abolition."*

Passing on to 1843 and 1844, up to which time the agitation of the subject of slavery was continued in Congress, we find the demands of the northern petitioners had been extended. They now required not only the abolition of slavery in the District of Columbia, but the prohibition of the sale of slaves by the citizens of one State to those of another; and also that Texas should not be admitted into the Union as a slave State. We have purposely avoided copying the discussions on the numerous points raised in the course of the controversy, and have aimed at affording a true conception of the views held on the main question.

On the 31st January, 1844, Hon. Andrew Johnson, of Tennessee, took the floor, and made a speech upon the subject. We quote from him, because no one can doubt the sincerity of the man, who, when the conflict came, and he was surrounded on all hands by enemies, still adhered to the flag of the Union, and fought under its folds in defense of the Constitution—willingly offering his life for its preservation.

---

* Congressional Globe, May 19, 1836, pages 386, 387.

Mr. JOHNSON, of Tennessee, said :

"He had a few plain inquiries to make of the abolitionists of the country, and their organs in this House. One was, if they had it in their power to abolish slavery now, were they prepared to turn over two million of negroes loose upon the country, to become a terror and burden to society, producing disaffection between them and their former masters, finally to be fanned into a flame, wearing into a servile war, resulting in the entire extirpation of the race in the United States, besides shedding much of the white man's blood? But as you have no right to abolish slavery in the United States, or anywhere else, are you prepared to tax the owners near ten hundred millions of dollars, and then give it back to them for their negroes, in the shape of purchase money? This would be legalized robbery. Are you prepared to tax the slaveholder and the non-slaveholder indiscriminately, ten hundred millions of dollars, to buy slaves, and send them to Africa, or anywhere else? This would be plundering one portion of the community to remunerate another. These inquiries are made for the purpose of bringing the minds of those wild enthusiasts to bear upon the immense importance of this subject. . . .

"Perhaps it will be considered uncharitable in me to come to the conclusion I have upon this subject; but the conviction fixes itself upon my mind irresistibly, and I will speak my sentiments, let the consequences be what they may. I do believe, and have believed for some time, that there is a deliberate design, on the part of some gentlemen, to effect, if possible, a dissolution of the Union. But when we of the South, who represent the interests of the slave States, contend for our rights, gentlemen say, 'O! you are too much excited—too much heated; your passion outruns your judgment; anything that you may say is not entitled to so much weight as that which proceeds from our calm and sober judgment.' Excitement! What is it which occasions that excitement? Is not the treatment which this question receives a sufficient cause for excitement? It becomes, in the hands of gentlemen on this floor, a question of dissolution—of Union or no Union—a question in which eleven States of this Union are vitally interested; States which possess upward of $1,000,000,000 of property in slaves. Yet when you are striking a blow which is to destroy that amount of property at once, to expel or exclude twenty-one of the ninety-three representatives of the eleven slave States from this House—nearly one-fourth of their entire dele-

gation—and thereby destroying the great compromise of the Constitution, agreed upon by the sages and patriots of the Revolution—
we are told, if we exhibit any feeling on this subject, it is southern
heat. O! no; we must not speak upon the subject, unless we are
perfectly calm and passionless. Let me tell agitators, the more they
press this question, the greater will be the excitement. It is worse
than nonsense to talk of making a calm, deliberate appeal to them;
it will not do; but when we come to examine the subject, I am
forced to the conclusion that there is a deliberate design to dissolve
the Union. (4.)

"Mr. Johnson here referred to an opinion formerly expressed by
Mr. J. Q. Adams's father, and read from the fourth volume of Mr.
Jefferson's Works, as follows : ' December the 13th, 1803. The Rev.
Mr. Coffin, of New England, who is now here soliciting donations for
a college in Greene county, Tennessee, tells me that when he first
determined to engage in this enterprise, he wrote a paper recommendatory of the enterprise, which he meant to get signed by clergymen, and a similar one for persons in a civil character, at the head
of which he wished Mr. Adams to put his name—he being the President of the United States, and the application going only for his
name, and not for a donation. Mr. Adams, after reading the paper,
and considering, said he saw no possibility of continuing the union
of the States ; that their dissolution must necessarily take place;
that he, therefore, saw no propriety in recommending to New England men to promote a literary institution in the South; that it was,
in fact, giving strength to those who were to be their enemies ; and,
therefore, would have nothing to do with it.'.

"He, Mr. Johnson, said he had referred to this merely as a starting
point at which to date the opposition of New England men to the
Union of the States, and their hostility to the institutions of the
South. He passed on to the Hartford Convention, spoke of its opposition to Mr. Madison's administration, asking a dissolution of the
Union, throwing every obstacle in the way of a successful prosecution of the war—Massachusetts even refusing to let her militia go
beyond the chartered limits of the State, to meet the invading foe.
Now, in this House, the same spirit of opposition is followed up by
J. Q. Adams, endeavoring to destroy the Union and the institutions
of the South, by the introduction of abolition petitions, and resolutions from the legislature of Massachusetts, asking an alteration of
the Constitution that amounts to a dismemberment of the northern

and southern States. Mr. J. Q. Adams's son is now in the legislature of Massachusetts, engaged in making reports, and procuring the passage of disorganizing resolutions, both endeavoring to split the Union in twain, thereby proving the father and grandfather to be true prophets. Mr. Johnson next referred to the Haverhill petition; also, one from the State of Ohio, asking a dissolution of the Union. He then read extracts from Mr. Adams's speech, made at the extra session of the 27th Congress, upon the 21st rule, prohibiting the reception of abolition petitions, to-wit:

" ' . . . He would say that, if the free portion of this Union were called upon to expend their blood and treasure to support that cause which had the curse and the displeasure of the Almighty upon it, he would say that this same Congress would sanction an expenditure of blood and of treasure, for that cause itself would come within the constitutional action of Congress; that there would be no longer any pretension that Congress had not the right to interfere with the institutions of the South, inasmuch as the very fact of the people of a free portion of the Union marching to the support of the masters, would be an interference with those institutions; and that in the event of a war, (the result of which no man could tell,) the treaty-making power become to be equivalent to universal emancipation. This was what he had then said, and he would add to it now, that, in his opinion, if the decision of this House, taken two days ago, should be reversed, and a rule established that the House would receive no petition on this subject, the people North would be, *ipse facto,* absolved from all obligation to obey any call of Congress.'

" Mr. Johnson asked, what the paragraph just read, meant; what effect was it calculated to have upon the abolitionists of the North and the slaves of the South? It is a stimulant to the one, a lure thrown out to the other. Is it not saying to the abolitionist of the North, Persist in your fiendish purpose; to the incendiary, who is standing with his torch ready lighted, prepared only for the destruction of the South—Proceed; touch the match; wrap the dwellings of your masters in flames; produce a servile war; make it necessary, for the preservation of your masters, to call upon the non-slaveholding States for assistance, 'and under the treaty-making power' you all shall be emancipated? Gracious God! are we prepared for scenes like these? are we prepared to surrender our homes and our firesides? are we prepared to see our fields, that now, in due season, yield luxuriant crops, relapse into their original state, or be converted

into fields of carnage? are we prepared to see the black hands of the
negro reeking in the blood of the white man? are we prepared to see
innocent women and children, virtue and beauty, all fall a helpless
prey? are we prepared to see the land that gave a brother birth,
drenched with a brother's blood? in fine, are we prepared to see
peace, prosperity, contentment, and happiness, converted into discord,
desolation, cries the most heart-rending, lamentations, producing, (to
use the language of the poet,) shrieks

> ————" 'So wild, so loud, so clear,
> Even listening angels stooped from heaven to hear;'

and yet to be calm and deliberate?

"Mr. Johnson said he wished to call the attention of the South
to a single sentence in a letter recently written by Mr. Adams to the
abolitionists of Pittsburgh, to-wit:

"'On the subject of abolition, abolition societies, anti-slavery societies, or the liberty party, I have never been a member of any of them.
But in opposition to slavery, I go as far as any of these; my sentiments, I believe, very nearly accord with theirs. That slavery will
be abolished in this country, and throughout the world, I firmly believe. Whether it shall be done peaceably, or by blood, God only
knows; but it shall be accomplished, I have no doubt; and, by whatever way, I say, let it come.'

"In the sentence he had just read, Mr. Adams says he is no abolitionist; but in opposition to slavery he goes as far as any of them;
and if the emancipation of the negroes in the South has to be effected
by the shedding of blood, he says, 'let it come?' Can the South be
mistaken as to the meaning of language like this? Is it not time to
be on the alert? Is it not time they were roused from their apathy?
He said this was a question that the South should unite upon: the
whole ninety-three members from the eleven slaveholding States
should come up on this question as a band of brothers, joining in one
fraternal hug; heart responding to heart; turning their faces toward
heaven, and swearing, by their altars and their God, that they will
all sink in the dust together before they will yield the great compromise contained in the Constitution of their fathers.

"In a speech made by the gentleman from Massachusetts, a short
time ago, he says he thinks the consummation of the Christian religion
will not take place until the emancipation of the negroes is effected.
And then, I suppose, we have the commencement of that glorious mil-

lennium which has been so long prophesied. I wish that day would come; but I do not wish to attain it by means of bloodshed and the sacrifice of thousands of lives. If I thought it would come in my day and generation, I would now be found standing on tip-toe, stretching my ken to the utmost tension, anxiously endeavoring to descry in the eastern horizon the first streaks of the glorious morning. How gratifying it would be to me to have the power to proclaim that the voice of the turtle was heard in the land; that the winter was past and gone; that the lion and the lamb had lain down together; when all could unite in that heart-felt chorus of glory to God in the highest, and peace on earth, and good will among men. But while thus indulging this pleasing illusion, while thus enjoying this happy aberration of mind, (at this moment Mr. Johnson turned his face to Mr. Adams,) what ill omen is that obtruding itself so abruptly upon our view? What evil genius is this hovering around this hall? Is it some demon, or a mortal man? What frightful specter do I behold, sending forth such unnatural sounds, predicting disunion, dissevered States, and the shedding of human blood! Frightful vision, this!

> " ' Black he stands as night;
> Fierce as ten furies ; terrible as hell ;
> And shakes a dreadful dart.' " *

Mr. GIDDINGS, of Ohio, said :

" . . . . I therefore lay it down as one of the principles on which our Federal Constitution was based, that each of the several States should retain to themselves and their people, the entire power over slavery which they previously enjoyed. In saying this, it is not my intention to deny the doctrine advanced by the venerable member from Massachusetts, Mr. Adams, ' that in case of war, when the existence of our government is threatened, we may then avail ourselves of that right of self-preservation which is based upon the law of nature ; ' and, if necessary to the public safety, may release any portion, or all, of the slaves in any of the States. It is a power that lies behind all Constitutional provisions, and is consequent upon a state of war only, but has no application in time of peace. It is, I believe, well understood by military men ; it was practiced by General Jackson, General Gaines, and General Jessup, and I believe by General Scott, while commanding our armies in the South. They did not hesitate to

---

* Appendix to Congressional Globe, Jan. 1844, page 97

sever the relation of master and slave, wherever the public good demanded it. In doing that, they merely exercised the power which is always attendant upon a state of war, and which is denied by few, if any. It therefore forms no exception to the doctrine which I have asserted, that each of the several States now holds and enjoys the same power over slavery, within its own territory, that it enjoyed under the old confederation; that Virginia, and each of the slave States, now holds her slaves as independently of the other States and of the Federal Government, as she does of Mexico, or of other foreign powers; that the Congress of the United States possesses no more right than the Parliament of Great Britain has to interfere with that institution in Virginia, or any other slave State. On this point, I think Southern men will agree with me. Indeed, I understand this to be the doctrine for which they contend, and on which, so far as I am acquainted with the views entertained by Northern men, there is an entire concurrence of opinion. . . . .

"I regard it as a perfectly clear proposition—one that is not to be doubted or denied—that slavery is entirely the creature of municipal law. It is unknown to natural law, and can only exist in direct violation of it.* In Ohio, our people go where they please, for the reason that no municipal law forbids the exercise of their natural right of locomotion. . . . . Not so with the five thousand slaves who are held in bondage here. They possess neither of those rights; and why not? Because the municipal law has forbidden them to exercise those rights which God bestowed upon them. . . . . Repeal those laws, and those vested rights would become divested. . . . . Let us throw as much obscurity as we can around this subject, it will remain perfectly clear to every intelligent mind, that this right of property and the whole power of the master over his slave is derived from statute law, which may be repealed at the pleasure of the legislature. . . . . But the repeal of those laws is objected to, on the ground that the abolition of slavery here will be likely to affect that institution in the adjoining States. That objection I regard as a strong argument in favor of its immediate extirpation from the District. I deny that we are under the least conceivable obligation to continue slavery here, in order that it may be prolonged in the States." . . . .

"Mr. Rayner, of North Carolina, said he wished to inquire whether

---

* The reader is referred to the argument of Charles O'Connor, and others, on this point, in the preceding section.

the gentleman from Ohio believes the Decalogue to be of divine origin?"

"Mr. Giddings. I do, but I would not if it sanctioned slavery."*

On May 21, 1844, upon the question of the annexation of Texas, Mr. GIDDINGS said:

"Now, Mr. Chairman, with all due respect to the legal talents and constitutional learning of those gentlemen, I may be permitted to deny that any guarantee in regard to slavery ever found a place in the Federal Constitution. . . . Sir, the idea that the Constitution contained a guarantee of slavery is an impeachment both of the sincerity and judgment of the framers of the charter of American liberty. . . . It was, therefore, a most wise and salutary object with the framers of the Constitution, to withhold all power from the Federal Government in regard to slavery, except that which has reference to fugitives, on which I have already remarked. The safety of the South and of the North consists in this wise and salutary absence of all power over slavery. It was foreseen by the framers of the Constitution, that the subject was of such a delicate character, that the Federal Government could not interfere with it in any form, without endangering the existence of the Union. I fully understand the excuse of Messrs. Upshur and Calhoun for attempting this unconstitutional support of slavery. They say that the continuance of slavery in the South would be endangered by the abolition of that institution in Texas. I answer, that the continuance of slavery in Texas will endanger the freedom of Ohio. . . . We have passed more than a half century under our present Constitution, and now the President assumes to himself the power of making slavery a national, instead of a State institution, and of extending the power, and influence, and funds, of the Federal Government to its support, and to a piratical commerce in mankind. In order to effect this unholy and nefarious plan, he attempts to bring into this Union a foreign slaveholding government, the effect of which is to place the balance of political power in the hands of foreign slaveholders, who have no feelings or principles, either moral, religious, or political, in common with the great body of the free States, and to transfer the descendants of our New England pilgrims to the political control and dominion of Texans and foreigners. Nor do his violations of the

---

* Appendix to Congressional Globe, Feb. 1844, pages 654, 655.

Constitution end here; he has gone farther, and brought our army
into the field in hostile attitude to a friendly power, with whom we
are on terms of perfect amity, and has sent a fleet to insult and
provoke that government to hostilities. In short, sir, he has, of his
own acts, by his secret orders, without the consent of the people of
the nation, or their representatives, and without deigning even to con
sult his constitutional advisers, suddenly plunged us into a war for
the openly avowed object and purpose of extending and perpetuating slavery. These profligate acts—these usurpations of power—
these violations of the Constitution—can be characterized by no
term of milder signification than treason—treason against the rights
of the people of this nation—treason against the Constitution, and
treason against humanity itself. I feel it my duty to declare it such
in the presence of the House, and of the country. . . .

"But we shall not surrender this Union, sanctioned and sanctified
by a half century of national prosperity, in order to try a new Union,
and that, too, with slaveholding Texas! Sir, every schoolboy must
see, that to form a new union with any foreign power, would be,
ipse facto, a dissolution of our present Union. Now I would say to
an imbecile President, and a demented cabinet, that they have not
the power to form a union between our people of the free States and
Texas. If such a union be ever formed, it will be by the voluntary
acts of the people of our States and those of Texas. The President
and his cabinet may enter into as many treaties as they please, and
make such stipulations as they please, and form such unions for
themselves as they please—we shall adhere to our present Union.
If they wish to leave this Union and go to Texas, I, for one, will bid
them 'God speed.' And if any of our southern sister States are
desirous of leaving our present Union, to form a new compact with
Texas, let them say so with generous frankness. But if northern
States prefer adhering to our present Union, and refuse to follow them
into such new confederacy, do not let them attempt to charge us with
dissolving the Union. I regret that any northern man should speak
of dissolving the Union, if Texas be annexed. Such expressions are
an abuse of language. The act of uniting with Texas would itself
be the dissolution; and refusal to unite with that government would
be to maintain the present Union. . . . I wish to call the attention of the committee to the expediency of the proposed annexation,
provided it were possible to effect it. The people of New England
are emphatically the moral, political, and religious antipodes of those

who reside in Texas. They are not homogeneous. Their interests are as widely separated as are their geographical locations, and can never be made to unite ! Their habits and their morals are distinct, as are their local situations. *The protective policy of New England can never be reconciled to the free-trade principles of Texas.** The love of universal liberty, so prevalent in New England, is wholly incompatible with Texan slavery. No act of Congress, favoring the interests or the views of New England, would be acceptable to the people of Texas. So, on the other hand, whatever law Congress may pass favoring the interests of Texas, will be unacceptable to the people of New England." †

On the question of the annexation of Texas, Mr. BUCHANAN, of Pennsylvania, said :

"Now, sir, annex Texas to the United States, and we shall have within the limits of our broad confederacy all the favored cotton-growing regions of the earth. England will then forever remain dependent upon us for the raw material of her greatest manufacture ; and an army of one hundred thousand men would not be so great a security for preserving the peace between the two nations as this dependence. . . . .

" It has been strenuously contended that the acquisition of Texas would be a violation of the Constitution of the United States ; and that no new State can be admitted into the Union, unless it formed part of our territory in 1789, when that Constitution was adopted.‡ On this point I shall be very brief. Mr. Van Buren, in his Texas letter, has demonstrated this objection to be wholly unfounded. The language of the Constitution is broad and general, embracing in its terms all new States, whether these be composed of foreign territory or not. It declares that ' new States may be admitted by Congress into the Union.' . . . It has been said, however, that, admitting this construction of the Constitution to be correct, yet, as Texas is an independent State, and not, like Louisiana and Florida, a terri-torial dependence of a foreign power, it would be a violation of the

* Here, in the sentence we have italicized, we have the true secret of the opposition of New England to the extension of slavery. This institution demands *free trade*—New England wants *protection*.

† Appendix to Congressional Globe, May, 1844, pages 706, 707.

‡ This was Mr. Chase's "Silver Pitcher" doctrine.

Constitution to ratify this treaty. And this in the nineteenth century, and in the American Senate! We had the honor, forsooth, to accept the cession of territories from Napoleon Bonaparte and the King of Spain, without ever consulting the wishes of the people whom they ceded; and yet we have not the power to accept such a cession from the sovereign people themselves of an independent State! I shall not waste time upon such an argument. It would prove that if ever (which God forbid) any of the States of this Union should shoot madly from their sphere, and establish an independent government, we would possess no constitutional power, upon their own earnest entreaty, to restore them to their ancient position." *

On the question of the annexation of Texas, Mr. WOODBURY, of New Hampshire, said:

"If I understand the substance of all the objections to the ratification of the present treaty, whether expressed in resolutions or debate, it is this: First, that the Government of the United States does not possess the Constitutional right or power to purchase Texas, and admit her people into the Union. Next, that the present Government of Texas, alone, has not the right or competency to make such a cession of her territory and sovereignty. And, finally, that it is not our duty at present to complete the cession, even were the right on both sides clear. . . . . The pretense that such a purchase and admission into the Union are unconstitutional, is the only plausible justification for the otherwise treacherous or fanatical cry of DISUNION, which so often deafens our ears. That cry originated on an occasion almost identical with this, when the act for admitting Louisiana as a State, in 1811, was pending.

"In the debate on that occasion, a member from Massachusetts overflowed with such threats, till he was called to order for his violence, and escaped censure on an appeal from the Speaker's decision against him, only from a conviction, in some of his opponents, that his threats would prove harmless. It was then the memorable saying was first uttered, which is now ringing again in our ears from the same class of politicians, and from the same State, but with less point and elegance in these degenerate days. Mr. Quincy said:

"'If this bill passes, it is my deliberate opinion that it is virtually a dissolution of the Union—that it will free the States from their

* Appendix to Congressional Globe, June, 1844, page 722, where Mr. Buchanan enters very ably into the refutation of abolition views of this question.

moral obligations; and that, as it will then be the right of all, so it will be the duty of some, definitely to prepare for separation—amicably if they can, forcibly if they must.' *

"It is true that the madness of faction can threaten disunion on the smallest, as well as greatest occasions, and may at times venture on it, unless deterred by a dread of the halter; but it is equally true that there is no more real occasion or justification for it now, than there was when so much vaporing passed off harmlessly in 1803 and 1811 about Louisiana, or than there was in the purchase of Florida, in 1819, or the admission of Missouri, in 1822. If those purchases and admissions were constitutional, so are these; and in order to allay the renewed excitement on this point, (honest with many, I have no doubt,) the patience of the Senate is asked a few minutes."

Mr. Woodbury proceeded with the discussion in a very statesmanlike manner, and with arguments that are conclusive, but we can not quote them at large. A few quotations only can be given:

"Every government that ever yet existed," said Mr. W., "possesses a competency to add to its territory. It ceases to have the functions of an independent nation, if it cannot, by treaty or discovery, obtain new boundaries for convenience, or new lands for culture, or new ports for commerce; and, as before suggested, it is stripped of the national function of acquiring territory, when assailed by unjust war, and holding it either for indemnity, or profit, or security. And if we can acquire it, reason, as well as the words of the Constitution, requires us, in due time, to make States out of it, and admit them into the Union.—(160.) Story says, in a note to this page, that the *Hartford Convention* proposed to prevent such admission, unless by a vote of two-thirds of both Houses; and by a report in that body, indirectly denied the authority to admit States or any territory without our original limits. But this doctrine has slept with that convention since, it is believed, till revived by Mr. Adams, in his Texas speech, in 1838, in Congress, and his political address in New York, in 1839.

---

* See National Intelligencer, Jan. 19, 1819, and Lambut on Rules, 74th page. Mr. Woodbury, in this connection, in a foot-note, takes notice of a whig anti-annexation meeting in Worcester, Massachusetts, which adopted a resolution "to separate the free States from the others, if annexation prevailed." He further alluded to the manifesto of Mr. Adams, Mr. Giddings, and others, copied on a succeeding page, declaring that annexation "would be identical with dissolution of the Union."

" How little ground exists for such doctrine, even in the opinion of the greatest constitutional lawyer of his own party, may be seen by looking to 3d Story, pages 160, 161: ' Sec. 1283. The more recent acquisition of Florida, which has been universally approved, or acquiesced in by all the States, can be maintained only on the same principle, and furnishes a striking illustration of the truth, that constitutions of government require a liberal construction to effect their objects; and that a narrow interpretation of their powers, however it may suit the views of speculative philosophers, or the accidental interests of political parties, is incompatible with the permanent interest of the State, and subversive of the great ends of all government, the safety and independence of the people.'

" This construction does not, as the senator from New Jersey argues, prevent the *blessings of liberty* from being enjoyed by the posterity of our fathers as they designed. Because there is enough at the bounteous table for all that posterity and any new associates. All such can participate with them in that freedom as they do in the air, water, and sun, without loss to either, and without exclusiveness and misanthropy.

"In truth, our whole history serves to illustrate the wisdom, on general as well as constitutional principles, of expanding our limits with the vast increase of our population and wealth. Such expansion prevents many of the evils of too dense a population, and secures the predominance of the safe, virtuous and republican pursuit of agriculture. It is said that we have a Sparta, and let us adorn it. But is there never to be an escape from the infant shell? nor any enlargement of the shell itself, to suit the growth of the animal within? Is our Sparta to be confined forever to a garden spot, or single plantation? a single city? or a few barren acres, as in Greece, with iron only for money, *black broth* only for food, and our *sons taught stealing* as an accomplishment—instead of spreading over half a continent, improving the sciences and the whole arts of the civilized world, covering remotest oceans with our commerce, and helping to spread abroad and at home superior education and a purer religion? Thank God! the scales fell from our eyes on this subject more than a quarter of a century ago, when Louisiana was purchased; and instead of trying to replace them, if we are able to preserve Oregon—gained both by discovery and purchase—and to recover Texas, we can, in another half century, not only gain, as has been done, double our States, and nearly quadruple our wealth, numbers, and power, but adorn, improve, and secure forever all the fair inheritance with which we are blessed.

" . . But these, and many formal exceptions, seem scarcely suitable to the magnitude of the subject, and the high duties and national honor and interests which are at issue. One of the most prominent of these interests is the importance of Texas to the United States, for security to the commerce of the West and Southwest, through the mouth of the Mississippi river. The freedom of that commerce was a topic which, as long ago as under the old confederation, agitated the whole country. It then introduced the first geographical division of parties between the South and the North, in which the latter, unfortunately, was quite as strenuous in resisting efforts and sacrifices to obtain that freedom, as it is now in resisting those to secure it, after having been obtained.

" A few circumstances in that age indicate strongly prejudices and contests not very unlike the present one.

" Mr. Gorham, of Massachusetts, 'avowed his opinion that the shutting the Mississippi would be advantageous to the Atlantic States, and wished to see it shut.' *

" But Virginia extended over Kentucky, and claimed all the Northwest; while North Carolina also crossed the Alleghenies into Tennessee. Hence, the South, at that early day, became the champions of western interests, no less than southern ones.

" And though Mr. Aymer, apparently concurring with Gorham, 'thought the encouragement of the western country was suicide on the part of the old States,† and though the vote of seven States was at first procured to proceed in the negotiations with Spain, without insisting on the free navigation of the Mississippi,'—yet Mr. Jefferson wrote that the navigation of the Mississippi we must have.‡ And Mr. Jay at last admitted our right to it was good.§ And the old Congress, before breaking up, in September, 1788, solemnly

" 'Resolved, That the free navigation of the river Mississippi is a clear and essential right of the United States, and that the same ought to be considered and supported as such.' ||

" In the Convention, while forming the Constitution, Governeur Morris frankly stated that ' the fisheries ' and the ' Mississippi ' security to them, were ' the two great objects of the Union.' ¶

" The whole question, as a national one, was then settled. That was the embryo of the present crisis. The duty to secure became

---

* Madison Papers, 609.   † 3 Madison Papers, page 1466.
‡ 1 Jefferson's Life, page 433.   § 4 Secret Journal, 451.
|| 4 Secret Journal, 453, Sept. 16, 1778.   ¶ 3 Madison Papers, 1523.

as imperative as had been the duty to obtain. A million and a half of square miles of territory, and what are now nine millions of people on the waters of the Mississippi and her tributaries, were foreseen, and were to be shielded in peace as in war; and tranquillity to their institutions, no less than safety to their property of every kind, were, in advance, solemnly guaranteed, and were never to be neglected. On this implied pledge your public lands have been sold there and settled. . . . . It is no new vagary, that, when our fathers, in 1786, finally resolved on their rights to the free navigation of the Mississippi, they, also, in the same act, and by the same dauntless spirit, meant to enforce that right till successful, and to defend it, also, when once acknowledged, as they afterward did in many an Indian war, as well as on the bloody fields of New Orleans. . . . .

"The treaty presents, at the same moment, a fortunate occasion to do that, as well as to enforce better the guarantees of the Constitution to promote '*domestic tranquillity*' in the South and Southwest, no less than the West and East. The property and domestic institutions of the former, however different from those at the North, were secured as amply under the old confederation as those of any other region; so are they by the present Constitution, so are they by all our legislative and judicial decisions; and so must they continue to be till the compromises of the Constitution are wantonly violated, or the Union dissolved. Hence the losses or capture of their property in slaves have often been indemnified; their escape into other States has been redressed by a surrender of them; and the *domestic tranquillity* designed for all the States, as set out in the preamble of the Constitution as one paramount object for its adoption, has again and again been sought to be secured, in times of excitement and peril, precisely as they are likely to be by the ratification of this treaty. . . . The South stood shoulder to shoulder with us in the Revolution, with this property and these institutions. They came into the Union with them on equal terms; they have so remained for half a century, and so must they continue, till injustice or fanaticism or treason violate all the sacred compromises of all we hold dear.

"The annexation has been opposed as not a duty, because inclining the balance of political power in our system too much in favor of the West and South. But the same course of reasoning would strip us of all our great domain on the Pacific Ocean—a country never to be surrendered while an American whaler visits its waters, or an

American emigrant chooses to fish, hunt, or plant on the banks of the Columbia. . . . It is resisted by many for the reason that slavery exists in Texas. That is an institution, to be sure, which most people born at the North are, like myself, averse to. But those who respect the Constitution and the Union, remember that it is an institution which our parent country, before the Revolution, forced upon both the North and South; which, after being more deeply interwoven through the social and political systems of the latter, the rest of the States did not hesitate to confederate with her in fighting the battles of independence; nor to counsel with her heroes, patriots, and statesmen, in forming the present Constitution, nor to associate with them in carrying out its great destinies; nor in guaranteeing their property and rights in common with the rest, then and during the half century since, in peace and war, and in weal or wo." *

REMARKS ON THE FOREGOING DISCUSSIONS.

(1) Mr. SLADE frankly avowed the principle lying at the foundation of the political agitation of slavery, to which allusion has been made in the introductory remarks to the present section. He said: "One of the objections he had heard strongly insisted on, was that abolition had a tendency to disturb the balance of the Constitution. He contended that the balance was disturbed on the other side by the gradual increase of slavery. It would not be long before the representation of the slaveholding States would far outweigh the proportions settled under the Constitution. . . . . This fact, he contended, would show that the progress of abolition was necessary to preserve the balance of the Constitution, or rather to restore it, for it had been already disturbed by the purchase of Louisiana."

The great object of politicians and statesmen, in all their movements, is to protect themselves and constituents against the increase of any element that may control, adversely to their interests, the legislation of the country. The New England people could only prosper as manufacturers, and required a tariff on foreign imports that would afford them protection. The South could only flourish as a planting region, and demanded free trade, so that

---

* Appendix to Congressional Globe, June, 1844, page 760, etc.

its productions might enter freely into the ports of all foreign nations. This placed New England and the South in a position of antagonism. The acquisition of Louisiana had unsettled the balances previously existing between the North and South, and given a preponderance to the planting States. The Louisiana territory had been subdivided into three States, instead of one, when Mr. Slade sounded the alarm as to the danger of acquiring additional territory by the admission of Texas. Mr. Slade, therefore, believed that "to preserve the balance of the Constitution, or rather to restore it," the successful prosecution of the abolition enterprise had become necessary. And why? The West, in its rapid growth, now held the balance of power. The South had shown it more favors than the East, and needed its support against the adverse action of eastern statesmen. While in the colonial condition, the South had enjoyed a free commercial intercourse with the British possessions, carrying its own products in its own vessels, and thus keeping in advance of the East in the extent of its foreign trade. The treaty of Mr. Jay with Great Britain, which came up for discussion in the Congress of 1795 and 1796, by its 12th Article, not only limited the size of American vessels, trading with the West Indies, to seventy tons and under, but gave up the carriage, in our own shipping, of cotton, sugar, indigo, and coffee.* The whole carrying trade of American cotton being thus placed in the hands of Great Britain, she could forbid all shipments of that article in her own vessels, and thus prevent American cotton from being exported to England.† Subsequently, Mr. Gorham, of Massachusetts, with others, had opposed the opening of the navigation of the Mississippi to the West, as an act suicidal to the Atlantic States. But the obnoxious feature of Jay's treaty was not confirmed; and, through the influence of Mr. Jefferson, the Mississippi question was settled favorably to the West and South; ‡ and by this means these two sections became intimately united in a bond cemented by their mutual interests.

---

* Benton's Abridgement of Debates in Congress, page 709.

† References elsewhere show that we had then only sent out our first exports, whereas the West Indies were then exporting largely.

‡ See Mr. Woodbury's speech, quoted in this section.

This result was the necessary consequence of the peculiar position occupied by the West, in her then infantile condition. In the absence of efficient means of transportation to the East, the West had long been dependent upon the Mississippi for the disposal of its surplus products, excepting the live stock, which could travel on foot to an eastern market. By this means the West found its interests identified with the South, and felt inclined to act with it in political measures. To interrupt this growing harmony, and dissever the West from the South, was long the policy of the East. The " American System," which was to create a home market, by the increase of manufactures, for the agricultural products of the North at large, had not received the universal acceptance of the people, as had been anticipated. To fail in controlling the vote of the West, was to leave the South in the possession of the National legislation, and to place the East in a position of great uncertainty as to the congressional protection it could secure for its manufactures. The *physical* obstacles forbidding the products of the West from being transported East seemed insurmountable; the only hope of success, therefore, in binding these two distant sections together, lay in the use of *moral* means. The opportunity of applying this remedy was at hand. The Churches at the North had been busied for many years in creating an anti-slavery sentiment among the people; and as a similar movement in Great Britain had secured West India emancipation, it was believed that equal success might attend the abolition movement in this country. But let that result as it might, the " progress of abolition," according to Mr. Slade, would tend "to preserve the balance of the Constitution." And how? If abolition should be successful in effecting emancipation, then the South would be prostrated at the feet of New England, and could no longer extend its cultivation westward; but, failing in this, the East, by means of the hatred of slavery that could be engendered at the West, would at least array the people of that section against the South, and thus put a check upon the progress of free trade legislation. Thus, in either case, New England would be the gainer, as she could then control the action of Congress.

But these two purposes were not the only measures contemplated by New England men, to secure to themselves the sectional advantages they wished to possess. A dissolution of the Union, as a last resort, was relied upon as a certain means of aggrandisement to their portion of the country.

This idea of " dissolution" was of early birth in New England. It broke forth from the classic lips of Mr. Quincy, of Boston, as early as 1811, in the Congress of the United States, when the admission of Louisiana was pending. His language, as will be seen by a reference to Mr. Woodbury's remarks, was clear and unequivocal, that its admission would virtually be a dissolution of the Union, as it would free the northern States from their moral obligations, and justify them in separating from the South, even by force, if necessary.

The right of secession was not held by Mr. Quincy alone. As early as 1839, Mr. J. Q. Adams, in an address before the New York Historical Society, gave the following deliberate opinion, not in the heat of debate, but as formed in the quiet of his study at home :

" Nations acknowledge no judge between them upon earth, and their Governments, from necessity, must, in their intercourse with each other, decide when the failure of one party to a contract to perform its obligations absolves the other from the reciprocal fulfillment of his own. But this last of earthly powers is not necessary to the freedom or independence of States connected together by the immediate action of the people of whom they consist. To the people alone is there reserved, as well the dissolving as the constituent power, and that power can be exercised by them only under the tie of conscience, binding them to the retributive justice of heaven.

" With these qualifications, we may admit the same right as vested in the people of every State in the Union, with reference to the General Government, which was exercised by the people of the United Colonies with reference to the supreme head of the British Empire, of which they formed a part; and, under these limitations, *have the people of each State in the Union a right to secede from the confederated Union itself.*

" Thus stands the RIGHT. But the indissoluble link of union between the people of the several States of this confederated nation is,

after all, not in the *right*, but in the *heart*.   If the day should ever
come (may heaven avert it) when the affections of the people of these
States shall be alienated from each other; when the fraternal spirit
shall give way to cold indifference, or collisions of interest shall fester
into hatred, the bands of political association will not long hold together parties no longer attracted by the magnetism of conciliated
interests and kindly sympathies; and far better will it be for the people of the *disunited* States to part in friendship from each other, than
to be held together by constraint.   Then will be the time for reverting
to the precedent, which occurred at the formation and adoption of the
Constitution, to form again a more perfect Union, by dissolving that
which could no longer bind, and to leave the separated parts to be re-
united by the law of political gravitation, to the center." *

But Mr. Adams was not without illustrious authority to sustain him in his opinion in relation to the right of secession on
the part of States.   The Virginia and Kentucky resolutions, so
familiar to public men, having been received unfavorably by many
of the other States, were referred to Mr. Madison for further consideration and defense.   In reporting upon them, he said:

"It appears to your committee to be a plain principle, founded in
common sense, illustrated by common practice, and essential to the
nature of compacts, that, where resort can be had to no tribunal
superior to the authority of the parties, *the parties themselves must be
the rightful judges, in the last resort, whether the bargain made has been
pursued or violated.*   The Constitution of the United States was formed
by the sanction of the States, given by each in its sovereign capacity.
It adds to the stability and dignity, as well as to the authority, of the
Constitution, that it rests on this legitimate and solid foundation.   The
States, then, being the parties to the constitutional compact, and in
their sovereign capacity, it follows, of necessity, that there can be no
tribunal above their authority, to decide, in the last resort, whether
the compact made by them be violated, and consequently, that, *as the
parties to it, they must themselves decide, in the last resort, such questions
as may be of sufficient magnitude to require their interposition.*"   .   .   .
"The resolution has, accordingly, guarded against any misapprehension of its object, by expressly requiring, for such an interposition,
'the case of a deliberate, palpable, and dangerous breach of the Con-

* Quoted in the speech of Mr. Benjamin, in U. S. Senate, Dec. 31, 1860.

stitution, by the exercise of powers not granted by it.' It must be a case not of a light and transient nature, but of a nature dangerous to the great purposes for which the Constitution was established."

These threats of secession, and these claims of a constitutional right in a State to secede, coming, as they did, in the first instance, from Northern statesmen, were well calculated, when taken in connection with the hostility existing in the East to the doctrines of free trade, to lead the South to the conclusion that a peaceful separation of the States might be effected, or rather, that it was really desired by the North. The Eastern representative men had so often advocated this right of secession, and its necessity, under certain contingencies, that, we have little doubt, the South, in its recent movements, anticipated no trouble in effecting a dissolution of the Union. Indeed, up to a very recent date, the right of secession by a State, or States, seems to have been held by prominent men on both sides of Mason and Dixon's line.

But this doctrine, often as it has been advocated, never received the assent of the people at large. It was the imputation of secession principles that secured the political damnation of Mr. Webster ;* and that will now damn every politician that has avowed the sentiment. The question is not whether, in a strict construction of the Constitution, the right of secession may not exist ; but the fact is, that the people, almost *en masse*, cannot be brought to contemplate favorably, even for a moment, the idea that the glorious Union, secured by the bravery and the blood of their fathers, shall ever be destroyed.

(2) Mr. MANN spoke the common sentiment of the North, at large, when he pledged himself and his constituents to the fulfillment of all the compromises of the Constitution. Mr. Calhoun and Mr. Preston, though making a strong statement of the alarm produced by the abolitionists at the South, did not present an exaggerated picture of the state of public feeling, in their section

---

* Mr. Webster was charged with having acted as a secretary of the Hartford Convention, and for this reason, perhaps, more than all others, his friends were always unable to secure for him the nomination to the Presidency. It was constantly urged, as a reason against him, that he could not succeed before the people, because of his connection with that band of supposed traitors to the Union.

of the Union, at that moment. The wholesale butchery attending emancipation in St. Domingo was then fresh in the recollections of the people; and the blood that was shed in the Virginia negro insurrection was scarcely yet dry upon her soil. Under such circumstances, none but fanatics, imbued with the rancorous spirit of demons, would have persevered in their attempts to fill the South with incendiary documents. Mr. Buchanan, in presenting the decision of Congress, of 1790, denying any power over slavery by the national legislature, showed conclusively, that the abolitionists, by interfering with slavery in the South, were acting in open violation of the compromises of the Constitution, as interpreted by those who framed it. To suppress the circulation of the incendiary publications of the abolitionists was no more an' interference with the rights of the citizen under the administration of General Jackson, than the prohibition of the circulation of secession documents is unconstitutional under that of Mr. Lincoln. Mr. Benton, in characterizing as diabolical the documents put in circulation by the abolitionists, made no unjustifiable charge against their authors. His notice of the causes that led to the San Domingo massacre, will serve a good purpose, as casting some new light upon that horrible tragedy.

(3) The appeal of Mr. Grundy to the people of the North, to arrest the progress of abolitionism, before its bitter fruits should come to maturity, was a reasonable request. But there was no legal means at the command of conservative men, by which they could interpose, directly, in the suppression of that movement. One thing only could have been done : the friends of the Union should have risen in their might, and protested against the doctrines and practices of the abolitionists. They should have spoken out, in thunder tones, the true sentiments of their hearts on the question of their constitutional obligations. But instead of adopting this course, they quietly suffered the fanatical abolitionists to assume a dictatorial position, both in religion and politics, until, emboldened by non-resistance, they imagined the field was won, and they were conquerors.

It was the great error of the conservative men at the North, that they allowed the enemies of the Constitution to give tone to public sentiment abroad, so as to create the impression that the free States had become thoroughly abolitionized. They are now paying the penalty of their remissness in duty; and when they succeed in restoring the Union, then wo to the fanatic, in future, who shall again dare to plot its overthrow.

Mr. PINCKNEY presents such facts as prove conclusively that the abolitionists were vastly in the minority, at the date of these discussions. But 34,000 persons out of 8,000,000 of population had attached their names to the abolition petitions. Mr. Pinckney was also right in another point. If the South had left the question of the suppression of abolition with the citizens of the North, it would never have attained the gigantic proportions it afterward assumed. But instead of leaving the matter to the North, every few months presented some new case of injury inflicted upon Northern citizens at the South, on account of their supposed abolition sentiments and designs. This, whether a deserved punishment or not, served as fresh fuel for the agitators at the North to feed their expiring fires; and had it not been for this, the abolitionists could never have maintained their ground. But there were conservative men at the South who disapproved of the mob violence used against Northern citizens; and so largely were they in the majority, that if they had used their influence, they could have prevented the scenes that occurred.* The conservative men of the South, therefore, were as much to blame as those of the North; nay, they were more to blame, because, had it not been for the cases of violence there, we could have acted with greater efficiency here. They tied our hands, and then complained of us for not fighting their battles.

---

* The case of the agents for the sale of " COTTON IS KING," at Enter rise, Mississippi, early in the year 1860, is one in point. The two young men were arrested, stripped of their clothing, and the tar and cotton standing ready to be applied, while eighty copies of the work were being burned as an abolition incendiary publication. The conservative men had sufficient courage to interpose, and by placing the agents in prison, under the plea of further investigation, thus rescued them from the mob. After eight weeks' imprisonment, they were tried, acquitted, and discharged—it having been determined that the object of the work was to demonstrate the absolute necessity of preserving the Union, as essential to the prosperity and happiness of both sections, and not designed to promote abolition and disunion.

(4) The charge made by Mr. Johnson, of Tennessee, that there existed a deliberate design, on the part of Northern men, to effect a dissolution of the Union, will startle some of our readers on account of its boldness. That such designs existed somewhere, no one can now doubt. But of the section of the Union in which they originated, few perhaps entertained a correct opinion; the facts now drawn out, therefore, must greatly interest the public, and will serve to disabuse the minds of many, in relation to the views they may have entertained heretofore. The opinion of the elder Adams, in 1803—based upon the Louisiana question, then agitated—" that he saw no possibility of continuing the Union of the States, and that their dissolution must necessarily take place," is referred to by Mr. Johnson only as a starting point from which to date the opposition of New England to the Union of the States, and their hostility to the institutions of the South. This hostility he found manifesting itself in the Hartford Convention, in the Halls of Congress, by the presentation of abolition petitions, and in the speeches of Mr. J. Q. Adams, in which he, (Mr. Adams,) not only announced his belief that the refusal to receive the abolition petitions would absolve the North from all obligations to the South, but, in case of war, the treaty-making power could declare emancipation.

This power to abolish slavery, in time of war, seems never to have been lost sight of by the abolitionists; and could they but bring on a collision of arms, either *civil* or *servile*, their mission would be accomplished. Reader, keep this in mind, and turn back to the quotations from the speeches of Mr. Giddings, which follow those of Mr. Johnson. While admitting that, under the Constitution, the North has no right to interfere with slavery, Mr. Giddings seems to dwell with evident satisfaction upon the fact that, in time of war, slavery could be swept away, as chaff before the wind, in defiance of the Constitution. But he goes further, and insists upon emancipation, by Congress, in the District, notwithstanding that to have a community of free negroes in such a central point as Washington might endanger the safety of slavery in the adjoining States. Nay, more, he urged emancipation in the District for that very reason; thus justifying the accomplishment of an object by indirect means, which can not be done constitutionally by direct means.

Again, in discussing the question of the annexation of Texas, Mr. Giddings denounces the project as nefarious, because it would " place the balance of political power in the hands of foreign slave-holders," and " transfer the descendants of our New England pil-grims to the political control of Texans and foreigners." Here we have a repetition of the fears entertained by Mr. Slade, that the balance of the Constitution would settle down to the injury of the people of New England, and the measures that would ef-fect this, Mr. Giddings pronounces treason. And why? " The protective policy of New England," says he, " can never be recon-ciled to the free-trade principles of Texas," and, therefore, " the act of uniting with Texas would itself be the dissolution " of the Union—*would be treason to New England.* That is to say, if New England could not have a protective tariff, in consequence of the extension of slavery, she would dissolve the Union.

But Mr. Giddings goes farther, and expresses his willingness that the President and his Cabinet, as well as our southern sister States, who were desirous of doing so, might leave this Union to form a new compact with Texas; and he would bid them God speed.

These views of Mr. Giddings fall in with the general opinions entertained by New England politicians at that day. During the preceding Session of Congress, March 3, 1843, a manifesto against the annexation of Texas was issued by the members whose names appear below, Mr. Giddings being one of the num-ber. A few extracts will show its true character, and the objects aimed at by its signers. In speaking of the annexation of Texas, they say :

" That a large portion of the country interested in the continuance of domestic slavery and the slave trade in these United States, have solemnly and unalterably determined *that it shall be speedily carried into execution,* and that by this admission of a new slave Territory and slave States, *the undue ascendency of the slaveholding power in the Gov-ernment shall be secured and riveted beyond redemption.* . . . . The same references will show, very conclusively, that the *particular objects* of this new acquisition of slave territory were *the perpetuation of slavery and the continued ascendency of the slave power.* . . . None can be so blind *now* as not to know that the real design and object of the South is to ' ADD NEW WEIGHT TO HER END OF THE LEVER.' . . We hold that there is not only ' no political necessity' for it, 'no advantages to be derived from it,' but that there is no constitutional power delegated to any department of the National Government to authorize it : that no act of Congress or treaty for annexation can impose the least obligation upon the several States of this Union to submit to such an unwarrantable act, or to receive into their family and fraternity such *misbegotten and illegitimate progeny.* We hesitate not to say that *annexation*, effected by any act or proceeding of the Federal Government, or any of its departments, WOULD BE IDENTICAL WITH DISSOLUTION. It would be a violation of our national compact, its objects, designs, and the great elementary principles which entered into its formation of a character so deep and fundamental, and would be an attempt to eternize an institution and a power of nature so unjust in themselves, so injurious to the interests, and abhorrent to the feelings of the people of the free States, as, in our opinion, *not only inevitably to result in a dissolution of the Union,* BUT FULLY TO JUSTIFY IT ; and we not only assert that the people of the free States ' ought not to submit to it ;' but we say, with confidence, THEY WOULD NOT SUBMIT TO IT."*

This was signed by the following abolition members of Congress :

JOHN QUINCY ADAMS,	NATHANIEL B. BORDEN,
SETH M. GATES,	THOMAS C. CHITTENDEN,
WM. SLADE,	JOHN MATTOCKS,
WM. B. CALHOUN,	CHRISTOPHER MORGAN,
JOSHUA R. GIDDINGS,	JOSHUA M. HOWARD,
SHERLOCK J. ANDREWS,	VICTORY BIRDSEYE.

Reader, what think you of this, when taken in connection with all the preceding declarations of Northern men which have been quoted? Were there treasonable designs toward the Constitution here ?

But we have said that the abolition controversy, in the hands of the few who aimed at controlling national events, was used as

---

* See Niles' Register, May 13, 1843, pp. 174, 175.

an element for the promotion of sectional interests. This was true of the South as well as of the East. After what has been presented in demonstration of the truth that it has been used for this purpose at the East, let us turn a moment to the South, and here we shall not multiply testimony, as no one doubts that the struggle of the southern States has been maintained to secure the balance of power in their own favor, that they might, under the guarantees of the Constitution, be able to protect their property in slaves.

Mr. Wise, in his speech on the Texas question, January 26, 1842, sums up the Southern view of the subject thus briefly:

"True, if Iowa be added on the one side, Florida will be added on the other. But there the equation must stop. Let one more northern State be admitted, and the equilibrium is gone—gone forever. The *balance of interests* is gone—the *safe-guard* of American property—of the American Constitution—of the American Union, vanished into thin air. *This must be the inevitable result*, unless, *by a treaty with Mexico*, THE SOUTH CAN ADD MORE WEIGHT TO HER END OF THE LEVER! *Let the South stop at the Sabine*, (the eastern boundary of Texas,) while the North may spread unchecked beyond the Rocky Mountains, AND THE SOUTHERN SCALE MUST KICK THE BEAM."*

Nothing can be clearer to the comprehension of intelligent men than that the war waged by New England against the South has been prosecuted for the purpose of sustaining her own sectional interests, and that the crusade against slavery has been only a secondary consideration, and employed as a means of accomplishing the real object in view. On the other hand, it is equally plain, that the South have resisted the aggressions of the North from motives of a similar nature. Both have been influenced by sectional interests; both have equally struggled to maintain the balance of power in their own hands. The North began the warfare, and the South accepted the challenge. The West, springing into existence with giant strength, was inclined to fight upon the side of her foster-mother, the South. Abolition came, with its foetid

---

* Niles' Register, May 13, 1843, p. 174, where it is quoted in the manifesto of Mr. Adams and his associates.

breath, to poison the atmosphere, and, under the influence of the temporary delirium produced, to array her on the side of the East. The question at issue, substantially, was, whether New England should multiply her spindles, or the South extend its slavery; and, as involved in the issue, whether the West should have a broadly extending market for its products, by the extension of cotton culture in the southwest, or be shut up to the meager demand created by .the parsimonious stomachs of New England. The opposition to the admission of Texas, if successful, would limit slavery to the States where it already existed. The natural increase of the slave population, under these circumstances, would soon be such as to render their labor unproductive to the planter, in consequence of their over-crowded condition; and his inability to make money from their labor would compel him to emancipate them, and thus the natural market for the products of the western farmer be ruined forever. That the West took this view of the question of securing Texas to the Union, is amply demonstrated by the eagerness with which her sons rushed to its rescue when Mexico threatened its subjugation.

The Legislature of Mississippi, during the agitation of the question of annexing Texas, gave an expression of opinion which may be taken as representing that of the South generally. It said:

" But we hasten to suggest the importance of the annexation of Texas to this Republic on grounds somewhat local in their complexion, but of an import infinitely grave and interesting to the people who inhabit the southern portion of this confederacy, where it is known that a species of domestic slavery is tolerated and protected by law, whose existence is prohibited by the legal regulations of other States of this confederacy; which system of slavery is held by all who are familiarly acquainted with its practical effects, *to be of highly beneficial influence to the country* within whose limits it is permitted to exist.

" The committee feel authorized to say, that this system is cherished by our constituents as the *very palladium of their prosperity and happiness;* and, whatever ignorant fanatics may elsewhere conjecture, the committee are fully assured, upon the most diligent observation and reflection on the subject, that *the South does not possess within her lim-*

its a blessing with which the affections of her people are so closely entwined, and so completely enfibered, and whose value is more highly appreciated than that which we are now considering. . . .

" *The northern States have no interests of their own* which require any *special* safeguards for their defense, save only their domestic manufactures; and God knows they have already received protection from Government on a most liberal scale; under which encouragement they have improved and flourished beyond example. *The South has very peculiar interests to preserve*—interests already violently assailed and boldly threatened.

"*Your committee are fully persuaded that this protection to her best interest will be afforded by the annexation of Texas; an equipoise of influence in the halls of Congress will be secured, which will furnish us a permanent guarantee of protection.*" *

It will be observed here, that the action of the South was not so much influenced by hostility to the tariff policy of New England, as it was by the existing necessity of protecting itself against the interference of the fanatics of the North with the institution of slavery. That there was extreme danger, every Southern man fully believed; and how could that belief be otherwise, when, as early as March, 1854, such language as the following was uttered on the floor of Congress? Mr. GIDDINGS said:

"Sir, I would intimidate no one; but I tell you there is a spirit at the North which will set at defiance all the low and unworthy machinations of this Executive, and of the minions of its power. When the contest shall come, when the thunder shall roll, and the lightning flash; when the slaves shall rise in the South; when, in imitation of the Cuban bondmen, the Southern slaves of the South shall feel that they are men; when they feel the stirring emotions of immortality, and recognize the stirring truth that they are men, and entitled to the rights which God has bestowed upon them; when the slaves shall feel that, and when the masters shall turn pale and tremble; when their dwellings shall smoke, and dismay sit on each countenance, then, sir, I do not say, 'We will laugh at your calamity, and mock when your fear cometh;' but I do say, when that time shall come, the lovers of our race will stand forth and exert the legitimate powers of this

---

* Niles' Register, May 13, 1843, as quoted in manifesto of Messrs. Adams, Giddings, etc., pages 173, 174.

Government for freedom. We shall then have constitutional power to act for the good of our country, and do justice to the slave.

"Then we will strike off the shackles from the limbs of the slaves. That will be a period when this Government will have power to act between slavery and freedom, and when it can make peace by giving freedom to the slaves. And let me tell you, Mr. Speaker, that the time hastens. It is rolling forward. The President is exerting a power that will hasten it, though not intended by him. I hail it as I do the approaching dawn of that political and moral millennium which I am well assured will come upon the world." *

We shall not pursue this subject farther than to make one more quotation, which, when taken in connection with what is said and quoted in the preceding pages, will throw a flood of light upon the schemes of the New England agitators. The *New York Anti-slavery Standard,* June 21, 1856, made the following revelation as to the office performed by the abolitionists, and the designs they had in view:

"The Whig party, five years ago in power, and with a reasonable prospect of maintaining it, now dispersed, is demolished to powder. . . . . The abolitionists saw that this must come to pass; but they did not dream of its accomplishing itself so soon. . . . . That the national parties should, sooner or later, divide on the only real matter of dispute existing in the country, was inevitable. . . . . But the lines are now drawn, and the hosts are encamped over against each other. The attempt to keep up a delusive alliance with natural enemies has been abandoned.

"The abolitionists have been telling these things in the ears of the people for a quarter of a century. *They have had a double part in what has come to pass, both by preparing the minds of the people of the North, and by compelling the people of the South to the very atrocities which have startled the North into attention.*† Nothing but the madness which ushers in destruction, and the pride which goes before a fall, on the part of the slaveholders, could have roused the sluggish North from its comfortable dreams of wealth, and made it put itself even into a posture of resistance. . . . . It is long since this paper took the ground that the first thing, though by no means the

---

* Political Text-Book, p. 23.
† The sentence we have italicised is an important declaration.

only thing needful, was the formation of sectional parties—of parties distinctly Northern and Southern, and, of necessity, slavery and anti-slavery. We rejoice that our eyes behold the day of that beginning of the end." *

Here we have a choice revelation! The office-holding abolitionists had declared that a *servile* or *civil* war, or both combined, would afford them an opportunity for abolishing slavery, irrespective of constitutional obligations to the contrary ; and had rejoiced at the thought that they could see the wished-for day approaching. On this ground they had taken their stand, and were only awaiting the sounding of the war-trumpet to hasten to the execution of their purpose. On the other hand, the abolition editors, clergymen, and civilians, after having educated the North up to this point, as they supposed, were perseveringly engaged in attempting, first, to promote servile insurrections among the slaves, and, second, in provoking the people of the South to the perpetration of the atrocities which would excite the North to resistance, and thus bring on the terrible collision of arms which would usher in the moral millennium of Mr. Giddings! A slave insurrection, or a rebellion, would equally promote their abolition schemes. Was not Mr. Johnson right in charging that there was a deliberate design, on the part of the abolitionists of the North, to dissolve the Union? We have it here confessed; and the scheme was to goad on the South to acts of resistance against the aggressions of the abolitionists, and then, when the collision came, and they had a sectional Executive, the abolition of slavery could be effected by a single dash of his pen. They have succeeded in the first, but, thank God, they have failed in the last.

But we shall pass on, and before completing our remarks on this topic, we must present the views of numerous individuals, so as to show the wide spread disaffection to the Union which prevailed at the North, and contributed so efficiently to the production of our present national calamities.

---

* Political Text-Book, p. 18.

SECTION III.—OPINIONS OF INDIVIDUALS, ETC., RELATING TO THE SUBJECT OF SLAVERY, AS ILLUSTRATING THE ABOLITION MOVEMENT.

As before stated, we are not preparing a connected history of the abolition movement, but presenting such facts as will serve to illustrate its character and objects. In addition to the productions of the political abolitionists, and the debates in Congress, we now turn to such of the leading incidents and opinions of individuals, or public assemblies connected with this fanatical crusade, as may best serve still further to illustrate its inner life.

At the opening of Pennsylvania Hall, Philadelphia, in 1838, a leading abolition lady, who had been recently married, and whose bridal attendants were composed of one half whites, and the other half blacks, offered the following resolutions, which were adopted:

"*Resolved*, That the prejudice against color is the very spirit of slavery, sinful in those who indulge it; and is the fire which is consuming the happiness and energies of the free people of color.

"That it is, therefore, the duty of the abolitionists to identify themselves with the oppressed Americans, by sitting with them in places of worship, by appearing with them in our streets, by giving them our countenance in steamboats and stages, by visiting them at their homes, and encouraging them to visit us, receiving them as we do our white fellow-citizens." * (1)

Among the letters received by the committee having charge of the proceedings connected with the opening of the Hall above referred to, is one from Hon. Thaddeus Stevens, of Pennsylvania, dated May 5, 1838, which reads as follows:

"*Gentlemen*:—I have delayed answering yours until this time, that I might be able to decide with certainty whether I could comply with your invitation to be present at the opening of the Pennsylvania Hall for the free discussion of liberty and equality of civil rights, and the evil of slavery.

"I regret that I can not be with you on that occasion. I know no spectacle which it would give me greater pleasure to witness, than

---

* Washington Globe, Extra, Sept., 1840, p. 203.

a dedication of a temple of liberty. Your objects should meet with the approbation of every free man. It will meet the approbation of every man who respects the rights of others as much as he loves his own. Interest, fashion, false religion, and tyranny may triumph for a while, and rob a man of his inalienable rights; but the people can not always be deceived, and will not always be oppressed."*

The Legislature of Ohio, during its session of 1840, passed a resolution, two only voting in the negative, that slavery is an institution recognized by the Constitution; and another, declaring that "the unlawful, unwise, and unconstitutional interference of the fanatical abolitionists of the North with the domestic institutions of the southern States was highly criminal."† That was then the sentiment of Ohio, and is still its sentiment, if fairly expressed.

On the 25th of February, 1850, Mr. Giddings, of Ohio, presented two petitions from citizens of Delaware and Pennsylvania, praying Congress, without delay, to devise and propose "some plan for the immediate, peaceful dissolution of the Union."

Mr. Webster suggested that there should have been a preamble to the petition in these words :—

"Gentlemen, members of Congress :— Whereas, at the commencement of the session you, and each of you, took your solemn oaths, in the presence of God and the holy evangelists, that you would support the Constitution of the United States, now, therefore, we pray you to take immediate steps to break up the Union, and overthrow the Constitution of the United States as soon as you can. And, as in duty bound, we will ever pray."

On January 16, 1855, Rev. H. W. BEECHER, in a lecture, in New York, on the subject of cutting the North from the South, said :

"All attempts at evasion, at adjourning, at concealing, and compromising, are in vain. The reason of our long agitation is not, that ministers will meddle with improper themes, that parties are disregardful of their country's interest. These are symptoms only, not the disease; the effects, not the causes.

* Washington Globe, Extra, October, 1840, p. 315.
† Niles' Register, February 8, 1840.

"Two great powers, that will not live together, are in our midst, and tugging at each other's throats. They will search each other out, though you separate them a hundred times. And if by an insane blindness you shall contrive to put off the issue, and send this unsettled dispute down to your children, it will go down, gathering volume and strength at every step, to waste and desolate their heritage. Let it be settled now. Clear the place. Bring in the champions. Let them put their lances in rest for the charge. Sound the trumpet, and God save the right!"*

At a public meeting held in his church, to promote emigration to Kansas, the Rev. H. W. Beecher made the following remarks, as reported in the *N. Y. Evening Post*:

"He believed that the Sharp rifle was truly moral agency, and there was more moral power in one of those instruments, so far as the slaveholders of Kansas were concerned, than in a hundred Bibles. You might just as well," said he, "read the Bible to buffaloes, as to those fellows who follow Atchinson and Stringfellow; but they have a supreme respect for the logic that is embodied in Sharp's rifles. The Bible is addressed to the conscience; but when you address it to them it has no effect—there is no conscience there. Though he was a peace man, he had the greatest regard for Sharp's rifles, and for that pluck that induced those New England men to use them." † (2)

SIMEON BROWN, Esq., of Massachusetts, the Free Soil candidate for Lieutenant-Governor, gave a statement, while canvassing the State, of the political objects in view by his party, as follows:

"The object to be accomplished is this: That the free States shall take possession of the Government by their united votes. Minor interests, and old party affiliations and prejudices must be forgotten. We have the power in number; our strength is in union." ‡

Mr. BURLINGAME, in one of his speeches, said:

"If asked to state specially what he would do, he would answer: - . . He would have judges who believe in a higher law, and an anti-slavery Constitution, and an anti-slavery Bible, and an anti-slavery God! Having thus denationalized slavery, he would not menace it in the States where it exists; but would say to the States, it is your

---

* Political Text-Book, p. 19.   † Ibid., p. 20.   ‡ Ibid.

local institution — hug it to your bosom until it destroys you. You must let our freedom alone. [Applause.] If you but touch the hem of the garment of freedom, we will trample you to the earth. [Loud applause.] . . . In conclusion, he expressed the hope that soon the time might come when the sun would not rise on a master, nor set on a slave." *

Rev. ANDREW FOSS, of New Hampshire, at the American Anti-slavery Society meeting at New York, May, 1857, said:

"If the angel Gabriel had done what their fathers did, he would be a scoundrel for it. Their fathers placed within the Constitution a provision for the rendition of fugitive slaves, and therein did a wicked thing. . . . Where slavery and freedom are put in the one nation, there must be a fight—there must be an explosion, just as if fire and powder were brought together. There never was an hour when this blasphemous and infamous government should be made, and now the hour was to be prayed for when that disgrace to humanity should be dashed to pieces forever." †

Rev. B. O. FROTHINGHAM, of New Jersey, at the American Anti-slavery Society meeting, New York, May, 1857, said:

"They demanded justice for the slave at any price—of Constitution, of Union, of country. This was the principle of the anti-slavery association. It was it which urged their next demand—the immediate emancipation of the slave—for the same reason as they would demand of a person pursuing a vicious course of drunkenness, gambling, or debauchery, that he should desist from it at once, at any cost of physical pain. Immediate emancipation presented no financial or political difficulty. He believed that this Union effectually prevented them from advancing in the least degree the work of the slave's redemption. . . . . The Northern people were beginning to see that the South was divided from them by its system of labor and by its ideas of human rights. They wanted to make that gulf of division deeper. . . . . As to the word 'Union,' they all knew it was but a political catch-word." ‡

The Hon. HORACE MANN,§ while representing Massachusetts in the 31st Congress, said:

---

* Political Text-Book, p. 20.   † Ibid.   ‡ Ibid., p. 21.
§ Late of Antioch College, Yellow Springs, Ohio.

"In conclusion, I have only to add, that such is my solemn and abid ing conviction of the character of slavery, that, under a full sense of my responsibility to my country and my God, I deliberately say, better disunion—better a civil or servile war—better anything that God in his providence shall send—than an extension of the bounds of slavery."* (3)

EDMUND QUINCY, of Massachusetts, at the meeting of the American New York Anti-slavery Society, at New York City, May, 1857, said:

"He wished for a dissolution of the Union, because he wanted Massachusetts to be left free to right her own wrongs. If so, she would have no trouble in sending her ships to Charleston, and laying it in ashes. (There was no State in the Union that would not contract, at a low figure, to whip South Carolina. Massachusetts could do it with one hand tied behind her back. He did not like such a republic as this. It was against his conscience. He hated and abhorred it. In order to hold any office under the Government of the United States, a man must swear to support the Constitution, and, consequently, to support slavery in its various phases. It was as as inevitable that this Union should be dissolved as that water and oil must separate, no matter how much they may be shaken. They could not tell how it was to be done, but done it must be." †

Hon. JOSIAH QUINCY, at Boston, August 18, 1854, said:

"The Nebraska fraud is not the burden on which I now intend to speak. There is one nearer home, more immediately present, and more insupportable. Of what that burden is, I shall speak plainly. The obligation incumbent upon the free States to deliver up fugitive slaves is that burden—and it must be obliterated from that Constitution at every hazard." ‡

The American Foreign Anti-slavery Society, in the resolutions passed at one of their meetings, revealed the foreign sources of the abolition strength in this country, by expressing their thankfulness for the munificent contributions they had received from the "earnest men and women" of Great Britain. These contributions, it must be noted, have been made in the midst of the

---

* Political Text-Book, p. 25.   † Ibid., p. 26.   ‡ Ibid., p. 26.

protestations of the abolitionists, that they were laboring for the overthrow of the American Union.   One of the resolutions reads thus :

"*Resolved*, That the discriminating sense of justice, the steadfast devotedness, the generous munificence, the untiring zeal, the industry, skill, taste, and genius, with which British abolitionists have co-operated with us for the extinction of slavery, command our gratitude.

"From the abolitionists of England, Scotland, and Ireland, we have received renewed and increasing assurances and proofs of their constant and enlightened zeal in behalf of the American slave.   Liberal gifts from all of these countries, falling behind none of the most bounteous of former years, helped to fill the scanty treasury of the slave." * (4)

A convention held in Boston, in 1855, adopted, by a unanimous vote, these resolutions :

"*Resolved*, That a constitution which provides for a slave representation and a slave oligarchy in Congress, which legalizes slave-hunting and slave-catching on every inch of American soil, and which pledges the military and naval power of the country to keep four millions of chattel slaves in their chains, is to be trodden under foot and pronounced accursed, however unexceptionable or valuable may be its other provisions.

"*Resolved*, That the one great issue before the country is, the dissolution of the Union, in comparision with which all other issues with the slave power are as dust in the balance ; therefore we will give ourselves to the work of annulling this ' covenant with death,' as essential to our own innocency, and the speedy and everlasting overthrow of the slave system."†

The Legislature of New Hampshire, in 1856, passed the following resolution, in reference to the repeal of the Missouri Compromise :

"*Resolved*, That the people of New Hampshire demand, as a right, the restoration of said Compromise, and the amendment of the Kansas Nebraska Bill, so-called, so as to exclude slavery from said territories, and will never consent to the admission into the Union of any State out of said territory with a constitution tolerating slavery."‡

* Political Text-Book, p. 26.   † Ibid., p. 26.   ‡ Ibid., p. 26.

Hon. W. R. SAPP, of Ohio, in the House of Representatives, 1st session, 34th Congress, said:

"Yes, with freedom and Fremont and Dayton emblazoned on the ample folds of our national banner, we will drive the base minions of slavery from their control of the Government, and we will use its powers to build up our new country free from the taints of slavery, and make America worthy of being the North Star of freedom, by which the eye of the exile can be guided with safety to the asylum of liberty."*

Senator WADE, of Ohio, in a speech at a mass meeting of the Republicans, held in Maine, in 1855, according to the *Boston Atlas*, said:

"There was really no Union between the North and the South, and he believed no two nations upon the earth entertained feelings of more bitter rancor toward each other than these two sections of the Republic. The only salvation of the Union, therefore, was to be found in divesting it entirely from all taint of slavery. There was no Union with the South. Let us have a Union, said he, or let us sweep away this remnant which we call a Union. I go for a Union where all men are equal, or for no Union at all, and I go for right."† (5)

Judge SPAULDING, of Ohio, in the Republican Conventoin, said:

"In the case of the alternative being presented of the continuance of slavery or a dissolution of the Union, I am for dissolution, and I care not how quick it comes."‡

Senator SUMNER, of Massachusetts, in a speech delivered in Faneuil Hall, Boston, on the 2d November, 1855, said:

"Not that I love the Union less, but freedom more, do I now, in pleading this great cause, insist that freedom, at all hazards, shall be preserved. God forbid that for the sake of the Union, we should sacrifice the very thing for which the Union was made."§

During the debate in the Senate, on the 26th June, 1854, Mr. Butler, of South Carolina, said:

"I would like to ask the Senator, if Congress repealed the fugitive

---

* Political Text-Book, p. 27. † Ibid., p. 29. ‡ Ibid., p. 28. § Ibid., p. 28.

slave law, would Massachusetts execute the Constitutional requirements, and send back to the South the absconding slaves?

" MR. SUMNER.—Do you ask if I would send back a slave?

" MR. BUTLER.—Why, yes.

" MR. SUMNER.—Is thy servant a dog, that he should do this thing?

" MR. BUTLER. Then you would not obey the Constitution. Sir,
standing here before this tribunal, where you swore to support it, you
rise and tell me that you regard it the office of a dog to enforce it.
You stand in my presence as a co-equal Senator, and tell me that it
is a dog's office to execute the Constitution of the United States!"

To which Mr. Sumner said:

" I recognize no such obligation."*

A convention was held in the city of Buffalo, in 1843, at which
the following resolution was unanimously adopted, with Mr. Chase
as chairman on resolutions:

"*Resolved*, That we hereby give it distinctly to be understood, by
this nation and the world, that, as abolitionists, considering that the
strength of our cause lies in its righteousness, and our hopes for it in
our conformity to the laws of God and our support of the rights of
man, we owe to the sovereign Ruler of the Universe, as a proof of our
allegiance to Him, in all our civil relations and offices, whether as
friends, citizens, or public functionaries sworn to support the Constitution of the United States, to regard and treat the third clause of
the instrument, whenever applied in the case of a fugitive slave, as
utterly null and void, and, consequently, as forming no part of the
Constitution of the United States, whenever we are called upon or
sworn to support it."† (6)

REMARKS ON THE FOREGOING EXPRESSIONS OF OPINION.

(1) This extreme view of negro equality was once popular
among the early abolitionists; but, for many cogent reasons,
founded upon the actual workings of the system, the social equality of the black man is not now practically recognized in respectable circles of the abolitionists.

(2) It is well to note the eagerness of Rev. H. W. Beecher, as

---

* Political Text-Book, p. 28.   † Ibid., p. 27.

early as 1855, for the conflict that was to cut the North loose from the South; and, in this connection, to put upon record the declaration of that clergyman, that "one Sharp's rifle" had more moral power "than a hundred Bibles." His assertion may probably be true, if restricted to that sacred volume as interpreted by himself.

(3) Passing by the extravagance of persons of minor consideration, we cite, as a representative man, the language of Hon. Horace Mann. He but gave utterance to the traitorous sentiments common among abolitionists, when he said: "Better disunion—better a civil or servile war—better anything that God in his providence shall send—than an extension of the bounds of slavery." In this, he but expressed the wishes of the Massachusetts lords of the cotton spindle, whom he represented. Edmund Quincy, of Boston, too, had to express his abhorrence of our republic, because of the compromises of the Constitution, and predicted the dissolution of the Union as inevitable. Hon. Josiah Quincy, of the same city, expressed the determination that the fugitive slave clause must be obliterated from the Constitution at every hazard. These traitorous sentiments passed unrebuked by conservative men, because no danger was apprehended from such insane ravings.

(4) It is instructive to find, in the midst of the labors of the abolitionists for the destruction of the American Union, that British gold was poured with "generous munificence" into their treasury to aid them in their unhallowed purposes. It is equally so, too, to find a convention in the city of Boston, without rebuke from its citizens, as long ago as 1855, pronouncing the Constitution of the United States "accursed;" and asserting that the one great issue before the country was "the dissolution of the Union."

(5) Hon. B. F. Wade, Hon. Charles Sumner, and Judge Spaulding, in expressing their desire for a dissolution of the Union, rather than that slavery should be continued, gave utterance to what, at the time, was a common sentiment among abolitionists.

(6) The convention at Buffalo, in resolving to repudiate the clause of the Constitution for the rendition of fugitive slaves,

notwithstanding their oaths to support the Constitution, is to be taken as a fair index of the extent to which the revolutionary sentiment of the North had progressed. It seems strange, in a civilized country, to hear men openly avow the determination to repudiate Constitutional engagements, when they could not but know that it must lead to civil war, whenever the sentiment became general, and was incorporated into legislative enactments.

How, then, did it come to pass that such opinions as these became prevalent among the people? How did they become educated up to the belief that they could, without perjuring their souls, deliberately violate their oaths to support the Constitution? In answering these questions we must remark, that, for a long while, there was no settled creed among abolitionists that would cover all the cases of conscience that might arise; and the neces sity for such a production became so pressing that the desider- atum was at length supplied. LYSANDER SPOONER, Esq., of New York, undertook the task, and though his production may not have been universally approved by abolitionists, in all its prin- ciples, it yet afforded the basis of the greater portion of all sub- sequent abolition action. It was published in 1845, just after the complete organization of political abolitionism; and its pre- cepts and reasonings are to be found ever afterward running throughout the productions of abolitionists. A synopsis of the teachings of this work, at large, can not be given, for want of space; but enough is presented to afford a true idea of its rad- ical and revolutionary tendencies. He chose for his title, "The Unconstitutionality of Slavery." We shall begin with what he says of law:

"Law is an intelligible principle of right, necessarily resulting from the nature of man; and not an arbitrary rule, that can be established by mere will, numbers, or power. . . . Natural law, then, is the paramount law. . . . And this natural law is no other than that rule of natural justice which results either directly from men's natural rights, or from such acquisitions as they have a *natural* right to make, or from such contracts as they have a *natural* right to enter into. . . . . Natural law, therefore, inasmuch as it recognizes the natural right of men to enter into obligatory contracts, permits the formation of government, founded on contract, as all our governments profess to be. But in order that the contract of government may be valid and lawful, it must purport to authorize nothing inconsistent with natural justice, and men's natural rights."*

"If the majority, however large, of the people of a country enter into a contract of government, called a constitution, by which they agree to aid, abet, or accomplish any kind of injustice, or to destroy or invade the natural rights of any person or persons whatsoever, whether such persons be parties to the compact or not, this contract of government is unlawful and void. . . . Such a contract of government has no moral sanction. It confers no rightful authority upon those appointed to administer it. It confers no legal or moral rights, and imposes no legal or moral obligation upon the people who are parties to it. The only duties which any one can owe to it, or to the government established under color of its authority, are disobedience, resistance, destruction.

"Judicial tribunals, sitting under the authority of this unlawful contract or constitution, are bound, equally with other men, to declare it, and all unjust enactments passed by the government in pursuance of it, unlawful and void. . . . No oaths, which judicial or other officers may take, to carry out and support an unlawful contract or constitution of government, are of any moral obligation. It is immoral to take such oaths, and it is criminal to fulfill them. . . . If these doctrines are correct, then those contracts of government, State and National, which we call constitutions, are void and unlawful, so far as they purport to authorize (if any of them do authorize) any thing in violation of natural justice, or the natural rights of any man or class of men whatsoever. And all judicial tribunals are bound, by the highest obligations that can rest upon them, to declare that these contracts, in all particulars, (if any such there be,) are void and not law. . . . Such is the true character and definition of law."†

"It being admitted that a judge can rightfully administer injustice as law in no case, and on no pretense whatever; that he has no right to assume an oath to do so; and that all oaths of that kind are morally void; the question arises, whether a judge, who has actually sworn to support an unjust constitution, be morally bound to resign his seat? or whether he may rightfully retain his office, administering justice,

---

* Unconstitutionality of Slavery, by Lysander Spooner, pp. 5, 6, 7.
† Ibid., pp. 9, 10.

instead of injustice, regardless of his oath? The prevalent idea is, that he ought to resign his seat; and high authorities may be cited for this opinion. Nevertheless the opinion is, probably, erroneous; for it would seem that, however wrong it may be to take the oath, yet the oath, when taken, being morally void to all intents and purposes, can no more bind the taker to resign his office than to fulfill the oath itself.)The case appears to be this: The office is simply *power*, put into a man's hands on the condition, based upon his oath, that he will use that power to the destruction or injury of some person's rights. This condition, it is agreed, is void. He holds the power, then, by the same right that he would have done if it had been put into his hands *without the condition*. Now, seeing that he can not fulfill, and is under no obligation to fulfill, this void condition, the question is, whether he is bound to resign the power, in order that it may be given to some one who will fulfill the condition? or whether he is bound to hold the power, not only for the purpose of using it himself in *defense* of justice, but also for the purpose of withholding it from the hands of those who, if he surrender it to them, will use it unjustly? It is clear that he is bound to retain it for both of these reasons."*

In illustration of the principle here stated, the author of the work from which we quote, puts the following case:

"Suppose A and B come to C with money, which they have stolen from D, and intrust it to him, on condition of his taking an oath to restore it to them when they shall call for it. Of course, C ought not to take such an oath to get possession of the money; yet, if he have taken the oath, and received the money, his duty, on both moral and legal principles, is then the same as though he had received it without any oath or condition: because the oath and condition are both morally and legally void. And if he were to restore the money to A and B, instead of restoring it to D, the true owner, he would make himself their accomplice in the theft—a receiver of stolen goods. It is his duty to restore it to D.

"Suppose A and B come to C with a captive, D, whom they have seized with the intention of reducing him to slavery; and should leave him in the custody of C, on condition of C's taking an oath that he will restore him to them again. Now, although it is wrong for C to take such an oath for the purpose of getting the custody of D, even

---

* Unconstitutionality of Slavery, pp. 147–150.

with a view to set him free, yet, if he have taken it, it is void, and his duty then is, not to give D up to his captors, but to set him at liberty —else he will be an accomplice in the crime of enslaving him." *

At this stage of the investigation, it is obvious that an anti-slavery man, aiming at attaining a seat on the bench of the United States Supreme Court, to operate against slavery, could not do so, excepting by committing a moral wrong in swearing to administer justice according to the Constitution and laws—these laws sanctioning slavery, and requiring the judge to order the return of fugitives from slavery back again into bondage.

Now, here comes in the distinction between the Garrisonians and the adherents of the Liberty party. The former believed that the Constitution authorizes and protects slavery, and that its destruction is necessary to the extinction of that institution. The latter believed that slavery might be abolished under the Constitution, by a strict construction of its provisions, and that anti-slavery men, therefore, may consistently vote and hold office under the Government. But this view demanded a totally new theory of interpretation of the Constitution; and this was at hand as soon as needed. Mr. Spooner, before quoted, supplied the desideratum, though others had been beforehand in some of the principles belonging to his system. We shall attempt to state his theory, and we do it the more willingly, because the quotations already made from Lord Stowell and Mr. O'Connor, and others, present a complete exposé of the fallacies and absurdities of his positions.

According to Mr. Spooner, slavery, probably, neither has, *nor ever had*, any constitutional existence in this country.† Our ancestors brought with them from England the common law, the writ of *habeas corpus*, the trial by jury, and the other great principles which have rendered it impossible that her soil should be trod by the foot of a slave. These principles were incorporated in all the charters granted to the colonies.‡ No one of all these charters contained the least intimation that slavery had, or could have, any legal existence under them. Slavery was, therefore, as

---

* Unconstitutionality of Slavery, p. 151. † Ibid., p. 20. ‡ Ibid., p. 21.

much unconstitutional in the colonies as it was in England.*
Lord Mansfield's decision, made before the revolution, settled the
question ·that slavery could have no existence upon British soil.
This decision was equally obligatory in this country as in England, and must have freed every slave here if the question had
been raised.† The fact that England tolerated the African slave
trade at the time, could not legally establish slavery in the colonies, any more than it did in England.‡ Besides, the mere toleration of the slave trade could not make slavery itself—*the right
of property in man* — lawful anywhere; not even on board the
slave-ship. Toleration of a wrong is not law.§ Even if a wrong
can be legalized at all, so as to enable one to acquire rights of
property by such wrong, it can be done only by an explicit and
positive provision.|| The English statutes, on the subject of the
slave trade, never attempted to legalize the right of property in
man, *in any of the thirteen North American colonies.*¶ But Lord
Mansfield said, in Somerset's case, that slavery was "*so odious
that nothing can be suffered to support it, but positive law.*" No
such positive law was ever passed by Parliament—certainly not
with reference to any of these thirteen colonies.** There was,
therefore, no *constitutional* slavery in the colonies up to the time
of the Revolution.††

So much for British legislation. Up to the time of the Revolution, according to Mr. Spooner, slavery had not been established
by positive law, by the mother country, in any of the North
American colonies; and, as it is contrary to natural law, slavery
could, therefore, have had no legal existence here, excepting
where it may have been established by colonial legislation. But
the colonial legislation, says Mr. Spooner, was not only void as
being forbidden by the colonial charters, but in many of the
colonies it was void because it did not sufficiently define the persons who might be made slaves.‡‡

" When slavery was first introduced into the country, there were no
laws at all on the subject. Men bought slaves of the slave-traders as

---

* Unconstitutionality of Slavery, p. 23. † Ibid. ‡ Ibid. § Ibid., p. 24.
|| Ibid. ¶ Ibid. ** Ibid. †† Ibid., p. 31. ‡‡ Ibid., p. 32.

they would have bought horses. . . . Yet all the while no act had been passed declaring who might be slaves. Possession was apparently all the evidence that public sentiment demanded of a master's property in his slave."*

Slavery not being established by positive statute, either by British or colonial legislation, it is argued by Mr. Spooner that, at the date of the Declaration of Independence, there could be no legal slavery in the country.

But admitting that slavery may have had an existence prior to the Declaration of Independence, either by British or colonial enactments, Mr. Spooner argues that the adoption of this instrument, as it absolves the people of the colonies from all allegiance to British law, so it freed every slave in the country—all former laws being thereby abrogated, and the principles of the Declaration only applying to the population. These truths, he insists, have never been denied or revoked by the American people, and are, therefore, in full force.† He then proceeds to say, that

"Our courts would want no other authority than this truth, thus acknowledged, for setting at liberty any individual, other than one having negro blood, whom our Governments, State or National, should assume to authorize another individual to enslave. Why, then, do they not apply the same law in behalf of the African? Certainly not because it is not as much the law of his case as of others. *But it is simply because they will not.* It is because the courts are a party to the understanding, prevailing among the white race, but expressed in no constitutional form, that the negro may be deprived of his rights at the pleasure of avarice and power. And they carry out this unexpressed understanding in defiance of, and suffer it to prevail over, all our constitutional principles of government — all our authentic, avowed, open, and fundamental law."‡

Mr. Spooner proceeds from the Declaration to the State Constitutions, and says, that of all of them that were in force at the adoption of the Constitution of the United States, in 1789, *not one of them established or recognized slavery;* and that all those parts of the old thirteen States that recognize and attempt to

---

* Unconstitutionality of Slavery, p. 33.   † Ibid., p. 38.   ‡ Ibid., p. 39.

sanction slavery, *have been inserted, by amendments, since the adoption of the Constitution of the United States.** In their original form, he says, they generally recognized the natural rights of men; and not one of them had any specific recognition of the existence of slavery.† And, after reviewing the Constitutions of the several States at length, he repeats what he had so often asserted, that

"Slavery is so entirely contrary to natural right; so entirely destitute of authority from natural law; so palpably inconsistent with all the legitimate objects of government, that nothing but express and explicit provision can be recognized, in law, as giving it any sanction."‡

In his examination, next, of the Articles of Confederation, as well as elsewhere, Mr. Spooner undertakes to prove that the word "free" is used as the correlative of "aliens," and not of "slaves," and that the negroes are thereby recognized as "citizens" and "inhabitants," but never as slaves.§

Lastly, the Constitution itself comes under consideration, and here Mr. Spooner says:

"We have already seen that slavery had not been authorized or established by any of the fundamental constitutions or charters that had existed previous to this time; that it had always been a mere abuse sustained by the common consent of the strongest party, in defiance of the avowed constitutional principles of their governments. And the question now is, whether it was constitutionally established, authorized, or sanctioned by the Constitution of the United States?"‖

In answering this question Mr. Spooner decides that it is perfectly clear that

"The Constitution of the United States did not, *of itself, create or establish* slavery as a *new* institution; or even give any authority to the State governments to establish it as a new institution. The greatest sticklers do not claim this. The most they claim is, that it recognized it as an institution already existing, under the authority

---

* Unconstitutionality of Slavery, p. 39. † Ibid., p. 40.
‡ Ibid., p. 43.   § Ibid., pp. 51, 52, 53.   ‖ Ibid., p. 54

of the State governments; and that it virtually guaranteed to the States the right of continuing it in existence during their pleasure. And this is really the only question arising out of the Constitution of the United States on this subject, viz., whether it *did* thus recognize and sanction slavery as an *existing* institution? This question. is, in reality, answered in the negative by what has already been shown; for if slavery had no constitutional existence, under the State constitutions, prior to the adoption of the Constitution of the United States, then it is absolutely certain that the Constitution did *not* recognize it as a constitutional institution; for it cannot, of course, be pretended that the United States Constitution recognized, as constitutional, any State institution that did not constitutionally exist. Even if the Constitution of the United States had *intended* to recognize slavery, as a constitutional *State* institution, such intended recognition would have failed of effect, and been legally void, because slavery then had no constitutional existence to be recognized. *

"We might here safely rest the whole question—for no one, as has already been said, pretends that the Constitution of the United States, by its own authority, created or authorized slavery as a new institution; but only that it intended to recognize it as one already established by authority of the State constitutions. This intended recognition—if there were any such—being founded on an error as to what the State constitutions really did authorize, necessarily falls to the ground, as a defunct institution.

"We make a stand, then, at this point, and insist that the main question—the only material question—is already decided against slavery; and that it is of no consequence what recognition or sanction the Constitution of the United States may have intended to extend to it.

"The Constitution of the United States, at its adoption, certainly took effect upon, and made citizens of *all* 'the people of the United States,' who were *not slaves* under the State constitutions. No one can deny a proposition so self-evident as that. If, then, the *State* constitutions then existing authorized no slavery at all, the Constitution of the United States took effect upon and made citizens of *all* 'the people of the United States,' without discrimination. And if *all* 'the people of the United States' were made citizens of the United States, by the United States Constitution, at its adoption, it was then forever too late for the *State* governments to reduce any of them to

---

* Unconstitutionality of Slavery, pp. 54, 55.

slavery. They were thenceforth citizens of a higher government, under a Constitution that was 'the supreme law of the land,' 'anything in the constitution or laws of the States to the contrary notwithstanding.' If the State governments could enslave citizens of the United States, the State constitutions, and not the Constitution of the United States, would be the 'supreme law of the land'—for no higher act of supremacy could be exercised by one government over another, than that of taking the citizens of the latter out of the protection of their government, and reducing them to slavery."*

Mr. Spooner next discusses the question of " THE UNDERSTAND-ING OF THE PEOPLE" in reference to the establishment of slavery by the Constitution, and comes to this conclusion :

"Now is it not idle and useless to pretend, when even the strongest slaveholding States had free constitutions—when not one of the separate States, acting for itself, would have any but a free constitution—that the whole thirteen, when acting in unison, should concur in establishing a slaveholding one? The idea is preposterous. The single fact that all the State constitutions were at that time free ones, scatters forever the pretense that the majority of the people of all the States either intended to establish, *or could have been induced to establish,* any other than a free one for the nation. Of course it scatters also the pretense that they believed or understood that they were establishing any but a free one."† . . . .

"At the adoption of the Constitution of the United States, there was no legal or Constitutional slavery in the States. Not a single State constitution then in existence, recognized, authorized, or sanctioned slavery. All the slaveholding then practiced was merely a private crime committed by one person against another, like theft, robbery, or murder. All the statutes which the slaveholders, through their wealth and influence, procured to be passed, were unconstitutional and void, for the want of any constitutional authority in the legislatures to enact them."‡

Having thus proved, as he supposes, that slavery is unconstitutional and illegal, Mr. Spooner proceeds to determine how the liberty of the slaves is to be secured; and this he decides is to be accomplished by the courts, under the writ of *habeas corpus*. He states the case as follows :

---

* Unconstitutionality of Slavery, p. 56.   † Ibid., p. 126.   ‡ Ibid., p. 271.

" This right of personal liberty, this *sine qua non* to the enjoyment of all other rights, is secured by the writ of *habeas corpus*. This writ, as has before been shown, necessarily denies the right of property in man, and therefore liberates all who are restrained of their liberty on that pretense, as it does all others that are restrained on grounds inconsistent with the intended operation of the Constitution and laws of the United States. . . . . As the government is bound to dispense its benefits impartially to all, it is bound, first of all, after securing ' the public safety, in cases of rebellion and invasion,' to secure liberty to all. And the whole power of the Government is bound to be exerted for this purpose, *to the postponement, if need be*, of everything else save, ' the public safety, in cases of rebellion and invasion.' And it is the constitutional duty of the government to establish as many courts as may be necessary (no matter how great the number,) and to adopt all other measures necessary and proper, for bringing the means of liberation within the reach of every person who is restrained of his liberty in violation of the principles of the Constitution.* . . . . The power of the General Government to liberate men from slavery, by the use of the writ of *habeas corpus*, is of the amplest character. . . . . If these opinions are correct, it is the constitutional duty of Congress to establish courts, if need be, in every county and township even, where there are slaves to be liberated; to provide attorneys to bring the cases before the courts, and to keep a standing military force, if need be, to sustain the proceedings."†

With such an interpretation of the Constitution as we have presented here, all obstacles to swearing to support it, on the part of Judges of the United States Courts, are fully removed; and with the bench filled with abolition judges, the work of emancipation could progress with rapidity. It was under the conviction of the truth of this interpretation of the Constitution, that Mr. Burlingame asserted that one of his aims, as a member of Congress, was to have judges who "believe in an anti-slavery Constitution;" and who would, consequently, use their official power in promoting emancipation; and it was in the same spirit that the Free Soil candidate for Lieutenant-Governor of Massachusetts, Mr. Brown, declared it to be the object of the free

---

* Unconstitutionality of Slavery, p. 275.   † Ibid., p. 277.

States to take possession of the Government by their united votes. To have succeeded in this would have enabled the Free Soil party to control the courts, and thus promote the work of abolition.

But the conservative men of the North rebuked this spirit of fanaticism by the defeat of the Free Soil party; and the present dominant party came into power under the pledge of non-interference with slavery where it exists. One wing of this party had other aims, we know, in giving it support; but the great mass of the people belonging to it repudiated the charge that they contemplated promoting the abolition of slavery.

The whole theory of the abolitionists, in reference to the unconstitutionality of slavery, and the consequent exemption of the citizens of the North from all obligations to recognize the right of the master to his slave, is based upon the fiction of Lord Manfield, in which he asserted that slavery can only exist as the creature of local law; and that, therefore, where no positive statutes exist, establishing slavery, there no slavery can prevail, if the courts do their duty. But the discussions of Lord Stowel and others, quoted in the present chapter, show that Lord Mansfield's opinion has not been recognized as correct; and the fact that American slavery has been treated as a legal relation by the American Congress, in various ways; by Great Britain, in paying for slaves illegally taken from their American owners; and by the Emperor of Russia, as an umpire in the case referred to him ;* all go to prove that slavery requires no positive statutes for its establishment; but that, at the time the Constitution was

---

* "RIGHT OF PROPERTY IN SLAVES RECOGNIZED BY GREAT BRITAIN.—The *London Courier* says: 'His Excellency, Mr. Stevenson, the American Minister, attended yesterday at the treasury department and Bank of England, and closed the negotiation which has been pending so long between the Government and that of the United States, relative to the number of slaves claimed by American citizens as their property, and which, having been shipwrecked, some eight or nine years ago, in the Bahamas, were liberated by the authorities of Nassau. The amount of compensation which we understand her majesty's Government finally agreed to pay, and was yesterday received by the American Minister, amounted to between thirty and forty thousand pounds sterling.' —*Niles' Register, February* 8, 1840."

adopted, African slavery was everywhere recognized as a lawful institution. The whole history of the country, so far as the African race is concerned, shows conclusively that no notice was intended to be taken of slavery by the framers of the Constitution, because, over that question the people did not intend to give the National Government any power whatever. The South so understood the compact; the North so understood it; and no one ever dreamed of giving the Constitution any other interpretation, until the rise of abolitionism. In no other sense than that in which it was adopted, can it be binding. Mr. Spooner's theories, therefore, are all *fudge;* and yet much of the action both in and out of Congress, on the part of the abolitionists, has been based upon his theories. Indeed, they are the only ones that can justify the treason of abolitionism—the only ones that will clear the conscience of the fanatic who attempts to resist the execution of the Fugitive Slave Law, or destroy the Union.

We might have extended the quotations in this section indefinitely; but as they are used only for illustration, it was not important that they should be multiplied. They show very clearly the feeling existing at the North against the Constitution and the Union, on account of slavery; and when taken in connection with the documents presented in the two preceding sections, prove conclusively that the right of secession, and even the dissolution of the Union, were questions favorably entertained at the North, even by men who had solemnly sworn to support the Constitution.

It will be noticed that the expressions of sentiment, which are quoted, date back several years, to a time when there was room for calm reflection; when deliberate purposes could be formed, and suitable measures to carry them out adopted. After the war began, individual opinions varied from day to day, and as these later opinions had no influence in producing it, they have no connection with the objects before us.

How far any of the opinions given were designed for mere local political effect, we shall not undertake to determine; the practical results at the South were the same as though the North was in earnest in these utterances. They were spread broadcast over the slave States, and produced that alarm which enabled the political leaders to precipitate the people of the South into acts of rebellion. Conservative men were as remiss in duty there, as they have been here. The penalty is now being executed upon them.

SECTION IV.—MOVEMENTS NORTH AND SOUTH PRECIPITATING CIVIL WAR.

A HISTORY, in detail, of the movements in the South, connected with counter-movements in the North, which precipitated the nation into civil war, is not necessary to the purpose we have in view. A few leading facts and incidents, in relation to the sectional contests resulting so fatally, will serve to convey a correct impression of the manner in which the actors brought on the final collision of arms, and compelled conservative men to rally for the preservation of the Union.

The year 1832 found South Carolina in the midst of her *nullification* measures. All the other slave States remained loyal to the Government; and even a large portion of the citizens of that rebel State continued true to the Union, and were most efficient agents in the work of restoring harmony when the proclamation of General Jackson appeared. At this period, therefore, the South at large were not contemplating secession and disunion.

But the peace of the country, secured by the energy of General Jackson, and by the statesman-like abilities of Henry Clay, who, in connection with the President, devised a compromise which satisfied both the discontented State and the General Government, was again to be disturbed. The pulpits and ecclesiastical councils at the North kept up the agitation on slavery. With two or three exceptions, every religious denomination stood pledged to labor on, and labor ever, for its overthrow. One of the most prominent Churches in the nation, at every succeeding conference, asked the question: "What can be done for the extirpation of the evil of slavery?" The clergymen who had become tainted with abolition sentiments, were crying aloud that they would give neither sleep to their eyes, nor slumber to their eyelids, until the last slave in the land should be proclaimed a freeman. Lecturers, commissioned and paid by abolition societies, swarmed over the North like the locusts of old, when, in judgment, they darkened the land of Egypt in their flight, and destroyed every green thing upon which they descended; and agents from Great Britain came to their help, to aid in the work of assailing the South.*   Abolitionists boasted that British gold was not lacking, but supplied with liberal hand, to promote the work of ruin which, it had been decreed in Exeter Hall, should overtake the American planter.

But the efforts of the abolitionists were not to be limited to moral means alone. New political parties were organized, expressly to lend their aid in promoting the work of abolition. The old established political parties reeled under the blows of the new, or, taking them to their bosoms, perished in the embrace. The original interpretations of the Constitution were set aside, and new ones adopted that would justify an aggressive warfare upon Southern institutions. Agencies were formed, extending into the slave States, to entice the slaves to escape from their masters; and provision was made in the free States, to enable the fugitives to flee in safety beyond the reach of their pursuers. The legislatures of many of the northern States passed enactments forbidding the execution of the original law of Congress for the return of runaway slaves; and the re-enactment of the Fugitive Slave Law, to meet the existing obstacles to the fulfillment of constitutional engagements, was made the occasion of renewed attacks upon the institutions and men of the South.

But, up to this date,† the balance of power between the slave and free States had remained undisturbed. Texas was in the Union, and its territory, though capable of being subdivided into five States, could not be made available to the South for an increase of power, as, according to the treaty of admission, two of the additional four States must be free, and the two remaining ones slaveholding.

---

* Englishmen seemed not to have forgotten the declaration of the Earl of Dartmouth, when, in opposing the abolition of the slave trade, shortly before the American Revolution, he said: "Negroes cannot become republicans; they will be a power in our hands to restrain the unruly colonists."

† The Fugitive Slave Law was passed in 1850.

A little previous to this,* an unsuccessful attempt had been made to extend the Missouri Compromise line to the Pacific, so that all territory acquired by the Mexican War, and lying South of that line, might be secured to slavery. This measure failing, left the South in a position of great uncertainty as to the future; and the fears entertained were well-grounded, as, in the subsequent organization of California, a large area of country lying South of the Missouri line was included in the territory of that State, and slavery excluded from the whole. The admission of California as a free State,† with more than one-third of its territory South of 36° 30′, was viewed by the South as a virtual abrogation of the Missouri Compromise, and as indicating an intention of putting the "Wilmot Proviso" into practical operation.‡

As the territories then remained, New Mexico alone lay South of 36° 30′, while immense regions were North of it, awaiting the westward flow of population, to come into the Union as free States.§ The South had no corresponding quantity of territory on its side of the line; and unless its institutions could be spread North of that line, so as to maintain the balance of power, it must soon be overwhelmed by the anti-slavery forces from the North. And even New Mexico, though South of 36° 30′, might share the fate of the Southern portion of California, and be wrested from the South by congressional enactment.

The Missouri Compromise had excluded slavery from all the territory North of 36° 30′ which was obtained by the purchase of Louisiana. The extension of slavery, therefore, to the North of that line, could not be effected except by the repeal of the Missouri Compromise. Minnesota and Oregon were preparing for admission into the Union, and Kansas and Nebraska were asking for territorial organization. In the Congressional bill for the

---

* August, 1848—the Mexican War having been closed in May previous.

† California was admitted in 1850.

‡ The "Wilmot Proviso," brought forward in Congress in 1846 and 1847, but never adopted, proposed to exclude slavery from all territories ever acquired on this continent.

§ It will be well for the reader to examine a map.

organization of these territories, the Missouri Compromise was repealed,* and the territories both North and South of 36° 30' thrown open to the competition of the opposing forces—slavery and anti-slavery. This brought on the Kansas troubles, in which the South was overwhelmed by the superior forces thrown into the territory from New England.

All this vast territory north of 36° 30', extending, we may say, to the Pacific, was included in the Louisiana purchase, and, consequently, slave territory.† But as the purchase had been made by the common funds of the nation, the North laid claim to a part of the territory, and, by the Missouri Compromise, took the lion's share of it. The South was looking toward Mexico to maintain the balance of power, by gaining territory better adapted to slavery, south of 36° 30', and submitted to the loss in patience.

But the developments of abolition principles at the North, by which it became evident the South would be denied access to the territories with its slave property, and that no more slave States would be admitted, left it but one resource to secure its safety. This was to protect itself against interference with slavery within the States where it existed; and this could only be effected by the insertion of a new clause in the Constitution. Such an amendment was the more necessary, as the new doctrines embraced at the North, that slavery is unconstitutional, and can be abolished by the courts, was entertained by not a few. No one could tell at what moment the small party holding this doctrine, and having the balance of power at the North, might gain the control of the Government, and force the question to an issue.

In the meantime, the results of emancipation in Hayti, Mexico, Bolivia, the British West Indies, and the French Islands, were manifesting themselves to the world, and demonstrating the utter worthlessness of a free negro population as a laboring force *in the cultivation of staple productions.* All these results were perfectly well known at the South, and its people fully believed that

---

* This bill was passed in 1854.

† John Quincy Adams, in his speech on the admission of Arkansas, said that slavery existed there at the time of the acquisition, and that he was, therefore, bound to admit her with slavery.

emancipation would result in ruin to themselves and their posterity, as well as in the extermination of the weaker race. They were not alone in holding this belief. "M. DE TOCQUEVILLE, who had judged America with so sure an eye,"* in speaking of negro slavery in the United States, had said :

"Hitherto, wherever the whites have been the more powerful, they have held the negroes in degradation and slavery; wherever the negroes have been the more powerful, they have destroyed the whites. This is the only account which can ever be opened between the two races."

Already the ground had been taken that no more slave States should be admitted, and that slavery should not be extended into the Territories. The manner in which these doctrines were met by the statesmen of the South, may be inferred from the debates in Congress during the session of 1855–56. A few extracts will serve as illustrations.

Mr. COX, of Kentucky, in the House, December 20, 1855, said:

"When you tell me that you intend to put a restriction on the Territories, I say to you that upon that subject the South is a unit, and will not submit to any such thing. You do not understand that, or you would not press it so pertinaciously."†

Mr. CAMPBELL, of Kentucky, in the House, Dec. 19, 1855, said:

"It is an interference with our institutions, when our citizens are denied the same rights in the new Territories with the citizens of the North; for that Territory belongs as much to us as it does to you. . . . We regard this confederacy as secondary in importance, and when a government falters in carrying out its guarantees for the protection of life, liberty, and property, it is no longer entitled to the fealty of its citizens. And in addition to that, I will avow this sentiment, believing that it will be indorsed by my constituency, that whenever this Government makes a distinction between a Southern and a Northern constituency or citizenship, then we shall no longer

---

* Count de Gasparin uses the quotation here made in his recent Essay on the "Co-existence of the two Races after Emancipation."

† Appendix to Congressional Globe, p. 30.

consider ourselves bound to support the confederacy, but will resort to the right of revolution, which is recognized by all."*

Mr. BROOKS, of South Carolina, in the House, Dec. 24, 1855, said:

" The gentleman from Massachusetts has announced to the world that, in certain contingencies, he is willing to 'let the Union slide.' Now, sir, let his contingencies be reversed, and I am also willing to 'let the Union slide,'—ay, sir, to aid in making it slide. . . . I hesitate not to say, that if his construction of the constitutional power of Congress over the Territories shall prevail in this country, I, for one, heartily indorse the sentiment."†

Mr. BOYCE, of South Carolina, in the House, Jan. 4, 1856, said:

" I have thought, and I still think, and I have expressed the opinion, that there are circumstances which are hurrying us almost irresistibly to disruption. . . . I have seen at the North the formation of a great party, based upon the single idea of hostility to the institutions of the South. The only question with me, then, as to the continuance of the Union is, whether that party will take possession of the North? If they do, in my opinion, the Union is at an end. . . . What is that party pledged to? The great boasting idea of that party is, that freedom is national, and slavery is sectional. That party, then, are obliged, if they come into power, as is recommended in the resolutions of the State of Maine, presented to the Senate yesterday, to abolish slavery in the District of Columbia, and to prohibit it in all the Territories, arsenals, and dock-yards in the United States. Well, then, it seems to me that if that party comes into power, pledged to those measures, we shall be in the midst of chaos, and anarchy, and revolution.

" This great sectional party at the North, goes upon the idea that, by uniting together at the North, they can obtain the control of this Government, and dispense its vast patronage among themselves, and reduce the people of the South to a secondary and subordinate condition. . . . That party which places itself upon the position of giving power to the North, will eventually succeed; and when that party does succeed, in my opinion, the Union will be at an end."‡

---

* Congressional Globe, p. 56. † Political Text-Book, p. 601.
‡ Congressional Globe, p. 143.

Mr. BOCOCK, of Virginia, in the House, January 19, addressing himself to the Republicans, said:

"You cheat yourself with the delusion that your platform makes you national. You declare war on the institution of slavery wherever the strong arm of this Government can reach it, and call that a national platform. To justify so absurd a position, you love to employ the specious phrase that 'freedom is national, and slavery sectional.' I tell gentlemen that it is a cheat and delusion. . . . When, in your platform, you come forward and say that your institutions alone are entitled to the protection of the Government, and that ours are to be discountenanced and restricted by its action, then you lay down a sectional platform, and array yourselves into a sectional party. You put us beyond the pale of the Constitution, and you force us to fight you by every fair and honorable means, and we shall do it."*

Judge BUTLER, of South Carolina, in the Senate, March 27, 1856, said:

"I say now, calmly, that when a Northern majority shall acquire such a control over the legislation of this country as to disfranchise the slaveholding States, in any respect in which they have an equality under the Constitution of the country, I will not agree to live under this Government, when the Union can survive the Constitution. . . All that I have contended for is, that the domain of this Government, acquired by the common blood and treasure of all parts of the United States, shall be just as free to one class of citizens as another. . . But, sir, if an insulting interference were to be made by a majority of Congress, or such an interference as would exclude a slaveholder on the broad ground that he was unworthy of equality with a non-slave-holding population, do you suppose I would stay in the Union if I could get out of it?"†

Mr. STEPHENS, of Georgia, in the House, Jan. 17, 1856, said:

"I was willing to divide, as an alternative only, but a majority of the North would not consent to it; and now we have got the great principle, established in 1850, carried out in the Kansas-Nebraska bill, that Congress, after removing all obstructions, is not to intervene

* Congress. Globe, p. 264.   † Ibid., p. 758, and Political Text-Book, p. 603.

against us. This is the old Southern Republican principle, attained after a hard and protracted struggle in 1850, and I say, if Congress ever again exercises the power to exclude the South from an equal participation in the common Territories, I, as a southern man, am for resisting it."*

Mr. JONES, of Tennessee, in the Senate, Feb. 25, 1856, said:

"We ask nothing but what the Constitution guarantees to us. That much we do ask. That much we will have. I do not wish to be excited about this matter. We do not mean to be driven from our propriety, but there is a fixed, immutable, universal determination, on the part of the South, never to be driven a single inch further. If we are not to enjoy our rights under the Constitution, tell us so; and if we may, let us separate peaceably and decently. . . . I tell you, in every hand there will be a knife, and there will be war to the knife, and the knife to the hilt." †

Mr. LETCHER, of Virginia, in the House, March 13, 1856, said:

"If you undertake to repeal the Fugitive Slave Law, and deprive us of the means of recovering our property when it is stolen from us. . . . If you undertake to abolish slavery in the District of Columbia, and prohibit it in the Territories of the United States by Congressional legislation, . . . you will find that the South, if it has a particle of self-respect—and I know that it has—will be prepared to resist any, and all, such measures." ‡

Mr. WARNER, of Georgia, in the House, April 1, 1856, said:

"We have been told by those who advocate this line of policy, that they do not desire to interfere with slavery in the States where it exists; and yet it is their intention to prevent the extension of slavery, by excluding it from the common territory. . . . It matters but little with me, whether a man takes my property outright, or restricts me in the enjoyment of it, so as to render it of but little or no value to me. . . . Slavery can not be confined within certain specified limits without producing the destruction of both master and slave; it requires fresh lands. . . . If the slaveholding

---

* Political Text-Book, p. 603, and Appendix to Congressional Globe, p. 60.
† Political Text-Book, p. 603, and Appendix to Congressional Globe, p. 95.
‡ Political Text-Book, p. 603, and Appendix to Congressional Globe, p. 230.

States should ever be so regardless of their rights, and their power, as co-equal States, to be willing to submit to this proposed restriction, . . . they could not do it. They ought not to submit to it on principle, if they could, and could not if they would.

"It is in view of these things, sir, that the people of Georgia have assembled in convention, and solemnly resolved that, if Congress shall pass a law excluding them from the common property, with their slave property, they will disrupt the ties that bind them to the Union. This position has not been taken by way of threat or menace. Georgia never threatens, but Georgia always acts."*

Mr. SHORTER, of Alabama, in the House, April 9, 1856, said:

"I believe in the right of a sovereign State to secede from the Union whenever she determines that the Federal Constitution has been violated by Congress; and that this Government has no constitutional power to coerce such seceding States. . . . I think South Carolina mistook her remedy—secession, and not nullification, ought to have been her watchword. . . . The extraordinary exertions made by Massachusetts . . . . to rob the South of her equal rights in the Territories has had one effect. You have thoroughly aroused the southern States to a sense of their danger. You have caused them coolly to estimate the value of the Union; and we are determined to maintain our equality in it, or independence out of it.

"The South has planted itself where it intends to stand or fall, Union or no Union, and that is, upon the platform laid down by the Georgia convention. . . . We tell you plainly that we take issue with you; and whenever you repeal the Fugitive Slave Law, or refuse to admit a State on account of slavery in her Constitution, or our equality in the territories is sacrificed by an act of Congress, then the star of this Union will go down to rise no more. . . . . Should we be forced to dissolve the Union in order to preserve Southern institutions and Southern civilization, we will do it in peace, if we can; in war, if we must; and let the God of Battles decide between us.

"The shadows, sir, of the coming storm already darken our pathway. It will soon be upon us with all its fury."†

Mr. BARKSDALE, of Mississippi, in the House, July 23, 1856, said:

---

* Political Text-Book, p. 604, and Appendix to Congressional Globe, p. 297.
† Political Text-Book, p. 604.

"Sir, I make no threats; but I tell the gentlemen on the other side of this House, plainly, as it is my solemn duty to do, as the representative of a hundred thousand freemen upon this floor, that we submit to no further aggressions upon us, ' there is a point beyond which forbearance ceases to be a virtue,' and that, for the future, 'we tread no steps backward.' We are done, gentlemen, with compromises. All that have been made you forced upon us; and while we have observed them in good faith, you have shamelessly disregarded and trampled them under foot. I hold up before you the Constitution as it came from the hands of its immortal authors, Northern and Southern men— itself a compromise; we claim our rights under that, and we intend to have them." *

In this connection it may be well to lay before the reader the opinions of Mr. Jefferson in relation to the dangers of the creation of sectional issues, and the domineering spirit of New England federalism. We copy from the *Political Text-Book*, page 336:

"In reference to the Missouri Compromise, Mr. JEFFERSON said:

"'The question is a mere party trick. The leaders of federalism, defeated in their schemes of obtaining power by rallying partisans to the principle of monarchism—a principle of personal, not of local division—have changed their tact and thrown out another barrel to the whale. They are taking advantage of the virtuous feeling of the people to effect a division of parties by a geographical line; they expect that this will insure them, on local principles, the majority they could never obtain on principles of federalism; but they are still putting their shoulders to the wrong wheel; they are wasting jeremiads on the miseries of slavery, as if we were advocates of it. Sincerity in their declamations should direct their efforts to the true point of difficulty, and unite their councils with ours in devising some reasonable and practical plan of getting rid of it.' †

"In a letter to Mr. ADAMS, dated Jan. 22, 1821, Mr. JEFFERSON says:

"'Our anxieties in this quarter are all concentrated in the question, What does the holy alliance, in and out of Congress, mean to do with us on the Missouri question? And this, by the way, is but the name

---

* Political Text-Book, p. 605.　　　　† Jefferson's Writings, vol. 7.

of the case; it is only the John Doe or Richard Roe of the ejectment.
The real question, as seen in the States afflicted with this unfortunate
population, is, Are our slaves to be presented with freedom and a
dagger?   For, if Congress has the power to regulate the conditions
of the inhabitants of the States within the States, it will be but another exercise of that power to declare that all shall be free.   Are
we, then, to see again Athenian and Lacedæmonian confederacies?
To wage another Peloponnesian war to settle the ascendancy between
them?   Or is this the tocsin of merely a servile war?   That remains
to be seen; but I hope not by you or me.   Surely they will parley
awhile and give us time to get out of the way.   What a bedlamite
is man!'

"In a letter to LAFAYETTE, dated Nov. 4, 1823, Mr. JEFFERSON
said:—

"'On the eclipse of federalism with us, although not its extinction,
its leaders got up the Missouri question, under the false front of
lessening the measure of slavery, but with the real view of producing
a geographical division of parties, which might insure them the next
President.   The people of the North went blindfold into the snare,
and followed their leaders for awhile with a zeal truly moral and laudable, until they became sensible that they were injuring instead of
aiding the real interests of the slaves; that they had been used
merely as tools for electioneering purposes, and that trick of hypocrisy
then fell as quickly as it had been got up.'

"In a letter to Mr. SHORT, dated April 13, 1820, Mr. JEFFERSON
said:—

"'Although I had laid down as a law to myself, never to write,
talk, or even think of politics, to know nothing of public affairs, and
had, therefore, ceased to read newspapers, yet the Missouri question
aroused and filled me with alarm.   The old schism of Federal and
Republican threatened nothing, because it existed in every State, and
united them together by the fraternism of party.   But the coincidence
of a marked principle, moral and political, with a geographical line,
once conceived, I feared would never more be obliterated from the
mind; that it would be recurring on every occasion, and renewing
irritations, until it would kindle such mutual and mortal hatred as to
render separation preferable to eternal discord.   I have been among
the most sanguine in believing that our Union would be of long du-

ration. I now doubt it much, and see the event at no great distance, and the direct consequence of this question; not by the line which has been so confidently counted on—the laws of nature control this—but by the Potomac, Ohio, and Missouri, or more probably the Mississippi, upward to our northern boundary. My only comfort and consolation is, that I shall not live to see it; and I envy not the present generation the glory of throwing away the fruits of their fathers' sacrifices of life and fortune, and of rendering desperate the experiment which was to decide ultimately whether man is capable of self-government. This treason against human hope will signalize their epoch in future history as the counterpart of the model of their predecessors.'

" 'I thank you, my dear sir, for the copy you have been so kind as to send me of the letter to your constituents on the Missouri question. . . . But this momentous question, like a fire-bell in the night, awakened me and filled me with terror. I considered it at once as the knell of the Union. It is hushed, indeed, for the moment; but this is a reprieve only, not a final sentence. A geographical line, coinciding with a marked principle, moral and political, once conceived and held up to the angry passions of men, will never be obliterated; and every new irritation will mark it deeper and deeper. . . . If they would but dispassionately weigh the blessings they will throw away, against an abstract principle, more likely to be effected by union than by scission, they would pause before they could perpetrate this act of suicide on themselves, and of treason against the hopes of the world.' *

" 'I am indebted to you for your two letters of Feb. 7th and 19th. The Missouri question, by a geographical line of division, is the most portentous one I ever contemplated; * * * is ready to risk the Union for any chance of restoring his party to power, and wriggling himself to the head of it; nor is * * * without his hopes, nor scrupulous as to the means of fulfilling them.' †

" 'The banks, bankrupt laws, manufactures, Spanish treaty, are nothing. These are occurrences which, like waves in a storm, will pass under the ship, but the Missouri question is a breaker on which we lose the Missouri country by revolt, and what more, God only

---

* Letter to Jno. Holmes, dated Monticello, April 22, 1820.
† Letter to Mr. Madison.

knows. From the battle of Bunker's Hill, to the treaty of Paris, we never had so ominous a question. It even damps the joy with which I hear of your high health, and welcomes to me the want of it. I thank God I shall not live to witness its issue.' *

" ' The line of division lately marked out between different portions of our confederacy, is such as will never, I fear, be obliterated, and we are now trusting to those who are against us in position and principle, to fashion to their own form the minds and affections of our youth. If, as has been estimated, we send three hundred thousand dollars a year to the northern seminaries for the instruction of our own sons, then we must have five hundred of our sons imbibing opinions and principles in discord with those of their own country. This canker is eating on the vitals of our existence, and, if not arrested at once, will be beyond remedy.' †

" ' The Missouri question is the most portentous one which ever yet threatened our Union. In the gloomiest moment of the Revolutionary War, I never had any apprehension equal to that I felt from this source.' " ‡

What Mr. Jefferson perceived in the distant future, Mr. Clay, twenty years afterward, saw as rapidly approaching. In addressing Rev. Walter Colton, his biographer, Mr. Clay expressed his opinions, in relation to abolitionism, as follows :

" ASHLAND, *Sept.* 2, 1843.

"*My Dear Sir :*—Allow me to select a subject for one of your tracts, which, treated in your popular and condensed way, I think would be attended with great and good effect. I mean abolition.

" It is manifest that the ultras of that party are extremely mischievous, and are hurrying on the country to fearful consequences. They are not to be conciliated by the Whigs. Engrossed with a single idea, they care for nothing else. They would see the administration of the Government precipitate the nation into absolute ruin before they would lend a helping hand to arrest its career. They treat worse, and denounce most, those who treat them best, who so far agree with them as to admit slavery to be an evil. Witness their conduct toward Mr. Briggs and Mr. Adams, in Massachusetts, and toward me.

* Letter to John Adams, December 10, 1819.
† Letter to General Breckenridge, February 11, 1821.
‡ Letter to Mr. Monroe, March 3, 1820.

"I will give you an outline of the manner in which I would handle it: Show the origin of slavery.   Trace its introduction to the British Government.   Show how it is disposed of by the Federal Constitution; that it is left exclusively to the States, except in regard to fugitives, direct taxes, and representation.   Show that the agitation of the question, in the free States, will first destroy all harmony, and finally lead to disunion—perpetual war—the extermination of the African race—ultimate military despotism.

"But the great aim and object of your tract should be to *arouse the laboring classes in the free States against abolition*.   Depict the consequences to them of immediate abolition.   The slaves, being free, would be dispersed throughout the Union; they would *enter into competition with the free laborer—with the American, the Irish, the German—reduce his wages, be confounded with him, and affect his moral and social standing*   And as the ultras go both for abolitionism and amalgamation, show that their object is to unite in marriage the laboring white man and the laboring black woman, to reduce the white laboring man to the despised and degraded condition of the black man.

"I would show their opposition to colonization.   Show its humane, religious, and patriotic aim.   That they are those whom God has separated.   Why do abolitionists oppose colonization?   To keep and amalgamate together the two races, in violation of God's will, and to keep the blacks here, that they may interfere with, degrade, and debase the laboring whites.   Show that the British Government is co-operating with the abolitionists for the purpose of dissolving the Union, etc.   You can make a powerful article, that will be felt in every extremity of the Union.   I am perfectly satisfied it will do great good.   Let me hear from you on this subject.

"HENRY CLAY."

But we must pass on.   The year 1859 found the prevailing excitement on the negro question quickened into new life, by the attempt of John Brown to raise a negro insurrection in Virginia; and his execution, near the close of the year, producing at the North many strong manifestations of sympathy for himself and the cause he had espoused, was the occasion of fresh alarm at the South.

And was there not cause for alarm?   One class of politicians had declared their intention to proclaim emancipation whenever a servile insurrection should occur, or a civil war break out.

John Brown had attempted to accomplish the task of arousing the slaves; and in the North his death was pronounced that of a martyr to a holy cause, and every token of respect shown to his memory in many pulpits, and in one legislative hall.* The courts of justice, too, in at least one case, were adjourned on the day of his execution, to signify an approval of his conduct.†

The abolitionists, having failed in exciting the slaves to insurrection, were still persevering in their attempts to provoke the South to acts of rebellion. John Brown had been but the embodiment of the spirit of this party; and Joshua R. Giddings had identified himself with it, when he thus wrote to the *Ashtabula Sentinel:*

"We have ourselves paid money to redeem Southern slaves until we have become disgusted with the practice, and prefer that our future donations shall be made in POWDER AND BALLS, DELIVERED TO THE SLAVES, TO BE USED AS THEY MAY DEEM PROPER."

The counter-movements in the South, to guard against the schemes of the abolitionists, progressed, from day to day, until it became evident that the safety of the Union was endangered. Reflecting men, both North and South, began to take the alarm, and to devise measures for the removal of the causes which threatened such a dreadful calamity.

And here, as elsewhere, we shall not attempt to trace with regularity the proceedings of the actors in this drama, because we wish to avoid coming into contact with the movements of political parties. This much, however, we can say, that the great majority of the two leading parties—Republican and Democrat—were determinedly hostile to a dissolution of the Union. But the Republicans, at the North, were powerless, except by the abolition vote; and the abolitionists, believing they had now

---

* Massachusetts.

† The court at Akron, Ohio, on motion of Attorney-General Wolcott, was adjourned on the day of the execution of John Brown, as a mark of respect to him, and of sympathy for the cause in which he lost his life. And what makes this latter case the more marked is, that Mr. Wolcott was afterward appointed a member of the Peace Congress, at Washington, by the Governor of Ohio, and aided in defeating the compromise of the national difficulties.

worked up the country to a point when a collision could be produced, and slavery abolished, were determined to push matters to the last extremity, and bring on the long-wished-for crisis. The Democrats, on the other hand, could not elect their candidate excepting by the united vote of the South. Less fortunate than the Republicans, they could not secure that united vote—could not affiliate with the secession party—and were, therefore, defeated. The event proved that the abolitionists held the balance of power at the North.

It does not fall in with our plan to give any detailed statements as to the views of the President upon the subject of slavery. That they have been conservative, in the main, appears from the assaults made upon him by the ultra abolitionists, immediately after his election. The *New York Times*, November 9, 1860, in noticing a speech of Wendell Phillips, in Boston, says:

"It is one of Mr. Phillips's sharpest and most stinging diatribes. Every sentence hisses with malignant scorn and indignation. LINCOLN, SEWARD, BANKS, and all the practical statesmen who concur in their opinions, are branded as traitors and hypocrites. . . . It is scarcely necessary to say, that the grounds on which Mr. Phillips denounces Mr. Lincoln are precisely those on which the country bases its hopes that he will have a successful and beneficent administration. Whatever Mr. Phillips may do, a President of the United States can not ignore the Constitution, nor disregard or evade its requisitions. Whatever he may think of slavery, he must recognize its existence in States over whose domestic affairs the Federal Government has no control, and give full weight to the rights and interests of those whose fortunes are identified with it. Mr. Phillips, some time since, paid Mr. Sumner the very damning compliment of saying that he thought him incapable of keeping the oath he had taken to support the Constitution of the United States. We are very glad to find that he has no such praise in store for Mr. Lincoln. He does him nothing more than justice in denouncing his purpose to abide by the Constitution in all its parts."

That the Republican party at large were very anxious to have it understood that Mr. Lincoln would occupy national ground in the administration of the Government, is further apparent from the remarks of Hon. Horace Greeley, at a Republican mass meeting, in New York City, on the evening of November 8, 1860, when the election of Mr. Lincoln had been ascertained. He said:

" It was not the fault of the Republican party if they had not been allowed to proclaim their principles in all sections of the country. Had they been thus allowed, the South would have been disabused of their errors in regard to the party, and he believed they could have fairly challenged the support of a majority of Southern men. As it was, he believed that when they come to be better understood, as they would be after the inauguration of Mr. Lincoln, their measures would be cheerfully acquiesced in by all the moderate men of the South."*

But these conservative views, attributed, we believe, justly, to Mr. Lincoln, did not stand alone among Republicans, or they would have contributed to the preservation of the peace of the country. At this very same meeting, William Cullen Bryant, who acted as chairman, and who was one of the electors on the Republican ticket, on taking the chair said:

" That they had met to-night to celebrate one of the most important moral and political victories that had ever been achieved. The youngest of his hearers might live till the next century, and not witness another election so pregnant with great results as the one through which they had just passed. And, best of all, they had triumphed. [Applause.] The enemy was conquered. At their feet lay the carcass of that odious slave oligarchy, which, for so long a period, had ruled our country, ruled Northern men, and tyrannized over both. [Tremendous applause.] And they, the young men he saw before him, had aided in dealing that terrible blow, which had, at length, struck the creature to the earth. [Renewed applause.] There it lay before them, dismembered, lifeless, dead, and from that death there was no resurrection. [A voice—' Thank the Lord !']."†

Thus, while conservative men in the Republican party were rejoicing over the election of a President who, in their opinion, would sustain the compromises of the Constitution, there were others, in that same party, who took a very different view of the

---

* New York Times, November 9, 1860.   † Ibid.

effects of the election.   Mr. Bryant may be taken as one of the opposite class, who anticipated the entire extirpation of slavery through the agency of Mr. Lincoln.   The truth is, that the abolitionists were now resolved to reap the harvest they had been so long engaged in sowing.

On the other hand, South Carolina was equally determined to carry out at once her long-cherished policy of secession.   Her politicians believed that compromises were no longer practicable, as they could not be relied upon to secure the objects for which they stipulated.   The Constitution itself had been a compromise, and yet, in some of its provisions, it had been repudiated, not only by political parties, but by States.   The parties claiming that slavery was unconstitutional, held the balance of power at the North, and, it was believed, could control the incoming administration.   South Carolina, therefore, persuaded herself that secession was the only safeguard for her institutions, and that, sooner or later, she must resort to that remedy; and that the longer it was deferred, the worse it would be for the whole South.   The North, by foreign immigration, was, year by year, growing stronger and stronger; while the South, having only its natural increase, was by no means able to keep up its numerical strength to an equality with the North.   The longer the delay, therefore, the less the chances of success—the less the ability of the South to resist the aggressions of the North upon its institutions.

Here, now, stood the champions in this conflict.   South Carolina, determined on secession as the only means of protecting her slave property, was arrayed on the one side.   New England, determined on the extinction of slavery, or the dissolution of the Union, stood upon the other.

But South Carolina stood alone—the other slave States believing that their rights could be best secured under the Constitution and in the Union.   As, however, it had been denied at the North that slaveholders had the same constitutional rights, as to property, which the non-slaveholders possessed, they demanded that proper guarantees should be given, so that, hereafter, no interference with slavery should be attempted.   Accordingly, the propositions were brought forward as a peace measure, which afterward took the name of the "Crittenden Compromise." But Congress failed to secure the necessary vote to carry this compromise. The "Peace Congress" was equally unsuccessful. Conservative men of both parties—Republicans and Democrats—tremblingly alive to the necessity of settling the controversy, and averting the impending civil war—united in entreating South Carolina to stay her incendiary hand, and not to apply the torch to the edifice which had cost, for its erection, the toil and the blood of their patriot fathers. They appealed, also, with equal fervor, to the fanatical abolitionist, to relax his zeal in a cause that must end in the ruin of the race he would benefit, as well as the destruction of the only free government on earth. But, no! Carolina stood ready to light the flame: the abolitionist, holding the legal control of the issue in his grasp, refused the guarantee to the South, and called for the effusion of blood.

We are not judging harshly. At the moment when it was thought that the "Peace Congress" might adopt measures to restore the Union, and prevent war, and when Michigan held back, and would not send delegates to that body, Senator Chandler wrote to Governor Blair, of that State, urging that the Legislature would retrace its steps, and at once send on its delegates. The following is his letter, and no other conclusion can be drawn than that the object was to prevent the passage of any compromise measures, so that civil war might be precipitated upon the country:

"WASHINGTON, *February* 11, 1861.

"*My Dear Governor:*—Governor Bingham and myself telegraphed you on Saturday, at the request of Massachusetts and New York, to send delegates to the Peace or Compromise Congress. They admit that we are right, and they wrong; that no Republican State should have sent delegates; but they are here, and can't get away. Ohio, Indiana, and Rhode Island *are caving in*, and there is *danger* of Illinois, and now they beg us, for God's sake, to *come to their rescue*, and *save the Republican party from rupture*. I hope you will send *stiff-backed* men, or none. The whole thing was got up against my judgment and advice, and will end in thick smoke. Still, I hope, as a matter of courtesy to some of our erring brethren, that you will send the delegates. Truly, your friend, Z. CHANDLER.

" His Excellency, AUSTIN BLAIR.

" P. S.—Some of the manufacturing States think that *a fight* would be AWFUL. *Without a little blood-letting, this Union will not, in my estimation, be worth a rush.*"

That a compromise would have been effected, and that the whole South would have accepted it, save South Carolina only, and the Union have been maintained, by the adoption of some one of the compromises proposed, is a truth that can not be disputed, and that was not denied when it was asserted upon the floor of Congress. Hear Mr. Douglas, in his speech in the Senate, January 3d, 1861, when urging the adoption of his compromise:

" I believe this to be a fair basis of amicable adjustment. If you of the Republican side are not willing to accept this, nor the proposition of the Senator from Kentucky, [Mr. Crittenden,] *pray tell us what* you are willing to do? I address the inquiry to the Republicans alone, *for the reason that, in the Committee of Thirteen, a few days ago, every member from the South, including those from the cotton States,* [Messrs. Toombs and Davis,] *expressed their readiness to accept the proposition of my venerable friend from Kentucky* [Mr. Crittenden] *as a final settlement of the controversy, if tendered and sustained by the Republican members. Hence, the sole responsibility of our disagreement, and the only difficulty in the way of an amicable adjustment is with the Republican party.*"

Again, we have the testimony of another Senator, Mr. Pugh, in his speech, March 2d, 1861, upon the Corwin resolution to amend the Constitution of the United States. He said:

" The Crittenden proposition has been indorsed by the almost unanimous vote of the Legislature of Kentucky. It has been indorsed by the Legislature of the noble old commonwealth of Virginia. It has been petitioned for by a larger number of electors of the United States than any proposition that was ever before Congress. I believe, in my heart, to-day, that it would carry an overwhelming majority of the people of my State; ay, sir, and of nearly every other State in the Union.

Before the Senators from the State of Mississippi left this chamber, I heard one of them, who now assumes, at least, to be President of the Southern Confederacy, propose to accept it, and to maintain the Union, if that proposition could receive the vote it ought to receive from the other side of the chamber. Therefore, of all your propositions, of all your amendments, knowing, as I do, and knowing that the historian will write *it down, at any time before the first of January, a two-thirds vote for the Crittenden resolutions, in this chamber, would have saved every State in the Union but South Carolina.*"

These declarations were made in the hearing of Messrs Seward, Wade, Fessenden, Trumbull, and all the Republican Senators, none of whom denied their truth; and Mr. Douglas also heard it, and confirmed its truth thus:

" *The Senator has said, that if the Crittenden proposition could have passed early in the session, it would have saved all the States except South Carolina. I firmly believe it would.* While the Crittenden proposition was not in accordance with my cherished views, I avowed my readiness and eagerness to accept it, in order to save the Union, if we could unite upon it. No man has labored harder than I have to get it passed. *I can confirm the Senator's declaration, that Senator Davis himself, when on the Committee of Thirteen, was ready, at all times, to compromise on the Crittenden proposition.* I will go farther, and say that Mr. Toombs was also."

But if more is wanting to prove that the South would have accepted the Crittenden Compromise, we have it in the language of Mr. Toombs himself, who, in his speech in the United States Senate, January 7, 1861, said:

"But although I insist upon this perfect equality, yet, when it was proposed—as I understand the Senator from Kentucky now proposes—that the line of 36° 30' shall be extended, acknowledging and protecting our property on the south side of the line, for the sake of peace—permanent peace, I said to the Committee of Thirteen, and I say here, with other satisfactory provisions, I would accept it."

The arrival of new delegates to the Peace Congress, upon the appeal made to the States not represented, placed the conservative Republicans and Democrats in a position which rendered them powerless for good. No compromise could be effected; and the die was then cast. The South had demanded protection or dissolution : the protection being refused, dissolution was attempted.

But there is another act in the drama, which must be noticed briefly, in order to have a better understanding of the causes contributing to our present national distress. Hon. Andrew Johnson, of Tennessee, had charged upon the anti-slavery men of the North the formation of a conspiracy to dissolve the Union. The right of secession had been claimed by Mr. Quincy, of Boston, in 1811; by J. Q. Adams, in 1838 and 1839; and by many other Northern men. As the present crisis approached, or toward the close of 1860, and after the Presidential election, one of the leading anti-slavery papers, and its editor a representative man among abolitionists, gave utterance to the following sentiments, perhaps as a *lure* to lead the South to hope that peaceful secession was practicable :

"If the cotton States consider the value of the Union debatable, we maintain their perfect right to discuss it. Nay, we hold with Jefferson, to the inalienable right of communities to alter or abolish forms of government that have become oppressive or injurious; and if the cotton States shall become satisfied that they can do better out of the Union than in it, *we insist on letting them go in peace*. The right to secede may be a revolutionary one, *but it exists*, nevertheless; and we do not see how one party can have a right to do what another party has a right to prevent. We must ever resist the asserted right of any State to remain in the Union and nullify or defy the laws thereof; to withdraw from the Union is quite another matter. And whenever a considerable section of our Union shall deliberately resolve to go out, *we shall resist all coercive measures designed to keep it in*. We hope never to live in a republic whereof one section is pinned to the residue by bayonets."*

"If the cotton States unitedly and earnestly wish to withdraw peacefully from the Union, we think they should and would be *allowed to do so.* Any attempt *to compel them, by force, to remain*, would be contrary to the principles enunciated in the immortal Declaration of

* New York Tribune, Nov. 9, 1860.

Independence—contrary to the fundamental ideas on which Human Liberty is based."*

"If the people of seven or eight contiguous States shall pretty unani mously resolve to secede and set up for themselves, we think they would do so, and that *it would be most unwise* to undertake to *resist such secession by Federal force.* Why is it that those who want to enforce this doctrine make their attack on something else ?"†

South Carolina opened her guns upon Fort Sumter, and a shout of exultation arose from the abolitionist. Listen to the *Anti-slavery Standard*, sounding the glad tidings over the land, and glorying in its treason to the Constitution :

"For the last ten years, yea, eleven, next seventeenth of March, the Hunkerdom of the North has been engaged in a constant effort to save the Union. The abolitionism of the North has been all the time busy in the opposite direction, trying to break it up.' *Well, we have beaten— the Union is dissolved, in spite of the Hunkers.* It is nothing odd that they should rage and imagine strange things. Nobody likes to be licked. That is just what they are. Let us be patient with them, and let them expend their froth and fury. Better times are at hand, and all the nearer, the worse they behave. *One thing is certain, the Union is dissolved.*"

The unceasing efforts of the abolitionists to secure emancipation by military proclamation, and their attacks upon every one— the President not excepted—who stood in the way of the execution of their policy, can now be understood. But in what way can we reconcile the declarations of Mr. Greeley, in favor of peaceful secession before the war, with his ferocious denunciations of the secessionists since its commencement, and his desire that the war shall be one of utter ruin to the South, excepting upon the theory of Senator Johnson, that there existed a conspiracy to effect a dissolution of the Union? Hear him, shortly after the war had commenced :

"Therefore shall we imitate the South no more in war than in peace. But, nevertheless, we mean to conquer them—not merely to defeat, but to *conquer*, to SUBJUGATE them—and we shall do this the most

---

* New York Tribune, Nov. 26.   † Ibid., Dec. 10.

mercifully the more speedily we do it. But when the rebellious traitors are overwhelmed in the field, and scattered like leaves before an angry wind, it must not be to return to peaceful and contented homes. They must find poverty at their firesides, and see privation in the anxious eyes of mothers, and the rags of children."

Mr. Greeley's language to the South, before its rebellion, was practically this : "Go on and secede, we do not longer want you, and we shall not molest you." But no sooner had the secession flag been fairly unfurled, than he calls for the direst vengeance to be executed upon all its inhabitants, mothers and children not excepted.

About the same time that Mr. Greeley called for destruction to the traitors, the *New York Independent*, the paper of Rev. Henry Ward Beecher, used the following language :

"The grand result — the only solution of the question — is fast coming up—the *emancipation of the slaves* by the nation. What other escape is there from our difficulties? Why should not our people and our statesmen look it fair in the face? The South is far stronger and better supplied than we suppose. She *is in earnest.* She believes herself bitterly wronged. She is not likely to think herself less so after a blockade and a campaign. She is encouraged by the base sympathy of England. She never could feel any surety for slavery in another Union with us. She *hates us.* . . . . . Evidently there is but one path to safety and victory—one to a permanent settlement—one to the quiet or subjugation of the South. Do not fear it! Look it boldly in the face—namely : the emancipation of the slaves.

"Let our armies, as a 'military necessity' and strategical act, declare 'freedom' to all, and in a moment we have an army of four million human beings on our side—allies in every house and on every plantation. The enemy is demoralized. Panic sweeps through the Southern land. Here is a foe more dreadful than Northern armies. Fighting so near our own forces, we may hope the revengeful feelings of these poor oppressed creatures would be restrained. Still, there would inevitably be desolation and destruction sweeping like a tempest over the Southern land. *And it would be just.* These men have borne the wrongs of centuries, and why should not their *uprising be bloody?* Let them have their freedom, if they can win it, even though it be over the corpses of their masters and the ashes of the ruined home-

steads.   After this tempest of fire and havoc, would arise a better era
for the South.   Free laborers would pour in; wasted fields would be
cultivated by new hands; ruined cities would be built up by Northern
capital and ingenuity, and the problem and the task for the civilization of the coming age would be the education and preparation of
4,000,000 of blacks—perhaps through some system of apprenticeship,
for the rights and the privileges of free laborers.

"*For such a glorious result, even if it come through tears and blood,
do we devoutly pray.*"

It would be an onerous task, indeed, to copy all the outpour-
ings of the gall and the wormwood of clerical abolitionists, on the
question of the subjugation of the South as a means of emancipation.   One or two only need be presented.   THE AMERICAN
REFORM TRACT AND BOOK SOCIETY,* an abolition association in
Cincinnati, in one of its Occasional Tracts, (No. 5,) undertakes
thus to frighten the Government into emancipation, by declaring
what is the will and purposes of the Almighty in the present condition of the country:

"*We shall fall before the rebels until the nation act as He demands
at our hands.   Defeat will attend our arms, corruption and mismanagement our affairs, destruction brood the nation,* the history of Pha-
raoh and Egypt be ours, unless we yield thus to His will.

"Then let the decree go forth from the nation, through its authorities; in obedience to the Word, and Spirit, and Providence of God;
in compliance with the enlightened sentiment of the civilized world;
in response to the moral convictions of our own people; in answer
to the emphatic demands of Public Safety, and in clear conformity
with a just Public Integrity—the decree that 'THIS SLAVEHOLDING
INTEREST, BEING IN REBELLION AGAINST THE NATION, AND THREAT-
ENING IT WITH DESTRUCTION, SHALL NO LONGER HAVE PROTECTION
UNDER THE NATIONAL LAWS; BUT IS FOREVER OUTLAWED AS A PUB-
LIC ENEMY; AND SLAVEHOLDING HENCEFORTH EXCLUDED WHEREVER
THE NATIONAL POWER EXTENDS.' "

Another Occasional Tract, (No. 6,) printed by the same society,
and delivered as a sermon by the pastor of the Ninth Street

---

* This Society and its tracts have been recommended by the General Assembly of the United Presbyterian Church.

Baptist Church, Cincinnati, December 8th, 1861, contains the following diabolical utterance :

"Let every city be razed to the ground, swept, sacked, and burned— let Washington, Baltimore, New York, Cincinnati and St. Louis lie in ashes, rather than we yield, or reconstruct, or *Compromise :* for *now* there is no compromise except in yielding."

We leave the reader to judge of the motives of Northern politicians, in first advocating the right of secession, and then demanding coercion, as soon as that right was asserted by the South.   In the quotations made, the opinion is openly avowed that abolitionism was necessary to preserve the balance of the Constitution; and that, in the event of that balance being made to turn in behalf of the South, by the extension of slavery, the North would dissolve the Union.   These oft-repeated threats, on the part of Northern politicians, were equally as criminal as any similar ones ever made at the South, so long as nothing but threats were employed.   They were conditional on both sides; those of the North threatening a withdrawal from the Union, should slavery be extended; those of the South threatening the same course of action, should any attempt be made either to destroy or limit that institution.   Both parties acted in a criminal manner, because such threats were familiarizing the people to the idea of the dissolution of the Union; and in allowing the parties using them to escape the most withering rebuke, scorn, contempt, indignation, has been the great sin of conservative men upon both sides of Mason's and Dixon's Line.   The only difference between these parties who talked so daringly about disunion, is, that while it was mainly employed as mere *bunkum,* for political effect, at the North, it was no unmeaning phrase at the South.   There, the value of property, the peace and safety of society, the lives of wives and children, were involved in the issue of the controversy which the secessionists of the South held with the disunionists of the North.   They were terribly in earnest, and, under such goadings as those quoted from Giddings and others, they have had the courage to carry out their threats into actual treason; and are now suffering the penalty justly due to the enormity of the offense they have committed. Had they waited, the conservative men of the North would have forced Congress to give them the guarantees they demanded under the Constitution. Of this there can be no question. But they are not suffering alone. We have more than once referred to the fact, that the conservative men of the country are responsible for the calamities brought upon the nation, by the opposing sectional factions who have used the slavery question as a means of promoting sectional interests. The penalty for their remissness is now being visited upon them; and these conservative men are at last aroused to a sense of the dangers that surround them, but which should have been prevented by them. They are at last taking a just view of the dangers of abolitionism, whether it presents itself in the pulpit, the press, or the ecclesiastical council. The disturbing influences of "pulpit politics," whether ringing from Southern pulpits in support of slavery, or from those of the North against it, have overwhelmed them in a mighty struggle to preserve the Constitution and the Union, and they are freely offering their property, their blood, their lives, to consummate that object. And when that task is done, they will have learned a more striking lesson than did the nation of Israel, under King David, when the three years of famine fell upon the land, as a judgment for the violation of its covenant with the Gibeonites, made centuries before the violation occurred.* And, here, we would remark, that it seems never to have occurred to the minds of the demagogues among the clergy, to study the history of the Gibeonites, and there to learn that covenants between peoples must be sacredly kept; because Heaven takes cognizance of the violation of covenant engagements among men.

But we must not pursue this subject. The roar of cannon sounding in our ears, the noise of the rush of armed men to the battle, the cries of the wounded, the groans of the dying, the tears and wailing of the widow and the orphan forbid it! A dreadful responsibility, before high Heaven, rests upon the authors of these woes.

---

* II Samuel, chapter 21.

CHAPTER XI.

THE COTTON CROP IN ITS RELATIONS TO AMERICAN COMMERCE.

Much misconception has existed in the United States in reference to the question of the production and supply of cotton, and
much misrepresentation, in relation to the facts in the case, has
been set afloat through the medium of the press. Were we to
pass this subject without notice, our investigations would be incomplete. In entering upon its examination, a historical review
of the movements of Great Britain will best serve to exhibit the
true relations which the American cotton planter has sustained to
the cultivation of this commodity throughout the world.

SECTION I. — EARLY MOVEMENTS OF GREAT BRITAIN TO RETRIEVE
HER LOSSES CONSEQUENT UPON WEST INDIA EMANCIPATION.

The death blow to cotton cultivation in the British West Indies
was given by the act abolishing the slave trade. At the beginning of the present century the exports of cotton from these
islands nearly equaled that from the United States — the one
exporting 17,000,000 lbs., the other 17,780,000 lbs. But upon
the suppression of the slave trade, and the consequent diminution
of labor in the islands, its cultivation began to decline, so that, by
1834, when the emancipation act went into operation, it had diminished to 2,296,525 lbs. This enormous decline in cotton culture,
in the West Indies, was a source of great alarm to British manufacturers. Emancipation was expected to remedy this great misfortune, on the principle that the labor of the negroes, when free,
would be much more productive than it had been while they were
slaves. This was the British theory of that day, as to the beneficial effects of emancipation; upon this theory Parliament based
its act for the abolition of West India slavery; and, as a consequence of this act, the English people confidently anticipated an

enlarged production of all the commodities usually cultivated in the islands.

Even as late as 1839 this theory was still held as true, as appears from an address delivered in Boston, by Mr. Scoble, a gentleman who had been secretary of the British and Foreign Anti-Slavery Society, which we find noticed in the *Christian Watchman* of that year. * Mr. Scoble had recently visited the West Indies, and professed to speak from actual observation. He represented the prosperity of the islands as on the increase, and this he "accounted for by saying that one free laborer would do more than two slaves."

All this, it is now well understood, was mere *bunkum*, designed to influence the people of the United States to follow the example of England in abolishing slavery. Æsop would have illustrated the designs of Mr. Scoble by his fable of the fox that lost his tail in the trap, and who urged upon a convention of other foxes the great convenience he experienced in having that bushy appendage out of the way.

The year 1839, in which Mr. Scoble came over to instruct us as to the benefits of emancipation, found the West Indies exporting but 928,425 pounds of cotton, and the year 1840 but 427,529 pounds as against 17,000,000 exported in 1800. Cotton cultivation was about at an end in the West Indies. The labor necessary for its production could not be commanded; and, even if it had been in sufficient abundance, prices had so fallen, in consequence of the immense production of the United States, then equaling, for export alone, 743,941,000 pounds that year, (1840,) that attractive wages could not be offered to the newly emancipated blacks.

The American planter had the monopoly of the supply of cotton to the markets of the Christian world; and the West India planter as far as he could command labor, chose to employ it in the production of sugar rather than upon cotton. This left the British manufacturer at the mercy of the slaveholder of the United States for his supplies of that commodity — a position that he chose not to occupy a moment longer than it could be avoided. We find,

---

* The article is quoted in the Christian Intelligencer, Hamilton, Ohio, October, 1839, page 284.

accordingly, that at the same time that Mr. Scoble was telling the American people about the increasing prosperity of the West Indies, and the greater efficiency of the free negro over the slave, a movement was set on foot, in England, to transfer the seat of cotton cultivation to the East Indies. George Thompson, Esq., the Abolitionist, was placed in the foreground in this movement, and, during 1839, in a course of lectures, undertook to prove that all the elements of successful cotton cultivation existed in India; and that the English people might soon obtain their supplies of cotton from that country, and thus be enabled to repudiate that of the United States. The appeal was made to Parliament to extend a helping hand to cotton culture in the East Indies; and the object to be gained by the measure proposed was the emancipation of the slaves of the United States, by destroying the markets for its cotton. In one of his lectures he thus exclaims:

"The battle-ground of freedom for the world is on the plains of Hindostan. Yes, my friends, *do justice to India;* wave *there* the scepter of justice, and the rod of oppression falls from the hands of the slaveholder in America; and the slave, swelling beyond the measure of his chains, stands disenthralled, a free man and an acknowledged brother." *

The introduction to the American edition of the lectures delivered by Mr. Thompson, on that occasion, which was written by William Lloyd Garrison, contains the following sentences. † They sufficiently indicate what were the anticipations of the advocates of the measure:

"If England can raise her own cotton in India, at the paltry rate of a penny a pound, what inducement can she have to obtain her supply from a rival nation, at a rate six or eight times higher? It is stated that the East India free labor costs three pence a day — African slave labor two shillings; that upward of 800,000 bales of cotton are exported from the United States annually to England; and that the cotton trade of the United States with England amounts to the enormous sum of $40,000,000 annually. Let that market be closed to this

---

* Lectures of George Thompson, Esq., 1839, page 121.
† Introduction to Thompson's Lectures, page 9.

slaveholding republic, and its slave system must inevitably perish from starvation ! "

In pursuance of this policy, cotton-seed from the United States was sent to India, and experienced planters from Mississippi, at high salaries, were employed to superintend its cultivation. But the enterprise was not successful, and the Mississippians, after several years' experimenting, returned home to their own plantations.

The public are fully informed on this subject, so that the history of the enterprise need not be traced at large.

Paragraphs like the following, from time to time, frequently met the eye of the general reader. It is taken from a reliable periodical :

"Late accounts from India, (through the English press,) represent that the attempts of the British capitalists, during the last two or three years, to cultivate cotton in the district of Dharwar, from which much was expected, have signally failed. In 1847-'48, about 20,000 acres were cultivated. It is now ascertained that the crop has rapidly decreased, only 4,000 acres having been under cultivation the past year."

Toward the close of this East India experiment, the *London Times*, under the head of "Cotton in India," said :

"The one great element of American success — of American enterprise — can never, at least for many generations, be imparted to India. It is impossible to expect of Hindoos all that is achieved by citizens of the States. During the experiments to which we have alluded, an English plow was introduced into one of the provinces, and the natives were taught its use and superiority over their own clumsy machinery. They were at first astonished and delighted at its effects, but as soon as the agent's back was turned, they took it, painted it red, set it up on end and *worshiped* it."

But this attempt of Great Britain, to secure her supplies of cotton from other sources than the United States, does not stand alone. Seeing, as if by prophetic forecast, that the attempt to cultivate the better qualities of cotton in India would prove a failure, a nearly simultaneous effort was made to extend its cultivation to Africa. The West Indies, as a field of cotton supply, seemed to be closed forever, as a consequence of emancipation. * It was the expectation of the British that the United States could be made to share the same fate, by the success of abolitionism; and that the monopoly of the American planter being thus destroyed, the price of cotton would necessarily rise, so that it could be grown and exported, at a profit, from more distant fields.

The circumstances which gave rise to the attempt to make Africa a field of cotton production are of very great interest, and must not be overlooked. They may be briefly given in a few extracts:

" The following table, extracted from Parliamentary documents, presents the average number of slaves exported from Africa to America, and sold chiefly in Brazil and Cuba, with the per cent. amount of loss in the periods designated:

DATE.	ANNUAL AVERAGE NUMBER EXPORTED.	AVERAGE CASUALTIES OF VOYAGE.	
		PER CENT.	AMOUNT.
1798 to 1805	85,000	14	12,000
1805 to 1810	85,000	14	12,000
1810 to 1815	93,000	14	13,000
1815 to 1817	106,000	25	26,600
1817 to 1819	106,000	25	26,600
1819 to 1825	103,000	25	25,800
1825 to 1830	125,000	25	31,000
1830 to 1835	78,500	25	19,600
1835 to 1840	135,800	25	33,900

" The late Sir Thomas Fowell Buxton devoted himself with unwearied industry to the investigation of the extent and enormities of the foreign slave trade. His labors extended through many years, and the results, as published in 1840, sent a thrill of horror throughout the Christian world. He proved conclusively that the victims to the slave trade in Africa amounted annually to 500,000. This included the numbers who perish in the seizure of the victims, in the wars of the natives upon each other, and the deaths during their march to the coast and the detention there before embarkation. This loss he estimates at one-half, or 500 out of every 1,000. The destruction of life during the middle passage he estimates at 25 per cent., or 125 out of the remaining 500 of the original 1,000. The mortality after landing and in seasoning he shows is 20 per cent., or one-fifth of the 375 sur-

* The coolie traffic was not then begun, and no means existed, apparently, for restoring the islands to their former productiveness.

vivors. Thus he proves that the number of lives sacrificed by the
system bears, to the number of slaves available to the planter, the proportion of *seven to three* — that is to say, for every 300 slaves landed
and sold in the market, 700 have fallen victims to the deprivations and
cruelties connected with the traffic.

"This enormous increase of the slave trade, it must be remembered,
had taken place during the period of vigorous efforts for its suppression. England alone, according to McQueen, had expended for this
object, up to 1842, in the employment of a naval force on the coast of
Africa, the sum of $88,888,888, and he estimated the annual expendi-
ture at that time at $2,500,000.

"The disclosures of Mr. Buxton produced a profound sensation
throughout England, and the conviction was forced upon the public
mind, and 'upon Her Majesty's confidential advisers,' that the slave
trade could not be suppressed by physical force, and that it was 'indispensable to enter upon some new preventive system calculated to
arrest the foreign slave trade.'

"The remedy proposed and attempted to be carried out, was 'the
deliverance of Africa by calling forth her own resources.'

"To accomplish this great work, the capitalists of England were to
set on foot agricultural companies, who, under the protection of the
Government, should obtain lands by treaty with the natives and employ them in its tillage ; to send out trading ships and open factories
at the most commanding positions ; to increase and concentrate the
English naval force on the coast, the rivers, and the interior. These
measures adopted, the companies formed were to call to their aid a
race of teachers of African blood, from Sierra Leone and the West
Indies, who should labor with the whites in diffusing intelligence in
imparting religious instruction, in teaching agriculture, in establishing
and encouraging legitimate commerce, and in impeding and suppressing the slave trade. In conformity with these views and aims, the
AFRICAN CIVILIZATION SOCIETY was formed, and the Government
fitted out three large iron steamers, at an expense of $300,000, for
the use of the company.

"Mr. McQueen, who had for more than twenty years devoted himself to the consideration of Africa's redemption and Britain's glory,
and who had become the most perfect master of African geography
and African resources, also appealed to the Government, and urged
the adoption of measures for making *all Africa a dependency of the
British Empire.* Speaking of what England had already accomplished,
and what she could yet achieve, he exclaims :

"'Unfold the map of the world: We command the Ganges. Fortified at Bombay, the Indus is our own. Possessed of the islands in the mouth of the Persian Gulf, we command the outlets of Persia and the mouths of the Euphrates, and consequently of countries the cradle of the human race. We command at the Cape of Good Hope. Gibraltar and Malta belonging to us, we control the Mediterranean. Let us plant the British standard on the island of Socatora — upon the island of Fernando Po, and inland upon the banks of the Niger; and then we may say Asia and Africa, for all their productions and all their wants, are under our control. It is in our power. Nothing can prevent us.'

"The African Civilization Society commenced its labors under circumstances the most favorable for success. Its list of members embraced many of the noblest names of the kingdom. Men of science and intelligence embarked in it, and when the expedition set sail, a shout of joy arose and a prayer for success ascended from ten thousand philanthropic English voices.

"But this magnificent scheme, fraught with untold blessings to Africa, and destined, it was believed, not only to regenerate her speedily, but to produce a revenue of unnumbered millions of dollars to the stockholders, proved an utter failure. The African climate, that deadly foe to the white man, blighted the enterprise. In a few months, disease and death had so far reduced the number of the men connected with the expedition, that the enterprise was abandoned." *

In 1844, Mr. McQueen again sounded the note of alarm in the ears of the people of Great Britain, and urged upon public attention the necessity of recovering the former advantages, in tropical productions, which the nation had possessed. The strong manner in which he put the case, will be seen from an extract or two:

" During the fearful struggle of a quarter of a century, for her existence as a nation, against the power and resources of Europe, directed by the most intelligent, but remorseless military ambition against her, *the command of the productions of the torrid zone*, and the advantageous commerce which that afforded, gave to Great Britain the power and resources which enabled her to meet, to combat, and to overcome her numerous and reckless enemies in every battle-field, whether by sea or land, throughout the world. In her the world saw realized the

* "Ethiopia," pages 12, 13, 14.

fabled giant of antiquity. With her hundred hands she grasped her foes in every region under heaven, and crushed them with resistless energy."

As remarked in a previous chapter, if the possession and control of tropical production gave to England such immense resources, and secured to her the superiority and such power, in the last century, then she would not yield them in the present, but in a death-struggle for their maintenance. That struggle had commenced when Mr. McQueen came forward with his appeals to the nation, to resort to Africa for the remedy. British philanthropy had wrought out its results in the West Indies, and demonstrated the futility of the schemes it had pursued. British tropical cultivation and the commerce it sustained both lay in ruins, while the slave trade and slavery laughed the nation to scorn. In urging immediate action upon the government and people, he proceeded to show that "the increased cultivation and prosperity of foreign tropical possessions is become so great, and is advancing so rapidly the power and resources of *other nations*, that these are embarrassing this country (England,) in all her commercial relations, in her pecuniary resources, and in all her political relations and negotiations."

In proof of his assertions, he presented the official returns of the exports from the British tropical possessions, as compared with those of a few only of those of other nations, in three articles alone of tropical products. The following are the results:

ARTICLES.	BRITISH POSSESSIONS.	FOREIGN COUNTRIES.*
Sugar, lbs., 1842	447,302,352	1,199,044,784
Coffee, lbs., 1842	27,393,003	337,432,84ᶜ
Cotton, lbs., 1840	137,443,446	981,206,903

This exhibition of figures is full of meaning. Nearly three-fourths of the products of these foreign countries had been created within thirty years of the date of the appeal of Mr. McQueen;

* The British Possessions referred to, include the East Indies, West Indies, and Mauritius; the foreign countries, the United States, Cuba, Brazil, Java, Venezuela.

and, aside from the United States, Java, and Venezuela, all were dependent upon the slave trade for the successful prosecution of their cultivation.   Mr. McQ., therefore, proceeded to say :

" If the foreign slave trade be not extinguished, and the tropical territories of other powers *opposed and checked by British tropical cultivation*, then the interests and the power of such states will rise into a preponderance over those of Great Britain ; and the power and the influence of the latter will cease to be felt, feared, and respected, among the civilized and powerful nations of the world."

From the foregoing facts it is easy to perceive that the slave trade had been very sensibly and very seriously affecting the interests of the British Government; * that it had been an engine in the hands of other nations, by which they had thrown England into the back ground in the productions of those articles of which she formerly had the monopoly, and which had given to her such power and influence ; and that she must either crush the slave trade, or it would continue to paralyze her.   Here is the true secret of her movements in reference to the slave trade and slavery.   Her first step — the prohibition of the slave trade to her colonies — gave to Spain, Portugal, and France all the advantages of that traffic ; and the cheaper and more abundant labor thus secured, gave a powerful stimulus to the production of tropical commodities in their colonies, and soon enabled them to rival and greatly surpass England in the amount of her production of these articles.   It was considered absolutely necessary, therefore, to the prosperity of Great Britain, that she should regain the advantageous position which she had occupied, in being the chief producer of tropical commodities, or, at least, that she should lessen her dependence upon other countries.

But the Government and its advisers now found themselves in the mortifying position of having blundered miserably in their emancipation scheme, and of having landed themselves in a dilemma of singular perplexity.   The prohibition of the slave trade, and the abolition of slavery in the West Indies, resulted so favorably to the interests of those countries employing slave labor, by enlarging the markets for slave-grown products, that the difficulty

* For details see Chapter V.

of inducing them to cease from it, was increased a hundredfold. In relation to the embarrassments under which the British nation was laboring, Mr. McQueen said:

"Instead of supplying her own wants with tropical productions, and next nearly all Europe, as she formerly did, she had scarcely enough of some of the most important articles for her own consumption, while her colonies were mostly supplied with foreign slave produce. . . . . . . In the meantime, tropical productions had been increased from $75,000,000 to $300,000,000 annually. The English capital invested in tropical productions in the East and West Indies had been, by emancipation in the latter, reduced from $750,000,000 to $650,000,000; while, since 1808, on the part of foreign nations, $4,000,000,000 of fixed capital had been created in slaves and in cultivation wholly dependent upon the labor of slaves."

The odds, therefore, in agricultural and commercial capital and interest, and consequently in political power and influence, arrayed against the British tropical possessions, were very fearful — six to one.

This, then, was the position of England from 1840 to 1844, and these the forces marshaled against her, and which she must meet and combat. In all her movements hitherto, she had only added to the strength of her rivals. Her first step, the suppression of the slave trade, had diminished her West India laborers 100,000 in twenty-three years, and reduced her means of production to that extent, giving all the benefits arising from this and from the slave trade to rival nations, who had but too well improved their advantages. But besides her commercial sacrifices, she had expended $100,000,000 to remunerate the planters for the slaves emancipated, and another $100,000,000 for an armed repression of the slave trade. And yet, in all this enormous expenditure, resulting only in loss to England, Africa had received no advantage whatever; but, on the contrary, she had been robbed, since 1808, of at least 3,500,000 slaves,* who had been exported to Cuba and Brazil from her coast, making a total loss to Africa, by the rule of Buxton, of 11,666,000 human beings, or one million more than the whole white population of the United States in

---

* McQueen.

1830, and more than three times the number of our present slave population. *

Now, it was abundantly evident that Great Britain was impelled by an overpowering necessity, by the instinct of self-preservation, to effect the suppression of the slave trade. It was true, no doubt, that considerations of justice and humanity were among the motives which influenced her actions. Interest and duty, therefore, combined to stimulate her to exertion. The measures to be adopted to secure success, were also becoming more apparent. Few other nations are guided by statesmen more quick to perceive the best course to adopt in an emergency, and none more readily abandon a scheme as soon as it proves impracticable. Great Britain stood pledged to her own citizens and to the world for the suppression of the slave trade. She stood equally pledged to demonstrate that free labor can be made more productive than slave labor, even in the cultivation of tropical commodities. These pledges she could not deviate from nor revoke. Her interests as well as her honor were deeply involved in their fulfillment. But she could only demonstrate the greater productiveness of free labor over slave labor, by opposing the one to the other, in their practical operations on a scale coëxtensive with each other. She must produce tropical commodities so cheaply and so abundantly by free labor, that she could undersell slave-grown products to such an extent, and glut the markets of the world with them so fully, as to render it unprofitable any longer to employ slaves in tropical cultivation. Such an enterprise, successfully carried out, she conceived, would be a death-blow to slavery and the slave trade. " But," says McQueen, " there remained no portion of the tropical world, where labor could be had on the spot, and whereon Great Britain could conveniently and safely plant her foot, in order to accomplish this desirable object — extensive tropical cultivation — but in tropical Africa. Every other part was occupied by independent nations, or by people that might and would soon become independent." Africa, therefore, was the field upon which Great Britain was compelled to enter and make her second grand experiment. †

---

* This refers to 1850.

† See " Ethiopia," pages 48, 49.

But even this field was not as fully open as it had been when the "Niger Expedition" was fitted out. The failure of that enterprise occurred while the Government was engaged in adjusting its difficulties with China, which grew out of the "Opium Question," and in conducting its war with the Sikhs of India. When, therefore, attention was again turned to Africa, it was found that much of its territory, also, had been occupied by other nations. Briefly, we must once more refer to the labors of McQueen for the main part of our facts:

"France, fully alive to the importance of the commerce with Africa, had, within a short period, securely placed herself at the mouth of the Senegal and at Goree, extending her influence eastward and southeastward from both places. She had a settlement at Albreda, on the Gambia, a short distance above St. Mary's, and which commands that river. She had formed a settlement at the mouth of the Gaboon, and another near the chief mouth of the Niger. She had fixed herself at Massuah and Bure, on the west shore of the Red Sea, commanding the inlets into Abyssinia. She had endeavored to fix her flag at Brava and the mouth of the Jub, and had taken permanent possession of the important island of Johanna, situated in the center of the northern outlet of the Mozambique channel, by which she acquired its command. Her active agents were placed in Southern Abyssinia, and employed in traversing the borders of the Great White Nile; while Algiers, on the northern shores of Africa, must speedily be her own.* Spain had planted herself, since the Niger expedition, in the island of Fernando Po, which commands all the outlets of the Niger and the rivers from Cameroons to the equator. Portugal, witnessing these movements, had taken measures to revive her once fine and still important colonies in tropical Africa. They included 17° of latitude on the east coast, from the tropic of Capricorn to Zanzibar, and nearly 19° on the west coast, from the 20th° south latitude, northward to Cape Lopez. The Imaum of Muscat claimed the sovereignty on the east coast, from Zanzibar to Babelmandel, with the exception of the station of the French at Brava. From the Senegal northward to Algeria was in the possession of the independent Moorish princes. Tunis, Tripoli, and Egypt were north of the tropic of Cancer, and independent tributaries of Turkey.

"Here, then, all the eastern and northern coasts of Africa, and also

---

* This has been accomplished.

the west coast from the Gambia northward, was found to be in the actual possession of independent sovereignties, who, of course, would not yield the right to England.   Southern Africa, below the tropic of Capricorn, already belonging to England, though only the same distance south of the equator that Cuba and Florida are north of it, is highly elevated above the sea level, and not adapted to tropical productions.   The claims of Portugal on the west coast, before noticed, extending from near the British South African line to Cape Lopez, excluded England from that district.   From Cape Lopez to the mouth of the Niger, including the Gaboon and Fernando Po, as before stated, was under the control of the French and Spanish.

"The only new territory, therefore, not claimed by civilized countries, which could be made available to England for her great scheme of tropical cultivation, was that between the Niger and Liberia, embracing nearly fourteen degrees of longitude."

Subsequently to the summing up of the facts here stated, Rev. Dr. Livingstone's discoveries, in the interior of Africa, have added much additional territory to the fields upon which Great Britain can enter.

SECTION II. — CONDITION OF THE COTTON QUESTION IN 1850.

Before attempting to show what has been done in Africa, or elsewhere, toward increasing the supplies of cotton to the English manufacturers, the exact condition of this question in 1850 must be given; as it will afford a starting point from which to estimate the true progress made by England in her efforts to become independent of the United States, for her supplies of this commodity.

For information on this subject we are indebted to the *London Economist*, January, 1850.   After a most elaborate investigation, the editor thus sums up the results:

"Now, *bearing in mind that the figures in the above tables are, with scarcely an exception, ascertained facts,* and not estimates, let us sum the conclusions to which they have conducted us: conclusions sufficient, if not to alarm us, yet certainly to create much uneasiness, and to suggest great caution on the part of all concerned, directly or indirectly, in the great manufacture of England.

"1. That our supply of cotton *from all quarters (excluding the*

United States,) has for many years been decidedly, though irregularly, *decreasing*.

"2. That our supply of cotton *from all quarters*, (including the United States,) available for home consumption, has of late years been falling off at the rate of 400,000 pounds a week, while our consumption has been increasing during the same period at the rate of 1,440,-000 pounds a week.

"3. That the United States is the only country where the growth of cotton is on the increase; and that there even the increase does not, on an average, exceed three per cent., or 32,000,000 pounds annually, which is barely sufficient to supply the increasing demand for its own consumption and for the continent of Europe.

"4. That no stimulus of price can materially augment this annual increase, as the planters always grow as much cotton as the negro population can pick.

"5. That consequently, if the cotton manufacture of Great Britain is to increase at all — *on its present footing* — it can only be enabled to do so by applying a great stimulus to the growth of cotton in *other countries* adapted for the culture."

The writer also presents the following historical sketch of the cotton trade of England, and closes with a statement of the reason why other countries have *diminished* their production of cotton. It will be seen that it is due to the fact that they are unable to compete with the United States in its production. We can supply the markets so much *cheaper* than they are able to do, that our cotton is driving theirs from the English market. The writer says:

"Within the memory of many now living, a great change has taken place in the countries from which our main bulk of cotton is procured. In the infancy of our manufacture our chief supply came from the Mediterranean, especially from Smyrna and Malta. Neither of these places now sends us more than a few chance bags occasionally. In the last century the West Indies were our principal source. In the year 1786, out of 20,000,000 pounds imported, 5,000,000 came from Smyrna, and the rest from the West Indies. In 1848, the West Indies sent us only 1,300 bales, (520,000 pounds.) In 1781, Brazil began to send us cotton, and the supply thence continued to increase, though irregularly, till 1830, since which time it has fallen off to one-half. About 1822, Egyptian cotton began to come in considerable quantities, its cultivation having been introduced into that country two years before.

The import exceeded 80,000 bales, (32,000,000 pounds,) in 1845. The average of the last three years has not been a third of that quantity. Cotton has always been grown largely in Hindostan, but it did not send much to England till about thirty years ago. In the five years ending in 1824, the yearly average import was 33,000 bales; in 1841, it reached 274,000; and may now be roughly estimated at 200,000 bales a year, (80,000,000 pounds.)

"Now what is the reason why these countries, after having at one time produced so largely and so well, should have ceased or curtailed their growth within recent years? It is clearly a question of price. Let us consider a few of the cases:

AT THE CLOSE OF THE YEARS,	Lowest price of Pernambuco.	Fall per cent	Lowest price of Maranham.	Fall per cent	Lowest price of Egypti'n	Fall per cent	Lowest price of Surat.	Fall per cent
1836–1839 inclusive......	9½*d*		8¼*d*		10¼*d*		4⅝*d*	
1840–1843	7*d*		5⅝*d*		7*d*		3½*d*	
1844–1848	5⅞*d*	36	4⅞*d*	42	5⅞*d*	43	2¾*d*	40

"Here, surely, may be read the explanation of the deplorable falling off in our miscellaneous supply."

But we may extend these examinations so as to embrace a range of facts that will show the true position of all Europe at this period, 1850, in relation to the cotton question.

	POUNDS.
The total consumption of cotton by England in 1849.........	624,000,000
By France	156,000,000
By the remaining Continental countries........................	129,920,000
To which add that of the United States........................	270,000,000
Total consumption of cotton in 1849	1,179,920,000

The sources from which these supplies were obtained reveals the extent to which slave labor and free labor, respectively, contributed of their products to make up the amount consumed. They were as follows: *

* These statistics are mainly taken from the London Economist, and the details may be found in "Ethiopia."

SLAVE LABOR COTTON CONSUMED IN 1849.

	POUNDS.
By England, from Brazil...	30,000,000
By England, from United States	522,530,800
By France, from United States ....:...............	147,000,000
By France, from Brazil, say..	3,000,000
By other Continental countries, from United States................	128,800,000
By United States, growth of United States	270,000,000
Total slave labor consumption.............................	1,101,330,800

FREE LABOR COTTON CONSUMED IN 1849.

	POUNDS.
By England, from all sources	71,469,200
By France, say...	6,000,000
By other Continental countries.........	1,120,000
Total free labor consumption	78,589,200
Grand total cotton consumption	1,179,920,000

This was the condition of the cotton supplies, so far as they depend upon slave labor and free labor respectively, upon the ushering in of the year 1850.

For the year 1859, the imports of cotton into Great Britain from all sources, excepting the United States and the East Indies, were only 50,125,000 pounds, while the monthly consumption of her looms was 46,600,000 pounds. Nor did India, at that moment, present any very encouraging prospects, as she furnished but 70,838,000 pounds of the 755,469,000 pounds that year imported into England.

Here had been a ten years' struggle on the part of England to render herself less dependent upon America for cotton. That the attempt failed is fully admitted, and that India could not be relied upon as a field in which to compete with the United States is reluctantly conceded. On this point the *London Economist*, after showing that Brazil, Egypt and the East Indies could not be made to meet the wants of the English manufacturers, said:

" Our hopes lie in a very different direction; we look to our West India, African, and Australian colonies, as the quarters from which, would Government only afford every *possible* facility, we might, ere long, draw such a supply of cotton as would, to say the least, make the fluctuations of the American crop, and the varying proportions of it which falls to our share, of far less consequence to our prosperity than they now are."

It was of vital importance to Great Britain that she should be able to promote the cultivation of cotton in her own territories. Thus far she had failed, and a renewal of her efforts was all that she could do, while, in the meantime, she remained hopelessly dependent upon the American planter.

SECTION III. — PROGRESS OF EVENTS CONNECTED WITH COTTON CULTURE AFTER 1850, AND THEIR RESULTS AT THE OPENING OF 1860.

The great leading interest of England — her principal dependence for the maintenance of her power and influence — is her manufactures.   Out of this interest grows her immense commerce, and from her commerce arises her ability to sustain her vast navy, giving to her such a controlling influence in the affairs of the world.   "Wealth, civilization, and knowledge add rapidly and indefinitely to the powers of manufacturing and commercial industry."   All these Great Britain possesses in an eminent degree.

"It is asserted that the manufacturers of England could in a short time be made to quadruple their produce — that so vast is the power which the steam-engine has added to the means of production in commercial industry, that it is susceptible of almost indefinite and immediate extension — that Manchester and Glasgow could in a few years prepare themselves for furnishing muslin and cotton goods to the whole world — that with England the great difficulty always felt is, not to get hands to keep pace with the demand of the consumers, *but to get a demand to keep pace with the hands employed in the production.*" *

We have seen that the low price of cotton — an average of 7 91-100 cents per pound — from 1840 to 1849 — was the principal cause of the decrease of its production in countries other than the United States; and that an increase of price was essential to the encouragement of its extended cultivation in the countries which had been supplying it, as well as in new fields where its growth might be introduced.   No permanent increase of price occurred,

* "Ethiopia," page 56.

however, until 1857, when it rose to 12 55-100 cents per pound;
but this was in consequence of the short crop made by the American planters, who exported that year 303,159,226 pounds less
than in the preceding year.   The years 1850 and 1851 had also
been unfavorable — the former supplying for export 391,220,665
pounds less than the exports of 1849, and the latter 99,365,180
pounds less than those of that year — the average price per pound
for the two years being 11 7-10 cents.   The five years succeeding
1851 furnished abundant crops in America, and the price averaged
only 9 12-100 cents per pound.   No increased production could
be secured under these prices; but the rise of 1857 brought England 250,338,144 pounds of cotton from India, being 69,841,520
pounds more than the imports from that country during the preceding year.   In 1858 and 1859, the United States produced her
usual abundant crops, and thus again resumed her monopoly of
the cotton markets — flinging to the winds the temporary prosperity of India, and reducing her supplies, in 1858, below those of
1857, more than 112,000,000 pounds.

But though the American cotton crops of 1858 and 1859 were
large — that of the latter year allowing an export of 1,372,755,000
pounds — yet owing to the increasing consumption on the continent and in the United States, the supply of England was not
equal to her wants; and the anxiety in relation to her cotton
supplies continued to engage attention.

The year 1859, it will be seen, supplies another point like
1849, from which to institute investigations as to the progress,
made by the English people, in developing the cultivation of cotton in fields not before devoted to that object.   The success attending their efforts — or rather the failure of their schemes —
will be apparent when the facts are fully presented.   Again we
quote from the *London Economist :* *

" We are not surprised that the future supply of cotton should have
engaged the attention of Parliament on an early night of the session.
It is a question the importance of which can not well be overrated, if
we refer only to the commercial interests which it involves, or to the
social comfort or happiness of the millions who are now dependent

---

* February 12, 1859.

upon it for their support. But it has an aspect far loftier, and even more important. At its root lies the ultimate success of a policy for which England has made great struggles and great sacrifices — the maintaining of existing treaties, and perhaps the peace of the world. Every year as it passes, proves more and more that the question of slavery, and even the slave trade, is destined to be materially affected, if not ultimately governed, by considerations arising out of the cultivation of this plant. It is impossible to observe the tendency of public opinion throughout America, not even excepting the free States, with relation to the slave trade, without feeling conscious that it is drifting into indifference, and even laxity. In every light, then, in which this great subject can be viewed, it is one which well deserves the careful attention equally of the philanthropist and the statesman."

The *Economist* then proceeds to say, that in 1840 the total supply of cotton imported into England was 592,488,000 pounds ; and that, with temporary fluctuations, it had steadily grown until it had reached, in 1859 and the two preceding years, an average annual amount of more than 900,000,000 pounds, showing an increase of fifty per cent.

"Nevertheless," continues the editor, " the demand had been constantly pressing upon the supply, the consumption has always shown a tendency to exceed the production, and the consequent result of a high price has, during a majority of these years, acted as a powerful stimulus to cultivation. But, practically speaking, we possess but two sources of supply, and both present such powerful obstacles to extended cultivation, that we are not surprised at the habitual uneasiness of those whose interests demand a continually-increasing quantity. Those two sources are the United States and British India. It is true that Brazil, Egypt, the West Indies, and some other countries, furnish small quantities of cotton ; but when we state that of the 931,847,000 pounds imported into the United Kingdom in 1858, the proportion furnished by America and India was 870,656,000 pounds, leaving for all other places put together a supply of only 61,191,000 pounds; notwithstanding the many laudable efforts both on the part of Government and of the mercantile community, to encourage its growth in new countries, it will be admitted that, as an *immediate* and practical question, it is confined to these two sources. They are not only the sources from whence the largest supplies are received, but they are also those where the chief increase has taken place."

Extending these investigations, we find that in 1859 the imports of cotton into Great Britain, from all sources, was 1,215,989,072 pounds, of which 1,154,038,144 pounds were from the United States and the East Indies, leaving but 61,951,928 from all other countries, or an increase from them of only 760,000 pounds during the year! The progress in Africa was too inconsiderable to merit much attention.

The powerful obstacles to extended cultivation in the United States, alluded to by the *Economist,* exist in the inability of the cotton planters to increase their labor forces in any greater ratio than that of the natural increase of the slave population. This increase is about three per cent. per annum, and the ratio of increasing production of cotton has generally been limited to that amount. From 1857 the prices remained more than two cents higher per pound than during the five preceding years, and thus a great stimulus was afforded to the American planter to increase his cultivation. But while the prices richly remunerated him, they were at least one cent per pound too low to allow of any serious competition from India. At 12 55-100 cents per pound, in 1857, the East Indies sent to England 250,338,000 pounds; but in 1858, at 11 72-100 cents per pound, only 138,253,000 pounds were forwarded from that quarter.

It was plain, therefore, that if the American planter could keep the price of cotton below about eleven cents per pound, he could retain the monopoly of the markets of Europe by preventing an increased supply from India. But here, at this very point, a difficulty presented itself. The increase of the demand for cotton, as has been estimated by a British writer, would equal *five* per cent. per annum, were it practicable to augment the production to that extent; and the American planter could only increase it in the ratio of *three* per cent.

An important question arose here, as to who should supply this increasing demand. The American planter could not do it, except by extending the area of slave labor; and the British people dare not attempt it, while cotton maintained the low prices which had prevailed. The English introduced the coolie system of labor, to revive their lost fortunes in the West Indies; and, fearing the Americans would renew the slave trade, they again commenced their efforts to prevent such a result. It was readily perceived, by English manufacturers and statesmen, that if the slave trade should be renewed by the United States — an opinion for which there never was any just foundation — all their hopes of regaining a monopoly of tropical cultivation, as well as their expectations of divorcing themselves from the cotton planters of the United States, would be at an end. It was of the utmost importance, therefore, that such a calamity to England, as the renewal of the slave trade by the United States, should be averted at all hazards.

In referring to this subject, the *London Economist*, of the date before quoted, says :

" But with what an enormous interest does this view of the case invest the cultivation of cotton in India? It is the only real obstacle we can interpose to the growing feeling in favor of slavery, and the diminishing abhorrence of the slave trade in the United States. It is the only field competition with which can, for many years to come, redress the undue stimulant which high prices are giving to slave labor in America." *

That the editor was well sustained in his opinions, by actual results, is apparent from the fact that no marked increase in the production of cotton had taken place excepting in the United States and East Indies. This was true not only as to late years, but has been true from the day that the American planters began their shipments of cotton in any considerable quantities. Here are the facts, as indicated by the imports into Great Britain, from all sources excepting the United States and the East Indies, for the years stated, in pounds :

YEARS.	POUNDS.	YEARS.	POUNDS.
1786	19,900,000	1848	28,670,712
1800	48,000,000	1849	50,126,447
1821	48,500,000	1850	51,591,007
1832	36,997,000	1851	58,113,811
1840	27,620,667	1852	79,229,472
1841	21,363,706	1853	54,978,793
1842	24,764,698	1854	35,345,794
1843	32,744,867	1855	64,943,312
1844	40,252,866	1856	63,349,664
1845	36,892,115	1857	64,172,704
1846	31,367,738	1858	61,189,856
1847	26,273,710	1859	61,950,928

* February 12, 1859.

These were startling results, truly, to those who had been flattering themselves that British capital and enterprise could force the cultivation of cotton in new fields of production, or augment it in the old ones from which the original supplies had been obtained.

Let us now look back for a moment to the state of the cotton supplies and cotton manufacture in Great Britain, a few years after the outbreak of the American Revolution. Her cotton manufactures were then in their infancy. In 1781 her imports of cotton were 5,198,778 pounds, nearly all of which was manufactured within the year. In 1786 the imports had increased to 19,900,000 pounds, and her consumption to 19,475,000 pounds. From that date to 1832, the year preceding the passage of the West India Emancipation Bill, the sources whence the cotton supplies were derived may be inferred from the following statement of the imports of that article into Great Britain, from the countries named, at the different dates given. The quantity is stated in pounds:

YEARS.	UNITED STATES.	EAST INDIES.	WEST INDIES.	BRAZIL.	TURKEY AND SMYRNA.	OTHER COUNTRIES.
1786.........			5,800,000	‡2,000,000	5,000,000	‖7,100,000
1791.........	*189,316		12,000,000	20,000,000		
1798.........	*9,330,000	1,622,000				
1800.........	*17,789,803	30,000,000	17,000,000	24,000,000		7,000,000
1821.........	*124,893,405	50,000,000	9,000,000	28,000,000	₰5,500,000	6,000,000
1832.........	*322,215,122	†5,178,625	1,708,764	20,109,560	₰9,113,890	964,933

From these statistics, we pass on to 1840, two years after final emancipation in the West Indies, and select the years that fairly represent the condition of the cotton supplies of Great Britain, from all sources, from that date to 1860:

Imports of Cotton into Great Britain for the years stated.

YEARS.	UNITED STATES.	BRAZIL.	MEDITER-RANEAN.	EAST INDIES	WEST IN-DIES AND GUIANA.	OTHER COUN-TRIES.	TOTAL.
1840.......	487,856,504	14,774,171	8,324,937	77,011,839	866,157	3,649,402	592,488,010
1845.......	626,650,412	20,157,633	14,614,699	58,437,426	1,394,447	725,336	721,979,953
1849.......	634,504,050	30,738,153	17,369,843	70,838,515	944,307	1,074,164	755,469,012
1856.......	780,040,016	21,830,704	34,616,848	180,496,624	462,784	6,439,328	1,023,886,304
1857.......	654,758,048	29,910,832	24,882,144	250,338,144	1,443 568	7,968,160	969,318,896
1858.......	732,403,840	16,466,800	34,867,840	138,253,360		9,862,272	931,847,056
1859.......	961,707,264	22,478,960	37,667,056	192,330,880		11,804,912	1,215,989,072
1860.......	1,115,890,608	17,286,864	43,945,064	204,141,168		9,666,048	1,391,929,752

* See notes on next page.

Here we have Brazil supplying less cotton in 1860 than in 1791; and the West Indies and all "other countries," a considerably less quantity in 1860 than the British West Indies alone was able to furnish in 1800. The increase from the Mediterranean — principally from Egypt — has been but slight as between 1856 and 1860, being only 9,329,000 pounds, or enough, merely, to supply the spindles of Great Britain for *three* days. There is, therefore, no disguising the fact stated by the *Economist*, that the East Indies and the United States are the only countries from which increasing quantities have been obtained to any important extent, notwithstanding the extraordinary efforts made to produce a different result. In relation to Brazil the *Westminster Review* for April, 1861, says:

" Since the abolition of the external slave trade in 1850, an increase in the available supply of labor sufficient to extend in any great degree the cotton cultivation has become impossible, and for that reason we have little to hope from this quarter."

In 1860, then, the United States and British India were the only prominent rivals in the great cotton markets of the world. The American planter had the decided advantage in the contest for supremacy in very many respects; but still he had obstacles to overcome of a very stubborn nature, among which, as already noticed, were the difficulties in the way of the extension of slave labor. To retain his monopoly of the cotton markets, he must not only increase his production, but, at the same time, keep the prices depressed below the rates at which it could be supplied from India. To allow any measures to be adopted which would greatly diminish the production of American cotton, would be to promote the interests of the East India planters, and enable them successfully to rival those of the United States. The existing difficulties in the way of the East Indies, at the opening of the year 1859, are thus stated by the *London Economist:*

---

* These figures include the total exports.
† East Indies and Mauritius.
‡ Reported as from Portuguese colonies, Brazil being a Portuguese colony.
§ Turkey and Egypt.
‖ From French, Spanish, and Dutch colonies.

"In some important respects the conditions of supply from India differ very much from those which attach to and determine the supply from America. In India there is no limit to the quantity of labor. There may be said to be little or none to the quantity of land. The obstacle is of another kind; it lies almost exclusively in the want of cheap transit. Our supplies of India cotton are not even determined by the quantity produced, but by that which, when produced, can be profitably forwarded to England. It is, therefore, a question of price whether we obtain more or less. A rise in the price of *one penny* the pound in 1857, suddenly increased the supply from 180,000,000 pounds in 1856, to 250,000,000 in 1857. A fall in the price in 1858 again suddenly reduced it to 138,000,000 pounds. It was not that the production of cotton varied in these proportions in those years, but that at given prices it was possible to incur more cost in the transit than at others. The same high price, therefore, which at present renders a large supply possible from India, creates an unusual demand for slaves in the United States. But would not the same corrective consequence be produced if we could diminish the cost of transit in India? Every farthing a pound saved in carriage is equivalent to so much added to the price of cotton. Four-pence the pound in the Liverpool market, for good India cotton, with a cost of two-pence from the spot of production, would command just as great a supply as a price of five-pence the pound if the intermediate cost were three-pence. The whole question resolves itself into one of good roads and cheap conveyance. Labor in India is infinitely more abundant than in the United States, and much cheaper; land is at least as cheap; the climate is as good; but the bullock trains on the miserable roads of Hindostan can not compete with the steamers and other craft on the Mississippi. . . . . . Whatever, therefore, be the financial sacrifice which in the first place must be made for the purpose of opening the interior of India, it should be cheerfully made, as the only means by which we can hope permanently to improve the revenues of India, to increase and cheapen the supply of the most important raw material of our own industry, and to bring in the abundant labor of the millions of our fellow-subjects in India, to redress the deficiency in the slave States of America, and thus to give the best practical check to the growing attractions of slavery and the slave trade." *

From all the facts and considerations before us it can no longer be disputed that the manufacturers of Great Britain, in 1860, as

---

* London Economist, February 12, 1859.

in 1850, were still dependent upon India and the United States for their cotton supplies; and that an increased production of cotton in the United States, at the low rates at which it had been previously furnished, would crush out all the hopes of enlarged exports from India, or extended cultivation anywhere else. It is easy to perceive, therefore, that Great Britain has long been deeply interested in the promotion of whatever policy would tend to diminish the production of American cotton, and enhance the price of that commodity, so as to stimulate its cultivation in her own provinces.

The following statement of the prices of cotton from 1821 to 1860, inclusive, will enable the reader to discover the causes which have produced the fluctuations in the production of cotton throughout the world, as far as its culture was controlled by the price of the article. The table of prices is taken from the Congressional Report on Finance, for 1860. The price stated is the average per pound for the year:

AVERAGE COST PER POUND IN CENTS.	AVERAGE COST PER POUND IN CENTS.	AVERAGE COST PER POUND IN CENTS.	AVERAGE COST PER POUND IN CENTS.
1821............... 16.2	1831............... 9.1	1841...............10.2	1851...............12.11
1822............... 16.6	1832............... 9.8	1842............... 8.1	1852............... 8.05
1823............... 11.8	1833...............11.1	1843............... 6.2	1853............... 9.85
1824............... 15.4	1834...............12.8	1844............... 8.1	1854...............9.47
1825............... 20.9	1835...............16.8	1845............... 5.92	1855............... 8.74
1826............... 12.2	1836...............16.8	1846............... 7.81	1856............... 9.49
1827............... 10	1837...............14.2	1847...............10.34	1857...............12.55
1828.. .... 10.7	1838...............10.3	1848............... 7.61	1858...............11.72
1829............... 10	1839...............14.8	1849............... 6.4	1859...............12.72
1830............... 9.9	1840............... 8.5	1850...............11.3	1860...............10.85

SECTION IV. — AGENCIES ENGAGED IN PROMOTING MEASURES TENDING TO DESTROY AMERICAN COMMERCE, BY LESSENING THE DEPENDENCE OF EUROPE UPON US FOR COTTON.

The question of the "cotton supplies," and who shall possess their monopoly in the future, is one of grave import to the Government and people of the United States. Let us look at the interests which it involves, and what it is that is risked to the nation in the loss of the cotton crop — a loss which many at the North have professed to believe would be no detriment to the prosperity of the country.

The quantity and value of our exports of domestic products is annually reported to Congress. The report on the finances for 1860, gives the total value of all the exports of the country since 1821. The several classes of products foot up as follows :

Breadstuffs and Provisions	$1,006,951,235
Rice	87,854,511
Tobacco	335,181,067
Cotton	2,574,834,091

Here the value of the cotton crop, to the foreign commerce of the country, stands out in its true proportions. And if to the value of the cotton we add that of the tobacco and rice, the entire exports of the Southern States, in these three products alone, reach a value of nearly *three billions of dollars*, or thrice the amount of the whole exports of all the other products of the soil.

These facts give us a clear idea of the character of our foreign commerce during the last thirty-nine years, and the extent to which the Northern and Southern States, respectively, have supplied the commodities exported — those of breadstuffs and provisions, mainly, being of Northern production, and the tobacco, rice, and cotton of Southern. To illustrate this point more fully, take the three years ending with 1860, as a means of comparison between the North and the South, in their present relations to our foreign commerce. The exports of the products of the soil, for the three years named, stood as follows :

PRODUCTS.	1858.	1859.	1860.
Breadstuffs and Provisions	$ 50,683,285	$ 38,305,991	$ 45,271,850
Tobacco	17,009,767	21,074,038	15,906,547
Rice	1,870,578	2,207,148	2,567,399
Cotton	131,386,661	161,434,923	191,806,555

The man of intelligence can now comprehend the extent to which the cotton crop enters into the foreign commerce of the country, and the ruinous consequences to our national progress and prosperity which must follow the discontinuance of its production, or its exclusion from foreign markets. Strike out the exports of tobacco, rice, and cotton, and the commerce of the United States, in the products of the soil, would at once dwindle down from *two hundred and fifty-five millions of dollars* per annum to less than *fifty millions of dollars*.   The history of the commercial operations of the country, for the last forty years, demonstrates the truth of this proposition.

But, again, by taking the monied value of all the commodities exported for the last *thirteen* years — from 1847 to 1860 inclusive — cotton will still be found occupying an imperial position in the commerce of the country.   The fiscal year ends June 30, and the several amounts were as follows :

Cotton	$1,489,859,591
Tobacco	172,319,772
Specie and Bullion	438,097,554
Products of the Sea	45,489,946
Products of the Forest	141,504,708
Breadstuffs and Provisions, including Rice	661,018,096
Manufactures	331,747,346
Raw Produce	28,107,594
	$3,308,144,607

Deducting the specie and bullion, and the cotton alone, throughout a series of thirteen years, is more than half the value of all the articles exported.

We can now comprehend the extent of the risks to the national prosperity of the United States which are involved in the diminution or destruction of the cotton crop, and the importance to the people of Great Britain of securing to themselves the monopoly of the cotton supplies.   From this stand-point, then, we can proceed with our examination of the agencies engaged in promoting the interests of Englishmen in their efforts to regain their monopoly of tropical cultivation.

The struggle, at present, for the monopoly of the cotton supplies, as we have seen, is narrowed down to a contest between the United States and India.   But, from the day that Hon. George Thompson lectured in old England, to induce its government and people to engage largely in cotton culture in the East Indies — from the day that this same gentleman undertook to lecture in New England, to promote the abolition of slavery in America — our country has maintained its advantageous position, and India has remained prostrate at the footstool of the American planter. Not only have the questions of price and transportation been against India, but the character of her staple, very inferior at the outset, has not been improved in quality to the present day. So long, therefore, as the production of cotton received no check in America, so long India failed to make any improvement in the quality of her product, or in the means of its transit from the interior; because this improvement was a matter dependent upon large investments of capital, and British capitalists shrunk instinctively from a contest with the monarch of America — King Cotton. · But the production of a better staple in India was dependent not simply upon an increased outlay of capital; the advanced civilization of the population was also necessary to the accomplishment of this object. On these points the *London Examiner* says, in a late issue :

" As for the opportunity, has it not been the same for India as for America for the forty-eight years of free trade which have elapsed since the year 1813, and what has been the result? Here it is from the unquestionable authority of Mr. Henry Ashworth :

" ' The proportion of India cotton consumed in this country last year (1860,) formed only seven per cent. in quantity, and only four and a half per cent. in value; and although 216,832,000 pounds were actually imported and brought to market, the great bulk — say more than two-thirds — was too poor to find buyers for English consumption.'

" Is it by bringing more of this trash into our market that India cotton is to prove a substitute for American? The cotton of India is just now exactly what it was when first imported seventy years ago, having in all that time sustained no improvement. It is probably now what it was four thousand years ago, and what it will continue to be for another four thousand years, if it shall continue to be cultivated by an ignorant, poverty-stricken Asiatic peasantry, to whom the death of a pair of bullocks is bankruptcy."

That India can not compete with us in the culture of cotton is apparent from the following facts in relation to the cost of its production in that country. The statement is taken from the *Calcutta Englishman* of 1861, a paper familiar with the subject it discusses :

" The following table shows the expense of cultivating an acre of land with cotton in the Raichore Doab, the yield of which will be 260 pounds, or when cleaned 70 pounds :

Government land tax	£0	5	0
Cost of preparing land	0	3	0
Weeding	0	1	0
Cost of 20⅜ pounds of seed	0	4	0
Sowing with drill	0	2	0
Picking the cotton	0	1	0
Cleaning the cotton	0	1	3
Carriage to seaport	0	4	8
Freight of £3 10s per tun	0	2	0
Screwing, baling, &c	0	0	11
	£1	4	10
Commissions at 2½ per cent., 7½d	0	0	0
Brokerage at ½ per cent., 1½d	0	0	9
Total	£1	5	7

Or nearly 4½d. per pound, exclusive of any profit whatever, either to the cultivator or shipper. It is thus clearly perceptible that the present price of India cotton in the Liverpool market is not sufficient to induce any increase in the cultivation, the more so as the charges here given are irrespective of the thousand and one demands made on the trader by every native agent through whose hands it passes."

But let us turn a moment from India to Africa. When, in 1850, it became obvious to the British people that India must fail in her competition with the United States, the most vigorous efforts were made to promote the cultivation of cotton in Africa, as a field more hopeful of favorable results. This enterprise, however, could be prosecuted only by the employment of slave labor; yet it was not discouraged on that account by the English people. It is known to every one familiar with the civil condition of Africa, that slavery everywhere prevails throughout all its territory, inhabited by the negro race. To cultivate cotton in Africa, therefore, is to establish slavery on a profitable basis, in a new field of tropical production. But to do so, it was argued, was justifiable on the ground of philanthropy, as it would tend to paralyze the slave trade, and prevent its renewal in America; that is to say, Englishmen assented to the establishment of slavery in Africa, provided its success there would destroy it in the United States.

"Once let the African chiefs find out, as in many instances they have already found out, that the sale of the laborer can be only a source of profit *once*, while his labor may be a source of constant and increasing profit, and we shall hear no more of their killing the hen which may lay so many golden eggs, for the sake only of a solitary and final prize."

Thus spoke the *London Economist* early in 1859. In commenting on the consequences of the movement for promoting cotton culture in Africa, the *American Missionary*, an anti-slavery publication, very truthfully remarks :

" There is, however, one danger connected with all this that can not be obviated by any effort likely to be put forth under the stimulus of commerce, or the spirit of trade. . . . . . The danger to which we allude is not merely that of worldliness, such as in a community always accompanies an increase of wealth, but that *the slavery now existing there may be strengthened and increased by the rapid rise in the value of labor*, and thus become so firmly rooted that the toil of ages may be necessary for its removal." *

As early as 1858, Lord Palmerston took ground in favor of the vigorous prosecution of the growing of cotton in Africa. He made no objection to the measure on account of the slavery which would be employed in its production. He said nothing about the *sinfulness* of slavery ; because the British Government had never adopted that belief as a rule of action. The theory that slavery is sinful, was designed for American use, and as a maxim that might overthrow American slavery. In referring to the encouraging prospects for cotton culture in Africa, during the debate of July 13, 1858, he said :

" I venture to say, that you will find on the west coast of Africa a most valuable supply of cotton, so essential to the manufactures of this country. It has every advantage for the growth of that article. The cotton districts of Africa are more extensive than those of India. The access to them is more easy than to the India cotton districts, and I venture to say, that your commerce with the western coast of Africa in the article of cotton will in a few years prove to be far

* American Missionary, March, 1859 · The italics are the author's.

more valuable than that of any portion of the world, the United States excepted." *

Details of the progress of cotton culture in Africa, and elsewhere, can not be given here without extending this chapter to too great a length.

It is only necessary, to a clear understanding of the subject of the cotton supplies, to state that, up to the close of 1860, no increased importations of cotton into Great Britain, from either the old or the new fields of production, had taken place, to such extent as would warrant her manufacturers in entertaining the least hope of freeing themselves from continued dependence for that staple upon the United States, so long as its production with us remained undisturbed. On the contrary, the imports of Great Britain, in the aggregate, from the West Indies, Africa, and " other countries," which were less by more than two million pounds in 1860 than they were in 1859, † have suffered a still further diminution in 1861.

Thus, for the year 1861, from every source, the imports of cotton into Great Britain, as compared with those of 1860, show an *increase* from Africa, the West Indies, and " other countries," of only 595,280 pounds; from Brazil, an *increase* of but 3,472 pounds; and from Egypt, a *decrease* of 3,061,978 pounds; being, from all sources, excepting the East Indies and United States, a total *decrease* below the imports of 1860, of 2,463,406 pounds. From the East Indies the *increase* has been 164,899,280 pounds over the imports of 1860, but only 118,702,304 pounds over the imports of 1857. These results must greatly disappoint those who were anticipating largely increased supplies from other sources than the United States. ‡

In reference to the extent of the recent supplies of cotton received in Great Britain, from new sources, Mr. William Cross, of Farnwarm, near Manchester, says in a communication in the *London Post*, June 21, 1861:

"It has been stated in several newspapers that 40,000 ' bales' of

---

* Westminster Review, April, 1861.

† See preceding tabular statement of imports into Great Britain.

‡ From Official Reports in the London Economist, March 1, 1862.

cotton have been received from fifty-eight new or revived sources. These statements are erroneous. A bale of cotton is about four hundred pounds weight, but a large proportion of the so-called bales are only small sample-bags, containing a few pounds of cotton. Of the remainder, 18,924 bales are from Tuticorin, the shipping port of the Tinnovelly District; and inasmuch as Tinnovelly cotton has been well known to the London and Liverpool cotton merchants during many years, it is false to describe that district as a new source of supply. Down to the present time, notwithstanding the assertions of the Cotton Supply Association, there has not been received as much cotton from new sources as would find employment for one moderate sized cotton-mill during the space of six months; and I believe I am quite within the mark when I assert that the several cotton-procuring companies which have been advertised in Lancashire are not in possession of as much paid up capital as would purchase a twelve month's supply of cotton for one cotton-mill of moderate dimensions."

It follows, as a logical deduction from the facts before us, that the successful development of the growth of cotton in the tropical possessions of Great Britain can only be secured by effecting a derangement of the labor forces engaged in its production in the United States, and that this derangement must be effected to such an extent as will diminish the production of American cotton, so as to give permanency to high prices for that commodity. This done, and British capital, in a proportionate degree, can be employed safely in both India and Africa for the improvement of the quality and the increase of the quantity of their cotton. But until this is done — until the American planter is crippled or prostrated — British capitalists, as we are assured by advices from abroad, will not venture upon extended cotton culture in any portion of the world. They had hoped to reverse this condition of things, and to have lessened the American production of that staple, by its increased cultivation in India, but this scheme was soon found to be impracticable, and its increased growth in India can only succeed by first interrupting its culture in the United States.

Now, on arriving at this point in our investigations, it is very easy to comprehend why the people of Great Britain have made such extensive and persevering efforts to promote the abolition of slavery in the United States. Emancipation, they very well know, would at once ruin the American planters, and completely destroy the production of cotton on their estates. It is also very obvious why the English abolitionists, on failing in their schemes in reference to the immediate abolition of slavery in this country, have, with such perfect unanimity, approved of the proposition of the American abolitionists, to confine slavery within the limits of the States where it now exists ; because, to prevent the extension of Southern slavery, is to diminish the production of our great commercial staple, and to allow the monopoly of the cotton supplies, ultimately, to pass from the hands of our own citizens into those of the subjects of Great Britain.

We do not complain of the English people for using peaceful means to place themselves upon an equal footing with those of the United States in the competition for the grand prize of supplying the cotton markets. But we can justly say that the Americans who are playing into their hands are no friends to the commercial prosperity of their own country. They should be able to see that the hostility of the British people, at large, to American slavery is not based on moral considerations — as is apparent from their being industriously engaged in establishing slavery in Africa, as a means of procuring supplies of cotton ; and that, therefore, in the present condition of the world, the abolition of slavery in the United States must, necessarily, force its establishment in Africa upon a footing commensurate with existing demands for tropical products, and humanity thereby reap no advantages by the abolition of slavery in America.

The tendency of the abolition movements in the United States are now easily discerned. The history of emancipation everywhere, *without exception,* proves that the great mass of the blacks will not work voluntarily, to any useful extent, beyond what is necessary to supply their absolute necessities. The blacks of the United States can form no exception to the general rule. Emancipation in our Southern States, therefore, would be the death blow to our cultivation of cotton, as it was in the West Indies to the production of both cotton and sugar. *

The crisis in American cotton culture is now upon us. The

---

* The reader will find the *facts* relating to the West Indies in Chapter V.

prices have gone up three hundred per cent. With these prices
prolonged, by the withholding of the American crop from the
markets for three or four years, but, especially, by the discontinuance of the culture of cotton in the South for want of hands to
perform the labor, the supplies of cotton from other countries may
be increased, so that the American crop may be no longer a desideratum to European manufacturers. Lord Palmerston seems to
understand the question in this light. At the late Lord Mayor's
dinner in London, the American minister, Mr. Adams, being present, the noble Lord, in alluding to the want of cotton from America, said :

"That temporary evil will be productive of permanent good—
(cheers)—and we shall find in various quarters of the globe sure and
certain and ample supplies, which will render us no longer dependent
upon one source of production for that which is so necessary for the
industry and welfare of the country."*

The extent of the dependence of Great Britain upon cotton,
will be understood when it is stated that the total value of all her
exports, for the year ending December 31, 1860, † estimating the
pound sterling at $5,00, was $679,214,085. Of these exports the
value of cottons, cotton yarns, etc., of all descriptions was, $260,-
067,410; raw cotton, 250,428,640 pounds exported, at say 11 cents
per pound, $27,547,150; to this add the British domestic consump-
tion of cottons, estimated at $120,000,000; making British in-
terests in cotton alone at $407,614,560.

Reader, can you now comprehend the question of the cotton
supplies as it affects Great Britain!

We do not say that the abolitionists of America desired to
destroy our cotton cultivation for the benefit of the colonial possessions of Great Britain. Their movements may be interpreted
on other principles. It has been conjectured, by a curious writer,
that Satan maintains his influence in the world, not by constant
attention to every man whom he is able to mislead—because he
is not omnipresent—but mainly by setting afloat such false max-

---

* New York Observer, November, 1861.
† London Economist, March 2, 1861.

ims in society as, on being accepted as rules of conduct, will corrupt mankind and mislead them to their ruin.

So it has been in reference to the abolitionists of the United States.   They have adopted, from time to time, one theory after another in reference to slavery, and all of which nearly are now demonstrated to be historically false.   These theories, mostly, were of foreign origin, and, like the false maxims of Satanic origin, were designed to mislead the simple and the unwary. *

As in the moral and religious aspects of slavery, false maxims have prevailed to a ruinous extent, so in reference to its economical relations, theories equally untrue and absurd have, from time to time, been set afloat, and as eagerly seized upon to promote the interests of abolition.   Who does not remember the labored attempts to prove that the Union, to the North, was of but little value, pecuniarily — about thirty-nine cents, perhaps, to each person in the North, according to one abolition organ — and that, therefore, the Northern States would be more prosperous were the Southern States cast off as a useless burden!   The story of the hay crop — not a pound of which is exported, as being of more value than the cotton crop, two hundred millions of dollars worth of which are exported — is still fresh in the memory of the intelligent reader.   Because, forsooth, we had three hundred millions of dollars worth of hay, we could very well do without the two hundred millions worth of cotton!   The mountaineer gentleman, as the joke runs, has a costly pair of spurs and a glossy shirt-collar, therefore he has no need of coat or other garments!

A few facts will set this point in its true light.   Hay, instead of being a standard of wealth, is but the indication of severity of climate and prolonged winters.   This proposition may be illustrated by examples taken from a few of the Northern States, which save large quantities of hay, as compared with the same number in the South, which save but little hay; and yet, the Southern States are able to subsist a much larger amount of live stock, from the fact that their climate is so favorable as to afford pasturage throughout the winter:

---

* The preceding Chapters are devoted to the exposure of the false theories of the anti-slavery men of the United States.

STATES.	HAY, TUNS.	HORSES, CATTLE, ETC.	SHEEP.	HOGS.
New Hampshire............	598,854	302,162	384,756	63,487
Vermont.....................	866,153	410,123	1,014,122	66,296
Maine	755,889	385,115	451,577	54,598
Connecticut	516,131	239,603	174,181	76,472
Michigan	404,943	333,073	746,435	205,847
Georgia	23,449	1,306,238	560,435	2,168,617
Alabama......................	32,685	915,911	371,880	1,904,540
Mississippi	12,504	903,977	304,929	1,582,734
South Carolina..............	20,925	912,340	285,551	1,065,503
Arkansas.....................	3,976	364,466	91,256	836,727

But we must not dwell upon the absurdities of these ruinous theories, gotten up to familiarize the public mind, at the North, with the idea of disunion.

Another topic claims attention, as illustrating, more fully, the facility with which errors on economical questions, as well as upon moral ones, may be propagated. When our national difficulties were approaching a crisis — with an object in view not requiring notice here — the attempt was made to create the impression that Europe was not so dependent upon American cotton as had been represented. Statements were set afloat which were calculated to deceive the careless thinker; and which did deceive tens of thousands of men, otherwise intelligent and guarded in their acceptance of theories and maxims. Take an example of a later date, as representing the whole, and which is as amusing to the public, as it must now be mortifying to its victim:

The senior editor of the *New York Observer* — a religious paper always in opposition to abolition — on retiring to his country seat, in the forepart of the summer of 1861, thus wrote:

"Ten years hence India will furnish as much cotton within a trifle as America will, even if the rate of increase continues in this country as rapidly in the next ten years as it has in the last decade of years."

This opinion of the editor was based on the statements made in an article in the *North British Review*, which contained the estimates of the *increase* alone in the British supplies of cotton, from the several cotton-growing countries, from 1850 to 1857. The *Review* says:

"During that period the increase of 300,000,000 pounds, in round numbers, in our imports of cotton was furnished by the following countries :

	POUNDS.
United States	161,604,906
Egypt	5,910,730
West Indies	1,184,667
East Indies	131,465,402
Africa and others	5,895,462

The article quoted appeared in the course of the summer of 1861. The deception practiced is in the selection of the seven years ending with 1857. The years 1850, 1851, and 1857, gave short crops in the United States, and there was consequently a largely increased importation from India, because of the increased prices. Had the contrast been made between India and America for the years 1858, 1859, and 1860, the *increase* of imports into England would have ranged so as to lead to a very different conclusion from that indorsed by the *Observer*. It was as follows:

	POUNDS.
United States, increase	383,486,768
East Indies, increase,	65,887,808
West Indies and other countries, *decrease*	196,224
Egypt, increase	9,077,224
Brazil, increase	820,064

These statistics tell a very different story, as to the present condition of the cotton supplies, from those quoted by the *New York Observer*.

Again, the *Observer* quotes from the *Review :*

" If we take the fourteen years from 1843 to 1857, we find that the cotton countries increased their shipments to England as follows :

	PER CENT.
United States	15
Egypt	140
Brazil	54
East Indies	288
Africa	300

A still greater deception is here practiced upon the careless reader, by giving results in *per cents.*, than even by the mode of contrast above noticed. The year 1843 gave 65,709,729 pounds of cotton from India—a much less quantity than in the two preceding years; while 1857 gave 250,388,144 pounds—a great increase over that of any year before or since, except 1861. The premeditated deception here practiced is apparent, when it is further stated, that, owing to our short crop, England received 125,281,978 pounds less from us in 1857 than she had the previous year, and 461,132,560 pounds less than in 1860. Had the contrast been drawn between the years 1857 and 1860, the result, instead of showing an increase from India, would have presented a *decrease* of twenty-three per cent. The increase from Africa may have been at the rate of three hundred per cent., but then the whole imports from the favored African districts of Lagos and Abbeokuta, in 1857, were only 35,000 pounds.

And, again, the *Observer* quotes:

"If we take the import of 1857 as the basis, and assume the increase of the fourteen succeeding years to be in the same ratio, the rate of increase in 1871 will be as follows:

	POUNDS.
United States	753,911,754
East Indies	720,973,853
Brazil	45,464,464
Egypt	31,216,849
Africa and others	23,758,480

It is only necessary, in noticing this formidable array of figures, to say that the imports of cotton into Great Britain from the United States, for 1860, were 1,115,890,608 pounds, or 362,297,-854 pounds in excess of what it was to be, according to the *Observer*, in 1871; and that the supplies from India, in 1860, instead of having increased at the rate of two hundred and eighty-eight per cent., were actually *decreased* below those of 1857, to the amount of 45,196,976 pounds! Brazil, too, instead of having had an increase between 1857 and 1860, supplied less in the latter year than in the former by 12,623,968 pounds. Egypt alone supplied *more* in 1860 than in 1857, but less in 1861 than in 1860.

These examples of the manner in which the most absurd and erroneous propositions may be set afloat and accepted as true, must suffice as illustrations of the mode in which the public mind in the United States has been misled on the subject of slavery.

A remark or two, and we have done.   It will be seen that the amount of cotton imported from India, by Great Britain, in 1861, though one hundred and sixty-four millions pounds larger than during the year 1860, is only a little over one hundred and eighteen millions more than her imports were in 1857.   Her imports from the United States during the year, have been 819,500,528 pounds, all of which, nearly, must have been shipped before the blockade of our ports.   As this is considerably more than she received from us in the whole of the year 1858, or any preceding year, it is evident that the loss of the American cotton crop is only beginning to be felt in its full force in England.   Indeed, the *London Economist*, in its estimates, showed that, by working short time, the manufacturers, with the supplies on hand, might avoid much suffering until the first of July of the present year; but that the strange counter-movement of reëxporting cotton largely from Liverpool back to New England, in consequence of the advantages gained by the American manufacturer through the Morrill tariff, would probably bring on the crisis by the first of May.

In relation to the chances that the East Indies might gain such advantages, by the American war, as to secure to itself the markets of Great Britain, the *Economist*, January 25, 1862, says:

"Such an entire misapprehension appears to prevail on this subject, and such strange and transparent delusions are daily propagated through the various organs of the Press as to the true merits of the controversy, that we must endeavor, even at the risk of repeating ourselves and wearying our more attentive readers, to explain once for all the real facts — or rather the one fact — which lies at the root of the competition between cotton the growth of the slave States of America, and cotton the growth of our own East India possessions. . . . . . . It is the more essential that the public should clearly understand the matter in hand, because we find among many sagacious persons the impression that if the India cotton can only *have a year or two's start*, so as to *establish itself* in the British market, it will be able to hold its strong ground and even to supersede the American; that this year or two will be secured to it by a continuance of the civil war and the blockade; and that, therefore, we ought rather to rejoice at than to deprecate that continuance.   The notion is so wholly fallacious, and so very mischievous, that no time ought to be lost in eradicating it. . . . . . .   The case is briefly this.   India cotton has for the last half century been as well known and as habitually used in this country as American cotton. It has been just as regular an article of import and consumption as its rival. . . . . . . It has always reached us in the quantities requisite to *supplement* the American crop. When the latter was abundant, comparatively little Surat* was used; when it was scanty, the demand for Surat increased. . . . . . The Orleans cotton was always worth *just half as much again* as the Surat, for nearly all purposes for which the latter could be used at all, *i. e.*, for the coarser yarns and fabrics. . . . . . When Orleans could be purchased at 3*d* or 4*d* a pound, the consumption of Surat almost ceased. . . . . . The explanation of this is very simple. The fibre of the Orleans cotton is much longer, more even, and more silky than that of Surat. . . . . . So much of the Surat cotton falls down as dust, or flies off as dust and flock, in the process of working it into yarn, that a pound of it *makes much less yarn or cloth* than a pound of Orleans. Being shorter in fibre, also, it requires more twisting to give it the required strength, and, therefore, can not be made into yarn *so fast*. From these two causes, its value to the manipulator is never more than *two-thirds* that of an equal weight of its American rival — and *never can be more*, whatever improvements and adaptations of machinery may be introduced, so long as its quality and character remain unaltered — for not only is its quality inferior, but its character is peculiar. . . . . . The plain, simple, conclusive truth is that the American cotton *has more in it* than the India. . . . . . *The moment the American cotton reäppears in Liverpool, it will resume its old position of superiority.* . . . . . The American and India cotton are *specifically* diffèrent. . . . . . The cultivation of the imported article *has never been able to spread*—the plain truth being that the one is a natural and the other an artificial cultivation. . . . . But of this we are confident — till Africa is settled and civilized, the Southern States of the Union will *always be the cheapest and best cotton field in the world*." †

The "cotton question" can now be comprehended by the reader; and the disastrous effects of either the prolongation of the war, or the emancipation of the slaves, upon the manufactures and commerce of Great Britain, as well as of France, can be easily discerned. In all other cotton producing regions, of any practical

---

* *Surat* is the trade name for India cotton, and *Orleans* for the American.
† The *italics* are the Economist's own, throughout the quotations.

importance, there has been a reduction of exports; and the East India cotton can not be made to supersede the American. These are the present facts.

Our government, therefore, by a wise policy, might have continued to enjoy the monopoly of the cotton markets, and to reap the rich rewards it secured. But there is a party in England, alluded to by the *Economist*, who believe that the British colonies can be restored to their former prosperity, and the owners of the ruined estates elevated from poverty to opulence, by the prostration of the American planter; and we have in our midst an association of men who boast that they are sustained, by the munificence of Englishmen, in their labors for the destruction of the Constitution and the Union, as a means of putting an end to cotton culture by slave labor; and they well know that the negro, when free, lies as an incubus upon the country which retains him. As to the colonization which they propose, it is all a delusion; it is wholly impracticable, except by force, and would be the destruction of the colored people subjected to the experiment.

We have also had a party in this country, who grieved over the loss, by the South, of the direct trade with Europe, and who imagined that they could, by a dissolution of the Union, secure to themselves not only the advantages of the commerce based upon the crops of tobacco, rice, and cotton; but that they would also, by political independence, become the most prosperous nation in the world.

These two parties may be considered as having had their chief seats in New England and South Carolina. Both were struggling for the same object, the overthrow of the Republic. The secessionist desired the dissolution of the Union, that he might retain and enlarge his slave labor forces, secure a direct trade with foreign nations, and maintain the monopoly of the cotton markets of the world. The abolitionist wanted the secessionist out of the Union, but not until he should be robbed of his slaves, so that the American cotton monopoly might be destroyed forever, and British subjects be enabled thereby to recover the losses arising from their philanthropic experiments with the negro. These objects were not all openly avowed; but that they formed a part of the designs in the abolition movement, has been apparent from the first to discerning men.

This, then, is the nature of the conflict in which we are engaged. The success of secession will lessen the foreign commerce of the nation, at once, to the extent of more than two hundred millions of dollars. The success of abolition will lessen it to an equal extent; and, at the same time, it will reduce the Southern States to the condition of Mexico, which is able only to raise its own bread, and has less than two millions of dollars of annual exports of agricultural products.

Now, a word here, as to the position of the Great West. The success of secession deprives us of the free navigation of the Mississippi, and presents us as humble suppliants at the footstool of the South, for a market for our surplus products. We must pay them tribute, or have the fruits of our labor left to rot upon our hands. The success of abolition leaves us in precisely the same condition, as to a loss of our Southern markets, excepting the payment of tribute. The South, with four millions of free negroes, can not carry on its cotton culture, as all past experience proves; and can not, therefore, continue to purchase the productions of the West. In either case, therefore, the West will be ruined.

And, here, those who laughed at Mr. Lincoln, for talking of giving "protection" to *Western corn*, will find, perhaps, that there was more meaning in it than at first appeared to the minds of the iron masters, who called out the remark. Illinois and Iowa understand, now, the necessity of protection to their corn. The Southern market cut off, leaves them with only the Eastern market, and many, many leagues of railroads between their corn-cribs and the purchasers of their corn. Sixty-five cents per bushel, in New York, they may get; but they must pay fifty-five for its transportation, besides commissions. Truly they need protection; and that protection can only be found in the preservation of the Constitution and the Union — in the recovery of the navigation of the Mississippi — and, for this, their sons are pouring out their blood like water.

The war now waged is a contest for the richest boon a nation ever possessed. The position of the Executive at Washington, is one of peculiar responsibility. On the one hand he has to contend against those who would destroy American commerce by emancipation; on the other he is combating forces who seek to wrench more than two hundred millions of dollars' worth of domestic exports from the nation by secession. The success of either party, for the present, sounds the knell of American greatness and glory. To the nation the question is, whether our foreign commerce, in the products of the soil, shall be fifty millions of dollars or two hundred and fifty millions; whether among commercial nations we shall become a second-rate power, or maintain our late position of one of the first class. It is a question whether fanaticism at the North or rebellion at the South, shall succeed in the destruction of the Union; whether the President shall yield to the one or to the other, and sink, along with his Government, into the depths of degradation and ruin; or whether, rising, like the true statesman, above the influence of faction, he shall plant himself upon the Constitution, and, rescuing the country from destruction, shall crown himself with immortal fame. May the nation in its majesty, and the army in its power, resolve to sustain him in his determination to preserve the Constitution and the Union!

CHAPTER XII.

WE can not select a better introduction to this closing chapter than the following extract from the eloquent Burke:

"Politics and the pulpit are terms that have little agreement. *No sound ought to be heard in the Church but the voice of healing charity.* The cause of civil liberty and civil government gains as little as that of religion, by this confusion of duties. Those who quit their proper character, to assume what does not belong to them, are, for the greater part, ignorant both of the character they leave, and of the character they assume. Wholly unacquainted with the world, in which they are so fond of meddling, and inexperienced in all its affairs, on which they pronounce with so much confidence, they know nothing of politics but the passions they excite. Surely the church is a place where one day's truce ought to be allowed to the dissensions and animosities of mankind."

SECTION I.—THE CLERGY OF NEW ENGLAND AND THE WAR OF 1812.

To afford the reader a correct idea of the extent to which clergymen may be roused by political controversy, and the reproach which they may bring upon religion by yielding to the excitements of the day, we need only refer to the character of the preaching in New England, in relation to the War of 1812.* The quotations are taken from sermons of New England clergymen who opposed the war, and threw the whole weight of their influence upon the side of the politicians who labored to embarrass the Government in defending itself against a foreign foe.

---

* We copy from the Olive Branch, a volume published by the venerable Matthew Carey, in 1815.

(592)

The bitterness of that controversy is little known to the people of the present day, but may be inferred from the violence of the pulpit productions which it elicited. A few extracts only can be given, as our volume is already swelled much beyond the size at first contemplated. It will be seen, from the very first sentences quoted, that New England clergymen were talking of secession—of "cutting the connection"—as early as 1812; and that Mr. Quincy, of Boston, before quoted, was not alone in his opinions of the duty of dissolving the Union.

The Rev. Mr. GARDINER, Rector of Trinity Church, Boston, July 23, 1812, in his sermon on Psalm cxx : 7, said:

"The alternative is, that if you do not wish to become the slaves of those WHO OWN SLAVES, and who are themselves slaves of French slaves, you must either, in the language of the day, CUT THE CONNECTION, or so far alter the national compact as to insure yourselves a due share in the government."

"Let no considerations whatever, my brethren, deter you, at all times, and in all places, from execrating the present war. It is a war unjust, foolish, and ruinous. It is unjust, because GREAT BRITAIN HAS OFFERED US EVERY CONCESSION SHORT OF WHAT SHE CONCEIVES WOULD BE HER RUIN."

"As Mr. Madison has declared war, let Mr. Madison carry it on."

"THE UNION HAS BEEN LONG SINCE VIRTUALLY DISSOLVED, AND IT IS FULL TIME THAT THIS PART OF THE DISUNITED STATES SHOULD TAKE CARE OF ITSELF."

The Rev. DAVID OSGOOD, D. D., Pastor of the church at Medford, said:

"If, at the command of WEAK OR WICKED RULERS, they undertake an unjust war, each man who volunteers his services in such a cause, or loans his money for its support, or, by his conversation, his writings, or any other mode of influence, encourages its prosecution, *that man is an accomplice in the wickedness*, loads his conscience with the blackest crimes—brings the guilt of blood upon his soul, and—IN THE SIGHT OF GOD AND HIS LAW, IS A MURDERER."

"My mind has been in a constant agony, not so much at the inevitable loss of our temporal prosperity and happiness, and the complicated miseries of war, as at its guilt, its outrage against heaven, against all truth, honesty, justice, goodness—against all the principles of social happiness."

" Were not the AUTHORS OF THIS WAR in character nearly akin to the deists and atheists of France; were they not men of hardened hearts, seared consciences, reprobate minds, and desperate wickedness, it seems utterly inconceivable that they should have made the declaration."

"One hope only remains, that this stroke of perfidy may open the eyes of a besotted people; that they may awake, like a giant from his slumbers, and WREAK THEIR VENGEANCE ON THEIR BETRAYERS, by driving them from their stations, and placing at the helm more skillful and faithful hands."

Rev. ELIJAH PARISH, in a discourse delivered at Byfield, said:

"Such is the temper of American republicans, so-called. A new language must be invented before we attempt to express the baseness of their conduct, or describe the rottenness of their hearts."

" New England, if invaded, would be obliged to defend herself. Do you not, then, owe it to your children, and owe it to your God, to make peace for yourselves?"

"A thousand times as many sons of America have probably fallen victims of this ungodly war as perished in Israel by the edict of Pharoah. Still the war is only beginning. If ten thousand have fallen, ten thousand times ten thousand may fall."*

" Should the English now be at liberty to send all their armies and all their ships to America, and, in one day, burn every city from Maine to Georgia, *your condescending rulers would play on their harps*, while they gaze at the tremendous conflagration."

" Here we must trample on the mandates of despotism! or here we must remain slaves forever."

" You may envy the privilege of Israel, and mourn that no land of Canaan has been promised to your ancestors. You can not separate from that mass of corruption, which would poison the atmosphere of Paradise. You must, in obstinate despair, bow down your necks to the yoke, *and, with your African brethren, drag the chains of Virginia despotism*, unless you discover some other mode of escape."

---

* "Those who take the trouble of multiplying, will find that ten thousand times ten thousand make 100,000,000, who are to perish out of a population of 8,000,000!"—*Olive Branch.*

" Let every man who sanctions this war by his suffrage or influence, remember that he is laboring to cover himself and his country with blood. THE BLOOD OF THE SLAIN WILL CRY FROM THE GROUND AGAINST HIM ! "

" How will the supporters of this anti-Christian warfare endure their sentence—endure their own reflections—endure the fire that forever burns—the worm which never dies—the hosannas of heaven—WHILE THE SMOKE OF THEIR TORMENTS ASCENDS FOREVER AND EVER ! "

We could multiply extracts, but here are enough to prove that clergymen, on political questions, are about as liable to be wrong as right. As these are some of the clerical gentlemen referred to in the writings of Thomas Jefferson, page 445, volume VI, we shall present his views upon the question of ministers preaching politics in the pulpit.

" On one question only I differ from him, (Rev. Mr. McLeod, of New York City,) and it is that which constitutes the subject of his first discourse, the right of discussing public affairs *in the pulpit*. I add the last words, because I admit the right in *general conversation* and in *writing;* in which last form it has been exercised in the valuable book you have now favored me with.

" The mass of human concerns, moral and physical, is so vast, the field of knowledge requisite for man to conduct them to the best advantage is so extensive, that no human being can acquire the whole himself, and much less in that degree necessary for the instruction of others. It has, of necessity, then, been distributed into different departments, each of which, singly, may give occupation enough to the whole time and attention of a single individual. Thus we have teachers of Languages, teachers of Mathematics, of Natural Philosophy, of Chemistry, of Medicine, of Law, of History, of Government, etc. Religion, too, is a separate department, and happens to be the only one deemed requisite for all men, however high or low. Collections of men associate together, under the name of congregations, and employ a religious teacher of the particular sect of opinions of which they happen to be, and contribute to make up a stipend as a compensation for the trouble of delivering them, at such periods as they agree on, lessons in the religion they profess. If they want instruction in other sciences or arts, they apply to other instructors; and this is generally the business of early life. But I suppose there is not an instance of a single congregation which has employed their preacher for the mixed purpose of lecturing them *from the pulpit* in Chemistry, in Medicine, in Law, in the science and principles of Government, or anything but Religion exclusively. Whenever, therefore, preachers, instead of a lesson in religion, put them off with a discourse on the Copernican system, on chemical affinities, on the construction of government, or the characters or conduct of those administering it, it is a breach of contract, depriving their audience of the kind of service for which they are salaried, and giving them, instead of it, what they did not want, or, if wanted, would rather seek from better sources in that particular art or science. In choosing our pastor we look to his religious qualifications, without inquiring into his physical or political dogmas, with which we mean to have nothing to do. I am aware that arguments may be found, which may twist a thread of politics into the cord of religious duties. So may they for every other branch of human art or science. Thus, for example, it is a religious duty to obey the laws of our country; the teacher of religion, therefore, must instruct us in those laws, that we may know how to obey them. It is a religious duty to assist our sick neighbors; the preacher must, therefore, teach us medicine, that we may do it understandingly. It is a religious duty to preserve our own health; our religious teacher, then, must tell us what dishes are unwholesome, and give us recipes in cookery, that we may learn how to prepare them. And so, ingenuity, by generalizing more and more, may amalgamate all the branches of science into any one of them, and the physician who is paid to visit the sick, may give a sermon instead of medicine, and the merchant to whom money is sent for a hat, may send a handkerchief instead of it. But notwithstanding this possible confusion of all sciences into one, common sense draws lines between them sufficiently distinct for the general purposes of life, and no one is at a loss to understand that a recipe in Medicine or Cookery, or a demonstration in Geometry, is not a lesson in religion. I do not deny that a congregation may, if they please, agree with their preacher that he shall instruct them in Medicine also, or Law, or Politics. Then, lectures in these, from the pulpit, become not a matter of right, but of duty also. But this must be with the consent of every individual; because the association being voluntary, the mere majority has no right to apply the contributions of the minority to purposes unspecified in the agreement of the congregation. I agree, too, that, on all occasions, the preacher has the right, equally with every other citizen, to express his sentiments, in speaking or writing, on the subject of Medicine, Law, Politics, etc., his leisure time being his own, and his congregation not obliged to listen to his conversation or to read his writings; and no one would have regretted more than myself, had any scruple as to this right withheld from us the valuable discourses which have led to the expression of an opinion as to the true limits of the right. I feel my portion of indebtment to the reverend author for the distinguished learning, the logic, and the eloquence with which he has proved that religion, as well as reason, confirms the soundness of those principles on which our Government has been founded, and its rights asserted.

" These are my views on the question. They are in opposition to those of the highly respected and able preacher, and are, therefore, the more doubtingly offered. Difference of opinion leads to inquiry, and inquiry to truth; and that, I am sure, is the ultimate and sincere object of us both. We value too much the freedom of opinion sanctioned by our Constitution, not to cherish its exercise even where in opposition to ourselves.

" Unaccustomed to reserve or mystery, in the expression of my opinions, I have opened myself frankly on a question suggested by your letter and present. And although I have not the honor of your acquaintance, this mark of attention, and still more the sentiments of esteem so kindly expressed in your letter, are entitled to a confidence that observations not intended for the public will not be ushered to their notice as has happened to me sometimes. Tranquillity, at my age, is the balm of life.

" While I know I am safe in the honor of a McLeod, I do not wish to be cast forth to the Marats, the Dantons, and the Robespierres of the Priesthood; I mean the Parishes, the Ogdens, and the Gardiners of Massachusetts.   "THOMAS JEFFERSON.

" MONTICELLO, *March* 13, 1815."

SECTION II.—THE THREE THOUSAND AND FIFTY CLERGYMEN OF NEW ENGLAND, AND THE CONGRESS OF 1854.

In 1854, during the Kansas-Nebraska controversy, three thousand and fifty clergymen of New England forwarded a protest to the United States Senate, against the passage of the Nebraska Bill.

This protest, on being presented to the Senate, led to much excitement and considerable debate. The opinions expressed by the senators who took part in the discussion, are of great interest, as embodying the sentiments of public men of eminence upon the question under consideration.　They are important also, as presenting a faithful index to the general sentiment of the public at large, on the question of the interference of clergymen in the political agitations of the country, and should be well considered by the spiritual teachers of the people.　The question is not, whether clergymen have the same rights, politically, as other citizens ; this no one denies ; but their indulgence in political preaching, or their separate action in reference to political topics, presents a subject for prudential consideration alone, as it affects their usefulness among those amidst whom they labor.　See how the matter presents itself in a practical way.　On none of the questions in relation to slavery, or any other one connected with party politics, are the clergymen united in opinion.　What, then, are the unevangelized portion of the community to think, when they see one party of ministers of the Gospel come before the legislative councils of the nation, demanding, in the name of Almighty God, the adoption of a particular course of policy ; while another party, equally respectable, present themselves before the same authorities, demanding, in the same sacred name, the very opposite policy ?　Surely, before the world at large, such a scene could be viewed only as a solemn farce !

PROTEST OF 3,050 NEW ENGLAND CLERGYMEN, OF ALL DENOMINA-
TIONS AND SECTS IN NEW ENGLAND, REMONSTRATING AGAINST THE
PASSAGE OF THE NEBRASKA BILL.

"*To the Honorable, the Senate and House of
　　　Representatives, in Congress assembled :*—

"The undersigned, clergymen of different religious denominations in New England, hereby, in the name of Almighty God, and in his presence, do solemnly protest against the passage of what is known as the Nebraska Bill, or any repeal or modification of the existing legal prohibitions of slavery in that part of our national domain which it is proposed to organize into the territories of Nebraska and Kansas.　We protest against it as a great moral wrong, as a breach of faith eminently unjust to the moral principles of the community, and subversive of all confidence in national engagements; as a measure full of danger to the peace and even the existence of our beloved Union, and exposing us to the righteous judgments of the Almighty: and your protestants, as in duty bound, will ever pray.

"Boston, Massachusetts, *March* 1, 1854."

The presentation of this document brought on a full and free discussion of the subject, from which we can make but a very few extracts.

Mr. Mason said:

"I trust I shall never see the day when the Senate of the United States will treat the authors of such petitions, upon any subject proper for legislation pending before the body, coming from the people of the United States, with aught but respect. But I understand this petition to come from a class who have put aside their character of citizens. It comes from a class who style themselves, in the petition, ministers of the Gospel, and not citizens. They come before us—I have not understood the petition wrong, I believe—as ministers of the Gospel, not citizens, and denounce prospectively the action of the Senate, in their language, as a moral wrong; and they have the temerity, in the presence of the people of the United States, to invoke the vengeance of the Almighty, whom they profess to serve, against us. Sir, ministers of the Gospel are unknown to this Government, and God forbid the day should ever come when they shall be known to it. The great effort of the American people has been, by every form of defensive measures, to keep that class away from the Government; to deny to them any access to it as a class, or any interference in its proceedings. The best illustration of the wisdom of that measure in our Government is to be found in this. Ministers of the Gospel, I repeat, are unknown to the Government. Of all others, they are the most encroaching, and, as a body, arrogant class of men. . . . If thirty thousand, or three hundred thousand citizens come from New England, let them be heard; but when they come here, not as citizens, but declaring that they come as ministers of the Gospel, and, as the honorable Senator from Texas declared them to be, vicegerents of the Almighty—so I understood him to declare, possibly he meant vice-regents to supervise and control the legislation of the country— say, when they come here as a class unknown to the Government, a class that the Government does not mean to know in any form or shape, not to recommend or remonstrate, but to denounce our action as a great moral wrong, because they claim to be the 'vicegerents' of the Almighty, we are bound—not from disrespect to them as citizens, not from disrespect to the cloth which they do not grace, but from respect to the Government, from respect to the sacred public trust which has been committed to us—to carry out the policy of the Government and refuse to recognize them. Sir, their object, as was well said by the Senator from Illinois, has been agitation—agitation; and I presume that their cloth and their ministry will enable them to agitate with some success."

Mr. Butler said:

"I have great respect, Mr. President, for the pulpit. I have such a respect for it that I would almost submit to a rebuke from a minister of the Gospel, even in my official capacity; but they lose a portion of my respect when I see an organization, for, I believe, the first time in the history of this Government, of clergymen within a local precinct, within the limits of New England, assuming to be, as the Senator from Texas said, the vicegerents of Heaven, coming to the Senate of the United States, not as citizens, as my friend from Virginia has said, but as the organs of God—for they do not come here petitioning or presenting their views under the sanction of the obligations and responsibilities of citizens under the Constitution of the United States, but they have dared to quit the pulpit, and step into the political arena, and speak as the organs of Almighty God. Sir, they assume to be the foremen of the jury which is to pronounce the verdict and judgment of God upon earth. They do not protest as ordinary citizens do; but they mingle in their protest what they would have us believe is the judgment of the Almighty. When the clergy quit the province which is assigned to them, in which they can dispense the Gospel—that Gospel which is represented as the lamb, not as the tiger or the lion—when they would convert the lamb into the lion, going about in the form of agitators, seeking whom they may devour, instead of the meek and lowly representatives of Christ, they divest themselves of all respect which I can give them. Sir, the ministers of the Gospel are the representatives of the lowly and poor lamb—of Christ; but when the men who have signed that paper—I do not know with what ends; I do not say a word against them as individuals, for I have no doubt they are good and respectable, and many of them Christians—assume to organize themselves as clergymen, to come before the country and protest against the deliberations of the Senate of the United States, they deserve, at least, the grave censure of the body."

Mr. ADAMS, of Mississippi, said:

"I trust I have as high a regard for their vocation as any other individual, and as much respect for the ministers of peace and good-will on earth as any other individual; but when they depart from their high vocation, and come down to mingle in the turbid pools of politics, I would treat them just as I would all other citizens. I would treat their memorials and remonstrances precisely as I would those of other citizens. It is so unlike the apostles and the ministers of Christ at an early day, that it loses the potency which they suppose the styling themselves ministers of the Gospel would give to their memorials. The early ministers of Christ attended to their mission, one which was given to them by their Master; and under all circumstances, even when the Savior himself was upon earth, and attempts were made to induce him to give opinions with reference to the municipal affairs of the government, he refused. These men have descended from their high estate to assail the action of this body. The Senator from Massachusetts, (Mr. Everett,) in presenting the petition, has done what he considered to be his duty; but I would remark, however, that with all the respect which belongs to the high character of those individuals as ministers of the Gospel, their petition should, under the circumstances, receive no more respect from us than if it came from any other private citizens."

Mr. DOUGLAS said:

"Now, sir, what is this remonstrance? These men do not protest as citizens. They do not protest in the name either of themselves or of their fellow-citizens. They do not even protest in their own names, as clergymen, against this act, but they say that 'WE PROTEST IN THE NAME OF ALMIGHTY GOD;' and in order to make it more emphatic, that they claim to speak by authority in their remonstrance, they underscore, in broad black lines, the words 'IN THE NAME OF ALMIGHTY GOD.' It is true, that they describe themselves as ministers of the Gospel, but they claim to speak in the name of the Almighty on a political question pending in the Congress of the United States. It is an attempt to establish in this country the doctrine that a body of men, organized and known among the people as clergymen, have a peculiar right to determine the will of God in relation to legislative action. It is an attempt to establish a theocracy to take charge of our politics and our legislation. It is an attempt to make the legislative power of this country subordinate to the Church. It is not only to unite Church and State, but it is to put the State in subordination to the dictates of the Church. Sir, you can not find, in the most despotic countries, in the darkest ages, a bolder attempt on the part of the ministers of the Gospel to usurp the power of government, and to say to the people: 'You must not think for yourselves; you must not dare to act for yourselves; you must, in all matters pertaining to the affairs of this life, as well as the next, receive instructions from us; and that, too, in the performance of your civil and official, as well as your religious duties.'

"Sir, I called attention to this matter for the purpose of showing that it involved a great principle subversive of our free institutions. If we recognize three thousand clergymen as having a higher right to interpret the will of God than we have, we destroy the right of self-action, of self-government, of self-thought, and we are merely to refer each of our political questions to this body of clergymen, to inquire of them whether it is in conformity with the law of God and the will of the Almighty, or not. This document, I repeat, purports to speak in the name of Almighty God, and then enters a protest in that name. We are put under the ban, we are excommunicated, the gates of heaven are closed, unless we obey this behest, and stop in our course and carry out these abolition views.

"The Senator from Texas says the people have a right to petition. I do not question it. I do not wish to deprive ministers of the Gospel of that right. I do not acknowledge that there is any member of this body who has a higher respect and veneration either for a minister of the Gospel, or for his holy calling, than I have; but my respect is for him *in his calling*. I will not controvert what the Senator from Massachusetts has said as to there being, perhaps, no body of men in this country, three thousand in number, who combine more respectability than these clergymen. Probably they combine all the respectability which he claims for them; but I will add, that I doubt whether there is a body of men in America who combine so much profound ignorance on the question upon which they attempt to enlighten the Senate, as this same body of preachers. How many of them, do you suppose, sir, have ever taken up and read the act of 1820, to which I allude? Do you think there is one of them who has done so? How many of them ever read the votes by which the North repudiated that act of 1820? Do you think one of them ever did? How many of them ever read the various votes which I quoted on that act and the Arkansas act? Do you think one of them knew anything about them? How many of them have ever traced the course of the compromise measures of 1850 on record? One of them? Yet they assume, in the name of the Almighty, to judge of facts, and laws, and votes, of which they know nothing, and which they have no time to understand, if they perform their duties, as clergymen, to their respective flocks.

"They do not pretend to judge from the knowledge of this world, from the records of the Senate, or from the statute-book, or from any of the sources of information on which Senators and citizens predicate their action; but by the will and the law of God, and in his name, and in consequence of their divine mission, they overrule all these, and prescribe a new test, and, in that name, they tell us that, by the passage of the bill which we have passed, we have committed a moral wrong. They tell us that it is subversive of all confidence in national engagements.

"Now, let me ask, are these men particularly tenacious of national engagements? Did they, in their pulpits, in 1850 and 1851, tell their followers that they were bound by their oaths, and by their religious duty, to surrender fugitive slaves in obedience to the Constitution? Did they tell their people that they must perform national engagements? Did they then tell their flocks that the Senate was right in carrying out the provisions of the Constitution? Have they been particularly in the habit of enjoining in the pulpit and from the sacred desk, as a matter of conscience, that the people should perform the national engagements contained in the Constitution of our country, and which we are all sworn to support? Sir, I do not remember that any one of these three thousand preachers, at the time when in Boston and other points of this country there were attempts to resist the Fugitive Slave Law by force, came forward and said it was a divine duty to perform national engagements. If they did, I have not seen the evidence of it. If they felt it was a matter of conscience and of duty on the part of the clergy to supervise the fulfillment of national engagements, to preserve the public faith, and the public honor, where were they then? when your Constitution was trampled upon, when oaths of office could not bind men to perform their constitutional duty, when public honor was being outraged, where then were these three thousand clergymen? We did not hear from them on that occasion. There was a national engagement which no man can deny; yet they did not raise their voices against its violation. But in this case, merely because some abolitionists from this body have said that an act of Congress constituted a national engagement, although the statement is contradicted by the record, they come forward at the bidding of an abolition *junta*, to arraign the Senate of the United States in the name of the Almighty!

"Sir, I deny their authority. I deny that they have any such commission from the Almighty to decide this question. I deny that our Constitution confers any such right upon them. I deny that the Bible confers any such right upon them. They can perform their duties within their sphere without my censure or my interference, and they are responsible to the Almighty for the manner in which they perform those duties; and I must be left to perform my duties within the sphere of my functions, with no other responsibility than to my constituents and to the Almighty, without the interference of those men. I do not acknowledge them as an intermediate tribunal. I do not acknowledge that they are, as the gentleman from Texas has called them, the vicegerents of the Almighty, and that they are to perform the duty of overlooking our conduct. I repudiate the whole doctrine as at war with the pure principles of Christianity, at war with the spirit of our institutions, at war with our Constitution, at war with every principle upon which a free government can rest."

SECTION III.—THE CLERGYMEN OF CHICAGO AND THE HON. STEPHEN A. DOUGLAS.

A FEW weeks after the 3,050 clergymen of New England forwarded their protest to Congress, the clergymen of Chicago and the Northwest, to the number of twenty-five, also sent on a similar protest "To the Senate and House of Representatives, in Congress assembled."

The Chicago document was identical with that of New England, with the exception of the addition of the words, "as citizens," and the difference in locality. Accompanying this protest were several resolutions, expressive of the sentiments of the protestors, and in one of which they passed a censure on Mr. Douglas and others. To this assault Mr. Douglas made a defense, and so effectually has he exposed the dangers of their assumptions of power, that we must copy a portion of it. Mr. Douglas says:

"With the exception of the description of your locality 'in the northwestern States' instead 'of New England' and of the interpolation of the words 'as citizens,' this protest is an exact copy of the one presented to the Senate from the clergymen of New England, upon which the debate occurred which you have condemned. After reading that debate, and seeing the nature of the objections urged to the New England protest, it seems that you determined to present youselves to the Senate in a two-fold capacity—the one 'as citizens' and the other 'as ministers of the Gospel of Christ.' Nobody questions your right; no one denies the propriety of your exercising the constitutional right of petitioning government for redress of grievances in your capacity as citizens; nor can there be any well-founded objection to your adding these other words, 'as ministers of the Gospel of Jesus Christ, if done only as illustrative of your relations to society and of your profession and occupation in life. This was not the obnoxious feature in the New England protest. The objection urged to that paper was, that the clergymen who had signed it did not protest in their own names, as clergymen, or citizens, or human beings, or in the name of any human authority or civil right, but they assumed the divine prerogative, and spoke to the Senate 'in the name of Almighty God!'

"With the full knowledge that Senators, in the debate to which you have alluded, understood the New England protest in this light—and as asserting a divine power in the clergy of this country higher than the obligations of the Constitution, and above the sovereignty of the people and of the States—to command the Senators, by the authority of Heaven, and under the penalty of exposing them 'to the righteous judgment of the Almighty,' to vote in a particular way upon a given question, you now re-adopt the protest, and repeat the command in the identical language in which it was originally issued. This looks as if it was your fixed and deliberate purpose, as clergymen, to force an issue upon this point with the civil and political authorities of the republic. If there were room for doubt or misapprehension, in this respect, on the face of the New England protest, you have removed all obscurity, and avowed the purpose distinctly and boldly in the resolutions which you adopted at the time you signed the protest:

"'Resolved, 1. That the ministry is the divinely-appointed institution for the declaration and enforcement of God's will upon all points of moral and religious truth ; and that, as such, it is their duty to reprove, rebuke, and exhort, with all authority and doctrine.'

"This resolution appears to have been adopted by you at an anti-Nebraska meeting (composed exclusively of clergymen, twenty-five in number), and called for the purpose of considering that question, and none other. It was adopted in connection with the protest, and forms a part of the same transaction. The protest denounces the Nebraska Bill 'in the name of Almighty God,' as 'a great wrong'—as 'a breach of faith eminently injurious to the *moral principle* of the community,' and 'as exposing us to the righteous judgments of the Almighty.' The resolution declares 'that the *ministry is the divinely-appointed institution for the declaration and enforcement of God's will upon all points of moral and religious truth !*' Do not the protest and the resolution refer to the same question, to wit, the Nebraska Bill, now pending before Congress ? Surely you will not deny that such was your understanding. You assembled to consider that question, and none other. You acted upon that subject, and that alone. Your resolutions were declaratory of the extent of your rights and powers as clergymen, and your protest was your action in conformity with those assumed rights and powers. I understand, then, your position to be this : that you are 'ministers of the Gospel;' that 'the ministry is the divinely-appointed institution for the declaration and enforcement of God's will upon all points of moral and religious truth;' and this 'divinely-appointed institution' is empowered 'to declare' what questions of a civil, political, judicial, or legislative character, do involve 'points of moral and religious truth;' that the Nebraska Bill does involve such 'points,' and is, therefore, one of the questions upon which it is the duty of this 'divinely-appointed institution' to 'declare and enforce God's will;' and that, clothed with 'all authority and doctrine,' this 'divinely-appointed institution' proceeds to issue its mandates to the Congress of the United States 'in the name of Almighty God.' This being your position, I must be permitted to say to you, in all Christian kindness, that I differ with you widely, radically, and fundamentally, in respect to the nature and extent of your rights, duties, and powers, as ministers of the Gospel. If the claims of this 'divinely-appointed institution' shall be enforced, and the various public functionaries shall yield their judgments to your supervision, and their consciences to your keeping, there will be no limit to your temporal power, except your own wise discretion and virtuous forbearance. If your 'divinely-appointed institution' has the power to prescribe the mode and terms for the organization of Nebraska, I see no reason why your authority may not be extended over the entire continent, not only to the country which we now possess, but to all which may hereafter be acquired.

"Nor do you propose to confine your operations to the supervision and direction of the action of Congress, in the organization of territorial governments, and the admission of new States into the Union. It is difficult to conceive of any matter of private or public concern, pending before Congress, or in the Legislatures of the different States, or in the judicial tribunals, which does not, quite as much as the Nebraska Bill, 'involve some point of moral and religious truth;' and we are informed, in your resolution, that 'upon all points of moral and religious truth' the 'ministry is the divinely-appointed institution for the declaration and enforcement of God's will. I do not wish to be understood as intimating that it is your present purpose, through the agency of this 'divinely-appointed institution,' to declare and enforce God's will in all matters affecting our foreign policy and domestic concerns, nor that you intend to direct the movements of the political parties, and control the local and general elections throughout the country. It is enough to fill with alarm the mind of every patriot, and to bring sorrow and grief to the heart of every Christian, that you have asserted the right to do this in all cases, and have, in one case, attempted the exercise of this divine prerogative 'in the name of Almighty God.' It is true that, while you assert the right in the broadest terms, and propose now to establish a precedent which will justify its exercise in all future time, in your second resolution you 'disclaim all desire' to do certain things, from which it might be inferred, on first view, that you do not intend to meddle with party politics, nor attempt to control the political movements of the day. This, however, turns out to be illusory, on a closer examination.

"'Resolved, 2. That while we disclaim all desire to interfere in questions of war and policy, or to mingle in the conflicts of political parties, it is our duty to recognize the moral bearing of such questions and conflicts, and to proclaim, in reference thereunto, no less than to other departments of human interest, the principle of inspired truth and obligation.'

"You do not 'desire to interfere in questions of war and policy.' Thus far I heartily approve. I rejoice to see that you are willing to leave the question of war where the Constitution has placed it—in the hands of Congress, as the representatives of the people and the States of the Union.

"You 'disclaim all desire,' also, 'to mingle in the conflicts of political parties.' This sentiment is admirable. It will meet the cordial approbation of every patriot and Christian. But you immediately follow it with the declaration that 'it is our duty to recognize the moral bearing of such questions and conflicts!' You do not desire to engage in war, nor to fight the battles of your country, but you do claim that it is your right, and, if you please, your duty, by virtue of your office as ministers, through the agency of this divinely-appointed institution, to declare, in the name of Almighty God, a war in which your country is engaged with a foreign power, to be immoral and unrighteous, although the representatives of the people and of the States, in pursuance of the Constitution, have declared it to be just and necessary. And this, not in the course of your ordinary pastoral duties to your several congregations, but as an organized body speaking to the constituted authorities of the nation. I can not recognize the principle that, while you are protected in the enjoyment of all your rights as citizens, of all your just rights as ministers, you are yet released, by virtue of your office as ministers, from your allegiance to your country during war, and from your obligation of obedience to the Constitution and laws, and constituted authorities at all times.

"You also say, that you consider it your duty to take cognizance of 'the moral bearing of the conflicts of the different political parties.' The moral bearing of the Democratic party, and of the Whig party, and of the Abolition party, are each to be recognized by your divinely-appointed institution; and you then add, that it is your duty 'to proclaim, in reference thereunto, the principle of inspired truth and obligation.' You propose, through your divinely-appointed institution, to apply the test of 'inspired truth' to each of the political organizations and to their respective conflicts, and 'to reprove, rebuke, and exhort with all authority and doctrine,' in the name of the great Jehovah. With all due respect for you, as ministers of the Gospel, I can not recognize in your divinely-appointed institution the power of prophecy or of revelation. I have never recognized the existence of that power in any man on earth during my day. . . . Your claims for the supremacy of this divinely-appointed institution are subversive of the fundamental principles upon which our whole republican system rests. What the necessity of Congress, if you can supervise and direct its conduct? Why should the people subject themselves to the trouble and expense of electing legislatures for the purpose of enacting human laws, if their validity depends upon the sanction of your divine authority? Why sustain a vast and complex judicial system, to expound the laws, administer justice, and determine all disputes in respect to human rights, if your divinely-appointed institution is invested with all authority to prescribe the rule of decision in the name of the Deity? If your pretensions be just and valid, why not dispense with all the machinery of human government, and subject ourselves, freely and unreservedly, together with all our temporal and spiritual interests and hopes, to the justice and mercy of this divinely-appointed institution?

"Our fathers held that the people were the only true source of all political power; but what avails this position, if the constituted authorities established by the people are to be controlled and directed —not by their own judgment, not by the will of their constituents, but by the divinely-constituted power of the clergy? Does it not follow that this great principle, recognized and affirmed in the Constitution of the United States, and of every state in this Union, is thus virtually annulled, and the representatives of the people converted into machines in the hands of an all-controlling priesthood?

"The will of the people, expressed in obedience to the forms and provisions of the Constitution, is the supreme law of this land. But your 'office as ministers' is not provided for in the Constitution. . . . The persecutions of our ancestors were too fresh in the memories of our revolutionary fathers for them to create, recognize, or even tolerate, a church establishment in this country, clothed with temporal authority. So apprehensive were they of the usurpations of this, the most fearful and corrupting of all despotisms, whether viewed with reference to the purity of the Church or the happiness of the people, that they provided in the Constitution that 'no religious test shall ever be required as a qualification to any office or public trust under the United States.' Still, fearful that, in the process of time, a spirit of religious fanaticism, or a spirit of ecclesiastical domination, (yet more to be dreaded, because cool and calculating,) might seize upon some exciting political topic, and, in an evil hour, surprise or entrap the people into a dangerous concession of political power to the clergy, the first Congress under the Constitution proposed, and the people adopted, an amendment to guard against such a calamity, in the following words:

" 'Congress shall make no law respecting an establishment of religion, or prohibiting the free exercise thereof.'

" The doctrine of our fathers was, and the principle of the Constitution is, that every human being has an inalienable, divinely-conferred right to worship God according to the dictates of his own conscience; and that no earthly 'institution,' nor any 'institution' on earth, can rightfully deprive him of that sacred and inestimable privilege.

" However, it is no part of my purpose to inquire into the extent of your authority in spiritual affairs. That is a question between you and your respective congregations, with which I have neither right nor wish to interfere.

" All I have said, and all that I propose to say, has direct reference to the vindication of my character and position against the unjustifiable assaults which you have made in regard to my official action in the Senate. I repeat, that your assumption of power from the Almighty, to direct and control the civil authorities of this country, is in derogation of the Constitution, subversive of the principles of free government, and destructive of all the guarantees of civil and religious liberty. The sovereign right of the people to manage their own affairs, in conformity with the Constitution of their own making, recedes and disappears, when placed in subordination to the authority of a body of men, claiming, by virtue of their offices as ministers, to be a divinely-appointed institution for the declaration and enforcement of God's will upon earth."

SECTION IV.—PULPIT POLITICS IN ITS PRACTICAL RESULTS.

We have now held up the mirror to *pulpit politicians*, as it comes into our hands from some of the ablest men of the nation. They can behold themselves as Jefferson beheld them, in 1812; and as the Senators of the United States beheld them, in 1854. If they do not like the portraits, they must not again place themselves before the daguerreotypist. It may seem defective to them, but it is, nevertheless, a true picture—a true reflection of the lineaments of their countenances.

But there is another aspect to this question. Suppose, for a moment, that the clergyman who delves into politics may accomplish some good for his party; is not the service thus rendered just so much of time, talent, and energy diverted from his legitimate duties? and are we not to expect that his congregation will suffer in proportion to his neglect of their spiritual interests? What was the argument used to justify the organization of the "Business Men's Prayer Meetings," but that the clergy had so far lost their hold upon the confidence of the people that their efficiency had become greatly impaired, and *laymen* must turn their talents and graces to account, or vital religion would continue to decay or totally expire?

It is well, therefore, to turn the attention of the class of clergymen to which we refer, to the results of the secularization of the pulpit upon the interests of religion itself; and in doing this we shall not ourselves draw up the statement, but profit by the labors of an abler pen. And as Massachusetts has been the chief seat of political preaching, it is very important to have one of her own sons to describe its effects, after fifty years' labor have been performed in that department of public teaching. About the first of February, of the present year, the *Boston Courier* contained the following article, under the head of "Political Preaching:"

"Our genial and amiable cotemporary, the *Saturday Evening Gazette*, says:

"'The fact is, from some cause or other, there seems to be a great falling off among our people in attending church services; as, comparing the number of our population with the seatings in our churches, the preponderance of the former over the latter is very marked. Some of the clergy are trying to solve the question, but have not yet found the remedy.'

"It is not remarkable that the clergy are not competent to solve this question; a man is not able to see anything which is on the top of his own head. The fact is true beyond all controversy, and a melancholy fact it is too. Not only in this city, but throughout this State—and, we fear, through most of New England—the interest in religion, and in the observance of religion, is declining. The attendance upon church services is comparatively meager. Practical, if not theoretical infidelity is spreading like a dry rot throughout the land. The number of men who are living virtually without God is on the increase. The heathen virtues of pride, self-esteem, self-reliance, active courage, are rising in estimation, and the Christian virtues of meekness, gentleness, patience, long-suffering, are declining. Among young persons, especially, of both sexes, there is a marked want of vital and practical Christianity, and a prevailing lack of interest in its ministrations and observances. The general characteristics of young persons are impatience of discipline, resistance to authority, a fierce assertion of assumed rights. To exact obedience is an outrage; to yield obedience is a weakness. Restraint of all kinds is resented as a wrong; and unchecked liberty—the power to do anything and everything that the natural and unregenerate heart prompts, without let or hinderance—is valued as the highest good of man.

"And what is the cause of this unhappy state of things? What has led to all this free-thinking, and to this lawless conduct, which is the legitimate child of free-thinking? No one cause can explain it all; but certainly the clergy themselves are in part to blame for it. In the tenth chapter of Leviticus, we read that Nadab and Abihu 'offered strange fire before the Lord, which he commanded them not. And there went out fire from the Lord, and devoured them, and they died before the Lord.' In these words, the narrative of a transaction, there is also a symbolical sense, and the expression of a vital and enduring truth. The clergy of New England have been offering 'strange fire before the Lord;' and the inevitable retribution has followed. And this 'strange fire' is the vulgar fire of secular politics—the fire of worldly passions—which wastes and consumes the heart on which it feeds. In such a heart the Christian graces can no more take root than roses and lilies will flourish in the slag and refuse of a furnace. Politics are usurping the place of religion, to a deplorable extent, in the pulpits of New England. Sermons are degenerating into stump speeches. The clergy are taking a more and more active part in political movements. You will hardly find a political convention in which one or more of the most active and noisy members are not clergymen. If you enter a New England church on any Sunday in the year, the chances are at least even that you will hear a political harangue, which part of the audience will be moved to applaud, and part to hiss.

"And the political opinions which are enunciated from the pulpit, are generally accompanied with a most offensive dogmatism and positiveness. This is natural enough. The clergyman is regarded with peculiar deference, as a man removed from secular struggles and secular stains, and set apart to break the bread of life to the people. He is rarely contradicted; he is treated by men as men treat women; he is never subjected to an intellectual rough and tumble; an atmosphere of respect surrounds him, which protects him as cotton protects diamonds. Upon sacred and religious topics he has a right to speak with authority; not only to soothe and heal and bless, but warn and rebuke and admonish; he is false to his trust, if he do not. But the habit of mind thus generated is easily transferred to secular themes. The priest's authoritative tone is easily assumed when he speaks on topics on which he and his parishioners stand on the same plane of observation, and where their vision is quite as likely to be as good as his. How common it is to see a young chick, just hatched from a divinity school, running about with the shell yet on his head, who will undertake to settle any question of administration or government as easily as he will pull off his glove! The mistake is in supposing that, in regard to those problems, you can come to a satisfactory solution by some short cut of inspiration, by the intuitive moral sense; whereas the contrary is notoriously the fact. There is often a ludicrous disproportion between the tone and manner with which dogmas are uttered from the pulpit, and the substantial value of the opinions themselves. To hear and see the preacher, one would suppose that he was enunciating the oracles of God, while what he is really uttering is some shallow, sentimental or mischievious nonsense, such as might have been picked up at an infant's school, a milliner's shop, or a lunatic asylum.

"What we have been saying has particular reference to the subject of slavery, on which this country has been growing stark mad for the last few years. The clergymen of New England are all, or nearly all, anti-slavery in sentiment and feeling. We don't object to this; it needs no ghost from the grave to tell us that slavery is a great social and economical evil, and that every patriot and every Christian should be glad to see it removed. But most New England clergymen are also Republicans, and here the trouble begins. Republicanism involves two very distinct elements: first, that slavery is an evil, wherein we are all agreed; and, second, that the Republican method of dealing with slavery is the true one; wherein we are not all agreed by any means. But the Republican clergymen can not or will not see the distinction. In this view, the man who is not a Republican is not opposed to slavery; is pro-slavery, in short. And this narrowness and intolerance comes from the fact that he mistakes emotion for insight—moral instincts for intellectual perceptions—a mistake under which the universal New England mind is now suffering.

"A religious congregation is not, and ought not to be formed on the ground of unity in political faith. The same religious truths—the same warnings, expostulations, encouragements, consolations—are to be addressed to Whigs, Democrats, Republicans, or Native Americans. Before the throne of God these distinctions melt away like those of station, wealth, or dress. It is one of the most beautiful elements in the Christian faith, that it brings together men who on secular topics differ most widely. In the congregation of the over-zealous Republican clergyman there will be, or may be, some persons who are not Republicans. They are just as conscientious in their anti-Republicanism, as he is in his Republicanism. But they are constantly exposed to the chances of hearing their convictions denounced, their motives impugned, and having their blood stirred by insulting insinuations. They are obliged to sit still, and hear a clerical dogmatist, from his vantage-ground of the pulpit, attack them with flimsy arguments, whose fallacy they have long since detected, and could easily show, if it were a proper place for discussion. They are sent home in a frame of mind anything but Sabbatical, if not muttering half-suppressed curses between their teeth. The natural result follows; they refuse to go to church where they are visited by denunciation, and exasperated by abuse.

"Nor do we put the objection to political preaching solely on the ground that such preaching offends the earnest political convictions of a portion of the congregation, and thus keeps them away from church. The objection exists in hardly less force as to that part of the congregation who may agree with the preacher in his views. The preacher's duty is to teach religion, and not politics. The general sentiment of the public would discountenance a clergyman who, instead of sermons, should give essays on banking or agriculture, on political economy, on dietetics, on the use and abuse of medicines. Why should such peculiar latitude be given to partisan politics? Laymen do not wish, on Sunday, to have their thoughts disturbed, and their tempers tried, by the heating discussions and jarring conflicts of the past six days. They go into the house of God to escape from them.

"'Sleep, sleep to-day, tormenting cares,
Of earth and folly born,'

is the heart's natural language. On Sunday a man seeks to clear the soul of the dust and soil of earth, and to garnish it with pure thoughts, tranquil aspirations, ethereal hopes—flowers that have sucked the dews of heaven—and how can he do this if his spiritual guide insists on shooting into the rubbish of politics?

" The effect upon the clergy themselves of this habit of preaching politics is most injurious. It acts upon the mind in much the same way as dram-drinking acts upon the body. It begets a craving for coarse, vulgar excitements, utterly inconsistent with a proper interest in the appointed functions and appropriate meditations of the pastoral office. The more engaged the clergyman becomes in political issues, and the success of this or that political party, the more coldly and languidly will he turn to religious themes and spiritual contemplations. Once upon a time, a worldly man, who was wholly absorbed in the accumulation of property, was gently remonstrated with by his clergyman, and reminded of the necessity of preparing for another world. ' Do n't talk to me of another world,' was the reply, ' one world at a time is as much as I can attend to.' There is a frankness, a freedom of hypocrisy, in this answer, which we like. It includes an obvious truth. No man, be he clergyman or layman, can be wholly absorbed in the interests and issues of this world, and leave due space in his heart for those of another. You can not serve God and politics, any more than you can serve God and mammon.

" To general strictures like the above there are, of course, reasonable qualifications and exceptions. They are not true of every sect; still less are they true of every clergyman in any sect. But we appeal to the great body of laymen in our community—especially those who are no longer young—if there be not too much truth in what we have said. That the spirit of religion is decaying, and the influence of the clergy is declining, are melancholy facts. We are sorry for both; as sorry for the latter as the former. Both facts are symptoms of the same disease ; and the same remedy is needed for both."

The author designs no unkind attack upon the clergy, in general, in the present work. Those who know him best, will believe him incapable of such an act; on the contrary, they know the better part of his life, and all his pecuniary means, have been devoted to a " well-meant effort" to supply the churches with sound theological reading ;* and that he commenced his efforts to afford a safeguard against the sad errors in religion which were coming in like a flood, in connection with the movements for

* The Calvinistic Family Library is here referred to, a work commenced and prosecuted by the author for several years.

PULPIT POLITICS.

social and moral reform in general, and of philanthropic effort in behalf of the African race in particular. His relation to the Churches, as a working layman, has afforded to the author the opportunity of investigating the general movements of Christians for the evangelization of the world; and has enabled him to trace their missionary movements, and bring out the results in the most interesting contrasts presented in the close of the third chapter.

But that relation has enabled him to do more than this. It has afforded him opportunities for observation as to the practical results of "political preaching" upon the usefulness of the clergymen who have indulged in the practice; and he must say, in truth, as a general thing, that the devil can not have been much alarmed at the rate in which they were making inroads upon his kingdom. They were, mostly, much better qualified to divide and distract congregations than to build them up; much more successful in generating angry disputes among their parishioners, than in promoting brotherly love and kindly co-operation in carrying on their Master's work. "By their fruits ye shall know them;" and lest some might suppose that the unfavorable opinion here expressed proceeds from personal dislikes or prejudices, a few quotations from the sayings of some of the clergy themselves, will show that we have not underrated their want of efficiency in the propagation of the Gospel. At a convention held at Xenia, Ohio, a few years since, composed of delegates from the Scottish American Presbyterian Churches, to lament over the ruins of Zion, and project measures for the rebuilding of her broken-down walls, the following declarations were made in the course of the remarks of the speakers:

"We have been watching sins in sister Churches more than those coming in on us from the world. . . . . We ought to watch the signs of the times more closely, and fall in more carefully and faithfully with the movings of Providence in the world around us. We have not done our duty."*

"We must wait on God, and not trust too much in self. We must

* Church Memorial, p. 234.

not go out of the means He has instituted, and substitute some ancient tradition or new invention."*

" That covetousness which is idolatry has reached the ministers of the Gospel as well as the farmers and business men of the land."† .

" Rev. * * * said, the want of an intelligent faith in God produces deadness in the Church. He mentioned several things in illustration of this, viz., ministers' distrust of God to give them a support or comfortable livelihood. . . . . The want of discipline, through fear that there will not be an increase in numbers. . . . . Immense multitudes of souls are going to perdition, and we are asleep."‡

" Religion has not been made a personal matter, and brought home with sufficient directness and earnestness to the consciences of sinners."§

" The Church, the ministry, and members of the Church, have been trying to serve both God and mammon."‖

" Schism is a sin of the day. A divided Church is a weakened society. The standard of piety is so low among us that if we did not see men baptized at the Church, or see them at the communion-table, we would not be able to tell who are Christians, and who are not. We can not distinguish them from the men of the world in the market or other places."¶

" One favorable symptom of the time is a general dissatisfaction both in and outside the Church. They feel that there is something wrong. This is the feeling, not of one, but of all—not in one locality, but in all localities. . . . Other nations, once enjoying the Gospel, have now given it up. . . . Fifty years ago, the Scotch Presbyterian influence had a controlling power; now rationalism, infidelity, and skepticism abound. What have we to meet this? Take all the Churches represented here, and Old and New School Presbyterians, if you please, and there is a decrease in the number of theological students, while our population is increasing. A famine, not of bread and water, but of hearing the Word. What is the cause? Some say, because ministers are kept at starvation prices. Parents turn their children to some lucrative employment. This is a very business-like view of the matter. One that is prevalent, and ministers give strength to it—the secular press takes it up, and even fiction lends its aid, all warning our youth against entering the ministry. After all, this is

---

* Church Memorial, p. 235.   † Ibid., p. 235.   ‡ Ibid., p. 236.
§ Ibid., p. 237.   ‖ Ibid., p. 237.   ¶ Ibid., p. 238.

not the cause. Offer them such salaries as bishops of England receive, all would be vain to raising up ministers in the Church. The cause is the declining, dead state of matters in the Church. Show us a revived Church, and you will find plenty offering themselves to the work of the ministry. See how it was after the day of Pentecost. They ordained elders in every city. Isaiah is an illustration — a seraphim touched his lips with a coal from the altar; that coal was love; when he had touched his lips, a voice from the throne on high said, Whom shall I send, and who will go for us? The Lord reads to him his commission. All terrors from poor salaries not to be compared to the terribleness of that commission. There was no drawback when the call had touched his lips and heart. \ Here is what we need; we need our young men prepared as Isaiah was. . . .

"Let me ask you to look at our want of success. The Gospel ministry is for the conversion of sinners, and for the perfecting of the saints. How little has it accomplished in our hands! You have felt this subject, every renewed heart has wept over it; sinners shun our ministry. How many in a year follow you to your closets? The most of us will have to say, not one. And what advancement in holiness in our respective congregations? In self-denial and that godly life which should distinguish the Christian? We have not been successful. What has been the cause? Will not the Spirit give the blessing? True, but can a ministry under the influence of faith be so unsuccessful? Look back to the day of Pentecost. As long as the Pentecostal spirit remained, there was continued success. When the reverse came, there came a reverse effect."

At a meeting of the same parties, subsequently, in Philadelphia, the following remarks were made:

"What are we doing? There are hundreds of young men in our congregations, but how many of them are brought forward to preach the Gospel? Perhaps not one! They dribble into God's treasury fifty or one hundred dollars for missionary operations, but not one soul for God's ministry."*

"Rev. * * * 's impression was, that the Church's sin was *the mind being withdrawn from the great principles of salvation.*"†

"I think it then of the first moment to get our minds affected with this truth, that *we*, not this or the other people, or the Church here

---

* Church Memorial, p. 296.   † Ibid., p. 297.

or there, but we ourselves, are in a spiritually lifeless condition. The evidences we have before us. A state of death is a state of inaction." *

"The rubbish must be removed, and Zion must be rebuilt. There will be a separating from the nations. So it was in the Pentecostal. Ministers disconnected themselves from everything else. They would not even consent to distribute gold and silver, but deacons must be chosen for this very work. Look at the result. The people came forward and laid their possessions at the Apostles' feet. A man would be accounted a madman in this land who would do as these did under the Apostles' ministry. Let us take up our cross and follow Jesus." †

But we must hold our hand. These penitential utterances are sufficient to subserve our purpose; which is to show that a prevailing sentiment exists that the Gospel ministry of the present day are failing to come up to the standard of efficiency required by the vows which are upon them. But in this, as in much else, there is, we believe, a great amount of misconception on the part of the ministry, as well as upon the part of the public. A minister considers his life unsuccessful, unless he can show such brilliant successes as shall demonstrate clearly that he is a bright particular star. This result may flatter his pride, but it is not God's plan of promoting the kingdom of Christ in this world. It is the quiet men who are the successful men, though they may die without being conscious of having wrought much good; and in thus dying, they demonstrate the great truth connected with God's moral government of the world. His rule of action is this: "My glory I will not give to another, nor my praises to graven images;" and the minister who aims at personal glorification in his ministry, must expect to be disappointed. He may do good; but, as a Paul may plant, and an Apollos water, yet it is God who giveth the increase, so God will take all the glory of the world's redemption to himself.

A remark here, and we have done. How does it come, that a body of men who exhibit so much humility in the practice of their sacred profession, should be so daring in their claims of a right to dictate in civil affairs?

* Church Memorial, p. 298.   † Ibid., p. 311.

CONCLUSION.

OUR labors are now terminated. Had not so many more pages than was anticipated been filled by the materials used, we should have closed with a somewhat extended representation of the points proved in our book. But, as the passing comments upon each subject discussed are often quite full, we must leave the intelligent reader to make his own generalizations. A few propositions, however, out of many that are fully demonstrated, may be noted, to serve as guides to those who wish to gain an intelligible view of the great problem before the country—the restoration of the Constitution, and the reconstruction of the Union, through the co-operation of the loyal population in the revolted States, and those who may return to their allegiance.

This, as we read events, is the great aim of the President, and is the only scheme for saving the country that has the merit of being both practicable and beneficent. A reference to a few of the points proved in this volume, will show that every other measure proposed can bring nothing but ruin in its train. Among other things, we have proved:

1. That the British theories on slavery are untrue, as applied to America; and that slavery is not necessarily a bar to the evangelization of the African race, but may be made greatly subservient to the promotion of that object.

2. That the ecclesiastical legislation, based upon the supposed truthfulness of the British theories, has been uncalled for, injudicious, and destructive to the harmony of the Church, and the peace of the country.

3. That, but for the ecclesiastical legislation at the North on the question of slavery, political abolitionism could never have had a basis upon which to found its action; and that, but for these

(620)

two causes combined—ecclesiastical and political abolitionism—the South would have had no cause of alarm for the safety of its constitutional rights, and would have felt no necessity of defending itself against aggressions from the North.

4. That the early anti-slavery writers, in their efforts to prove that slavery was sinful, were driven to the necessity of denying that the Apostles of Christ understood their duties in relation to Roman slavery; and that, by denying that the teachings of the Apostles are a proper guide to us now, on American slavery, they were laying the basis for the rejection of the Scriptures as infallible guides upon other moral questions, and thus promoting doctrines of infidel tendency.

5. That the converts to Christianity among the African race, in all the mission fields outside of the United States, are more than two hundred thousand less than the colored converts within the slave States; and that the Christian character of the converts in the slave States is at least equal to that of the converts in the Protestant missions anywhere throughout heathendom.

6. That the colored church-membership, in the slave States, is nearly ten times greater in number than the converts in all the foreign missions of all the American Protestant churches; and that it is almost double the whole number of converts in all the heathen missions under the care of all the churches of Protestant Christendom.

7. That the whole of the white membership in both branches of the General Assembly Presbyterian Church, in 1859, fell short of the number of the colored church-members in the slave States, to the extent of more than fifty thousand; and that the membership in the Scottish American Presbyterian Churches, in 1861, fell short of the number of the colored membership by more than three hundred and eighty thousand; and yet, these Churches were the first to pronounce slavery a barrier to African evangelization!

8. That emancipation does not necessarily improve the moral and physical condition of the colored race, but, on the contrary, in many instances, it has been injurious and ruinous; that careful moral training alone, under suitable constraint, can elevate

the colored people, whether in bondage or in freedom; and that as the Gospel is extensively preached to the slaves of the South, and with eminent success, the Churches can find no justification for attempting to interrupt that work by emancipation.

9. That the African race, wherever fully emancipated, and left free to act—though capable of fitful labor to the extent of supplying the actual necessaries of life — have proved themselves *wholly unreliable in the cultivation of staple productions,* such as now enter so largely into the commerce and manufactures of the world; that when thus set free, and left unaided by the superior race, they invariably show themselves incapable of making any intellectual or moral progress; and that this result has been so uniform, and so universal, that emancipation, in the southern States, must necessarily be expected to lead to an almost total suspension of the culture of their staple products, and the relapse of the colored population itself back again toward its original barbarism.

10. That the southern States have been increasing the annual exports of the products of their soil, until it had reached, in 1860, the value of more than two hundred millions of dollars, while the northern States supplied, of similar products, for export, not more, at any time, than fifty millions of dollars; and that the dissolution of the Union, or the emancipation of the slaves, would be equally fatal to the prosperity of the country, as it would deprive it of this immense amount of the elements of its foreign commerce.

11. That the success of abolitionism would prostrate, for generations to come, the agricultural interests of the West, by depriving its people of the only practicable market they have ever possessed; that the success of secession, in addition to affecting this market injuriously, would leave the Western agriculturist liable to the payment of tribute to the Confederacy, for the use of the Mississippi, and subject the country to the frequent recurrence of civil wars; and that neither emancipation nor secession can be allowed, as either would bring ruin upon the Northwest, as well as upon the country at large.

12. That with the light we now possess on the "Cotton Question," there can no longer be any doubt that the restoration of